The Politics of Antipolitics

The Politics of Antipolitics

The Military in Latin America

Second Edition, Revised and Expanded

Edited by Brian Loveman

and Thomas M. Davies, Jr.

University of Nebraska Press

Lincoln and London

This book is dedicated to
Bernard J. Loveman and
Thomas M. and *Faith Arnold Davies*

Acknowledgments for permission to
reprint copyrighted material appear on pages 515–17.

Library of Congress Cataloging-in-
Publication Data

The Politics of antipolitics: the military in Latin
America/edited by Brian Loveman and Thomas
M. Davies, Jr.—2nd ed., rev. and expanded.
    p.   cm.
Includes bibliographies.
    ISBN 0-8032-2884-8. ISBN 0-8032-7928-0 (pbk.)
    Civil-military relations—Latin America. 2. Latin
America—Armed Forces—Political activity. 3. Latin
America—Armed Forces. 4. Latin America—Politics
and government. I. Loveman, Brian. II. Davies, Thomas M.
JL956.C58P65   1989
322'.5'098—dc19   CIP 88-10226

Contents

Preface to the First Edition

When we set out several years ago to prepare an interdisciplinary graduate seminar on the military and politics in Latin America, we found that the available materials were widely dispersed among journal articles, country monographs, government documents, personal memoirs, and military journals in Spanish, Portuguese, and English, as well as several well-known books written in the period 1960–74 (particularly the pioneering efforts of Edwin Lieuwen and John J. Johnson). We also found several anthologies on the military in Latin America and the Third World, but none of these had attempted to bring together these diverse Latin American and United States sources nor had there been any attempt to compile a reader on military politics in a representative selection of Latin American countries.

This book seeks to fill that void and, in so doing, to provide a volume which will be of use in a variety of courses on Latin America, inter-American affairs, and the role of the military in Third World nations. The central theme of the book is the underlying similarities in outlook, ideology, and practice of military governments in Latin America. Combining historical, thematic, and case-study approaches, the volume traces the origins of these similarities—which we term "antipolitics"—back to the Hispanic political tradition and follows the development of military antipolitics through the century and one-half of Latin American independence.

Focusing on five Latin American nations—Argentina, Bolivia, Brazil, Chile, and Peru—we begin with a theoretical essay on antipolitics and then treat, in turn, the age of the caudillos, the creation of modern military establishments through European military training missions, the role of the military from 1919 to 1945, the United States and military antipolitics in the twentieth century, particularly after World War II, and the policy consequences of military rule in the five countries. We have also included a section of speeches and documents by military leaders where the military is allowed to "speak for itself."

We have tried to treat these themes in a logical historical sequence and have sought to achieve continuity through our introductory essays to each section of readings as well as by treating the same five nations for each historical period and each thematic focus. We chose these particular countries after a great deal of consideration and for a variety of reasons including, of course, the availability of materials from which to select. The historical role of the military in the nations that we have chosen ranges from the Bolivian and Peruvian cases of almost constant direct intervention into politics to (with exceptions) the less overtly political behavior of the Chilean military. The countries themselves range from the poorest to the wealthiest, from those with significant Indian and black populations to those with predominantly European or mestizo populations. Lack of appropriate published and documentary materials forced us, regretfully, to exclude case studies of the Central American republics. We have omitted Cuba and Mexico because in our opinion the unique revolutionary conditions in both led to the emergence of quite different political-military relationships.

In order to avoid excessive length, we were forced to omit all but a few of the footnotes which appeared in the original essays, leaving a few descriptive notes and adding several editors' notes for purposes of clarity. Moreover, we have edited all the essays, some quite heavily, but have always sought to retain the tone and thrust of the original. The spelling, punctuation, and capitalization of reprinted articles have been regularized, and ellipses indicate our own deletions of material.

No book of this nature can ever be completed without the aid and assistance of a great many people. In our case, we are particularly indebted to the students in our graduate seminar. Through their incisive analyses of the military phenomenon and their constant questioning of previous theories and positions, they helped us to rethink and refocus many of our ideas. Thus, to Michael T. Argüello, Mary Berson, Jo Della-Giustina, Penny Hill, Robert Kagon, Steve Kantes, Jim Kennedy, John Mahedy, Fabio Martínez, Gary Page, Marco Antonio Rodríguez, Gloria Stone, Duane Thornton, and Rob Valentine we offer our thanks.

Various Latin American and United States colleagues also contributed their time and knowledge. Foremost among them are Julio Cotler, Frederick M. Nunn, and Víctor Villanueva who cooperated with us in revising and updating several of his essays. Davies's father-in-law, General (r) José Monzón Linares of the Peruvian Guardia Civil, through his vast knowledge of military affairs and language contributed much to the various translations. We alone, of course, are responsible for any errors of fact or interpretation.

Cecilia Ubilla translated the speeches by Humberto Castello Branco and Ernesto Geisel, and Marion Leitner patiently typed and retyped what must have seemed to be an endless number of revisions.

Finally, we owe a large debt of gratitude to our wives, Sharon Loveman and Tita Monzón de Davies, for their support and encouragement, and to our children, Taryn, Mara, and Carly Loveman and Jennifer Davies.

Preface to the Second Edition

The second edition of this book appears at a time when most of the military regimes which dominated Latin America in the 1960s and 1970s have given way to civilian governments proclaiming their commitment to democratization. In some cases, for example, Brazil and Peru, this transition to civilian government took place as a result of gradual, orchestrated extrication of the military institutions from the visible centers of government. In other cases, disintegration of the military regimes due to internal difficulties or, in the case of Argentina, a disastrous war, led to a more abrupt and somewhat more thorough reduction of direct military participation in everyday policy making. Nowhere, however, has military influence and participation in policy making disappeared. In all cases, the military regimes of the 1960s and 1970s have left an enduring legacy in the political, economic, and social fields. This legacy and the continuing influence of the military in politics are examined in the last section of the present edition.

In addition to a consideration of the consequences of military antipolitics in Latin America, this second edition includes material on two Central American countries, Guatemala and El Salvador, where variations of the antipolitical military regimes have played a major role in national life in the post–World War II period. This expanded coverage extends the discussion to seven countries—Argentina, Brazil, Bolivia, Chile, Peru, Guatemala, and El Salvador—providing historical background for each from the early independence years until the present. In addition, this second edition includes new speeches and declarations from the military leaders in those countries, allowing them to further "speak for themselves" in outlining the rationale and objectives of the military governments in the region.

Finally, though the apparent demise of the military regimes has led to a large number of books and articles since 1980 on the theme of democratization in Latin America, the immediate political setbacks of antidemocratic forces in the region do not imply the acceptance of liberalism, pluralism, or constitutionally limited government by the majority of the military elites, nor by their civilian allies. Neither do they imply a decline in contempt for the civilian politicians or democracy itself. Antipolitics survived the military regimes, just as traditional Hispanic political culture and institutions and modernized versions of Hispanic authoritarianism have resisted democratization of the region throughout the twentieth century.

Perhaps the recent experience of systematic and institutionalized government terrorism and torture, brutalization of opposition, and repression of political parties, labor organizations, media, and even some religious groups will provide strong incentives for civilian leaders to overcome the legacy of antipolitics. President Alfonsín of Argentina suggested in his book *La Cuestión Argentina* (1980), "We have emerged from a blood bath. The most painful experienced by modern Argentina. And the curtain has not yet fallen. All of us, without exception, must act in the future with the cost of this enormous burden in mind." Peru's president, Alan García, told the Peruvian Congress in July 1985, "What Peru needs is a democratic revolution, a historical restructuring that reactivates the depths, that frees the social forces that have been ignored up till now." Whether President Alfonsín and President García, or their colleagues in Bolivia, Brazil, El Salvador, and Guatemala, can achieve a long-term transformation of politics and society in their nations remains to be seen. What is clear, however, is that there exists the possibility that democratization may fail and that antipolitical regimes may reassert authoritarian ideological and political visions throughout the region. We hope this second edition will clarify both the experiences of these last years and the rationale, justification, and consequences of military antipolitics in Latin America.

In the preparation of this second edition, we have incurred several new debts. We want to express our appreciation to Teddy Ralph for her patience in typing and retyping new drafts, to Rosa M. Hippler-Perry for translating the speech by João Figueiredo, and, most important, to Michael Stanfield, who, while in Central America, collected most of the new material on Guatemala and El Salvador.

1 Military Rule and the Latin American Tradition

The Politics of Antipolitics

Military leaders successful in anticolonial wars founded the Spanish American republics in the early nineteenth century. Military elites were also responsible for the creation of the Brazilian Republic in the late nineteenth century. In the 1960s and 1970s professional military officers in Latin America scanned the panorama of Latin American history and blamed the ineptitude and corruption of civilian politicians as well as the imported institutions of liberal democracy for the wretched conditions in Latin America. In much of Latin America, professional military officers concluded that only an end to "politics" and the establishment of long-term military rule could provide the basis for modernization, economic development, and political stability. This determination, strengthened by events in Brazil after 1964, led to explicitly antipolitical military regimes in most of Latin America.

Military antipolitics originated both in military understanding of Latin American history and military assessment of the Latin American dilemma in the mid-twentieth century. Throughout most of the nineteenth century, "politics," that is, conflict among personalist factions and, later, political parties, over ideological formulas and the spoils of rule, submerged most of the Latin American nations in bloody civil strife. In the late nineteenth and early twentieth centuries, however, military leaders sought to end the chaos and impose stability and order amid the social conflict and dislocation caused by the process of modernization. "Politics," including the demagogic appeals by civilian politicians to the emerging proletariat, promoted class conflict and instability which "forced" sectors of the military to intervene to restore order and cleanse the body politic of political corruption.

The years following World War I witnessed not only the failure of civilian experiments with political democracy, but also the collapse of the Latin American export economies, a collapse which demonstrated to many military officers the folly of total dependence on foreign capitalists. When the military leaders again intervened in the 1920s and 1930s to restore order and deal with the problems that civilians refused or were unable to resolve, they pointed to civilian bungling, ineptitude, and corruption as the primary motivating factors in their decision.

In Chile in 1924, one civilian minister was told:

Even though you now represent to us the most disgusting element in our country—politicians—all that is corrupt, the dismal factional disputes, depravity and immoralities, in other words, the causes of our national degeneration, we recognize that you, despite the fact that you must defend sinecures, hand out public jobs, support avaricious ambitions, that you are one of the few honest politicians.[1]

Three years earlier, a statement signed by seventeen Peruvian army officers contained the following words:

Comrades:
For some time now, since politics infiltrated the army, we military officers have been serving as steppingstones for unscrupulous politicians. They use our services, and then they promote us. This must stop. Promotions must be based upon professional competence and not on political activity. . . . *We [must] assume the reins of government of the country in order to root out political influence, the worst of all plagues, and we shall shape Peru's destiny with our own hands and our own initiative.* . . . Our fatherland suffers daily from the partisan struggles of politicians who care nothing for the development and progress of the nation. It is our task to normalize the institutional life of the country. . . . *The army, drawn from all social classes of the nation, must intervene directly in the management of the affairs of state.*[2]

As the twentieth century wore on, the hopes of career military officers for modernization and industrialization were increasingly frustrated. The attitudes and aspirations imparted by the European training missions that professionalized many Latin American military establishments in the late nineteenth century conflicted with the obvious inability of Latin American civilians to create viable institutions for directing national development. Thus, while many young military officers retained kinship and class ties to the traditional elites, they harbored an ever growing disdain for civilian politicians and for politics in general.

One widely held assumption of Latin American military officers, and one also shared by many conservative civilian groups, was that "politics" was largely responsible for the poverty, instability, and economic backwardness of their nations. This assumption was not new, nor did it originate in all cases within military circles, but the depolitization of "politics" and the establishment of an administrative regime to forge an organic, hierarchically structured polity provided a crucial ideological link between civilian propertied interests and military modernizers.

Acceptance of this ideology of antipolitics also entailed the denial of the legitimacy of labor protest, strikes, political party claims of representing diverse interests, and, more generally, of opposition to government authority, policies, and programs. Order, obedience, authority, and stability—cherished values of the Hispanic socioeconomic elites—not only dovetailed neatly with the spirit of military training, but also provided easy rationalizations for military rule. With slight alteration, these values and assumptions formed the ideological core of military antipolitics and military rule in the 1970s.

Latin American Antecedents of Antipolitics

Widespread instability and economic deterioration in early nineteenth-century Latin America contrasted markedly with the special case of Chile, where, after 1833, an institutional predecessor of military antipolitics provided the basis for economic expansion, territorial aggrandizement, and regime stability. Thus, the legal and political practices introduced in Chile during those years are useful benchmarks for the organizational assumptions of antipolitics, the political practices of antipolitics, and, from the perspective of conservative civilians and military leaders intent on "modernization," the economic successes of antipolitics.

The Chilean Constitution of 1833 concentrated authority in an all-powerful executive, the president, who was permitted to serve two five-year terms. The legislative branch was subordinate to the executive. For example, when the legislature was in recess (most of the time), the president could declare a state of siege in any part of the country, thereby suspending constitutional government in that region. The administrative officers in each province and department (*intendentes* and *gobernadores*) were named directly by the president as his "natural and immediate agents." Thus, the constitution made operative the organizational premises of antipolitics: (1) centralization of authority; (2) hierarchical rule through administrative (nonparliamentary) agencies at the provincial and local levels; (3) a "flexible" constitution, that is a constitution that offered little effective constraint on the exercise of governmental authority; and (4) official recognition of governance through a state of siege.

These assumptions about the structure and scope of governmental authority were combined with political practices that epitomized the ideological commitment to antipolitics: (1) systematic persecution of opposition elements, including the press; (2) pragmatic repression of the regime's opponents expressing overt resistance to official policy or programs; and (3) nonrecognition of the legitimacy of active opposition or of political bargaining, negotiation, or compromise.

Repudiating the liberal principles used to justify the Latin American independence movements, the leaders of Chile's autocratic republic made no pretense of accepting a noninterventionist state mediating among conflicting pluralist interests. The Chilean state, following the classic Hispanic tradition, sought to impose order, direct and regulate economic enterprise, and maintain the "proper" relationships among the elements of an organically conceived society. These basic tenets concerning the role of government authority and the state apparatus were perhaps best summed up by Diego Portales, founder of the Chilean autocratic regime: "One can never understand lawyers: and, *¡Carajo!* what use are constitutions and bits of paper unless to remedy an evil that one knows to exist or is about to exist. . .? An accursed law, then, [if it] prevents the government from going ahead freely at the opportune moment."[3]

The principles and practices of Chile's autocratic republic—an interventionist, centralized state; a flexible, "suspendable" constitution allowing for government through state of siege at executive discretion; intolerance of opposition; repression of opponents of the regime; and maintenance of order, which is understood to include hierarchical social and class relationships—provided the ideological underpinnings for Latin America's first successful experiment with a deliberate policy of economic expansion founded upon international commerce, foreign capital, and stimulation of the nation's primary sectors, mining and agriculture.

From 1830 to 1860, in sharp contrast to the economies of most of Latin America, Chile's economy grew and prospered. Agricultural output increased, new roads were constructed, and foreign trade mushroomed. American and European entrepreneurs brought modern transport and navigation systems to Chile, which contributed, in part, to the notable expansion in the mining sector. Precepts of liberal economic doctrine, particularly free trade, dominated economic policy, thereby encouraging imports at the same time that Chilean wheat found its way to California markets. Antipolitics produced both stability and economic growth.

The Spread of Antipolitics
In the late nineteenth century, the social and economic implications of positivism offered a philosophical rationale for authoritarian governments' efforts to stimulate economic modernization. The main features of the Chilean autocratic republic were increasingly evident in Mexico, Guatemala, and across much of South America. As with Chile in the years 1830–60, the combination of authoritarian rule, pragmatic (nonideological) repression, and Hispanic capitalism[4] in an international economy demanding Latin America's primary products produced stability and economic growth. Antipolitics worked—for those who ruled. It produced stability, concentrated the benefits of economic growth in the hands of a

small elite, and forced the emerging urban and industrial working classes and the rural poor to bear the costs of "development."

The United States and Antipolitics in Latin America

Then came the Mexican Revolution, the Russian Revolution, and World War I, all of which contributed to a general questioning of traditional values and governmental systems and to the emergence of new concepts about societal relationships. Civilization came to mean democracy, and Latin American elites wanted to be included in the civilized world. Unfortunately, democracy did not work very well, certainly not as well as antipolitics. Democracy, after all, required the tolerance of opposition, placed constraints on executive authority, meant mobilization of the rural and urban poor, and entailed demands for income redistribution. The potential threats to the existing order contained in liberal democracy, and after World War I, Marxism, concerned United States policy makers as much as Latin American elites. Foreshadowing the military assistance programs of the Alliance for Progress years, the United States began to create military constabularies whose leaders (for example, Rafael Trujillo in the Dominican Republic and Anastasio Somoza in Nicaragua) recognized the viability of a new version of antipolitics founded on the coercive force of professional military establishments.

On the other hand, the professional military created by United States intervention or earlier German and French military missions posed a contradiction as nationalist sentiments and the desire for economic development aroused both admiration and hostility toward Western European and American ideology and society. Eventually, however, these military officers devised a developmental orientation highly consistent with the Latin American tradition, with the added touch of assigning the predominant governmental role to the military itself. Patriotism, nationalism, self-sacrifice, and absolute commitment to the national welfare and security distinguished military officers, in their own opinion, from the self-seeking, venal civilian politicians, who served special interests rather than those of the nation. The perfection of antipolitics required nonpolitical leadership and the negation of partisan strife. It required, in fact, the military.

Economic Development as a Military Mission

Speaking to the Argentine Círculo Militar in 1926, Colonel Luis Vicat told his colleagues:

The real meaning of national defense is vast and complex; it can be defined by saying that it includes all those activities and security measures necessary to assure the tranquillity, prosperity, and independence of a nation, as well as rapid victory in case of conflict.[5]

Fifty years later, the notion that economic development is synonymous with national defense and national security, that is, a military mission, was widely held by Latin American military officers. One of the theoreticians of the Brazilian Revolution of 1964 contends:

At the beginning of the century it was enough to maintain armed forces capable of ensuring the integrity of national boundaries and overcoming the military might of possible enemies. But this idea has [now] been replaced by another, which recognizes that national security includes everything that in one way or another affects the life of the nation.[6]

That this concept was hardly novel in Brazil can be seen in a statement made in 1952 by one of the founders of Brazil's Superior War College (ESG): "National security lies in the battle for production, in the tranquillity of the population, and in the provision of stability and a reasonable standard of living."[7]

Increasingly, there seemed to be a common assumption among military officers that only through an end to "politics" and the imposition of military rule could any developmental mission be accomplished. Officers no longer intervened merely to restore order or to act as caretakers; in the 1960s and 1970s they adopted a revised version of antipolitics to justify military rule.

Counterrevolution and Antipolitics

The internal rationale for military antipolitics was also heavily influenced by the United States's response to revolutionary change in Cuba. Convinced that communism flourished where people lived in poverty, the United States committed itself to an Alliance for Progress for Latin America. This so-called alliance featured economic and military assistance programs designed both to induce economic growth and to support, finance, and "advise" Latin American civic action and counterinsurgency programs designed to combat those forces which opposed incumbent regimes.

Summing up the objectives of American assistance programs to Latin America, former Secretary of Defense Robert McNamara declared in 1967:

The specific objectives of military assistance are the development of Latin American forces capable of maintaining internal security against threats of violence and subversion, whether Communist-inspired and supported or "home grown"; encouraging the armed forces to support and strengthen democratic institutions and to undertake civic action projects which both contribute to the social and economic development of the country and bring the armed forces and civilian populace closer together. . . .[8]

Despite McNamara's reassertion of the Kennedy administration's thesis that Latin American armed forces would support and strengthen democratic institutions, by 1967 it had already become evident that the Alliance for Progress's counterrevolutionary inspiration intensified the contempt of the military's "new professionals" for civilian politicians. Furthermore,

UNITED STATES MILITARY ASSISTANCE FUNDS FOR CIVIC
ACTION PROGRAMS, FISCAL YEAR 1962 THROUGH FISCAL YEAR 1966
(In Thousands of Dollars)

	Fiscal Year 1962	Fiscal Year 1963	Fiscal Year 1964	Fiscal Year 1965	Fiscal Year 1966
Latin America					
Argentina	—	—	298	1,253	539
Bolivia	—	1,817	397	239	114
Brazil	2,200	2,156	2,097	2,386	1,961
Chile	860	2,019	1,279	391	634
Colombia	—	1,488	1,655	550	696
Costa Rica	—	—	222	13	*
Dominican Republic	—	596	59	64	122
Ecuador	1,500	323	709	476	104
El Salvador	—	534	145	99	65
Guatemala	—	863	567	133	343
Honduras	—	84	20	240	71
Mexico	—	—	—	8	20
Nicaragua	—	59	—	3	—
Panama	—	—	2	44	22
Paraguay	—	840	1,111	596	576
Peru	1,135	2,794	1,271	2,411	2,871
Uruguay	—	546	431	286	103
Venezuela	—	—	23	47	59
Region†	—	—	—	—	72
Area total	5,695	14,119	10,286	9,239	8,372

NOTE: Fiscal year 1962 was the first year that civic action assistance was so identified in MAP. Fiscal year 1967 is estimated to have a worldwide total of $11,810.

* Less than $500.

† Probably refers to funds not dedicated to a particular country but to region "overhead."

the failure of the United States to distinguish clearly between "Communist" and "homegrown" insurgents fit neatly with the Hispanic tradition of antipolitics in dealing with opponents of the regime.

Still, some military officers were uneasy about the "new professionalism" that cast military officers in the role of the only force capable of resolving national problems in a disinterested and patriotic fashion. This uneasiness resulted from the lack of a systematic ideological and doctrinal rationale for prolonged military rule. Gradually this void was filled by the emergence of specialized military universities that not only developed an appropriate rationale for military rule, but also took it upon themselves to train civilians as administrators in the antipolitical military state.

Prototypical Institutions of the New Professionalism of Military Antipolitics: CAEM (Peru) and ESG (Brazil)

In the 1970s, military antipolitics became a predominant political form in Latin America. No longer did military officers feel obliged to insist that intervention in politics was temporary or even undesirable. To a great extent, the openly political ambitions and activities of military elites stemmed from a new emphasis in professional training that provided a rationale for and a stimulus to the creation of military governments as instruments of development.

Prototypical in this respect were the Center for Advanced Military Studies (Centro de Altos Estudios Militares—CAEM) in Peru and the Superior War School (Escola Superior de Guerra—ESG) in Brazil. Interestingly, the military governments in Peru and Brazil, led chiefly by graduates or instructors from these institutions (and also assisted by civilian graduates), have been seen as both "rightist" (Brazil) and "leftist" (Peru) because of the policies and programs adopted in their countries. In fact, however, the basic paradigm of both regimes, "military antipolitics," is consistent either with mobilizational inclusionary programs of economic modernization (Peru, 1968–75) or with politics that demobilize social and political groups and limit political participation to encourage modernization through regressive income distribution and capital accumulation (Brazil, 1964–73, Chile, 1973–).

Historical and environmental factors greatly influenced the particulars of public policy under the new military regimes. Where quasi-feudal land tenure systems, ethnic and cultural diversity, and relatively weak industrial economies existed, efforts to modernize through antipolitics appeared to be reformist, populist, or even "leftist." In nations with more developed capitalist economies, or more militant and well-organized labor movements, military antipolitics seemed more reactionary. In either case, law and order, restraints on autonomous popular mobilization, press censorship, restrictions on civil liberties, and intolerance of opposition underlie apparent differences among the military regimes.

Although some have labeled the orientation of these institutions the "new professionalism,"[9] neither their orientations nor their attitudes are, in fact, new. Rather, the explicit concern with internal security, economic development, and social services; the ineptitude of civilian politicians; and the inadequacy of politics is the result of an amalgamation of traditional Hispanic antipolitics with the influences of military professionalization from 1880 to 1930, the Cold War ambience, the United States–influenced counterinsurgency and Alliance for Progress programs, and, importantly, the doctrinal justification for military rule contained in the CAEM, ESG-type military educational experience. But even this doctrinal justification, including the expansion of the concept of national security to encompass all those political, economic, and social conditions that affect the power of a nation, was merely an elaboration upon the sentiments of Latin American military officers in the early twentieth century (see the remarks of Colonel Luis Vicat, cited above).

The educational experience at CAEM, for example, reinforced the long-held disdain and contempt that officers felt for civilian politicians and for "politics." Since the civilian governments had failed to stimulate development, it followed therefore that they were responsible for all of Peru's social and economic ills. Moreover, since the civilians who had governed Peru belonged to the traditional elites representing agro-commercial interests, the military's anticivilian orientation coincided nicely with leftist critiques of the Peruvian landed oligarchy. The military saw itself as being patriotic, self-sacrificing, and dedicated to national—not class—interests, unlike the self-interested civilians.

Thus, the Peruvian military was "leftist." Yet the basic assumptions about the role of the state, the nature of authority, and the uses of constitutions bore a much greater resemblance to Diego Portales than to Karl Marx. The military's mission, to provide internal security, required that the state have "freedom of action and the necessary resources to achieve social well-being. . . . [The state must have] the authority to adopt measures considered necessary for achieving its objectives. . . . The state is supreme within its territory."[10] If the Peruvian officers disliked their dependence upon the United States and seemed to attack certain sectors of the private economy, the philosophical basis of these measures reached back to colonial Hispanic capitalism and military nationalism, not to Marxism. CAEM merely provided a modern rationale for antipolitics under military direction.

In Brazil, a larger and much more industrialized society than Peru, the socioeconomic dilemmas of political leadership by the military were even more complex. Political experience under civilian regimes had been more varied and the failure of liberalism and populism more recent and more directly menacing to the military. Thus, the Brazilian variant of antipolitics included rabid anti-Marxism. Yet, allowing for Brazil's somewhat unique history in Latin America, the basic assumptions of rule held by the ESG graduates were quite familiar: the need to centralize authority, the intolerance of opposition, the contempt for civilian politics and politicians, the refusal to be constrained by constitutional limits, the propensity to govern by decree, and the censorship or closure of opposition mass media.[11]

Brazilian practice added a relatively new element to antipolitics (an element anticipated by George Orwell): government use of torture and terror as a routine instrument of rule. Variants on the Brazilian version of antipolitics, notably after 1973 in both Chile and Uruguay, incorporated terror into the arsenal of the public policy instruments of Latin American antipolitics.

In Argentina, after 1976, the military declared and waged a war against the internal enemy—politicians and "subversives"—which left thousands dead or "disappeared" in the late 1970s and early 1980s. Meanwhile, in Guatemala and El Salvador, thousands more died in civil wars and counterinsurgency operations as death squads, secret police, and counterintelligence units detained, arrested, and attacked labor leaders, peasants, journalists, politicians, students, clerics, and other regime opponents in efforts to extirpate the "cancer of politics" from national life.

Policy Consequences of Military Antipolitics

The assumptions of antipolitics allow for a great diversity of policy initiatives by military rulers. Antipolitics is committed neither to capitalism nor to socialism. It is antiliberal and anti-Marxist. It assumes repression of opposition, silencing or censoring of the media, and subordinating the labor movement to the objectives of the regime. It does not willingly tolerate strikes by workers or the pretensions to aristocratic privilege by traditional elites. It seeks order and progress; the latter assumed contingent upon the former. It places high priority on economic growth and is usually little concerned with income distribution except insofar as worker or white-collar discontent leads to protest and disorder. It can pragmatically emphasize either concessions or repression in obtaining its objectives. It can even use "elections," pseudopolitical parties, and plebiscites in order to give a veneer of "democratic" legitimacy to authoritarian direction of the state and society.

Military antipolitics adds several elements to those general characteristics: military leadership, a more evident linkage between the state and coercion, a more insistent demand for order and respect for hierarchy, a less tolerant attitude toward opposition, and an outright rejection of "politics," which is perceived as being the source of underdevelopment, corruption, and evil.[12]

Thus, whether military antipolitics includes programs for land reform or industrialization, expanded public-health services, urban housing, or new educational facilities, the other policies of antipolitics tend to be shared. And, above all, military antipolitics produces a regime of masters and "proles," of rulers and the ruled. Sometimes the masters use torture and other forms of repression to enforce their will and maintain their power; sometimes prosperity permits the use of more pleasant instruments of persuasion. Nevertheless, the military version of antipolitics remains tied to the Portalian notion: "The stick and the cake, justly and opportunely administered, are the specifics with which any nation can be cured, however inveterate its bad habits may be."[13]

Notes

1. Raúl Aldunate Phillips, *Ruido de sables* (Santiago de Chile: Escuela Lito-Tipográfica, "La Gratitud Nacional," n.d.), p. 87.

2. Quoted in Víctor Villanueva, *Ejército peruano: del caudillaje anárquico al militarismo reformista* (Lima: Librería-Editorial Juan Mejía Baca, 1973), p. 177. The emphasis is in the original.

3. Simon Collier, *Ideas and Politics of Chilean Independence, 1808–1833* (Cambridge: Cambridge University Press, 1967), p. 345.

4. In contrast to the European liberal tradition of laissez-faire capitalism, Hispanic capitalism views private enterprise as a concession of the state. Thus, in the Hispanic system, monopoly is not the end product of capitalist development, but rather the starting point of private enterprise. The old slave monopoly, or *asiento,* of colonial days and the various concessionary monopolies, or *estancos,* of the republican period are merely two examples of this system.

5. Luis Vicat, "El desarrollo industrial como empresa militar," in Jorge Alvarez, ed., *Ejército y revolución industrial* (Buenos Aires: Talleres Gráficos Verdad, 1964), p. 25.

6. Quoted in Víctor Villanueva, *El CAEM y la revolución de la fuerza armada* (Lima: Instituto de Estudios Peruanos, 1972), p. 233.

7. Quoted in ibid.

8. U.S. Congress, House, *Foreign Assistance and Related Agencies Appropriations for 1967, Hearing before a Subcommittee of the Committee on Appropriations,* 89th Cong., 1st sess., 1967, pp. 605–6.

9. For a discussion of "new professionalism," see Alfred Stepan, "The

New Professionalism of Internal Warfare and Military Role Expansion," in Alfred Stepan, ed., *Authoritarian Brazil: Origins, Policies, and Failures* (New Haven: Yale University Press, 1973), pp. 47–65.

10. Villanueva, CAEM, p. 156.

11. Stepan, "New Professionalism," p. 55.

12. It must be noted that there remain military officers who wish to return to a narrower professional role. Important divisions within the Latin American officer corps developed (in each of the countries upon which we focus in this book) precisely over the desirability of prolonged military rule or even military intervention. Yet in the 1970s the officers who desired an end to military rule or a return to anything approximating liberal domestic politics were clearly out of step with the dominant doctrines in the military academies and the reality of the Latin American scene. In the 1980s, this trend was, at least temporarily, reversed.

13. Collier, *Ideas and Politics of Chilean Independence,* p. 359.

2 *Antecedents of Military Antipolitics*

Instability, Violence, and the Age of the Caudillos

The roots of the antipolitical military regimes of the 1960s, 1970s, and 1980s stretch far back into Iberian and colonial Latin American history. There exists a plethora of theories about and explanations for the form of Spanish colonial government and for the rise of the caudillos in the nineteenth century. One of the most popular, particularly as developed by Américo Castro, holds that the Spanish, and consequently the republican, mentality was decisively shaped by the *Reconquista* experience: El Cid and the warrior priest. Others have pointed to the institutional contributions of the highly developed Amerindian civilizations and particularly to the submissiveness of the lower orders present in Aztec, Maya, and Inca cultures. Still others explain the rise of the caudillos and the political chaos of the nineteenth century in terms of the heritage from the Spanish conquistadores.[1]

More important for the study of antipolitics, however, is the approach adopted by Professor Richard W. Morse in his classic essay "Toward a Theory of Spanish American Government."[2] Morse points to the dualism and philosophical polarization present in Spanish thought. On the one hand, there was the medieval Thomistic philosophy embodied in the *Siete Partidas* (the basic source of Spanish law during this period) and practiced by Queen Isabella. The *Siete Partidas*, according to Morse, "assumed the nuclear element of society to be, not Lockean atomistic man, but religious societal man: man with a salvable soul (that is, in relationship with God) and man in a station of life (that is, having mutual obligations with fellow humans, determinable by principles of Christian justice). The ruler, though not procedurally responsible to the people or the estates, was bound through his conscience to be the instrument of God's immutable, publicly ascertainable law."[3]

Isabella's husband, Ferdinand, on the other hand, by virtue of the nature of the Aragon Empire, with such diverse components as the Balearic

Islands, Sardinia, Sicily, and Naples, was forced to adopt a strikingly different political philosophy for his regime. As Morse notes:

Ferdinand was committed to the shifting, amoral statecraft of competing Christian princes in maintenance and expansion of a domain which, within its Christian context, was diversely composed. Ferdinand ruled under transitional conditions which precluded resorting for authority to Isabella's Thomistic sanction or to statist apologetics. Managing with sheer personal verve and cunning, he was, in the fullest sense, Machiavellian.[4]

Thus, Spanish colonial government had from the outset a "dual heritage: medieval and Renaissance, Thomistic and Machiavellian." The role of the king in this colonial system was crucial, for he was the ultimate unifying symbol. As Morse states:

The king, even though he might be an inarticulate near-imbecile like Charles II, was symbolic throughout his realm as the guarantor of status. In Thomistic idiom, all parts of the society were ordered to the whole as the imperfect to the perfect. This ordering, inherently the responsibility of the whole multitude, devolved upon the king as a public person acting in their behalf, for the task of ordering to a given end fell to the agent best placed and fitted for the specific function.[5]

The stated objectives of this system—order, obedience (both to God and king), authority, and stability—are in many respects identical to those of the caudillos and of the later military regimes. However, the system was fragile, relying almost entirely for its continuance on subject loyalty to the crown.

Napoleon Bonaparte's invasion of Spain in 1808, the placing of his brother Joseph on the throne, and the subsequent criollo revolts in the colonies all had the effect of destroying the delicate political equilibrium. Gone was the supreme moral force provided by the crown, and the subsequent power struggles that emerged represented efforts to find a new basis for political order. For a time, the great liberators, such as Simón Bolívar and José de San Martín, served as surrogate kings, but with the end of the wars, the liberators either retired from the political arena or were forcibly ejected.

In the early nineteenth century, criollo leaders attempted to rule by applying the new, alien concepts of constitutionalism and liberalism, but they failed to stem the tide of personalism and localism which swept the land. "With the breakdown of the moral authority of the crown, lawlessness became widespread and was overcome not necessarily by a substitute moral authority, but rather by the personal magnetism of a given charismatic leader. Personalism rather than principle tended to prevail."[6]

Argentina's first president, Bernardino Rivadavia, summed this up best when he wrote in 1830:

In my opinion what retards regular and stable advance in those republics stems from the vacillations and doubts that deprive all institutions of that moral force which is indispensable to them and can be given only by conviction and decision. It is evident to me, and would be easy to demonstrate, that the upheavals of our country spring much more immediately from lack of public spirit and of cooperation among responsible men in sustaining order and laws than from attacks of ungovernable, ambitious persons without merit or fitness and of indolent coveters.[7]

This leadership crisis was further compounded when most upper-class criollos also withdrew from the active direction of their newly created nations and returned to their great landed estates. The absence of these men created a tremendous vacuum, not only political but also military and moral. The old Thomistic order was truncated and replaced by a new order ruled not by statesmen or professional soldiers, but by prototypical Machiavellian leaders—the caudillos. For fifty years, the caudillos, with varying degrees of success, attempted to fill the vacuum caused by the lack of effective, legitimate political institutions—an attempt which invites comparison with today's military antipoliticians.

The nineteenth-century caudillo, whether Juan Manuel de Rosas, in Argentina, Ramón Castilla, in Peru, Andrés de Santa Cruz, in Bolivia, or Rafael Carrera, in Guatemala, had much in common with twentieth-century military elites, despite a lack of professional credentials. Neither the caudillo nor today's professional soldier is committed to political movements or interests based on traditional ideological questions of liberal or conservative, left or right. Both caudillos and professional soldiers usually justify their rule in nationalist terms of saving and maintaining the fatherland, although this appears more frequently among the latter than the former. Neither the caudillo nor today's professional soldier tolerates dissent, much less formal opposition, and both react quickly to stifle it. Finally, both the caudillo and the professional soldier employ force as the basis for their political rule.

But there are important differences as well. The professional soldier stresses military education, strict obedience to a hierarchical authority, and submission of personal desires to the well-being of the military institution and the nation. The caudillo, on the other hand, was highly individualistic and hated all laws and authority except his own. The professional soldier, then, adopts many of the precepts of the Thomistic tradition, while the caudillo opts instead for an extreme form of atomism.

The adjectives employed to describe the caudillo are as varied as they are colorful: crude, vulgar, barbaric, cruel, daring, sadistic, strong, fearless, and illiterate. As Domingo Sarmiento noted about the Argentine caudillo Juan Facundo Quiroga, his was a type of "primitive barbarism" which knew no bounds or restraints. The caudillo relied not only upon force to maintain his power, but also, more importantly, on his charisma and his unfailing ability to dominate those around him.

In contrast to the nationalistic professional soldier, most caudillos were committed only to a locality or a region. They possessed a limited sense of nationalism, and when a caudillo did become president of his nation, he still thought in regional terms, often seeking to dominate only the capital city. He ruled the remainder of his country through a rather loose alliance with other regional caudillos or *caciques*. As Hugh Hamill puts it: "Given geographic isolation and the vastness of the region, the scattered power nuclei, controlled by *caciques,* were fundamental to the emergence of a national caudillo. Whereas a *cacique* is a ruler among men, a caudillo is a ruler among *caciques*."[8] The success of his rule depended upon personalism and charisma, not on institutions. Thus, there was little or no institutional development in the period, be it in the civilian political arena or in the military sector.

During the Wars of Independence, the officer corps were drawn principally from the upper classes. After the wars they withdrew and were replaced by men of much lower social status for whom, in the words of Edwin Lieuwen, "an army career provided the opportunity to break through the arbitrary restrictions of the old social order, to shoot one's way into a share of the power, wealth, and social prestige enjoyed by the landed oligarchy and the church hierarchy."[9] Thus the upper classes lost effective control over the military establishments which, in conjunction with regional civilian caudillos, became the arbiters in what amounted to a political system of chaos.

These so-called national armies had almost nothing in common with today's Latin American military establishments. The officers and men alike were ill trained and poorly equipped. As John Johnson has noted, the service academies which did exist were poorly organized, and attendance was not a prerequisite for professional advancement. Moreover, neither the cadets in the academies nor the enlisted men in the ranks were taught any skill that might be of use in national development, despite the fact that the various militaries consumed over half of their nations' yearly budgets.[10] In addition to being poorly trained and equipped, the enlisted men never felt part of a nation or a national institution. What loyalty they did feel was to their commander, who in turn was loyal only to himself or to another caudillo.

Although the creation of the Latin American nations was to a large extent a military achievement, in many cases it was only through the ventures of nationalistic caudillos that the territorial units of Latin America were forged and maintained against European as well as Latin American enemies. As the age of caudillos gave way to that of civilian politics, the successors of the caudillos— the professional military—often saw in the venality and incapacity of civilian elites a betrayal of nations which the military had founded.

In contrast, these modern-day military officers view with respect the regimes of the great caudillos in their nations' past. Not only did the caudillos shape and defend the fatherland, but they also did it with firmness (even violence) and with dedication. They alone prevented the national disintegration which would have resulted from "politics." In short, they successfully applied the politics of antipolitics and in so doing served as vital links between traditional Hispanic politics and the antipolitical military regimes of today.

One of the best known and most successful of all Latin American caudillos was the Argentine strongman Juan Manuel de Rosas. Breaking with his family at an early age, Rosas went to the interior, where he soon gained fame for his daring and skill as a gaucho. He became wealthy in cattle ranching and later expanded into the complementary businesses of salt and slaughter houses. In 1829, he was appointed governor of Buenos Aires province and charged with ending the chaos created by the politicians of the legislature. His solution was as efficient as it was prototypical of *caudillismo*—the carrot or the stick. Rosas totally dominated Buenos Aires province but allowed the regional caudillos to retain control of their respective provinces in return for their absolute loyalty to him. Recalcitrant caudillos were dealt with quickly and severely.

In the early years of his rule, Rosas was enormously popular with all strata of the population. The upper-class ranchers supported him because he had restored internal order and because he emphasized the cattle industry in his economic policies. The lower classes admired his prowess as a gaucho and responded to his tremendous charisma. In 1832, Rosas stepped down as governor and went south with his army to fight the Indians. He succeeded in pushing them almost to Patagonia, thereby adding to his reputation as a fierce warrior. He increased his support among the great ranchers (*estancieros*) by distributing to them the newly opened Indian lands.

The period 1832–35 saw Argentina slip back into the chaos that had been characteristic of "politics" before. Finally, in 1835, after much pleading and a rigged plebiscite, Rosas agreed to accept the governorship again. He quickly reestablished internal order, whipped the regional caudillos back into line, and repressed all opposition. Rosas tolerated no dissent, and those who dared challenge him were either jailed, exiled, or killed, while thousands more fled into voluntary exile. Even the Catholic church was brought into line and forced to hang Rosas's portrait next to the altars in the churches. His was a regime of terror and personalist rule. Argentina was not a true nation, rather a series of provinces held together by the power and charisma of the dictator. Still, it did survive as an entity as it might not have under the rule of "politics."

Rosas sought to rule his neighbors as he did his gauchos. He refused to accept the independence of Uruguay or even of Paraguay and was constantly meddling in the internal affairs of the former. He declared war on his Bolivian counterpart Andrés de Santa Cruz in 1837 in an effort to prevent Santa Cruz from uniting Bolivia and Peru into a strong confederation. He also successfully defended his regime and Argentina from attack by Europeans. In 1838, the French captured Martín García Island and instituted a blockade which lasted until 1840. In 1845, the French returned, this time with the British, and blockaded the entire Río de la Plata estuary. Although the blockades caused severe economic dislocations in Argentina, Rosas held out and forced the two powers to withdraw by 1848.

In 1851, Rosas sought to renew his pact with the regional caudillos, but this time his long-time supporter Justo José Urquiza, the strongman of Entre Ríos province, declared against him. Urquiza succeeded in winning over the other caudillos, in addition to getting support from both Uruguay and Brazil, and defeated Rosas's army in 1852.

Rosas had ruled for almost a quarter of a century, but his sudden defeat is indicative of the fragility of the caudillo system. Nevertheless, Rosas did establish internal order (despite the high social and political costs), and he did defend the nation against both South American and European challengers. In contrast to the weak, corrupt, and inept civilian regimes which followed, the nationalism of the Rosas regime was viewed favorably by subsequent military officers.

In Peru, one finds much the same political situation in the years following independence as that which existed in Argentina. In 1826, Simón Bolívar departed Peru, leaving behind a constitution and a caretaker government headed by Andrés de Santa Cruz. Both were overthrown in 1827, and for the next seventeen years Peru was in almost constant chaos. The principals were military caudillos, veterans of the independence wars, who traded the presidency back and forth by means of *golpes* and counter *golpes*.

Finally, in 1845, Ramón Castilla assumed the presidency for the first time (he served two terms, 1845–51 and 1855–60) and initiated an era of economic prosperity, military preparedness, and political order. He was so successful that he ranks first in the pantheon of Peruvian heroes and is revered by the military today for his honesty, patriotism, and firm commitment to national defense.

Castilla was a mestizo with relatively unsophisticated manners, and this contributed to his popularity with the lower classes. Like most caudillos, he had led an active and eventful life, serving on both sides in the Wars of Independence, being captured and taken to Buenos Aires, escaping and walking back to Peru across South America. He was daring, resourceful, and charismatic.

Upon taking office he faced the monumental task of restoring internal order, both politically and militarily. He quickly suppressed the bandit bands which had flourished between Lima and Callao and on the coastal highway to the north. He ended the political strife between Liberals and Conservatives by using both but joining neither. He used the revenues from guano exploitation to promote business and regularize the economy and the civil service, thereby inaugurating an era of unprecedented prosperity. He built the first railroad in South America, wrote the Constitution of 1860, which lasted for sixty years (longer than any other before or since), and sought to instill a new patriotism in the young nation. Like Rosas, Castilla used the carrot-and-stick technique with opponents, but he did so in a much less violent fashion. He neither executed nor jailed his enemies; rather he sent them into exile with the understanding that they could return under very favorable circumstances anytime they decided to cooperate. In this way he avoided making any really dangerous enemies. Finally, he subdued the various regional military leaders and centralized the military command structure.

More than anyone else in the nineteenth century, Castilla was responsible for the creation of a national military force, stating that: "Our military forces are not the instrument of tyranny or the enemies of society. . . . Imbued with a sense of the importance of their noble destiny, they are the conservers of the public tranquillity, the custodians of external and internal peace, and the loyal defenders of the constitution and the laws."[11]

Castilla greatly increased the size of the army, reopened the military academy, and purchased modern armaments. He also concentrated on improving and expanding the navy and built it into the most powerful naval force on the west coast of South America. His long-remembered thesis was that if Chile bought one ship, Peru should buy two. The fact that a civilian president, Manuel Pardo, canceled an order for two warships, which were subsequently purchased and used by Chile in the War of the Pacific (1879–83), provided added weight to Castilla's judgment, a judgment which has become an almost religious principle among today's professional soldiers in Peru.

Castilla is also remembered for his success in foreign affairs and in defense of the national boundaries. He was among the leaders of the opposition to the abortive attempt by Spain to retake Ecuador in 1845. He was also an outspoken critic of the United States's aggression against Mexico, and he sought to create a united Latin American front against the Colossus of the North. In 1859, Castilla attacked Guayaquil, Ecuador, in retaliation for the Ecuadorian government's attempt to placate European creditors by ceding them land claimed by Peru.

Finally, in 1865, Castilla, though no longer president, was the first to denounce the Vivanco-Pareja Treaty between Spain and Peru as being insulting to the national honor. The treaty was aimed at ending Spanish occupation of Peru's principal guano deposits on the Chincha Islands, which had been seized by the Spanish fleet some months earlier. What incensed Castilla was that Peru agreed to pay not only Spanish claims dating back to the War for Independence, but also the cost of the Spanish occupation of the Chinchas.

Thus, from a military point of view, Castilla stands as one of the greatest leaders in Peruvian history. He established internal order, brought about economic prosperity, enlarged and improved the armed forces, assumed a leadership role for Peru in foreign affairs (including challenging the United States), and vigorously defended the national boundaries against both South American and European opponents. If one compares Castilla with subsequent civilian presidents, both in the nineteenth and twentieth centuries, one might conclude, as have thousands of Peruvian military officers, that what Peru needs is not civilian "politics," but the antipolitics of Ramón Castilla.

Bolivia suffered a bewildering succession of caudillo presidents in the nineteenth century, a situation which continued to plague her in the twentieth. As with Castilla in Peru, however, one caudillo, Andrés de Santa Cruz, stands above all in terms of leadership and national vision. Born in 1794, Santa Cruz, like Castilla, was a mestizo and initially fought with the royalist forces in the Wars for Independence, later joining the rebels. Santa Cruz was an outstanding military commander, who quickly gained the attention of Simón Bolívar. In 1826, Bolívar appointed him provisional president of Peru, but he was overthrown one year later. He went to Bolivia, where he assumed the presidency in 1829 and held it until 1839.

It is generally agreed that Santa Cruz was the best president that Bolivia has ever had. His ten-year term not only was one of the few stable periods in Bolivian history, but also was characterized by its economic productivity. Santa Cruz was an honest and capable administrator who sought to complete the nation-building task begun by Antonio José de Sucre.

He first established internal order by ending the incessant feuding between factions in the military and in the civilian political arena. He organized the Bolivian national army and the national police force—the *Carabineros*. He founded trade and art schools, as well as the two major universities, in La Paz and Cochabamba. Moreover, he reorganized the judiciary, improved the economic state of the nation, and took the first steps to alleviate the educational and economic plight of the great mass of illiterate, non-Spanish-speaking Indians.

His fatal flaw was one common to many caudillos of the age—an all-consuming ambition, which in his case took the form of redrawing the map of South America. His dream was to combine Peru and Bolivia into one great nation ruled by himself, and he did in fact succeed in creating the Peru-Bolivian Confederation, which lasted from 1836 to 1839. Such a confederation, however logical from either an economic or geographic standpoint, upset the balance of power in South America, and thus provoked the wrath of Rosas, in Argentina, and Diego Portales, in Chile.

Defeated in battle in 1839, Santa Cruz returned to Bolivia, where he was deposed as president and sent into exile. Though he failed in his grand scheme of confederation, Santa Cruz deserves credit for having organized the various components of the Bolivian state. To present-day Bolivians, the ambitions, dreams, and deeds of Santa Cruz compare favorably to the tragicomedy of Bolivian politics in the twentieth century. And like their counterparts in Argentina and Peru, Bolivian military officers look back on their great caudillo with pride and admiration.

Several thousand miles to the north, in Central America, a remarkably similar scene was being played out. By 1835, the United Provinces of Central America, launched in 1823 with dreams of achieving Central American unity, was in ruins. As with the confederations of Gran Colombia and Peru-Bolivia, the seeds of disunity and destruction had been sown centuries earlier by the structure of Spanish colonialism, seeds which sprouted anew in the Liberal-Conservative conflicts of the late colonial and early independence periods.

Ideological divisions between Liberals and Conservatives in Guatemala and the rest of Central America differed little from those prevalent in the rest of Latin America. Conservatives, for the most part, wanted a strong centralized government with traditional ties to the Catholic Church, that is, a continuation of the Hispanic tradition. Liberals, on the other hand, intermittently held sway in some of the provinces and looked favorably upon a United States–type model of federation. Most Liberals also sought to curb the influence of the Church and move toward the establishment of a more secular state.[12]

Although the Liberals and their leader Manuel José Arce had controlled the federation since its inception, Conservatives never accepted the legitimacy of their rule. Constant infighting and skirmishing finally erupted in a bloody civil war in 1826. By 1829, the Liberals and their new leader, Francisco Morazán, had overcome the Conservative forces and immediately embarked upon a program of far-reaching change. These reforms all but guaranteed the outbreak of a new civil war. As Ralph Lee Woodward has written, "The grassroots reaction against the Liberals was especially violent against foreign elements and against efforts to change traditional lifestyles and patterns of rural life."[13]

Convinced that the economic and political backwardness of their region was the direct result of Hispanic culture, institutions, economic models, land tenure patterns, and legislation, Morazán and the Guatemalan governor, Mariano Gálvez, along with their Liberal allies, sought to emulate the Lockean tradition of England and the United States, a tradition which proved totally antagonistic to the communal tradition of the region's Indian peoples and to the power of the Church and of many colonial elites.

Like their Andean counterparts, José de San Martín and Simón Bolívar, the Liberals of Central America held a rather simplistic view of the "Indian problem" and rural land tenure structures. Imbued with the ideals of the French Revolution and of Thomas Jefferson, they not only misunderstood Indian culture, but also mistakenly assumed that communal landholdings necessarily inhibited economic development and limited agricultural production.[14] Their solution was the parcelization of communal lands and the granting of individual land titles to Indians. Almost everywhere these types of proposals led to massive appropriation of communal lands by nearby haciendas and other favored beneficiaries at the expense of Indian peasants.

Peasant anger over this Liberal land "redistribution" was exacerbated by government policies which encouraged and supported foreign colonization projects in sparsely populated regions. The Liberals, on the other hand, felt that lumber and agricultural concessions to foreigners, primarily British, would provide a much-needed impetus to modernization and economic progress.

Liberal attitudes toward the Catholic Church and education further inflamed the antagonism of many Indian and rural groups. Not only were most peasants deeply religious, but they also had tremendous respect, even adoration, for many local priests who were thus able to rally them against the government, particularly after a cholera epidemic swept the region in 1837. In time-honored fashion, the Church preached that the cholera was God's retribution for Liberal anticlericalism. Likewise, Liberal attempts to destroy Indian culture through mass-education programs, including the removal of children from their parents, provoked additional anger.

Added to this were Liberal policies which established a head tax [reminiscent of the old Spanish Indian tribute] and a labor draft for the construction of roads (reminiscent of the variety of Spanish forced labor systems during the colonial period). Both fell heaviest on the rural masses.

Out of this milieu emerged José Rafael Carrera, the greatest of the mid-nineteenth-century Central American caudillos. Born in 1814 to a family of very modest means, Carrera has been variously characterized as "an illiterate Guatemalan Indian," a "primitive," and a "religious fanatic of strong will and messianic aspirations."[15] In fact, Carrera was a *ladino* who received no formal education, served briefly in the army as a youth, and then moved to the countryside where he married and settled down to raise pigs. In 1837, he joined the rebellion against the Liberals and organized a peasant guerrilla army, quickly gaining fame for "fearlessly leading his forces in fanatical charges against troops with better arms and training."[16] After heavy fighting, Carrera's peasant forces entered Guatemala City in January 1838 and overthrew Gálvez. Throughout 1838, chaos reigned in Guatemala as Conservatives and Liberals continued to fight and the United Provinces of Central America collapsed. Finally, in early 1840, Carrèra routed the Liberal forces and took control of the nation. For the first four years, 1840–44, Carrera controlled the government through the army; in 1844, he assumed the presidency, which he held, with a brief interlude (1849–51), until his death in 1865.

Like Rosas in Argentina, Carrera possessed an enormous ego and often compared himself to Napoleon Bonaparte. He was also an astute politician who skillfully played Liberals and Conservatives against each other. His lower-class origins, mixed ancestry, and fame as a warrior made him immensely popular with the masses. Although rejected initially by the elites, Carrera's increasing commitment to Conservative ideals and his ability to maintain internal order ultimately won him much upper-class support as well.

Under his long regime, most of the Liberal policies were reversed or abandoned. He centralized all government operations in his hands, restored to the Church its confiscated lands, the tithe, and control of education, abolished the head tax, reinstated the colonial land tenure system, and abandoned the Liberal's attempts to Westernize the Indians and integrate them into "national" life. Moreover, Carrera sought to create a national, professional military and to foster economic growth through subsidies, tariffs, and the reactivation of the old colonial Economic Society.

Carrera also took steps to monitor and control foreigners in the country and in general adopted a highly nationalistic stance. This nationalism was most evident in his active participation to oust the filibustering William Walker from Nicaragua, an act similar to the role of Rosas against European invaders in Argentina and the role of Castilla in Peru. He also actively intervened in the affairs of his neighbors, as exemplified by the installation of one of his lieutenants, Francisco Malespín, as dictator of El Salvador.

In sum, Carrera consolidated national government in Guatemala, imposed order from the chaos of the early independence period, resisted the incursion of foreign ideas and influence, and made efforts to create a more modern military. He reestablished a centralized political system based on the traditional values of Hispanic society and the blessing of the Catholic Church—a nationalistic government which prided itself on law and order, the carrot and the stick, which would serve as a model for future military leaders of Guatemala.

Unlike Guatemala, El Salvador did not produce one outstanding nineteenth-century caudillo. In the half century from 1821 to 1872, the Liberals held power for twenty-nine years and the Conservatives for twenty-one. The reasons for this were many, but one of the most important was the omnipresence of Carrera in Guatemala. On three separate occasions (1840, 1851, 1863), Carrera intervened openly in El Salvador to dislodge Liberal governments. Nevertheless, partially as a response to Carrera's intervention in El Salvador and the rest of Central America, Liberal caudillos in El Salvador gave rise to a heroic military tradition in the first part of the nineteenth century. Among the most colorful of these, General Gerardo Barrios began his career as a youthful follower of Morazán. During the 1840s and 1850s, after a brief exile in Peru, Barrios fought against the armies of Carrera in Costa Rica, Nicaragua, and El Salvador. In 1858, as interim president, Barrios had the remains of Morazán returned from Costa Rica to El Salvador and during the next seven years challenged Carrera's forces in Central America.

In one of the many losing efforts, Barrios won the everlasting adulation of Salvadoran nationalists with his oft-quoted response to demands for his surrender: "Tell them I will not surrender. I will be buried with my soldiers." Barrios brought Colombian General José María Melo to El Salvador in 1859 to reorganize the army. For the first time, discipline and drill, along with standard uniforms, were introduced. In 1862, a French mission of four officers replaced the Colombians, and the beginnings of a proud military tradition in El Salvador were being forged amongst the struggles of the Central American caudillos.[17]

Seven years later, Barrios was captured in Nicaragua, taken to El Salvador, "tried" by his opponents, and then executed. Carrera himself died only months later, ending the era of early nineteenth-century caudillos in the region. In El Salvador, however, the memory of Barrios lives among the nation's twentieth-century military leaders, including those like Oscar Osorio, who initiated the era of modernizing military regimes in the late 1940s. In 1949, El Salvador's military government commemorated the anniversary of Captain General Gerardo Barrios's death with a homage and erection of a statue which would be "a model for all Salvadorans who aspire to ennoble the fatherland, with sword, struggle, and deeds."[18]

Both Carrera and Barrios must be viewed in national as well as regional terms. For the embattled military officers in Central America of the 1980s, José Rafael Carrera and Gerardo Barrios embody the virtues of patriotism, honor, courage, military discipline, and economic development which they seek to impose upon their societies today—conflicting in their view, with the malevolent forces of "politics," venality, and subversion which threaten the fatherland. In these circumstances, as the military leaders make clear, it is their sacred duty to save *la patria* from disorder and destruction.

The nineteenth-century political experiences of both Brazil and Chile stand in sharp contrast to those of Argentina, Peru, Bolivia, and Central America. Unlike the Spanish American republics, Brazil was spared the violence, bloodshed, political chaos, and economic dislocation of a struggle for independence. Instead, Emperor Pedro I abdicated in favor of his son, and the transition was a smooth one. From 1831 to 1889, Pedro II ruled Brazil peacefully, and therefore the Brazilian military establishment developed out of a totally different milieu.

As outlined in the introductory essay, the age of the caudillo was extremely short-lived in Chile, being replaced after 1830 with a highly centralized, autocratic republic which maintained internal order and greatly expanded the economy of the nation, but which tolerated no opposition or dissent. Thus, Chile also avoided the economic and political chaos associated with the age of the caudillos.

In most of Latin America, the age of *caudillismo* gradually came to an end after 1870. National economies demanded national policy making. National policy making implied effective national leadership, which in many cases meant the dominance of a truly national caudillo like Porfirio Díaz, in Mexico. In other cases, such as Chile and Argentina, national political institutions developed which allowed legal transfers of power and implementation of public policy through national administrative agencies.

A key to the formation of real nation states was the emergence of national military institutions. Control of national politics required the reorganization, modernization, and professionalization of the national military establishments, which in turn meant the destruction of the old regional and personalist armies. This professionalization process did not mark an end to the military as political elites, but rather to the formation of a new national military-political elite to replace the regionalistic caudillo commanders. Latin America and Latin American military officers in particular had begun the slow road back to what Morse has called the Thomistic tradition, a road which was to culminate in the military antipolitics of the 1960s, 1970s, and 1980s.

Notes

1. For a succinct discussion of these and other causal factors, see the Introduction by Hugh M. Hamill, Jr., in his *Dictatorship in Spanish America* (New York: Alfred A. Knopf, 1965), pp. 3–25.
2. Originally published in the *Journal of the History of Ideas* 15 (1954),

pp. 71–93, the essay was reprinted in abridged form in Hamill, *Dictatorship*, pp. 52–68. All citations are from the latter.

3. Morse, "Toward a Theory," pp. 53–54.

4. Ibid., pp. 54–55.

5. Ibid., p. 56.

6. Hamill, *Dictatorship*, p. 21.

7. Quoted in Morse, "Toward a Theory," p. 60.

8. Hamill, *Dictatorship*, p. 11.

9. Edwin Lieuwen, *Arms and Politics in Latin America*, rev. ed. (New York: Frederick A. Praeger, 1961), pp. 19–20.

10. John J. Johnson, *The Military and Society in Latin America* (Stanford, Calif.: Stanford University Press, 1964), pp. 50, 53.

11. Quoted in Fredrick B. Pike, *The Modern History of Peru* (New York: Frederick A. Praeger, 1967), p. 92.

12. For a cogent description and analysis of Liberal-Conservative conflict in Central America in the early nineteenth century, see Ralph Lee Woodward, Jr., *Central America: A Nation Divided*, 2d ed. (New York: Oxford University Press, 1985), pp. 92–119.

13. Ibid., p. 99.

14. See Thomas M. Davies, Jr., *Indian Integration in Peru: A Half Century of Experience, 1900–1948* (Lincoln: University of Nebraska Press, 1974), pp. 19–23; and ibid., pp. 100–101.

15. Howard I. Blutstein et al., *El Salvador: A Country Study* (Washington, D.C.: American University, 1979), p. 12; John Edwin Fagg, *Latin America: A General History*, 3d ed. (New York: Macmillan Publishing Co., 1977), p. 411; and Richard F. Nyrop, ed., *Guatemala: A Country Study* (Washington, D.C.: U.S. Government Printing Office, 1983), p. 16.

16. Woodward, *Central America*, p. 105.

17. See Pedro Zamora Castellanos, *Vida Militar de Centro América*, 2d ed., 2 vols., 1967, 2:193–205.

18. *Diario Oficial*. San Salvador, 29 August 1949, 147, no. 188, p. 3011.

The Latin American Nation State and the Creation of Professional Military Establishments

One of the great illusions in post–World War II thought on Latin American development was the hope that the Latin American military establishments would be professionalized, thereby ending their periodic intervention into national politics. North American observers in particular equated military professionalism and professionalization with apolitical military establishments. In practice, however, military professionalization in the Latin American milieu actually accelerated institutional and officer involvement in the political arena.

This result surprised many North American and European specialists on Latin America. To a great extent, their surprise stemmed from a misreading of the history of Latin American military professionalization during the latter part of the nineteenth and early part of the twentieth centuries, as well as of the quality and direction of this professionalization after World War II. In contrast to what North Americans expected, the introduction of professional training, organization, and staffing of Latin American military establishments by European training missions led to the creation of political as well as military elites. Indeed, key political actors in the first three decades of the twentieth century were graduates of the German or French military professionalization programs or later of the programs run by German-trained Chilean personnel. Examples are Carlos Ibáñez in Chile, José F. Uriburu in Argentina, Luis M. Sánchez Cerro in Peru, and Leitão de Carvalho in Brazil.

In the first selection of part 2, Frederick Nunn presents an overview of the effects of European military training missions in Latin America around the turn of the century. Nunn concludes: "The overriding impact of fifty years of European military training or orientation on Latin American armies was to stimulate rather than lessen political interest and to motivate elitist, professional army officers to assume responsibility for the conduct of national affairs."

Marvin Goldwert's discussion of the rise of modern militarism in Argentina supports many of Nunn's generalizations concerning the effects of professionalization while at the same time providing a historical background to the role of the military in Argentine politics. As Goldwert notes: "For those who believe that military professionalization is an antidote to militarism, the Argentine case offers serious doubts."

In the third selection, Warren Schiff analyzes the influence of the German training missions and war industry on Argentina, including the military socialization of José F. Uriburu, who led a successful military coup in 1930. Uriburu's career—a top graduate of the Argentine War Academy in 1902, service with the Imperial Guard in Germany, and director of the War Academy from 1907 to 1913—made him a model professional officer and a highly political one. As Schiff concludes, the German military instructors left a deep impression on the increasingly influential officer corps, an impression which hardly depoliticized the Argentine military.

Frederick Nunn reviews the "Prussianization" of the Chilean army. In Chile, the German military mission actually participated in the Chilean Civil War of 1891, helping to oust constitutionally elected president José Manuel Balmaceda. As in Argentina, the products of German professionalization programs (men such as Carlos Ibáñez, Juan Pablo Bennett, Marmaduke Grove, and Bartolomé Blanche) were hardly apolitical and significantly influenced Chilean national politics in the 1920s and later.

As in Chile, the beginnings of military professionalization in Peru followed Chile's victory against Peru and Bolivia in the War of the Pacific (1879–83). Former Peruvian army officer Víctor Villanueva describes late nineteenth-century developments in Peru, the role of the French military mission in professionalizing the Peruvian military, and the impact of professionalization on the political activities of army officers.

Bolivian military professionalization in the early twentieth century had the benefit of both French and German training missions. The documents transcribed and edited from the State Department Serial Files on Bolivia make clear how the German military mission, and particularly its leader Major Hans Kundt, affected Bolivian national politics. From 1912 into the 1930s, with only brief absences from Bolivia, Major Kundt, whose official charge was to professionalize the Bolivian armed forces, became the arbiter of Bolivian politics.

In Brazil, the influence of European military training missions before World War II was slight. Nevertheless, the move toward professionalization of the Brazilian military played a significant political role in the late nineteenth and early twentieth centuries. As in Argentina, Chile, Peru, and Bolivia, professionalization in Brazil meant the development of a politicized, anticivilian military elite anxious to "cleanse" the Brazilian polity and lead Brazil to continental hegemony. Frank McCann traces the evolution of the professionalization and concomitant politicization of the Brazilian military in the late nineteenth and early twentieth centuries.

In Central America, European military missions and the process of military professionalization occurred somewhat later, as liberal and conservative caudillos led conflicting armies throughout the region during most of the nineteenth century. In Guatemala, where no systematic study of the European military missions has yet been completed, Spanish officers helped to create the Escuela Politécnica in the early 1870s and continued to provide staff for the military school into the 1880s. Later, French officers served as advisers to the army and, after World War I, the air corps. Although the small French mission remained the dominant influence in the Guatemalan military schools, Guatemalan officers also attended Spanish military institutions during the 1920s, and a small number were sent to the United States. In the 1930s, United States officers replaced the French and Spanish influence; American officers were also designated to head the country's military academy.

Development of foreign and European influence in the military institutions of El Salvador began even earlier than in Guatemala. As Robert Elam indicates, Colombian, Spanish, French, and Chilean officers (the latter trained by Germans) all contributed to El Salvador's military tradition—and to the central role military officers and the military institutions have played in Salvadoran politics. Generals ruled the country from 1887 to 1903; professionalization in the first decades of the twentieth century set the stage for development of one of the most politicized military institutions in Latin America from the 1930s until the present.

Taken together, these descriptions and analyses of military professionalization in Latin America in the late nineteenth and early twentieth centuries suggest that, instead of creating an apolitical military, professionalization actually produced a politicized officer corps, with its own ideology of modernization, industrialization, corporate elitism, nationalism, and antipolitics.

Frederick M. Nunn

An Overview of the European Military Missions in Latin America

The presence of military organizations in Latin American politics is a reality of the twentieth century just as it was of the past. Scholars are in unison on this point but disagree on the reasons for the behavior and political outlook of twentieth-century political officers. Obviously "changing times," nationalism, and middle-class origins of officers are insufficient causes for the nationalist, reformist-authoritarian strain of contemporary military attitudes in Latin America.

One of the most important causes for the development of contemporary Latin American military attitudes toward state, nation, and society is the creation of a professional army officers corps undertaken late in the last century and early in this century by the more advanced countries and by some of the lesser republics as well. Military professionalization was undertaken in Latin America for a variety of reasons, depending on time and place. In those countries where pre–World War II professionalization was guided by Europeans—French and Germans, chiefly—it resulted in the creation of a powerful political interest group. That group, the officers corps, completed the laying of the foundations for professional militarism. And professional militarism in Latin American countries where French and German officers served wears the indelible stamp of their presence. It is the purpose of this essay to point out the significance of that presence.

For some time now we have assumed that military professionalization did not achieve the desired results—that is, depoliticization—in Latin America because of such endemic factors as fiscal problems, weak economies, political conflict, and social change. But endemic factors may be the least important reason for the failure of professionalization to preclude political activities by the military in Latin America. The overriding impact of fifty years of European military training or orientation on Latin American armies was to stimulate rather than lessen political interest and to motivate elitist, professional army officers to assume responsibility for the conduct of national affairs. This is by no means a monocausal interpretation; it is, rather, an additional explanation for military interest in Latin American politics.

Abstention from politics, then, did not result from professional training. What did develop first was a state that can be called military professionalism, and more. For the end of military professionalism—expertise, corporateness or sense of career, and responsibility—in Latin America during the age of modernization was professional militarism: a set of attitudes that may result in the resort to political action in an attempt to find solutions for social and economic distresses by methods based on a military ethos.

A careful historical examination of the professional armies selected by Latin American military leaders and statesmen to be models for their own armies indicates that they in fact were highly political. The French and German armies were highly political, not in the sense that they intervened in the affairs of the state time and time again, but in the sense that they were professions, corporate entities, immune in theory but not in practice from civilian meddling. And they were loyal to the state and the nation more than to a specific government or administration. They were vital and potent ingredients of the political process in France and Germany at the same time they were involved in the training of Latin America's armies.

Although the histories of the German and French armies from 1871 to 1914, and then from 1918 to about 1940, are those of a high degree of professionalism, they are also histories in which partisan political issues were of vital importance to the military profession per se. To review the Dreyfus Affair, the Catholic-Radical-Masonic conflict, and the catastrophe of 1914–15 in France, or the German army and the empire, . . . and the rise of Nazism would be redundant here. History has yet to record more politicized armies than those of pre–World War II France and Germany.

It can be tentatively posited that Latin Americans who learned their military science in the classroom, in war games, and on maneuvers learned other things from their mentors. If the French and Germans were exemplary in a professional way, they cannot have been less exemplary in an extraprofessional way.

European military influences—professional and extraprofessional—were most keenly felt in South America, where the military buildup was a facet of traditional international rivalries on the one hand and a component of the overall modernization process on the other between 1890 and 1940. By 1914 German missions and individual instructors were training the armies of Argentina, Bolivia, and Chile. Chileans, who had studied under the retired German Captain Emil Körner (who rose to the rank of general in Chile) and his cohorts, in turn laid the foundations for the modern armies of Colombia, Ecuador, and El Salvador. Cadets and young officers from Central America, Venezuela, and Paraguay studied in Santiago. German-trained Argentines were prominent in that country's army by 1914, and students from Bolivia, Paraguay, and Peru came to study in Buenos Aires. Colonel Hans Kundt, probably the best known of all German officers in Latin America, put in several fruitful years prior to 1914 at the military school in La Paz, Bolivia. He would later prepare and lead that country's army to disaster in the Chaco War.

The Peruvian army was under French influence through a series of missions from 1896 until 1940, except for the 1914–18 interim. And, in 1919, a French mission led by General Maurice Gamelin, later chief of the French general staff, was contracted by Brazil. With the exception of those of the countries in the Caribbean area under heavy United States influence, no Latin American army was without an attachment to French or German (and in certain specialized fields, Spanish, Swiss, or Italian) influence during the half century before World War II.

In those countries most heavily influenced by French or German military training the armies were intensely political, in a professional sense and for professional reasons, as early as 1920 and by no later than 1930. Added to the incredible difficulties of shattered economies, disrupted commercial patterns, political disharmony, and social ferment in the interwar years was the rise of the professional military as a political interest group. By the end of 1930, Argentina, Brazil, and Peru were under army-led or created regimes. Chile was entering its sixth year of military-influenced rule. Bolivia was girding for war; so was the French-trained Paraguayan army.

The integrity of the profession and professional expertise were supposed to have been guaranteed through professionalization by consent of civilian authority, but they were not. Thus, members of the professional officer corps in Argentina, Bolivia, Brazil, Chile, Paraguay, and Peru blamed social disorder, economic collapse, and professional shortcomings on civilians and their politics long before the Cold War, Castro, and Che Guevara. And in doing so, they often displayed attitudes assimilated from France and Germany.

Having been Europeanized, they aped their mentors by holding themselves above the rest of society and by considering themselves superior to their non-Europeanized commanders. They were, they believed, models of modernity and members of a truly national institution. We know this is true in Argentina, Brazil, Chile, and Peru. As junior officers in these countries rose to positions of influence, they naturally favored alternate political systems of organizations that might guarantee them the prerequisites for professional progress.

In Chile and Brazil, European orientation had both similar and diverse results. First, French or German training tended to solidify the profession but did not make it monolithic by any means. Second, political motivation and action were tempered to the point where the status of the profession became both causal and inhibitive to flagrant overthrow of a fragile civilian regime or system. Third, both armies were led by elitist officers who believed they represented the only true national institutions—impartial, apolitical (nonpartisan), pure, and morally superior to civilian interest groups. Fourth, virtually all professional shortcomings were blamed on civilians; the "impotent" Old Republic in Brazil and the "irresponsible" Parliamentary Republic in Chile. Fifth, Franco-German professional "differences of opinion" kept political action from taking on a personalist tone: in Chile the appeal of *Ibañismo* was more pronounced among civilians than among military men; in Brazil the officer class spawned no *manda chuva* (military caudillo) after the demise of Marshal Hermes in 1923. There are civilian "corollaries" to each of these assumptions, which should not be overlooked in an overall assessment of civil-military relations.

Among the major Latin American nations (excluding Mexico), Brazil and Chile are among the few held up as exemplary in the field of civil-military relations. Not until 1964 did the Brazilian armed forces, led by the army, actually overthrow a government with the idea of holding on to power. Even then the maintenance of power was debated fiercely within the services for some months. Since 1932 the Chilean army has refrained from such conduct until 1973, and except for isolated movements in 1935, 1938, 1939, 1945–46, 1953–55, and 1969, it has stayed "in the barracks." Here one might tentatively posit that professionalization achieved its objective purposes at least until 1964 in Brazil and until 1973 in Chile. Obviously, the existence or lack of strong national civilian political or socioeconomic groups is significant. But the fact remains that owing heavily to European training and orientation, the armies of these two nations became more capable of being intensely political for professional reasons. The nature of their political action was molded by environment as well, but their propensity for it was, and is, an inheritance based on their early twentieth-century experiences.

This is also the case in Argentina and Peru; but inherited and environmental factors vary, despite apparent similarities. German military training in Argentina, like Chile, was a pre-1914 phenomenon, but there the army was successful in eventually casting off the stigma of Germany's defeat by virtue of having asserted earlier that it was quite capable of continuing the professionalization process on its own. Also, the favored position of the army under Gen. Julio A. Roca (president, 1880–86, 1898–1904), then its politicization at the hands of Hipólito Irigoyen (president, 1916–22, 1928–30), was unequaled at the time in South America.

Argentines perpetuated the outlook of the pre–World War I German officer class themselves, and in a roughly similar milieu. Like their counterparts in Brazil, Chile, and Peru, Argentine military elitists were highly critical of civilian politics, particularly during the Radical Era (1916–30). Unlike their counterparts, the Argentine army officers functioned within a cult of personalism, exaggerated by then extant Latin American professional military standards and akin to personalism à la Seeckt and Hindenberg. Generals Agustin P. Justo and José F. Uriburu represented the politics of military factionalism in the interwar years. Uriburu represented the continuation of German military orientation fused with chauvinistic Argentine and Fascist-elitist ideas. Justo associated himself with the anti-personalist Radical faction. Despite factionalism, though, the military attitude toward civilian politics retained an authoritarian, elitist character in Argentina from World War I through and beyond the Perón years (1943–55).

As early as 1900, war minister Gen. Pablo Riccheri established limitations on foreign (German) penetration of the Argentine army by stating that the army would not copy any European military organization but would instead adapt what best suited its needs. Argentina, he reasoned, was not European, but American. Nevertheless, until 1914, German officers were in charge of the Escuela Superior de Guerra and trained all Argentine staff officers. Instruction, education, tactics, and strategy were German oriented, whereas for fortification techniques, the artillery and engineers depended more heavily on post-1871 French concepts. By 1914, Argentina's staff school instructors and administrators were strident Germanophiles. During this period, the German theory of all-out offense became the principal doctrine of the Argentine army. This, when coupled with professional attitudes toward military needs, soon took the form of army demands made in public for a national program to support mass mobilization (with two fronts always in mind!). When war appeared improbable from 1904 on, this philosophy became a demand for industrialization and economic development, not for the sake of making war but as a prerequisite to overall national greatness.

At the beginning of the twentieth century, Peru, like Argentina and Brazil, was an unintegrated nation. Geographically and socially, Peru was divided, and from the earliest stages of French military indoctrination, the army officer corps looked upon itself as the agency most capable of bringing the country together.

After the War of the Pacific (1879–84) Peru was not only lacking integration and unity, but it was in political and economic collapse. Chile had eclipsed Peru as the leading Pacific power of the continent and had begun the military reform program under German leadership in order to maintain that position "by reason or force"—the motto on the Chilean escutcheon.

Peru's contracting of a mission in 1896, like Argentina's resort to German training, was primarily in response to the Chilean military buildup. The Peruvian government, however, did not look to Germany for assistance, but to France. France had suffered defeat at the hands of the Germans, to be sure, but the reorganization of the French army in the 1880s impressed the decision makers in Lima. Furthermore, the French army, owing to a large number of Catholic and Monarchist officers, was removed (or so it appeared) from politics. French expertise in fortification, frontier defense, and military engineering appealed to Lima. Forswearing any military designs on lost territory, Peru sought to apply French defensive doctrines to her own situation. In 1896, Capt. Paul Clément was appointed a colonel in the Peruvian army and took up his duties as instructor, inspector, and reorganizer. Some seventy-five French officers served in Peru between Clément's arrival and 1940. Until the 1920s, the French had great freedom in reorganizing the Peruvian army, but, as with the Germans in Argentina, held no command positions.

One of the first things Clément called for was a rigid promotion system that would allow only academy graduates to rise above the rank of *subteniente* (second lieutenant). This became law in 1899, but, unfortunately for discipline, was not rigidly applied. Other French-inspired proposals, dating in many cases from 1899, presaged by a half century proposals emanating from the now twenty-three-year-old, elite Centro de Altos Estudios Militares (CAEM). In his report of 1899, for example, Clément noted that frontiers must be accessible from the capital in time of peace as well as war, that internal lines of communication would aid the development of national unity as well as defense. He further stated that regionalism necessitated a flexibility in training, armament, tactics, and strategy, and that the officer class should seek close association with civilians. These are themes reiterated time and again in this century.

Clément also suggested that staff officers serving in the provinces should study the history, economy, politics, and society of their region in order to know all possible in case an emergency arose. "Peru has not one topographic map," he wrote, "not even of the area surrounding Lima. . . . It will be the army's job to supply one." Just above his signature to the seventy-five-page 1899 report are the words, "Throughout the country, one can sense the desire to see the army move ahead along the road to progress and obtain the prestige that corresponds to the military profession." For nearly forty years, Peruvian cadets, staff aspirants, and colonels who attended special advanced courses (which ultimately evolved into CAEM) had a steady dose of such heady stuff.

Neither Clément nor those who came after him were able to make the army immune to political issues and pressures. But because of their pervasive influence there existed no apparent divisions within the officer corps on professional issues, save those emanating from the old versus the young rivalry.

Unlike their Brazilian counterparts, however, Peruvian political officers (Col. Luis Sánchez Cerro, for example) appealed in a personalistic way to civilians as well as army officers. This lasted well into the second half of the twentieth century. Nevertheless, French emphasis on territorial unification and the awareness of having to deal with a large aboriginal population, based on French experiences in Africa and Indochina . . . laid groundwork for the emergence of the technocratic nation builders of the 1960s. In an article published in 1933, Lt. Col. Manuel Moria wrote of the *misión civilizadora* of the army in Peru, where nationhood had yet to flourish. Transportation, communications, education and health programs for Indian conscripts, patriotism, discipline, and national economic development could all be provided by army service and supervised by the officer corps, he concluded.

Early in this century, therefore, Peruvian army officers saw themselves as nation builders in a backward and divided land. Based on published materials in military journals and given the emphasis on French training, it is possible to trace the origins of the present Peruvian *mentalidad militar* ascribed by Víctor Villanueva to French influences. Army officers today readily cite the French emphasis on communications in remote areas, frontier defense, and flexible organization in the provinces as contributory to the assumption of political responsibility. CAEM, which since 1950 has turned out a number of "intellectual officers," is a direct result of French emphasis on continued education for high-ranking officers.

Examined together, Argentina and Peru appear superficially dissimilar rather than similar. But in more detail, the similarities are evident. First, personalism continued in both armies despite professionalization and because of early politicization. In both countries the "military modernization" issue was hotly debated in civilian circles, and much published material exists that is highly critical of the alleged need for a modern military: defense of the profession by civilians did not go unrewarded in times of national crisis.

Second, both Peru and Argentina originally sought European missions out of fear—Chile being the immediate danger, so they thought, from about 1885 until 1905. Once the heavy emphasis on war subsided, though, the profession did not wither. Instead, in both countries the professional army became a political pressure group with its own mission: national integration, education, nationalization of indigenous and immigrant conscripts, and overseer of internal economic development.

Third, the army became hostile to the civilian center-left. In Argentina, some professional officers blamed the Radicals for the lack of military progress towards professionalism, but others were coopted by that party. The end result was the smashing of traditional civilian institutions, perhaps beyond repair. The disenchantment with *Peronismo*-labor politics is a continuance of this attitude in Argentina. In Peru, the army became anti-Aprista, primarily as Luigi Einaudi says, "based on the perception of APRA as 'another unreliable civilian political entity,'" and because of Aprista attempts to subvert military discipline. Finally, the status of the profession tempered political activities less in Argentina and Peru than in Brazil and Chile, as long as European influences were prevalent. As with Brazil and Chile, these conclusions do not stand alone and cannot be separated entirely from civilian influences.

Because of the nature of civilian politics, and owing to the socio-economic dilemma, European-trained Argentines and Peruvians did become political, but apparently less for professional reasons than in Brazil and Chile, until World War II. This may be because of politicization and the fact that civilians sought out military allies and promised them much more in Argentina and Peru than they did in Brazil and Chile. Professional training by Europeans plus the environmental factors helped to make involvement of the profession more a constant in Argentina and Peru than in Brazil and Chile.

The Argentine, Brazilian, Chilean, and Peruvian officers who spent time in France or Germany, and Spain and Italy also, after academy and staff training at home, rose to elite status rapidly upon their return. Uriburu, Klinger, Leitão de Carvalho, the Chileans Bartolomé Blanche and Marmaduke Grove, and Luis Sánchez Cerro owed much to their French and German training.

Marshal José Felix Estigarribia of Paraguay, who directed the Chaco campaign for his country, had studied in Chile and in France at the Ecole Supérieure. Without a doubt his French staff training made him a national figure in remote, backward Paraguay.

In summary, nearly all armies in Latin America were influenced in some ways by European training in the first half of this century. Six of South America's ten countries (Bolivia and Paraguay in addition to those treated herein) had significant military missions or instructors. In Argentina, Brazil, Chile, and Peru the contracting of French or German missions was part of the overall modernization process, continental power politics, and military rivalry. War-making potential was minimal, nevertheless, with the exception of the Bolivia-Paraguay conflict. But the European impact on military activities in other spheres was great. Military professionalism in a developing Latin America was also affected by civilian meddling, financial limitations, human resources, and political instability; but the concept of professional integrity and status was very real. The concept stimulated, rather than precluded, political action in the manner called professional militarism.

Reprinted and edited from *Military Affairs* 39 (February 1975), pp. 1–7.

Marvin Goldwert

The Rise of Modern Militarism in Argentina

The striking characteristic of modern Argentine militarism is that it evolved in one of the most highly professionalized armies in Latin America. For those who believe that military professionalization is an antidote to militarism, the Argentine case offers serious doubts. By professionalization is meant the formation of a technically trained army officer corps comprised of paid career men dedicated solely to professional matters. This objective necessitated the establishment of academies for advanced training in modern methods and weaponry, along with the adoption of objective criteria for promotion based on merit and seniority. Paradoxically, professionalization in Argentina, with its emphasis on strict subordination to civilian authority and dedication to military matters alone, proved to be a necessary condition for the rise of modern militarism.

The process of military professionalization began with President Domingo F. Sarmiento, who in 1869 established the Colegio Militar to train officers for the Argentine army. Sarmiento looked to the formation of a professional army as the answer to the improvised gaucho militias of provincial caudillos who had spread havoc in Argentina during the long conflict between the port and the province of Buenos Aires. After this conflict ended in 1880 with the federalization of the city of Buenos Aires, the national army began to play a new role in Argentine history. It became the praetorian guard of an all-powerful president representing the landed oligarchy. From 1880 to 1886, President Julio A. Roca established the *unicato,* the one-man rule of the president, largely through the use of an army now well equipped with the new Remington rifle and capable of swift transport on recently constructed railroads. Using the power or the threat of army intervention, Roca transformed the once powerful provincial governors into docile instruments of the president. Through these governors, in turn, and the Ministry of the Interior, charged with electoral supervision, Roca controlled elections to the congress. Thus it was that the armed forces, the provinces, and the legislature, were all subordinated to the *unicato.*

While Roca was converting the army into a tool of the president he also pressed for military professionalization in the late nineteenth and early twentieth centuries. His protegé, General Pablo R. Riccheri, was also a major figure in transforming the "Old Army" into the "New Army." What had been an ill-disciplined cavalry force of impressed soldiers led by amateur officers became a conscript army with modern arms and a professional officer corps. According to military historians, the "three basic columns" which served as the foundation of the "New Army" were the modernization of weaponry and war material, the establishment of the Escuela Superior de Guerra, and the law of obligatory military service.

In 1884, during his first administration, Roca converted the Argentine general staff from a simple bureau for the transmission of orders into a major institution intended to prepare the nation for war. During the 1890s, Riccheri headed an armaments commission in Europe which purchased modern German weaponry on a large scale for the Argentine army. Both developments led to the creation of a war academy to train general staff officers in new military methods and weaponry. In 1899, Roca, then in his second term (1898–1904), engaged the first German training mission to organize such an academy on the Prussian model. On January 29, 1900, the Escuela Superior de Guerra was created by general order of the Ministry of War. One year later, the famous law no. 4031, sponsored by Minister of War Riccheri, established obligatory military service in Argentina.

Military professionalization was destined to have a profound impact on the course of Argentine political history. Professionalization heightened the corporate consciousness of the army officer corps, especially its determination to acquire and maintain autonomy on vital matters such as promotion. By 1910, the criterion for promotion had shifted from political or presidential favoritism to mastery of the techniques of modern warfare. Officers of the "Old Army" were being retired in large numbers to enforce the new criterion. A related development was the shift in the control of promotions from the presidency to the professional army, represented by a Tribunal de Clasificación. The tribunal was comprised of commanders of army divisions headed by the highest-ranking general. This shift meant that able officers could rise in the profession and acquire military prestige apart from that formerly bestowed by the president. In other words, a peacetime military establishment had become the first institution of state to escape the shadow of presidentialism. Should the presidency falter in a grave crisis and the state cease to operate, as happened in 1930, the army officer corps was prepared to provide not only the force but also the leadership needed to define political change.

Reprinted and edited from *Hispanic American Historical Review* 48, no. 2 (May 1968), pp. 189–205.

Warren Schiff

The Influence of the German Armed Forces and War Industry on Argentina, 1880–1914

Discreet German participation in the Argentine arms trade dated back to the beginning of Argentina's nationhood. Paraguay's army, then Argentina's foe, introduced Krupp cannons into the Plata region during the Paraguayan War, between 1865 and 1870. Argentina, with a typical deep suspicion of Chile's intentions, ordered her first Krupp cannons in 1873 under the cloak, just as typically, of an officially inspired press silence.

Soon, prospering but unstable Argentina became increasingly interested in adopting German military methods as well. Her government shared the worldwide respect for German military successes. It felt itself beset by the increasingly German-oriented Chilean army. And it was anxious to use growing quantities of modern German weaponry effectively. In addition, Argentina and Germany shared not only the experiences of a recent national unification and a common European tradition, but also those of authoritarian governmental structures, domination by elites, and a desire for rapid economic modernization. On the other hand, the German government became aware that it had to balance its interests in Argentina against those in Chile.

Reflecting the close link between the purchase of modern weaponry and the adoption of modern training methods, Argentina established military institutes and sought the advice of a few German and other European military technicians while General Julio A. Roca was serving his first presidency between 1880 and 1886. An admirer of the German military establishment and a man of arrogant and martial airs, Roca, for years to come, served as one of his nation's most influential advisers on matters of national defense. Soon a handful of German specialists proved their competence and began to rise to key line positions in the Argentine army.

By 1894, the Argentine government had become sufficiently concerned about the possibility of a violent confrontation with Chile to request special credit for military defense in an urgent congressional session which was kept so secret that the press was prohibited from alluding to it under penalty of the immediate suppression of any offending newspaper. At a time when Chile seemed bent on upsetting the South American balance of power, the conservative newspaper *La Nación* observed how Germany's efficient army was worth its immense cost. It was indeed a tense year, as Chilean reconnoitering parties began to violate Argentinian territory. They included several Germans, who claimed to be astronomers but were really preparing strategic maps for Chile.

Germany's military influence continued to grow despite worry over the effects of the heavy arms expenditures, which could be only partially disguised, on Argentina's budget and credit rating. At one point a number of applications by German officers for service in Argentina had to be temporarily rejected because of budgetary difficulties. Nevertheless, a German military orientation became pronounced during Roca's second presidency between 1898 and 1904. Chile, after all, had been enlarging her contingent of German officers since 1895 and seemed to be preparing for war against Argentina.

Argentina's military leadership determined to provide greater homogeneity, training in modern warfare, and an efficient organization for its own army. Reform measures seemed all the more urgent when Argentina, following Chile, adopted a system of compulsory military service. But unhappily, even the German-inspired Argentine general staff found it almost impossible to handle the frequently inept, overly large, and miscellaneous officer corps. Some of its members had been trained along traditional lines with an adherence to ancient and rigid Spanish regulations. Others followed gaucho guerrilla tactics. Still others had been trained in a number of European countries, in each of which they had been taught to believe that that country's system was the most effective. Many of them, especially political appointees, were hardly trained at all. Roca and his military entourage concluded that a powerful, centralizing war academy would remedy these conditions. It was to be directed and staffed by distinguished military specialists from Germany, the exclusive model country, and serve also as a training institution for senior and general staff officers. An alternate measure, the formation of an Italian Legion, which was supported by members of the growing Italian colony, had to be dropped by Roca in the face of protests by both the Italian government and Chile's Italians.

Official consideration of a German-dominated war academy turned out to be highly controversial. Sharp nationalistic opposition forced Roca to reduce to a mere handful the number of German officers to be invited. Certain misgivings of the nationalists were not entirely unjustified, as at least some German officers appeared to be more concerned with their rank and status in Argentina than they were with their salary. Important newspapers spearheaded the opposition to the War Academy. *La Nación* questioned the need for specialists, feeling that firmness and energy by the military leadership might suffice to shape a well-trained and disciplined army. It worried that the war minister would become a puppet of foreigners and observed that the "Prussianization mania" had reaped the Chileans little but headaches. And only months before the War Academy's inauguration in 1900, *La Prensa* still persisted in its own line of criticism by expressing dissatisfaction with the new institution's curriculum and admission requirements.

Under the circumstances, the War Academy's first director had to be both an effective military planner and a skillful diplomat, requirements that were not fully met by General Alfredo Arent, a former German general staff officer and decorated veteran of the Franco-Prussian War. A competent military man, Arent was also loquacious, politically naive, and vindictive. The latter characteristics not merely curtailed his personal effectiveness, but almost ruined the German military program as well. Arent began by offending Argentine political sensibilities with some comments made during a speech at the War Academy's inaugural ceremony. Somewhat later his overeagerness probably delayed rather than expedited the program for training Argentine officers with the German army. Arent's personal relationship with War Minister Pablo Riccheri was stormy to the extent that Arent repeatedly asked Roca to intervene against this member of Roca's own cabinet.

Another quarrel finally sealed Arent's fate. In 1899, Arent invited his friend Major Rolo von Kornatzki to accompany him to Argentina. Kornatzki had pleaded with Arent to extract him from an unpleasant assignment in Germany, which he had received for having married a Jewess. In Argentina, Mrs. Kornatzki's driving ambition, glamorous appearance, unpopular opinions, and distinguished friends quickly stirred the resentments of Mrs. Arent and other members of the rather parochial-minded German colony in Buenos Aires. Before long, Arent tried and failed to persuade Kornatzki to cancel his contract, then denounced his former friend in his confidential annual report to the war minister. His report was leaked, in turn, to *La Prensa,* whose editors used this new opportunity to hold the German military system up to popular scrutiny by printing it. In view of the subsequent general publicity, the general was induced, within less than a month, to leave Argentina on a temporary basis. But after an Argentine military investigating commission exonerated Kornatzki publicly, the German emperor personally barred Arent's return to Argentina.

Arent, who was now succeeded by Argentine officers, had already managed to pattern the infant War Academy after its prestigious counterpart in Berlin. This standard was modified from time to time, but never abandoned. As planned, the institution gradually extended its influence over the officer corps. Being well acquainted with his own country's concept of a nation in arms, Arent had also furnished important recommendations for the implementation of the new law of obligatory military service. Among the most urgent goals that the general had set himself at the War Academy were the formation of a competent general staff and the inauguration of thorough combat training, with an emphasis on joint maneuvers by large bodies of troops to be drawn from several branches of the army, who would copy the training exercises of elite model units.

The German military advisers or instructors who worked with and succeeded Arent performed their tasks on the basis of reasonably consistent attitudes on ethical values, pedagogy, military organization, and politics. These could be generally traced back to the precepts of a nation in arms and the spirit of a close identification between a people and its army. With this motivation, German officers on assignment with the Argentine army galvanized reforms in military legislation, organization, and methods of instruction. Their efforts evoked ideological support from within the Argentine officer corps. In 1909, for example, an Argentine general arranged that a captain who had served with the German army for two years address a select and receptive circle of officers. The captain eulogized the German army and presented an idealized image of it as a body of thinking and well-trained soldiers. This was meant to counteract the impression of the German army as a giant war machine bent on conquest. More concretely, the exacting German officers were resolved to inculcate in their students and disciples the severe principles of constant professional dedication and unity, obedience, simplicity, efficient flexibility, and personal discipline.

Articulate, pragmatic, and gregarious José F. Uriburu, the War Academy's director between 1907 and 1913, and, ironically, subsequent president of Argentina by virtue of a military coup d'etat, emerged as a key figure among the often younger and "progressive" officers who were eager to implement German military doctrine. Born in 1868 into an aristocratic family, he early chose a military career, but developed a political consciousness as well. Soon he joined the type of officers' lodge that was to affect Argentine politics significantly in later years, in this case the idealistic Lodge of the Thirty-Three, which backed largely middle-class-inspired revolutionary activities in 1890. Like a number of his fellow conspirators, he quickly rose to military prominence as a stringent advocate of the army's modernization, which he came to equate with Germanizing. In 1902 he was one of the first graduates of the War Academy, with top honors. Anticipating the introduction of a formal Argentine-German exchange program, the then Major Uriburu thereupon served a lengthy tour of duty with the artillery section of the German Imperial Guard, and personally impressed Emperor William II.

Employing the maxim of the concurrence of military axioms, Uriburu consciously related military pedagogy to discipline: "The War Academy is not destined to supply incoherent knowledge," he noted, "quite the contrary, it is planned that the instruction in each new field of studies be based on previously understood and well-assimilated principles."

Beyond this, German-type military training suggested to some the standard of a truly national army in the role of a great civilizing instrument. It transformed uneducated and uncultured draftees into literate and articulate citizens, who were aware of their moral and social obligations and who recognized the necessities of hygiene and a healthy way of life. Such men would eventually be able to improve their standards of living. An overall achievement of such goals, it was hoped, would lead to a final recognition by citizen soldiers that nothing could be accomplished anywhere, from school to factory, without recognizing that an individual sense of discipline must prevail in even instinctive social relationships. Particularly in the field of politics, far from implanting militarism, a German-trained army would intervene in the affairs of government only as a stabilizing element in order to safeguard the honor, liberty, and prestige of Argentina's republican institutions.

A rationale was likewise developed to justify Argentine receptiveness to German instruction. It was intimated that, since certain national characteristics of South American countries resembled those of France and Italy, some of the more dissimilar German perspectives and institutions should complement those prevalent in Argentina. A blind imitation of German practices could be avoided easily. It was pointed out in this connection that, in contrast to the highly centralized Argentine military organization, the powerful German general staff enjoyed virtual autonomy and that the German high command and general military administration were decentralized. Especially German military pedagogues, it was also noted, emphasized not specific doctrines but only the acceptance of a fundamental sense of duty and basic education or training. Finally, the German officers themselves taught that, rapid movement by railroad notwithstanding, the advent of weapons of great destructive capacity had placed the individual soldier in greater isolation in any case and had forced him to become more self-reliant.

Defenders of German influence denied that an acceptance of certain German ideas or methods degraded Argentina's national heritage because, after all, Argentina had been affected by the European tradition throughout her history. Even if one did admit that an exclusive imitation of German methods offended Argentina's self-esteem, a Germanophile like Uriburu pointed out, then it was precisely by such emulation that Argentina could catch up most quickly with the more advanced European nations.

Argentina's top command wished to assure, at minimum expense, the long-range survival of its modern training system. But it preferred to be more careful than the Chileans had been to avoid the army's domination by a haughty coterie of foreign advisers. In 1906, with this end in mind and after initial German, as well as Argentinian, misgivings had been overcome, it was decided, ironically, to imitate still another Chilean experiment by assigning Argentinian officers for training in Germany. They were to gradually supplement and, perhaps, eventually replace the approximately thirty German officers who taught in Argentina between 1900 and 1914. The fact that an impressive number of the from one to five dozen annual trainees later reached top command positions in the army bears testimony to the program's success. In 1908, the German officers who served at the War Academy gained, at least temporarily, a controlling voice in the decision-making process for officer promotions to senior ranks. In addition, Uriburu involved himself and his institute energetically in the selection of Argentine officers for training in Germany.

German and other foreign armaments interests pursued their intrigues within the Argentine government to the eve of World War I. While the often unemotional Germans were, as before, more respected than loved, German military instructors and German-trained Argentine officers in key commands were gradually succeeding in shaping a relatively more cohesive, better disciplined, and somewhat less rebellion-prone officer corps at the head of a more modern and better-equipped national army. Even in the face of persistent Argentine nationalistic assertiveness, close relations continued to be nurtured between the aristocratic German officer corps and Argentine commanders tied to the landed elite, like Uriburu. Capable young officers from middle-class backgrounds, who tended to benefit generally from the new German-inspired emphasis on professional ability, were given new opportunities for promotion as a result of the military reform legislation that had been initiated by Uriburu. Furthermore, in line with German suggestions, more emphasis had been placed on practical training.

Only months before the German advisers took their final leave in order to fight for their own country, German military and naval interests were represented through a distinguished "unofficial" visitor to Argentina. He was Prince Henry, the emperor's brother and a top commander in the German navy. Prince Henry bore witness to another at least tentative German accomplishment when, in the company of Uriburu, he reviewed troops en route to large-scale military maneuvers.

With the encouragement of members of the Argentine government and officer corps, increasing German weapons sales had helped to bring about a significant German participation in the molding of a modern Argentine army. In the forefront of those who opposed this type of German penetration had been nationalists, traditionalists, pacifists, and a number of supporters of other foreign interests and tendencies. In response, the German government, armed forces, and war industry, at the turn of the century, began to defend their new and growing vested interests with determination. On the whole, activities related to the sale of weapons and warships had a largely passing but corrosive impact on Argentina, a nation in search of a strong sense of national cohesion. But the teachings of the German military instructors, controversial as they had been, left a deep impression in the increasingly influential officer corps. They had, therefore, contributed to the forging of Argentina's national heritage.

Reprinted and edited from *Hispanic American Historical Review* 52, no. 3 (August 1972), pp. 436–55.

Selected Documents on Military Professionalization in Bolivia

This is a letter written by the U.S. diplomatic mission in Bolivia.

January 24, 1913

To the Honorable
    The Secretary of State,
        Washington.
Sir:

I have the honor to refer to Department's Instruction No. 76, dated October 10, and to my despatch No. 200 of December 10, 1912.

On the subject matter of the said instructions I had yesterday a very interesting and satisfactory conference with the Minister of War who was not only very willing to give me all the information I desired, but expressed pleasure to see for the first time that our Government shows some interest in the Military affairs of Bolivia and South America.

The present German Military Commission was engaged in 1910 under contract for a period of three years beginning January 1, 1911. The method of its selection was the Bolivian Government made a formal request of the German Government for such a commission. The German Government recommended Colonel Hans Kundt as the Chief of the Commission who was accepted by the Bolivian Government and has proved to be a most excellent selection. The Chief was authorized to choose his staff which is composed of four captains, one each for the Military College, the Artillery, the Infantry and Cavalry and eight Sergeants. The head of the Commission, who has been made Major-General of the Bolivian Army, receives a monthly salary of 2000 marks and in addition a residence, light for the same, servants and two horses. The monthly salaries of the others are as follows: Captain of Artillery, 1416 marks, the other three captains, 1250 marks each and the eight sergeants 300 marks each.

The Military Commission is in full charge of the Army.

It has done very good work considering the material it has had to work with and the conditions. It is said by those competent to express such an opinion that the Bolivian Army has the highest standard and is the most efficient in proportion to its size of any Army of South America.

The influence of the German Commission has been and is very considerable and extends into commercial and social circles. An instance of that is that it has induced the Bolivian Government to buy in Germany within the last year nearly $500,000 of army material and supplies—clothing, shoes, saddles, harness, etc.

It seems to me that it has been a great oversight on our part to permit such European Commissions to come to these South American Countries. Such a policy has caused us to suffer greatly in both prestige and commerce and has held back our forming a closer union and more friendly relations with these valuable countries. I hope our Government has at last recognized our mistaken policy and has decided to make a change.

I have the honor to be, Sir,
>   Your obedient servant,

Source: United States Department of State, Serial Files on Bolivia, 1910–29, Records relating to the Internal Affairs of Bolivia, National Archives, 824.20/3.

This is a letter from Jesse S. Cottrell, a U.S. diplomatic representative in Bolivia to the secretary of state.

June 1, 1925

No. 721

The Honorable
>   The Secretary of State,
>   Washington.

Sir:

I have the honor to report that the rumors which have for sometime prevailed in Bolivia that General Hans Kundt, the German Chief of Staff of the Bolivian Army, would resign reached a definite status May 27th, when the General submitted his resignation to President Saavedra, asking that he might be released at once and return to his native country. His resignation was promptly declined.

General Kundt stated in his brief renunciation of his charge that the local press had made references reflecting upon his personal dignity. He referred to brief editorial comments in the opposition press which insinuated that General Kundt was being overpaid for his services.

The President in declining the resignation paid General Kundt a high tribute and stated that his salary had not in fact been sufficient and that had the treasury of the country permitted he would have been paid more. He also assured General Kundt that he had the confidence of the Government and that he would, when he did retire, receive a pension whereby he could pass his old age in his native land in comfort and peace. The President incidentally mercilessly excoriated those who have made critical references to General Kundt. Spanish and translated copies of the resignation and the reply of the President are attached.

General Kundt came to Bolivia in 1912, the head of the German Military Commission of sixteen. He was given the rank of colonel in the Bolivian Army and remained here until Germany started the World War. He returned to Germany with the entire commission except Sergeant Kutzner, who remained on account of his age. Of the fifteen German soldiers who went home and entered the Army, only three survived, General Kundt, who during the World War was a member of General Ludenberg's staff, Colonel Fritz Muther, who is now a professor in the "Colegio Militar" (Military College) in La Paz, and an aviator who is an invalid in Germany from permanent injuries received in the service.

Soon after the Armistice and before the Versailles Treaty had been finally terminated, General Kundt managed to leave Europe, came to Buenos Aires and made his way through the interior of the Argentine and Bolivia to La Paz. Under the laws of Bolivia two years' residence in the country is a prerequisite to naturalization. Such is effected by a municipal council or through the Ministry of Colonization. General Kundt was naturalized over night by the La Paz city council on his statement that he had intended during his previous residence to become a Bolivian citizen. He was immediately placed in the station of "el Jefe de Estado Mayor General," or Chief of Staff, on a three-year contract at a salary of Bs. 40,000.00 per annum (now about $14,000.00 U.S. Cy.) with a proviso that if killed while in the discharge of his duties his widow would receive Bs. 160,000.00, and at the end of six years if he desired to retire he would receive a pension of "jollification" such as given superannuated Bolivian soldiers, Kundt's pension to be the equivalent of about $300.00 U.S.Cy., per month.

During the six years he has been here as Chief of Staff, General Kundt has served the Liberal party one year and the Republican party five. He had only limited authority during his year's tenure with the Liberals and it is a recognized fact that had he been in complete control of the Army in 1920, the coup d'etat which placed the Republicans in control of the Government would never have been accomplished.

No sooner had the Republicans come into power than they gave General Kundt absolute authority and control of the Army with orders to keep the Republican party in power. He at once weeded out the "Montesistas" (followers of ex-President Montes, Liberal President), eliminated from "El Colegio Militar" all cadet appointees named during the Liberal regime before they were graduated, lest they would enter the Army and foment Liberal propaganda, and saw to it that no more cadets from families of Liberal persuasion were nominated to the Military College. He gradually dropped from the Army all officers and soldiers of Liberal ideas and began building up an army of 8,000 to 10,000 soldiers of Aymara and Quechua Indians. He established schools in all "quarteles," or barracks, stopped the use of coca and alcohol, provided sustaining food and comfortable quarters, with the result that today Bolivia has the best army in her history,— the first in fact scientifically trained.

That General Kundt desires to leave Bolivia is well recognized. During the six years he has been here he has made investments in Germany and dealt in securities in London until he is recognized as wealthy. His wife and daughter have already left for his home, where he has extensive properties, and now that he is past fifty-five he desires to retire.

Should General Kundt leave, the future welfare of the Republican party would be jeopardized. Several native applicants for his position would appear and a bitter contest would ensue.

It is currently reported that when President Saavedra retires from the executive chair he will immediately thereafter become Minister of War. It is on these conditions, it is understood, that General Kundt would remain. This combination would insure peace in the country, because President Saavedra (by means fair or foul) has made the Republican party the dominant power in Bolivia, with General Kundt meanwhile enabling him to have complete sway by putting down repeated revolutions and building up a well trained army.

General Kundt is an affable and agreeable personality who is very popular with the foreigners of all classes as well as with Bolivians, and withal a soldier at all times.

I have the honor to be, Sir,

> Your obedient servant,
> > Jesse S. Cottrell.

Source: United States Department of State, Serial Files on Bolivia, 1910–29, Records relating to the Internal Affairs of Bolivia, National Archives, 824.20/31.

Frank D. McCann, Jr.

Origins of the "New Professionalism" of the Brazilian Military

. . . In the course of Brazilian military history, since at least the beginning of the century, there have been debates and even violence revolving ultimately around questions of self-definition. Why have an army? What was it for? The answers as to what the army's missions were and hence what it meant to be an officer and a soldier varied across time; the variance produced conflict within the institution. This resulted from the deliberate ambiguity of the military's constitutional status. The constitutions of the Empire (1824) and the Republic (1891, 1934, 1937, 1946) specified that the military were to defend the country against foreign attack and, as the constitution of 1891 phrased it, to "maintain the laws in the interior." The political leaders wanted the military squarely between the two poles of external and internal security, so not surprisingly some officers defined their profession in terms of an exclusive external or internal orientation, while others mixed the two. Clearly such men as the Duke of Caxias in the Empire, Marshals Deodoro da Fonseca, Floriano Peixoto, Hermes da Fonseca, Pedro A. de Góes Monteiro, and Eurico Dutra fall into the latter category because they exercised both external defense and internal political roles. There appear to have been relatively fewer officers who were totally external defense oriented and therefore apolitical. A few who do come to mind are José Caetano de Faria, Estevão Leitão de Carvalho, and João B. Mascarenhas de Morais because these adhered to the legalist position that the army must obey the lawful orders of the government and because they were concerned with shaping the army into a fighting force of European quality. Yet, though their orientation was basically professional, they were drawn into internal affairs because of their desire for a modern, European-style, external defense army.

Perhaps it is best not to seek hard and fast definitions of professionalism but to examine currents of thought that mix and blend over time. José Murilo de Carvalho discerned three currents: that of the citizen-soldier, the professional soldier, and the corporative soldier. The first made its appearance in the 1880s serving as a means of unifying the officer corps for reformist intervention to replace the tottering monarchy with a renovating republic.

The Citizen-Soldier

The officer corps had been split since the Paraguayan war into two antagonistic groups, the *tarimbeiros* and the *doutores*, who nevertheless shared a common disdain for the political elite. The tarimbeiros were those who had come up from the ranks without attending the military school. The term referred to the *tarimba,* the hard wooden soldier's bunk that was common in old forts and barracks. They favored intervention only to strengthen the military institution, that is to say their own positions vis-à-vis the civilian elite. Their desires revolved almost exclusively around power and prestige. The doutores were the graduates of the military school, who glowed with the light of Colonel Benjamin Constant's positivist teachings. In their view, soldiers should be regarded as armed civilians, rather than as a separate caste, because industrial progress would retire armies and their weapons of destruction to the museums and pages of history. The distinction between the concepts of citizen and soldier should be extinguished in favor of a broadened view of citizenship. But they acknowledged that a weakened army could not bring about political reform and so before it could disappear, the army had to be strengthened. Given the generational fissures of the era and the differences between tarimbeiros and doutores, simultaneous reformist intervention and institutional strengthening were incompatible. The first decade of the republic did little to improve the army's martial abilities until the rude awakening of the Canudos campaign of 1897, and efforts to secure the Amazon during the Acré affair (1903–4) forced a reassessment of values.

The interventionist sentiment that flowed from, or perhaps even created, the concept of the citizen-soldier was based on resentment against an elite that ignored the officer corps, keeping salaries low, promotions slow, and arms scarce, while seeking to minimize the army's political power via increases in police and National Guard forces in and around Rio de Janeiro. Lieutenant Sebastião Bandeira, Captain Antônio Adolfo de Mena Barreto, and General Tibúrcio de Sousa were typical of officers convinced that not only was the imperial government hostile to the army, but, in a broader sense, all civilian politicians were the enemy.

Psychologically, the officers compensated for their inferior status by counterposing it with a belief in their spiritual superiority. "There was a generalized conviction that the men in uniform were *pure,* were *vigorous,* were *patriots*; whereas the civilians were *corrupt*, were *vice-ridden*, without any public sentiment." The officers saw themselves as "saviors of the *patria*," with the obligation not only to defend their own rights and interests, but to rescue the fatherland from the civilian politicians who corrupted it. Floriano Peixoto wrote that a military dictatorship was necessary because only a "government of the sword" could "purify the blood of the social body." The vision of the officer corps as a priesthood of national purification blended with republican terminology to give form and substance to the citizen-soldier and his role in Brazilian society. But after overthrowing the imperial government, the officers discovered that running a country was not as easy as it looked from the barracks window. The civil war, the continued disagreements between tarimbeiros and doutores, resurgent regionalism, and the Canudos affair shook the officers' self-assurance, and they stepped aside for civilians.

The Professional Soldier

In the first two decades of the new century, the professional soldier embraced the citizen-soldier idea as a vehicle to reform the army. This reform in turn would lead to a widening of the army's influence, power, and roles. The professionals, whose family backgrounds and premilitary education were apparently similar to the more politically involved citizen-soldier and corporative soldier types, desired a European-style army. Nineteenth-century Brazilian history demonstrated little need for such an army. The major experiences had been internal affairs in which officers either fought against government forces as rebels or battled to suppress rebellion. The list is impressive: uprisings in Rio de Janeiro in 1831 and 1832; the *Cabanagem* in Pará from 1835 to 1840; the Sabinada in Bahia in 1837–38; the Balaiada in Maranhão in 1831–41; the Alagôas revolt of 1844; the Praieira revolt of 1848–50 in Pernambuco; and, of course, the Farroupilha in Rio Grande do Sul from 1835 to 1845. By comparison, the foreign combat had been against the United Provinces of the Rio de la Plata, 1825 to 1828; Buenos Aires' Rosas in 1852; and Paraguay's Solano López from 1865 to 1870.

This last was "The War" for the senior officers who commanded the army at the turn of the century. The experience left its mark in a distrust of politicians who would declare war without providing adequate means or forces to fight with, and who would ignore and deprecate the victors, the wounded, the widowed, and the orphaned. Officers came to believe that only they were concerned about Brazil's defense. Another legacy of the war was a lingering bitterness between the former Argentine and Brazilian allies regarding the treaty arrangements. In the years before World War I, as Buenos Aires modernized its forces with German equipment and instructors, the Brazilian army held up their southern neighbor's energetic activities as a warning against complacency. To make matters more nerve-wracking, the undefended Amazon, with all its supposed riches, seemed a likely target for a repetition of what the powers had done to Africa and Asia. Even the great republic of the north had recently acquired an overseas empire, and the nightmare of the powers sitting around a table in some faraway chancellery dividing the Amazon and the underpopulated interior seemed possible if the nation did not create a sufficiently martial facade.

In 1904, Minister of War Marshal Francisco de Paula Argollo complained that Brazilians placed too much faith in "the principles of international jurisprudence and the efficacy of diplomatic notes" to protect their territory. But without military force—the *ultima ratio*—the diplomats would not be able, he argued, to make their logic prevail. "The weak countries lived condemned to the degrading tutelage of the strong, who feel that they possess the right to counsel them, direct them, and even to admonish them, transforming, de facto, their independence and autonomy into a true fiction." Japan was treated with respect, he observed, because it had demonstrated military prowess. Brazil must do likewise. But how? Civilian and military enthusiasm for army reform rose and fell with equal speed. "The army is in the condition it finds itself," he lamented, "not because we ignore its necessities ... but only because of the lack of firmness, resolution and courage on our part to realize that which we recommend and avow to be indispensable."

So the military problem of the new century was twofold: A European-style army would have to be created because the likely enemy would employ such a force; and basic attitudes inside and outside the army would have to change. The professionals knew that Brazil was too poor to maintain a large standing army and so they placed their hopes in developing a cadre army with large trained reserves. The easily expandable force was convincing on paper, suited the economic realities, and did not appear to threaten the political power of the regional elites.

Because the past did not provide the models that they needed for the future, the professionals did tours of duty as junior officers in the imperial Prussian army (1910–12) and later accepted a French Military Mission (1919–39) to organize and teach their advanced officer and general staff courses. Since their geopolitical views were shared by Foreign Minister Rio Branco and his diplomats, they had support for obtaining new foreign-made armament. But how to alter the attitudes of civilian society?

Here the professionals found ready allies in the growing urban middle class. These people were appalled at the stunning ignorance, poverty, and filthiness of the masses, and burned with resentment at the rural landowners, or *coroneis*, whose armed hangers-on and elaborate alliance system kept the masses and the central government subservient. If the middle class could control an invigorated army, they might be able to impose their vision of Brazil. But they lacked the will for conflict and knew from experience in the civil war of 1893–95 that they would suffer from such internal warfare. And because they had little ability, or perhaps taste, for unified political action, they sought to reform the prevailing system from within: In historian Edgard Carone's phrase, "instead of struggle, collaboration: in place of its own ideology, the vague glorification of citizenship (*civismo*)."

Through spokespersons such as the patriotic poet Olavo Bilac, the middle class supported the establishment of a national draft lottery in 1916 to provide annual levies of recruits to be given a year of training and then returned home as reservists to spread the good work of citizenship. Bilac saw the lottery as "a promise of salvation" for Brazil. Reflecting the prevalent middle-class view that Brazil was not a cohesive, unified nation, he saw the privileged classes wanting only self-pleasure and prosperity, the lower classes living in "inertia, apathy, and superstition," and the foreign immigrants isolated from others by language and custom. The "militarization of all civilians" was the way to impart middle-class virtues to society and thereby give it the cohesion necessary to preserve itself. Military service was to be the means of massive social uplift; however, from the middle-class point of view, it was also important that it act as a leveling force bringing the upper classes down to a more reasonable level. For Bilac, "generalized military service" was:

the complete triumph of democracy; the leveling of the classes; the school of order, discipline, cohesion; the laboratory of individual dignity and patriotism. It is obligatory primary instruction; it is obligatory civic education; it is obligatory cleanliness, obligatory hygiene, obligatory muscular and psychic regeneration. The cities are full of lazy, barefoot, ragged enemies of the "ABC's" and of bathing— brute animals, who have only the appearance and wickedness of men. For these dregs of society the barracks will be salvation.

Military service would purify them and return them to society as "conscientious, worthy Brazilians." The military would provide the discipline and order to reconstruct Brazil by lifting up the downcast millions. And because he held the rural oligarchies to be primarily responsible for the people's distressing state, he argued that only the middle class possessed "complete intellectual and moral culture," "high-mindedness," and capacity to place themselves above self, class, or partisan interests, and so they were destined "to the sacred mission of governing and directing the multitude." The military, already possessing these high qualities, would help the middle class take power peacefully. The nation, that is, the remade people under middle-class leadership, would be the army; and the army, reformed, restructured, redirected, would be the nation. The officer corps in Bilac's view was the army, its soul—"all the sensibility, all the intelligence, all the will of the corporation of soldiers." The officer was the priest of the cult of the nation, and as such should flee from political ambition and involvement. The officer would be the regenerator and disciplinarian, the middle class would govern and direct. The draft lottery may have meant to the reformist professional a modern army, with a growing reserve that would be mobilized to support Brazilian dreams of greatness and desire for security, but to the middle class it had a key role in developing their social vision of Brazil. For such a division of roles to work, they would have to be clearly defined and accepted. Such was not the case. The "militarization of all civilians," which Bilac called for, was not possible, and the effort to achieve it via the draft lottery served to intensify the army's inward orientation. So in the 1920s while the army was acquiring all the trappings of a professional force, it was becoming steadily more involved internally via the very means it sought to use to professionalize itself.

The draft lottery provided the mechanism and justification for the army's physical expansion and contributed to its increasing involvement in society and politics. Instead of opting for one or two national training camps, with subsequent distribution to posts throughout Brazil, the army wished to keep the soldiers in their own regions. This would avoid the cost and administrative burden of transporting large contingents hither and yon, and would give the army a local image. But to effect this required at least one army unit in each state to receive and train the draftees and volunteers, and to do that would necessitate the increase of effectives from an authorized 18,000 men to 25,000, which was the smallest figure which would allow the army to deal with "questions of internal order" and also serve as a "nucleus of instruction." The expansion in turn also involved a higher level of military spending. After Brazil entered World War I in October 1917, the pace of expansion increased to the point where by mid-1918 every state had at least one federal army unit to serve as a reception and training center for draftees. Commanding an army that now embraced 52,000 effectives, War Minister José Caetano de Faria expressed the belief that the war demonstrated the dangers of returning "our army to the insignificant effectives that we had." Once the expansion had occurred, it would not be possible to deter the pace of growth. According to General Eurico Dutra, the number of effectives rose from 30,000 in 1920 to 50,000 in 1930, and had reached 93,000 in the midst of the Estado Nôvo in 1940. Though the proportion of soldiers to population would remain low in comparison to other countries, that is, about 1.1 soldiers per thousand, the army's size increased at a faster rate than did the population. José Murilo de Carvalho has shown that while the population increased 162 percent between 1890 and 1930, the army grew 220 percent. And while Alfred Stepan may well be correct in asserting that "political variables are frequently far more important for determining the role of the military in society than the absolute size of the armed forces," still we are confronted with the parallel developments of the army's numerical growth and its greater political involvement. Surely, by itself, the former was not the cause of the latter, but it is hard to imagine the army of 1905 providing the muscle for the Estado Nôvo or the 1964 to 1979 governments.

While the lottery and the war provided the justification for expansion in size and space, the army used the necessity for reserves to extend its influence over state police forces and the national guard. Under a January 1917 law, it made agreements with the state governments whereby state police and firemen would be considered auxiliary army forces. Complete control would not be secured until the Estado Nôvo in 1937–45, but this was the first step. The national guard was denominated the army's second line and by a 1918 decree was to be remodeled. Considered a rival force by many officers, it would be abolished before the next decade was out. As a result, for the "first time among us," as Caetano de Faria happily pointed out, the army came to control "all the forces which ought to constitute the military power of the nation."

It fell to the republic's only civilian minister of war, João Pandiá Calógeras, to consolidate the numerical and spacial expansion by an ambitious building program in 1920–21—the largest before the Estado Nôvo. Taking over the ministry, he traveled throughout the country to see firsthand the army's condition. He was dismayed. "Brazil owes it to itself," he declared, "not to consent to its sons . . . being quartered in filthy *senzalas* (slave quarters)." From North to South, telegrams rained on the ministry describing the army's precarious situation—troops were without blankets, ponchos, uniforms, barracks, wagons, and, worse still, their pay was behind schedule. The expansion had taken place too precipitously, units were dangerously under strength, and as for training, Calógeras summed it up—"Instruction nil. Training areas nonexistent. . . . No training at all." With that, he inaugurated the construction of 56 new barracks in 49 locations throughout Brazil and the repair and enlargement of some 45 others in 41 places at a cost of approximately $20 million 1920 U.S. dollars. In addition, regional headquarters, powderhouses, deposits, hospitals, and infirmaries were remodeled and expanded at a total cost of approximately 1920 U.S. $2.5 million. Considering that the army's regular 1919 budget had been roughly the equivalent of U.S. $20 million and that of 1920, U.S. $27 million, these expenditures were truly extraordinary.

Not only was the army larger and present in some form in every state, but its pattern of distribution changed. Under the empire, the largest garrisons were in the frontier provinces of Rio Grande do Sul and Mato Grosso and in the capital. In 1889, the large provinces/states of Minas Gerais, São Paulo, Bahia, and Pernambuco had few national troops. The Caetano de Faria–Calógeras expansion radically altered the pattern. There was a clear tendency to place military forces "where political power was concentrated." The change was especially noticeable in Minas Gerais, São Paulo, Paraná, and Bahia. Federal troops in the first two rose from 113 and 386 in 1889 to 3.787 and 3,675 in the 1920s. Significantly, by 1933, army effectives outnumbered state police forces in Rio Grande do Sul, State of Rio de Janeiro, Paraná, Pará, and Mato Grosso. At the same time, the large states that were still attempting to cling to their old autonomy— Bahia, Minas Gerais, Pernambuco, and São Paulo—had felt compelled to increase their police forces relative to federal garrisons. Given the army's local recruitment of common soldiers, it may be, as Stepan suggests, that "the loyalty of local units is often open to question during times of great national political conflict." Even so, it is certain that the army's expansion set the stage for increasing federal involvement in the states in the 1930s.

Along with the physical expansion, the officer corps improved its technical ability to plan, coordinate, and carry out assigned missions, thanks to improved French-advised general-staff course and the reformed general staff itself. The *tenente* uprisings of the 1920s were devisive, but they provided combat experience, exposed weaknesses in military institutions, and helped draw ideological lines. The result was a growing determination to avoid future divisions within the institution and a heightened sense of membership in a separate corporate entity. The citizen-soldier and professional soldier had given the army a new self-image and the ability to carry out its tasks. But what tasks, what mission? The answer was being developed gradually since the turn of the century, and would be given expression and put into practice by the corporative soldier.

The Corporative Soldier

In his 1905 report to the president, War Minister Marshal Francisco de Paula Argollo had worried that if the army did not avoid partisan struggles, ignoring the "lying and ephemeral applause of exploitative politicians," it would lose the confidence of, and become an object of fear for, "the conservative classes of society, of whose interest it ought to be the best solid guarantee." In the first issue of the reformist young Turk journal *A Defesa Nacional* in 1913, Bertholdo Klinger, who certainly had the proper professional credentials, wrote that the army needed to be equipped for its "conservative and stabilizing function" and "prepared to correct the internal troubles [*perturbacões*] so common in the tumultuous life of societies in formation."

If Argollo, who won his commission on the battlefield in Paraguay, represented the old army, and Klinger the new, then it appears that there were no substantial differences between them concerning the army's ultimate role; both saw it as maintaining social stability. Both could accept the legitimacy of military intervention providing it was an armywide effort and not just lieutenants and captains inciting units to mutiny and rebellion. The corporative soldier disagreed with the early version of citizen-soldier only over the form and substance of intervention. His basic requirement was that it be armywide under the direction of the general staff. In 1930, for example, Klinger was chief of staff of the so-called Movimento Pacificador that deposed President Washington Luís. The initial intention was to promote new elections to resolve the impasse between the government and the revolting Vargas forces, and Klinger saw the army's role as that of arbitrator. In a message to the president, Klinger noted that the government's use of the armed forces to solve political conflicts had only produced ruin and that "public salvation" and "the integrity of the nation" required delivery of "the destinies of Brazil in the present moment to its general officers of the land and sea." His attitude was further defined in a *Defesa Nacional* article, published after the military junta had turned the government over to Getúlio Vargas, which argued the right of the military to intervene in the political system, declaring that the presidency was a "general staff problem."

Perhaps the most skillful practitioner among the corporative soldiers was Pedro A. de Góes Monteiro. A highly regarded general staff officer, who, as a student in the staff school had won great praise from the French instructors, Góes acted as Vargas's chief of staff in 1930. He embodied many of the ideas and attitudes of the citizen-soldier and the professional soldier. But he saw the army's role in a wider context. The armed forces [a curt nod to the navy!] were the only national organizations and so ought to develop their own policies, their own politics. For him the army was an "essentially political instrument" whose "collective conscience" should produce a "politics *of* the army" to avoid "politics *in* the army." Its sole objective was "the greatness of the common *patria*." He saw the army, the people, and, in the 1930s, the Vargas regime, as being in "a crusade of national regeneration" that included "developing the physical and spiritual health of our people," improving education, both technical and moral, building highways and railroads for strategic and economic purposes, and encouraging the collaboration of private industry "in the work of our defense." The army's efficiency was intimately linked to the harmonic development of all the vital forces of the nation. And just as the army should be concerned with "National Security" [*Sergurança Nacio-*

nal:] always capitalized in army literature) in its widest sense to ensure a solid base for Brazil's greatness, so too should one of the first concerns of good Brazilians be the army.

But while Góes's writings show a deep involvement in internal affairs, they also demonstrated a preoccupation with discipline, with anything that would prevent presenting a united front to society. Because the order of the day was the development of and the presentation of an army policy, a "politics *of* the army," then the army had to be "immunized against partisan seductions." Officers must not be tainted with the slightest suspicion of being involved in factious movements or having partisan concerns "alien to the policy (*política*) of the Army." Further, they must develop a "conscience capable of rejecting everything that would be against and accepting everything that would be useful to the principles and purposes of the Army." The individual officer was to function politically only in concert with his fellow officers and only at the direction of the general staff. This attitude would be turned into policy by 1939, when Minister Eurico Dutra reported that "the law of social conformity and the elimination of non-conformists forms the moral base of the Army's disciplinary structure and justifies the severe repression of dissident elements or rebels."

The citizen-soldiers' reformist intervention (including *tenentismo*) merged with and utilized the work of the professional soldiers to produce "the interventionism of the generals, or of the general staff, the intervention of the organization as a whole." From the 1930s onward, intervention would be controlled from above so that the army could fulfill its "immense historical responsibility of maintainer (*mantenedor*)" and "guardian of federative unity, of order and of internal progress and of national sovereignty." This self-definition supported the Estado Nôvo, then rejected the dictator when he attempted to change his political base, and underlay the various postwar administrations and the direct military rule of the past fifteen years. It may well be a new professionalism, but its roots are deep in the Brazilian past.

Reprinted and edited from *Journal of Interamerican Studies and World Affairs* 21, no. 4 (November 1979), pp. 505–22.

Frederick M. Nunn

Emil Körner and the Prussianization of the Chilean Army

In 1885 the Chilean government appointed Captain Emil Körner of the Imperial German Army to train its officers. When Körner arrived in Chile he found an experienced officer corps composed of veterans from the War of the Pacific and the Indian campaigns in Araucania. They were men who took pride in being the heirs of Bernardo O'Higgins and Manuel Bulnes, but they had little experience in the rigors of the classroom. Chile wanted a modern professional army; Körner molded one; and when he retired in 1910, he left behind the best-equipped land fighting force and the best-educated officer corps in Latin America. But by the time Körner died, ten years later, that same army found itself enmeshed in politics, a professional organization within an anachronistic political and social order and almost a distinct political institution.

Chile emerged victorious from the War of the Pacific. Established as the dominant state on the Pacific coast of South America, she faced potential enemies on each of her three borders. To the north and northeast, Peru smarted from the loss of Tarapacá, Tacna, and Arica; Bolivia became a landlocked nation with the Chilean annexation of Antofagasta; and across the Andes, Argentina, always suspicious, viewed the territorial cessions with envious concern. Chile's victory in the War of the Pacific merely heightened the need for a modern, powerful fighting machine and for increased sea power.

But South American "power politics" was not the sole reason for the Chilean military buildup of the late nineteenth century. Historians, over-emphasizing this factor, may have obscured the true role of the army and (to a lesser extent) the navy in Chilean history. In 1904 a Costa Rican major studying in Santiago cited certain factors, endemic to Chile, which should be carefully considered when viewing the Prussianization of the Chilean army. In the beginning, war created and maintained the national identity, as the Chileans defeated the Spaniards, carried the campaign to Peru, and then eliminated the confederation of Peru and Bolivia in 1837. When Chile's position and integrity were menaced again in 1879, war made her preeminent on the west coast of South America. Despite the relegation of the armed forces to a nonpolitical role after 1831, military might (for external use) was traditional in Chile. During the nineteenth century, Chilean military men had great prestige; they earned it.

. . . Further, by 1885 the existence of a professional, educated army was an established if poorly observed tradition. In 1817 Bernardo O'Higgins founded the Military School, the oldest such national institution in Latin America. However, it did not function effectively during the troubled times between the fall of O'Higgins in 1823 and the Battle of Lircay seven years later, in which the Conservatives defeated the Liberals and assumed complete control of politics.

Diego Portales, the *éminence grise* of Chilean conservatism in the 1830s, undertook to remove the military organization from politics. He purged or exiled officers who had sided with the liberal faction in the civil conflict of 1830 and some Conservatives whose loyalty to the new government of President Joaquín Prieto was questionable. Well aware of the army's potential threat to civilian control of politics, Portales also set up a civil militia as a counterpoise to ambitious officers. While he directed Chilean affairs, the militia performed this function. Portales himself commanded a militia infantry battalion quartered in La Moneda, the presidential palace, and paraded in uniform with the group on festive occasions. After Portales's assassination in 1837 the exclusion of the army from politics continued, except for short-lived revolts in 1851 and 1859. The Military School continued to function, as did the militia.

The forty-year period between the death of Portales and the final confrontation with Peru and Bolivia was one of great progress in Chile. Kept busy externally by the war of 1837–39 and by sporadic Indian uprisings on the southern frontier, the army eschewed political activities. At the end of the War of the Pacific, however, military education was antiquated; organization and ordinances had changed little since the days of O'Higgins; organically, the Chilean army was essentially the same as the forces which had struggled for independence. By 1885, tradition, discipline, and experience were not enough for Chile's needs. The government, therefore, turned for inspiration to Germany, the military titan of Europe.

President Domingo Santa María instructed Guillermo Matta, head of the Chilean legation in Germany, to find a qualified officer who might be engaged as military instructor, and Matta selected Körner. Actually Körner was Matta's second choice, for his first selection, Major Clemens Meckl, had already accepted a position with the Japanese army. In August 1885 Körner agreed "to serve in the Military School . . . as professor in artillery, infantry, cartography, and military history and tactics." The salary agreed upon was 12,000 marks a year, payable in Chilean gold.

Körner assumed his new duties early in 1886, with the rank of lieutenant colonel and the title of instructor and subdirector of the Military School. He immediately began to plan the organization of Chile's own *Kriegsakademie*. The Chilean government officially founded the War Academy on September 9, 1886, only thirteen months after Körner had agreed to serve in Chile.

The government created the academy for the purpose of "elevating, as much as possible, the level of technical and scientific instruction of army officers, in order that they may be able, in case of war, to utilize the advantages of new methods of combat and modern armaments in use today."

In its first years the War Academy offered a three-year program. The first-year class studied tactics, fortification, cartography, ballistics, military history, geography, military science, inorganic chemistry, physics, a choice of either mathematics or world history, and German. The second-year curriculum consisted of further training in tactics, fortification, cartography, geography, military science, physics, chemistry, mathematics or world history, and German, plus topography and war games. The third year consisted of Chilean military history, war games, Latin American military geography, hygiene, international law, general staff service, either mathematics or world history, and German. The first class (originally limited to fifteen select officers) began its courses on June 15, 1887, under the supervision of the academy's first director, Brigidier General Marco A. Arriagada. After graduation in 1890, five of its members went to Europe for further study.

On January 1, 1891, parliamentary leaders challenged the executive branch and, supported by conservative navy chiefs, pronounced against Santa María's successor, President José Manual Balmaceda. Though the bulk of the army remained loyal to Balmaceda, Körner and his followers did not. Balmaceda formally dismissed Körner from his position, and the German, accompanied by other dissenting officers, sailed north on May 9, 1891, to join the congressional forces in Iquique, the revolutionary capital. According to General Francisco Díaz, Körner fully appreciated that a congressional victory would facilitate the reform of the army and joined the revolutionary forces, not because of political ideas, but to open new military horizons and to lead those who had been his students. In less than six months Körner trained an army of 10,000 officers and troops which ultimately defeated the regular army.

On the cessation of hostilities in 1891 Körner set out to implement Prussianization as he conceived it. The immediate problem facing the victors was what to do with officers of the defeated Balmaceda's army. This problem was resolved in several ways. A decree of September 14, 1891, gave to Colonel Estanislao del Canto, commander in chief of the congressional army, the power to prosecute any officers from captains to generals who had served the Balmaceda government at any time during 1891. That same day Canto named a four-man court-martial to try the accused.

Balmacedista officers were divided into four groups: (1) Those who were guilty of nothing more than having served in the army; (2) those accused of war crimes or breaches of civil law; (3) those who had committed war crimes under orders; and (4) those who, failing to appear, were tried in absentia. A second official decree of September 14 stated that only those who had joined the congressional army or who had at least refused to serve under Balmaceda would be allowed to continue in service. In this way, high-ranking Balmacedista officers were to be purged, clearing the path for Körner's Prussianized professionals. In October, 118 Balmacedista captains went on trial for treason by virtue of the fact that they had obeyed commands of a man who had ceased to be president for his violations of the constitution. The accused based their defense on loyalty to the president as commander in chief and on the apolitical nature of the army, established by the constitution, but they were not allowed to testify or to obtain legal advice. All but two were removed from service for a period of six years and were denied the right to hold public office as citizens for an equal period. Some who escaped this harsh verdict at first were retried later and found guilty.

At the end of 1891 Brigidier General Emil Körner became chief of the general staff. The following year he returned to his original mission and served as professor of applied tactics and military geography in the War Academy as well as heading the general staff. He filled both positions until April 1894, when he went to Europe to supervise completion and shipment of coastal artillery batteries being built by the Krupp armaments factory in Essen.

Körner returned to Chile in October 1895, resumed his post as chief of staff, and on November 1 was promoted to division general. With him came thirty-six German officers, who were to play key roles in the Prussianization of the Chilean army. Lieutenant Colonel Wilhelm Ekdahl directed the War Academy from 1904 to 1907, after having served on its faculty for nine years. Majors Edward Banza and Carl Zimmermann taught at the War Academy. Captain Günther von Below taught at the Military School, as did Majors Alfred Schönmeyer and Herman von Bieberstein. Three Germans and an Irish colonel, Robert O'Grady, served in the War Ministry's fortification section; two Germans served in the technical section; two served on the Chilean armaments commission and one on the general staff. Two Germans were instructors in ballistics at the artillery school; four served in the Escuela de Clases, an institution for the training of noncommissioned officers. Two had staff positions in provincial garrisons. One German was a member of the presidential cavalry escort; three served in cavalry regiments, four in infantry regiments, three in the artillery, and one in the engineers. Two years later twenty-seven more Germans came to Chile.

As the German officers began to arrive in Chile, the first of many Chilean officers went to Germany for further training. Until the end of World War I these men studied with distinction at Charlottenburg and served with the elite Imperial Guard. After returning to Chile many of these Prussianized Chileans distinguished themselves in military and other government service, becoming the nucleus of a Chilean army elite. Led by General Carlos Ibáñez del Campo (who attended the academy but did not study in Europe), this elite involved the army in politics from 1924 until 1932. All important military positions and many political positions during that time were held by graduates of the War Academy or by Prussianized officers. Prominent among these foreign-trained soldiers were Colonel Arturo Ahumada Bascuñán, General Juan Pablo Bennett Argandoña, General Bartolomé Blanche Espejo, and Colonel Marmaduke Grove Vallejo.

. . . On May 12, 1906, Chile adopted a reform program intended to make the military organization a creole copy of the Imperial German Army. Körner had proposed this reform seven years earlier, but it soon proved disappointing to him and his followers. The administrative reorganization reduced the powers of the inspector general and increased those held by division commanders. This decentralization was supposed to make administration more efficient and flexible but did not. Consequently the administration of the War Ministry was also decentralized and a German-style general staff created for planning and coordination.

The government might create new administrative units on the order of the German army, but it soon found that there were not enough qualified officers to serve as administrators. Divisions functioned with skeleton staffs. Younger officers, lacking experience but pressed into higher administrative ranks, clashed with superiors whom they considered unfit to serve because they lacked German training. The hasty reorganization also created havoc in the War Ministry, for when division commanders found that they could not deal with all problems, they bombarded the ministry with requests for solutions. In the crush to fill all administrative positions, political pressure was used, so that friends of high-ranking civilians or officers got coveted posts, while those without connections did not. In the haste to fill up the skeleton divisions, too many untrained subalterns commanded new, untrained troops. One officer later wrote that the changeover of 1906 was outright adoption when it should have been adaptation and that the government was at fault for basing a peacetime reform on extreme wartime needs, rather than on the country's financial and manpower capabilities.

Twenty years after he had begun the task of Prussianization Körner saw it carried to the extreme in 1906. During the last four years before his retirement in 1910 he was no longer overseer of Prussianization, for the reforms of 1906 had limited his power as inspector general. Nevertheless, he continued to be an influence on the officers who had trained under him or in his system. In his 1908 report to congress he pointed out that politically influential but poorly trained officers in important positions would endanger discipline and morale: "The ease of jumping in rank predisposes the favored one to become restless in a short time, and if his aspirations to be promoted even further are not satisfied, his energy and his enthusiasm diminish, no doubt justifiably."

In 1910 the War Ministry's official report to congress supported Körner's complaint that there were not enough trained and experienced officers to fill posts created by the 1906 reforms. The 1910 report called for changes in the promotion system (which was still based on 1890 legislation) as a solution to the problem of unfit or "political" officers in key positions. Two years later the ministry's report repeated this view and disapproved outright adoption of the German model for Chilean army organization.

Even from the standpoint of the German-trained professional officer the reforms of 1906 were singularly unsuccessful. Despite a superficial glitter, the Chilean army was Prussianized beyond the capacities of the nation and suffered from serious internal problems. From the official point of view these were structural and administrative; as the government, with its anachronistic parliamentary system, creaked on, the complaints of military men became a blend of professional grievances and political interest. Even before Körner retired the army had become a "state within the state."

But German influences did not stop with Chile. They extended to officers of other Latin American armies trained at the Military School at Santiago; and the Chilean army carried "second generation" Prussianization directly to El Salvador, Ecuador, and Colombia. In the latter two cases the Chilean government was motivated by a desire for friends in the power structure of the Pacific coast.

In 1903 the government of El Salvador requested a Chilean military mission to improve army instruction. On September 4 Chile designated Captains Juan Pablo Bennett (as chief) and Francisco Lagreze and Lieutenants Julio Salinas, Armando Llanos, and Carlos Ibáñez to staff the mission. The Chilean mission stayed in El Salvador for six years. At the same time, three Chilean officers were also sent to Ecuador as army instructors, Captain Estanislao García Huidobro and Lieutenants Arturo Montecinos and Luis Negrete. Three Chilean army captains had already been acting as advisers in Ecuador for nearly a year and helped an Ecuadoran officer, Major Luis Cabrera, to write a new military code in 1902. In 1907 General Rafael Reyes, the president of Colombia, reopened the military school, which had been closed during the civil war of 1899–1902 and on six other occasions in the past century. Reyes wanted the Colombian army to be led by apolitical professional officers and chose the Chilean army as his model because of its reputed success with German training. . . .

While some of the Prussianized Chilean army officers went abroad to train other Latin American armies, others stayed home to form pressure groups and influence the Chilean government. The army had long resented meddling politicians, the cumbersome parliamentarism, and the government's inability to find long-range solutions to social and economic problems. This inability forced the army to improvise short-range solutions, as when it used force in putting down numerous strikes during the first twenty years of this century.

In 1907 a group of army officers in Santiago organized a secret lodge, the Liga Militar. Liga members, exasperated at a government which they considered "disorganized and undisciplined," swore under oath "to work for the progress of the army." Their primary objectives were professional—new promotion, salary, and retirement systems for army officers—and the Liga undoubtedly owed its creation to the effects of Prussianization, especially the reforms of 1906. According to a contemporary member of Chile's officer corps, the Liga blamed civilian political disorganization for the army's problems.

By 1910 the Liga was nationwide. Ramón Barros Luco, who assumed the presidency on the death of Pedro Montt in that year, knew of its existence, but did nothing about it. In the same year the Club Militar opened its doors in Santiago. This national social center for army officers became the seat of Liga activities and made Santiago the preferred location for politically minded officers during the next two decades.

The creation of a modern army in Chile had serious long-range consequences, both professional and national. Prussianization set ambitious professional officers against their superiors, against their incompetent colleagues, and against politicians who meddled in army affairs or who failed to support the military's legislative requests. Prussianization created an army elite which magnified its role in Chilean society and politics during the second decade of this century. The aping of the Prussian army became a curse for government and military alike when officers began to challenge the traditional power structure from 1907 forward. As long as that structure remained outwardly solid the army was kept in its place. But the shattering experiences of 1919 and 1920 ended one chapter in Chilean civil-military relations and prepared for another, even more dramatic—the outright military intervention and domination from 1924 to 1932 by those who had shared in the experience of Prussianization.

Reprinted and edited from *Hispanic American Historical Review* 50, no. 2 (May 1970), pp. 300-322.

Víctor Villanueva

Military Professionalization in Peru

The government of Nicolás de Piérola (1895–99) provided ample opportunities and incentives for the industrialization of the country. New factories and commercial enterprises appeared, mineral production increased, and in 1895, with the opening of an electrified alum plant in Lima, the first industry employing electric power began functioning. But this industrial boom, mineral and commercial, resulted from the introduction of foreign capital which appropriated the principal production sectors, thereby reinforcing the economy's dependence on the export of primary products.

One would presume that accomplishments would not have been achieved if Piérola had not first reorganized the army and then placed it under civilian control. He understood that if the personal ambitions of the men in the barracks were not curbed, the result would be political instability and economic chaos. It was essential to subordinate the military officers (to civilian control) and in order to achieve this, it was also necessary to create new and different attractions, apart from politics.

But returning for a moment to the eighteenth century, the triumph of the French Revolution in Europe made it possible, up to a point, to displace the Spanish nobility in the colonial army and replace them with members of the bourgeoisie who had previously received military training. The new profession, once the exclusive property of the aristocracy by virtue of their privileged birth, passed into the hands of those who had some expertise—although the government at first demanded purity of blood (*limpieza de sangre*) [for a man] to be an officer, a requirement which gradually lost its importance.

In Peru, the army was not under the control of a noble class, but rather in the hands of aristocratic caudillos who were dedicated political adventurers, hungry for power, but who lacked basic military skills. It was necessary, therefore, to replace them with true professionals, something which various governments in the nineteenth century had encouraged but at which all had failed. Piérola tried, once more, to resolve this acute problem and to change the soldier into a technician, a true professional who had no desire other than to serve in an institution dedicated to specific tasks such as the defense of the nation, its laws, and its legally constituted government.

In order to attain this end, it was of course necessary to provide the military officer with career stability and to bureaucratize him within a military organization which would require academic studies to enter and within which it would be possible to achieve the highest ranks without recourse to extraprofessional activities.

Piérola adopted two procedures to ensure the complete success of his program. He reduced the regular army to 2,000 men, thereby making any military insurrection almost impossible. The drastic reduction in numbers of regulars decreased even further the possibilities for promotion, a situation which undoubtedly caused widespread discontent. However, the increasing loss of morale which the military was suffering forced them to accept with resignation the new government policies.

During the Piérola administration exports tripled and government revenue doubled. The boom benefited public functionaries, whose salaries were increased between 15 and 50 percent in some cases, but military salaries remained unchanged. Such a situation was accepted by the military with patience and submission, not only for the above-mentioned reasons, but also because of their lack of arms. Moreover, the disastrous loss to Chile in the War of the Pacific [1879–83] still smarted, and civilians eagerly took every opportunity to remind the military of it. The classic haughtiness of the old officer had to yield to the insolence of the upper class.

By the end of the Piérola administration, the military occupied an economic position within the national bureaucracy which was very inferior to what it had been before. Taking the four highest ranks of the judiciary, the administrative bureaucracy, the church, and the military, according to that part of the budget which they each received, we have constructed the following index: clergy 550, judicial and public administration 330, army and navy 212. Ministers of state had an index of 600 and the president of the republic 3,000. This is the period in Peruvian history in which the military officer slipped to his lowest point not only economically but also in terms of his political influence and social position.

Despite owing to Piérola its transformation into a modern institution, it may be these events, and the memory of 1879 and 1895, that have generated the hatred which the military feels for Piérola. Jorge Basadre expressed it this way:

It is possible to state that, consciously or unconsciously, many members of the Peruvian armed forces have a deep hatred for the memory of Piérola, recalling that by accident, without belonging to the military profession, he tried to direct the defense of Lima against the Chilean invasion with dismal results, but that as the head of bands of guerrillas, he successfully faced professional soldiers [the Peruvian military] on March 17, 1895.

In addition to impoverishing the army in a material sense, the victor of 1895 adopted another procedure for removing the military from politics: the reorganization of the institution on a technical basis which would be directed by a military mission contracted in Europe. In 1871, the Prussian army inflicted a serious defeat on the French army, thereby demonstrating the inferior professional quality of the French officers, who were surrounded in the Sudan and forced to surrender. From that moment the Prussian army was considered to be the best in the world. It would have been logical, therefore, for Piérola to choose it as a model for the Peruvian army, particularly if one remembers that Piérola had a German military adviser in the 1895 campaign.

In spite of these reasons, however, Piérola contracted with French officers to reorganize and train the Peruvian military. The motives behind the president's action are unknown. The fact that the Chilean government had hired a military mission in Germany some years before[1] may have been one reason why Piérola did not turn to the same country in search of military assistance. Perhaps, as has been suggested by Klaus Lindenberg, the German government might have refused to lend technical aid to two rival countries at the same time.

The fact that France was a republic and not an empire like the new Germany might have been another motive; perhaps also the fact that France was a Catholic country rather than Lutheran might have had certain influence. One might also point to the activities and probable influence of Auguste Dreyfus, the guano monopolist and probable financier of Piérola in the revolution against Pardo, and also (and why not?) the romantic memory of the French widow who accompanied him during his first revolutionary activities.

It could have been these motives or even others that led Piérola in 1896 to hire a French military mission to direct the restructuring of the Peruvian army. Under the command of Lt. Col. Paul Clément, three captains, one each from the branches of artillery, cavalry, and infantry, arrived in Peru with the new rank of Lt. Col.—Clément now held the rank of colonel. All of them had participated in the colonial campaigns of Tunisia, Algeria, Madagascar, and the Sudan. Moreover, Clément was a staff officer.

These army officers had been shaped professionally during the Third Republic, a time when the bourgeoisie had consolidated its power and had pushed the nobility out of high public office. The nobility sought refuge in the army, in the clergy, in the arts, and in scientific study, that is to say in those activities where it was not necessary to work with one's hands—something considered undignified for persons of their lineage. . . .

Since the French army had been professionalized, some officers did not belong to the nobility, but they also quickly identified with the aristocratic spirit of the institution. An officer who remained aloof from the ideological foundation of the army was an officer who lacked esprit de corps, a black sheep who had no possibility of advancing. And the members of the bourgeoisie who joined the army did not do so for the same reasons as the old nobility. Rather they entered with the desire of making the military a career; they were careerists—what Morris Janowitz calls those military men who join the army with a bureaucratic spirit, as a means of living, a vehicle for economic security, both personal and familial, now and in the future. These officers, then, if they wanted to have a career, had to accommodate themselves to the norms of the institution, including its ideology.

To the traditional military virtues of valor, courage, and honor, the bourgeoisie inculcated in the military new virtues, such as poverty and patriotism, by which they replaced the old loyalty to the monarch with loyalty to and identification with the nation. With these new ideas, the dominant class succeeded in dislodging the military from its previously class-oriented vocation and from its love of power.

As the army was badly paid—France [was] a poor country—poverty was elevated to a military virtue. The military profession, the bourgeoisie said to the officers, does not have profit as its purpose; wealth is the property of the bourgeoisie and therefore contemptible. The bourgeoisie substituted for the old military privileges the "honor of dressing in the military uniform," with certain economic concessions such as the education of the children and dowers for the wives. With the uniform in which they dressed and the honor which it signified, the officer was converted into a "priest of the fatherland," dedicated exclusively to its service, without any interest other than the nation—elements which generated a special mysticism. Imbued in the officer was the desire to be appreciated by posterity, a sentiment lacking in the mercenary, who is only interested in pay.

The French officers were to serve with pleasure in the colonies and enlist with enthusiasm in wars of conquest, even though their salaries were not raised, because such operations provided the opportunity to gain glory and also because they provided a psychological outlet for the loss of power in the Metropolis. The colonial officer acted as an administrator, almost independent of the civilian government of France. The lower-ranking officers had certain autonomy within the colonial division governed by a senior officer. In addition, they wielded power over the indigenous population. These officers "describe in offensive terms the civilian officials and petty politicians, whom they despise. As administrators, they are crude, but they boast of knowing the indigenous population well, of respecting their customs, and of not subjecting them to a given ideology."

Marshall Lyautey, the famous Gallic colonial, wrote in Indochina, in 1882, that he did not aspire to be "more than a warrior, a good cacique. . . a young feudal chieftain."

It was in that period in France that the Dreyfus Affair exploded, a period in which the army openly identified itself with the most reactionary elements in the country. Almost all the officers were anti-Semitic, anti-liberal, antirepublican, and proclerical. This feeling of autonomy manifested itself during the affair. Whether Dreyfus was innocent or guilty did not matter; what did matter was that the army had made its decision, and there was no excuse for civilian interference.

After the innocence of Dreyfus had been established and the sentence of the military tribunal annulled, the autonomy of the army was destroyed, and it experienced a crisis. The dower for the wives was abolished, and candidates for the military school of St. Cyr were required to spend a year in the ranks. Moreover, military protocol was modified to give subprefects preference over colonels and prefects preference over generals, minutia that had great importance for military pride. Thus, militarism suffered a serious decline in France as a result of the sacrifice of Dreyfus.

Such was the ideological background of the French officers who arrived in Peru at the end of the last century, with their burden of frustrations ranging from their subordination by the bourgeoisie to their defeat by Prussia and their loss of institutional autonomy. I have presented these details because I deem it important to understand the ideological baggage of those who came to shape professionally the Peruvian military, which had itself suffered similar crises—the defeat by Chile, the loss of political power, and the forced subordination of the military to civilian authority.

The French officers were to influence seriously the minds of their Peruvian colleagues and to collaborate effectively with the governments of the *civilista* aristocracy in the attainment of their political goals. The Gallic officers inculcated their ideology which, in its principal aspects, coincided with that of the earliest Peruvian officers, who were shaped by the Spanish army—monarchist and colonial—since the French army was also colonial and antirepublican at the end of the century.

Owing to these similarities, the intellectual task of the French was an easy one. All they had to do was revive old ideologies and antiquated institutional habits which were perhaps dormant because of military defeats, the indiscriminate recruitment of officers during the war, the loss of prestige suffered by the army in losing the war, and the deplorable economic situation they had been placed in as a result of the fiscal collapse of the nation.

The French mission succeeded in isolating the Peruvian army and reinforced its historic belief that it was an institutional repository of the honor and dignity of the nation, with a monopoly on patriotism. This belief, together with the fact that they dressed in a military uniform, made them see themselves as a superior class. At the same time, the mission lent its influence to maintain the official aloofness from "that dirty thing which is politics," manifested in the army's total contempt for politicians and therefore the entire parliamentary system.[2] In a word, the mission contributed to the depolitization of the army.

In a general way, the Gallic instructors achieved their principal goals. Perhaps they even succeeded in temporarily assuaging the political appetite of the military. However, when the threat of new social upheaval presented itself, the bourgeoisie again called the soldiers out of the barracks to resolve their problems. The evangelization of the army that converted it into "the tutelary institution of the fatherland" came very shortly afterwards. The dominant class elevated the military institution to this level to alienate it from the people so that it would continue to defend the traditional social structure, which was particularly vital in the early years of the century when there was a new wave of working-class activity and organization directed by the anarcho-syndicalists.

The messianic sense acquired by the military officer (or perhaps it was just reinforced) undoubtedly was a direct consequence of bourgeois deification of the army. When the bourgeoisie, terrified of a popular uprising, calls upon the army to silence labor protest and when the military succeeds in bringing peace and tranquility, the Peruvian military officer has to believe that his institution is predestined, if not to win international wars, then at least to triumph in the social arena. That self-confidence has lasted until the present in that the armed forces honestly believe, without doubt, that they possess the capacity to establish harmony between antagonistic classes without eliminating the causes of that antagonism.

French officers continued arriving in Peru in successive missions until 1922. In 1932, French military officers were again hired, this time on an individual basis, but they were withdrawn by their government in 1939 with the outbreak of World War II. In all, more than fifty officers were hired. Most held the rank of general or lieutenant colonel, but there were some lower-ranking officers, generally specialists.

The influence of these officers on the Peruvian army was decisive, as much in professional and technical aspects as in ideology and politics. French influence increased when large numbers of Peruvian officers began studying in French academies. According to as yet unpublished research by Luigi R. Einaudi, between 1916 and 1940, every Peruvian general had spent some time studying in France. By 1950 that figure had dropped to 59 percent and finally to 30 percent in the period 1960–65.

. . . The French military mission began its work in 1897. In April of the following year, the School of Applied Military Science was inaugurated, "destined to improve the professional knowledge of line officers and to pass that knowledge onto bright young men who wish to follow a military career. . . ."

The first goal was transitory and received little attention; at the same time instruction began of the newly accepted students. The first class of six officers graduated in February of 1901. This primitive School of Applied Military Science evolved, changed its name and organization, and became the Chorrillos Military School of today.

The Chorrillos Military School became the alma mater of the Peruvian army. From its founding until the present, 5,144 officers have graduated, including sergeants who enter in the third year of studies. In addition to these, some 807 officers came from the ranks, until, in 1963, it was decreed that the Chorrillos School would be the only source for officer recruitment.

Translated, reprinted, and edited from *Ejército peruano: del caudillaje anárquico al militarismo reformista* (Lima: Librería-Editorial Juan Mejía Baca, 1973), pp. 122–33.

Notes

1. See the preceding selection by Nunn. [ED.]

2. During the present century, the armed forces have dissolved the Congress on the following occasions: with Augusto B. Leguía in 1919; with Luis M. Sánchez Cerro in 1930; with Oscar R. Benavides in 1936; with Manuel A. Odría in 1948; and by military coup in 1962 and 1968. In 1963, there was an evident desire to proceed in the same way, but the coup was thwarted by the opposition of President Fernando Belaúnde Terry. In 1914, the coup by Oscar Benavides had as its declared goal the defense of the parliament, but that was not really a military coup; rather it was an oligarchical coup in which the army was used as a mere tool.

Robert V. Elam

The Army and Politics in El Salvador, 1840–1927

From the dissolution of the Central American Union in 1839 to the presidential victory of Pío Romero Bosque in 1927, El Salvador experienced more than its share of militarism. Frequent armed uprisings at home, together with a dozen invasions from across its frontiers, kept the tiny republic in a state of constant turmoil and rendered the development of stable political institutions all but impossible. However, El Salvador's failure to provide stable central government did not produce regional divisions, as was the case in many of its sister republics. San Salvador remained throughout the period the undisputed capital and the center of all national activities. The diminutiveness of the country constrained the local caudillos, and the constant fear of invasion enhanced the need for political unity. Furthermore, racial, linguistic, or economic regionalisms never developed.

El Salvador sustained no particular ideological character during the last century. It vacillated between liberal and conservative leadership, accepted and rejected the idea of union, in much the same fashion as its neighbors. What remained constant in politics was the reliance upon military force. No sooner did the Constituent Assembly meet in January 1841 than it was threatened with military domination. Each subsequent political conflict, regardless of the nature of the issue, gave rise to armed hordes—hardly could they be called armies—and the brief periods of peace were used for the preparation of new rebel forces.

Because of the violent nature of Salvadorean politics, no enduring military institution developed and the division of civil and military authority remained obscure and confusing. The constitution of 1841, in effect until 1864, provided the president with the authority to use troops, and the congress with the power to raise them, for the defense of the nation. The armed forces were declared apolitical. Active officers were prohibited from serving in congress, though no such prohibition was applied to the presidency. A more serious omission was the failure to provide the chief executive with the powers of commander in chief. As a consequence, civilian presidents often found themselves wholly dependent upon the country's senior officer. The fact that generals held the presidency for a combined period of little more than two years between 1841 and 1859 is evidence that military leaders normally contented themselves with retaining real power rather than titular power.

After General Gerardo Barrios took control of the government in 1858, new emphasis was given to the task of building a formal military organization. On his request, Colombian General José María Melo arrived in 1859. As inspector general of the newly emerging army, Melo emphasized discipline and drill, issued the first standard uniforms, and organized and equipped a special squadron for the president. A French mission of four officers, which replaced Melo in 1862, introduced cavalry and artillery instruction and provided new codes and military ordinances. Prior to this, all codes and ordinances approximated those in use before independence. Not until 1864 and the promulgation of a new constitution were the presidential office and the position of commander in chief combined. Three years later, the first officer school opened in San Salvador under the direction of Spanish General Luis Pérez Gómez. However, mismanagement and limited funds prevented it from having much effect for nearly a decade.

Further reorganization was accomplished in 1879. For the first time, a fixed numerical strength was established for the army. The forces were divided into four divisions, each containing five thousand men.

Increased interest in the development of a stable military institution and greater concern with the promotion of harmonious civil-military relations were less the result of professionalization than of a changing social and economic environment. El Salvador's volcanic soil was found to be highly suitable for growing coffee, and its production was greatly encouraged by General Gerardo Barrios. His successors not only continued the policy of favoring coffee growing but also provided the newly emerging elite with further opportunity for economic and political power. Expropriation of communal lands and the development of large estates characterized the period after 1859, and the process of land concentration was nearly complete by 1912. Moreover, after 1860 the government gave up ownership of rural real estate not used for public facilities with the express condition that the land be planted in coffee.

Other measures were taken to promote economic development and political stability. General Santiago González (1871–76) initiated the building of a modern communications network with army garrisons established at key points. Port facilities were vastly improved, and commodities necessary for coffee production and industrial development were exempted from import taxes.

Little recognition was given to the inherent dangers of a one-crop economy or to the ill effects of encouraging the development of a socioeconomic system dominated by a handful of wealthy families. Those making policy saw themselves as having overcome the burdens of the nation's colonial past by developing a truly modern economy. Plantations resembled factories more than farms, and the new elite was more interested in capital investment and improved agriculture than in family traditions and local politics. Vital to the continuation of these trends was the maintenance of political harmony.

A balance between the needs of the new commercial aristocrat and those of the old conservative generals, long schooled in political intervention, was difficult to achieve, since the desire for wealth and power on the part of ambitious officers often proved insatiable. Generals held the presidency from 1887 to 1903, and not until 1911 was an understanding between civilian and military factions established. That the conflict could take on the characteristics of a barroom brawl is revealed in a dispatch to Washington, D.C., written by a United States representative in Central America: "July 10, 1906. On the 5th, General Regalado, Commander of the Salvadorean army, commenced one of his drunken orgies, ordered out a Hotchkiss gun, and fired two shells into the Presidential Palace, loudly proclaiming his Government a den of thieves whom he desired to wipe out. . . . The morning of the 6th he left for the Guatemalan border where he previously had stationed 1,400 troops, and attacked a Guatemalan outpost. [President] Escalon did all in his power to get him to return to the capital. . . ."

So long as wars with neighbors threatened, the new elite resigned itself to the idea that strutting generals and strong-arm tactics were the price for national protection. But after the 1907 Washington treaty of peace and amnesty, this view began to change. Deprived of the opportunity for foreign campaigns and confronted by a powerful oligarchy determined to achieve order, the military constrained its more disreputable officers and accepted civilian political leadership. The resulting stability, which would continue until 1931, proved even more profitable for the armed forces than had the predatory struggle of the past. Defense expenditures normally absorbed over 20 percent of the total government budgets. Modern garrisons were constructed throughout the republic and the latest European arms were imported.

Indicative of the military's new role was the change in military missions and the creation of the National Guard in 1912. Beginning in 1905, a Chilean mission of five officers spent six years organizing and instructing El Salvador's army. Emphasis was given to tactics and discipline befitting a force designed for external warfare. Then, in 1912, a Spanish mission arrived to establish the National Guard and to organize the armed forces into an internal peace-keeping institution. Under the dual control of the ministries of war and government, this new corps operated as an adjunct to the army, drawing its officers from the Escuela Politécnica and its armaments and ordinances from the Ministry of War. Assignments for the National Guard were determined by the Ministry of Government, and its duties included the patrolling of agricultural estates, the surveillance of roads and ports, and the policing of remote villages and towns. By 1924, the National Guard numbered one thousand guardsmen and ninety-six officers, divided into three infantry regiments and one cavalry regiment stationed throughout the republic.

The National Police, created during the presidency of Rafael Zaldivar (1880–84) was subjected to a thorough reorganization after 1919. Like those of the new National Guard, officers of the National Police were trained in the Escuela Politécnica. Under the jurisdiction of the Ministry of War, the police served to insure order within the urban areas of the republic.

The results, at least on the surface, were impressive. American expert Dana Munro thought that El Salvador's army was the best trained in Central America, though considerably larger than was necessary. The new National Guard, smartly dressed in pith helmets and Sam Browne belts and sporting a battery of motorcycles, added to the overall impression that the nation's armed forces had at last achieved a degree of professionalism. "Really an admirable organization," reported United States military attaché Garrard Harris to the United States Department of Commerce in 1916.

Conservative in matters of social reform, suspicious of mass political participation, and always wary of civilian authority, El Salvador's military cooperated with the government so long as its own sentiments were given ample consideration. The Meléndez-Quiñónez family, which provided the presidents from 1913 until 1927, satisfied the military. By sharing the presidency, the oligarchy avoided the danger of open political campaigns while providing the nation with order and stability. Occasional public protests were met with swift military repression, and the armed forces continued to be well paid for their efforts.

3 The Military and Latin American Politics, 1919–45

Modernization, Instability, and Military Leadership, 1919–45

In the years between the end of World War I and the end of World War II, much of Latin America experienced a period of intensified urbanization and industrialization. These socioeconomic developments were accompanied by hopeful turns toward formal democracy, which were occasionally interrupted by civilian or military dictatorships.

With the onset of the economic depression of the 1930s, even the seemingly most "democratic" Latin American governments saw military elites, by themselves or in alliance with civilian allies, put an end to the post–World War I experiments with liberal democracy. In these years, military elites were still not willing to become permanently involved in "politics," and caretaker regimes or temporary restorationist movements followed coups. Still, divisions were developing within the military establishments themselves over the viability and utility of democratic institutions in Latin America.

Not until two decades after World War II, however, did the military factions committed to long-term military rule emerge triumphant. Nevertheless, in the period 1920–45, military officers attracted to corporate, fascist, or military populist political models temporarily dominated governmental institutions in all seven of the countries upon which we focus in this book: Argentina (1930, 1943, 1946); Bolivia (1936–39, 1943–46); Brazil (1937–45); Chile (1927–31); Peru (1930–39); El Salvador (1931–44); and Guatemala (1931–44). Whether their programs were rightist or leftist, the military elites usually made antipolitics a basic foundation of their programs. They broke with or subordinated traditional political parties and repressed leftist parties or movements. They sought to administer national policies without the distraction of "politics" or the inconvenience of a tolerated opposition. Ironically, these antipolitical officers often belonged to secret societies or lodges—for example, the Logia General San Martín and the GOU (Grupo de Oficiales Unidos) in Argentina, and the RADEPA *(Razón de Patria)* in Bolivia—which engaged in intrainstitutional politics.

In Argentina, Bolivia, Brazil, Chile, and Peru, the appeals of European corporatism or fascism allowed the nationalist, hierarchical, and antipolitical inclinations of the military elites to combine with conservative or reactionary civilian sectors in new political experiments. Frequently the patronage and partisan politics characteristic of formal democracy were used as a pretext for military intervention. Leading officers blamed civilian politics for the consequences of the economic collapse of the 1930s, as well as for the intromission of party politics into the supposedly sacrosanct realm of military promotions, budget decisions, and military education.

The selection by Robert Potash in this chapter describes an archetypal case of this phenomenon in Argentina, where after more than a half century of legal transfers of government, a military coup in 1930 set the stage for restoration of oligarchic rule and then for the reign of Juan Domingo Perón. Of particular interest are the types of justifications provided by the military officers for their action against President Hipólito Yrigoyen as well as the prominent role of the most highly professionalized military elites in Argentina (including Generals Uriburu and Justo) in the reaction against the results of fourteen years of government by the middle-class Radical party.

Also to be noted are the divisions within the military professional elites over the proper role of the military in politics and the substantive character of public policy once the military found itself in control. Clearly, civilian political cleavages had affected the Argentine military establishment, as officers, like civilians, were divided over the policies of the Radical politicians, economic nationalism, populism or oligarchic restoration, and the Argentine constitution itself. Professionalization had done much to improve the Argentine military, but it also made politics and public policy an intimate concern of the professional officer corps. The eventual emergence of Juan Perón as a military populist with a highly political antipolitical appeal was a product of the events of the 1930s in Argentina.

In Bolivia, the tutor of military professionalization, Hans Kundt, led Bolivian soldiers in the disastrous Chaco War against Paraguay. From this debacle came a new military elite which blamed civilian corruption and ineptitude for their losses on the battlefield. While Bolivia never really experienced, even in limited form, the formal democratic experiments of Argentina, Brazil, or Chile, the military reaction to civilian ineptitude spawned nationalist military lodges (RADEPA), military "socialists," such as Toro and Busch, and alliances with fascistlike civilian movements, including the MNR, which later carried out the Bolivian National Revolution of 1952. These Bolivian movements shared with Uriburu, Castillo, and Perón of Argentina the anticivilian, hierarchical, nationalist, and "integralist" orientations antithetical to the liberal democratic beliefs of the post-Versailles world. The essay by William Brill describes the Toro and Busch governments in the late 1930s and events leading up to the Revolution of 1952.

Likewise in Brazil, the 1930s saw an end to an era of liberal democratic experiments. Getulio Vargas in alliance with modernizing elements of the armed forces (including the *tenentes*) and civilian industrial interests took power with a military movement and sought to forge a truly national political regime in a Brazil still dominated by local and regional notables with private armed retainers or state militia. The article by Ronald Schneider describes the coming to power of Vargas. Despite the fact that Vargas himself was a civilian leader, it is clear that military political thinking and military support formed the foundation for the Vargas experiment in Brazil.

In Chile, military antipolitics dominated the years 1924–32. From 1932 until 1973, no successful military coup interrupted the evolution of Chilean formal democracy. Frederick Nunn analyzes the background and consequences of the "honorable mission" of the armed forces in Chile in the period 1924–32. The lack of successful military movements in Chile from 1932 until the coup which overthrew President Salvador Allende in 1973, however, does not mean that the Chilean military was completely devoid of antipolitical officers, as periodic military protests or "strikes" from the late 1930s onward made clear.

In Peru, a civilian dictator, Augusto B. Leguía, ruled from 1919 to 1930 with the complete support of the armed forces. The role of the military in the Leguía administration and in the numerous coups and countercoups until 1945 is dealt with by Víctor Villanueva. As with the German advisers in Bolivia, officers of the French military mission in Peru played a significant role in post–World War I Peruvian politics.

In 1930, one of the officers trained by the French, Lt. Col. Luís M. Sánchez Cerro, led a successful revolt against Leguía. Owing to divisions within the military establishment, Sánchez Cerro was first elected head of the military junta and later, by popular vote, president of the republic. Sánchez Cerro allied himself with the traditional landed oligarchy against the center-left reformist elements in the Alianza Popular Revolucionaria Americana (APRA) party led by Víctor Raúl Haya de la Torre.

Sánchez Cerro's regime was characterized by extreme violence, including the bloody Trujillo massacre of July 1932 and two assassination attempts against his person (the one of April 1933 being successful).

General Oscar R. Benavides, who had led a coup in 1914 and served briefly as president, assumed power and sought to end the bloodshed and establish internal order. He first tried to achieve this through a policy of liberalization and traditional politics (that is, maintaining the Constituent

Congress and calling for presidential elections in 1936). When this policy failed, he resorted to antipolitics, which in the Peruvian case meant annulling the elections of 1936, dissolving the Congress, and repressing political parties, both rightist and leftist.

It is also in this period (1936–39) that the influence of fascism began to spread among the Peruvian officer corps and among certain civilian elites who were closely allied with the military. The new ideology seemingly offered a panacea for ending the chaos and bloodshed which many officers blamed on civilian politics.

In both Guatemala and El Salvador, personalist military dictatorships dominated politics from 1931 to 1944. In the cases of both General Maximiliano Hernández Martínez in El Salvador and General Jorge Ubico in Guatemala, the economic and political crisis of the 1930s provided justification for an increased militarization of politics and a rejection of democracy. The articles by Robert Elam and Kenneth Grieb describe the growing role of the military in national politics in El Salvador and Guatemala during this period.

Robert A. Potash

The Military and Argentine Politics

Increasing professionalism, even when accompanied by physical growth and expanded budgetary allocations, did not necessarily make for greater unity, contentment, and morale within the Argentine officer corps. Quite the contrary, a series of strains developed in the 1920s between rival groups of officers and between parts of the corps and the governing authorities. These strains were all related in one way or another to the rise of Hipólito Yrigoyen and the Unión Cívica Radical (Radical party) to political power. The process of professionalization had coincided with, and to some extent was a response to, the efforts of the Radical party to gain access to power for its growing number of middle-class adherents. From its founding in 1891, the party had been frustrated by electoral fraud from legally achieving its goals; and under Yrigoyen's leadership it had demanded electoral reform, while engaging in a series of conspiracies and revolts. These culminated in the unsuccessful revolution of February 1905, in which numerous officers took part even at risk to their professional careers. Partly in reaction to their involvement, the revised military statute enacted later that year restated the standing regulations prohibiting officers who held troop commands or any assignment under War Ministry control from participating directly or indirectly in politics, even by exercise of the franchise, and warned that "military men who do not comply with [these] prescriptions . . . will be punished for disobedience."

Such regulations did not prevent individual officers from joining the Radical cause, and even General Ricchieri, who as war minister in 1901 had authored the original prohibition on political activity by troop commanders, is said to have offered support in 1909, when serving as a field commander, in Yrigoyen's struggle for electoral reform. Conspiratorial activity involving civilians and military men continued, but no new uprising took place. The guarantees of electoral reform offered to the Radicals in 1910 by the newly elected Conservative president, Roque Sáenz Peña, initiated instead a peaceful process of change that culminated in the election of Yrigoyen to the presidency in 1916.

The calm with which the military accepted the peaceful revolution inherent in the Radicals' rise to national power was subsequently disturbed by the policies of the new administration. The military apparently had little criticism of the international policies of Yrigoyen, especially of his determination not to break relations with Germany in World War I. On the domestic scene, however, the numerous provincial interventions had definite repercussions. Yrigoyen justified the interventions as a means of extending the honesty of the ballot to provincial government and of ending political corruption, a policy of atonement for past wrongs that he liked to call *reparación política*. But these interventions made extensive use of the army to maintain order, and critics noted that the diversion of army units to police duties seriously interfered with the training of conscripts. Moreover, the use of military forces to enable Radical party provincial politicians to take over the offices of rival political groups must have been disturbing to those officers who thought of their mission in professional military terms.

In applying the concept of *reparación* to the army itself, Yrigoyen also aroused resentment in the professional-minded officers who regarded military regulations as sacrosanct, or at least not to be disregarded at the whim of the civil authority. The president, for his part, quite naturally wanted to reward those men whose military careers had suffered because of involvement in the "cause." Acting through a civilian minister of war—in itself a break with the usual practice of appointing a high-ranking officer—Yrigoyen passed over officers eligible for promotion in favor of ex-revolutionaries and issued decrees altering the rank lists, promoting retired officers, and granting pensions regardless of the stipulations of existing law and regulations. The alienation of many officers was increased by a 1921 legislative proposal, whose enactment President Yrigoyen urged, declaring that participation in the Radical revolts of 1890, 1893, and 1905 constituted service to the nation. This bill proposed the reincorporation into the retired list and the granting of retirement benefits for those ex-officers who had been dropped from military service, and one-grade promotions for all those now on the retired list who had been passed over because of their involvement in the revolts. Although the beneficiaries of the bill, after its enactment in modified form in 1923, proved to be relatively few, this attempt to reward personnel who, to paraphrase the words of the bill's author, placed civic obligations above military duty, was an assault on the consciences of those who had remained loyal to that duty. In arguing that there were "primordial obligations to country and constitution far superior to all military regulations," Yrigoyen's supporters unwittingly offered a rationalization for future military uprisings, of which they were to be the first victims. The tragedy was that in looking backward and trying to redress past inequities, Yrigoyen was helping to undermine the none-too-strong tradition of military aloofness from politics and to weaken the sense of unity in the officer corps.

Indeed that unity all but disappeared in the 1920s as differences between officers hardened and factionalism grew. Evidence of this was the organization in 1921 of a secret society of officers alienated by the administration's handling of military matters. This society originated in a merging of two groups of officers, one a group of captains largely from the cavalry, the other, field grade officers of various services. The society took the name Logia General San Martín and eventually comprised some 300 officers, or about one-fifth of the total line officer strength.

A recent study of the Logia ascribes its formation to five basic factors: the toleration shown by the War Ministry to politically minded officers who used their positions to campaign for public office or to generate support for Yrigoyen; favoritism and arbitrariness in the handling of promotions; the development of deficiencies in the training of conscripts; the failure of the administration to act on army requests for adequate arms and equipment; and a general deterioration of discipline within the army that was reflected in enlisted and noncommissioned ranks as well as among the officers.

To these essentially professional concerns leading to the creation of the Logia must be added the apprehension with which certain officers viewed the spread of left-wing activities in Argentina. Still fresh in mind was the week-long breakdown of order in Buenos Aires in January 1919, the so-called *Semana Trágica,* when a minor labor dispute gave rise to bloody clashes with the authorities, mob violence, and what some regarded as an abortive attempt at social revolution. The subsequent discovery that soldiers and noncommissioned officers in at least two garrisons had been forming "soviets" exerted a direct influence on several of the officers, who two years later took the initiative in forming the Logia General San Martín. The Logia's members looked on the organization, therefore, not only as an instrument for correcting professional ills but also as a means of pressuring the government to be less tolerant of the political left. . . .

The appointment of Agustín Justo as Alvear's minister of war in 1922 was a victory for the Logia but no less so for the persistence of factionalism. The gulf between officers who had been critical of Yrigoyen's military measures and those who had profited from them grew wider than ever, the major difference being that it was the former critics who were now the ones to enjoy positions of power. Logia members received many key assignments, including chief of the war ministry secretariat, chief of the president's military household (Casa Militar), and director of the military and war academies. Moreover, the promotion list for superior officers, which the outgoing administration in its final weeks had submitted to the Senate, was recalled before it could be approved, and a new one was prepared.

The Logia members waged relentless war against those officers who in their view were engaged in political activity. Not only did they secure an official decree calling for enforcement of the statutory prohibition on such activity, but they resorted to ostracism of officers who continued to violate it. The leaders of the Logia devised what they termed a blacklist of such officers and called on their members to refrain from any personal contact with those blacklisted except as required by acts of the service. The Logia's existence as a formal organization ended early in 1926. A majority of its governing committee had reached the conclusion that its mission was accomplished, and to prevent its being used for personal ambitions, they moved to dissolve it, a step that was supported by the bulk of the membership. Nevertheless, the procedures used by the Logia in its five years of existence had not eliminated factions in the officer corps. Among some of the former "*logistas*" there was built up a special bond that was to manifest itself in the politics of the future, while on the part of those who had suffered from the Logia, a determination developed to seek revenge against Logia members.

. . . The inauguration in October 1928 of Hipólito Yrigoyen marked the return to the presidency of a charismatic leader, the most popular figure in Argentine history before Perón. Neither the limited achievements of Yrigoyen's first administration (1916–22) nor his six years out of office had dislodged him from the special place he enjoyed in the hearts of average Argentines. Unlike other leaders with mass followings, Yrigoyen was neither a spellbinder nor a crowd-pleaser. Indeed, he had rarely appeared in public and had carefully avoided making speeches, even during the recent electoral campaign. His strength lay rather in his personal persuasiveness, in his ability to convince those who came into direct contact with him to accept his leadership. Strong-willed, tenacious, a firm believer in his own historic mission to redeem the downtrodden, Yrigoyen projected at once a sincerity of purpose and a weight of authority that was difficult to resist. Reinforcing his appeal was the air of mystery he maintained about himself and the austerity of his private life. Even while serving in high office he avoided ceremony as much as possible and continued the ascetic life that had been his norm for the past half century. In his predilection for conversing in low tones in shaded rooms, his preference for wearing dark, nondescript suits, and his reluctance to pose for photographs, he revealed the continuing effects of his early career as a political conspirator. . . .

The Yrigoyen administration's handling of the military construction and armaments program in its first eight months in office was the source of considerable dissatisfaction within military circles. At the close of July

1929 the U.S. ambassador, in a message devoted to analyzing the general situation observed, "The officers of the Army and the Navy are said to be generally disgruntled with the Government because work has stopped, through failure to make payments, on barracks and many other improvements undertaken by sanction of the previous Government."

The military malaise that developed under the Yrigoyen administration had other roots than its mishandling of the capital outlay program. Much more serious from the viewpoint of the ordinary officer was the display of political favoritism in the treatment of military personnel. This favoritism took various forms: the reincorporation into the officer corps of personnel long since discharged with full credit for serving the intervening years; retroactive promotion of retired officers, contrary to explicit provisions of the military laws, with the right to collect the differential in retirement pay; and alteration in the date-of-rank of favored active-duty officers, giving them greater seniority than their contemporaries and consequently an advantage for promotion. . . .

President Yrigoyen's role in the promotion process and in other personnel decisions was not a passive one. He felt free to request changes in the lists submitted by army promotion boards, and he ordered additional promotions in response to personal appeals by individual officers. Indeed, his propensity to respond generously to individuals seeking changes in status introduced a chaotic note in personnel administration. As *La Prensa* observed in July 1930: "It is well known today in the entire national administration, even in the navy and especially in the army, that the military man or his relatives who can secure access to the president of the nation gets everything he wants, even if it is unjust or illegal.". . .

Early in the new administration, officers who were identified with the Logia or with the outgoing war minister, General Justo, were relieved of their posts and placed in an unassigned status (*disponibilidad*). This status, which some officers endured for more than a year, resulted in enforced idleness, as well as loss of the supplementary pay that went with specific assignments. Eventually many of these officers were given assignments, but others preferred to ask for retirement. Among the latter was Colonel Luis García, onetime head of the Logia and former director of the Colegio Militar, who used his retired status to fire salvo after salvo at the War Ministry from the editorial columns of the conservative Buenos Aires daily, *La Nación*. His 137 articles, published from mid-July 1929 to September 5, 1930, spelled out in convincing detail the administration's military mismanagement, seeking thereby to undermine officer corps loyalty.

Working toward the same end was General José F. Uriburu, whose retirement from active duty in May 1929 freed him of inhibitions against participating in a conspiracy. In December 1927, when approached by young nationalists to consider a military movement that would prevent the return of Yrigoyen, his reply is said to have been, "Aren't you forgetting that I am an officer on active duty?" Now, on the occasion of his retirement, he made plain his hostility to the Yrigoyen government in a speech that denounced its influence on the army. After noting that an armed force is a reflection of the nation, having the same virtues and defects, he observed:

The weaknesses of command, which in themselves are usually an expression of the decadence of character, take on a catastrophic aspect the moment that the political power undermines its innards, by destroying through favor or threat what is most respectable in the soul of the officer: his disinterestedness. And it can be asserted without fear of error that from the very moment this sentiment begins to weaken, intrigue and base servility substitute for the common ideal of serving the country with disinterest.

. . . As the Argentine winter of 1930 set in, the administration of the aging president was being buffeted from all sides. Within his own party, disillusioned elements questioned his leadership and that of the men who surrounded him, but Yrigoyen made no move to change either his style or his advisers. Instead, he contented himself with criticism of the critics, including intemperate remarks about the role of foreigners and young people in the party. Outside the party, the barrage of criticism reached unprecedented heights. In the latter part of August, with reports that Yrigoyen was planning to intervene in Entre Ríos province, the atmosphere became explosive. Leaders of all opposition parties called on the president to change his course. A series of mass meetings sought to mobilize public opinion against the administration, while certain political figures on the right began conspiring with army officers. The stage was being set for the military intervention of September 6. . . .

General Uriburu's assumption of power in September 1930 as president of the provisional government marked the beginning of a seventeen-month period of de facto rule. In its own day and ever since, the Uriburu government has been described variously as a military regime, a civil-military government, and a personalist dictatorship. The confusion in terminology derives from the contradictory makeup of the regime. To understand its true character and the place of the military in it, it is necessary to examine the persons who made up the administration, the procedures by which it governed, the groups that supported it, and finally the policies it pursued. . . .

The Uriburu regime rested primarily on the support of the armed forces, which, as we shall see, was not unqualified; on the support of vociferous nationalist groups, including the paramilitary Legión Cívica Argentina (Argentine Civic Legion) described below; and on certain provincial political organizations, of which the Conservative Party of Buenos Aires was the most important. At the very beginning of his administration, however, as a result of the euphoria produced by the very success of revolution and by the pledges given to respect the constitution and work for national harmony, General Uriburu enjoyed the support, or at least the goodwill, of much broader sectors of Argentine opinion. Not only were the political parties that had worked to bring on the revolution, notably the Independent Socialists of the Federal Capital, the Democrats of Córdoba (a conservative group), and the Anti-Personalista Radicals, prepared to cooperate with the government, but parties that had opposed military intervention, the old-line Socialists and Progressive Democrats, showed a willingness to go along with the regime. Even an important sector of the divided labor movement made a public declaration of support.

Had the revolutionary government been content to serve simply in a caretaker capacity while preparing the country for early general elections, these various groups would have supported it in this task. But Uriburu's determination, publicly acknowledged early in October, to promote a series of constitutional reforms that would, among other things, alter the existing electoral and representation system, precipitated a process of political alienation. To the natural and open opposition of the Radicals was added the tacit opposition of several of the parties that had opposed the Radicals. In the absence of any public enthusiasm for his reforms, Uriburu's support was eventually narrowed to the military, the nationalists, and small conservative groups.

Military support for the Uriburu government, while sufficient to enable Uriburu to stay in power for a year and a half, was not unconditional. He had to contend not only with the threat of officers still loyal to Yrigoyen, but also with the influence and ambitions of General Justo and his supporters, who disagreed with Uriburu on the goals of the revolution. . . .

Although the Uriburu administration was able to conduct its economic policies with relatively little concern for military reactions, its political policies involved it in a dialogue with armed forces officers. The war and navy ministers were the normal channels of communication, but President Uriburu frequently spoke before military audiences to build support for his policies. Paradoxically, some of his most important political announcements were made in speeches at military installations, where politics was supposed to be regarded as a threat to morale and unity.

General Uriburu's political objective, as has already been noted, was the adoption of constitutional changes that would, in his view, prevent a repetition of an Yrigoyen-type government. While some of these changes embodied long-standing proposals to strengthen the legislative and judicial branches in relation to the executive and to shore up provincial autonomy against domination from the center, the heart of the proposed reform was alteration of the existing system of universal manhood suffrage and geographical representation. Never spelled out in detail, the proposals aimed at some sort of restricted vote and direct representation of functional groups. . . .

The Uriburu government did use its decree powers, however, to make one far-reaching innovation, the creation of the Escuela Superior Técnica, the technological counterpart of the War Academy. This institution, replacing the advanced course given at the Colegio Militar, trained military engineers and was the logical corollary of the efforts already underway to develop an armaments industry, including the production of aircraft. Under its first director, Lieutenant Colonel Manuel Savio, the Escuela Superior Técnica was to become the center for studying technical problems related to heavy industry development and the promoter of economic nationalist doctrines within the army.

The impact of the Uriburu era on the Argentine army of course transcended questions of size, promotions, training, and regulations to affect the very morale and outlook of the officer corps. Professional values tended to be subordinated to political issues, and what had once been regarded as beyond their competence became matters of daily discussion. The harmful effects on professional standards were evident even to officers who had supported the revolution. Writing in April 1931, Captain Perón observed to Lieutenant Colonel Sarobe, then far removed from the Argentine scene:

I think this revolution has done great harm to the officer cadre. It will be necessary for the men who govern in the future to return things to their place. There is no other solution than to multiply the tasks. The year 1932 at the least ought to be for officers in general a year of extraordinary work of every sort; only in this way can we avoid the harm produced in the army by idleness, backbiting, and politics. Every officer will have to be kept busy in professional tasks from reveille to retreat. Otherwise this will go from bad to worse.

. . . Deterioration of discipline and intensification of rivalries within the officer corps were the inevitable consequence of the September revolution. Another result was an increased disdain for civilians and civilian politicians. Uriburu's speeches to his comrades-in-arms repeatedly denigrated politicians and inculcated the view that patriotism was somehow the monopoly of the armed forces or of special groups like the Legión Cívica. How many officers were persuaded of this view cannot be determined, but it seems likely that a good many junior officers accepted as their own the scornful attitudes of their commander in chief.

The damage inflicted on Argentine society by the revolution worked two ways. On the one hand, it made many officers unwilling to accept completely the idea that political party activity is normal and essential in a democratic society. On the other hand, it lowered civilian confidence in the armed forces as a national institution above politics and spread skepticism about its aims. As Alfredo Colmo put it, "The army will have difficulty, henceforth, in convincing anyone that it is the patrimony of the entire country, that alien passions are not playing in it nor self-centered or irresponsible elements meddling in it. It will have to work to recover its prestige and good name."

An enormous burden was thus thrust upon the Justo administration when it took control in 1932, a burden that its very pursuit of power had helped to create. Not only did it have to cope with the alienation of the Radicals and face the economic and social problems of the deepening depression, but it had to work out, in an atmosphere of considerable distrust, a viable relationship between the army and a goodly part of Argentine society. . . .

From the very beginning of his administration President Justo was extremely sensitive to the problem of military support. The bulk of the officer corps, he was well aware, was politically neutral. However, there were two potential sources of danger: on the one hand, those officers who belonged to, or sympathized with, the Radical party and who subscribed to its view that the Justo government was illegitimate in its origin; and at the other extreme, and bitterly hostile to the Radicals, the authoritarian-minded officers who had been close to Uriburu and who after the latter's death developed the myth that Justo had betrayed the ideals of the September revolution.

Justo's response to the problem was a mixture of measures designed to reduce the likelihood of further alienation of officers while safeguarding him against the subversive activities of unreconstructed elements. Perhaps his shrewdest move was the appointment of Manuel Rodríguez to the War Ministry. As already noted, Rodríguez was a prestigious officer known for his deep commitment to professional standards. As minister of war, Rodríguez undertook to isolate the military from politics and to restore the discipline that had been shattered by the events of 1930–31. For one thing, he deliberately intensified the daily training schedules so as to leave little time for other activities. For another, he constantly emphasized the concept of professionalism and the primacy of military duty over other considerations. The sincerity with which General Rodríguez was able to proclaim these values undoubtedly helped maintain the loyalty of the bulk of the officer corps.

To protect his government against the politically minded officers, however, President Justo employed other means. A surveillance system was developed that included monitoring long-distance telephone calls placed through Buenos Aires and maintaining a close watch on contacts between officers and politicians. With information supplied by military intelligence personnel and by the Federal Capital Police, Justo was in a position to deal quietly with would-be conspirators, in some cases transferring them to innocuous positions, in other cases using the promise of promotion to wean them away from their allies. Arrest and retirement, however, were the usual penalties for those active-duty military personnel who carried their opposition into the open.

Justo much preferred to use indirect methods for thwarting military opposition. This is seen in the promotion of superior officers. In the list he submitted to the Senate in July 1932, the first to be approved since 1928, the grade of colonel was requested for forty-three officers, including Uriburistas and Radicals as well as members of the "Justo group." There is some reason for believing, moreover, that the president tried to exploit the mutual hostility of Radical and Uriburista officers as a means of keeping both in check. His overtures to the former through a proposed amnesty for pro-Radical officers penalized by the Uriburu regime and his concession to the former Uriburistas in not shutting down the paramilitary Legión Cívica support such an interpretation. The discontent of both groups persisted, but neither was able by itself to upset Justo's position.

The most determined efforts to overthrow him in the first two years of the administration came from the Radical side. A small group of officers and noncommissioned officers, of whom Lieutenant Colonel Atilio Cattáneo was the driving spirit, tried to organize a civil-military revolution in conjunction with leaders of the Radical party. Opposition from the Alvear wing of the party and rivalries among the military and civilian elements pledged to take part plagued the effort, as Cattáneo's memoirs attest. The first attempt, which was to consist of coordinated uprisings in the capital and several provinces, never came off because an accidental explosion a week before the planned day in December 1932 alerted the authorities and resulted in Cattáneo's arrest.

A few weeks later two Radical officers tried, unsuccessfully, to raise a regiment in Concordia, Entre Ríos, but the next major effort was scheduled to coincide with the holding of the Radical party's national convention in Santa Fe, in December 1933. This time the authorities knew the timing of the uprisings in advance, although not exactly where they would take place. Waiters on the river vessel that carried Radical party members to Santa Fe had been replaced by police agents, and on the basis of their reports, the president and his advisers waited up on the night of December 28–29 for the blows to strike. The main fighting took place in Santa Fe and Corrientes, with other disturbances in Buenos Aires province, but federal forces were easily able to restore order. A nationwide state of siege was proclaimed, and President Justo now took advantage of the situation to crack down on the entire Radical party, arresting Alvear and other moderate leaders who wanted a return to electoral politics, as well as those who frankly favored revolutionary methods.

With the failure of the 1933 movement, conspiratorial activity among the pro-Radical officers was confined to a few diehards. The party itself, recognizing the impossibility of regaining power by force, decided, despite vigorous internal dissent, to resume contesting elections in 1935. Thereafter, its contacts with the military were designed primarily to persuade the officer corps that a Radical victory at the polls would not threaten their careers. . . .

By 1937, President Justo had gained sufficient control of the political process to rig the election for his successor without fear of military intervention. Radical appeals for the army to supervise the balloting received no visible response from the officer corps, which obeyed Justo's injunction, repeated at the annual armed forces dinner on July 6, to stay clear of politics. The politically minded nationalist officers, who had as little use for the official candidate as they did for his Radical opponent, were in no position to act. Instead, they decided to await Justo's exit from office before making a new attempt to take power.

The willingness of the officer corps as a whole to leave politics to the president was undoubtedly influenced by their approval of Justo's handling of military affairs. Under his administration the modernization of the armed forces, which had been interrupted after 1928, was renewed and outlays of funds for military purposes reached unprecedented heights. . . .

The support given the Justo administration by the armed forces obscured but did not prevent the intensification of nationalistic sentiment in the officer corps and of the accompanying belief that the military should play a larger role in shaping public policy. Evidence of this trend may be seen in articles published in semiofficial and official military organs during and after the Justo era. Although the views expressed were those of individual authors, it is evident that the military men who edited the *Revista Militar* and the *Revista de Informaciones* were not opposed to having such views associated with the military establishment. A favorite theme of these articles was the great destiny that awaited Argentina and the need for the nation to prepare for an important future international role. Typical of this view was the flat assertion of a military engineer, Major Ricardo Maraimbo, that "the Argentine Republic ought to be and must be a great world power." The preparation that he and like-minded fellow officers proposed included nationalization of foreign investment, promotion of industrial self-sufficiency, intensification of patriotic sentiment through the repudiation of "utopian, internationalist, pacifist, and exotic ideas," and a substantial strengthening of the peacetime army. . . .

Not content with setting forth general goals, some officers insisted on the army's right to a major voice in foreign policy decisions. Colonel Carlos Gómez repeatedly advocated that the general staff chiefs participate in a national defense council concerned not just with defense plans but with the entire process of international relations. With reference to bordering countries, he specifically claimed the right for the military to say "With this neighbor we ought to be friends or allies; with this other it does not matter whether we are." Strategic considerations alone, he felt, should determine the nature of Argentina's relations with her South American neighbors.

From the belief that the military had a natural right to determine foreign decisions, it was no great jump to the conclusion that this competence extended also to the domestic field. Civilian nationalists like the poet Leopoldo Lugones had long been advocating military influence in domestic matters, of course, and had seen their ideas translated into approximate reality during the Uriburu interlude.

As the Justo administration came to an end, the gap was widening between the official view of the army's role and that held by an indeterminate but increasing number of individual officers. Officially, the army was depicted as an institution without interests apart from those of the nation, one that accepted subordination to the constituted authorities, one that contributed to the general progress of the republic. Justo's first war minister had once summed this up by stating to the Congress that he was "a representative of the interests of the nation in the War Department, and not the representative of the interests of the army." But even though General Rodríguez had spoken of the army as "a weapon to be used by the civilians who have responsibility for the governments of the nation," military skepticism about the ability of such civilians to conduct its affairs was very much alive at the time the fraudulently elected Ortiz-Castillo government took power. The six years of the Justo administration had postponed, not resolved, the delicate question of the place of the military in the political process. . . .

The Army in Power, 1943–44

The substitution of military for civilian government [again] in June 1943 took place under conditions quite distinct from those prevailing at the time of the first takeover thirteen years before. Missing was the atmosphere of public excitement that had preceded the Uriburu-led coup, an atmosphere deliberately fomented by Yrigoyen's opponents. The June uprisings, in contrast, came as a surprise to the general public and even to those politicians who were aware of the widespread discontent within the officer corps. The politicians were anticipating a move in September, not in June.

Still, it would be erroneous to claim that the military acted without regard for the civilian sector, or indeed without encouragement from it. The officers shared the universal concern over President Castillo's electoral plans even while they disagreed among themselves on the wisdom of his foreign policies. Moreover, the belief that it was their responsibility to take action was strengthened by their increasing contacts with political leaders, especially those of the Radical party. Without this stimulus, it is questionable whether the liberal, pro-Allied sector of the army would have risen, and without their participation the movement could not have succeeded. The inability of the nationalist sector to mount a successful coup by itself had been demonstrated time and time again in previous years.

In acting to oust the Castillo government, the military was responding to a harsh axiom of Argentine politics: that no constitutional authority is strong enough to prevent a determined president from imposing his will, even if this involves violation of the laws and the constitution itself; and that only the withdrawal of military support can call a halt to such an administration. With his control over the Senate, Dr. Castillo could be unconcerned about impeachment proceedings, and he had shown by his continued extension of the state of siege his determination to ignore hostile opinion. The belief that it was up to the military to intervene was by no means limited to military circles; many civilians would have agreed with General Rawson when he told his comrades-in-arms: "When the nation, as a result of bad rulers, is put into a situation where there are no constitutional solutions, [the military] has a duty to fulfill: to put the nation in order." But here was the rub. Could an officer corps as deeply divided as that which existed in 1943 "put the nation in order"?

Adapted from chaps. 1, 2, 3, 4, and 8 of *The Army and Politics in Argentina, 1928–1945: Yrigoyen to Perón,* by Robert A. Potash, with the permission of the publishers, Stanford University Press (January 1977). © 1969 by the Board of Trustees of the Leland Stanford Junior University. Footnotes are omitted.

William H. Brill

An Overview of
the Bolivian Military
in National Politics to 1952

The armed forces in Bolivia have a long history of political involvement. It was the military that carved the republic out of the remnants of the Spanish empire and provided it with its early leaders. Unlike the revolutionary army of North America, which willingly laid down its arms and surrendered its power to well-developed civilian institutions, the Bolivian military assumed both by intent and by default the proportions of a ruling institution. Along with the church, the military became the bastion of conservatism and assured the landowning and merchant class that the revolution would not go beyond the achievement of independence.

With the decline of the powers of the church in the late nineteenth century, the military came to wield even greater power; it was limited only by the advent of the liberal movement of the early twentieth century. But even during this era, the military continued to exert a powerful influence on Bolivian politics and was always a force to consider. After senior officers had opposed the take-over of the government by the Republicans in 1920, [Bautista] Saavedra, the new president, felt it necessary to organize his own army, the Guardia Republicana (Republican Guard), and to remove the firing pins from the rifles issued to regular army soldiers stationed near the capital city of La Paz. And in an effort to block the political artery that led from the top of the armed forces to the presidency, a former German military adviser, Hans Kundt, was made chief of the general staff. Although respected as a military officer, the fact that Kundt was a German also recommended him, for it precluded his ever taking over the government.

The working relationship that had been crudely and imperfectly fashioned between the military and civilian leaders in the early part of the twentieth century broke apart under the impact of the Chaco War. This bitter, agonizing experience was a defeat not only for the German-trained Bolivian Army—but also for the entire nation. As Robert Alexander has pointed out, "the four-year conflict with Paraguay from 1932 to 1936 disorganized the economy, discredited the army, spread new ideas among the urban workers and miners, and sowed discontent among the intelligentsia."

The social disorganization which followed the Chaco War led to the formation of new political parties. In 1937, the Falange Socialista Boliviana (Bolivian Socialist Falange, or FSB) was created, patterned after Franco's falange in Spain, and in 1940 a Marxist-oriented Partido de la Izquierda Revolucionaria (Party of the Revolutionary Left, or PIR) was formed, along with a Trotskyite Partido Obrero Revolucionario (Revolutionary Workers Party, or POR). It was not until 1941 that the most important party of all was born—the Movimiento Nacionalista Revolucionario.

To its founders, such as Víctor Paz Estenssoro, Hernán Siles Suazo, José Cuadros Quiroga, and Augusto Céspedes, the MNR was intended to be something more than a "party" in the traditional Bolivian sense. According to Céspedes, and explicit in the name of the organization, the MNR was to be a "movement"—a broadly based structure that linked miners, peasants, and middle-class intellectuals under a banner that was revolutionary and nationalistic and thus against the members of the established oligarchy, such as the large landowners and the foreign mine owners. Although never able to fashion a definitive ideology, the MNR did ultimately translate the symbols of nationalism and revolution into a program which called for the nationalization of the mines, land reform, and universal suffrage and education.

In the years that the new political parties were forming, the military was far from idle politically. Shaken, bitter, and humiliated at its defeat by the lightly regarded Paraguayans, it promptly elevated a series of military officers to the presidency of Bolivia. A few of these men proved to be adventuresome. Colonel David Toro, for example, nationalized Standard Oil, established the first Ministry of Labor, and initiated some workers' legislation. But his otherwise casual approach to the presidency, characterized by heavy drinking and other festivities in the palace, led to his downfall, and he was succeeded by Colonel Germán Busch. Busch intensified Toro's liberal political policies. Before his death in 1939, he established a federation of miners and even encouraged the formation of trade unions.

At the same time that the military was maneuvering on the national level, another force was at work within the institution. This was the RADEPA (Razón de Patria), a secret society formed by young officers in the prison camps of Paraguay during the Chaco War. Sworn to secrecy and vowing to save Bolivia, these officers in the years following the Chaco War slowly moved up through the ranks of the Bolivian army. Some of them were sent to Germany and Italy, where their need for pride and identity was fully exploited by their hosts—even to the point of granting the Bolivians audiences with Der Führer and Benito Mussolini. Upon their return, these officers, by now majors, joined their RADEPA brothers and for the first time became an active force in the military.

It was the RADEPA that opened the dialogue between the MNR and the army. The year was 1943. The popular Busch had been succeeded by General Carlos Quintanilla and then by General Enrique Peñaranda, an honest, simple man by all accounts, who had gained the presidency by a popular election in 1940. Once in power, Peñaranda was beset by falling tin prices and trouble in the mines. In December 1942, government troops fired on rebellious miners at the huge mining complex of Catavi, and the MNR made the ensuing massacre its rallying cry. At the same time, RADEPA leaders were charging the government with corruption and with mismanagement of Bolivia's natural resources. Advocating a strong, authoritarian government, RADEPA gained the support of the young officers and began casting about for a revolutionary ally. According to one of the founders of RADEPA, the leadership of the society made contact with all the major political parties of the day after deciding that they needed a "political base." At one point, the RADEPA leaders even thought of trying to make the Marxist-oriented PIR more nationalistic but rejected the idea in favor of the MNR. Whether the MNR was selected simply because of its growing political strength or whether there was a perceived ideological similarity is difficult to say. Both the MNR and the RADEPA have been charged with fascist leanings during this period, and both have denied it.

In any case, the year 1943 brought the RADEPA and the MNR to power after a bloodless coup against the feeble Peñaranda. Gualberto Villarroel, a young major and member of the RADEPA, was made president, and Víctor Paz Estenssoro, the MNR leader, became minister of finance.

The Villarroel regime lasted a little more than two years. During this time several opposition leaders were murdered, the United States charged the coup with being fascist-inspired and withheld recognition for six months, and the MNR and the army frequently found themselves at odds. But despite the friction and the intense opposition to the regime, this brief period allowed the MNR to consolidate its support. Trade unions were formed, and Villarroel and his ministers called and attended a national Indian congress. Moreover, the Villarroel government gave the MNR its first experience with power, and it was during this period, it should be noted, that the MNR and the army first took each other's measure.

The circumstances of the fall of Villarroel are shrouded in mystery. Both the army and the MNR charge each other with betraying the president. The MNR cites the failure of the army to defend Villarroel against the mob that dragged him from his office in the palace and hanged him from a lamppost;

and the army charges that the MNR cut the telephone lines to the palace. In any case, Villarroel is something of a hero to each of his former supporters. According to Colonel Ponce, a RADEPA leader who talked to Villarroel hours before his murder, the president "preferred to be dead rather than misunderstood" and refused to issue orders for the army to take action against the mob. The MNR, for its part, made a monument out of the lamppost upon which Villarroel was hanged.

With the end of Villarroel, the army and the MNR parted. It was to be six years before they were to meet again—this time in mortal combat. In the interim, the MNR suffered the fate of the opposition in Bolivia, while the army, purged of the RADEPA, backed the new government which was headed first by Enrique Hertzog and then by Mamerto Urriolagoitia.

Reprinted and edited from *Military Intervention in Bolivia: The Overthrow of Paz Estenssoro and the* MNR (Washington, D.C.: Institute for Comparative Study of Political Systems, 1967), pp. 5–9.

Ronald M. Schneider

The Military and Brazilian Politics to World War II

Since the establishment of the republic, there have been very few periods in Brazilian history that have not been marked either by military revolts or by heavy armed forces tutelage of the government. In the recurrent struggle between legalism and political activism within the Brazilian military, the latter has long been substantially stronger than depicted by most historians and many contemporary observers. Neglect of this fundamental fact and the corresponding overemphasis of the role of civilian politicians and political movements have distorted interpretations of Brazilian political development. While a series of civilians from São Paulo did govern the country with reasonable security after the initial years of military domination under Marshals Deodoro and Floriano, two of these three presidents faced military crises that in the context of the times posed threats to their continuance in office. Prudente de Morais (1894–98) was plagued by dissatisfaction over his handling of the Canudos "insurgency" problem and in November 1897 was saved from assassination by a veteran of that campaign only because War Minister Machado Bittencourt sacrificed his own life to save the president. Following Campos Salles's quite peaceful term (1898–1902), Rodrigues Alves survived the November 1904 revolt of the Military School at the midpoint of his administration. The first *mineiro* president, Afonso Pena (1906–9), died in office of a "moral traumatism" soon after being thwarted in his preferences for a civilian as his successor and being forced to accept the candidacy of War Minister Hermes da Fonseca. Nilo Peçanha's year in office was little more than an opportunity to preside over the marshal's election, and Hermes himself was barely settled in the presidency when the naval revolt of 1910 broke out. His regime was also plagued by protracted insurgency in the northeast and south by dissident politicians. The latter problem extended into the term of Wenceslau Braz (1914–18), who otherwise enjoyed stability, although the nation's political king-maker, Senator Pinheiro Machado, was murdered (to the ill-concealed satisfaction of some officers). The military's involvement in World War I temporarily reduced its political interference and left Braz a good bit freer than he might otherwise have been.

Military involvement in politics resurged during the interwar period. Epitácio Pessoa (1919–22) was involved in rather constant friction with the armed forces because of his insistence on appointing civilians to head the war and navy ministries. By the last year of his term a grave military question had arisen as the army, behind Marshal Hermes da Fonseca, adamantly opposed the choice of Arthur Bernardes as president for the 1922–26 term. Indeed, the entire decade of the 1920s was one of repeated military uprisings, culminating in the successful 1930 Revolution. [Getúlio] Vargas himself, although heavily backed by, and to a considerable degree dependent upon, the armed forces, faced civil war in 1932 and a communist revolt in 1935, in both of which movements regular army elements were involved, before staging his own dictatorial coup in 1937. Like Wenceslau Braz, a quarter of a century earlier, Vargas also benefited from the military's concern with its wartime obligations. But with the end of World War II, Vargas was unceremoniously removed from office by the armed forces.

The transition from dictatorship to a constitutional, competitive regime after 1945 did not place undue strains upon the political process shaped by Vargas, at least so long as it received predominantly support rather than demands from the armed forces. Subsequently, however, the problems of aftermath politics in a period of emerging populism and resurgent traditional clientelism, aggravated by dislocations caused by the external influence of postwar international adjustments, gave rise to increasing tensions and a "revolution of rising frustrations." Under these conditions, Vargas's return to power through popular elections took place in 1950, only to encounter the full brunt of the participation crisis. Governing within the constraints of a constitutional system that had been consciously devised to thwart a president who might try to operate in his old style, Vargas found his tried-and-true techniques of manipulation and conciliation inadequate. His response involved a shriller demagoguery and intensified exploitation of nationalism rather than evolving a more serviceable substitute political style. In this situation, the majority of the officer corps withdrew their support from his regime.

Thus, the military's repeated intervention in the political arena in the postwar era had behind it a substantial tradition. Indeed, the relative political peace under Juscelino Kubitschek (January 1956–January 1961) was as long a recess from major political-military crisis as the republic had yet witnessed. When Kubitschek turned over the presidential office at the end of his full term to an elected successsor in a climate of normalcy, he was accomplishing something achieved only by three previous civilian presidents (Campos Salles, Rodrigues Alves, and Wenceslau Braz). Moreover, three governments fell by force in the single constitutional term between [Eurico Gaspar] Dutra and Kubitschek, while the five-year presidential period after Kubitschek saw the emergence and decline of three distinct regimes in a process of nearly continual crises that interred the old pattern of civil-military relations and brought the armed forces back to the direct exercise of power they had experienced in the infant years of the republic.

In a very similar sense to the continuity of *tenentismo* (the political militance of the junior officers entering the service after World War I) and even of the *tenentes* themselves from the 1920s through the 1960s, *Florianismo* in the form of advocacy of military rule as practiced by Marshal Floriano [Peixote], spanned the 1890s to the early 1920s. First with the "Consolidator of the Republic" himself, then through the political career and presidency of his aide and favorite nephew, Marshal Hermes da Fonseca (1910–14), and finally with the bridge between *Florianismo* and *tenentismo* in the form of the 1921–22 campaign of the Military Club against the government under Hermes's leadership, this interventionist current left its impact on the military generation born after the establishment of the republic. Thus, if events before 1910 were just faint memories to the senior officers of the early 1960s, the same was not true of the Hermes da Fonseca administration and the period of World War I. For with few exceptions, the generals of the post-Vargas era were already cadets at this time, enrolled in military preparatory school (Colegio Militar) if not already in the academy (Escola Militar). Hence, for example, the naval revolt that broke out after Hermes's inauguration appears to have left an imprint that disposed them to react strongly to the navy insubordination in March 1964.

While the earlier military interventions and revolts were part of the armed forces' historical memory, the developments of the 1920s were directly related—through the Revolution of 1930, the 1937 coup, and the ouster of Vargas in 1945—to the developments of the 1954–64 decade.

Throughout this period, military figures were actively involved in the political life of the states, albeit more often behind the scenes than in the spotlight. In point of fact, between 1900 and 1930 the Brazilian armed forces were an even more active factor in the politics of the nation than were their Argentine counterparts—conventional wisdom to the contrary. The Brazilian armed forces differed from the Latin American norm during the first three decades of the twentieth century more as a result of the nature of the Brazilian political system as a whole than in terms of their own particular characteristics as an institution. As the system underwent a process of change, so did the military subsystem, in response to many of the same dynamic factors.

With the beginning of the political decay and institutional deterioration of the Old Republic at the end of World War I, the military was at the center of every crisis. The increasing division within the armed forces along generational lines, which placed them on both sides of the conflict between the established order and the forces of change, nourished a continued belief, strongest within the military but accepted by much of the public, that it was national rather than institutional interests or personal ambitions that motivated their political actions, and to a considerable degree this was true. As their predecessors were the midwives of the republic in 1889, the younger officers—those emerging from the Military School toward the end of the war and after—were its gravediggers.

By 1928, the republican regime in its nearly four decades of existence had reached the same point of deterioration, and the oligarchic system a parallel degree of political decay, as had been the case with the empire in the mid-1880s. Institutions and processes that might have been suitable for the first years of republican self-government had failed to evolve beyond an amalgam with traditional practices carried over from the monarchy. Indeed, they became entrenched through the federal government's willingness to let state power structures alone as long as they cooperated in Congress and created no undue difficulty over presidential succession. The electoral process was highly fraudulent; national parties were nonexistent; and protests against the inequities of the established order were increasingly met with repression rather than compromise and evolutionary reform. The federal executive, while frequently arbitrary, often lacked the compensatory merit of strength and effectiveness. The political representatives of the patriarchal and "oligarchic" regime could not point with pride to outstanding accomplishments to justify their continued stewardship of the nation. Or rather, when they sought to do so, they were convincing only to themselves, while appearing hypocritical and self-seeking to an increasing proportion of the politically conscious public.

As long as elections might lead to change, there was no strong popular base for revolution. But the people were aware that never in the history of the republic had the government's candidate lost. Moreover, only on two widely separated occasions had the electorate been given even the shadow of a real choice rather than just an opportunity to ratify the decision of the powerful state machines (and this only when the bargaining process among the president and the governors of São Paulo, Minas Gerais, and Rio Grande do Sul had broken down). Indeed, to all intents and purposes, the selection of São Paulo's governor for the 1926–30 presidential term had taken place in 1919, when the election of Epitácio Pessoa to the presidency was understood within the political class as a temporary "emergency" interruption of the pattern of São Paulo–Minas Gerais alternation, which would give the young state executive four more years to mature. In this context, the presidential succession of 1930 turned out to be the last chance for the old republican system to demonstrate significant flexibility or adaptability. But the course of events from late 1928 on demonstrated that Brazil's political crisis was one both of men and of institutions.

The core of the revolutionary movement that eventually triumphed in October 1930 was composed of the *tenentes*, who had gained conspiratorial experience as well as a degree of popular renown during the four years of their armed struggle against the government of Arthur da Silva Bernardes (1922–26). During 1928–29, they were able to win additional adherents to their cause within the officer corps, exploiting the growing dissatisfaction with the regime's policies. The successful revolution became possible only after they formed an alliance with a broad coalition of political forces possessing a significant power base in the key states, but their proselyting and infiltration of military units throughout the country were essential to the achievement of this purpose. Indeed, without the assurance of widespread military adhesions, the generally cautious political leaders would not have risked a revolutionary venture, particularly the coldly calculating Getúlio Vargas, in whose name the 1930 revolt was ultimately launched and who had delayed his commitment until the movement was far advanced.

Tenentismo paralleled in many respects the positivistic republicanism of the young officers in the last decade of the empire. On the intellectual side, its origins can be found in the Military Academy, reopened in 1911–12 at Realengo after being closed in the wake of the 1904 cadet revolt. There during World War I such future leaders as Eduardo Gomes, Luís Carlos Prestes, Siqueira Campos, Oswaldo Cordeiro de Farias, Stenio Caio de Albuquerque Lima, and Ciro do Espírito Santo Cardoso (to name but one group among several who maintained a significant exchange of ideas) studied and lamented a "Brazil laden with problems, beneath the weight of the crisis and in the hands of politicians [who are] inept as well as unscrupulous and instruments of oligarchies." The leaders of the academy made a conscious effort to keep the education essentially technical rather than highly theoretical, with a taste of the humanities, or at least of positivist philosophy, as had been the case at the old academy at Praia Vermelha during the years when its instructors were still the disciples of Benjamin Constant. The goal was to develop competent professional soldiers, well disciplined and obedient to constituted authority. This orientation was successful with many. But in light of the lower-middle-class origin of a large proportion of the young officers, the example of their superiors' often mixing in politics, the siren call of renewed *Florianismo* through the person of Hermes da Fonseca, and the magnitude of national problems (contrasted with the "selfish" interests of the "boss"-dominated political system), it is not surprising that a significant minority questioned the military's institutional role as a support of the established order.

The militants of both the legalist and reformist theses were greatly outnumbered at the time (as they would be three decades later) by the vast majority of officers for whom the two sides of the nation's motto, "Order and Progress," had equal importance. Since the 1891 Constitution enjoined the armed forces on the one hand to be "essentially obedient, within the limits of the law" to the president, but on the other hand declared them "obligated to support the constitutional institutions," it virtually consecrated ambivalence in ambiguous situations when the threat to the constitution's integrity appeared to come from the executive. Moreover, the increased emphasis upon study and training advocated so vigorously by the champions of professionalism and embodied in the 1920 military regulations, along with the arrival in the same year of a French training mission, which was destined to have a heavy impact upon the army's mentality, appears to have made young officers more aware of national problems than before. Growing numbers came to believe: "On the national scale, the army, and only the army, was the organized force which could be placed at the service of democratic ideals and popular demands, against the interests of the bosses and oligarchies which increasingly aggravated the burdensome conditions of survival for the unprivileged."

The spread of this reformist-activist sentiment among the military coincided with the increasing alienation of urban progressive groups who found the establishment unresponsive to their demand for a significant voice in policy making and not at all disposed to yield to demands for any type of reform, including that of the electoral system. As had been the case forty years earlier, nearly all of the preconditions for revolution existed. Dissension within the political elite over presidential succession combined with the impact of the world economic crisis made the regime vulnerable and provided additional impetus to the formation of a revolutionary coalition capable of overthrowing the established order.

The successful revolutionary movement of 1930 was a heterogeneous amalgam of groups desiring sweeping political changes if not a new social order, with elements, which although violently opposed to the incumbent administration and the president's hand-picked successor, were devoid of any wish for more than modest political and administrative reforms. In both its civilian and military components—each crucial to its success— the revolutionary coalition was essentially, indeed almost exclusively, bourgeois in nature. The Communists, considering the October 1930 revolt to be narrowly concerned with regional rivalries within the existing system, refused to participate or support it—a fact that was to have significant implications for the postrevolution political struggles.

Presidential succession was the issue that coalesced the fragmented opposition forces into a single movement cohesive insofar as its immediate objective—attainment of power—was concerned. In 1929, the world market crisis combined with a record coffee harvest to thwart government price-support policies and trigger an economic recession. Elements linked to industry, finance, commerce, and services began to react strongly against economic policies favoring export-oriented agricultural producers. Against this background, an unusually strong opposition coalition was forged to contest the 1930 presidential election. When outgoing President Washington Luis, of São Paulo, broke with tradition and sought to impose another *Paulista* as the official candidate, Minas Gerais political leaders threw their support to the "Liberal Alliance" slate headed by Getúlio Vargas, the governor of Rio Grande do Sul. Júlio Prestes was announced the winner, but the Liberal Alliance refused to accept the allegedly fraudulent results and launched a revolt in October 1930. Alarmed at the prospect of civil war and impressed with the visible decay of the old regime in the face of this challenge, the high command of the armed forces, after a good deal of maneuvering by generals with key commands, stepped in and forced the president to resign in favor of a junta, which it was hoped by some participants might prove a viable alternative to the revolutionary forces.

Vargas became provisional chief executive at the head of a very heterogeneous movement. Although the *tenentes* and some "young Turk" politicians desired a real social revolution, they lacked any coherent plan; other groups wished only to correct the evident deficiencies of the old political system. They agreed only upon a new electoral code incorporating the secret ballot, proportional representation, a system of electoral courts, and extension of the franchise to include women. Following an unsuccessful "Constitutionalist" revolt centered in São Paulo in July 1932, a constituent assembly was elected and in 1934 conferred a four-year presidential term upon Vargas. During this time both the communists and the local fascists (known as Integralists), thriving in a situation where less ideological parties failed to take root, sought Vargas's overthrow by violent means. In November 1937, Vargas staged a coup with the acquiescence of the armed forces' leaders, assuming dictatorial powers and decreeing a semicorporate "New State" *(Estado Nôvo)*. By absorbing into his regime important elements of the dominant state machines, he was able to bend the existing political system to his wishes and adapt it to his needs. Thus, he was able to govern without a formal party structure while maneuvering to neutralize critical military elements.

Vargas's fifteen-year stay in power, although interrupting Brazil's tradition of constitutional government, helped to break the hold of the traditional elite groups and brought new elements into the political arena.

Moreover, Vargas gave impetus to social and economic developments that subsequently tended to give a broader base to Brazilian experiments with representative regimes in the 1946–64 period. Yet more than anything else the *Estado Nôvo* reinforced authoritarian tendencies and corporatist structures which proved barriers to the development of a pluralist system.

Reprinted and edited from *The Political System of Brazil: Emergence of a Modernizing Authoritarian Regime*, 1964–1970 (New York: Columbia University Press, 1971), pp. 37–48, by permission of the publisher and the author.

Frederick M. Nunn

The Military in Chilean Politics, 1924–32

Prior to 1973, political orientation and motivation of Chilean army officers in the twentieth century was generally confined to the 1924–32 period. During those eight years the military functioned as a politically deliberative body in four distinct ways. First, in September 1924 the actions of junior and middle-grade officers caused President Arturo Alessandri Palma to resign his office, whereupon a junta composed of two generals and an admiral assumed executive functions. Four months later, in January 1925, a coup led by the progenitors of the 1924 movement deposed the junta and recalled Alessandri, allowing him to serve out the remaining few months of his five-year term.

Second, during the two tense years that followed, the army, under the control of a clique of colonels, steadily increased its influence in national politics while observing constitutional procedure. From the pose of an obedient, objectively controlled military organization the Chilean army moved to a position of dominance. It was the army which provided impetus for civilians to write a new constitution in 1925. In September 1925 the recalled Alessandri resigned his office a second time because of military pressure. His elected successor fared no better and by early 1927 was a pawn in the struggle between reform-minded military men and recalcitrant and antimilitarist political leaders. The army's insistence on full exercise of constitutionally provided executive powers forced him to resign. When he did so, it was only a matter of weeks before the military reform leader Colonel Carlos Ibáñez del Campo became president, the first military man to occupy the presidential chair in three-quarters of a century.

Third, Ibáñez and his civilian and military supporters governed Chile for four years, until July 1931. Applying the socioeconomic reforms called for in the new constitution, Ibáñez paid only lip service to civil liberties and democratic procedures of governance embodied in the same document. He was not a true dictator, but a rigid authoritarian, elevated to power constitutionally, who had grave doubts about traditional liberal democracy and constitutionalism.

Fourth, after the fall of Ibáñez in 1931 army officers continued to engage in intrigue and plotting for nearly fifteen months. In this last period the prestige of the armed forces suffered greatly. Plotting and effecting the overthrow of three administrations within three months in 1932 assumed an almost Parnassian quality and showed little orientation toward national issues at stake during the previous three epochs.

It is in the second of these clearly delineated periods that an aberrant civil-military relationship came to fruition. In the 1925–27 period the leaders of the Chilean state within the state were not concerned with the classic freedom from budgetary powers of parliament or with the refusal to accept democratic controls. Their concept hinged upon a refusal to accept what they considered to be an outmoded form of democracy per se. They adopted such a stance in order to see to it that a new form of democracy be realized in state and society. More than a mere withdrawal of "the most vital military matters" from all civilian controls, Chilean political officers desired to alter the very basis of those controls by changing the form of civilian administration. They partially achieved this in September 1924 when Alessandri agreed (temporarily) to designate only military men as war and navy ministers.

These politicomilitary aspirants adhered to no ideology; as politicomilitary participants they had no programmatic approach to reform. They paid prime allegiance to Chile, not to the parliamentary system of government or its adherents; not to Alessandri, its leading foe or his civilian colleagues; not to any political party or coalition, social sector or economic group. In word and action they paid allegiance to the nation.

Only twenty-five years earlier the Republic of Chile was the supreme military and naval power on the Pacific coast of South America. Economically, the country was in the midst of a nitrate boom brought about by the successful termination of the War of the Pacific against Peru and Bolivia (1879–83). Socially and politically, Chile was stable, its homogeneous society being remarkably free from immobility (by Latin American standards) and its politics modeled after those of Great Britain in a pseudo-parliamentary regime.

Within a quarter of a century, however, Chile fell under the influence of army leaders who looked with distaste on politics, believed that serious social problems were going unattended, and who realized that the effects of the post–World War I recession had ruined their country's economy. Chilean politics encased in parliamentarism did not prove representative of society in a changing Chile. The country was on the threshold of social change being brought about by urbanization and increasing personnel changes at all levels of government. "Middle-class" and provincial elements were important in politics, but their voices were those of the minority until 1924. The army identified more with new social and political elements than it did with those of the past, but this did not necessarily mean that it would serve their interests.

Chile's crisis of the 1920s was essentially one of leadership. The Chilean advocates of change—who held that government action and/or constitutional reform were necessary for social and economic modernization—were a divided lot. The "social reform" parties, the Radicals and Democrats, were not at all committed to sweeping constitutional reforms proposed by the man they helped elect president in 1920. That man, Alessandri, fervently worked for a return to the presidential system (or at least an executive-legislative equilibrium) through constitutional reform as the way to provide necessary leadership and solutions for national problems. For the first four years of his presidency he failed.

Finally a ray of hope met Alessandri's gaze. In March 1924 he arranged for army officers to oversee congressional elections in certain key districts. It was this maneuver which enabled him to establish a shaky coalition majority in both houses of Congress. The 1924 elections so compromised the army that it was unable to dissociate itself from politics for over eight years. Nevertheless, it was not until early 1925 that the army became a disciplined and united political force.

Involvement of the army in the crucial March elections brought cries of intervention from all quarters. The conservative opposition to Alessandri (composed of Conservatives and many Liberals) accused the army of intervention. Even Alessandri's cohorts were uneasy about military collaboration. When Congress failed to act on Alessandri's legislative proposals, the army, already torn between old and new leaders, reacted. In September 1924 Alessandri left office because of the pressure exerted on him by both elements, and military rule was imposed on Chile. But the high command's answer to Chile's crisis (the provisional junta) was unsatisfactory to those junior- and middle-grade officers who had initiated the pressure tactics on Alessandri and Congress in September.

By January 1925 Chile's new army leaders took the initiative themselves. Led by the Comité Revolucionario (headed by Lieutenant Colonel Carlos Ibáñez del Campo and Lieutenant Colonel Marmaduke Grove Vallejo), they overthrew the interim government headed by General Luis Altamirano. Ibáñez, a cavalry officer, and Grove, an artillery officer, were long-time friends and former colleagues in the Academia de Guerra, Chile's army staff school. The clique of elite officers responsible for important political decisions in the 1925–27 period and during the subsequent presidency of Ibáñez (1927–31) were all products of the "Generation of 1912–14," the last class to enter and leave the Academia prior to the outbreak of World War I. While bent on recalling Alessandri, they let it be known that the army would, by no means, allow a restoration of traditional parliamentary politics. Ibáñez became war minister on January 23 and did not relinquish the post until 1927 when he rose to the Interior Ministry.

The coup met with little opposition except for objections from the conservative anti-Alessandri Consejo Naval, Chile's admiralty, based in Valparaíso. Once this opposition was overcome, however, nothing stood in the way of the president's return.

The next step in ensuring that the army would have its way was the creation of a transition government to administer Chile until Alessandri returned. The transition government was a junta handpicked by Ibáñez and his collaborators. From his desk in the War Ministry, Ibáñez began acting a king-maker's role even before Alessandri arrived home. He was aided by Grove and another long-time friend and Academia cavalry colleague, Colonel Bartolomé Blanche Espejo, the subsecretary of war. In the hiatus between January 23 and March 20, when Alessandri arrived in Santiago, Ibáñez made several moves designed to strengthen his grip on the army; hence the army's position as a political force.

To preclude intra-army rivalries he transferred loyal cavalry elements from the provinces into Santiago and gave Blanche a free hand to deal with recalcitrant infantry officers who, particularly, objected to the new influence of the cavalry. He transferred the rural carabineros from the Interior Ministry and brought them under control of the War Ministry to eliminate the possibility of any armed conflict between them and the army. Included in all transfers and shifts were key promotions or assignments for Ibáñista officers.

Army influence in restored politics was evident from the outset. Fearing a civilian reaction to military intervention, Ibáñez bluntly let Alessandri know that he owed his reinstatement to the army Comité as much, or more, than to civilian resistance to the Altamirano government. In short, the army still eschewed actual political control, but demanded its just due for allowing Alessandri to finish his term in office.

Alessandri had struggled with Congress since 1920 for constitutional reform to provide a balance between the executive and legislative branches, to reform the Chilean fiscal system, separate church and state, and establish a governmental role in the labor and welfare fields. He realized these goals with the promulgation of a new constitution on September 18, 1925, but not without considerable help from the army. Though written by civilians, it is doubtful that the Constitution of 1925 would have become a reality without military pressure. It is doubtful if that military pressure could have been applied had Ibáñez and the new leaders not taken an adamant stand on the need for reform.

Doubtless Chile would have been provided with a new constitution at this time in its history. The precise time, manner, and form of this provision, however, was dependent on the politics of the army, specifically the politics of the war minister Ibáñez.

Ibáñez and Alessandri clashed numerous times during the winter of 1925, during and after the constitution-making process. In May and June the nitrate port of Iquique was convulsed by continuous labor agitation. Ibáñez ordered carabineros to forcibly break up demonstrations in which the red flag was shown and refused to rescind the order when ordered to do so by Alessandri. Ibáñez received numerous telegrams congratulating him for maintaining order and discipline, but Alessandri accused him of aiding the forces of reaction and violating civil liberties. When demonstrations turned to violence, Alessandri ordered General Florentino de la Guarda, commandant of the First Division, to crush resistance to the government and placed the provinces of Antofagasta and Tarapacá under a state of siege and martial law. Guarda carried out his order to the letter and tried all agitators as "communist revolutionaries." Concomitantly, rumors circulated in Santiago that Ibáñez had political ambitions. These rumors were summarized ably in official despatches written by United States Ambassador William Miller Collier. Alessandri's enforced reliance on the army as an internal police force and rumors of a political future for the army's chieftain led to an Alessandri-Ibáñez estrangement and made the army even more a political force.

On September 29 a group of party and independent leaders presented Ibáñez with a petition requesting his declaration of intent. Ibáñez accepted the petition and declared his candidacy. The next day the cabinet resigned en masse, a customary act when a minister of state became a candidate. But the war minister's name was missing from the list of resignations. When Alessandri demanded his resignation, Ibáñez refused in an open letter to the president published October 1. Referring to himself as "chief of the revolution," he stated that his tenure in the cabinet was vital to the maintenance of public order. He then informed Alessandri that as the only cabinet member in service his signature had to appear on any executive decree. Alessandri's response to this was his own resignation and transfer of the government to Luis Barros Borgoño.

The obdurate stand of Ibáñez in the face of Alessandri's demand for his resignation has been interpreted as evidence of his own presidential ambitions. Whatever his personal ambitions may have been at this point, they were frustrated.

Reaction to the Ibáñez-Alessandri showdown came from both the military and the civilian realm. An ill-conceived putsch attempt of October 3 failed to restore Alessandri, but some of the political leaders who petitioned Ibáñez on September 29 now expressed doubts about his motives. Further, there was military pressure exerted on him to bow out of the incipient presidential contest in favor of a civilian unity candidate. Admiral Juan Schroeders, director general of the navy, and Inspector General Navarrete both urged him to do so. Just four days after Alessandri resigned, party leaders agreed to support a colorless aristocrat, Emiliano Figueroa Larraín of the Democratic Liberal party. Ibáñez promptly withdrew his candidacy, so did the Radical Quezada.

The Rise of Ibáñez, October 1925–February 1927

Clearly, the impact of the military on Chilean internal affairs depended on the actions of Ibáñez. Equally clearly, the political effectiveness of Ibáñez and his cohorts depended on their control (or lack of control) of the army. Ibáñez's ambivalence during October reflected the delicate politicomilitary position into which the perhaps over hasty "acquiescence to a presidential draft" had temporarily lodged him. He stated that Figueroa was a reactionary. When José Santos Salas announced as a candidate of the Republican Social Union of Chilean Wage-Earners (Unión Republicana de Asalariados de Chile, or USRACH), Ibáñez supported him. Then he changed his mind on Figueroa; finally he called for postponement—but not cancellation—of the elections. The elections were held as scheduled, with Figueroa the victor.

Congressional elections, held a month later, resulted in gains for the reform parties, the Radicals and Democrats; but the new leaders of Congress showed no immediate willingness to yield to presidential prerogatives established in the new constitution, and President Figueroa showed a similar lack of will to exercise them. This dual unwillingness to adjust lasted throughout 1926 and served to renew military doubts about the viability of Chilean liberal democracy.

That this attitude became dominant in the army, and then the navy, can be seen in the gradual reestablishment of Ibáñez's strong position during 1926. From the nadir of October 1925, Chile's war minister rose to a new zenith by February 1927. Figueroa retained him in the cabinet, for it was apparent that he was less a threat if kept inside the government. The state and the state within remained in conjunction once normal constitutional processes were restored and extraordinary conditions ceased to be. Because of this, military influence continued to grow.

Politics drifted to the right during 1926, but it was not until April that Ibáñez showed his obdurate side again. On April 16 he addressed the Chamber of Deputies, whose presiding officer, Conservative Rafael Luis Gumucio, the editor of *El Diario Ilustrado,* was an outspoken critic of the army since the overthrow of 1925 and opposed the new constitution.

Ibáñez debunked charges that there was new plotting in the army and defended the army's (and his) actions since 1924. He said that military men were concerned about the nation's postwar difficulties and characterized the army's role since September 1924 as one of a national institution which acted for the good of the country, not for any single political faction. He reminded the deputies of the army's role in securing legislation long stalled in Congress and in the constitution-making process. The war minister concluded by stating that if Congress could not carry on the work begun by the military, the military might be forced to assume the burden.

The April 16 confrontation did nothing to bring about executive-legislative harmony; if anything, it exacerbated an already existing conflict. During the Chilean winter of 1926, the Alessandri-Congress impasse of 1920–24 was replayed with new personnel. Administration spokesmen were heckled in the Senate and chamber, and Radicals and Conservatives refused to compromise with the executive branch on any major items of legislation. Meanwhile, Chile's economic situation continued to deteriorate. By the time Congress adjourned for the September 18 independence festivities, the Radicals led by Senate president Enrique Oyarzún and party president Pedro Aguirre Cerda had broken all relations with the administration. The Radical party, receptive to social and economic reform, would not support measures introduced by an administration it considered reactionary and would not cooperate with it even in the face of growing pressure from Ibáñez.

Ibáñez accused the chamber and the Senate of irresponsibility and lack of concern for national needs. These, he claimed, made the people susceptible to extreme leftist propaganda. He closed by challenging the right of senators and deputies to criticize the army, in or out of congressional session. In late October 1926, Chilean politics entered a new crisis stage.

For six weeks Chilean politics remained static, and relations between Ibáñez and the parliament continued strained. On November 13, Chile's emerging strong man tried a new tactic; he demanded that the cabinet be reconstituted because it had proved powerless to cope with Congress, unable to realize its reform programs, and incompetent in dealing with the communist menace. Ibáñez turned his attention temporarily from the legislative to the executive branch. The cabinet resigned en masse on November 14; Ibáñez resigned in a separate document, but in his quest for a successor, Figueroa met with no success. So solid was Ibáñez's position by this time that no officer would accept the War portfolio. A new cabinet (with Ibáñez retaining his post) was sworn in on November 18. At this point, the traditional Chilean civil-military relationship inverted.

Carlos Ibáñez del Campo attained an "unassailable position" in November 1926, a position which allowed him a free hand to represent the interests of the state within the state and of the tight clique of staff officers who had aligned themselves with him in January 1925 before the civil authorities of Chile. This "unassailable position" was enhanced in January 1927 when leaders of a new naval reform movement appealed to him for support. When Ibáñez feigned ignorance of the navy affair, the new interior minister, Manuel Rivas Vicuña, resigned in disgust. On February 9, 1927, President Figueroa appointed Ibáñez interior minister and allowed him to form a new cabinet.

In February 1927, the Chilean state within the state ceased to be, for its leader had become a political figure with civil authority. Within two months of his appointment to the Interior Ministry, Ibáñez became vice-president when Figueroa took a leave of absence for "personal reasons." On May 5 Figueroa officially resigned, and on May 22 Ibáñez was elected to the presidency. The Chilean army elite, whose advocacy of social, political, and economic reform and whose hostility toward traditional liberal democracy were first made obvious in the crisis of 1924 and the overthrow of 1925, had succeeded in imposing its version of reform and democracy on the state. Once this was done military influence continued, to be sure, but in a slightly less obvious manner until the desperate days of 1931–32.

No valid appraisal of modern Chilean democracy can be made without bearing in mind the impact of the military on the internal affairs of Chile from 1924 to 1932. No valid appraisal of that octennium can be made unless the 1925–27 period is understood, for it was in that period that the Chilean army figuratively marched the nation toward reform and provided the necessary national leadership to do so.

Reprinted and edited from "A Latin American State Within the State: The Politics of the Chilean Army, 1924–1927," *The Americas* 27, no. 1 (July 1970), pp. 40–55.

Víctor Villanueva

The Military in Peruvian Politics, 1919–45

In 1919, Augusto B. Leguía launched his campaign for the presidency against Antero Aspíllaga, a large landholder from the north who was backed by outgoing president José Pardo and the Civilista party. The Pardo administration, however, had lost a great deal of prestige due to its bloody repression of the general strike, which had been called to demand an eight-hour day. Moreover, the traditional oligarchy was in decline, with the general populace completely opposed to it, and Leguía easily won the army-supervised elections. It was rumored that the government would refuse to accept the election results, so Leguía immediately began to conspire.

He searched for a "man on horseback," making offers to various officers with all the savoir faire he had learned from his years of business experience. Finally, he obtained the support of an officer of the Palace Guard who promised to open the doors of the National Palace at an opportune moment.

The army had seen Leguía win at the ballot box, but more importantly they had seen Pardo cut the military's share of the national budget from 25.21 percent in 1915 to 17.87 percent in 1919. Thus, they quickly decided to support Leguía, who wielded a chauvinistic slogan: "Recover the Bluff of Arica," which Peru was forced to surrender to Chile in the War of the Pacific.

In the early morning hours of July 4, 1919, the Lima garrison revolted, arrested President Pardo, and put Leguía into power. Leguía entered the palace accompanied by the legendary Andrés Cáceres, symbol of the resistance against the Chilean invasion and principal guarantor of Leguía's future military policy—the recuperation of Tacna and Arica.

Despite the fact that he was a civilian, Leguía quite frankly initiated a new militarist and dictatorial period in Peru, a period that had its antecedents in the insurrection of February 4, 1914. Now the term *militarism* referred not only to specific military governments but also to military influence in a nation's politics and to the use of the military as a tool for capturing and maintaining power.

Leguía gained the presidency by means of a military coup. He had himself reelected twice without any popular backing, relying instead on the exclusive support of the armed forces, and succeeded in remaining in power against the popular will for eleven years (the *Oncenio*). The Leguía government paid very little attention to the army as an institution, but it did obtain the individual support of many officers, due principally to the concessions and gifts provided them. Military discipline kept the remainder in line. By carefully selecting loyal officers and giving them key posts, Leguía was able to elude all kinds of dangers and even to control the discontent within the army's own ranks. . . .

As a means of rewarding the sergeants who took part in the July 4 coup, Leguía promoted them to officers, thereby violating the Promotions Law. He did the same for all the officers who had participated in the barracks revolt. The process of demoralization of the army, begun by Benavides in 1914, was accelerated by Leguía's 1919 action. The illegal promotions caused a profound disquiet among military officers. Those who had been so promoted were nicknamed "horse thieves" and were looked down upon, but since they enjoyed official approval, those officers continued their careers undaunted. Not a few achieved high rank in the officer corps, and a few even succeeded in donning the embroidered uniform of a general.

Leguía then was responsible for reimplementing the system of paying for political favors with military promotions, a throwback to the previous century. A popular joke held that military officers were like gasoline—sold by the gallon. The loss of prestige engendered by this caustic joke lasted for a very long time. The army, made up of true professionals, was contaminated by the "horse thieves," who, since they were regime men, were given the highest positions. The other officers, either through discipline or prudence, obeyed these new officers, thereby giving the impression that the entire army supported the Leguía regime, which quickly changed into a dictatorship. Many officers, who had never had much moral stature, accommodated themselves easily to the system of offering their political allegiance to the dictator in return for being favored in the promotion lists. The sops to the "cooperative" officers also took other forms such as "educational trips to Europe" for undeserving men and salary increases and corresponding perquisites in a period characterized by fiscal penury. Moreover, in addition to military backing, Leguía enjoyed the decided approval of United States imperialism, which provided him with numerous loans.

In spite of the unconditional allegiance which the army gave to the dictator, it received very little in return, except for the gratuities offered to selected military personnel. Indeed, Leguía even tried to diminish the importance of the army. In order to create a military equilibrium and counterbalance the army, Leguía organized the Guardia Civil [Civil Guard], granting to the officers of the new institution the same prerogatives, remuneration, and even the same uniforms as army officers. The Guardia Civil even succeeded for a time in having more regular troops than the standing army.

It seems that the military officers of that period were not concerned with the state of the army. They received promotions and stipends, and they did not ask for more. Leguía neither acquired new armaments nor increased the size of the army nor tried to reorganize and modernize it. When Leguía came to power he found a military budget which absorbed 17.87 percent of the national budget. In the first year, he abruptly increased it to 22.1 percent but then steadily decreased it to 17.59 percent by 1930, the year he was overthrown. The budget of the Ministry of Government and Police, on the other hand, rose from 807,234 Peruvian pounds in 1919 to 2,090,896 pounds in 1930, a threefold increase.

Leguía did more for the navy than he did for the army, acquiring four submarines. He also supported the air force, purchasing a number of planes and founding the Palmas Aviation School. Leguía named his son Juan Leguía to be commander of the air force, with the rank of colonel even though his only qualifications were his relationship to the president and the possession of a private pilot's license from England.

Though Leguía was not a military caudillo, militarism dominated the period. The army principally, but also the other military services, acquired great political importance, with the opinions of high-ranking officers carrying more weight than those of a senator or minister. Nevertheless, that was the period in which they invented or reactivated the slogan: "The military should not intervene in politics." The intention was not to remove officers from politics, but rather, since it was now "illegal" to play politics inside the army, to give those officers loyal to the regime a better opportunity to impose their will.

It was said, as it always has been, that an officer was playing politics when he uttered one critical word against the government. On the other hand, he was applauded for attending "official receptions" in order to praise whatever action the government had taken. Thus, eulogizing what the government had done was not "playing politics," according to that curious regime logic.

To maintain his regime, Leguía depended on the continued support of the military and the availability of foreign loans, the combination of which created a false impression of internal tranquillity and economic prosperity. The economic crisis of 1929, however, decisively brought to a close the

"Leguía Century" which had lasted eleven years. The leader of the revolt was Lieutenant Colonel Luís M. Sánchez Cerro, a man with a reputation for both bravery and conspiracies and a captive of the intellectual bourgeoisie of the provinces. He was the commander of a sapper battalion in Arequipa, and that became the core of the military uprising.

Once the Arequipa revolt was known, the government adopted the necessary measures to put it down; but the economic crisis had undermined the regime, and the army found itself morally defenseless, with its high command in crisis because of the prolonged support it had lent to the dictatorship. In addition, popular pressure against the regime was mounting and antiregime propaganda by the oligarchy became insistent.

At the beginning, Sánchez Cerro enjoyed authentic popular support and the unanimous backing of the citizenry. Of a decidedly mestizo background, in fact a *cholo*, the insurrectionist of Arequipa could have become a true caudillo by virtue of his great charisma, his personal valor, and the fervor he was able to awaken in the masses; but he lacked political experience, he lacked a coherent ideology, and he fell victim to vanity.

An analogous thing happened to Luis Carlos Prestes in Brazil. The "Knight of Hope," who roamed all over Brazil fighting against the regular army and defeating it in more than one hundred battles over a two-year period, never found the road to attainment of his ideals. But then it is necessary to put that into proper perspective. Prestes, an army captain, was a legitimate *tenente*, a member of the *tenentismo* movement, an expression of Brazilian militarism, yes, but a progressive militarism which arose in defense of the people's rights. Prestes was the heir of Marshall Hermes de Fonseca, who had tried to stop the army from shooting at the population of Pernambuco. [See selection on Brazil in this section, pp. 110–17.]

Sánchez Cerro, on the other hand, lacked the democratic "pedigree" of which one could be proud. His predecessors had only fought for their own interests at the beginning and for the interests of the oligarchy afterwards; his successors did not do anything except shoot at the populace until a new type of militarism arose in Peru in 1962.

During the Sánchez Cerro period, militaristic attitudes proliferated to the extent that they assumed the characteristics of an epidemic. In the lapse of one month, six military uprisings broke out. At one point there was a government in Lima and another in Arequipa, and five different juntas followed in quick succession. The period compared favorably with the most tumultuous times of the past century.

Sánchez Cerro was elected president and took office on December 8, 1931. Though he failed to remain in power (he was assassinated in 1933), he did succeed in consolidating a third period of militarism in Peru. Except for a brief period ruled by a civilian-led junta, military regimes controlled the destinies of the nation throughout the 1930s. From 1948 to 1956, there was another military dictatorship, and the two administrations of Manuel Prado (1939–45, 1956–62) were contrary to the popular will, being maintained only by the armed forces. In 1962, a new military junta ruled for one year, and in 1968 the armed forces returned to power and have ruled to the present [1978].

With the death of Sánchez Cerro, the oligarchy, terrified of the social struggle which threatened their interests and powerless to take power on their own, prudently pulled back and gave power to another general [who] hopefully would know how to defend their interests and continue the struggle against APRA, the political party most hated and feared by the oligarchy, which was not aware of, or perhaps did not believe in, the venality of its leaders.

The oligarchy did not realize that through the use of bribes, it could have converted the APRA movement into the best tool for defending the bourgeoisie, as Manuel Prado succeeded in doing some years later.

With the body of the tyrant still warm, the Constituent Assembly elected General Oscar R. Benavides, then inspector general of national defense, as president of the republic to finish Sánchez Cerro's term. The election violated the newly promulgated Constitution of 1933, which prohibited, in Article 137, the election as president of "a member of the armed forces on active duty." But the infringement of the constitution mattered little to them. Stopping the enemy was the primary concern; putting a halt to the social revolution they saw coming was basic. And Benavides was chosen for the task because of the qualities he had already demonstrated in the pro-oligarchy coup of 1914. Moreover, his background was completely acceptable.

In 1936, Sánchez Cerro's term ran out, and Benavides was supposed to step down. He called for elections and proposed the candidacy of Jorge Prado for president—as he had done years before with Javier Prado and would do later with Manuel Prado, whom he finally succeeded in putting in power. The Aprista party, incapable of launching a revolution and legally prevented from running their own candidate, threw its support to Dr. Luis Antonio Eguiguren, an honest and upright, but very conservative, lawyer.

As the election returns came in, the bourgeoisie viewed with dread the victory of the Aprista candidate. Benavides, in a totally dictatorial decision, ordered the Congress to annul the elections inasmuch as Eguiguren's victory was due to Aprista votes, that is to say, votes of an "international party" which was prevented by the constitution from taking part in politics. Benavides also ordered the Congress, whose legal term had likewise ended, to recess and delegate all legislative powers to the president.

Benavides first used these new powers to name three vice-presidents:

General Ernesto Montagne as first vice-president, General Antonio Rodríguez as second vice-president, and General Federico Hurtado as third vice-president. Benavides had become an all-powerful dictator, and the most curious thing is that his dictatorship was "constitutional" and "legal" in that it had been approved by the Congress which, at least in theory, represented the will of the people. The armed forces not only accepted passively the trampling of democracy and the violation of the constitution, they went even further and congratulated the dictator on his actions and promised him their complete support.

The military dictatorship continued along the road of oppression and bloodshed. To the end of improving on the means of repression, Benavides contracted a fascist Italian police mission which brought and implemented the most modern systems of repression and torture. He created the Assault Battalion, a motorized unit which specialized in breaking up demonstrations, equipped it specially for its mission, and assigned its command to several civilian politicians.

The campaign of Nazification of the army was effectively carried out. Magazines in Spanish, seemingly technical in nature but full of political propaganda, circulated freely. The military services adopted German techniques, and Hitler's rantings were well received within the army, which had always been inclined to applaud certain types of attitudes, particularly when they were backed up with brilliant and spectacular military deeds.

Benavides approved of this campaign of penetration and pushed it throughout the country. The principal newspapers of the capital, although they were enemies of the regime, played the same game. Carleton Beals lists the headlines of one Lima daily to show how it exalted the totalitarian powers and eulogized their activities. Beals also details the diverse activities of Nazi-fascist penetration in the Benavides dictatorship.

At the same time, APRA, realizing that it could not come to power by means of a popular uprising, turned to the army as a possible vehicle for achieving power. The first officer they approached was General Antonio Rodríguez, second vice-president and minister of government in the Benavides administration. Convinced he was the "chosen man" to lead the country out of oppression, Rodríguez and a few friends revolted in the early hours of February 19, 1939, taking advantage of the absence of the president, who was on board a navy ship taking a pleasure cruise off the coast. The conspirators captured the National Palace, something which was relatively easy because of Rodríguez's high position. They then obtained the support of the Guardia Republicana [Republican Guard], which in turn captured the Lima penitentiary and freed all the political prisoners. But then all action ceased.

The movement, well-planned from a political point of view, was not equally well-planned militarily. The conspirators remained in the palace without taking any further action until the Assault Battalion arrived and killed Rodríguez with a burst of machine-gun fire. The other officers did not know what to do; they were incapable of taking any action at all. The Aprista party, which according to the agreed-upon plan should have taken to the streets as soon as the palace was captured, likewise did nothing. The "popular support" offered by APRA never materialized.

From that moment, when they persuaded General Rodríguez to revolt, the Apristas have continued to interact with military officers. The anti-militarist party that APRA originally was henceforth had to praise the generals, apparently submit itself to their will, and approve of army intervention in politics. APRA has openly urged the armed forces to leave their barracks and take power, many times begging that they do so "in defense of the constitution." Aprista newspapers, pamphlets, and speeches are full of such calls.

Thus, the militarism that had long counted on the complacency and tolerance of the oligarchy, then on the consent of the rich bourgeoisie, henceforth could count on the support and cooperation of a party which called itself "antimilitarist" and "of Marxist extraction," and which was popularly based even though it was directed by a sector of the petit bourgeoisie.

Benavides was president on three occasions: in 1914, when he took power by force; in 1933, when the Congress gave it to him; and in 1936, when that same Congress extended his term. In none of these cases was he elected by the people, nor did he ever enjoy any popular support. Benavides never counted on any party to back him nor did he try to organize one. It was enough that the armed forces supported him, together with his own background and experience as a dictator.

These were the times in which Hitler and Mussolini shone like stars of the first magnitude in the world arena. These were the times in which a Peruvian author wrote: "We are walking triumphantly on top of the decaying body of the god of liberty." These were the times in which dictatorship was considered to be the best system of government ever invented by man and democracy only an obstacle to the progress of civilization. To imitate those men of the Old World was the dream of all the apprentice dictators of Latin America.

But Benavides demonstrated that he was not an apprentice; his period of apprenticeship had already passed. He was a man of his time, a dictator in every sense of the word. He was also the last great man of Peruvian militarism.

Despite the fact he was a military man and had governed with the exclusive support of the armed forces, Benavides reduced military expenditures during his administration from 24.11 percent of the national budget to 21 percent, increasing instead expenditures on public works and social programs.

However, there were several reasons why the military dictator did not give much importance to the armed forces. Not one of the Aprista conspiracies against his government ever crystallized; all were smothered at the outset, so he never had to call upon the armed forces. In order to sustain his slogan of "Order, Peace, and Work," in order to put down uprisings, and in order to uncover conspiracies, Benavides never had to go beyond the police, particularly the investigative police and his own well-paid secret police. The armed forces served only as guarantors of the stability of the dictatorship, not as an active instrument of repression.

The recurrence of militarism in Peru with the coup of Sánchez Cerro and its consolidation under Benavides were not isolated incidents in Latin America. On the contrary, they constituted what we might say was characteristic of the period. During these years, there were only four countries ruled by popularly elected civilians: Colombia, Uruguay, Chile, and Costa Rica.

Europe was dominated by Hitler, Mussolini, Franco, and Salazar—four dictators backed by their respective armed forces. The dictatorship of Stalin in the Soviet Union completes the picture of an epoch that was characterized by the crisis of bourgeois democracy on a worldwide scale.

In 1939, Manuel Prado became president of the republic. APRA came out of hiding, the Aprista prisoners were set free, and there was a type of undeclared amnesty. It was not what APRA wanted, however, for semi-legality hardly suited them. Prado did not fulfill his part of the political bargain, and APRA moved into open opposition and subsequently back into hiding.

The Prado government was constitutional in origin, but it lost its claim to constitutionality by violating statutory guarantees. The armed forces, in obedience to that same constitution, had to defend the government. It is said that the Prado government was oligarchical and consequently the military supported the oligarchy. This is true, but it is also true that the army, according to the constitution, does not question, it only obeys. It could also be said that if the oligarchy is in power that the armed forces are not responsible, but rather the people who elected it. Nevertheless, the army did uphold that tyrannical regime.

On the one hand, the armed forces were accused of collaboration with tyranny, and, on the other, they were urged to revolt. APRA did both at once. In some clandestine publications, APRA invoked the constitution and reminded the armed forces, with frequent insistency, of their duty to respect the constitution. In other flyers and broadsides, APRA blamed the armed forces for the state of the country. At the same time, Apristas sought contacts with high military officers and tried to conspire for the overthrow of the Prado regime. Those same officers, however, were satisfied with the government and invoked the classic slogan used when they want to remain passive: "We do not get involved in politics."

The Aprista party held a leadership convention in 1942 and among other things issued a "Political Declaration," which held that the Prado regime was carrying out "an antidemocratic policy of persecution of APRA and a policy of denying citizen rights." The party also issued a call to the armed forces to come out in defense of the constitution, an action which "would not constitute subversion of the public order, but rather would mean the preservation of constitutional order and of the democratic norms of the nation which every Peruvian has the civic duty to respect and defend."

But the ranking officers of the armed forces remained deaf to Aprista demands. Only when the party shared power in 1945 did those same officers declare their long-standing sympathy for *Aprismo*. It should be noted, and many observers have already written on the subject, that this phenomenon is common in Latin America. The high command of the armed forces always identifies with the oligarchy that governs their respective nations, while the younger officers, on the other hand, try to get closer to the people and support them in their struggle for social change.

At any rate, the armed forces are constantly pressured by the bourgeoisie to leave their barracks and intervene in the political process of the country. The Aprista party, representing the petit bourgeoisie, acted the same way with the two military strata: officers and enlisted men, and within the first, senior and junior officers. To the first they talked about the necessity of respecting the constitution, of returning to the democratic course, and of fighting against communism, which is to say they emphasized conservative positions.

To the younger officers and to the enlisted men, the Apristas spoke of establishing social justice, of the great changes needed by the country, and of the destruction of the oligarchy. The Aprista preachings had a greater impact among the junior officers than on the senior ones. In addition, the Apristas knew of the honesty of the younger officers, so they talked to them of the fatherland, not of the party, of the people and not of *Aprismo*. What APRA wanted was to take power, but they wanted someone else to do it for them. Therefore, they encouraged the militaristic attitudes of the army. . . .

At the beginning of 1945, the end of the Axis Powers was in sight, the fall of German Nazism and of Mussolini's fascism was imminent. The fervent admirers of those ideas in Peru were crestfallen. The generals who before had had no objections to heaping praise on the totalitarian dictators now preferred to turn their attention to the Allied officers and speak of the advantages of democracy, including in that term, the Red Army which had succeeded in resisting Hitler's army.

Translated, reprinted, and edited from *El militarismo en el Perú* (Lima: T. Scheuch, 1962), pp. 52–107. Víctor Villanueva slightly revised this article in September 1976 for publication in the first edition of this volume.

Robert V. Elam

The Military and Politics in El Salvador, 1927–45

The elections of 1927 deviated from the traditional political pattern. The elite erred in transferring its power to Dr. Pio Romero Bosque, an outsider, for this marked the end of its political control. Faithful to his inaugural pledge, the new president unmuzzled the press, raised the general state of siege, restored constitutional rights, and granted the university autonomy. He declared amnesty, and most political exiles of the previous six administrations returned. Though he had served as war minister (1923–25), Romero Bosque did not hesitate to indict the former president for financial malfeasance. In particular, Romero Bosque accused him of entering into an unwritten agreement with senior officers which transferred funds to the Ministry of War that were officially assigned to other ministries. A three-month investigation failed to uncover proof but did create fear and suspicion in the armed services.

In addition, Romero Bosque initiated a reform of the officer training system and of the laws regulating officer promotion. The efforts of Chilean and Spanish missions had been only partially successful in modernizing the military. Overlapping laws, vaguely written regulations, and inadequate systems of advancement and retirement still prevailed. Part of the problem stemmed from the overabundance of senior officers who had gained their rank and office through service in the campaigns of 1906 and 1907. The lack of a reserve corps before 1912, the absence of a regularized system of promotion before 1913, and the inadequate retirement law of 1916 allowed older, ill-trained officers to establish themselves so firmly in control of the armed services that they remained long after structural reforms had taken place. It was not uncommon as late as 1920 to find regimental commanders sufficiently influential to dictate the selection of their staffs or to move their officer corps with them when they were transferred to another regiment. Graduates of the Escuela Politécnica either attached themselves to one of the provincial military chiefs or found their professional opportunities sharply curtailed. When an insurrection of cadets resulted in the closing of the Escuela Politécnica in February 1922, the integration of new and old officers ceased to be a problem. During the next five years, as civilian influence increased and as old-time officers were retired, El Salvador found itself in the unusual position of having too few officers to direct its military. As a consequence, a new school, the Escuela Militar, was founded in January 1927. Between August 8, 1927, and December 30, 1930, 125 second lieutenants were graduated, and the process of integrating the new with the old began once again.

Much had taken place between the closing of the Escuela Politécnica in 1922 and the founding of the Escuela Militar in 1927 to alter the process of integration. The experiences of World War I resulted in new methods of military organization and a changed view of the role of the officer. The new school, free from the accumulated traditions so burdensome to the old Escuela Politécnica, reflected these experiences. Instruction now emphasized the importance of small-group action directed by individual officers to implement the strategy of high command.

Texts and manuals stressed the need for qualified personnel in the lower echelons of the officer corps and detailed the duties and responsibilities of each rank. Specialization further minimized tradition by establishing for each grade a prescribed program of study. The objects were to insure recognition and respect from superior officers as well as those of inferior rank and to destroy the tendency to equate senior rank with superior knowledge in all fields of military activity.

Opposition to Romero Bosque's military reorganization was inevitable. On December 6, 1927, Colonel Juan Aberle and Major Alfaro Noguera took possession of the capital's central police barracks in an attempt to force the president's resignation. Poorly planned and executed, the uprising was quickly repressed. The following April, a group of senior officers protested the new promotion laws and threatened to withdraw their support of the government. Romero Bosque responded by transferring all the conspiring officers to regiments of unquestionable loyalty. However, the maneuver did not hush rumors that the protest was aimed at the president's overall civil-military policy rather than at the specific issue of promotion. Another source of irritation was the resignation of the highly respected minister of war, Dr. Alberto Gómez Zárate, and the appointment of Romero Bosque's son to that high post.

A further cause of dissatisfaction with the new administration was Romero Bosque's lack of concern over the growth of left-wing extremist groups. By mid-1930, terrorism in the rural areas had reached alarming proportions, and confiscated propaganda indicated that it was being initiated and directed by a hard core of foreign Communists. Ranking officers claimed that it was impossible to maintain order in an atmosphere of governmental indifference and requested that Romero Bosque take a strong stand against all subversive activities. He replied in August by ordering the expulsion of all foreigners found "employing Communist subversion." A request to use army troops was denied, and the National Guard continued to carry the responsibility for rural order.

Clearly, the relationship between the military and the government, essentially static for thirteen years, showed signs of fundamental change during the presidency of Pio Romero Bosque. Wisely avoiding a direct challenge to the older officers whenever possible, the president undermined their power by establishing the Escuela Militar and rewriting the promotion laws. Also, he assured the advancement of junior officers by insisting upon the strict application of the new law of officer retirement. That he was successful in maintaining junior officer support is evident in their attitude toward the presidential campaign of late 1930 and the election of early 1931.

To crown his achievements in the area of civil liberties, Romero Bosque guaranteed that his successor would be the choice of the people. The three days of balloting in January 1931 represented the first free presidential elections in the nation's history. In response to the presidential orders, officers took up positions in each population center to act as observers and coordinators of the balloting. Other military personnel formed an election center in the presidential house to register calculations as the votes were telegraphed from outlying polls. Everything seemed to suggest that Romero Bosque had succeeded in his policy of military reorganization.

A Relapse in Civil-Military Relations

On March 1, 1931, labor candidate Arturo Araujo was sworn into office on the basis of a clear victory at the polls. Proposing broad social and economic reforms, the wealthy engineer and his supporters had barnstormed the country in an unprecedented fashion, promising land to the peasants and the elimination of taxes. The day after Arturo Araujo moved to the presidential palace, his supporters began forming queues outside in the hope of collecting their share of the promised land. Each day the crowds came and were turned away, and each day the newly elected president lost support.

To be sure, the troubles that marred Araujo's nine-month administration were not all his own doing. The Great Depression affected the entire nation as the bottom fell out of the coffee market. Conditions of the workers, instead of improving as Araujo and his party workers had promised, became worse. Incidents of violence broke out everywhere.

The new president's handling of the military was uncommonly harsh. In

February a group of officers gathered in the Círculo Militar to draft and sign a memorandum asking Araujo to abolish certain injustices which existed in the armed forces. Their demands were simple and direct: first, that pay be equalized among both officers and enlisted men of all fourteen departments; second, that the military be paid on a monthly instead of a daily basis; and third, that pay be received during the first days of each month. When the memorandum was placed in front of Araujo, he praised it but failed to put its suggestions into practice.

In the month of July, another incident increased tensions between the army and the government. Araujo ordered the eleven officers enrolled in the medical, engineering, and law schools of the National University to resign their commissions and remain as students or leave the school for posts in active service. As officers, stated Araujo, they were part of the military profession and had no place in a civilian program of studies.

Although the above-described incidents are admittedly isolated, they do point out some of the reasons for the growing resentment felt by many army officers toward the Araujo administration. They also reveal the new president's incapacity to understand the military's political role during the preceding eighteen years. Consequently, when the government sharply reduced the military budget in August and called for the elimination of the positions of a number of officers, who were on the payroll but who had not actively served for years, it did so in a climate of suspicion. Though eventually rescinded, the order irreparably damaged civil-military relations, and plans for a revolt were soon under way.

Worst of all, Araujo neglected the first requisite for a Latin American president, which is to assure prompt payment of the military. From September through November 1931, officers in every department went without their salaries. Then, on November 30, after a series of appeals, Araujo promised that the government would pay all salaries. The promise, however, was broken, and a revolt began two days later.

Araujo was a political newcomer without firsthand knowledge of the power relationships developed since 1913. Incapable of exerting informal influence like his predecessor, Araujo relied upon formal patterns of authority that had remained largely unchanged and ignored since the nineteenth century. As a result, officers in revolt in December 1931 justified their actions not only on grounds of public discontent with Araujo's administration but also on grounds of preservation of their institution.

In addition, because of grave economic hardships, the frequency of peasant uprisings increased. The military's inability to quell rural violence placed the army in a poor light. Newspaper articles questioning the capabilities of the army began to appear in early 1931, and civilian criticism mounted. In defense, the officers claimed that the administration's failure to curb Communist infiltration and the imposition of restrictions upon the military made it impossible for them to act decisively. Given the freedom to consider the situation strictly in military terms, they argued, the army could quickly restore peace and order.

On the second day of the revolt, the Military Directorate transferred full executive powers to the vice president, General Maximiliano Hernández Martínez, who had been released the previous day, December 3, after having been held prisoner in Fort El Zapote since the early hours of the revolt. Contrary to popular opinion, the vice president had not taken part in the planning of the revolt. The directorate made the decision only after careful deliberation with prominent lawyers. As is commonly the case following the establishment of a government by force, those in command saw the need to legitimatize their powers. Legitimacy, they reasoned, would insure recognition as well as cause dissident elements to hesitate before acting against the new regime, hence the appointment of Hernández Martínez to administer a caretaker government. The directorate, however, retained the power to make military appointments until its disbandment on December 12.

A worrisome issue for the new government was the question of diplomatic recognition. The United States, initiator and major supporter of the Treaty of Washington of 1923, viewed the new government with suspicion. Specific criteria as to the manner in which a revolutionary government must proceed when organizing itself had been agreed upon. The United States State Department immediately requested its minister to Colombia, Jefferson Caffery, to go to El Salvador to study the situation. Since Hernández Martínez had been a part of the overthrown government, Caffery concluded that the government would require a new president if it expected to comply with the treaty of 1923 and thus gain recognition. Generally, civilians found this position unacceptable. Some Salvadoreans argued that the treaty was not applicable, since their National Assembly had withheld ratification of various clauses of the 1923 treaty, particularly those clauses relating to the functions of the vice president of the republic. *El Espectador* viewed the problem in another way:

The movement of the second should neither be classified as a revolution nor a *Golpe de Estado*, because in reality it was neither one nor the other. Juridically speaking, its true name or denomination in Spanish political terminology, already generally accepted, is that of *pronunciamiento militar*. This differs from the above types in that it does not include the breaking of Article II of the General Treaty of Peace and Amnesty ... which is *now being used* to negate the possibility of recognition for the government of Martínez.

Finally, the suspension of diplomatic relations was viewed as a kind of subtle imperialism such as the United States had employed in Nicaragua, and the new president used growing anti-U.S. feeling to enhance his own position. Whereas Hernández Martínez viewed nonrecognition as a source of strength, political opponents saw it as a basic weakness. Liberals hoped that the desire for recognition would compel the new regime to initiate sweeping political reforms and to usher in a period of genuinely democratic government. Revolutionists believed that nonrecognition would sufficiently weaken the government to allow them to establish a socialist government in its place. Consequently, the suspension of diplomatic relations helped to turn sporadic outbreaks of rural violence into a general peasant uprising in the early months of 1932.

The causes of the massive 1932 revolt are not difficult to find. Like most Latin American countries before World War II, El Salvador had for years suffered from a bottom-heavy social structure based upon subsistence and export agriculture. Burdened by economic problems generated beyond the frontiers, the family dynasty sought ways to protect the nation's elite, often at the expense of the lower classes. No pressure groups existed that were willing or able to represent the masses, whose living conditions grew steadily worse.

In 1925, with the assistance of Mexican and Guatemalan agents, the first organized Communist group was established in San Salvador. The following year, under the direction of this group, the Regional Federation of Salvadorean Workers was founded. Not until 1929, however, did labor leaders consider their movement anything but urban, and Communist labor propaganda was confined to San Salvador and other population centers. But after a congress held in the capital in mid-July of that year, labor's platform was redirected to include rural workers. Increasingly, the Federation's publications encouraged the class struggle and emphasized the important role of the peasant.

In late December 1929, leaders of the Federation established the first national Communist Party. Though the labor and Communist organizations appeared to act independently after 1929, their leadership was in fact provided by the same men. The Regional Federation now urged the establishment of worker cells in all factories and places of business, and both organizations broadcast an intense stream of propaganda directed toward the overthrow of the government.

President Bosque's efforts to curb the movement's growth, and the weak opposition afforded by his successor, seemed only to strengthen the labor-Communist alliance and to increase foreign assistance to the movement. Even before the 1931 presidential elections, the movement had won substantial support from intellectuals and workers. However, it was not until the last weeks of Araujo's presidency that a conscious effort was made to infiltrate the military. Two objectives characterized this phase of the movement: first, a broad campaign to subvert the rank and file; and second, an effort to cultivate a hard core of Communists and Communist sympathizers among the officer class. Manifestoes now began by addressing the "workers, peasants, and soldiers of the nation" and called for an all-out struggle against the existing government. One circular dated January 14, 1932, reminded soldiers:

Above all, the soldier is a worker or a peasant whom the rich exploit in factories, shops, and fields. When he is still a youth, he is taken to the barracks where he is forced to bear arms in defense of the wealth which he has produced for the rich as a worker or peasant.

The discontent which the soldier feels in the barracks from the oppression by which he lives is the result of the fact that a soldier, enduring the lies of chiefs and officers, feels that they are his enemies, because these same chiefs and officers belong to the same class which exploited him in the factories, shops, and fields.

Then, on the twenty-first, a sequel was published: ". . . COMRADE SOL-DIERS: Don't fire a single shot at the revolutionary workers and peasants. Kill the chiefs and officers. Place yourselves under the orders of the Comrade Soldiers who have been named Red Comrades by this Central Committee." Loyal officers soon grew aware of the deep inroads being made in the ranks of the military. In some instances, soldiers went to their superiors with reports of Communist activity. In one case, a report by an enlisted man led to the discovery and elimination of a plot to assassinate all the commissioned officers of a barracks and to use the military arms to equip a civil-military "red army."

Despite precautions, barracks revolts did break out and had to be quelled by force. After one such outbreak, in the First Regiment of Cavalry, the government declared a state of siege in six of the fourteen departments, restricted the press, and ordered the arrest of the directors of the Communist mouthpiece, *Red Star*. The hardest blow to the movement, however, came with the execution of Augustín Farabundo Martí on February 1, shortly after his arrest for the third time. Without his leadership, and with the capture of a number of his lieutenants, the rebel organization broke into discordant factions. Without leadership, peasant bands struck out in wanton and blind destruction of anything resembling the traditional order.

Under the guise of meeting a national emergency, President Hernández Martínez replaced civilian bureaucrats with military officers at both the national and provincial levels. Little objection was heard. In an article entitled "Para que el pueblo sepa y no se confíe," a student publication boldly noted that the majority of public administrative offices had been filled with military officers: "assaulted," in a word, "by a pack of robbers." But such sentiments never reached the regular press.

In addition, the conflict demanded the utilization of a large share of the nation's armed services and provided a long-needed outlet for the officers' military desires. The majority of officers had seen no previous field service, and they eagerly looked forward to the opportunity to direct military action. Furthermore, those who served best proved by their actions a willingness to support the new regime. Officers who opposed the December coup and who failed to make their peace with the new government were eliminated as burdensome baggage in the drive for order.

Hernández Martínez's government, as a consequence, emerged from the revolutionary experience of 1932 supported by a more devoted and united armed force than had existed in the nation for many years. In addition, the government could boast having gained the following of most of the urban populations, as well as the wholehearted support of the landowners, some of whom owed their lives to government protection. In late January the government recommended that the "honorable laboring men of every population center of El Salvador organize themselves . . . into militias patterned after the Italian *Fascio,* the Spanish armed corps (*somatenes*) or the patriotic youth groups of *Acción France,* for the defense at any time of our families and homes against the deadly and ferocious attacks of the gangs of villains that fill the ranks of the Red Army that hopes to drown in blood the free and generous nation left to us by our ancestors." Though militias were never established, groups of upper-class citizens of the capital were armed by the military to patrol the streets. On the suggestion of a prominent banker, these citizens were given carte blanche to shoot any "Communist" on sight.

Both in material and in psychological terms, the Communist-inspired revolution of 1932 proved costly. Six population centers, together with the capital, had been affected. So great was the death toll in rural areas, and through mass executions staged in the capital, that the chief of the department of sanitation feared a major epidemic would result from the slowly decomposing bodies. By the end of January, the number of deaths had risen to the point where burial became impractical, and the chief of operations ordered the incineration of bodies. Night after night San Salvador was disturbed by the rumble of military trucks carrying the captured into the city and by bursts of machine-gun fire as "justice" was hurriedly rendered. It remains impossible to render an accurate count of the number killed during January and February of 1932. Estimates as high as twenty-five thousand are not uncommon.

By mid-February, the country was beginning to return to normal. Clearly, the new regime was in firm command and further displayed its strength and character by naming three army officers as president designates. To remain in opposition to or moderate toward government policy was impossible. All adversaries were labeled Communist or Communist sympathizers. Opportunity for the development of loyal opposition did not exist.

Despite the passing of more than five decades, horrifying details of terrorism still remain clear in the minds of many El Salvadoreans, and fear of a similar occurrence has in part shaped the legislation and policies of governments ever since 1932.

By dealing successfully, if brutally, with the question of disorder, Hernández Martínez acquired the right to advance the process of militarization. The waning of anti-military sentiment, which had been growing under Romero Bosque and Araujo, provided the new president with a free hand to build a loyal military establishment. By spring 1934, little doubt existed as to the character of the regime. Civilians had been gradually replaced by army officers. Three generals added glitter to the cabinet, the treasury minister was a captain, and the director of the government printing house was a colonel. All but one of the governors of the fourteen departments were military men. The subordinate offices of all government branches were filled with loyal officers. The armed forces became the "dictator's praetorian guard."

By fall 1934, the dictator was ready to exhibit his military's strength, and a crowd of some ten thousand witnessed the first modern war maneuvers in the nation's history. A total of two thousand men participated, including cavalry, artillery, and air force. Demonstrations in aerial bombardment, artillery and machine-gun fire, and mass troop movements were conducted. Hernández Martínez proudly unveiled the first domestic-made tank, equipped with six heavy machine guns.

Related to the establishment of military dictatorship was the increasing identity of El Salvador with the Axis powers. The brief experiment in party politics and representative democracy had failed. It was now the military's mission to redeem the country. The economic crisis during Araujo's administration only deepened the military's distaste for political liberalism and heightened its desire for a more elitist form of government. Communist subversion in 1932 strengthened this view. As early as 1936, Salvadorean officers began training in Italy and Germany. Pro-Axis officers held key military and government posts until late in 1941. In March 1938, a contract was signed whereby Italy agreed to supply El Salvador with four Caproni fighters and spare parts in exchange for $200,000 worth of coffee. The following October, six Caproni bombers arrived, as well as three Fiat tanks and three heavy tractors capable of being quickly converted into armored cars. To assist in the training of drivers and mechanics, a group of Italian technicians accompanied the equipment.

Significant too was the appointment of General Eberhardt Bohnstedt as director of the Escuela Militar in 1938. With the rank of colonel in the German army, Bohnstedt replaced Colonel Ernesto Bará, of French descent and a veteran of French campaigns in World War I.

Little doubt remained as to Hernández Martínez's policy when, in June

1940, it was decreed a national crime to express sympathy for the Allied cause. When Italy declared war the same month, three hundred Blackshirts paraded through downtown San Salvador. The unfavorable reaction on the part of spectators was quickly suppressed by the police.

By fall 1940, the nation was clearly suffering from the high price of Axis sympathy. Unreliable trade with Italy and Germany produced severe shortages. Sharply declining exports to the Axis nations and a corresponding decrease in production caused the unemployment of 20 percent of the work force. In the face of growing hostility at home and pressure from abroad, Hernández Martínez reversed his policy by publicly denouncing European totalitarianism and praising the Allied cause in October 1940.

One cause of the change in foreign policy was the sharp increase in military opposition to the Axis powers. Even though officers remained divided on ideological grounds, armament shortages and the unavailability of European materiel made the abandonment of the pro-Axis stance appear to be the most profitable course of action. Furthermore, the United States had clearly shown itself willing to replace Europe as El Salvador's major arms supplier. When Defense Minister General Salvador Castañeda Castro requested thirty-five thousand rifles from the United States military attaché in June of 1940, Colonel J. B. Pate informed him that he was confident that a way would be found "to help our exceptionally loyal friends in this matter." Castañeda boasted that his country could raise an army of forty thousand men and added that the armed forces were overwhelmingly in favor of the Allies. It was only a matter of time, he continued, before his government would denounce German and Italian aggression.

Despite a willingness to change his international views, Hernández Martínez remained uniform in his approach to domestic politics. Throughout his rule, the overriding principle was the retention of power. In August 1934, the presidency was transferred to General Andrés Ignacio Menéndez, minister of war, to enable Hernández Martínez to campaign for the March 1935 elections. According to the arrangement, Menéndez's first act was to appoint Hernández Martínez as his minister of war to insure his own resumption of that office after the election. To mark the occasion, amnesty was decreed for all minor crimes against the state, and sentences were reduced for serious crimes committed by military personnel.

Preparations for Hernández Martínez's campaign began in late 1933, though newspapers were prohibited from carrying political news until December 1934, when the National Assembly belatedly announced the election. Opposition candidates had little time to campaign, and Hernández Martínez was inaugurated the following March.

The 1939 election presented a more difficult problem. Reelection was prohibited by the constitution, and civilian opposition to *continuismo* was widespread. Citizens prided themselves on the fact that no president had held consecutive terms since the nineteenth century. Nonetheless, Hernández Martínez clearly had no intention of relinquishing control, and campaigning for a "reform" of the electoral laws was well advanced by the middle of 1937. Every conceivable device was used to convince the country of the wisdom of constitutional change and the need for Hernández Martínez's reelection. Well-planned campaigns were conducted by the government-controlled radio stations, as well as by the press. Motion pictures of organized demonstrations were employed, and thirty thousand Hernández Martínez supporters were reported to have welcomed convention participants when they convened in November 1938 to write a new constitution. The new constitution, effected January 20, 1939, extended future presidential terms from four to six years, and the convention itself elected Hernández Martínez to a second term. Further, to insure political order, military courts were granted the right to try all intended or committed crimes against the peace, and additional measures were taken by the defense ministry to tighten public surveillance.

No amount of military might or constitutional maneuvering could stay the tide of growing national discontent. The state of siege remained in effect until Hernández Martínez's fall in 1944. Periodic uprisings reflected the profound social and economic changes which had taken place since World War I. Following the trend of the whole of Latin America, El Salvador had become a partially urbanized nation, and by 1936, over a third of the population were city dwellers. This group, cognizant of national events, demanded better living standards and formed a hard core of discontent not easily controlled by oppressive measures. Increasingly, the population realized the need for basic political and economic reform, and few people were willing to accept the world depression as the sole reason for their ills.

Occasional efforts to dislodge the military dictatorship were met with swift military repression. A strong army, a National Guard to control the rural sectors, and a secret police force that was reported to be the best in Central America insured that revolts rarely went beyond the planning stage. Malcontents had a way of simply disappearing, and every available jail in San Salvador was kept full.

Ostensibly, the Constitutional Assembly which convened in January 1944 assembled for the purpose of amending the constitution to permit the expropriation of German property, but its main business was to alter the election laws to allow Hernández Martínez a fourth term. March 1 marked his inauguration, and the dictator celebrated the event in a gala evening of toasts and well-wishing. Opposition groups, however, concluded that the time to act had arrived.

Leading civilian opponents knew that the foundation of military support constructed by the dictator was showing serious signs of wear. In late 1943, members of the clandestine Acción Democrática Salvadoreña had met with seven junior and senior officers of the army and air force to choose a director for the anti-Martínez movement. Civilians consciously fanned unrest within the army's officer corps by pointing to the inequity of division of spoils and the arbitrary system of promotion. Their hope, of course, was that the overthrow of Hernández Martínez would end personal aggrandizement on the part of all officers. Even the dictator had lost faith in the army's willingness to support him. Despite his efforts to transform the army into a personal guard, every unsuccessful revolt during his administration had included army officers. As a consequence, the dictator increasingly devoted more attention to the other services. After 1937, the air force and National Police received larger percentages of the defense budgets, and the National Guard was given the largest share of the new equipment.

Much of the advantage Hernández Martínez gained by building the National Guard, the National Police, and the air force to offset the army was lost in September 1941, when the government called for the creation of a civilian militia. Fashioned from the membership of Hernández Martínez's Pro-Patria party, this group came to be recognized as a counterbalance to the armed forces. The fact that the civilian militia remained small and poorly armed did not keep it from being a source of concern for all the military services.

Under these circumstances, it was no surprise that when a revolt was staged on April 2, 1944, many of those involved were members of the armed forces. By April 3, all resistance in the capital had been crushed. On the following day, troops under the command of Subsecretary of Defense General Fidel Cristino Garay reestablished government control in Santa Ana, the only place outside the capital to enter into open rebellion.

Though short in duration, the revolt had been costly in lives and property lost. Although sources vary as to the number of fatalities, a cautious estimate would place the total in excess of two hundred. At least half this number were civilians. The worst tragedy occurred when twenty-two truckloads of civilians, heeding the rebel call to arms, were ambushed by troops under the command of General Garay about midway between Santa Ana and San Salvador. Earlier in the day, fire caused by rebel bombs aimed at the police barracks had spread in the downtown area, and two square blocks were completely destroyed. Six planes that had fallen into the hands of rebel pilots were also destroyed. These six, together with three planes that escaped, constituted 75 percent of the planes registered in the country.

Hernández Martínez had been successful in riding out the first stage of revolt, but it appeared that the dictator had lost faith in his capacity to control the nation. Repeatedly in the days that followed, statements from the presidential palace emphasized the return of tranquility, the insignificant number of "traitors" who had taken part in the abortive revolt, and the fact that the armed forces of the nation steadfastly supported the government. The reign of terror now imposed had all the earmarks of a government uncertain of its ability to remain intact. If there were those who stood in horror of the events of April 2, it was the entire nation that was repulsed by the inhumanity that followed. No sooner had a semblance of order returned than the dictator named a Council of War to judge and prosecute those who had led the rebellion. By its orders, ten officers were executed on the morning of the tenth, whereas nine others were sentenced to death in absentia. Of this number, only two held the rank of colonel and one the rank of general. The following day the executions included the first civilian. To make it clear that continued subversion was futile, the executions were held on a downtown street in full view of the public, and martial law was proclaimed throughout the republic. All newspapers were suspended with the exception of the government-owned *Diario Nuevo* and *El Gran Diario*.

By the last week of April, eighteen more officers and civilians had been condemned or executed, bringing the total to forty-three. Civilian opposition to the regime's heavy-handedness continued to mount. Initially, university students declared themselves on strike in protest to the continued bloodshed. They were followed by secondary students and employees of the banks and commercial houses of the city. By the end of the month, most of the professionals in San Salvador, and many subordinate personnel in several ministries, were staying at home, and the city's activities were slowing to a halt. On the evening of May 5, President Hernández Martínez spoke over the two government-owned radio stations. He lamented the poor coverage by foreign newspapers of the events of April 2 and then announced that the nation was at peace and working, with the exception of the capital, where "seditious elements were carrying on a war of nerves." Even to those in opposition, it was a pathetic speech. It revealed the dictator's resolute belief that the people, in truth, still supported him.

Hernández Martínez had reason to plead. Nothing he had done had persuaded the capital to return to work. That morning banks had closed their doors. For the fifth consecutive day, jeering, taunting crowds filled the streets, obviously hoping to incite police action. In a last effort to maintain his power, Hernández Martínez gave up hope of regaining the allegiance of the professional and business community and directed his appeal to the workers and peasants. With the assistance of loyal landowners, eight hundred peasants armed with machetes had been transported to the capital on April 6 and quartered in various military barracks.

The combination of radio and printed appeals to the lower classes, and the appearance of armed peasants in the streets, aroused memories of the 1932 revolution. These memories were sufficient to inspire grave fears and to prompt some government employees and businessmen to return to work.

Still, the strike continued and rumors of impending uprisings spread freely through the city. On April 7, Hernández Martínez had called a meeting of his cabinet in the salon of the Ministry of Foreign Relations. The dictator requested a continuation of power until the end of the month. He was certain that order could be restored, and though he admitted opposition by the armed forces, he spoke of the small number involved and the divisions that separated them. Despite his assurances, only the minister of the treasury, Escobar Serrano, agreed. The rest of the cabinet remained silent. That same afternoon, having already resigned himself to abdication, Hernández Martínez called a second meeting which included cabinet members and also a handful of loyal followers. Five designees to the presidency were chosen and their names left with the dictator.

On May 8, Hernández Martínez spoke over the government's radio stations and announced that he was resigning. The following day, as the strike brought the capital to a complete standstill, it was announced that the Legislative Assembly had chosen General Andrés Ignacio Menéndez to succeed to the presidency.

Just prior to this announcement, but anticipating the selection of Menéndez, a group of junior officers had approached General Luis Andreu and proposed that he assume control of a military directorate and thus guarantee continued military control. Andreu, a recognized wheelhorse of the Hernández Martínez regime and probably better informed about the circumstances of the coming selection, refused. It was common knowledge that many junior officers had for years found Menéndez to be too absolutely honest, too much of a disciplinarian, a soldier who would do nothing that did not conform to the strict letter of the military law.

Menéndez, above intrigue and without political aspirations, had probably been selected by Hernández Martínez as a safe compromise. The old dictator favored Menéndez, since he could be trusted to hand over the presidency if Hernández Martínez managed to return. Military equipment had been dispatched to strategic areas throughout the republic. The assignment of devoted followers to the governorships of those areas during the first week of May suggested the use of such equipment to regain the country for Hernández Martínez.

Whether or not Hernández Martínez could regain political control was of little consequence to most senior officers. They had enjoyed extramilitary power and ample budgets too long to take their chances under a civilian regime. The failure of the April 2 rebellion had the effect of cleansing from the military all officers who might have shown a willingness to accept civilian government. The few that escaped execution either remained outside the country or returned in support of Menéndez. As a consequence, liberal civilians urged that the strike continue until fundamental rights were restored and the nation freed of military control.

No one could doubt that the country remained in the hands of the military. Trucks loaded with troops patrolled the capital, and manifestoes from the defense ministry circulated daily. The only remaining question was whether Menéndez or a military directorate was in charge of the country.

On May 10, the provisional president named his cabinet, which included representatives from the various political factions operating in the nation. At the same time, the National Congress, still dominated by friends of Hernández Martínez, extended amnesty to all political refugees and prisoners. Liberty of the press was reestablished. A manifesto was circulated to the effect that the new chief executive offered his word of honor as a soldier that all "noble aspirations would be sympathetically received" by him and his government.

At the very least, liberal civilians had successfully challenged Hernández Martínez and had introduced a period of expectation and adjustment. However, at best, the nation still remained under military control and still lacked a truly constitutional framework.

Kenneth J. Grieb

The Guatemalan Military and the Revolution of 1944

Under the watchwords honesty, efficiency, and progress, General Jorge Ubico held Guatemala in the firm grip of a highly *personalista*, progressive-military dictatorship for thirteen years. The platform of his Liberal Progressive Party emphasized development, and the stern caudillo devoted much of his attention to public works projects, particularly a vast expansion of the transportation and communications facilities. A highly successful road construction program gradually helped create an essential element of the economic infrastructure, opening new areas to settlement and cultivation, while encompassing a greater portion of the population in the money economy. These efforts resulted in a considerable expansion and transformation of the economy during Ubico's thirteen-year rule, with the effects increasing during the later portion of his tenure. This upsurge of commerce naturally brought attendant opportunities for small industry and the service professions, and resulted in the expansion of the government bureaucracy. These factors led to the establishment of a considerable number of middle-level managerial, sales, clerical, and other white-collar positions, which vastly expanded the middle class. The impact of this phenomenon was greatest in the capital, where industry, commerce, and governmental offices were concentrated. Economic development thus greatly enlarged the middle class in the capital, creating a potentially new political force. Since Guatemala was run by and for a tiny oligarchy composed of the military officer caste and the owners of the estates that produced the country's export crops, the regime ignored the newly emergent middle class. Although the economic expansion brought undeniable benefits, the expanding middle class became increasingly frustrated with its systematic exclusion from positions of political power.

Since the army has traditionally constituted one of the principal elements of the power structure throughout Guatemalan history, it is scarcely surprising that General Ubico's regime was military in character. The economic progress he fostered had its price in an immense security apparatus which maintained careful surveillance over all activities. Press censorship stifled criticism, while political opponents were exiled or harassed, and election control assured a subservient Congress. Perceiving that support of the officer caste was essential to maintaining himself in power and as a product of this caste himself a partisan of its predominance, Ubico judiciously cultivated this group to such an extent that his government became increasingly militarized during its protracted tenure. Gradually, officers replaced civilian governors in the provinces, and eventually the posts of *jefe político* and governor became synonymous. This process became more evident during the latter portion of his rule, since the effect was cumulative, as supporters rose to higher rank. By 1944, the Guatemalan army boasted 80 generals to command its 15,000 men. Inevitably these promotions fell to old line, politically appointed officers, but like other benefits of the Ubico regime, these rewards had their price. Since generals considerably outnumbered commands, it became customary for the "surplus" generals who did not occupy active command positions to assemble daily at the National Palace, in the President's outer office, where they awaited the Chief Executive's pleasure. Many of the generals thus became virtual "errand boys," whom Ubico employed to handle any situations that arose during the course of the day. Ubico required complete subservience from his officials, and placed the entire security apparatus under his personal control. The police reported directly to the Chief Executive rather than to the Minister of Gobernación, and the President conferred daily with his Minister of War, an aged officer selected primarily for his loyalty. While promotions and decorations were frequent, Ubico applied his austerity program to the army, with the result that the average conscript was paid a mere $3 per month, and even the generals had to settle for a modest salary of $125, far below the standards of other Latin American armies.

Just as with the economy, part of Ubico's program to strengthen the military sowed the seeds of dissent. In the case of the army, this stemmed from the President's efforts to increase professionalism among the officers through upgrading the Escuela Politécnica, the Guatemalan military academy. At Ubico's personal request, a United States Army officer assumed command of the school, and in accordance with Ubico's directive to "make the Escuela Politécnica as near like West Point as was possible under conditions here," stiffened requirements and discipline, introducing a system based on merit. The academy was thus drastically reformed during Ubico's tenure, with a modernized curriculum, a merit system, and a considerable expansion in size. These reforms gradually produced an expanding corps of well-trained, professionalized junior officers. Since they owed their graduation solely to merit, they included some individuals of middle-class origin, thus introducing a new element into the officer corps.

The events of 1944 become understandable only when viewed in this perspective. In both the civilian and the military spheres, the government failed to recognize the situation created by its own programs, and attempted to continue administering the nation as if no changes had occurred. The result was the disaffection of the young professionals in civilian and military life, which increased as the regime clung to office, gradually producing an explosive situation.

A revolt in Salvador, which unseated another long-standing dictatorship during May 1944, increased the tension in Guatemala. The winds of change had swept into a neighboring country, and the parallel between the regime of General Maximiliano Hernández Martínez in Salvador and that of Ubico was obvious. United States Ambassador Boaz Long reported that Ubico was disturbed by the Salvadoran turn of events. Significantly, the Guatemalan President was extremely critical of Martínez' attempts to suppress the rebellion, condemning the resulting bloodbath. Ubico stated that such a situation "would not happen" in Guatemala. The success of the Salvadoran uprising emboldened the Guatemalan opposition, and provided exiles with a base of operations on the border. Student leaders promptly announced plans to boycott the June 30 celebration commemorating the founding of the official Liberal Party. In an effort to counteract the discontent, Ubico decreed a 15 percent increase in all salaries to alleviate the pressures caused by wartime inflation, but this token came far too late.

Protests by university students regarding internal campus grievances provided the spark that ignited the volatile situation. A small coterie of law school students had begun meeting several years earlier, and in 1942, had revived the defunct Law Students Association. The Medical Students Association was resurrected at the same time, and other campus elements followed suit. By late 1943, the groups had coalesced to form the University Students Association to coordinate their activities. In June 1944, medical and law students petitioned for the removal of their Deans. To the surprise of all, the government yielded. This unusual gesture was interpreted as a sign of weakness, and campus leaders immediately determined to press for further concessions to gain political leverage. As one of the few organized sectors of the populace, the students constituted almost the only group capable of initiating a challenge to the administration. The fact that a considerable number of the students came from middle-class families denied political power increased their frustration with the regime's rigid control of intellectual activity. With the normal rashness of youth, they were more willing to risk political activity to redress the grievances their parents were content to decry in private. Upon receiving word of the government concession, the University Students Association endorsed sweeping demands for educational reforms and dismissals throughout the entire university and called for a general university strike. Attempting to placate the dissidents, the President's private secretary, Lic. Ernesto Rivas, summoned protest leaders to the palace and offered concessions in return for a pledge to terminate the demonstrations. Sensing their new-found political power, the students refused. Their ultimatum caused Ubico to convene the first cabinet meeting of his thirteen-year regime. The ministers concluded that further concessions would encourage demands by other sectors, and decided to suppress the student factions.

A presidential decree suspending constitutional guarantees, issued in accordance with the cabinet decision, converted the internal campus problem into a national political issue. Despite the government's announcement that the measures were directed exclusively at campus dissidents and its pledge to rescind the decree as rapidly as possible, lawyers and other professional men interpreted the suspension of constitutional guarantees as a general threat. Although student demonstrators surging through the capital were quickly dispersed by troops and police, driving the leaders to asylum in the Mexican Embassy, several small, clandestine associations of lawyers emerged, and promptly marshalled widespread support. By June 24, a student-sponsored general strike, endorsed by some labor groups and a substantial portion of the middle class, brought the capital to a standstill. A group of 311 professional men petitioned the government for restoration of constitutional rights and a general liberalization of restrictions. The demonstrations and the broad support they elicited caught the administration completely by surprise. Responding instinctively with harsh measures, the government decreed martial law, sealed the nation's borders, and rushed reinforcements to the capital, stationing troops at strategic points throughout the city. The regime also adopted the novel expedient of announcing immediate payment of the entire foreign debt, totaling $8 million, to empty the treasury and remove what officials considered a "temptation to the opposition." Even these desperate measures failed to alleviate the situation. While the security forces effectively dispersed large demonstrations, they proved unable to cope with the new tactics that moved small groups of people to the Central Plaza, where they suddenly combined. Army units ringing the palace eventually fired on these mobs, furnishing the movement with martyrs. Passive resistance became the order of the day, in view of the government's preponderance of force, and demonstrations were abandoned in preference for a general strike supported by the capital's businessmen, which paralyzed the city. Militarization of the railroad and transportation workers failed to break the strike. . . . Perceiving that his own continuance in office was impossible, Ubico opted for preserving military control by stepping aside. . . . If the President was to relinquish his post, however, his successor must be someone whose selection would placate public opinion. . . . Consequently, Ubico decided to form a military junta. . . .

Hasty selection of the junta indicated that all concerned considered military control the only important aspect. None of the three [Federico Ponce Vaides, Eduardo Villagrán Ariza, and Buenaventura Pindea] were confidants of Ubico, or had played a pivotal role in his regime. . . . The three were simply available—and that was all that was considered necessary. The generals, collectively, constituted the real repository of the presidency, with the junta officers as figureheads.

Ubico's resignation produced widespread jubilation, but the resulting turmoil, coupled with the relaxation of government controls, merely exacerbated the political crisis. While waiting for Congress to assemble, the junta acted to remove the principal legal irritants by terminating the stringent measures imposed during the outbreak. The decree suspending constitutional guarantees was immediately revoked, along with various other measures generally blamed for the burgeoning inflation, such as restrictions on the sale of agricultural products and the slaughter of cattle. To complete the evidence of change, the military commanders withdrew the troops to fixed positions around the palace and other governmental installations, terminating patrols within the city and abandoning efforts to prevent street demonstrations. These policies were designed to emphasize the end of the Ubico era and create an appearance of revolutionary victory, while masking the army's continued dominance. . . .

Installation of General Ponce as provisional president confirmed the military control, and indicated that the change in government was more apparent than real. . . .

It quickly became apparent that the military was still in control, and governmental transfer resembled a changing of the guard rather then a significant alteration of the power structure. Although a new general occupied the presidential chair, it was still firmly in the hands of a military "strong man," Despite several new cabinet appointments, a substantial portion of the Ubiquista officials continued in office on a "temporary" basis, including such key individuals as Minister of Foreign Relations, Carlos Salazar, Military Commander of the Plaza General, Roderico Anzueta, and Private Secretary to the Presidency, Ernesto Rivas. Although Ubico had refused to participate in the selection of the junta or the provisional president, once Ponce assumed office, Ubico received a constant stream of visitors at his home, including several members of the government, causing speculation that the ex-president was still in control. While Ubico and Ponce were not on close personal terms, holdover administrators might well have turned to their old mentor for "advice." The former chief executive and his generals had shrewdly created the appearance of yielding to popular pressure, while effectively maintaining power in the hope that this maneuver would placate the discontented masses.

Agitation continued, and although the opposition leaders initially refrained from condemning Ponce, they launched a major effort to organize the masses in preparation for the forthcoming elections. *El Imparcial* bristled with articles relating experiences of individuals imprisoned by Ubico and of students injured in clashes with police during the recent demonstrations, in an attempt to elicit support and sympathy from the populace by emphasizing the harshest aspects of the old regime. Direct criticism of the provisional president was initially limited to editorials urging him to renounce any intention of becoming a candidate in the forthcoming elections, as rumors to this effect were already circulating. Ponce immediately obliged, declaring that he would not enter the elections under any circumstances. The dissidents formed several peasant and labor unions, attempting to channel the widespread popular support into disciplined groups. A plethora of minuscule political movements emerged, with new parties surfacing weekly. American embassy officials prefaced their reports with the comment that the rapid proliferation of parties rendered all analyses transmitted by mail obsolete by the time they reached Washington. . . .

It became obvious to the generals that a mere change of presidents would not be sufficient to enable "business as usual," and that the free rein granted to popular feeling was increasing discontent. The military leaders and the oligarchy had hoped that merely substituting another general for Ubico, and then installing a civilian oligarch as a facade, would calm public sentiment and stifle the surge for social reform. They apparently calculated that removing restrictions would permit a brief orgy of popular enthusiasm which would exhaust itself and dissipate the energies of the opposition leaders. Instead of fading, however, the dissidents continued to gain strength.

With the emergence of an opposition that posed an effective electoral threat, the generals edged toward the familiar tactics of repression. The decision was apparently reached late in August, when American officials learned that a representative of the regime visited Salvador, to confer with military leaders who had regained control of that country after suppressing a similar outbreak. Rumors that Ponce would enter the lists as a presidential aspirant increased, and by mid-September, many Guatemalans were convinced that the General intended to retain power. Ponce began to sound out the Assembly regarding passage of a constitutional amendment permitting the provisional executive to become a candidate without resigning. Manuel Melgar, the new secretary to the President, summoned the Deputies in small groups, asking them to inscribe their names on lists supporting the constitutional amendment, but encountered considerable resistance. The regime also prepared to employ the rural Indian masses to counter the agitation in the capital. This strategy became apparent when several hundred Indians, armed with machetes and clubs, were transported into the city in government trucks to participate in a national holiday on September 15. They paraded through the streets with photos of Ponce pinned to their clothes, and then were quartered at the government-owned finca "La Auora" on the edge of the capital for several days. The presence of this group terrorized the entire city. It was evident that the government intended the measure as a warning.

Following these preparations, the Ponce regime began to suppress its opposition ruthlessly. During the latter part of September, a radio station and several newspapers were ordered closed, and attempts were made to persuade others to temporarily suspend operation "voluntarily." On October 1, Alejandro Cordova, the owner-editor of *El Imparcial*, the leading anti-administration periodical, was assassinated by "unknown individuals." The crime occurred a few days after the minister of war summoned him and warned him to cease his attacks on the regime, while offering him a substantial sum of money to close his paper and "take a vacation" until after the election. A few days later, Cordova's successor was compelled to jump out his office window to escape pursuing police, fleeing to the protection of the Mexican Embassy. . . . Some thirty-six hours after the publisher's assassination, ex-president Ubico called at the United States Embassy to provide his personal analysis of the political situation. The former executive . . . stated that the situation rendered it essential that Ponce continue in office. The following day, Ponce visited the ambassador, who noted that the provisional president's analysis of the situation was identical with Ubico's. Results of the October 13 elections to fill vacancies in Congress confirmed Ponce's determination to retain power. In the words of the American chargé, the official returns indicated that the government-supported slate "won by a handsome, not to say fantastic, margin, garnering 48,530 votes out of a total of 44,571" ballots cast. Invigorated by its "success," the regime ordered the arrest and deportation of Juan José Arévalo [who had returned from exile in Argentina to become the leading civilian candidate for the presidency with the support of the various revolutionary groups].

The generals were not the only component of the military, however, and the revolutionaries found a fertile field for their propaganda among the disgruntled, professionalized junior officers. The student and middle-class leaders had learned from painful experience that although passive tactics could compel the resignation of the executive, their effects were purely negative. Working outside the power structure, they could exert no influence over the choice of a successor. It was evident to the dissident leaders that the revolution had been aborted by the generals, and that only possession of sufficient force to counteract the army could bring a change in the power structure. Given the realities of Guatemala, this force could come from only one source—inside the very military the revolutionaries sought to overthrow. Consequently, during the weeks following Ponce's installation, the revolutionaries launched a new strategy—seeking to subvert the army from within. They quickly discovered that ample opportunity to split the military existed. Expansion of the polytechnic school had produced a substantial corps of well-trained, professionalized junior officers, who considered themselves better prepared than their commanders, many of whom had begun their careers prior to the establishment of the military academy, and owed their rank to political maneuvering. The rigidity of the regime and the social system denied the younger officers opportunities they felt they deserved. Since Ubico stressed austerity, military wages were extremely modest. If a general's salary of $125 a month looked meager to the senior commanders when compared to those in other countries, it appeared absolutely princely to the subalterns. The newly commissioned lieutenant found upon completing the arduous course at the academy that his stipend was a mere $24 a month. Naturally the junior officers chaffed at such scales. In addition, Ubico was extremely reluctant to send officers abroad for advanced training, thus barring a potential "fringe benefit." Approaching the junior officers coincided with the civilian emphasis on a youth movement. Revolutionary propaganda also stressed the superior training of the junior officers, and the political origins of the generals. Junior officers were informed that Ubico, Ponce, and their cohorts had besmirched the name of the army by corrupt practices, thus reducing its standing within the nation. Finally, the revolutionaries found it necessary to produce a counter-argument to military loyalty, which had been instilled in the young officers. In doing so, the rebel leaders ironically were compelled to espouse the theory that the army had a duty not merely to defend the government, but also to uphold the constitution. The concept of the army as the custodian of the constitution was the only possible rationale to counter the military loyalty, as it appealed to the officers' sense of duty. To overthrow a military regime, it proved necessary to propagate the notion that the military was above the government, and had a duty to oust corrupt, unrepresentative, and unconstitutional regimes.

The resulting split in the military ranks proved to be the key to the overthrow of the Ponce regime, which became possible only after the revolutionaries had secured the support of a substantial portion of the army. By October 1944, the American chargé reported that only six of the officers who had graduated from the military academy during recent years were on duty in the capital, and those six included the President's sons. Even with such stringent dispersal of recent academy graduates, the chargé noted "decided mistrust" between those junior officers stationed in the capital, and the senior commanders.

On October 20, a few days after Arévalo and several of his key supporters had issued a manifesto calling for revolt, the Ponce regime fell abruptly when the presidential guard rebelled under the leadership of junior officers. While all other garrisons in the capital initially remained loyal, the government's previous decision to concentrate heavy armaments in the hands of the *guardia de honor* proved decisive, for, in addition to being well-supplied with artillery and machine guns, the guard had control of the country's twelve tanks. The revolt was essentially military in character, led by Major Francisco Javier Arana, commander of the tank battalion, and Captain Jacobo Arbenz, who had recently been dismissed from the service. Both Arbenz and Arana had long been considered leaders of the junior officers, and Arbenz had been particularly popular with the cadets while serving as a professor at the military academy. A fierce battle ensued, but government forces were hopelessly outgunned, and the tank battalion enabled the rebel troops to seize most of the capital. Ponce's efforts to borrow weapons and ammunition from neighboring countries proved futile, and a lucky hit by an artillery shell on the magazine of one of the loyal forts completed the debacle. Negotiations were initiated shortly after the fighting began, culminating in the surrender of the government forces. The departure of numerous leaders of the oligarchy for exile, including cabinet members and senior army officers, indicated the scope of the turnover. Unlike the resignation of Ubico, this transition produced a sharp break.

The successful revolt ousted the old military elite, and placed the younger officers in control. The new junta consisted of Major Arana, Captain Arbenz, and a civilian, Jorge Toriello Garrido. Despite the civilian representative, Arana and Arbenz held the effective power. The military regime had been ousted only by a military revolt, and it was replaced by a predominantly military junta, although the latter was pledged to install a civilian, Arévalo, as eventual president. The new junta promptly purged the bureaucracy and the senior army commands to remove adherents of the old regime, thus completing the transfer of power. Of course, the purges also opened places for the young rebel leaders. Military pay was immediately increased substantially. Although the new regime enjoyed considerable popularity, it found it necessary to proceed cautiously, and the junta ruled "with an iron hand in a silk glove." Supporters of Arévalo swept the November Assembly elections, and a presidential ballot was immediately scheduled for December. As expected, Arévalo scored an overwhelming triumph. His installation in office completed the transition begun by the junta.

There was, of course, a price for the support of the young officers, which had enabled Arévalo to take office. Despite the idealistic rhetoric, the leaders of the revolt received the traditional rewards. Arana rose from Major to full Colonel, and Arbenz from Captain to Lieutenant Colonel. Arana also became Minister of Defense, and hence, effective commander of the armed forces. The officers and men who had supported the uprising had already received their share—higher salaries, an opportunity to study abroad, and promotions resulting from vacancies created by the purge of supporters of the old regime. More importantly, the new Constitution made the armed forces virtually independent of the government. This autonomy measure appeared on the agenda which the junta prepared for the Assembly in what the American ambassador described as "a Constitutional curiosity" attempting to "dictate by executive action the provisions of a new Constitution." The Assembly accepted the proposal, which was strongly endorsed by Arévalo. Its avowed purpose was to divorce the army from politics by terminating political promotions based on loyalty and preventing manipulation of the army for political purposes. Hopefully, it would cause the army to devote its concern to professional matters and remove itself from politics. But autonomy could also have the reverse effect, particularly when combined with the idea that the military was the guardian of the Constitution. Throughout his term of office, Arévalo was careful to praise the army effusively, and champion its autonomy. This was the cost of military support, and granting favors and praise to the army differed little from the policy of previous regimes. There was little friction because of the alliance between young officers and young intellectuals who shared ideals about improving the country. But the implications for the future remained, and reform was dependent upon the commitment of the professionalized officer corps.

Reprinted and edited from *The Americas* 32, no. 4 (April 1976), pp. 524–43.

4 The United States and Latin American Military Politics

The United States and Military Politics in Latin America

After World War II, the United States sought to incorporate Latin American military establishments into the Western defense alliances against the expansion of international socialism. The Río Pact of 1945 bound Latin American nations, at least formally, to a collective security arrangement explicitly oriented against "Communist" intervention. But just as only Brazil had actually sent armed forces to fight against the Axis Powers in World War II, only Colombia participated in the war to "contain Communism" in Korea. Thus, the Latin American military establishments remained largely without a serious professional mission to perform in regard to defending their nations against external threats. Then came the Cuban Revolution. On January 27, 1959, shortly after the victory of Fidel Castro over Fulgencio Batista's dictatorship, Ernesto "Che" Guevara outlined the implications of the Cuban Revolution for the rest of Latin America:

The example of our revolution for Latin America and the lessons it implies have destroyed all the café theories; we have shown that a small group of resolute men supported by the people and not afraid to die if necessary can take on a disciplined regular army and completely defeat it. This is the basic lesson. There is another, which our brothers in Latin America in economically the same position agriculturally as ourselves should take up, and that is there must be an agrarian revolution and fighting in the countryside and the mountains. The revolution must be taken from there to the cities. . . .

It did not matter that Batista's army was hardly disciplined or that Fidel's *guerrilleros* never "completely defeated" a regular army in pitched battle. The Cuban experience was to provide an inspiration to Latin American revolutionaries such as Chilean presidential candidate Salvador Allende, who proclaimed in 1960:

Cuba's fate resembles that of all Latin American countries. They are all underdeveloped—producers of raw materials and importers of industrial products. In all these countries, imperialism has deformed the economy, made big profits, and established its political influence. The Cuban Revolution is a national revolution, but it is also a revolution of the whole of Latin America. It has shown the way for the liberation of all our peoples.

If many on the political left saw Cuba as a hope for the future, policy makers in the United States and traditional power holders in Latin America came more and more to fear the spread of the Cuban Revolution or its principles to the rest of Latin America. Furthermore, the fate of the Cuban officer corps was not lost on the military establishments in the rest of the hemisphere.

From 1961 onward, the United States, in cooperation with Latin American governments and military elites, organized a counterthrust to the Cuban Revolution: the "Alliance for Progress." The Alliance, however, came more and more to be an alliance between United States policy makers and Latin American counterrevolutionaries and military elites.

Theorists and policy makers drew attention to the threat of communist subversion and the need for United States counterinsurgency programs to prevent the spread of revolution throughout the hemisphere. The article reproduced below by Walt Rostow, one of the U.S.'s best-known intellectuals and policy makers advocating these programs in the 1960s, illustrates clearly the underpinnings of United States policy during this period. Entitled, "Guerrilla Warfare in Underdeveloped Areas," this article notes emphatically the view that guerrilla warfare in the Third World represents "a systematic attempt by the Communists to impose a serious disease on those societies attempting the transition to modernization."

During 1962 and 1963, the United States expanded its counterinsurgency programs and training capabilities. These included the army's special forces, the Southern Command in the Panama Canal Zone, and the center at Fort Bragg, North Carolina. The Agency for International Development (AID) established the Inter-American Police Academy in the Canal Zone in 1962. From 1962 to 1968, United States military missions provided training, support, and personnel to assist Latin American regimes in the destruction of guerrilla movements and other opposition (at times even banditry) to incumbent governments. These combined United States–local military efforts were overwhelmingly successful, culminating in 1967 with the deaths of Che Guevara and his guerrilla band in Bolivia.

The training received by Latin American military officers and police officials as part of the counterinsurgency programs had more than simple technical substance and implications. This training not only prepared officers to lead troops against insurgents, but also led them to ask questions about why such operations were necessary in their countries. The answers to these questions involved complex relationships among (1) international communism, (2) Cuba, (3) the lack of economic development in their countries, and (4) the ineptitude and corruption of civilian politicians.

In the United States, there were some policymakers who resisted the United States' role in fomenting counterrevolution and military rule in Latin America. Despite such objections, however, the United States role in assisting, training, and buttressing military expansion and rule in Latin America continued.

As guerrilla forces and revolutionary political movements became more sophisticated, especially after the death of Che Guevara in 1967, there was growing concern about urban as well as rural-based guerrilla movements. By 1975, over seventy thousand Latin Americans had been trained in the United States, in the Canal Zone, or in various Latin American countries by United States military instructors.

Most of the Latin American guerrilla movements failed or were defeated. But in Nicaragua in 1979, the Sandinista revolutionaries spearheaded a popular insurrection which toppled the Somoza dictatorship. Meanwhile, government forces, supported by United States military assistance, were stalemated in El Salvador. Renewed concern for communist subversion brought a new focus on what came to be called "low-intensity warfare." In 1985, Colonel John D. Waghelstein, an officer recently responsible for direction of U.S. military programs in El Salvador, published an appeal in *Military Review* for the United States military establishment to develop further its low-intensity warfare capabilities to deal with the existing threats. Thus, his "Post-Vietnam Counterinsurgency Doctrine" provides a significant insight into the definition of the politico-military mission of United States military forces in Latin America in the 1980s.

In the 1980s, United States policy focused more and more on the Caribbean and Central America. Even as the gradual transition from antipolitical military regimes to moderate civilian coalitions occurred in the Southern cone, United States policy accompanied a militarization of domestic and foreign politics in Central America and the Caribbean. This process is well described by Jorge Rodríguez Beruff in the final selection of Part 4.

W. W. Rostow

Guerrilla Warfare in Underdeveloped Areas

It does not require much imagination to understand why President Kennedy took the problem of guerrilla warfare seriously. When this administration came to responsibility, it faced four major crises: Cuba, the Congo, Laos, and Vietnam. Each represented a successful Communist breaching—over the previous two years—of the Cold War truce lines which had emerged from World War II and its aftermath. In different ways, each had arisen from the efforts of the international Communist movement to exploit the inherent instabilities of the underdeveloped areas of the non-Communist world, and each had a guerrilla-warfare component.

Cuba, of course, differed from the other cases. The Cuban revolution against Batista was a broad-based national insurrection. But that revolution was tragically captured from within by the Communist apparatus, and now Latin America faces the danger of Cuba's being used as the base for training, supply, and direction of guerrilla warfare in the hemisphere.

More than that, Mr. Khrushchev, in his report to the Moscow conference of Communist Parties (published January 6, 1961), had explained at great length that the Communists fully support what he called wars of national liberation and would march in the front rank with the peoples waging such struggles. The military arm of Mr. Khrushchev's January 1961 doctrine is, clearly, guerrilla warfare.

Faced with these four crises, pressing in on the President from day to day, and faced with the candidly stated position of Mr. Khrushchev, we have, indeed, begun to take the problem of guerrilla warfare seriously.

To understand this problem, however, one must begin with the great revolutionary process that is going forward in the southern half of the world, for the guerrilla-warfare problem in these regions is a product of that revolutionary process and the Communist effort and intent to exploit it.

What is happening throughout Latin America, Africa, the Middle East, and Asia is this: Old societies are changing their ways in order to create and maintain a national personality on the world scene and to bring to their peoples the benefits modern technology can offer. This process is truly revolutionary. It touches every aspect of the traditional life—economic, social, and political. The introduction of modern technology brings about not merely new methods of production, but a new style of family life, new links between the villages and the cities, the beginnings of national politics, and a new relationship to the world outside.

Like all revolutions, the revolution of modernization is disturbing. Individual men are torn between the commitment to the old, familiar way of life and the attractions of a modern way of life. The power of old social groups—notably the landlord, who usually dominates the traditional society— is reduced. Power moves toward those who command the tools of modern technology, including modern weapons. Men and women in the villages and the cities, feeling that the old ways of life are shaken and that new possibilities are open to them, express old resentments and new hopes.

This is the grand arena of revolutionary change, which the Communists are exploiting with great energy. They believe that their techniques of organization—based on small disciplined cadres of conspirators—are ideally suited to grasp and to hold power in these turbulent settings. They believe that the weak transitional governments that one is likely to find during this modernization process are highly vulnerable to subversion and to guerrilla warfare. And whatever Communist doctrines of historical inevitability may be, Communists know that their time to seize power in the underdeveloped areas is limited. They know that, as momentum takes hold in an underdeveloped area—and the fundamental social problems inherited from the traditional society are solved—their chances to seize power decline.

It is on the weakest nations, facing their most difficult transitional moments, that the Communists concentrate their attention. They are the scavengers of the modernization process. They believe that the techniques of political centralization under dictatorial control—and the projected image of Soviet and Chinese Communist economic progress—will persuade hesitant men, faced with great transitional problems, that the Communist model should be adopted for modernization, even at the cost of surrendering human liberty. They believe that they can exploit effectively the resentments built up in many of these areas against colonial rule and that they can associate themselves effectively with the desire of the emerging nations for independence, for status on the world scene, and for material progress.

This is a formidable program, for the history of this century teaches us that Communism is not the long-run wave of the future toward which societies are naturally drawn. But, on the contrary, it is one particular form of modern society to which a nation may fall prey during the transitional process. Communism is best understood as a disease of the transition to modernization.

What is our reply to this historical conception and strategy? What is the American purpose and the American strategy? We, too, recognize that a revolutionary process is under way. We are dedicated to the proposition that this revolutionary process of modernization shall be permitted to go forward in independence, with increasing degrees of human freedom. We seek two results: first, that truly independent nations shall emerge on the world scene; and, second, that each nation will be permitted to fashion out of its own culture and its own ambitions the kind of modern society it wants. The same religious and philosophical beliefs which decree that we respect the uniqueness of each individual make it natural that we respect the uniqueness of each national society. Moreover, we Americans are confident that, if the independence of this process can be maintained over the coming years and decades, these societies will choose their own version of what we would recognize as a democratic, open society.

These are our commitments of policy and of faith. The United States has no interest in political satellites. Where we have military pacts, we have them because governments feel directly endangered by outside military action and we are prepared to help protect their independence against such military action. But, to use Mao Tse-tung's famous phrase, we do not seek nations which "lean to one side." We seek nations which will stand up straight. And we do so for a reason: because we are deeply confident that nations which stand up straight will protect their independence and move in their own ways and in their own time toward human freedom and political democracy.

Thus, our central task in the underdeveloped areas, as we see it, is to protect the independence of the revolutionary process now going forward. This is our mission, and it is our ultimate strength. For this is not—and cannot be—the mission of Communism. And in time, through the fog of propaganda and the honest confusions of men caught up in the business of making new nations, this fundamental difference will become increasingly clear in the southern half of the world. The American interest will be served if our children live in an environment of strong, assertive, independent nations, capable, because they are strong, of assuming collective responsibility for the peace.

The diffusion of power is the basis for freedom within our own society, and we have no reason to fear it on the world scene. But this outcome would be a defeat for Communism—not for Russia as a national state, but for Communism. Despite all the Communist talk of aiding movements of national independence, they are driven in the end, by the nature of their system, to violate the independence of nations. Despite all the Communist talk of American imperialism, we are committed, by the nature of our system, to support the cause of national independence. And the truth will out.

The victory we seek will see no ticker-tape parades down Broadway, no climactic battles, no great American celebrations of victory. It is a victory that will take many years and decades of hard work and dedication—by many people—to bring about. This will not be a victory of the United States over the Soviet Union. It will not be a victory of capitalism over socialism. It will be a victory of men and nations that aim to stand up straight, over the forces that wish to entrap and to exploit their revolutionary aspirations of modernization. What this victory involves, in the end, is the assertion by nations of their right to independence and by men and women of their right to freedom as they understand it. And we deeply believe this victory will come—on both sides of the Iron Curtain.

If Americans do not seek victory in the usual sense, what do we seek? What is the national interest of the United States? Why do we Americans expend our treasure and assume the risks of modern war in this global struggle? For Americans, the reward of victory will be, simply, this: It will permit American society to continue to develop along the old humane lines which go back to our birth as a nation, and which read deeper into history than that—back to the Mediterranean roots of Western life. We are struggling to maintain an environment on the world scene that will permit our open society to survive and to flourish.

To make this vision come true places a great burden on the United States at this phase of history. The preservation of independence has many dimensions.

The United States has the primary responsibility for deterring the Communists from using nuclear weapons in the pursuit of their ambitions. The United States has a major responsibility for deterring the kind of overt aggression with conventional forces that was launched in June 1950, in Korea.

The United States has the primary responsibility for assisting the economies of those hard-pressed states on the periphery of the Communist bloc, under acute military, or quasi-military pressure, which they cannot bear from their own resources; for example, South Korea, Vietnam, Taiwan, Pakistan, Iran. The United States has a special responsibility of leadership in bringing not merely its own resources, but the resources of all the free world to bear in aiding the long-run development of those nations which are serious about modernizing their economy and the social life. And, as President Kennedy made clear, he regarded no program of his administration as more important than his program for long-term economic development, dramatized, for example, by the Alliance for Progress, in Latin America. Independence cannot be maintained by military measures alone. Modern societies must be built, and we are prepared to help build them.

Finally, the United States has a role to play in learning to deter the outbreak of guerrilla warfare, if possible, and to deal with it, if necessary.

It is, of course, obvious that the primary responsibility for dealing with guerrilla warfare in the underdeveloped areas cannot be American. There are many ways in which we can help—and we are searching our minds and our imaginations to learn better how to help; but a guerrilla war must be fought primarily by those on the spot. This is so for a quite particular reason, A guerrilla war is an intimate affair, fought not merely with weapons, but fought in the minds of the men who live in the villages and in the hills, fought by the spirit and policy of those who run the local government. An outsider cannot, by himself, win a guerrilla war. He can help create conditions in which it can be won, and he can directly assist those prepared to fight for their independence. We are determined to help destroy this international disease, that is, guerrilla war, designed, initiated, supplied, and led from outside an independent nation.

Although, as leader of the free world, the United States has special responsibilities which it accepts in this common venture of deterrence, it is important that the whole international community begin to accept its responsibility for dealing with this form of aggression. It is important that the world become clear in mind, for example, that the operation run from Hanoi against Vietnam is as certain a form of aggression as the violation of the 38th Parallel by the North Korean armies in June 1950.

In my conversations with representatives of foreign governments, I am sometimes lectured that this or that government within the free world is not popular; they tell me that guerrilla warfare cannot be won unless the peoples are dissatisfied. These are, at best, half-truths. The truth is that guerrilla warfare, mounted from external bases—with rights of sanctuary—is a terrible burden to carry for any government in a society making its way toward modernization. For instance, it requires somewhere between ten and twenty soldiers to control one guerrilla in an organized operation. Moreover, the guerrilla force has this advantage: Its task is merely to destroy, while the government must build, and protect what it is building. A guerrilla war mounted from outside a transitional nation is a crude act of international vandalism. There will be no peace in the world if the international community accepts the outcome of a guerrilla war, mounted from outside a nation, as tantamount to a free election.

The sending of men and arms across international boundaries and the direction of guerrilla war from outside a sovereign nation is aggression; and this is a fact which the whole international community must confront and whose consequent responsibilities it must accept. Without such international action, those against whom aggression is mounted will be driven inevitably to seek out and engage the ultimate source of the aggression they confront.

In facing the problem of guerrilla war, I have one observation to make as a historian. It is now fashionable to read the learned works of Mao Tse-tung and Che Guevara on guerrilla warfare. This is, indeed, proper. One should read with care and without passion into the minds of one's enemies. But it is historically inaccurate and psychologically dangerous to think that these men created the strategy and tactics of guerrilla war to which we are now responding. Guerrilla warfare is not a form of military and psychological magic created by the Communists. There is no rule or parable in the Communist texts that was not known at an earlier time in history. The operation of Marion's men in relation to the Battle of Cowpens in the American Revolution was, for example, governed by rules that Mao merely echoed. Che Guevara knows nothing of this business that T. E. Lawrence did not know or that was not practiced, for example, in the Peninsular campaign during the Napoleonic Wars, a century earlier. The orchestration of professional troops, militia, and guerrilla fighters is an old game, whose rules can be studied and learned.

My point is that we are up against a form of warfare that is powerful and effective only when we do not put our minds clearly to work on how to deal with it. I, for one, believe that with purposeful efforts, most nations which might now be susceptible to guerrilla warfare could handle their border areas in ways which would make them very unattractive to the initiation of this ugly game. We can learn to prevent the emergence of the famous sea in which Mao Tse-tung taught his men to swim. This requires, of course, not merely a proper military program of deterrence, but programs of village development, communications, and indoctrination. The best way to fight a guerrilla war is to prevent it from happening. And this can be done.

Similarly, I am confident that we can deal with the kind of operation now under way in Vietnam. It is an extremely dangerous operation, and it could overwhelm Vietnam if the Vietnamese—aided by the free world—do not deal with it. But it is an unsubtle operation, by the book, based more on murder than on political or psychological appeal.

When Communists speak of wars of national liberation and of their support for "progressive forces," I think of the systematic program of assassination now going forward in which the principal victims are the health, agriculture, and education officers in Vietnamese villages. The Viet Cong are not trying to persuade the peasants of Vietnam that Communism is good; they are trying to persuade them that their lives are insecure unless they cooperate with them. With resolution and confidence on all sides, and with the assumption of international responsibility for the frontier problem, I believe we are going to bring this threat to the independence of Vietnam under control.

My view is, then, that we confront in guerrilla warfare in the underdeveloped areas a systematic attempt by the Communists to impose a serious disease on those societies attempting the transition to modernization. This attempt is a present danger in Southeast Asia. It could quickly become a major danger in Africa and Latin America. It is our task to prevent that disease, if possible, and to eliminate it where it is imposed.

Every American should be aware of the military and the creative dimensions of the job. Those with whom I have the privilege of working are dedicated to that mission with every resource of mind and spirit at our command.

Reprinted and edited from *Marine Corps Gazette* 46, no. 1 (January 1962), pp. 46–49.

Colonel John D. Waghelstein, U.S. Army

Post-Vietnam Counterinsurgency Doctrine

In the post-Vietnam era, counterinsurgency has virtually become a non-subject in the U.S. military educational system. The term *counterinsurgency* has been replaced by the less controversial *low-intensity conflict*. A recently proposed definition of low-intensity conflict for the revised Army field manual on that subject reads:

The limited use of power for political purposes by nations or organizations . . . to coerce control or defend a population, to control or defend a territory or establish or defend rights. It includes military operations by or against irregular forces, peacekeeping operations, terrorism, counter-terrorism, rescue operations, *and military assistance under conditions of armed conflict*. This form of conflict does not include protracted engagements of opposing regular forces. [Emphasis added, ED.]

The problem with this is that low-intensity conflict is a description of the level of violence from a military viewpoint. This kind of conflict is more accurately described as revolutionary and counterrevolutionary warfare. It is *total war* at the grass-roots level—one that uses *all* of the weapons of total war, including political, economic, and psychological warfare with the military aspect being a distant fourth in many cases. The subordination of the military in counterinsurgency has always created problems for the U.S. military establishment. This kind of conflict is fundamentally different from the American way of war.

Low-intensity conflict and counterinsurgency involve two distinct uses of the U.S. military. The first, as demonstrated in the Grenada operation, is the surgical application of force—a role for which U.S. units are trained and equipped. The second use involves assisting an ally in politico-military operations to combat armed insurgents, a role for which the U.S. military is unprepared. The state of preparedness for this second role is at its lowest point in twenty years.

Low-intensity conflict instruction at the U.S. Army Command and General Staff College [USACGSC], Fort Leavenworth, Kansas, includes an analysis of insurgency—the causes, the catalysts, and the role of the sponsor in generating insurgency, as well as ways the United States can best *assist* besieged friendly governments in countering insurgencies. Developmental or consolidative campaigns aimed at the root causes of insurgency are studied, as well as methods of mobilizing human and material resources and ways of neutralizing the armed guerrilla threat. In short, the doctrine stresses a balanced approach of development, mobilization, and neutralization.

Additionally, there is a careful analysis of various types of insurgencies and the social groups and political forces existing in each. Case studies are used (for example, Venezuela, 1959–63), as well as the macro approach. The situation-specific aspects of each insurgency are stressed to preclude another "cookie cutter" disaster—for example, trying to apply a Malayan strategic hamlet solution to Vietnam. What little doctrine there is is sound and provides some useful tools to those officers who may be called upon to operate in a counterinsurgency environment.

The real problem is not the doctrine but the amount of emphasis that the services place on the subject. For example, by 1977, a paltry forty hours of the one-year-course core curriculum were devoted to the study of low-intensity conflict at the USACGSC. Two years later, the low-intensity conflict course had been reduced to eight hours. In the branch schools, the subject was discontinued altogether. The U.S. Army still does not regard guerrilla warfare, insurgency, and counterinsurgency as being unique and is unwilling to devote substantial resources to preparing for our most likely form of involvement.

A recent study by Captain Andrew F. Krepenevitch of the Department of Social Sciences, U.S. Military Academy, West Point, New York, details the Army's failure in the early 1960s to make any serious attempt at developing counterinsurgency doctrine and training. Many of the same criticisms are being leveled today:

The Administration's emphasis on developing a counterinsurgency capability impacted heavily on the Army brass. They were, in effect, being told to alter radically the Army's method of operation, a method that had been eminently successful in prior conflicts. The notion that a group of novice civilians ([John F.] Kennedy, [Robert S.] McNamara, and the "Whiz Kids") should require the Army to de-emphasize what had been its strong suit (i.e., heavy units, massed firepower, high technology) in favor of stripped-down light infantry units encountered strong organizational resistance. [Emphasis added.]

Statements from the Army's leadership bear out the organization's disinterest in the President's proposals and their conviction that the concept [the conventional approach to war] could handle any problems that might crop up at the lower end of the conflict spectrum:

General Lyman Lemnitzer, Army Chairman of the JCS *(Joint Chiefs of Staff),*

1960–1962: stated that the new administration was "oversold" on the importance of guerrilla warfare.

General George Decker, Army Chief of Staff, 1960–1962: countered a presidential lecture to the Chiefs on counter-insurgency with the reply "any good soldier can handle guerrillas."

General Earle Wheeler, Army Chief of Staff, 1962–1964: "The essence of the problem in Vietnam is military." [Emphasis added.]

General Maxwell Taylor. Chairman of the JCS, 1962–1964: recalling his reaction to JFK's proposals: "It (counterinsurgency) is just a form of small war, a guerrilla operation in which we have a long record against the Indians. Any well-trained organization can shift the tempo to that which might be required in this kind of situation. All this cloud of dust that's coming out of the White House really isn't necessary. [Emphasis added.]

. . . .

The Army's disinterest with regard to the development of counterinsurgency capability was demonstrated not only in that mechanistic approach in which it addressed this requirement in the 1960s, but also in the manner in which once the "aberration" of Vietnam ended, the organization discarded what had always been an unwanted appendage to its concepts. [Emphasis added.]

Given the proposition that low-intensity conflict is our most likely form of involvement in the Third World, it appears that the Army is still preparing for the wrong war by emphasizing the Soviet threat on the plains of Europe [fondly called the "Fulda Gap" mentality]. This concern should not preclude preparations to assist our allies in meeting the threat of internal subversion and guerrilla warfare.

The triumph of the Sandinistas in Nicaragua, the insurgency of El Salvador, and Cuba's renewed efforts in the Caribbean Basin have conspired to force the Army to reevaluate its priorities and, like St. Paul on the road to Damascus, many have become converts and begun to reassess our capability. The USACGSC curriculum is now back to a modest thirty-two hours, and old counterinsurgency lesson plans are being dusted off at the service schools. And serious work, albeit modest, is beginning in the service schools, staff colleges, and senior service schools.

The Special Forces, faced with drastic personnel cuts in 1979, have been resuscitated and are expanding modestly. Somewhat surprisingly, senior naval officers were instrumental in saving the Special Forces as they questioned the diminution of their "unconventional warfare" assets in the Pacific and Caribbean regions. The 8th Special Action Force (SAF) for Latin America was deactivated in 1973, and the Latin-American counterinsurgency capability was reduced to a single Special Forces battalion at Fort Gulick, Panama. The 7th Special Forces Group (Airborne) at Fort Bragg, North Carolina, is now oriented toward that region and presently provides the bulk of the training assistance for Honduras and El Salvador.

Apparently, the nadir of our Special Forces capability has been reached and is being expanded slightly to meet the new challenge of the 1980s and 1990s.

What concerns many of us is that these welcome changes stop far short of a serious commitment by the services to devote the personnel and curriculum hours that are needed for adequate instruction *throughout the various educational systems*—the place where long-term changes are made. Thirty-two hours at the Army's mid-level staff college hardly constitute a renaissance for low-intensity conflict. And a few hours of counterinsurgency-related tactical training do not adequately prepare our junior officers for this most likely arena.

Nor are the other services any better prepared than the Army. The Air Force devotes twenty-six hours to low-intensity conflict and counterinsurgency at the Air Command and Staff College, Maxwell Air Force Base, Alabama, and there are no units today with the training and capabilities that would be equivalent to those of the Air Commandos of the 1960s. The Navy and the Air Force still do not have foreign area officer programs that adequately prepare officers for duty in advisory or training assistance roles. The Air Force officers sent to El Salvador during my tenure there were fine pilots and administrators. However, they were totally lacking in language qualification and regional preparation, not to mention the unique aspects of insurgency and counterinsurgency.

Fortunately, the Navy was able to find two superb sea-air-land team (SEAL) officers for duty in El Salvador, but the personnel managers constantly attempted to push "blue water" conventional sailors into what was essentially a brown water, low-intensity conflict situation. All of the services are having difficulty providing counterinsurgency-trained, area-oriented, and language-qualified senior officers for El Salvador. The psychological operations and civil affairs capabilities needed to support our advisory effort in Central America are inadequate. It may be that the U.S. defense establishment is still wary of becoming involved in another Vietnam.

I recently heard two comments from more conventionally oriented colleagues: "Who gives a damn about a bunch of chili-dip countries?" and, "It smells like NUC-Mam to me." While these comments may not reflect Department of Defense policy, they do portray some traditionalists' indifferent and "gun-shy" attitudes toward small wars which we are unprepared to fight.

Given today's realities, however, failure to adequately prepare for low-intensity conflict is inexcusable. I remember the attitude of the Army personnel wallahs early in the 1960s. They did everything they could to discourage combat arms officers from serving at the Vietnamese unit and subsector levels. "What you need is troop duty in Europe with a 'Regular' (for example, conventional) unit." After U.S. troop units were committed to Vietnam, duty with the Military Assistance Command, Vietnam, was still considered to be less "career-enhancing" than duty with a U.S. unit. Despite the lessons of post–World War II insurgencies and the experiences of officers, such as Generals William B. Rosson, Edward Landsdale, or John K. Singlaub, we are essentially where we were when Kennedy became president.

Our track record in dealing with insurgencies in Latin America may account, in part, for our present indifference. In the 1960s, with our help, most guerrilla movements in the region were effectively neutralized by Latin American armies. In 1964, the peak year of the mobile training team effort, we provided 275 of these teams from the 8th SAF in Panama alone. By 1970, the number was down to 70, and most of those were technical assistance teams of one or two specialists each. Our Latin American allies had by then established their own training centers and cadres, and they were capable of putting rural guerrillas and urban-based terrorists supported by Fidel Castro out of business. In 1967, for example, a fifteen-man Special Forces mobile training team trained the Bolivian Rangers that made short work of Ernesto "Che" Guevara's adventure. By the late 1960s, it appeared that Castro would have to look elsewhere for excitement.

Nicaragua (1979) changed all that. The Marxist-Leninists used a popularly based insurgency to achieve power. Castro has finally convinced Moscow that revolution in Central America is possible without waiting for *all* objective conditions to exist. The changed role of the Latin American church since the Medellín Colombia Conference (1968) and the subsequent radicalization of some churchmen and women have added a new dimension to insurgency.

Most importantly, the effective orchestration of U.S. public opinion by sympathetic interest and front groups and their impact on congressional security assistance support has given new life to Castro-supported, Marxist-Leninist insurgencies. More sophisticated planning and coordination is evident in El Salvador, in Grenada, and throughout the region. While Castro has learned from the mistakes of the 1960s, we still appear to have difficulty recovering from our Vietnam hangover.

A recent book on Central America, *Rift and Revolution: The Central American Imbroglio*, contains a superb chapter on "Revolutionary Movements in Central America" by Ernest Evans. Evans concludes:

For both doctrinal and organizational reasons revolutionary warfare goes deeply against the grain of the U.S. military. The doctrinal problem is that in the U.S. military there has always been a widely shared belief that military issues are and should be kept separate from political issues. The organizational problem is that the U.S. military is a big-unit, high-technology military. Wars against guerrillas, however, for the most part, require small units and fairly simple technology.

Although the U.S. military could, of course, modify its organizational patterns, the war in Vietnam demonstrated that the U.S. military is extremely reluctant to modify its big-unit, high-technology orientation.

The fear of becoming involved in another quagmire is evident everywhere in the Department of Defense and, as a result, we are not adequately prepared for any involvement short of commitment of U.S. combat units. Security, training, and advisory assistance are the keys to success in counterinsurgency and, if utilized early enough, will preclude the need for the deployment of U.S. troops in a role for which, given our present conventional preoccupation, we are inadequately trained and doctrinally unsuited. The U.S. counterinsurgency effort, to be effective, must have security, advisory, and training assistance experts who can assess the situation, advise the host country forces on the proper counterinsurgency techniques and training, and equip those forces to do the job. They must be supported by theater and unified command staff officers who understand that counterinsurgency is not just the application of high technology, more logistics, firepower, and mobility.

In many respects, real counterinsurgency techniques are a step toward the primitive (for example, *less* firepower that is more surgically applied). The keys to popular support, the sine qua non in counterinsurgency, include psychological operations, civic action, and grass-roots human intelligence work, all of which runs counter to the conventional U.S. concept of war. To be effective in our advice, we should be sending our best trained counterinsurgency experts to assist our allies. We should not, as has generally been the case, send conventionally oriented officers to create a miniature U.S. defense establishment.

Snarled security assistance legislation, arbitrary restrictions on numbers of trainers (for example, a fifty-five-man level in El Salvador), constraints on the trainers' in-country activities (terms of reference), as well as a lack of emphasis in the Army's educational system and a paucity of fully qualified officers in the services, indicate that we still have a long way to go to meet the challenge.

Reprinted and edited from *Military Review* 65, no. 5 (May 1985), pp. 42–49.

Jorge Rodríguez Beruff

United States Caribbean Policy and Regional Militarization

The prominence of military measures (direct military presence, military intervention, aid, training, arms sales, intelligence, strengthening of the police forces, etc.) within the new United States regional policy has promoted a process of militarization of Caribbean societies of far-reaching implications. By militarization, we mean (1) the growing diversion of economic resources, internal or external, from social to military expenditures; (2) the expansion of the state security forces; (3) the enhanced political weight of the military in articulating state policy; (4) the penetration of traditionally civil spheres of the state bureaucracy (e.g., the police, customs, immigration) by the military, or the organization of these spheres along military lines; (5) the growing resort to force as a means of buttressing the dominant position of the ruling classes; (6) the revision of the legal framework to respond to the military's interest or outlook (e.g., State Security legislation); and (7) the promotion of military forms of organization and values in civil society. All these dimensions may not be present in specific countries, but they do represent general trends in the Caribbean as a whole.

This process has been set in motion with the active support of the conservative political forces which have risen to power throughout most of the countries due to their fragile base of social support. One of the most notable aspects of this process has been the rapid growth of the small, or even nonexistent, military establishments of the Eastern Caribbean. The process has also promoted the growth and the internal weight of the military in countries such as the Dominican Republic, Jamaica, and Haiti and has produced a dramatic increase in United States military activities in Puerto Rico. Cuba has not escaped this regional militarization, due to a greater concern for security, having launched a costly program of military expansion which diverts resources from economic development.

The Caribbean in the Late Seventies: The Emergence of the Popular Movements and the Erosion of United States Power

It could be argued that a United States Caribbean policy—in the sense of a distinct strategy based on an evaluation of specific interests and trends in the region—is a relatively recent development, if we take into consideration the post–World War II period. We would like to suggest that the Carter administration was the first to recognize the need for formulating a coherent regional strategy. This need was derived from three central concerns: (1) the urgent question of how to deal with the emergence of popular mass movements and progressive or reformist regimes throughout the Caribbean and Central American region, (2) the equally pressing and related issue of redefining and "modernizing" the traditional forms of the United States presence in the region (particularly in the military sphere) in the context of the post-Vietnam military and political crisis, and (3) the perceived urgency of overcoming the also traditional "Cuba-centered" view of the Caribbean which was now considered an obstacle to developing effective policies geared to the new regional situation.

In short, the main problem facing the Carter administration was how to neutralize or integrate, through negotiation or pressure, the popular movements to bring the process of change in the Caribbean under control and to channel it in directions that were not antagonistic to United States interests while generally proceeding with a reduction of direct military presence and of traditional forms of military influence. The reductions were deemed necessary not only for economic reasons, but also because of the ideological persuasion (generally derived from the Vietnam defeat) that military means were ineffective in containing revolutionary movements and provoked long-term contradictions that further radicalized popular struggles.

The paramount importance attached to the Caribbean during the Carter administration was reflected in the president's April 1977 speech to the OAS delineating his policy toward Latin America. Three of the most important points (support for the Central American Common Market, resolution of the Panama Canal status, and improvement of United States–Cuba relations) dealt with regional problems. He also stressed "flexible" bilateral relations based on respect for the "individuality" and national sovereignty of each country, which can be understood as an implicit acceptance of ideological and political pluralism in the region. This emphasis on the Caribbean was also reflected in high-level visits to the English-speaking Caribbean, an expansion of the diplomatic presence in the Eastern Caribbean, and a sharp concern for developments in the Dominican Republic and Jamaica. As we know, this initial policy was clearly abandoned in 1979—when it was felt that regional developments were getting out of hand and a wave of conservative revivalism was threatening to electorally engulf "soft" reformism—in favor of a harder line which placed greater emphasis on military instruments of power and served as a convenient transition to the Caribbean Basin policy of the Reagan administration.

During the years 1979 and 1980, a series of events in the region brought into sharp relief the erosion of United States power. Clearly, the two most dramatic were the New Jewel Movement ascent to power in Grenada (March 13, 1979) and the Sandinista victory in Nicaragua (July 19, 1979). But these were not isolated occurrences; rather they were part of a pattern that indicated the ascent to power of new political forces. In that same year, the conservative government of Patrick John in Dominica was removed and replaced by a Committee of National Salvation which included left figures. The St. Lucia Labour Party won a resounding electoral victory against John Compton on the basis of a progressive program. The PNP government in Jamaica appeared to be steering a left course by reinstating D. K. Duncan in the leadership and denouncing the IMF agreements. In El Salvador, the armed struggle was beginning to gain momentum. The Arron government in Surinam was toppled in 1980 by a movement of discontented military which initially included left officers. Finally, the massive emigration of Haitians indicated the precariousness of the Duvalier regime, whereas, more generally, the increased flow of Caribbean migrants focused United States attention on Caribbean developments.

In addition, these developments appeared favorable to the broadening of relations between Cuba and the other countries in the region, thus undermining the United States policy of isolation. Cuba had been able to establish relations with Jamaica, Nicaragua, Grenada, and Surinam, in addition to its links with Guyana. Belize also indicated its willingness to establish ties, and the issue of relations with Cuba became hotly debated in the Eastern Caribbean. The United States could hardly impose a policy of no relations while itself seeking to improve relations with Cuba.

It was in this political context that the new regional policy, including its military aspects, began to be articulated by Carter in 1979, and subsequently by Reagan.

From Carter to Reagan: The Formulation of the New Military Policy

The shift in military policy toward the Caribbean must be located in the second half of 1979, when the original foreign policy premises of the Carter administration were revised. As has been noted, the revision of foreign policy was not limited to the Caribbean, but rather formed part of a new orientation toward revolutionary processes in the underdeveloped world in general and was conditioned by events (such as the Soviet involvement in Afghanistan) that went beyond the region. However, the main concern at that time was related to developments in two regions: the Caribbean and Central America, and the Middle East. For all practical purposes, the geopolitical and cold war ideological orientation of the New Right began to inform foreign policy even before Reagan's electoral victory. On this basis, a new consensus began to emerge among United States ruling groups that trends in those two regions were unfavorable to United States interests and required a more aggressive response.

The adjustments made in regional policy were explained by Robert Pastor, staff member of the National Security Council who was responsible for Latin American and Caribbean policy in the Carter administration:

Changes in the region and the world in 1979 and 1980 made the Carter administration more sensitive to traditional military concerns. The coup in Grenada in March 1979, and the collapse of the Somoza dynasty in July brought new leaders to power, who tended to see Castro's Cuba as the answer. . . and the U.S. as the problem. . . . Simultaneously an economic decline in the region and more aggressive Cuban posture—exemplified by the obtrusive role played by the Cuban Ambassador in the 1980 Jamaican elections—further unsettled the region. This instability naturally was viewed in the U.S. in the context of more ominous international developments—the invasion of Afghanistan, hostages in Iran, uncertainty in the Persian Gulf, and Soviet threats against Poland. The U.S. cooled the relationship (with Grenada) and sought to expand aid to Grenada's neighbors as a signal that only democracy would be rewarded in the region. In the security area, a task force was established in Key West to coordinate naval exercises in the region, and there was a modest increase in security aid. Economic assistance also continued to increase, as did the numbers and quality of official personnel stationed in the area.

The artificial crisis created by the presence of a "Soviet Brigade" in Cuba, September 1979, served to legitimate the new orientation toward the region. The following month, simultaneous announcements were made of an increase in economic aid for the Caribbean and the creation of a Joint Caribbean Task Force in Key West. Subsequently, intense military activity began with an increase in military maneuvers and with numerous visits by high-level Pentagon officials to the region to offer military aid and seek access to new bases.

Toward the end of 1979, Admiral Harry Train, Atlantic Fleet Commander, visited Venezuela and other countries to discuss regional security. In a 1980 visit to the Dominican Republic, Major General Robert L. Scheitzer offered "all types of military aid to combat communism." A later visit by Admiral Train to the same country provoked street disturbances. United States attempts to obtain additional military bases in Haiti and the Dominican Republic were revealed in the framework of these visits.

Even though the overall picture of military assistance for the Caribbean (without taking into account Central America) was not dramatically altered between 1979 and 1980, there was a growing interest in the Eastern Caribbean. By 1980 and 1981, a sharp increase had occurred in all types of security assistance, particularly marked in those countries considered strategically important, such as Barbados (and others of the Eastern Caribbean) and Jamaica.

With the Reagan administration, revision of United States foreign policy accelerated, and the goals to be pursued in the region were clearly delineated. The order of priorities established by Thomas Enders (former assistant secretary of state for Inter-American Affairs) in his June 1981 address was significant. Of the four points relating to the new regional policy, only the third point refers to economic aspects. The first and second emphasize the need for military assistance and preventive measures in "threatened countries." The fourth point commits the United States to increase military pressures against Cuba. This emphasis on military aspects of external policy has been a central feature of policy documents and official pronouncements of the Reagan administration. For example, although Reagan did not mention military measures in his 1982 address on the Caribbean Basin Initiative, he did underscore that its leitmotiv was security considerations.

The main lines of the new military policy toward the Caribbean—in this case including Central America—are contained in an important study of the Strategic Studies Institute of the United States Army War College. This study was concluded on October 26, 1981, several months before Reagan's Caribbean Basin Initiative speech. It was ordered in December 1980 by the Army Office for Operations and Plans in coordination with SOUTHCOM. Among other things, the study directive mentioned that "emerging nationalism, increased radicalization, Cuban activism, and expanding Soviet interest in the region pose direct challenges to U.S. security interests." It requested the Institute to "identify, assess, and recommend alternative uses of military resources as part of a coordinated and comprehensive policy response to secure U.S. strategic interest in the region. . . .The study will emphasize the development of military alternatives designed to reduce the occurrence of destabilizing events. . . ."

The final document was a comprehensive evaluation of the regional situation, including country-by-country analysis and recommendations in all policy areas. Some of the economic proposals (e.g., increase in economic aid and commercial concessions) were later incorporated in the Caribbean Basin Initiative package. Among the recommendations on military policy specifically relating to the Caribbean, the following stand out:

Promote the capabilities and professionalism of friendly regional military forces and their self-confidence in handling both external and internal threats. Promote collective security arrangements, interoperability and common military doctrine with regional military establishments. . . . Establish a network of military-to-military relationships which can: (1) gain for the United States an understanding of the current position and future direction of the various Caribbean militaries and leadership elites; (2) foster increased access to decisional elites in order to enhance U.S. influence; and (3) serve as a bridge between regional military elites in order to encourage intraregional cooperation and the peaceful solution of conflicting interest. . . . Increase the overall size of the security assistance effort. In the Insular Caribbean, provide assistance for maritime security, navigation safety, and for law-and-order forces: police, constabulary, and Coast Guard forces. . . . Increase IMET spending for the region. . . . Expand the role of the U.S. Coast Guard. . . .

The study also advocated a reorganization of the United States direct military presence in the region, with particular emphasis on the role of the "military diplomat" (i.e., advisor) and on the strengthening of SOUTHCOM. A policy of "indirect confrontation" with Cuba was discussed, but conclusions regarding Cuban policy were not found in the document due to extensive deletions of relevant parts.

Another important and heavily deleted document reflecting the new military policy was a review of war plans against Cuba begun in March 1979 (significantly coinciding with the Grenada revolution) by the Atlantic Command and concluded in August 1981. This review was obviously necessary if an intervention in Grenada, and a possible confrontation with Cuba, were being considered. The plan considered as an option in a general war situation massive air strikes and naval actions against a "sample" of forty-one targets designed to neutralize Cuban air and naval capabilities. According to the document, this option was considered "acceptable, but not optimal." A "defensive-deterrent" option (distinct from a status quo but not defined in the parts made public) was apparently preferred, as "the primary Cuban strategic objective in a general war between NATO and Warsaw Pact may be their ultimate survival and independence."

This military planning was accompanied by an increasingly aggressive rhetoric aimed at Cuba, threatening to make that country "pay the cost" of the revolutionary upsurge in the region. Even the apparently "reasonable" proposal advanced by Edward Gonzalez of Rand Corporation—that of compelling the "Finlandization" of Cuba through indirect confrontation— had ominous implications, as it is difficult to envisage that design outside the context of an all-out war.

The New Regional Military Policy and the Militarization of Caribbean Societies

The revision of military policy toward the Caribbean initially found expression in a series of large-scale military maneuvers which virtually transformed the region into a war games scenario. These massive exercises, which took place during the period 1981–84, had the purpose of bringing military pressure to bear on Cuba (e.g., Operation Safepass in 1982), preparing and planning an invasion of Grenada (e.g., Ocean Venture in 1981 and 1982, and Universal Trek in 1983), and generally increasing the level of training of United States forces, particularly of components of the Rapid Deployment Force. The intensity of the exercises was unprecedented in postwar history. Ocean Venture 81, for example, included 120,000 troops, 240 ships, and 1,000 airplanes. In Ocean Venture 1984, B-52 planes flew nonstop from their California bases to Puerto Rico to carry out bombing exercises.

An indication of the Grenada focus of these maneuvers has been the prevailing tendency since 1984 toward a reduction of the scale of the exercises. Recent exercises have been mainly small-scale events designed to train the security forces of the Eastern Caribbean and to develop what the United States military calls "coalition warfare" capabilities (i.e., acting together with regular United States forces in auxiliary roles). The exercise Exotic Palm held in September 1985, for example, involved five hundred Caribbean effectives drawn from the newly created Special Service Units and Coast Guard of St. Lucia, St. Cristopher-Nevis, Dominica, and Grenada and the "defense forces" of Antigua, Barbados, and Jamaica, together with United States and British regular military forces. The exercise was, significantly, an invasion of an island modeled after the Grenada operation. In November 1985, the operation Upward Key was carried out in Antigua, with one hundred United States effectives and Antigua's Special Service Unit and Defense Force. The impact of these "modest" war games in small islands having little previous experience with military structures and having strong civilist traditions should not be underestimated.

The United States military buildup has also had the effect of increasing Cuban military preparations in all fields. This trend has been particularly marked since 1981, when arms shipments from the Soviet Union increased sharply, and has led to a significantly higher level of military expenditures. Though we do not have post-Grenada invasion figures, the actual confrontation of Cuban personnel (with about forty deaths and over fifty wounded) and United States forces must have sharpened that country's concern with security.

SECURITY ASSISTANCE TO CARIBBEAN COUNTRIES
(SELECTED YEARS IN THOUSANDS OF DOLLARS)[a]

	1979	1980	1985	(Requested) 1986
Bahamas	—	—	50	50
Barbados	6	58	b	b
Belize	—	—	4,600	5,100
Eastern Caribbean[c]	—	4,000	25,300	45,400
Guyana	—	—	50	50
Haiti	375	1,127	5,750	130
Jamaica	—	—	75,250	78,280
Dominican Republic	984	3,450	53,750	60,800
Panama	1,399	291	40,000	59,100
Surinam	—	26	80	50
Trinidad-Tobago	—	—	50	50
Total	2,764	8,952	204,880	249,010

SOURCE: Department of Defense, *Congressional Presentation, Security Assistance Program,* 1982 and 1985; and Langhorne A. Motley, "Aid and U.S. Interests in Latin America and the Caribbean," *Caribbean Today,* 2, no. 2, p. 26.

[a] Includes MAP, IMET, FMS, and ESF.
[b] Included in Eastern Caribbean.
[c] Antigua, Barbados, Dominica, Grenada, St. Lucia, St. Vincent, and St. Kitts-Nevis.

The level of assistance and training to regional military and police forces has grown explosively since the late 1970s. Total military assistance to countries in the region has increased from $8 million to about $250 million in the requested budget for 1986. Particularly sharp increases have occurred in the cases of Jamaica, Panama, and the Eastern Caribbean. Similarly, the number of Caribbean military officers trained under IMET has also increased. This expansion of military training to consistently high levels during the mid-1980s will mean that most of the officers in the Caribbean will undergo some form of United States training. For example, 318 Jamaican officers have been trained in the period 1983–85 alone. The creation of a new training center in Antigua will ensure that middle- and lower-ranking military and police effectives are incorporated in this process.

Arms sales have followed the same trend as military assistance and training. Commercial sales to the Caribbean have increased from $1.7 million in 1979 to $7.6 million in 1985. Sales to the Bahamas, Belize, the Dominican Republic, Guadeloupe, Guyana, Haiti, Jamaica, and Trinidad-Tobago have increased at an extremely rapid pace.

Although reliable figures for military expenditures in the Caribbean

STUDENTS FROM CARIBBEAN COUNTRIES TRAINED UNDER THE INTERNATIONAL
MILITARY EDUCATION AND TRAINING PROGRAMS (SELECTED YEARS)

	1979	1980	1983	(Estimated) 1984	(Proposed) 1985
Bahamas	—	—	—	—	10
Barbados	1	13	a	a	a
Belize	—	—	19	49	49
Eastern Caribbean[b]	—	—	62	136	120
Guyana	—	—	10	27	27
Haiti	17	11	32	51	53
Jamaica	—	—	73	98	124
Dominican Republic	113	51	157	200	200
Panama	187	204	304	269	346
Surinam	67	195	—	17	26
Trinidad-Tobago	—	—	—	—	10
Total	385	474	657	847	965

SOURCE: Department of Defense, *Congressional Presentation, Security Assistance Program,*
1982 and 1985.

[a] Included in Eastern Caribbean.
[b] Includes Antigua, Barbados, Dominica, St. Lucia, St. Vincent, Grenada, St. Kitts, Anguilla,
British Virgin Islands, and Montserrat.

region are difficult to obtain, it would be safe to assume, particularly
taking commercial arms sales as an indicator, that the military budgets of
most countries have tended to grow. This clearly has been the case of
Trinidad-Tobago, which has significantly expanded its military establishment. If so, then a portion of increased United States aid funds, such as the
resources transferred under the Economic Support Fund, are being absorbed by the military.

Of particular importance has been the impact of United States military
policy in the English-speaking Caribbean, since the policy has promoted
militarization in countries with small or nonexistent military structures.
This process was begun in the pre-Grenada invasion period through
training of Jamaican, Dominican, and Barbadian effectives in Puerto Rico
and through the promotion of an anti-Grenada military pact among
Eastern Caribbean states in 1982.

During the period 1982–84, it seemed that the United States was
moving toward the formation of a regional defense force based in Barbados. However, the marginal importance attached to the Caribbean
multinational force during the Grenada invasion (included in the invasion
plan almost as a political afterthought) indicated the lack of United States
interest in this arrangement. These forces, the Caribbean Peacekeeping

Force, mainly performed postinvasion police functions. Cost considerations (estimated at about $100 million) also seem to have played a role.

The United States instead chose the option of building up the national military, police, and Coast Guard forces through bilateral assistance while coordinating these forces in what is now called a Regional Security System. In those Eastern Caribbean countries where no military forces existed, eighty-man Special Service Units have been created within the existing police forces and trained in countersubversive tactics by one hundred Green Berets advisors. Special Service Units have been established in Dominica, St. Lucia, Grenada, and St. Christopher-Nevis. The United States has also sought, and obtained, Canadian and British support in training Eastern Caribbean police forces.

The Caribbean: A New Pax Americana?

Caribbean policy has been presented as a glowing success of Reagan's foreign policy, in contrast to the evident stalemate in Central America and as an example of what "determination" can achieve. The militarization of the region, the Grenada invasion,and the buttressing of a constellation of conservative pro-U.S. governments seem to have stemmed the tide of popular movements which began in the mid-1970s. The Grenada invasion, particularly, led to an upsurge of modern jingoism and self-congratulation by the Reagan administration. More recently, the apparently smooth departure of Duvalier and the installation of a *duvalierista* military junta in Haiti seemed to indicate that the United States is still in full control of the situation.

This, however, may be superficially true, as actual trends indicate that the new regional policy may have only postponed necessary changes toward democracy, self-determination, and social justice in the region. The incapacity of the Haitian military to contain popular democratic demands through repression was evidenced in the fall of the original junta. The cry of "down with the leopards" voiced by Haitian masses indicates the new contradictions created by the process of militarization. In the Dominican Republic, the governing PRD suffered a significant erosion of popular support in the aftermath of the bloody repression (ninety killed) of the April 1983 popular protests. Support for the Seaga regime in Jamaica is at its lowest since the 1980 elections, and conservative Eastern Caribbean leaders, such as Eugenia Charles, are confronting similar political difficulties.

The erosion of democratic rights and the militarization of Caribbean societies has generated increasing internal opposition, whereas the growing diversion of economic resources to a bloated military establishment will hardly help overcome the prolonged economic and social crisis of the region. That is why the conservative neocolonial leaders promoted to power by the Carter and Reagan administrations are clamoring for results—hitherto meager—in the economic aspects of the Caribbean Basin Initiative.

Viewing the Caribbean from this perspective, the United States may have to increasingly resort to military regimes in the future (as it has done in Haiti), leading to a further erosion of democracy in the region and deepening the crisis of legitimacy of regional states.

5 The Military Speaks for Itself

Military Spokesmen for Military Rule

In the years following the Cuban Revolution, the military antipolitics which dominated Latin America took on distinctive policy agendas from country to country. Differing policy emphases flowed from national political legacies as varied as *Peronismo* in Argentina and the Peruvian military's seeming commitment to destroy the vestiges of neofeudalism in the Peruvian Andes. Despite national idiosyncrasies, however, the following selection of speeches and policy statements by prominent military leaders in Argentina, Bolivia, Brazil, Chile, Peru, El Salvador, and Guatemala make clear an underlying unity of commitment to economic developmentalism and to antipolitics. Whether we turn to Onganía in Argentina, Ovando in Bolivia, or Velasco in Peru, we find civilian corruption, deceit, or even treason blamed for the ills of the Latin American nations. We also hear military officers promising to restore law, order, stability, and social discipline—and to repress opposition elements, whether rightist or leftist, who oppose the military program.

Without ignoring the diversity of viewpoints and ideological orientations within the military establishments of Latin America, we have chosen the selections herein in order to provide (1) an initial statement by military leaders of the rationale for military rule in each country and (2) an assessment by those responsible for military rule of the evolution of the military regimes and their public policy initiatives. Our choice of speeches or policy statements was also influenced by the peculiarities of each case. In Argentina, Chile, and Peru, where military antipolitics was initially associated with the extended influence of a particular military officer, the choice was relatively easy. In Bolivia, Brazil, El Salvador, and Guatemala, where a succession of military officers exercised authority, we have included selections from several different officers. An effort has been made to illustrate the differences and similarities among the military leaders in each of these countries.

Argentina

SPEECH BY PRESIDENT JUAN CARLOS ONGANÍA
1966

Armed Forces of the Nation:

Again on the eve of the birth date of the Argentine Republic, her men in arms come together around a common table in all the barracks of the country. Once again we come to renew our old bonds of friendship and camaraderie with a profound love for the fatherland oveflowing our hearts.

In the past, this great celebration was always an occasion to reaffirm, with simple eloquence, our common ideals and our common profession of service to the country. But never as today have we so profoundly felt the responsibility that the historic national process has conferred upon the armed forces. . . .

The Recent Revolution

A number of serious events led to a deceitful and decadent social situation in which we Argentines witnessed the perversion of everything that in other times had been the source of our pride. It is because of this that the revolutionary action of June 28, 1966, finds its irrefutable principles in the defense of the essential values of the republic and in the removal of those causes [of the decadent social situation thus] opening a hopeful future for the tenacity and imagination of our people. In this way 1816 and 1966, so distant in time, merge into the same revolutionary significance, with transcendental aims.

Argentina has completed a historic cycle. In the future, no one will be able to excuse his aberrancy by appealing to the legacy of some anonymous past which [once] existed. Our political and institutional resources have been exhausted. The time has come to live to our fullest capacity and to create a new nation for ourselves and for our posterity. The future will be the inexorable result of the common efforts of all of today's Argentines.

The armed forces have been the instrument of the Argentine Revolution and because of that our celebration is filled with a sense of history and responsibility. We feel as never before the essence of the *patria* overflowing our spirits because the determination of her future has coincided with the strict fulfillment of our mission.

Institutionally fixed within Argentine society, the armed forces actively participate in the national business. Their disciplinary system, which ensures a subordination and hierarchical order, does not constitute an inhibition to accepting the consequences that political leadership entails, within the social body of which they form a part. Their profound spiritual constitution, the result of an education which is inspired by our historic roots, confirms the dominance of moral values over material ones and their strict acceptance by the Argentine people.

Contradictions

During the last few years, we have been witnesses to a contradictory process between the conduct of politics and the exigencies of the national reality. With the mechanism for representation damaged, the popular will was rendered impotent and the far-reaching changes so vitally needed became merely wishes. The armed forces constituted the medium of legitimate expression of that popular will which had been isolated through cunning. From that point, this revolutionary unanimity and consent were expressed in our history only when it was necessary to make a decision about the national destiny. . . .

The armed forces have begun the revolutionary process, and it is now up to the government to act to satisfy fully the pressing needs of the country. The cohesion of our institutions, which made this historically important act possible, ought to be our permanent concern because that cohesion is the maximum guarantor of the spirit that gave rise to the republic.

We will protect that unity, avoiding the moral erosion inherent in the exercise of public office, firmly convinced that an authentic and honest administration is the only means of maintaining the support and participation of the citizenry in the governmental endeavor which we are undertaking.

The modern concept of national defense also requires us to adopt a productive and intelligent system of cooperation which will permit the armed forces to overcome [their] . . . financial difficulties and to have at their disposal the means necessary to fulfill their mission. One could not conceive of any military operation without the strict cooperation of the three service branches. Therefore, we should put into professional practice this profound spirit of comaraderie that brings us together today and this unity of purpose that has made possible the legitimate interpretation of the aspirations of the citizenry.

We will integrate ourselves into a solid and efficient military entity, highly qualified to lay out the modern methods and doctrines that will allow us to carry out completely the exigencies of defending the moral and material patrimony of the nation. This contribution to the nation's transformation will be just as important as the other deeds which you have accomplished with decision and discipline, thereby earning you the respect and devotion of our citizens.

On this solemn occasion, I want to express our gratitude to all the sailors, aviators, and soldiers (who) came before us; to our old comrades who contributed their effort to the growth of the spiritual and technical character of the armed forces; to those who made our profession an apostleship of Sanmartinian virtues and bequeathed to us, with the abnegation and sacrifice of their lives, this instrument of order and liberty that has just lent such signal service to the republic; and to all the men of the air, sea, and land who today guard our frontiers and who are present in spirit at this glorious celebration of the birth date of our fatherland.

As president of the nation, I pray that this unity which we reaffirm today will inspire the solidarity of the Argentines and make us deserving of their respect and everlasting gratitude.

Translated and reprinted from *La Prensa* (Buenos Aires), July 7, 1966.

THE ARMED FORCES' DECISION TO ASSUME THE DIRECTION OF THE STATE
1976

Since all constitutional mechanisms have been exhausted and since all possibility of rectifications within the institutional framework has ended and since the impossibility of recovery through normal processes has been irrefutably demonstrated, the armed forces must put an end to the situation which has burdened the nation and compromised its future.

Our people have suffered a new frustration. We have faced a tremendous political vacuum capable of sinking us into anarchy and dissolution. We have also been faced with the national government's inability to call the people together; with the repeated and successive contradictions evidenced by the adoption of all kinds of measures; with the lack of a government-directed strategy to confront subversion; and with the total lack of solutions for the basic problems of the nation which have resulted in the steady increase of extremism; with the total absence of ethical and moral examples which the directors of the state should exhibit; with the manifest irresponsibility in the management of the economy which has exhausted the production apparatus; and with the speculation and the generalized corruption—all of which translates into an irreparable loss of greatness and of faith.

The armed forces have assumed the direction of the state in fulfillment of their unrenounceable obligation. They do so only after calm meditation about the irreparable consequences to the destiny of the nation that would be caused by the adoption of a different stance. This decision is aimed at ending misrule, corruption, and the scourge of subversion, but it is only directed at those who are guilty of crimes or abuse of power. It is a decision for the fatherland and does not suppose, therefore, to discriminate against any civic group or social sector whatever. It rejects, therefore, the disruptive actions of all extremists and the corrupting effect of demagoguery.

During the period which begins today, the armed forces will develop a program governed by clearly defined standards, by internal order and hard work, by the total observance of ethical and moral principles, by justice, and by the integral organization of man and by the respect of his rights and dignity. Thus, the republic will succeed in unifying all Argentines and will achieve the total recuperation of the national sovereignty. . . . To achieve these goals, we call upon all the men and women, without exceptions, who inhabit this land, to join together in a common effort.

Besides those shared aspirations, all the representative sectors of the country ought to feel clearly identified with and committed to the common undertaking that will contribute to the greatness of the fatherland.

This government will never be controlled by special interest groups, nor will it favor any one group. It will be imbued with a profound national spirit and will only respond to the most sacred interests of the nation and of its inhabitants.

Upon incurring such a far-reaching obligation, the armed forces issues a firm summons to the . . . citizenry. In this new stage, there is a battle post for each citizen. The task before us is both arduous and pressing. It will not be free of sacrifices, but it is undertaken with the absolute conviction that this example will be followed from top to bottom and with faith in the future of Argentina.

This process will be conducted with absolute firmness and with a spirit of service. Beginning now, this newly assumed responsibility imposes on the authorities the rigorous task of eradicating, once and for all, the vices which afflict the nation.

To achieve that, we will continue fighting, without quarter, all forms of subversion, both open and clandestine, and will eradicate all forms of demagoguery. We will tolerate neither corruption nor venality in any form or circumstance, or any transgression against the law, or any opposition to the process of restoration which has been initiated.

The armed forces have assumed control of the republic. And we want the entire country to understand the profound and unequivocal meaning of our actions so that the responsibility and the collective efforts accompanying this undertaking, which seeks the common good, will bring about, with the help of God, complete national recovery.

Signed:

Lt. Gen. Jorge Rafael Videla, commander in chief of the army

Adm. Emilio Eduardo Massera, commander in chief of the navy

Brig. Gen. Orlando Ramón Agosti, commander in chief of the air force

Translated and edited from a text of the radio announcement by the three conmanding generals of the armed forces (March 25, 1976), published in *La Nacion* (Buenos Aires), March 29, 1976.

A TIME FOR FUNDAMENTAL REORGANIZATION OF THE NATION SPEECH BY GENERAL JORGE RAFAEL VIDELA 1976

To the people of the Argentine Republic:

The country is passing through one of the most difficult periods in its history. With the country on the point of national disintegration, the intervention of the armed forces was the only possible alternative in the face of the deterioration provoked by misgovernment, corruption, and complacency.

. . . The armed forces, conscious of the fact that the continuation of this process did not offer an acceptable future for the country, put forth the only possible answer to this critical situation. Such a decision, predicated on the mission and the very essence of the military institution, was planned and executed with temperateness, responsibility, firmness, and a balance that has earned the gratitude of the Argentine people.

But it should be abundantly clear that the events which took place on March 24, 1976, represent more than the mere overthrow of a government. On the contrary, they signify the final closing of a historic cycle and the opening of a new one whose fundamental characteristic will be manifested by the reorganization of the nation, a task undertaken with a true spirit of service by the armed forces.

This process of national reorganization will require time and effort; it will require a broad capacity for living together; it will exact from each one his personal quota of sacrifice; and it will necessarily count on the sincere and complete confidence of all Argentines. The attainment of this confidence is, above all else, the most difficult of the endeavors which we have undertaken.

For many years, so many promises have been unfulfilled, so many plans and projects have failed, and so deep has been the national frustration that many of our fellow citizens no longer have faith in the word of their government leaders, even to the point of believing that public employees do not serve the people but only serve themselves. Thus, they were convinced that justice had ceased to exist for the Argentine citizen.

We will begin then by establishing a just order within which it will be incumbent upon each to work and [to] sacrifice; in which the fruits of this effort will be transformed into better living conditions for all; in which the honest and exemplary citizen will find support and encouragement; in which those who violate the law will be severely punished regardless of their rank, their power, or their supposed influence. In this way, the people will regain confidence and faith in those who govern them, and we will have established that point of departure indispensable for confronting the grave crisis which afflicts our country.

It is unnecessary to list the tragic conditions under which the country lives; each inhabitant of the fatherland knows and suffers intensely from them day after day. Nevertheless, it is worthwhile to point out some of the most important components of this situation.

The management of the state had never been so disorderly, directed with inefficiency [because] . . . of general administrative corruption and accompanying demagoguery. For the first time in its history, the nation came to the point of suspending all payments. A vacillating and unrealistic economic leadership carried the country toward recession and the beginnings of unemployment, with its inevitable sequel of anguish and desperation, a condition which we have inherited and which we will seek to alleviate.

The indiscriminate use of violence by all sides engulfed the inhabitants of the nation in an atmosphere of insecurity and overwhelming fear. Finally, institutional stagnation, manifested in the unsuccessful attempts to produce in time the urgent and profound evolution which the country required, led to a total paralysis of the state, with a power vacuum incapable of revitalizing it. . . .

Profoundly respectful of constitutional powers, the natural underpinning of democratic institutions, the armed forces, on repeated occasions, sent clear warnings to the government about the dangers that existed and also about the shortcomings of their senseless acts. Its voice went unheard, and as a consequence not one essential measure was adopted. Therefore, every hope of institutional change was completely dashed. In the face of this dramatic situation, the armed forces assumed control of the national government.

This conscious and responsibly taken action was not motivated by an interest in or a desire for power. It was in response to the demands of an indispensable obligation emanating from the armed forces' specific mission to safeguard the highest interests of the nation.

Faced with that imperative, the armed forces, as an institution, have filled the existing power vacuum and also as an institution, inspired by an authentic spirit of service to the nation, have provided a response to the national crisis by establishing objectives and guidelines for the government to develop. For us, respect for human rights is not only born out of the rule of law and of international declarations, but also it is the result of our profound and Christian belief in the preeminent dignity of man as a fundamental value.

And it is precisely to ensure the just protection of the natural rights of man that we assume the full exercise of authority; not to infringe upon liberty but to reaffirm it; not to twist justice but to impose it. After reestablishing an effective authority, which will be revitalized at all levels, we will turn to the organization of the state, whose performance will be based on the permanence and stability of juridical norms which will guarantee the primacy of law and the observance of it by the governors and governed alike.

. . . Even though the armed forces have suspended all political party activity in order to achieve internal peace, they reiterate their decision to guarantee freedom of opinion in the future to those movements authentically national in expression and [having] a proven spirit of service.

A similar attitude determines our policy in the area of labor relations, directed as much at management as at labor. Both labor and management should confine their activities to defending the legitimate aspirations of their members and avoid intruding into areas foreign to their competence.

Likewise, we trust that both workers and businessmen will be conscious of the sacrifices required in these early days and also of the unavoidable necessity of postponing requests that are just in periods of prosperity but which are unattainable in times of emergency. . . .

This immense task which we have undertaken has only one beneficiary: the Argentine people. All the government measures are aimed both at achieving general well-being through productive labor and at developing a genuine spirit of social justice in order to form a vigorous, organized, and unified society that is spiritually and culturally prepared to forge a better future.

No one should expect immediate solutions or spectacular changes in the present situation. The armed forces are cognizant of the magnitude of the task to be performed: they are aware of the profound problems to be resolved; and they know of the special interests that will oppose them on this road that everyone should travel together. But we have to travel this road with firmness, a firmness that is expressed in our decision to complete the process with a profound love of nation and without concessions to anyone. . . .

Speech by Gen. Jorge Rafael Videla. Translated and edited from *La Nación* (Buenos Aires), April 5, 1976.

SPEECH BY GENERAL LEOPOLDO FORTUNATO GALTIERI
1980

Five years ago, on February 9, 1975, the Argentine Army had to go to the mountains of Tucumán in order to halt and destroy a threat which jeopardized the very existence of the Fatherland. It happened because at that time representatives of foreign doctrines, based on a religion with neither God nor priests, whose goal was destruction for destruction's sake, tried to install here, in our Argentina, in our Tucumán, in the cradle of freedom of South America, a regime which blasphemed that freedom, the family, private property, and the nationality of mankind. They arrogantly believed that terror and cowardly assassination were proper methods for breaking the will to fight and the beliefs of an entire people and its armed forces. They wanted to make these sinister elements decisive and conditioning factors in the life of the nation. The entire country knows and should not forget, I repeat, the entire country knows and should not forget, that in that dark period of terror and crime—during which sons were indoctrinated to assassinate their parents—parents abandoned their children in order to engage in criminal nihilism, and Argentine families were the innocent victims of an unmerciful aggression and a systematic attempt at dissolution of the family.

Any calm observer of Argentine reality in those years knows that that generalized societal aggression required a prompt response before the maladies reached a level which would be irreparable in the future. The severe gravity of that painful picture . . . can be totally understood only by those who lived it and who knew that strange phenomenon.

Thus, it was necessary for the Argentine Army and the other armed security and police forces to come together to eradicate that scourge and to reestablish order and security, engaging with the people in an undeclared war. As in every war, and as has always occurred in every part of the world, the results, apart from triumph and defeat, can be nothing else but destruction and tears. Moreover, as in any war, there is a victor and a vanquished, and it is precisely from the seat of honor of the victor that we return to make our voice and our thoughts heard in answer to those who, from the position of the ignoble vanquished, seek to constitute themselves accusing prosecutors of a nation which they betrayed and submerged in chaos. Today, that nation repudiates them.

That maxim, already known by the entire country, was clearly expressed in a speech which the commander in chief delivered last year on the anniversary of the Argentine Army. We repeat, therefore, one more time, in the hope that it will be understood once and for all, that in this country there was not, and could not have been, any violation of human rights. There was a war, an absurd war, unleashed by a treacherous and criminal barbarism, a war which, in spite of the fact that it was directed not only against the people but also against a way of life which is supported by a large number of the nations of the world, had to be confronted and resolved by Argentines alone.

The war ended with the flight from the country of the leadership of the terrorist nihilism, a handful of traitors who today are attempting to achieve, with the conscious or unconscious complicity of their foreign sympathizers, that which they could not achieve in the struggle the Argentine people carried out and legitimately won.

With the economic resources produced by their criminal acts (robberies, kidnappings, and torture to the very limits of cruelty), and making use of the deliberate support which, out of ignorance or at times good faith, they receive from political and social sectors, they have organized a campaign to discredit this heroic and suffering Argentina, which they accuse of having violated the human rights that they themselves trampled upon in the cruelest manner possible.

Those who today discuss the results of the war in forums distant from the Fatherland, with a biased view of the events based on the tales of those traitors who provoked it and were defeated, ought to understand that, all things considered, the country must keep vigil over that which belongs to it. The country is not disposed to accept tutors. It has understood and assimilated on its own the inevitable burden of a struggle which it had to shoulder alone.

It should also be clear that for this country of free men, lovers of peace and pioneers in the defense of the rights of man, calumny and lies mean nothing.

The truth and the complete answer are to be found in one single concept: the defense of liberty, of our convictions, and of our traditions. As citizens, as fathers of families, and as military men, we can and we should understand the legitimate pain of those compatriots who, to this day, can find no explanation for the death or disappearance of a loved one. We understand this and it concerns us because we have our own wounds and because the nation has conferred upon us the right and the honor of using arms to prevent violence.

Nevertheless, we cannot explain the inexplicable. We cannot account for the irrational. We cannot justify the absurd. It is impossible to do so because the inexplicable, the irrational, and the absurd of this war originated in ambiences foreign to ours. It was not the Argentine Army which inaugurated that dark period.

Since 1810, the armed forces of the Fatherland have always been able to explain all their actions: within the framework of an open struggle, they must participate in order to safeguard our most important interests.

In this war, in which the organized, homicidal madness reached levels far beyond human comprehension, in which the elements of destruction were directed at persons indiscriminantly, in which the aggressors hid their designs, their faces, and their identities in the shadows, there are no explanations possible.

Within this general context, finding our very existence to be at stake, the armed forces were faced with the alternative of accepting the challenge of the struggle or of risking the dissolution of Argentine society, of aiding in the disappearance of a Fatherland as a state, or of fighting, with all the determination necessary—and winning.

Nor do we have answers for the questions asked of us, any more than the questioners would be able to answer us, if from the place of the vanquished, we would ask for the reasons for the disintegration of our Fatherland, of our system, of our way of life. On this point, all Argentines should reflect, and from that perspective, we should continue healing our wounds.

In our reflections, we must remember our dead, because the blood shed here has no price; it is because of the memory of this loss that we will never accept anything which will ruin or pervert the military victory or make us forget the clear and tremendous cost.

Second, we must be on guard against those who, with distinct goals, take advantage of another's grief and despair in order to advance their own ends, and against the useless review, far from our country, of what we have suffered in the flesh and of what only we are capable of grasping in its true dimension.

This is a synthesis of what the Argentine Army thinks about the theme of human rights and about this war in which the forces of order achieved a victory; but that does not mean that the final objective has been attained.

This idea has not varied, nor will it vary, because it is the product of reflection, of reason, and of truth.

As a part of that idea, we came here today, to this town, whose founding was proof of the tremendous Argentine desire to travel a road toward the present day of order and tranquility, in order to remember that part of the pain which belongs to us, to remember our dead, and to honor our heroes.

Soldiers carrying out the law, simply because they refused to deny their principles and traditions were stripped of the supreme human right—life itself. We do not ask for explanations for that, but we do base our opinion on it in order to strengthen our conviction that neither violence nor death is the preferred means to settle differences among opposing ideas.

Because of that, we find ourselves engaged in another struggle with very distinct characteristics, whose objective is the illumination of the new historic cycle of the nation.

That objective has to be achieved with two basic premises, the first being national unity. Said unity's result should be the agreement of all Argentines regarding the fundamental foundations of our system, today more than ever, Western and Christian, and on the historic tradition inherited from our forefathers which should govern the future life of the republic. It is in defense of that union and of the republic that the army met here, struggled, triumphed, and will continue moving toward the final objective. The other premise is the political will, which should inspire us to accompany our people in the effort to achieve for it a rightful place in today's world. There can be no greatness without political will any more than there is victory without the will to fight.

For the sake of that objective, our heroes from this war and previous ones rest here in Tucumán soil and in many other places of the national territory. Their memory should serve as an example, so that we understand and engrave in our consciousness that war is not the road we wanted for ourselves; nor do we desire it for our sons. Our struggle today is for the peaceful progress of the nation.

For those ideas, those objectives, entreating the protection of God, we summon all Argentines and demand of their sons here present—members of the 5th Infantry Brigade, and in their voice the entire Argentine Army—subordination and valor.

Translated and reprinted from *Clarín* (Buenos Aires), February 10, 1980.

FINAL DOCUMENT OF THE MILITARY JUNTA REGARDING THE WAR AGAINST SUBVERSION AND TERRORISM: THE FUNDAMENTAL CONCEPTS
1983

Introduction

This historical synthesis of a painful, yet still near, past is intended to be a message of faith and a recognition of the struggle for liberty, justice, and the right to life.

It is addressed, first of all, to us, the people of a nation, a nation victim of an aggression it did not deserve, invaluable and dedicated participant in the final victory. Second, it is addressed to the world of free men who belong and will continue to belong to the republic, loyal to its historical destiny.

An experience which the nation must never repeat is presented for the reflection of the Argentine people and of the world with the deep desire that, by the grace of God, the brothers of our America and the peoples of other continents will pick up and understand the message, and avoid a similar experience.

The Facts

After the mid-1960s, the Argentine Republic began to suffer the aggression of terrorism, which sought both to modify the concept our community holds regarding man and the state and to capture power through violence.

Thefts of arms, assaults on banks and other institutions, kidnappings, extortion, and assassinations on a growing scale made the public aware of the criminal activity of the three most powerful terrorist groups. The actions of these groups, designed to paralyze the population, were characterized by a permanent and indiscriminate violation of the most fundamental human rights: assassinations, tortures, and prolonged detentions, incontrovertible proofs of their criminal acts and intentions,

Their victims came from every social stratum: workers, priests, intellectuals, businessmen, journalists, public employees, military judges, public safety agents, political leaders, union members, and even children.

Active members and decided sympathizers of the terrorist organizations occupied eminent positions in the national cabinet, in the provincial legislatures, and in the judicial branch. Not even the religious organizations nor the police were immune from this infiltration.

Their insidious activity caused the deviation of thousands of young people, many of them still adolescents, incorporated into bands through various recruitment techniques or simply through fear. Many died facing the forces of order; others committed suicide to avoid capture; others deserted trying to hide themselves from both the authorities and their own bands.

In order to have a clear idea of the magnitude of the terrorist activity in terms of numbers, it is worth emphasizing that in the year 1974, there were 21 surprise attacks against units of the legal forces, 466 attacks with explosive devices, and 16 robberies of large sums of money; 117 persons were kidnapped and 110 were assassinated. The year 1976 marked the apex of the violence. Kidnappings reached 600 and assassinations 646, with an average of two victims daily from terrorism; 4,150 terrorist actions were registered, including attacks on localities, actions of armed propaganda, intimidations through extortion, and attacks with explosives.

An examination of newspapers for the years 1973–79 reveals that in that period there were 742 confrontations, resulting in the deaths of 2,050 persons, a figure which does not include the casualties suffered by the government forces.

Between 1969 and 1979, 21,642 terrorist acts were registered. This figure is in direct relation to the magnitude of the subversive structure, which at its height included 25,000 subversives, of which 15,000 were combatants, that is to say, individuals who were technically trained and ideologically fanaticized to kill.

The nature and characteristics of these systematic and persistent surprise attacks forced the adoption of classified procedures in the spreading war. The strictest secrecy had to be imposed on all information regarding military actions and successes, as well as on recent discoveries and planned operations. It became imperative not to alert the enemy, not to reveal our own intentions, thereby recapturing the initiative and the element of surprise which, until that moment, was in the hands of our opponents.

During all these operations, it was practically impossible to establish with precision either the total number of casualties suffered by the bands of criminal terrorists or the identities of their members, even when the cadavers remained behind after an episode. This was due both to the fact that they participated using false names, or using nicknames known as "war names," and to the fact that their structure of cells, method of operation, and division of labor made it impossible to have at our disposal a more complete picture of the events.

The efforts made by the armed security and police forces to reestablish peace and order produced increasingly positive results. Terrorist aggression slackened and Argentine society began to recuperate, in terms of peace and security, the ground it had lost. Thus, a painful and cruel period was ended in which the victory finally achieved held the same meaning as that of the defeat of the subversives. This was because Argentine society remained loyal to its traditions, faithful to its conscience, and firm in its decision. For each social sector, the subversives had drawn up and set in motion distinct methodologies, all of which converged on the final goal of destroying those sectors, but this, too, failed to affect the most solid values of a peaceful and free people.

The Principles and Procedures

The exceptional conditions under which the country lived during the period of terrorist aggression meant that the essential elements of the state were affected to such a degree that their very survival was made difficult.

The exercise of human rights was left to the mercy of the selective or indiscriminate violence employed by the terrorist actions. These took the form of assassinations, kidnappings, "revolutionary trials," forced departures from the country, and compulsory contributions.

The government's ability to act was seriously compromised by subversive infiltration and by the political vacuum caused by the death of President Juan Perón. In that crucial, historic moment, the armed forces were summoned by the constitutional government to confront the subversion (Decree No. 261 of January 5, 1975, and Decree No. 2772 of October 6, 1975).

In order to procure the common good, the national government, via its legal mandate and through the armed forces as intermediary, ordered the reestablishment of the rights of every inhabitant and of the essential conditions guaranteeing the inviolability of the national territory and of the social contract, thereby facilitating the government's ability to function. The armed security and police forces acted in defense of the national community whose essential rights were not secure, and contrary to subversive actions, the armed forces did not use their power directly against innocent third parties, even though these might have suffered consequences indirectly.

The actions undertaken were the result of assessments of what had to be done in an all-out war, with a measure of the passion which both combat and defense of one's own life generate, within an ambience stained daily by innocent blood, and by destruction, and before a society in which panic reigned. Within this almost apocalyptic framework, errors were committed which, as always happens in every military conflict, could have passed, at times, the limits of respect for fundamental human rights. These errors are subject to God's judgment, to each person's conscience, and to the comprehension of man.

The armed forces hope that this painful experience will enlighten our people, so that we all can find the means compatible with the ethics and the democratic spirit of our institutions.

The Results of the Conflict

It is necessary to point out clearly that there are many unhealed wounds in Argentine society: long years of profound insecurity, frequent moments of terror, loss of family members and loved ones who fell as a result of an attack as unjustified as it was cunning, mutilations, lengthy detentions, and disappearance of people. All this, individual and collective, physical and spiritual, is the result of a war which Argentines must overcome.

The armed forces, faithful to the goal of seeking to heal the wounds left by the struggle and desirous of clarifying the points of doubt which could exist, place in the Ministry of the Interior, at the disposition of everyone, the following information:

—A list of the members of terrorist organizations at present convicted and processed by the federal courts and the councils of war, as well as of those detained by orders of the national executive branch by virtue of Article 23 of the national constitution

—Requests for the whereabouts of persons (presumably disappeared) registered by the Ministry of the Interior from 1974 to the present

—Requests for the whereabouts of persons whose cases have been resolved either juridically or administratively

—Casualties produced by terrorist activity

It is the theme of disappearances which most strongly batters legitimate humanitarian sentiments, and it is that theme which is employed so insidiously to shock the good faith of those who neither knew about nor lived under the events which took us to the brink. The experience of living through it permits us to affirm that many of the disappearances were a consequence of the terrorists' method of operation.

The terrorists changed their true names. They knew each other by what were called "war names," and they prepared abundant forged personal documents. These same people are tied to what has been called the "passage to clandestinity," where they decide to join terrorist organizations in a surreptitious manner, abandoning their families, work, and social mediums. This is the most typical case: The family members report a disappearance whose reason they cannot explain, or, if they know the reason, that they do not want to explain.

Therefore, some "disappeared ones" whose absence has been reported appear later carrying out terrorist activities. In other cases, the terrorists secretly leave the country and live in the exterior under a false identity. Others, after exiling themselves, return to the country with forged papers.

And finally, there also exist fugitive terrorists, either inside or outside the republic.

There are also cases of deserters from the various organizations who live today with false identities, inside or outside the country, in order to protect their own lives.

Many of those who died in confrontations with the legal forces either carried no identification at all or had false documents and, in many cases, had their fingerprints obliterated. Faced with imminent capture, other terrorists committed suicide, normally by swallowing cyanide pills. In these cases, the bodies were not claimed, and given the impossibility of identifying them, they were buried legally as "unknowns."

Moreover, whenever possible, the terrorists carried the bodies of their dead from the site of the battle. These bodies, as well as those of the wounded who died later, were either destroyed or buried clandestinely by the terrorists themselves.

The struggle for hegemony among the terrorists led to assassinations and kidnappings among the distinct organizations. The terrorists, in compliance with a pseudorevolutionary code, made a parody of justice and assassinated those of their members who defected or failed in their assigned missions. The bodies were buried with false identities or in unknown places and circumstances.

During the struggle, the legal forces infiltrated men into the terrorist organizations. If discovered, they were killed, and their burial place was never made known.

Moreover, there have been cases of persons reported as missing who later appeared and led normal lives without this fact having been made known to the proper judicial or administrative authorities.

Finally, the list of disappeared ones may be artificially increased by including those cases not attributable to the terrorist phenomenon but rather to events which habitually occur in all large urban centers.

It is appropriate to emphasize that the reports of supposed kidnappings are the subject of judicial investigation and that a large number of trials for the presumed crime of illegal deprivation of liberty have been initiated officially by the appropriate judges.

The possibility that persons considered "disappeared" might be found buried as unknowns has always been one of the principal hypotheses accepted by the government. We agree with the judgment in the report drawn up by the Inter-American Commission on Human Rights, which visited the country in 1979, when it states that, in certain cemeteries, one can verify the internment of unidentified persons who died in a violent manner, most of them in confrontations with the legal forces.

It is also said of the "disappeared ones" that they will be found detained by the Argentine government in unknown sites in the country. This is nothing more than a lie used for political ends. There no longer exist in the republic secret detention sites, nor are there in the prisons persons clandestinely detained.

It should be made definitively clear that those who figure in the lists of disappeared ones, and who are not in exile or underground, are considered to be dead, in judicial and administrative terms, even when it has not been possible to determine either the cause or place of the death or the site of burial.

Final Considerations

The victory achieved at such a high price depended upon the general assent of the citizenry who understood the complex phenomenon of subversion and expressed, through its leaders, its repudiation of violence. From this attitude on the part of the population, it is clear that the desire of the entire nation is to put an end once and for all to a painful period in our history, in order to begin, in union and liberty, the definitive constitutional institutionalization of the republic.

In order to achieve success on this road, it is absolutely essential that we have the equilibrium sufficient to comprehend that which has happened, without forgetting the circumstances which carried us to the very edge of disintegration or the responsibilities which, by commission or omission, will correspond to the distinct sectors of the community, to not traveling again that painful road.

Those who gave their lives to combat the terrorist scourge merit our eternal homage of respect and appreciation. Those who knew how to sustain the principles of a style of life based on respect for the fundamental rights of people and on the values of liberty, peace, and democracy, risking their personal security and that of the families (political leaders, priests, businessmen, labor leaders, magistrates, or simple citizens), merit the recognition of the nation.

Those who placed their intelligence, goodwill, solidarity, and piety, indeed, the whole weight of their being, at the service of the reconciliation of the Argentine family are worthy of recognition and respect. . . .

Going beyond ideological differences and joining with them by virtue of being children of God, we say to those who lost their lives by enrolling in the terrorist organizations which attacked the very society that had nurtured them, you will receive your pardon.

Those who have recognized their error and have atoned for their mistakes deserve help. In its generosity, the Argentine society is willing to take them back into the fold.

Reconciliation constitutes a difficult beginning of an era of maturity and responsibility realistically assumed by everyone. The scars represent not only a painful memory, but also the foundation of a strong democracy, of a united and free people, a people which learned that subversion and terrorism constitute the inexorable death of liberty.

The armed forces are delivering this information to the citizenry so that they, in common, can judge this sad period of our history, which as such is a problem which touches all Argentines and one which all Argentines should resolve in common if we want to assure the survival of the republic.

Because of all of that expressed above, the military junta declares the following:

1. That the information and explanations furnished in this document represent the sum total of everything the armed forces have at their disposal to inform the nation about the results and consequences of the war against subversion and terrorism

2. That within this frame of reference, one that was not desired by the armed forces, who had it forced upon them in order to defend the system of national life, only history can judge with exactitude who bears the direct responsibility for unjust methods and innocent deaths

3. That the activities of the members of the armed forces in operations carried out during the successful war constitute acts of military service

4. That the armed forces acted, as they will every time that it is necessary, in obedience to an emergency order from the national government, taking advantage of all the experience gleaned from this painful circumstance in national life

5. That the armed forces submit to the people and to the judgment of history these decisions, which translate into an attitude having as its goal the common good, identified in that instance with the survival of the community, and whose content they assume with the authentic sorrow of Christians who recognize the errors which could have been committed in the carrying out of the assigned mission.

Bolivia

JUSTIFICATION OF THE REVOLUTION OF NOVEMBER
SPEECH BY GENERAL ALFREDO OVANDO CANDÍA
1966

Honorable Gentlemen:

At the end of the Chaco War [1932–35], the new generation was confronted with the necessity of transforming the traditional society. Today, we again find ourselves obligated to resume that uncompleted task and rectify the errors of those who made a mockery of the Bolivian people's longing for liberation.

When the armed forces of the nation took charge of the government in November 1964, they found the country submerged in a desolate and chaotic situation. Nevertheless, in spite of the errors of the last regime, errors for which they will have to account before this honorable Congress and before future generations, it would be unjust to attribute all the defects of the economic, social, political, and administrative structure of the country to the political system which was ousted in November 1964. In truth, the presence of such a corrupt party at the top level of public life can only be explained in terms of the power vacuum produced in 1952 in the country as a tragic result of circumstances accumulated over decades and as an unequivocal sign of the end of a political era.

All the problems of the past were aggravated by the presence of inept and venal politicians, conspirators for the possession of power. Masters of the art of destruction, they turned out to be incapable of establishing the foundations of the Second Republic called for by the Bolivian Revolution.

Under different banners, power was always highly concentrated in the presidency, to the detriment of the other branches of government, but the despotism of the last twelve years finally transformed the republican system into a type of absolute monarchy with total power and authority. The suffrage that, as in all incipient democracies, did not have the minimum breadth or decorum that is needed to be classified as democratic, was converted into a grotesque parody of universal suffrage, which precluded all citizen participation in the determination of public affairs. In the past there had been problems regarding the length of the presidential term and the pretensions of continuism, but never had the people been so stunned by the institutional means used to maintain the political leaders in power.

The ... constitution of the state, amended to serve that end, did violence to the constitutional traditions of the country. The cabinets, which in the past had not always been constructive, now were characterized by ineptitude and servility. The all-powerful authority to select government functionaries reached every level to such a degree that the legislative branch, the judicial branch, the local governments, and the rest of the vital organs of the republic lost their institutional integrity, thereby cancelling the principle of separation of powers.

In such a state of disintegration, it was understandable that subservience would be rewarded. How painful it was for the armed forces to see the symbols of Bolívar and Sucre, of Santa Cruz, Ballivián and Linares, of Frías, Campero, Pando and Montes; of Busch and Villarroel in such unworthy hands.

The contradictions between a backward social structure and the political forms of a liberal, representative democracy were evident from the early days of the republic. The effects of that conflict were felt in many ways in the institutional life of the country. Because of that, faced both by the demand for reform and the burden of the decrepit structure, the Revolution of 1952 took place. But since the improvising leaders of the great process either did not know how or did not want to create the new vehicles for structural change, all the evils of the past were accentuated and the virtues of the people ignored.

With the inordinate growth of the executive branch, the legislative branch steadily declined. The parliament lost its majesty and functioned inefficiently. Full of revolutionary verbiage, it never did anything to develop the country. Bolivians were so humiliated that they almost seemed to lose hope of returning to representative democracy. The tribunal of the great legislators of our history surrendered in shame without playing its high and noble institutional role. In truth, very few men dignified the Parliament with their valor in those twelve years. One-partyism suffocated democracy and paralyzed the opposition. The despotism ignored the parliamentary jurisdiction. Never before then had the legislative branch sunk to such abject levels. And what about the judiciary and the municipalities? Justice was replaced with prevarication, and the municipalities, with very few exceptions, were converted into solicitous and inoperative appendages of the central government.

... It disturbs us to recall this assembly such painful events, but in order to analyze the twenty-one month administration, it is necessary to remember the economic state of the country in 1964. COMIBOL [the Bolivian Mining Corporation], the Central Bank of Bolivia, and the State Petroleum Corporation, to mention only a few of the most important national agencies, were all in a state of bankruptcy.

The process of social disintegration reached a critical point; very few institutions were spared its effects. It is enough to remember how a bureaucratic caste took over the leadership of the nation's labor organizations in order to undermine the principles of authority, democracy, and union independence.

The campesino strife, unleashed by interests of the ruling party, the labor anarchy, the administrative corruption, the incredibly low educational indices, and the growing unemployment and misery of the people were unmistakable signs of the desperate situation that prevailed.

The political parties were almost completely destroyed. Functioning only intermittently, not one party had a significant number of members because terror inhibited the active participation of the citizenry. The majority of the parties suffered both from a lack of organization and a lack of press coverage. Heavily infiltrated by spies, they were subjected to a steady campaign of vilification.

With few exceptions, the private businessmen were victims of extortion. Terrorized by the regime, they barely succeeded in surviving, abandoning all dynamic and creative drive. The muzzled press saw its freedom curtailed by censors.

Education at all levels was left helpless; both teachers and students were treated as enemies by the regime. The universities also existed under tragic circumstances, to oppression was added the burden of financial asphyxia.

Year after year, a growing number of professionals, laborers, and campesinos left the country in search of better living and working conditions. The flight of talent and human capital reached astronomical proportions, but even more serious yet was the flight of material wealth. Since the regime deemed obsequiousness to be one of the highest of ethical norms, intellectual ability was viewed with suspicion, and negativism reached such a point that it was inadvisable to strive for excellence.

This process of disintegration soon affected the ruling group itself; it ceased to be a political party and became instead an instrument of power and oppression. That process culminated in the creation of political fiefdoms located in the federal administration and distributed regionally. In this way, the most extreme forms of pressure were institutionalized. Instead of promoting the national interest through legitimate channels and through the dialogue and analysis that are the essence of democracy, they turned to threats, corruption, sabotage, and direct action which in many cases ended in crimes that went unpunished. . . .

A monstrous apparatus of political repression and demagogic practices, without precedent, was installed, converting the regime, despite its instability, into something seemingly omnipotent. Only a cold analysis of the realities, with an ardent patriotism, permitted the armed forces, seconded by the people, to destroy the artificial base of that regime and make possible again the institutional life of the country through law and progress. The state of our foreign relations was equally bad and, as a consequence, the frequent blunders endangered our national honor.

The spirit of reform which had moved the Bolivian people for decades lost its true significance because of bad leadership. The nation's sovereignty, instead of being strengthened, was compromised by the increasing dependence upon external power groups. Not even the national budget depended upon Bolivians alone. After twelve years, the nationalization of the mines continued to be an empty gesture because it was not complemented by the installation of foundries. The agrarian reform was at a standstill, with no hope of effective progress. The so-called plan for economic diversification never moved beyond talk. Universal suffrage was a myth, and educational reform merely [an unimplemented] law. Per capita income declined from 123 dollars to 97 dollars. Mining exports declined from $120 million to $40 million and more than seven hundred factories closed, thereby decreasing the number of employed persons by 25 percent.

During this period of disintegration, the only organism that maintained a unity of doctrine strengthened by a truly national outlook was the . . . armed forces. The Bolivian military officer possesses neither a reactionary mentality nor a sense of caste. On the contrary, resulting as much from their origin as from their tradition, the armed forces of Bolivia embody the national and democratic essence. This fact allows us to comprehend the need for profound change in the confused world created by the Bolivian Revolution.

Honorable Gentlemen, I must solemnly state before you that the armed forces took power in 1964 to make the Bolivian Revolution a reality and to establish the foundations of the Second Republic. For that reason, we ask that all social groups and institutions work in solidarity for the social and economic development of Bolivia. We want a vigorous union organization which is conscious of its rights and its obligations; we want a youth full of healthy rebellion, optimistic, studious, and honorable; we want the citizenry to act freely and the political parties to be organized on a solid doctrinal base; we want the Christian ideal to light our way and democracy to strengthen our institutions; we want happiness for all; and we want culture and progress to flourish, and our thinkers, artists, workers, and soldiers to make the life of man in our fatherland even more beautiful.

The armed forces believe that the revolution belongs to the people, and because of that we contend that the Bolivian Revolution means the slow and steady liberation of the national economy from its semicolonial dependence upon foreign markets. This means controlling our national resources and marketing and distribution of our products under the conditions most favorable to internal development and to the expansion of Bolivian power. In sum, we seek state planning and dominance in the principal areas of production in order to avoid the excessive concentration of power and the absentee ownership of wealth enjoyed in the past by financial monopolies more powerful than the state. That is the road chosen by the armed forces. That is our philosophy of economic development, of popular action, of national unity, and of sovereignty.

Bolivia is faced with a social complexity that has erected a multitude of obstacles to her progress. The objective of the Second Republic is to accelerate the social integration now under way, respecting the will of all groups, employing technology to relieve the demographic pressure on the Altiplano, and promoting literacy and culture to the fullest extent for the campesinos. In that way we are proud to declare that the Indian population of our country will achieve undreamed-of levels of progress. . . .

Translated, reprinted, and edited from "Informe a la nación por el general Alfredo Ovando Candía, Presidente de la H. Junta Militar dal Gobierno," August 6, 1966, in Guillermo Lora, ed., *Documentos Politicos de Bolivia*, pp. 584–93.

THE PATH OF DUTY
SPEECH BY HUGO BANZER SUÁREZ
1971

When I spoke at the commencement of the Military College last year, the state of the nation was very different from that of today. The agents of anarchy and extremism were preparing to take the country by storm in order to place it at the service of interests foreign to the fatherland and to destroy our institutions and our cultural heritage.

Those agents were embedded in the government itself and in the state security agencies. With funds from the National Treasury, contributed by all Bolivians who pay taxes, they financed extremist organizations like the so-called People's Assembly, where they replaced the portraits of our heroes and our founding fathers with those of adventurers [like Ernesto "Che" Guevara] who came to our country to kill and to try to impose on us doctrines and systems foreign to our culture. Our glorious tricolor was replaced by another flag which waved over the buildings of the agencies of extremism.

In the university, which should be a temple dedicated to scientific and technological research and to the formation of professionals qualified to direct the development of Bolivia, they paid homage to violence and redirected energies and resources toward the attainment of goals contrary to the highest interests of the fatherland. We have now confirmed that, fortunately, the promoters of disorder were in the minority and that the great majority of the university students, deceived and supplanted by a handful of agitators, only wanted to dedicate themselves to study and research in order to place their energy and knowledge at the service of Bolivia. We will soon fulfill those legitimate and positive aspirations of Bolivian youth.

Similar conditions were causing the paralysis of all creative initiative and the strangulation of the economy and were causing the army of unemployed and desperate to grow enormously. Nevertheless, in the breasts of the armed forces of Bolivia, the sacred fire of love of the fatherland and of dedication to defend it at all costs, was never extinguished.

It was in those critical and difficult hours, in which all appeared lost because of vacillation and weakness, that I had the privilege of delivering the commencement address at this military college. Denouncing, in the name of the armed forces, the intolerable state of affairs, I asserted that the bastard ambitions, the political and administrative corruption, the demagoguery, the lies, the hate, the rancor, and the institutional disorder had come to rot the very heart of the fatherland. We are living, I said, in permanent frustration, and wherever you look, you will see only division.

I added that we had, with a passive and indifferent attitude, been witnesses to the appetites of extranational ideologies. The extreme left and the extreme right had sunk their teeth into the nation's guts, causing the mental subservience of some Bolivians. It was time to put a stop to that national disgrace; it was time that we realized that the fatherland will rise again as the result of . . . peace, . . . labor, and the understanding of the citizens. It was time to put an end to the attitude of those traffickers of foreign ideas, of demagogues who thousands of times had cheated their brothers the campesinos, the miners, the workers, and their fellow citizens. I said this had to be the moment of truth; either we go with the fatherland or against it, respecting the laws or trampling on them, with order or with chaos and anarchy, with sincerity or with fraud and deceit, with peace or with war, with courage or with servility, with honesty or with systematic robbery. That then was the hour of reckoning, and we military men, trustees of the national honor, with the people, ought to have demanded it of those who commanded and governed us.

Those were difficult words to say in those moments in which the dignity of men who were upright and respectful of law and order was at the mercy of veritable hordes of fanatics who were ready to utilize any means to silence criticism and quash any form of opposition to their abuses and misbehavior.

As a dramatic confirmation of the veracity of my judgment, a judgment and belief shared by a majority of the armed forces, they did not delay in taking reprisals against me, seeking to teach the entire (military) institution a lesson through the example made of the commandant of the Military College. First, I was removed from this command, which I served with singular affection and devotion, then retired, and finally forced into exile, which is the cruelest of punishments for an honorable military officer.

But my warning had the effect of alerting the armed forces to the true nature of the regime that oppressed us and to the hidden designs for the destruction of the fatherland and the annihilation of its institutions. . . .

Soon the spark became a firestorm of national fury that swept away forever the agents of extremism and hate, returning to Bolivians their right to liberty, work, peace, and security. The heroic movement of August of this year . . . was begun in this same place, exactly a year ago, in the presence of many of you who attended the commencement exercises and the graduation of new officers in 1970. It was through that opportunity that I had the honor of being selected to plant the seeds of rebellion and to calm the spirits of those who, months later, returned our flag and our sacred symbols to their place of honor on the national altar.

Today the country has returned to normal and . . . to more propitious conditions. With the institutional backing of the armed forces, a solid alliance of civilian political forces has been produced, and large contingents of people are preparing to enter this pact in order to construct, for the first time in Bolivian history, an organization representative of the majority of the Bolivian people.

The mission of the military in Bolivia today, apart from its specific functions of maintaining internal peace and defending the national sovereignty, has been expanded in scope: to be the unifying and cementing factor of the nation. The role that the armed forces played in the patriotic uprising of August has conferred upon them the perfect right of protecting the national institutions and has, in fact, confirmed their status as the vanguard institution (of national development). . . .

Speech by Hugo Banzer Suárez. Translated, reprinted, and edited from *El Pensamiento del Presidente CNL, Hugo Banzer Suárez* (La Paz: Ministero de Información y Deportes, 1971), pp. 107–12.

TOWARD THE CONSTITUTIONALIZATION OF BOLIVIA
SPEECH BY GENERAL HUGO BANZER SUÁREZ
1977

Bolivians:

In the course of the evolution of humankind, those who change with the greatest rapidity are those peoples who know their own imperfections and have the capacity to overcome them in the search for ever more perfect forms of organization.

Within the framework of this concept, Bolivia is cognizant of the limitations which impede her total development. She knows how much poverty and dependency affect her, and she knows as well the causes of that situation. Beginning with the knowledge of her reality, she has decided to transform and to create. She has decided to organize a just society, based on man and his grandiose destiny.

During the events of August 1971, the Bolivian people became very determined. Out of the confrontation of alternatives which took place at that time, and by action of the majority of the people, reason triumphed over instinct, peace over violence, and the fatherland over foreign imposition.

Since that date, the system chosen by Bolivians has constantly evolved. A new spirit animates all the activities of the country. The different social groups have united to face the future. The myth of poverty has been overcome forever.

The economic advances are, in themselves, highly significant. Foundries, factories, highways, airports, and schools cover the national territory, giving Bolivia a progressive image, full of vitality.

Social peace and political stability, the fruit of the general consensus and of the militant backing which the population offers to the system, have made our country an ideal medium for diverse human activities.

The respect and consideration which we have won from the international community is the direct result of our conduct as a sovereign and independent nation, as well as of the responsibility and deliberation with which we have carried out the obligations we have with the rest of the world.

The hope which animates the population is part of the security in the social area and in the ever more broad and profound developmental area.

With respect to the political transformations, what has happened over the last six years is part of a plan which has been carried out within the limitations of our own reality. The programmed processes have taken place in conformity with the forecasts of the first few years. Nothing has been left to chance or to improvisation. . . .

As a consequence of these ideas, and after a profound study—which went beyond the considerations of a personal or group nature—of the new conditions which exist inside and outside the country, the government over which I preside has consulted with the armed forces regarding the possibility of modifying the plans, approved three years ago, for the institutionalization and constitutionalization of the country. . . .

The Government of the Armed Forces considers democracy in the political arena, as well as growth in the economic arena, to be nothing more than means for achieving the great objectives of the Bolivian people. As a consequence, there is no significance whatsoever in a democracy or in a growth which sacrifices man or debilitates the nation.

The general elections will have to be accommodated to the conditions which emerge from the role which Bolivia should play with regard to her own people and to the obligations and exigencies of the age in which we live. But it would be an error to consider the plebiscitary act as an end in itself or to foster the hope that only a political opening will resolve the problems which currently affect the lives of Bolivians. We ought to be fully conscious of the tremendous challenge presented by the period the country is entering. This period will be neither free nor easy.

Indeed, from this moment on, each Bolivian is called upon to behave in a serene, intelligent, and patriotic fashion. . . .

We need a set of institutions which, in different places in the republic and among the distinct sectors and levels of national life, will function with the precision of a watch, with the discipline of a soldier, and with the wisdom of a sage.

Neither the time at our disposal nor the resources we can count upon are sufficient in and of themselves to close the gap which separates us from the level of evolution we must achieve in order to satisfy the true needs of the Bolivian people. Such a reality obliges us to augment the material factors through the efficiency of human behavior. After all the experience we have accumulated over the last few years, there would be no justification whatsoever for wasting resources, duplicating efforts, improvising decisions, or subordinating the fate of the nation to the successes and satisfactions of isolated political parties or of special-interest groups.

The Armed Forces of the Nation, when they return to the field of their specific duties, will in no way renounce their position as the titular institution of the fatherland [emphasis added, ED.]. Today, more than ever, the armed forces have sufficient moral strength to prevent interest groups, sectarians, or agents of anti-national tendencies from sacrificing the progress of the nation in favor of their petty designs.

This is the time to understand clearly that government, before a source of privileges and advantages, is now a place of struggle and of work. It is a place where the revolution should be carried out with sacrifice, with discipline, and with honesty. Those who think otherwise are mistaken, but they still have time to change their mentality, as well as their behavior. . . .

Relative to our ideas regarding the organization and development of the State, we proclaim the need for a new public order. No longer are we trying to maintain things as they were, to assume the defense of a public order which protects privileged or unjust situations. The order which should be conserved is that which benefits the collectivity. A peace which is not the result of a collective consensus, of a conscious adherence to the system, of popular participation, as much in the rights as well as the obligations of development, is not the peace we are seeking,

Over the course of this new period in our history, we will initiate the implementation of an authentically Bolivian democracy, of a participatory social process, and of a development based upon a common, united effort. . . .

The Government of the Armed Forces moved up the date of the constitutionalization of the country because it believes that this is the opportune moment for the people, starting from the levels of development which we have achieved, to decide for themselves the direction for their future. Surely, this is one of the few times that a voluntary transfer of power has occurred, a generous and patriotic act which constitutes a brilliant example for the future of the continent.

In November 1974, we stated that the responsibility assumed by the Armed Institution had definite objectives. Those objectives have been achieved. Bolivian society is predisposed to organize itself democratically. Those, among others, are the reasons why my government, this morning, resolved to lift the political recess which was imposed three years ago.

Nevertheless, it should be made very clear and firmly established that the Titular Institution of the Fatherland guarantees the tranquility of the citizenry, the security to which businessmen, students, and researchers have the right. It guarantees the continuance of an institutional, juridical framework of mutual respect and of civilized cooperation. It guarantees continued development. It guarantees the holding of democratic elections and the transfer of power to the government anointed by the national majority.

The fundamental premise is the constant strengthening of the fatherland. For the armed forces, no isolated factor, no sectarian or individual right, can be above that concept. For that reason, the armed forces have a clear conscience regarding the role they must play under circumstances when social excesses, political deformations, or irrational actions place the integral development of the nation in danger.

To the businessmen who contribute to the industrialization of the country, to the workers who increase the national wealth, to the professionals who cultivate and enrich science, to the youth who wait for a better world, we say to you that there exists no force, interests, or tendency capable of destroying that which we are building, of disturbing or impeding progress, or of generating chaos once again. The Bolivian people, together with their armed forces, will not allow liberty to be destroyed by arbitrariness or licentiousness, or democracy to be perverted by deliberately provoked chaos. . . .

We military men, who during these years have occupied the posts of national government, declare with satisfaction that we have fulfilled our duty. We also declare that we have had difficulties and have committed errors, but what we are sure of is that we have served the people with honesty, with valor, and with a profound sense of justice.

After lifetimes dedicated to fulfilling our duty, we aspire only to live in the simple confines of our profession. But, at the time of selecting a military career, we swore, before the fatherland, to be permanently at its service. From such a sublime obligation, honorable military men are relieved only by death. . . .

Workers and businessmen, students and professionals, men and women of Bolivia, the conquest of a great fatherland has its price. We will pay it without fear of the sacrifice, convinced of the inevitable victory.

Translated, reprinted, and edited from *Hacia la Constitucionalización de Bolivia* (La Paz: Secretaría General de Informaciones de la Presidencia de la República, 1977).

NATIONAL RECONSTRUCTION: A MISSION OF THE ARMED FORCES SPEECH BY GENERAL LUIS GARCÍA MEZA TEJADA 1981

Under the present circumstances, when Bolivia has begun along the road to transforming her structures, accelerating her development, and constructing a society compatible with the concepts and advances of the modern world and of human evolution, the armed forces, as an essential part of the nation, have the high and difficult duty of assuming the direction of our people.

Their unity is the unity of the Bolivian people, their conduct is the patriotic conduct of the nation, and their discipline is the new mystique which, today, nurtures the spirit of Bolivians. . . .

The armed forces are an active part of the process of national reconstruction which was begun last July, and they are also responsible for ensuring its fulfillment, for guaranteeing its institutional continuity. Thus it is that their degree of cohesion, the disciplined fulfillment of duty, the conscientious obedience, and the opportune and adequate processing of national events also form part of the service dedicated to the fatherland.

Any dispassionate analysis of the Republic of Bolivia could not ignore the fact that, in 1980, the country was suffering from one of the greatest frustrations of all time. There existed an immense and dangerous power vacuum, characterized by a state of affairs which included the absolute incapacity and paralysis of the government accompanied by chaos, anarchy, disorder, corruption, generalized subversion, and, the most serious of all, an accelerated economic and social deterioration.

Our country was confronted with a continuous state of institutional crisis which was carrying the nation to the extreme of dissolution and which was forming a sociopolitical picture of permanent dissociation.

The social and political forces in power, who claimed, paradoxically, to be representatives of the people, demonstrated more interest in promoting terrorist delinquency and social chaos than in saving the country from the disaster toward which it was being pushed.

This is a summary of the general picture of the country up to July 17, 1980, and the entire Bolivian population knows perfectly well that it was real and not a fiction invented by the armed forces.

It is for that reason that the Titular Institution of the Fatherland, in accordance with its constitutional mandate and faced with the resignation of the then president of the republic, who resigned in favor of the armed forces of the nation, assumed the responsibility of directing the State.

Many selfish and unscrupulous people ingenuously seek to undermine us by asserting that the process of national reconstruction lacks objectives. Undoubtedly, this assertion is tendentious and false, and because of this it is necessary to understand it in its true dimension.

The Objectives

So that they will remain definitively established, I want to take this opportunity to reiterate the ends and objectives of the process of national reconstruction, the same ones which were clearly expressed in the basic documents the armed forces made public, together with their historic determination.

Within the framework of a national project destined for a political, economic, and social reordering, Bolivia requires profound changes which will modify her decrepit institutions in order to achieve levels of progress compatible with the development of the most advanced countries of the contemporary world, as well as to achieve the well-being of her people, realizing, in the shortest time possible, the following national objectives:

1. Return to the sea—a national desire long linked with the aspirations of our people, and an inalienable and irrevocable right of the nation

2. National development—to achieve goals which will contribute to the

improvement of material, social, and spiritual conditions capable of providing the Bolivian people with a process of change designed to forge a community in which the inhabitants will be able to satisfy completely their needs and their aspirations

3. National integration—to consolidate the union of the Bolivian family and strengthen the national spirit as an innovative force proud of itself, and to achieve a complete territorial vertebration in order to secure a harmonious, balanced, and concerted regional development which will allow us to guarantee the civic, spiritual, and moral affinity of the national being

4. Economic independence—to allow us to have the national wealth at our disposal in accord with the legitimate interests of progress, well-being, and development, free of pressures and impositions from the centers of world power who try to impose new forms of colonialism on the countries which produce strategic, primary products, such as is the case of Bolivia

5. National security—to also guarantee the territorial integrity and the political, social, and economic stability of the country, assuring the conditions basic for the peaceful living and security of all Bolivians

Clear Ideological Definition

Now that they have been established, these objectives require for their implementation political goals which will attest, in a clear and unequivocal manner, to the motives and aims that inspire the conduct of the government. Primary among those is the intention of installing an organic, republican, and stable democracy which will be authentic and in accord with the sociocultural reality of the Bolivian people. . . .

In Bolivia, we can speak no more of liberal democracy, with the political parties shut down and proscribed, when social movements tend to dissolve the multitude of small political factions which have been obstacles to the political activity of recent times.

The democracy to which the great majority of the Bolivian people aspire is that which permits the active and real participation of the popular sectors of the country, of the peasants who, even today, still live outside the national decision-making process. The people want a democracy which is based on social justice, on the people's access to culture and production, on the humanization of labor and capital, and on an increase in income levels and the improvement of the standard of living of the Bolivian people.

Democracy cannot be imposed by decree, nor achieved by a simple act of will. Its effective validity depends upon the execution of unavoidable structural prerequisites, such as social peace, internal security, the integration of the peasantry into active, national life, the presence of representative political parties, and the common acceptance of living together peaceably.

The democracy of our time cannot remain static, nor can it continue developing within closed groups, elites who gained their status through inheritance or fortune. Rather, this democracy must be continually expanding to provide space for the growing multitudes who inevitably must come from the majority sectors of the national population.

For that reason, liberal and bourgeois democracy should give way to a democracy which is the expression of the will of the people and of its own adequately organized characteristics, a democracy of total participation, where men intervene in the realm of decision making without intermediaries and where the political, economic, and social decisions are not made by miniscule minorities. . . .

Comrades:

The politician of the moment never stops thinking about mere electoral matters or about himself, and he thinks only in present terms. That is the error of politicians, and because of that, we lament the lack of statesmen who think first about the fatherland and about future generations. It will be precisely those generations who will turn their eyes to the past and both demand that history render an accounting and judge that which the rulers did to bequeath them a dignified and developed fatherland.

In the face of the failure of the politicians, what the process of national reconstruction wants to leave Bolivians is an honest doctrine and a program of effective action in order to build a nation which is socially just, economically free, and politically sovereign.

At this moment, we are convinced that not one national problem can be isolated from the world context. There is no time more opportune than the present to call upon all Bolivians to preserve the moral patrimony which the liberators left us.

Bolivia is growing and will grow greater through the solid work of her sons. We are beginning to build a new fatherland, a common task which neither military nor civilian can shirk.

A great mystical patriotism is shaking the national soul. We are walking to meet our destiny, and we are sure that Bolivia will recover her seacoast and be strong and great, both in America and in the world. Bolivian nationalism unites the majority of the people, and in spite of the dissociative actions of the extremists, the nation will continue to advance with a firm step toward achieving the goals we have proposed, which, in short, will mean happiness, peace, and prosperity for each and every Bolivian.

These considerations regarding the national reality will surely move the spirit of this important meeting of the commanders of the largest military units in the country, and their measured conclusions will orient the actions of the government in the great task of transforming our nation into a modern, civilized country capable of forging its own destiny.

Translated, reprinted, and edited from Bolivia, *Documentos del Gobierno de Reconstrucción Nacional* (La Paz: Secretaría General de Informaciones de la Presidencia de la República, n.d.), pp. 101–17.

Brazil

SPEECH BY HUMBERTO CASTELLO BRANCO
1967

Gentlemen Members of the National Congress:

When I addressed the nation for the first time as president of the republic, I promised all Brazilians that I would relentlessly promote the general welfare. I did not ignore, at that moment, either the responsibility attached to such a gesture, nor the magnitude of the tasks ahead. I was also convinced that the whole nation would respond to my dramatic call to collaborate, even with some sacrifice, in order to resume the development process and to achieve true social justice.

After almost three years, I bring before your Excellencies an account of my government, as a testimony of how much has been demanded from the Brazilian people so that they could regain confidence in the ideals of their government.

There was no break in this process, and the struggle included all areas of activity. The initial steps of the program called for implanting radical structural reforms, a stoical and permanent inflationary decompression, along with the overriding objective of boosting the national economy and revitalizing the country's management.

But no social change can take place without having [an] effect on the balance of political forces. The defects of the infrastructure always incite the former privileged groups to resist the new laws promoting equality; the new institutions still arouse stubborn opposition . . . and the memory of old habits stirs up discontent and regret in a permanent struggle to retake the government.

For that very reason, the rupture of the juridical order existing until March 31, 1964, called for the adoption of certain political measures in order to provide an adequate transition according to the terms and the ideas of the revolution.

I want to emphasize, of course, the application of Articles 7 and 10 of the First Institutional Act, strengthened later by Articles 14 and 15 of Institutional Act number 2.

In the exercise of such prerogatives, some legislative measures were canceled and the political rights of persons indicated by the members of the National Security Council, were suspended. I repeat, these decrees were political measures of the revolution. They were not inspired by a simplistic whim to punish. On the contrary, a rigorous verification of responsibilities was conducted in every case. And it must be remembered that every revolutionary process presupposes, in its own context, measures of a repressive nature. Very few, however, have proceeded with as much justice and moderation as the March 1964 movement. . . .

Since 1945, the legislation and dynamics of the representative system has deeply misguided and profoundly distorted the will of the people. A multiplicity of parties and the abuse of economic power in the electoral campaigns were two of the basic causes.

. . . In turn, the effects of multipartyism on the administrative life of the country provoked a continuous instability, with the obvious consequences. As an example, let it be remembered that the average term in office for the ministers of state, from 1946 to 1964, did not reach 224 days.

. . . [In this context] it is once more fitting to review the serious weakening of democratic institutions in the phase prior to the revolution. A social and political crisis, which reached unbearable levels, became a factor in the deteriorating internal and external economic situation, then already very critical.

As an unavoidable consequence, there occurred a decline in the efficiency of all aspects of national activity. Confronted with the need to reveal the implications of such a situation in relation to national development, we shall now undertake a brief analysis of the Brazilian situation as of March 1964, focusing especially on the socioeconomic aspects.

Despite the various structural limitations that tended to conspire against self-sustained and rapid development, the Brazilian economy experienced satisfactory performance in the period from World War II to the year 1961, and especially between the years 1947–61. During that period the gross domestic product grew at an average annual rate of 5.8 percent (equivalent to 3 percent per capita). The . . . expansion of the industrial sector through the substitution of domestic products for imported goods was the most important stimulus.

However, this process of development took place against the backdrop of a social and economic structure unfavorable to lasting economic progress. Alongside the rapid growth of the manufacturing sector, the conditions of the agrarian sector—in which more than 50 percent of the national population existed at a low standard of living—remained almost unchanged, victim of the reigning technical backwardness in the rural sector and of the unsatisfactory levels of education, health, and hygiene.

Likewise, an archaic financial structure, highly sensitive to inflationary pressure, persisted along with a lack of basic services (transportation, energy, silos and warehouses, and communications), aggravated over and over by incorrect economic policies. An opportunistic and myopic view of the economic relations of the country with the rest of the world led to neglect of exports, which constituted the main determining element of the external purchasing power of the country. As a consequence, the Brazilian capacity to import stagnated.

Finally, during the entire above-mentioned period, that is, from after the war to 1961, the Brazilian economy developed within an atmosphere of continuous inflation of variable but bearable intensity, to the point of having permitted the satisfactory evolution of the gross domestic product, at least until 1961. In the meantime, the presence of those inflationary pressures, with partial control by government officials, was harmful enough to produce undesirable distortions in the system of relative prices and to give way to speculative activities, one consequence of which was the weakening of the money and capital market and the rates of savings and exports. The extraordinary growth of the Brazilian population and the resulting increase in the demand for new jobs, linked to the vulnerability of the public administration to political pressure, encouraged the transformation of employment in the public sector into "political spoils." This undermined operational efficiency and generated increasing deficits. The consolidated deficits of the government in turn were traditionally financed with currency issues, a source of new inflationary pressures. It ended in a vicious circle. . . .

Starting in 1962, several circumstances tended to increase the government expenses, independent of the comparative increase in the fiscal revenues, with a consequent progressive evolution of deficits in the case of the National Treasury and an increase of the rate of inflation. There were also serious signs of a worsening of the balance of payments situation and the reduction of import capacity. The deficiency of the economic infrastructure became more acute, creating a climate of uncertainty and uneasiness. As a consequence, the level of investments and the growth rate of the economy declined, and the weaknesses of the national economy became more evident.

As a result of all this, increases in the general level of prices, which had reached an average of 15 percent per year between 1941 and 1946 [and] rose to 20 percent in the period from 1951 to 1958, suffered a rapid acceleration starting in 1959. The rate of increase in the cost of living rose in that year to 52 percent in Guanabara, and, after going down in 1960, started rising progressively until reaching 55 percent in 1962 and 81 percent in 1963. In the first quarter of 1964, it reached 25 percent and, given its rate of acceleration, it could have very well reached 150 percent by the end of the year. . . . The social and political atmosphere of the previous administration could not have been more unfavorable; the following factors should be underlined: the constant political tension created by the disharmony between the federal executive on the one hand and the national Congress and the state governments on the other, distrustful of the anticonstitutionalist intentions and desires of the old regime [to maintain itself in power]; a penchant toward state property and control that created a continuous discouragement and threat to private investors; the communist infiltration, generating apprehensions about the overthrow of the social and economic order; the successive paralysis of production by the "strike commands." Not only did urban activities suffer but also investment in farming and cattle raising were discouraged. . . . Political instability and administrative improvisation prevailed, producing a lack of national direction . . . the entrepreneurial classes suffered from a crisis of distrust; the working classes found themselves frustrated because of the impossibility of their realizing the demagogic promises; finally, certain, more restless groups, such as the students, not finding an outlet for their idealistic impulses slipped into the error of subversive solutions. . . .

To summarize, when this government took power, the financial and economic situation was truly gloomy. To the structural deficiencies of the national economy had been added temporary troubles which underscored these [deficiencies], disrupted internal markets, pushed the increase in prices to the verge of extreme inflation, generated a crisis of confidence [and] a slowdown in the flow of investments and in the rate of economic development. [These troubles also] increased the level of unemployment, and, finally, they damaged the country's credit abroad. The most urgent task, therefore, was to contain the extraordinary rise of the general level of prices, to recover the minimum necessary order for the functioning of the national economy, to overcome the crisis of confidence, and to return to the entrepreneurs and to the workers the tranquillity necessary for productive activities. . . .

Reprinted and edited from Mensagem ao Congresso Nacional Remedita pelo Presidente de la República Na Abertura da Sessão Legislativa de 1967 (Message to the National Congress at the Opening of the legislative session of 1967). Translated by Cecilia Ubilla.

SPEECH BY PRESIDENT ERNESTO GEISEL
BEFORE THE BRAZILIAN CABINET
1974

. . . In a previous public statement I have already pointed out that the modernizing Revolution of 1964 bases all of its strategic doctrine on the two pillars of development and security, recognizing, of course, that in essence the first of the two is the dominant one. In more precise terms, one can say that the strategic action of the revolution has been and will continue to be exercised in such a way as to promote for the Brazilian people at all levels, at every stage, the maximum possible development with a minimum of indispensable security.

Likewise, in the area of national security the process is also essentially integrated, since this process is the same as national development, though applied to a more specialized and more restricted area. The minimum of indispensable security results, therefore, from an interaction duly balanced . . . in each of its integrated components.

. . . It is clear that we have received a valuable heritage from the governments of the revolution, which in these last ten years managed to raise Brazil to an outstanding position among the new world powers, with an internal market which places Brazil among the ten largest of the western world, and a gross domestic product, this year, on the order of $66 billion. After a phase of pressing sacrifices, during which combating inflation, remodeling economic institutions, and reestablishing internal credibility became priorities, and, parallel to this, the creation of a climate of order, stability, dedication to work, and faith in the future—we begin to see indications of highly satisfactory performance: rates of growth of actual product, since 1968, between 9 percent and 11.5 percent a year; inflation on the decline and neutralized in regard to its major distortions, because of corrections in monetary policy and the system of minidevaluations; balance of payments surpluses, permitting the accumulation of reserves, [which amounted] in December 1973 to more than $6 billion.

Thanks to the impressive dynamism of the economy under President Medici, the country recorded the highest level of prosperity in modern history, with expectations that per capita income will exceed 600 dollars in 1974.

The great expansion and diversification of our external sector, accomplished in those ten years, increased foreign trade to a value of $12 billion in 1973, which will enable the country to face the most serious challenges of the future confidently.

It is not less certain, however, that the drastic changes which have taken place in the world scene—such as the serious energy crisis, the shortage of basic foods and raw materials in general and the shortage of oil and its by-products in particular; the instability of the international monetary system, already in a painful search for a new order; the inflation which has spread over the entire world at alarming rates; the political and social tensions, aggravated by the ferment of the irresponsible calls to violence, which disturb the life of many nations, in a setting of transition toward the still not well defined new international order—all of these have serious repercussions on the national scene, especially in a year of intense political activity such as 1974. . . .

The great success achieved and the spirit of unity of the governments of the revolution . . . suggest that the major thrusts of government policy be continued.

Continuity, however, does not mean immobility. And if we intend to adapt to those new external circumstances, which represent a serious challenge, we must not only improve the institutional mechanisms for the coordination of development and security policy, but also to take care of new objectives and of new priorities which derive, naturally, from the high level of progress already attained by the country.

. . . In regard to domestic politics, we shall welcome sincere movements toward gradual but sure democratic progress, expanding honest and mutually respectful dialogue and encouraging more participation from responsible elites and from the people in general . . . in order to create a climate of basic consensus and to proceed to the institutionalization of the principles of the Revolution of 1964. I am anxious to see the extraordinary instruments with which the government has armed itself to maintain an atmosphere of security and order which is fundamental for socioeconomic progress, . . . used less frequently [and] . . . made unnecessary by a creative political imagination which will install, at the opportune moment, efficacious safeguards . . . within the constitutional context.

It is evident that this will not solely depend on the federal executive power, since, to a great extent, it calls for the sincere and effective collaboration of the other powers of the nation as well as that of the other government organs in the state and even municipal centers, including conscientious discipline and their own ironing out of difficulties. It will necessarily depend on the spirit of debate of the restless and disoriented minorities, disturbers of the country's life, irresponsible or demagogic, resorting even to deceit, intrigue, or violence—[and their] recognition of the general repudiation [of their doctrines] and the full recognition of today's unquestionable reality: the definitive implantation of our revolutionary doctrine.

One must not accuse this doctrine of being antidemocratic when . . . it is essentially aiming at perfecting, in realistic terms, democratic practices and adapting them in a way better suited to the characteristics of our people and to the current stage of the social and political revolution of the country, yet safe from the attacks—overt or covert—of those who in the name of liberal democracy only wish, in fact, to destroy it or to corrupt it for their own benefit. . . .

Reprinted and edited from *O Estado* (São Paulo), March 20, 1974. Translated by Cecilia Ubilla.

SPEECH BY ERNESTO GEISEL TO MILITARY COMRADES 1976

Gentlemen:

I thank you for the welcome that you have given me at this barracks today, in this garrison of Vila Militar. I thank you for the wishes for my personal happiness proposed in the toast by his Excellency the secretary of the army and answered by all of you.

My visit here today is for me a source of special satisfaction, for it gives me the opportunity to share this day with my highly esteemed army comrades, and, with them, the representatives of the navy and air force.

It is not only the feeling of an old soldier who returns to military life, to the place where he worked and toiled for many years and where, at an early age, he began his education. It is not merely a sharing with his fellow soldiers or [a chance] to exchange impressions, to taste their successes, their aspirations, and the anxiety under which they live. It is not merely the return to this Vila Militar, where I served for many years, in my youth and also as an adult, with energetic professional activity, totally dedicated to the army: it is truly much more than that. It is because, in fact, there is no more appropriate surrounding in which to commemorate our Revolution of 1964 than the site of an army barracks. In fact, the armed forces—and among them the army—played a principal role in the Revolution of 1964, by taking the initiative to combat a situation of anarchy and havoc which was spreading throughout the nation.

And it was the armed forces which, through their efforts, made this revolution successful, gave stability to it, and gave order to the country, an order with which it was possible to ensure the progress that Brazil has enjoyed since 1964. Furthermore, it was the armed forces which confronted and fought the subversive movements. These movements, which aimed at the destruction of our nation, had, to a great extent, been inspired from abroad.

It was also the armed forces which were able to overcome intrigue, lack of understanding, slander, and insults, and made possible—I must repeat—this stability in which we have been living for the last twelve years. And these armed forces are today united, cultivating the ideals of our revolution, wholly fulfilling their constitutional duties, which allow the government favorably and on a large scale to undertake at the present time an evolution [toward progress]. A gradual evolution certainly, aiming at the improvement of our social and political institutions, based on the economic development that we are continuing, despite the critical international situation.

These are, then, the extraordinarily important motives which bring me on this visit here today. Undoubtedly the contacts that I had and my presence here constitute an extraordinary source of encouragement for those who, like me, shoulder an exceptional responsibility in the leadership of the Brazilian nation and who try honestly and with integrity to find the way, or the road that we must take, which will undoubtedly be difficult . . . It is a path troubled by intrigue, by harmful information, by meddling of all sorts that we must untangle in order to see the true direction that we must follow. . .

I must also say that I shall carry out this most noble, however difficult, task which has been laid upon my shoulders. I shall comply with my duty with all my strength and using all the means and resources which the government has available. I think that I shall successfully carry out this task. With all the delights and difficulties that government life implies, I still have the zeal and the hope to say sincerely that we shall carry out our task to a successful end—a success which means well-being for the Brazilian people, a success which means the aggrandizement of the Brazilian nation.

My good wishes are expressed in this direction, and I ask you to join me in a toast for the fulfillment of them all.

Reprinted and edited from *Journal do Brasil,* April 1, 1976. Translated by Cecilia Ubilla.

SPEECH BY PRESIDENT JOÃO FIGUEIREDO
TO THE BRAZILIAN NATION
ON THE SIXTEENTH ANNIVERSARY OF THE REVOLUTION

On this date sixteen years ago, the Armed Forces of the Nation were confronted with the historic mission of halting the most menacing political threat to the aspirations of our people ever experienced by us. The Brazilian family reacted with resolution and vitality against that imminent destruction of our traditional political institutions.

Under the pretext of protecting the poor and needy, democracy's enemies actually sought to exploit a peace-loving and orderly people by negating their rights as well as the social progress already achieved.

Furthermore, they attempted to subjugate Brazil to interests which were ideologically, politically, and economically opposed to our own.

However, the nation was not as passive as those who wished to destroy it imagined. Throughout Brazil, a vehement outcry came forth and grew against the attempted denial of our values and the disrespect for law and order. In the barracks, on our ships, and in our air force, a unified view solidified our determination. We could not leave the nation to the mercy of subversion, demagogy, civil hatred, distrust, and class struggle.

These concerns were as profound as they were universal. We knew and felt that most Brazilians also shared these concerns. We also knew and felt how superficial was the uproar of those who said they spoke for the people but in fact were repudiated by them.

The "Nation in Arms" responded in concrete terms to all the appeals heard throughout Brazil.

Marshall Castelo Branco described the revolution [the coup of 1964] as "an inevitable stage in our evolution." Brazil's commitment to democracy led the nation to "progress without damaging our people's fundamental characteristics and feelings."

Only those who oppose the revolution for the sake of opposition itself would deny our firm determination to achieve the goals we first announced some sixteen years ago. In fact, we should not worry about the opposition, because they fail to acknowledge the evidence. They are blind and mute, refusing to see or to answer. They are less perceptive than rocks.

The course that we are taking in order to create a more just, politically open, and pluralistic society is the same course chosen by the revolutionaries of 1922, 1924, 1930, and 1945. Such a society is founded upon personal and civil rights written in the constitution. Man's progress and the fulfillment of his political aspirations are the only and final objectives of every State action.

Therefore, in the lawful State, order is a necessary, a priori, and undeniable requirement. Marshall Costa e Silva affirmed that order is "a projection of the spirit upon an external reality which disciplines it, gives it meaning, and makes it possible for social groups to flourish."

Derived from liberty itself, order is thus distinct from the silence imposed by the tyrant's intransigent hands. Order does not call for a monolithic conformity with official truth. It is from within the legal order that different opinions are expressed; this attribute characterizes genuinely free societies.

For these reasons, I say that democracy, justice, equality, and the rule of law, respect for the will of the majority, are the foundations for the political and social structure. And let us not deceive ourselves. If one of these basic elements is missing, then none will exist.

At the same time, the revolution occurred in order to address the impasses that were rapidly accumulating and threatening to destroy the nation's chances for economic development. For the first time, we had experienced negative growth in our per capita national product. Our credit abroad was in shambles; almost all our exports faced a crisis. In addition, there appeared to be no future or incentives for our industry, commerce, and agriculture.

Faced with this gloomy picture, the revolutionary governments brought progress despite the economic difficulties. Today, we face the difficulties produced by economic growth, rather than those of stagnation and despair. In the words of President Emilio Medici, the revolution "will be considered by history as the period in which the nation's greatness was constructed."

The statistics confirm the development experienced by all sectors. In many respects, Brazil has grown more during these sixteen years than during the seventy-five years since the Proclamation of the Republic [1889].

Yet, if it was not possible to achieve even more, or if in certain cases the actual results did not meet our expectations, it is essential to recognize that this is due to the difficult international situation we experience: the petroleum crisis and imported inflation. The historical circumstances, known to all Brazilians, prompted mistakes or forced us to change our plans.

All this would not matter in a totalitarian regime. These regimes would change the historical records or alter history itself. The central goals of our revolution, in contrast, are to reform (and always as quickly as possible) and to realize the ideals of supporting, defending, and sustaining democracy as the legitimate political form of government.

With this same frankness, I recognize that we were only partially successful in fighting inflation and in improving the foreign trade balance. To this end, the Brazilian people have been making great sacrifices, especially wage earners and the less fortunate classes in general. We must recognize, however, that this indispensable sacrifice should be divided equitably, with the greatest share relegated to the wealthy.

As I have already stated on other occasions, the producers, industrial and commercial, will need to accept lower profit margins in order to maintain lower prices for consumers. I hope that they do this voluntarily.

In the face of all these difficulties, we continue as resolute today as we were in the first minutes of the revolution. If the political opening consciously initiated by my honorable predecessor appears to emphasize the occasional errors rather than the great and permanent accomplishments, then I suggest that we should not forget President Ernesto Geisel's warning. He affirmed that we have the duty to remind those who had not lived through the inauspicious times of the nightmare and affliction which shrouded our well-intentioned hearts during the prolonged vigil over the nation's agony." Those times were "the abyss of incapacity, vacillation, corruption, and disorder that were subverting all of Brazil's institutions."

Brazilians:

The revolutionary process has not ended; it continues with the implementation of the goals we have proposed. Naturally, the revolutionary methods will not be as evident as before, but the ideals are permanent, or we would not be "in the beginning of a new era," to use the words of President Emilio Medici.

As I have already promised to make this country a democracy, I now affirm to all Brazilians that we, the 1964 revolutionaries, shall not deviate from our course of pursuing the normalization of the political process.

Every day, one can see that democratic privileges are more evident among us. This is proof of the government's uncompromising intention to struggle for a democracy founded upon our moral and spiritual values. In accordance with the desires of Brazilians, the government rests upon Christian principles that have accompanied us since our formation as a people.

Translated, reprinted, and edited from João Figueiredo, *Discursos, 1980* (Brasília: Presidencia da República, 1981), vol. 2, pp. 39–44.

Chile

THE REASONS OF THE JUNTA
1973

In Order of the Day No. 5, the Junta outlines for the public benefit the reasons which moved it to assume control of the country.

The text of the order is as follows:

Order of the Day Number 5

Whereas:

1. The Allende government has exceeded the bounds of legitimacy by violating the fundamental rights of liberty, of speech, and of education; the right to congregate, to strike, and to petition; the right to own property and, in general, the right to a worthy and stable existence;

2. the government has destroyed national unity, encouraged sterile and, in many cases, cruel class wranglings, disdained the invaluable help which every Chilean could give to preserve the country's welfare, and engendered a blind fratricidal struggle based on ideas alien to our national heritage which have been proven false and ineffective;

3. the government has shown itself to be incapable of assuring a peaceful association among Chileans by nonobservance of the common law on many occasions;

4. the government has placed itself outside the law on multiple occasions, resorting to arbitrary, dubious, ill-intentioned, and even flagrantly erroneous interpretations of it, which, for various reasons, have escaped sanction;

5. by the use of subterfuge, which the government was pleased to call *resquicios legales* (legal recourses), some laws have not been promulgated, others have been flouted, and a situation of illegitimacy engendered;

6. the government has repeatedly failed to observe the mutual respect which one power of the state owes to another, disregarding decisions approved by Congress, by the courts of justice, and by the comptroller general of the republic, offering unacceptable excuses for so doing or none at all;

7. the supreme authority has deliberately exceeded its attributes. . . gravely compromising the rights and liberties of all;

8. the president himself has been unable to disguise the fact that the exercise of his personal authority is subject to decisions taken by committees of the political parties which support him, impairing the image of maximum authority which the constitution confers upon him;

9. the agricultural, commercial, and industrial economies of the country are in a state either of stagnation or recession and inflation is rampant, but there are no signs whatever that the government is interested in them, except as a mere spectator;

10. anarchy, stifling of liberties, moral and economic chaos, and, as far as the government is concerned, absolute irresponsibility and incapacity have led the country to ruin, preventing it from occupying its proper place among the leading nations of the continent;

11. the foregoing justify our opinion that the internal and external security of the country is in dire peril, that our very existence as an independent state is in danger, and that the continuance in power of the government is fatal to the interest of the republic and the welfare of its people;

12. that, moreover, the foregoing, viewed in the light of our national and historical idiosyncracies, is sufficient to justify our determination to oust an illegitimate, immoral government, no longer representative of national sentiment, in order to avoid the greater evils which threaten the country, there being no other reasonable method holding out promise of success, and it being our objective to reestablish normal economic and social conditions in the country, with peace, tranquillity, and security for all;

13. for the foregoing reasons the armed forces have taken upon themselves the moral duty, which the country imposes upon them, of deposing the government, which, although legitimate in the early exercise of its power, has since fallen into flagrant illegitimacy, assuming power for ourselves only for so long as circumstances so demand and counting on the support of the vast majority, all of which, before God and history, justifies our action; and hence whatever regulations, norms, and instructions we may think fit to lay down for the attainment of our objectives aimed at the common good and the maximum patriotic interest;

14. Consequently, the very legitimacy of the said norms obliges all, and especially those in authority, to abide by them.

Signed: Government Junta of the Armed Forces and Carabineros of Chile.

Santiago, September 11, 1973.

Reprinted and edited from *Three Years of Destruction* ASIMPRES (Chilean Printers Association, n.d.).

This speech was given on the second anniversary of the military coup.

SPEECH BY AUGUSTO PINOCHET UGARTE
1975

Today Chile commemorates the recent achievement of its national liberation.

Barely two years ago, sombre misgivings filled the air, and the general feeling of anguish knew no bounds. Chilean women instinctively feared the destruction of their homes, realizing the extent to which violence had undermined their children's most elemental safety. Our youth rebelled against the sinister aims and alien ideas of a minority who endeavored to control their consciences and curtail their freedom. When it became evident that the country was in a state of chaos, workmen of all types protested by putting an indefinite stop to their activities.

In this atmosphere, an unsuccessful and corrupt government forfeited its last traces of legitimacy by neglecting its functions as the established authority and, seeking to divide Chileans by means of systematically fomented hatred, prepared a civil war which would have inflicted a death blow to our beloved nation.

Yet the proud, indomitable Chilean spirit rose again with renewed vigor. From the bottom of their hearts our people demanded their liberation, and on a morning such as this, our armed forces and carabineros, in complete unison, and, in fact, representing the last reserve of a juridically organized state, took over the government of the nation.

Our flag once again waved proudly, dignified and victorious, and the date of September 11 took its place among the most glorious periods of our independence.

I shall outline today the task which our government has undertaken. It has not been an easy path to follow, but on this second anniversary we face a nation which lives in peace, order, and respect, after three years of chaos and Marxist-Leninist violence; a nation which threads its way among many stumbling blocks, but is convinced that it advances towards a definite goal; a nation which daily becomes more united, with renewed confidence in its own destiny. What a contrast this is to the desolate picture of a world universally submerged in spiritual oppression, moral confusion, and physical violence!

For this reason, my words this morning are those of a president of the republic who, in spite of fully assessing the difficult situation we still confront, can point with satisfaction to the ground we have already covered and invite the Chilean people to continue treading the path of progress in order and justice.

. . . One of the most difficult aspects in the task of national reconstruction, which directly affects every Chilean, is the socioeconomic field.

For this reason, rather than going into a very detailed and technical account of the matter, I would simply prefer to outline the fundamental objectives pursued by the government and the steps taken to achieve them.

One must not forget that the country's economic and productive systems were so severely damaged, that it is no exaggeration to compare the conditions to those of a war-ridden nation.

All the symptoms for runaway inflation were present. The principal cause of this situation was the unprecedented increase in money issued by the Central Bank in order to pay for the fiscal deficit deriving from the excessive growth of the public sector. To this we must add the large losses suffered by the approximately 500 state enterprises, either seized, requisitioned, or bought by CORFO [Chilean Development Corporation, created in 1939 by a popular front government], and the combination of immorality and inefficiency with which unemployment was disguised by means of hiring unproductive political activists, all of which was financed by the state.

The situation of the productive sector was chaotic. It is enough to recall that agricultural production had fallen 30 percent, thus forcing the country to multiply its food imports by more than four; in 1973 these ascended to over 600 million U.S. dollars.

. . . Never had we been so dependent or suffered such an economic disaster, which compromised social peace and national security, as through the deliberate action of the worst government in our history; the socialist regime, which had promised so-called economic independence.

The new government's first preoccupation was to take the necessary measures to allay the impending collapse. In order to prevent extreme inflation, fiscal expenditure has been rationalized, taxes have been increased, and the situation of "intervened" [a legal-administrative term in Chile referring to "temporary" government management of a firm] or requisitioned business enterprises has been normalized. On the other hand, we have adopted a strategy of freedom of prices, fixing these only for those essential goods in which there is insufficient competition. In order to correct the crisis in our balance of payments, a policy of liberalization has been adopted for international commerce, and we have effected one of the largest currency devaluations in recent history.

Some of these measures have aroused understandable criticism, but the fact remains that it has been possible to reestablish the normal functioning of a ruined economy, definitely removing the danger of runaway inflation and putting a stop to the existing chaos.

Only then could the present government turn to the deeper and more permanent problems which have affected our economy, to a greater or lesser degree, for over three decades and whose solution is essential for solid future development.

Viewed in perspective, the government's economic and social policy has three main objectives:

The first of these is the rechannelling of our productive resources, that is, their progressive displacement toward those products which can be more efficiently produced.

It seems inconceivable—and unthinkable for the future—that for entire decades, and in benefit of an often artificial and overprotected industry, Chilean agriculture has been neglected, and full use has not been made of the country's mining possibilities. The fact that we possess a comparatively great mining and agricultural potential obliges us to channel our resources preferably in that direction. This does not mean a restriction of our industrial development, but rather its orientation towards fields which seem more advisable, such as agricultural industry, among others.

This by no means implies an artificial manipulation of our economy. On the contrary, only a proper redistribution of our productive resources can do away with this long-standing absurdity and guarantee a rapid, solid, and stable growth.

The socialist trends in our economy during the past decade have provoked the uncontrolled growth of the public sector, so that in 1973, fiscal expenditure was 26 percent of the product, and the state financed 80 percent of investment. The second objective of our economic and social policy is therefore to reduce this public sector.

When we maintain that the state should only retain those productive activities or business enterprises which are of strategic or vital importance for national development and hand over the rest to the responsibility of the private sector, we are by no means minimizing the functions of the state. Precisely because it is the state's supreme obligation to promote the common good, and its mission is so fundamental, it should not be driven to neglect its inherent and irreplaceable duties by performing tasks which can be adequately handled by private citizens. With respect to the state's intervention in the national economy, we are not guided by rigid dogmas. There is no doubt that the modern era requires a state which engages in the active planning and flexible regulation of the economic field, but current factors should indicate how far it can go. What we do proclaim as a fundamental principle, however, is that this intervention should keep its subsidiary character and should not annul or invade the framework of private initiative, for the latter is essential for collective progress in a . . . free economy.

. . . Having detained hyperinflation by means of the initial measures already described and laid the foundations for our economic future, the government has now devoted itself toward controlling inflation, which last April was still very high, with an added deficit of 1 billion U.S. dollars resulting from the low price of copper.

A plan for economic recovery has been devised and put into practice, with the main purpose of defeating inflation. Otherwise we cannot expect the necessary degree of new investment, and what is even worse, the great efforts made by the government, as well as by the country in general, would have been wasted.

. . . However, the application of this plan for economic recovery has meant lowering the income of our countrymen to that which our present economic capacity can really afford.

A great part of the so-called social cost of the economic program is merely the acknowledgement of the effects of the international crisis on the persistently low price of copper. On this account alone each Chilean family receives a monthly average of 105,000 escudos less than during 1970.

This impoverishment of the country, produced by factors which lie beyond our control, has necessarily meant a reduction in consumption, as well as the open manifestation of a higher rate of unemployment, particularly in the great urban centers. You will note that I say "open manifestation of unemployment," because it is common knowledge that in 1973 the enormous existing rate of unemployment was disguised by means of creating useless and unproductive jobs in the public sector, which required constant currency issues.

It is the government's duty to warn the public that as a consequence of the temporary state of economic contraction resulting from the country's straitened circumstances, and from the agreements of CIPEC (copper-producing countries) in order to defend the price of copper in 1975 production will decline approximately 10 percent compared with last year. This should not be disheartening or produce confusion, since it is contemplated in the economic plans and will be recovered in the near future.

To have eluded this "social cost" would have meant once more deceiving the people by allowing them to continue living on false hopes for a time, but within a few months Chile would have faced an even worse social and political situation than that of 1973.

It is far from agreeable for any government to assume the obligation of taking such drastic measures, especially when not personally responsible for the causes involved. But when power has been attained not through one's own will, or personal political ambition but by a moral, historical, and patriotic imperative, the exercise of authority only makes sense in the strict compliance with moral duty. I feel that the reason for the generous support which I, as well as the entire government, am constantly shown throughout the whole country, [is the result of] the people's instinctive conviction that this is the case.

. . . The world beholds today a generalized crisis of the traditional forms of democracy, whose failure and exhaustion, at least as far as Chile is concerned, should be considered definitive.

This situation is particularly favorable for totalitarian regimes of differing ideologies, [having in] common scorn for the spiritual values of mankind, to take advantage of this weakness and seize power.

Those of us who believe that the concept of democracy essentially contains a sense of man's dignity are duty bound to face this problem with decision and resolutely advance towards the creation of a new democracy by means of a new political and institutional regime.

The profound crisis of contemporary democracy finds its deepest cause in the loss of the basic spiritual unity of the peoples of the world. The free play of [opposing ideas] in both the generation and exercise of power offers no major institutional obstacles if at least certain fundamental principles are accepted by the whole community, but when this minimal [consensus] is lost, society can no longer be ruled by the same mechanisms, whose efficiency has been damaged at its source.

The existence and propagation of Leninist-Marxism in the world today represents the destruction of the basic moral foundations from which the Western and Christian civilizations derive. Under the euphemism of alleged "Leninist morals," communism destroys all notion of good and evil, cynically judging acts according to whether or not they are convenient for totalitarian revolution. And thus, in the name of that entirely immoral doctrine, we have witnessed the assassination of millions of beings; the slavery of entire nations; hatred, lies, and slander as an habitual line of conduct; and all kinds of aggression against man, his rights, and liberties. It is evidently impossible to live in democratic harmony with such a doctrine.

Reality has laid bare the inadequacy of the concept of liberty as understood by classic liberalism and has placed us in the position of having to redefine it in its authentic significance. True liberty is not simply each individual's right to do or say as he pleases. Freedom is an innate attribute of man which enables the human being to defend the inviolability of his own conscience, as well as to exercise the right of unconfined choice for himself and his family, free from the oppressive interference of the state.

Since liberty derives from man's inherent spirituality and is therefore justified if put to use for his moral and intellectual development, it is unacceptable if employed for the weakening and destruction of those very same values. However, social environment and a correct juridical order require certain restrictions on individual liberties, not only to preserve the personal freedom of others, but for the common good.

Facing today's novel circumstances, it is imperative to react in a vigorous and alert manner. In this day and age, a state's sovereignty not only depends on its territorial integrity, [but] its political, economic, and social organization must also constitute an efficient guarantee against another graver peril: the attempt of international communism, as the instrument of Soviet imperialism, to seize states, infiltrating them from within by means of the local Communist parties, aided by other groups who favor or condescend to Marxism by paving the way or ensuring their [freedom to act].

Direct territorial conquest is thus replaced by the penetration of the vital centers in free countries which naively permit the access of Marxism to the control of labor unions, universities, and the mass media. Even the churches, which by definition should provide the most solid protection against this avalanche, have suffered Marxist infiltration in their ranks.

The world today faces an unprecedented form of war. Communism penetrates society ideologically and at the same time, from its various centers of power, imposes upon democratic governments a line of action which favors its own advancement. The universal character of the Leninist-Marxist revolution fits in perfectly with the imperialistic hegemony of the Soviet geopolitical school.

In this war, nothing can be of greater use to communism than the declaration of ideological neutrality by states which are not yet under its control. How can a state possibly defend itself in an ideological war if it officially declares its neutrality in the ideological field? To this, we must add that communist control of a country not only means the end of all personal liberty and state sovereignty, but, it also involves the destruction of the very essence of nationality. The latter is inadmissible in the name of liberty. The fatherland, with its traditions and historical-cultural identity, cannot be the patrimony of any given generation, for it also belongs to those who built it in the past, and those who have a right to its future inheritance. Nor can any generation so consider itself the sole possessor of its nationality as to feel authorized to destroy it.

Our country temporarily forgot these truths and experienced the bitter consequences. To begin with, communism was allowed direct or indirect control of fundamentally influential media and was given ample facilities for political action and propaganda. Later its vocabulary and ideas were gradually adopted by democratic sectors, who from the habit of dialogue inadvertently became imbued with its myths and slogans. Thus the "non-capitalistic road to development," "community socialism," "Christians for socialism," and other such manifestations appeared, which, when it comes to the definition of their doctrines, were either devoid of meaning or could only answer to Marxist ideology.

It is not surprising then that these sectors never quite realized the virtual suicide they were committing by allowing Marxism access to power when they could have avoided it constitutionally. And not content with this, they officially introduced the most unrestricted ideological pluralism into our constitution, by declaring that to sustain or spread any political idea would not constitute offense. Thus, guerrillas, terrorism, or the organization of paramilitary forces could go unpunished if endowed with the protective cloak of "political ideas."

Now that we have risen from the bottom of the abyss to which this attitude led us, Chile has resolutely proclaimed its nationalistic and Christian definition, by means of a Declaration of Principles, laying down the foundations for the future state which our regime is endeavoring to build, [which will include] a sense of duty to defend our national sovereignty and tradition in a manner suited not only to conditions fifty or one hundred years old, but also to those of the present time.

Not to permit the enemy access to the control of the mass media, universities, or trade unions, does not in any way curtail the legitimate freedom of expression of cultural thought or of labor organization. On the contrary, it implies preserving these from the destruction they would be exposed to if the very forces who intend to annihilate them are allowed to grow freely.

We Chileans have recently had proof of these harsh realities and are firmly determined not to repeat the same mistakes.

The classic concept of punishment is often defied nowadays by the appearance of terrorism, a contemporary iniquity by means of which small minorities commit criminal offenses against innocent people who generally have no connection whatsoever with the objectives of the delinquents. Because of the danger and cruelty involved, society is under the obligation of drastic self-defense, thus giving birth to new restrictive measures in the exercise of personal liberty or lawful rights, in order to reconcile these with the imperative of security which every community justly demands.

The aforementioned is directly related to the problem of human rights, on which I wish to dwell for a moment, since it is still being used all over the world as an instrument to oppose our government and our country. Human rights, in the measure that they are truly such, are universal and inviolable, but they are certainly not unrestricted or of equal hierarchy. As outward manifestations of liberty, they are, without exception, subject to the restrictions imposed upon them by the common good. In this respect, it is curious to observe that those who admit without hesitation that the right to private property is limited by its social function, are often the first to protest the restriction of other rights and liberties, even if also applied for the sake of common good.

Nor are all rights of the same hierarchy. Even among natural rights, some are more fundamentally important than others. They may usually all be exercised simultaneously, but this is impossible when society becomes sick. The latter situation is precisely a symptom of political abnormality requiring an exceptional juridical regime in which the exercise of some rights is limited or can even be suspended in order to ensure the free exercise of other more important ones.

Those who condemn the juridical restrictions essential for the present state of emergency in which we are living should definitely understand the reason why their arguments go against the mature conviction of the Chilean people. The vast majority of our fellow countrymen accept and support these restrictions because they are aware that [such restrictions] are the necessary price to be paid for the peace and social order which make our country a veritable island within a world convulsed by violence, terrorism, and general disorder.

The greatest possible enforcement and highest respect of all human rights implies that these must not be exercised by those individuals who spread doctrines or commit acts which, in fact, seek to abolish them.

. . . If we feel ready today to reduce by one degree the state of siege, it is thanks to the efficient action which the government has taken to dismember organized extremist groups. But while any kind of significant subversive action still exists, whether overt or covert, we are obliged to maintain the necessary restrictions to ensure social peace and prevent the return of chaos.

. . . Chileans:

Soon after our independence, Chile was one of the first countries in the world to abolish slavery. Now our country has broken the chains of totalitarian Marxism, the great twentieth-century slavery, before which so many bow their heads without the courage to defeat it. We are thus once again pioneers in humanity's fight for liberation.

Our victory over communism is especially significant because of the geopolitically strategic importance of our country in the defense and security of the continent, but even more so for its deep spiritual content.

Today Chile will ignite the flame of liberty, as a living symbol of its faith and hope for a world which at present labors in darkness.

As president of Chile, I feel certain that this flame will be lit with the support of the entire Chilean population, whose hearts beat in unison with the highest and purest patriotism.

I devotedly implore Our Holy Lord, with deep humility before the magnitude of our task, never to allow this flame to die down and that Chile may always face, with renewed vigor, the tempests which may arise and keep its patriotic oath of forever being "the tomb of the free or else the shelter against oppression."

Edited from *Chile Lights the Freedom Torch* (Santiago: Editora Nacional Gabriela Mistral, 1975), pp. 1–68.

CHILE SHOULD NOT FALL INTO THE VICES OF THE PAST
SPEECH BY GENERAL AUGUSTO PINOCHET
1983

I want to put those politicians who are anxious to recoup power on notice that we will not tolerate either limits or conditions being put upon the exercise of authority beyond those established by the legitimately approved constitutional provisions, which are an expression of an authentic consensus which no one can ignore.

On September 11, 1980, the country opted for a renovated democracy, one distinct from that defenseless system which carried us to the very edge of a confrontation between brothers and one which, also to differentiate it from that system, is fundamentally inspired by traditional national values which, throughout our history, gave our fatherland its own physiognomy.

This nationalistic democracy does not accept international ideological commitments, or economic linkages with these ideologies, which, in the end, preclude liberty and self-determination.

On numerous occasions, I have pointed out that the democracy which we approved cannot be confused with the traditional democracy which we knew until 1970; that sectors which are confused or have unstated designs are seeking to reestablish it, knowing that such conduct will cast the country headlong into *politiquería* and the chaos we have already known; and, that we are repelling and will continue to repel the permanent aggression of Soviet imperialism.

Our historical experience confirms that political parties, as they were called under the old constitutional framework, tended to transform themselves into monopolistic sources for the generation of power; that they made social conflict more acute; and that in the electoral struggle in which they engaged, ethical limits disappeared, thereby allowing for any maneuver whatsoever to injure their adversaries, including the defamation and dishonoring of individuals and of families.

Moreover, that concept of political parties accepts those who obey foreign orders and who even receive economic support from the outside, constituting themselves as true advancemen of international ideologies foreign to our reality.

As a result, there exists a profound difference between the constitution approved by the citizenry and the political plan elaborated by one of the opposition groups on the occasion of the 1980 plebiscite.

Through an intensive campaign, those opposition groups have insisted upon the reestablishment of the old democratic system with only minor adjustments which maintain its defects and vacuousness.

It is my duty to call to the attention of my fellow citizens that which, without doubt, would lead to a fatal confusion.

When the government and the opposition speak of "returning to full democracy," they are not referring to the same thing. Between the one philosophy and the other, there are profound differences which no one should ignore.

In the face of a totalitarian threat, and in order not to return to the vices of the past, the government over which I preside is delineating, within the framework established by the constitution, a political system which will give to the intermediate bodies of the society (those no longer contaminated by the disease of partisanship) the administration and government of the regions and municipalities, a system whose goal is the establishment of an authentic and effective democracy.

The foregoing does not mean the elimination of political parties, but rather the placing of them in their true role as currents of opinion framed within a juridical order which will save the country from excesses, as parties whose bases are those consecrated by the people of Chile in their new constitution.

Only in this way will we preserve our most sacred republican traditions, avoid the distortions which an unbridling of partisanship would bring, and give to democracy an authentically representative dimension.

In order to avoid falling anew into the vices of the past, we will continue, with a firm stance, in the work of renovating completely our institutional system to the end of banishing forever the inveterate habits which are an inevitable consequence of the excesses which Chilean partisanship brought down upon itself during various generations.

There is no doubt that we Chileans will not allow ourselves to be dragged down either by false ideals of apparent salvation or by the hallucinatory demagogy of a few politicians from the past.

Translated and reprinted from *Pinochet: Patria y Democracia* (Santiago: Editorial Andrés Bello, 1983), pp. 27–29.

Peru

MANIFESTO OF THE REVOLUTIONARY GOVERNMENT OF PERU—1968

Upon assuming power in Peru, the armed forces want to make known to the Peruvian people the underlying causes for their far-reaching and historic decision, a decision which marks the beginning of the definitive emancipation of our fatherland.

Powerful economic forces, both national and foreign, in complicity with contemptible Peruvians motivated by [the desire for] unbridled speculation and profit, have monopolized the economic and political power of the nation. These forces have frustrated the people's desire for basic structural reforms by maintaining the existing unjust social and economic order which allows a privileged few to monopolize the national riches, thereby forcing the great majority to suffer economic deprivation inimical to human dignity.

The economic growth rate of the country has been poor, creating a crisis which not only adversely affects the financial condition of the nation, but which also weighs heavily on the great mass of our citizens. The contracts for our natural resources have been ruinous, thereby forcing us into a dependent relationship with the great economic powers, compromising our national sovereignty and dignity, and postponing indefinitely the reforms necessary to overcome our present state of underdevelopment.

Overwhelming personal ambition in the exercise of the responsibilities of the executive and legislative branches in the discharging of public and administrative duties, as well as in other fields of the nation's activities, has produced immoral acts which the public has repudiated. This selfishness has also destroyed public faith and confidence in the government, a confidence which must be restored if the people are to overcome their feeling of frustration and the false conception of government that has come about because of the lack of action and responsiveness on the part of those charged with rectifying this unfortunate situation and with improving Peru's present world image.

In 1963, the Peruvian people went to the polls with a profound democratic faith and voted for the recently ousted regime in the belief that that government's program of reform and revolutionary change would become a reality. Our history will record the overwhelming popular support enjoyed by that now defunct government, as well as the loyal and dedicated cooperation offered by the armed forces, support with which it should have been able to implement its program of action. But instead of dedicating their efforts to finding executive and legislative solutions to the nation's ills, that government's leaders, with other corrupt politicians, scorned the popular will and moved to defend those powerful interest groups which had thwarted the aspirations of the people. They subordinated the collective welfare to their . . . ambition for personal aggrandizement. Proof of this can be seen in the government's lack of direction, its compromises, its immorality, its surrender [of natural resources], its corruption, its improvisation—in the absence of any social sensitivity, characteristics of a government so bad that it should not be allowed to remain in office.

The armed forces have observed with patriotic concern the political, economic, and social crisis which has gripped the nation. The armed forces had hoped that a combination of good judgment and hard work would enable the nation to overcome the crisis and to improve the lot of the people through the democratic process, but that hope too was shattered.

The culmination of all these blunders came with the fraudulent and unbridled use of extraordinary powers which were granted unconstitutionally to the executive. One example was the pseudosolution, a national surrender, in the La Brea y Pariñas affair, a surrender which clearly demonstrated that the moral decline of the nation had reached such. . . extremes as to jeopardize Peru's very future. It was because of this that the armed forces, fulfilling their constitutional obligations, is acting to defend one of Peru's natural sources of wealth, which since it is Peruvian, should be for Peruvians.

As the people come to understand better the revolutionary stance of the armed forces, they will see it as the road to salvation for the republic and the way to move definitively toward the attainment of our national goals.

The action of the Revolutionary Government will be shaped by the necessity of transforming the structure of the state in such a manner as to permit efficient governmental operation; of transforming the social, political, and economic structures of the country; of maintaining a definitively nationalist posture, a clear, independent position internationally, and a firm defense of national sovereignty and dignity; of reestablishing fully the principles of authority, of respect for and obedience to the law, and of the predominance of justice and morality in all areas of national endeavor.

The Revolutionary Government promises that it will respect all the international agreements that Peru has ratified, that it will remain faithful to the principles of our Western, Christian tradition, and that it will encourage foreign investment that subjects itself to the interests and laws of the nation.

The Revolutionary Government, clearly identified as it is with the aspirations of the people, issues a call to work with the armed forces to achieve social justice, dynamic national development, and the reestablishment of those moral values which will assure our fatherland of its greatest destiny.

Reprinted and edited from Peru. Comando Conjunto de la Fuerza Armada, *3 de Octubre de 1968. ¿Por Qué?* (Lima: n.p., 1968).

This speech was given on the first anniversary of the military takeover in Peru.

SPEECH BY JUAN VELASCO ALVARADO
1969

Fellow Citizens:

Upon completing the first year of government, I am here tonight, on behalf of the armed forces, not only as the chief of state, but also principally as the chief of the revolution. But this title carries with it a meaning radically different from those of the past. . . . To be chief of the revolution is to be the leader of a team of men who are profoundly identified with the revolutionary spirit of the armed forces, on whose behalf was initiated a year ago the process of transforming our country.

This is not a personalist government. There is no one preordained nor irreplaceable among us; nobody has a monopoly on either wisdom or power. We are a team that is carrying out the revolution that Peru needs, the revolution that others proclaimed, only to betray once they were in power. But we know that this will not be understood by those who in reality are no more than simple *caciques* of a new breed, extremists of personalism, vanity, and political fraud.

During the year that ends today, we have begun the process of national transformation that the armed forces promised the country on October 3, 1968. In this brief period, we have completed an enormous task, but it has only been the beginning of the revolutionary process. There still remains an immense job which will require long years of effort and struggle. We will finish it regardless of the obstacles because that is what the urgent needs of our people demand and because that is what the armed forces committed itself to doing when they assumed the responsibility of governing the country.

Faced with this duty, on whose fulfillment the very destiny of Peru depends, we assign little importance to the selfish cries and false protests of those who always used power for their own profit and benefit. Today there is a chorus of voices, known to everyone, that demands the immediate return to constitutionality, that aspires to encourage a vanity which we do not possess, in order to suggest our sudden retirement and our participation in an electoral contest through which they hope to restore that formal democracy which they debased to the point of converting it into a great hypocrisy—speaking of liberty to a people victimized by exploitation, misery, hunger, corruption, surrender, and venality.

Because of that, I want to repeat that not one of us has political ambitions. We are not interested in competing in the electoral arena. We have not come to play the game of politics. We have come to make a revolution. And, if in order to make it we are required to act politically, we should not be confused with those criollo politicians who did so much damage to the country. . . .

Certainly those people do not want to understand what has happened in Peru, but we are living a *revolution,* and it is time that everyone understood it. Every genuine revolution substitutes one economic, political, and social system for another which is qualitatively different. Just as the French Revolution was not made to shore up the monarchy, ours was not launched to defend the established order in Peru, but rather to alter it fundamentally in all of its essential aspects.

Some people expected very different things and were confident, as had been the custom, that we came to power for the sole purpose of calling elections and returning to them all their privileges. The people who thought that way were and are mistaken. One cannot ask this revolution to respect the institutional norms of the system against which it revolted. This revolution has to create, and is now creating, its own institutional structure. . . . Our proposals have nothing to do with the traditional forms of criollo politics that we have banished forever from Peru.

For that reason, our legitimacy does not come from votes, from the votes of a rotten political system, because that system never acted in defense of the true interests of the Peruvian people. Our legitimacy has its origins in the incontrovertible fact that we are transforming this country, precisely to defend and interpret the interests of that people, who were cheated and sold out with impunity. This is the only legitimacy of an authentic revolution like ours.

Of what value to the true man of the people was the liberty they spoke of and then traded away in the back rooms of the National Palace and the Congress? What did these defenders of formal democracy and constitutional rights ever do to resolve, once and for all, the fundamental problems that afflicted Peru and her people?. . . Where are the profound reforms that they promised so often at election time and then, once in power, whisked out of sight in order to serve the oligarchy?. . .

Nevertheless, do not think we have any interest whatsoever in refuting the charges that are hurled against the revolution. The best defense of the revolution lies in its accomplishments. . . . We do not talk of revolution; we are making one. That is our best justification before Peru and before history. All honorable Peruvians are conscious of the fact that, for the first time, we have begun to attack in toto the fundamental problems of the country.

There is plenary proof of our deeds. There is that handful of far-reaching accomplishments that greatly surpass everything that was achieved by past governments. There is the recovery of our petroleum from the hands of a foreign company which previously, because of bribery or fear, influenced the politicians that governed this country from both the [executive branch] and the Congress. There is the new Agrarian Reform Law that benefits the campesinos and breaks the back of the oligarchy, which until recently was all powerful. There is the General Water Law that at last fulfills the dreams of thousands of farmers whose rights were always trampled upon to benefit the *latifundistas*.

There is the new mining policy which ends the old practices which were prejudicial to the interests of Peru. There is the law which puts a stop to the abusive speculation in lands for urban expansion and which will contribute, in a very important way, to remedying the problem of urban housing. There is the initiation of a policy of state control over the Central Reserve Bank, which now does not represent private interests but the interests of the nation. Finally, there is the new international policy, not of submission but of dignity, whose course is limited solely to the interests of Peru.

All of this, and much more, has been achieved in scarcely one year of government action. There are those who assert that the power of propaganda is very great, and possibly this is so. But no propaganda can erase from the minds of all Peruvians the conviction that this government is doing the things that no other dared to attempt, either because of fear or selfishness. Nevertheless, it is completely understandable that incredulity and skepticism still persist in this country where so often promises were betrayed and where political chicanery was substituted for politics. . . .

We have wanted to do much more than we have done for the good of Peru, but there exist monumental obstacles that the citizenry ought to know about. We found Peru in a profound economic crisis; we did not inherit a bonanza situation. The last administration left an external debt of more than 37 billion soles [more than $860 million]. What great or important thing for our people was done with this immense sum of money? Which great reforms were financed by that enormous debt, which the past government borrowed from other countries? It is necessary to speak plainly: a large part of those 37 billion soles was squandered in the unparalleled corruption that devastated this country during the last regime. Where are those who trafficked in the misery of the poor? It is necessary to make known that some of them escaped justice by taking refuge in the international organizations which they always served with no care for the reputation or the future of their fatherland. The day will come when we will settle accounts with those who betrayed the trust of the people. We have no reason to speak in euphemisms. A revolution implies also a different language without halftones and without subterfuge.

But the limitations that the revolution has to overcome are not based solely on the heavy burden of the huge foreign debt that the last government contracted and that Peru has to repay. There is another very important limitation. The oligarchy that has seen its interests affected by the Agrarian Reform Law is not investing its money in the country. This is the great conspiracy of the economic right, its great antirevolutionary strategy, its great treason to the cause of the Peruvian people. It persists in this manner in order to create a fictitious economic crisis that will endanger the stability of the government. The excuse for not investing is that there does not exist in the country a "climate of confidence." This venal phrase is the refrain, as well as the psychological weapon, that the right uses day after day to cover with a smokescreen its true, antipatriotic intentions.

What type of "confidence" do the great proprietors of wealth demand? A "confidence" that permits them to maintain the luxury and the privileges that are not justified except by the bad habits of inveterate exploiters of the Peruvian people?. . . This type of confidence they are not going to have while we are governing because on this type of confidence are based the injustices that submerged the great majority of our people in misery and exploitation.

But there are conditions of authentic confidence for all those who understand that wealth should also fulfill a constructive social responsibility. There is confidence and government backing for investment that promotes the economic development of the country within a framework of respect for the just expectations of capital and for the legitimate rights of the workers. There is confidence because there is total political stability in the country, because social violence no longer exists, and because the people clearly support this government. . . . There is confidence because private investment enjoys all the guarantees that any modern business requires.

From the beginning, the Revolutionary Government declared its support of and encouragement to private investment, including the foreign investment that complies with the laws of the country. There exist then all the conditions of legitimate confidence that honorable investment requires. Many businessmen now understand this, and there are very clear indications of a new and positive tendency in the investment field. But the oligarchical sectors of national capitalism are plotting against the revolution through their control of the economic apparatus, assisted by an ultra reactionary press. . . . The Peruvian people ought to have a very clear idea of the oligarchy's true economic conspiracy because the revolutionary government will not maintain forever its serene attitude of waiting for these people to recover their sense of reality and abandon their pernicious, anti-Peruvian position.

The immense task of realizing effective changes is being carried out by this government without violence and without bloodshed. Ours is the only revolution that, having succeeded in initiating profound transformations, is executing them peaceably. In other countries, agrarian reforms less advanced than ours cost thousands of lives over years of brutal, fratricidal struggle. Until now, Peru has escaped that fate of blood and death, and we are confident that this will continue to be the case in the future. But we understand that the experience our fatherland is living through today represents a conquest without precedents. Without any doubt, this revolution is a radically new phenomenon; it cannot be understood within traditional models. For that reason, the Peruvian example excites interest, expectation, and admiration in the rest of the world and particularly in our Latin American continent.

. . . There are, to be sure, very powerful forces behind the campaign to confound the ongoing revolution. These forces dictate the course of that propaganda which, on one side, demagogically urges deceitful extremism and, on the other, insinuates that our revolution has entered a mellowing phase. Both antirevolutionary postures have the same source of inspiration—the purses of those who pay for them. These two strategies are clearly perceivable. One of them holds that the revolution has gone too far, too fast. But we will not commit that error. The other antirevolutionary strategy persists in presenting us as a movement overcome by complacency, without energy, and incapable of moving beyond that which we have done. Naturally, to halt the march of a revolution which has only recently begun would be another regrettable error, [one] which we are not going to commit. We know very well that, in order to succeed, the reforms initiated must necessarily be complemented by others that are equally indispensable. For us, the transformation of this country is a complex and integral process which will have to be attacked from distinct fronts and with different plans of action. Because of this, the revolution has a program, and that program will be carried out methodically and in its totality.

The two strategies of the oligarchy move in unison, in perfect concert, from within and from without. The conspiratorial action of the adversaries of the revolution functions at these two levels. One of their principal instruments is the synchronized propaganda and twisting of the truth that operates through certain foreign news agencies, through some internationally circulated magazines, and through the majority of the newspapers printed in Peru, newspapers that represent and defend the interests of the Peruvian oligarchy and its foreign accomplices.

The vast majority of Peruvian newspapermen have little or nothing to do with this insidious campaign of lies because they are not responsible for the editorial policies adopted by the majority of newspaper owners. In general, that immense majority of newspapermen really sympathize with the revolution. But those who control and monopolize the ownership of the press are members of the oligarchy, enemies of the transformation we are realizing.

... The revolution will go forward until it achieves its objectives, without haste and without hesitancy, by its own route and with its own methodology. We have learned how to resist pressures. We will not be provoked, but we will be implacable in the defense of the revolution on whose success depends the future of Peru. Do not confuse tolerance with weakness. In the Peru of today, the lines are clearly drawn. This revolution will be defended whatever the price. Its adversaries, within and without, should understand this with no room for error. The armed forces will sustain it, and the people will daily defend it more because they will feel it to be theirs.

... Thus, if we feel our duty and commitment is to the revolution, we have to be vigilant that it always be an example of purity, honesty, efficiency, sacrifice, and generosity. We have to create an awareness of the immense task that a revolution entails. It will be necessary to correct, from day to day, the errors that are inevitably committed in the mundane operation of the revolution. We have the honesty, the humility, the wisdom, and the valor that others have never had to recognize our errors and correct them.

Far from weakening the revolution, this will strengthen it because it will give it added moral authority. But we will be supremely demanding of ourselves; we will aspire to be a bit better each day; and we will encourage the honest criticism which is an invaluable contribution in every creative effort. Above all, we will never forget the sacred duty of always being loyal to this revolution on which depends the future of our fatherland.

... I want to close by directing myself first to those who are not yet involved in the revolution and, second, to the campesinos of the country. To the first group I want to say, in the name of the Revolutionary Government, that in this national mission there is a place for every Peruvian who sincerely desires a profound change in our country. Only those who identify with the oligarchy or with the hated past against which we revolted will be excluded from the revolution. This is a minority in Peru. The great majority of the blue-collar and white-collar workers, the intellectuals, the industrialists, the students, and the professionals, that is to say, the true people of Peru, have no reason to identify with the past nor to defend the interests of the enemies of the revolution. It is for them and with them that we are making this revolution.

My final words this evening will be for the campesinos because the revolution has begun the agrarian reform, the agrarian reform that many dreamed of but very few believed would some day be realized in our country, the agrarian reform that is awakening the campesino and exciting the admiration and respect of the whole world. Nevertheless, as we predicted the day it was promulgated only three months ago, it is now the target of sabotage and obstructionism.

To those campesinos, for whom we effected the agrarian reform, today we say that you should not be deceived, that you should remember those who when in power dictated a reform law designed to defend the great landowners, that you should understand that the propaganda of those who seek to confound and create confusion cannot be sincere, and that you should be ready to defend with your own lives, if necessary, the lands and water that are and will be yours.

In great part, the future of the revolution depends upon the efforts and the responsibility of the campesinos to make the agrarian reform a success. There exist, and there will continue to exist, problems of implementation. But the campesinos should be alert to the enemies of this reform because they are the enemies of the revolution. The campesinos should never forget that this reform and this revolution are being carried out for all the people, for all the poor of Peru. The benefits of the agrarian reform will be felt in other sectors of our society that were equally exploited by the same oligarchy that submerged the peasantry in misery. The revolution began in the countryside, but it will not stop there. The horizon of the revolution is the same horizon of the fatherland.

If we are in power, we have to accept the responsibility for both triumphs and defeats. On us depends the future of the revolution, but it will succeed. We have on our side the might of right, but we also have the right of might.

Reprinted, translated, and edited from *Peru. Velasco: La Voz de la Revolución* (Lima; Ediciones Participación, 1972), 1: 89–108.

SPEECH BY FRANCISCO MORALES BERMÚDEZ
1976

My dear countrymen:

There are many ways in which the chief of state can set forth the guidelines and policies of the Revolutionary Government of the Armed Forces which he represents.

During this second phase of the revolution, we have addressed you many times through statements, speech, press conferences, and direct dialogue with the people both at the palace and in the different regions of our country.

Today I want to avail myself of another means of communication— television and radio—in order to come into your homes for a while and deal in a most sincere manner with matters that concern our beloved country. . . .

Today's speech or talk, on this the last day of summer, has the purpose of outlining the main problem areas and situations that our country and the revolutionary process are experiencing. One hears repeatedly that the government's authority is weakened, thereby weakening authority at all levels.

This is a confused situation which should be fully clarified by calmly identifying the real causes. In the first place, we have to admit that there obviously has been a change in the methods and political management of the government, as we stated publicly on August 29. [On this day Morales Bermúdez replaced Juan Velasco Alvarado as president of Peru.]

We have opened the channels of dialogue and of freedom of expression which were very limited during the first phase of the revolution. This has enlarged the scope of political debate, a characteristic of the "Revolution with Freedom" that we practice. But we are also facing a typical situation wherein the intense propaganda of leftist and rightist opponents, who can now express their opinions, with the psychological fear of many of being considered "less than revolutionary," has led to a confusion between the need to establish authority and the need for repression and rightist fascism. The result is to endanger the revolutionary process, to which contribute, paradoxically, through their lack of lucidity and clear political vision, not only the opponents of the process but also its supporters who still do not comprehend the essence of revolutionary humanism.

. . . Another cause of this apparent weakening of governmental authority can also be identified. It has been barely seven months since we initiated the second phase of the revolution and assumed the responsibility of leading the country. We did so at the request of the armed forces in conjunction with the police forces, fully conscious of the great political and economic difficulties which this responsibility would entail. In the areas of economics and finance, my five years' experience as minister of economy and finance [1969 through 1973] and my assumption of the premiership in 1974, where I devoted most of my time to the economic affairs of the country, made it evident to me, as I announced publicly, that an economic crisis was approaching. . . .

As there was no hiatus between the first phase and the second phase of the revolution, because we followed a strict norm of revolutionary ethics, we have in fact absorbed all the virtues and defects of the revolution since its inception. The Revolutionary Government is now suffering a natural attrition after exercising power for over seven years, seven years of profound structural changes within a model that seeks to be original and unique and that has the problems of identification and attitude to which we referred above. But this phenomenon does not have its origin in the second phase, because credibility was already lost in the latter part of the first phase. We now have the obligation and the moral and patriotic duty to regain that credibility. We should acknowledge frankly and humbly the mistakes which undoubtedly have been made, for to err is human. Moreover, it would be impossible to hide them, for any period of time, just by denying them. . . .

I would now like to convey to you some reflections on the doctrinary and political-doctrinary aspects of the revolution. In order to leave no possible doubt, we ought to set forth the present and immediate political objectives. In short, these are: to consolidate the revolutionary process, avoiding its degeneration into communist statism or its return to already outdated forms of prerevolutionary capitalism, and to complete the structural reforms in order to turn Peru, in time, into a humanist, socialist, Christian, solidary, pluralist society, truly democratic and fully participatory. That is to say, to attain the final objectives of a fully participatory social democracy. This objective runs parallel to the development of the country, to make it a great, strong, and prosperous nation. Therefore, the corresponding plan for the achievement of these goals will, without any shadow of a doubt, be conceived in such a manner as to merit the enthusiastic support of the majority of the Peruvian people. . . .

And when in order to eliminate all doubts we must practice self-criticism, we shall do so; and we shall begin doing so now in this speech. Since the first phase of the revolution, we have had the tendency of not stating in a clear, simple, and unmistakable fashion what we believe, what we seek, and what we stand for. In order to avoid being accused of not being sufficiently revolutionary, or of being petit bourgeois defenders of privilege, or of not wanting to free ourselves from the past, or of thinking with certain prejudices, we frequently adopted attitudes which consisted of either dressing up or toning down our real thoughts. We then hid these thoughts behind a certain type of jargon, which interested and committed propagandists, both foreign and domestic, termed *revolutionary*. However, if we are right, and we are; if our revolutionary objective is superior, and it is; from the moment we affirm the validity of our actions and from the moment we no longer fear to state in a clear and unequivocable manner, for example, that we disagree with certain measures that are considered "revolutionary" only because Marxists preach them, we will dispel this fear that has been imbued from within and abroad, and we will affirm ourselves and reaffirm our own superior ideology. In the end what will endure is not what is thought of us today, but rather what we finally achieve, and for that reason it is essential to define everything clearly.

. . . The principles of the Peruvian Revolution are humanistic and Christian. Nothing can be clearer than this or the consequences derived therefrom. The essence of both principles is that man is the end and not the means or the instrument of others. The human condition is a constant, and therefore no one has the right to manipulate or use human beings as objects for profit or power.

If we want to achieve justice, justly, and freedom, freely, we must. . . use proper methods. For this reason, our revolution cannot be imposed by blood and fire because that would mean the manipulation of the masses and the sacrifice of many people for the sake of an uncertain future. This fact reveals that in the realm of practical politics, the most acute problem which a movement such as ours has to face is how to carry out profound structural change while still guaranteeing personal freedom. The solution we have found is gradualism. Gradualism should not be confused with reformism because reformism places a limit on the amount of change and also because reformism, in reality, only demands palliatives to prevent the traditionally privileged groups from losing power. Gradualism does not mean stopping halfway down the path, but rather means advancing by stages, with each stage being characterized by effective solutions to the problems within the limits of existing resources. . . .

We want to make this perfectly clear because if we do not proceed in this manner the economic system will collapse and we will be left with only two alternatives: either the revolution will be truncated and [will] die, or an implacable socialist dictatorship will have to be imposed by violent means, which will preclude the people from having true participation in the collective decisions. If anyone knows of another way in which the problem of harmonizing structural transformation while maintaining people's freedom can be solved, please let us know, as we shall be very grateful indeed.

. . . My dear fellow countrymen: the armed forces, with the police forces, are and always will be bound to the revolutionary process and will defend this revolution to the end.

It should be remembered that this revolutionary process is the creation of the armed forces, who initiated the revolution on October 3, 1968, and who now direct the process in this second phase. The armed forces, guardians of the nation, are a permanent institution. The rulers are representatives of their institutions, but while men change, the institutions live on. There is no difference in either our principles or our objectives; what has changed are our methods and procedures of governing.

It was the armed forces that decided to change the political leadership last August 29. The armed forces understood long ago that the desire of our country to be free and sovereign abroad necessarily required that the people be free from all forms of domestic exploitation. The armed forces also understand that national dignity begins by acknowledging and respecting the dignity of each citizen.

Therefore, the progress of this revolutionary process is indissolubly and unshakeably linked to the armed forces. Its zealous efforts to avoid distortions and to frustrate attempts to thwart it are therefore understandable. Thus, the revolution is the very embodiment of our military conscience, and when its goals and objectives are achieved, it will make every officer, every soldier, every man in uniform feel satisfaction in having accomplished his mission and will maintain each one of them in constant vigil to prevent the original design from being distorted.

A revolution which thus exalts justice, freedom, work, participation, solidarity, creativity, honesty, and respect for human dignity is a revolution which deserves [our] living for, deserves defending and dying for. . . .

Reprinted, edited, and translated from *La Revolución Peruana: Consideraciones, Políticas y Economicas del Momento Actual* (Lima: Empressa Editora Perú, 1976), pp. 3–43.

SPEECH BY GENERAL FRANCISCO MORALES BERMÚDEZ CERRUTI ON THE 158TH ANNIVERSARY OF NATIONAL INDEPENDENCE, JULY 28, 1979

The goal of a presidential message should not be confined merely to informing the public, but rather, above all, should be to orient, to offer the citizenry the opportunity to interpret and to judge the administration. It should not, therefore, be reduced to a compendium either of data which can be found in statistical volumes or of deeds which are enumerated in government annals. Rather, a message should highlight that which is truly significant, that which falls back upon the dynamic of national life, conforms to the present, and will have an influence upon the future. For that reason, a message should represent a pause on the journey, which allows us to contemplate the route we have already traveled and makes possible a glimpse of the road yet to be traveled.

Meditation of this sort is all the more necessary today because we are approaching that moment when the Revolutionary Government of the Armed Forces will have completed the process of transferring power back to the civilians, completely independent of personal interests or of institutional contingencies.

In beginning a review of the most significant accomplishments of our governance, we would point to our foreign policy, an area in which Peru initiated a process of genuine world understanding predicated upon new foundations, committing her most sincere and positive efforts, as behooves a country in the international arena that espouses a highly independent, sovereign, and universalist foreign policy. Within this broad and unrestricted perspective, our priority task, born out of an integrationist vocation and flowing from common historical and cultural values, has been directed toward the nearest and most intimate nations within the Latin American context. In this area, new dimensions have been offered to Peru, as much in the bilateral field as in the integrationist process. . . .

For the next twelve-month period, the government has prepared a plan which maintains the objectives established in the 1978–80 Economic Program, harmonizing the achievement of these objectives with the political goal established for July 1980. All our efforts will be directed toward carrying out the plan in that time frame.

With this plan, the government intends, in its last year, to make the external sector of the economy completely healthy, restoring stability to the financial situation and establishing the foundations for a rapid reactivation of domestic economic activity once the goals of stabilization have been achieved.

We are confident that, by 1980, worker incomes will have greater purchasing power than in 1978 and that we will have eliminated the bottleneck of scarcity of resources for international payments. This will be possible by having persevered in the implementation of the four programs already mentioned, whereas the present sacrifice will be compensated by the fact that the nation will be able to continue along the road to development with a better distribution of wealth, which is the goal we are seeking to achieve.

The election of the Constituent Assembly and the promulgation of a constitution, which will take effect once the new government takes power, are steps already taken toward the transference of power, on July 28, 1980, to the government which the people will legally elect, with neither conditions nor hindrances. Thus, the country will have one more proof that the armed forces keep their word.

We recall that when the Túpac Amaru Plan[1] was published, there was skepticism; moreover, there was criticism that the transference of power and the installation of a representative democracy would truncate the revolutionary process begun in 1968, because we would be retiring without having achieved our fundamental objectives. In order to respond to these criticisms and to demonstrate that our decision to initiate the transference to civilian rule is based on the conviction that the essential goals of the process have been achieved, it is necessary to offer a brief examination and analysis of the situation before and after ten years of revolutionary activity.

We can state, without being unjust, that our country before 1968, apart from being an underdeveloped country, which it still is, was more dependent, was less integrated socially and economically, and had greater social marginality and concentration of wealth than today. To this was added a weak State, less capable of confronting the exigencies imposed by the necessity of overcoming underdevelopment and dependency.

We want to make it very clear, however, that we are not denying the worth of those in the past who struggled against this situation, or of those who, with valor, intelligence, and integrity, contributed to the glorification of the fatherland. Nor are we denying the worth of the institutions, or of the social, economic, or political groups. Peru is distinguished by the extraordinary quality of its cultural production and is distinguished particularly by the courage of its sons who in fateful moments of national life knew how to offer their lives in carrying out actions of incomparable heroism.

In spite of being freed by our founding fathers from the colonial yoke, historical conditions made it very difficult for this political liberation to be, at the same time, social, cultural, and economic liberation. The colonial state had created a rigid society with rigid social estates and with a series of values, legal dispositions, and social and mental structures which made profound change impossible.

Because of that, over the course of the past century and the first half of the present one, there was a series of what only appeared to be changes: Economic power began to change hands and a national bourgeoisie began to be formed, but always within the general framework which we had inherited from the colonial period.

In spite of the facts that the social structure itself made it impossible to see things as they were and that, therefore, there did not exist a collective consciousness of the situation, or a national demand for change, numerous persons and some political groups saw these things clearly and proposed models of transformation. This consciousness intensified, and the moment arrived when the desire for social transformation was generalized.

The political parties began to propose political platforms which included the changes that would have to be effected to overcome the underdevelopment, the marginality, and the lack of integration which afflicted our country. But when they came to power and had the opportunity to apply their programs, they could not carry them out. The rigidity of the structure, the nature of the political system—a formal democracy without the flexibility necessary to effect socioeconomic transformations—prevented it. What also prevented it were the characteristics of partisan rivalries and the external pressure from the great powers who were accustomed to the state of dependency of our country.

The armed forces of Peru were conscious of the fact that this situation constituted an impasse. On the one hand, order had to be maintained, but on the other, there was no doubt that this order did not represent the interests of the people of the nation. To continue accepting it would impede development and national cohesion, place our sovereignty in danger, make it impossible for our system of national defense to achieve the efficiency which the security of the country required, and allow the marginality of the national majority.

Therefore, the armed forces, conscious of the situation, concluded that it was urgent to initiate a new order, one more just, more humane, and also more efficient, in order to overcome the obstacles which prevented development, integration, independence, and the participation of the majority of the population in the national dynamic.

Assuming such a broad responsibility meant entering into certain areas and problems which in a way are foreign to the specific military function, for example, confronting the angry opposition of those who wanted to maintain their privileges, overcoming the inertia of many indifferent groups, stemming the outpouring from the ignored sectors who, many times manipulated by outsiders, aspired to an immediate solution to all their problems even though that is impossible, and struggling against extremist groups who were fighting to derail the revolution or who were substituting demagogic preachments for the real work of transformation.

We knew, therefore, that these were the problems we were going to face and that in carrying out our plan we necessarily would have to pay the price of debilitating ourselves. Nevertheless, on balance, clearly most important was the unavoidable obligation of a disinterested sacrifice for the cause of the fatherland, facing the task of initiating the structural transformations in a peaceful manner different from foreign experiences because of our need to respond to circumstances distinct from other places and other epochs.

Through these transformations, a process of national integration has been initiated. It is impossible to achieve total integration in only one decade because this would imply that we had achieved a high level of economic and cultural development. But, among other actions, redistributing the land to those who work it and modifying the structure of private companies by granting greater participation to the workers in their management and in the benefits of the wealth they produce do allow for the attainment of the conditions necessary for integration. It has not been possible to achieve definitively our proposed goals because that would require much more time, but we have created the conditions necessary so that they can be achieved.

Within this same process, and thanks to the transformations already mentioned, it was possible to confront successfully the problem of dependency. Following always her Latin Americanist line, Peru modified the traditional policy which moved her in only one direction and joined the group of nonaligned nations. Maintaining a correct friendship with all of the countries of the world and particularly with those of our continent, we have succeeded in establishing an independent line in international decisions.

It cannot be denied that these accomplishments are authentic achievements of the Peruvian Revolution. The fact that they have been carried out makes the Peru of today a Peru different from that of yesterday, a Peru more integrated, in which the majority has a greater participation in the national life, a greater share in the determination of its own destinies, in which have emerged new protagonists of our history. The peasantry, for so long marginalized, has emerged as a new and powerful force, not only politically, but economically as well. The industrial workers today have much more importance, are more organized and cohesive, than just a few years ago. But it is not just the labor forces. New groups of professionals, technicians, merchants, and businessmen who explore new possibilities, routes, and nontraditional methods have arisen with the revolution. The power of the landed oligarchy has disappeared. Today, there no longer exist latifundios with their own ports, or gigantic companies which constituted a state within the State. Today, Peru belongs more than ever to each Peruvian; it is more his; it is closer to him.

Naturally, there have been errors throughout this process, and we have pointed them out on numerous occasions. There were inevitable errors and errors which could have been avoided. But, above all, they were errors which were due to the difficulties of the road along which we traveled. At times, there was improvisation. At other times, we wanted to advance too rapidly; we proceeded without calculating exactly the effects.

Perhaps the most difficult thing of all and that which has caused the greatest number of errors is the difficulty of duly harmonizing the process of social justice with that of liberty. In every revolution, there are stages during which it is necessary to break rigid structures, clashing with multiple interests which still have power and which tenaciously oppose the transformations. When one takes into account the goal pursued, in our case a humanized society, one should never lose sight of the precept of liberty. But, at times, in the heat of the battle, there are methods which can be avoided. The degree of liberty can be greater. In other moments, however, the energy is absolutely inevitable. If one does not proceed in that way, one runs the risk of falling into social chaos. In spite of this, we never passed a certain limit, and we succeeded in preserving the bloodless essence of the revolutionary process.

The balance sheet allows us to arrive at an undeniable conclusion: We have succeeded in carrying out deep and important structural transformations, and we have created the conditions necessary for achieving the goals of development and national integration. These accomplishments have been achieved through a dynamic process in which a broad and lucid national consciousness has been generated. Thanks to the revolutionary process, there exists today in our country a new consciousness which demands that Peru follow one way and not another. Because of that, the Revolutionary Government arrived at the firm conclusion that the principal conquests had been achieved. Therefore, the government could be sure that its task had been completed and that it could now consider the transference of power to a representative democracy. . . .

The new Constitution, in accord with the judgment and desire of the Institutions of the Armed Forces and the Police Forces, affirms the participation of these groups in the economic and social development of the country, and in civil defense. This manner of living, which is not just for now but for always, is demonstrated by the daily work of the men in uniform.

We see, then, that essential aspects of the transformations have been incorporated into the Constitution. There have been certain adjustments with certain anticipated limitations, but in essence, there they are embodied in the Fundamental Law of the nation, like sentinels of the Peruvian people who are conscious of the conquests that have at last been achieved and which should never again be abandoned. We are dealing, thus, with a process that has been institutionalized. The armed forces have carried out their mission. . . .

We now have one year left before the transfer of power, a year during which the Government of the Armed Forces ought to meet the challenge of the immediate objectives which we have outlined: complete the process of transfer of power and continue the economic reactivation. These constitute our responsibility and assume the character of a faithful and strict promise to the country.

It is clear that even if each of these objectives requires a specific treatment, both are so intimately related that, in practice, they should be viewed as the two faces of one single problem. If the transfer of government is not accompanied by advances in the area of economic recuperation, then the stability necessary for the future constitutional regime will be jeopardized.

It is necessary to state as emphatically as possible that even though these two objectives form part of our Plan of Government, they cannot be the exclusive responsibility of the Revolutionary Government of the Armed Forces. Moreover, we could not carry them out through our efforts alone, no matter how much determination and dedication we gave to them. These objectives can be achieved only to the extent that the entire citizenry assumes them as a transcendental commitment to organize its democratic life. . . .

Today, more than ever before, it is imperative that the political organizations demonstrate that they have achieved the maturity which the situation demands. There are in today's context ingredients which give specific characteristics to the present situation: On the one hand, the presence of an economic crisis has generated an understandable discontent, and on the other, the political parties, in the face of the approaching electoral process, are striving to win support from the diverse social sectors for their programs, platforms, or doctrines. The confluence of these factors constitutes a singular situation, and if the problems which derive from it are not treated successfully, we run the risk of falling into a situation which will be very difficult to manage.

In issuing this call for maturity on the part of the political parties,we are not seeking backing for or acceptance of the policies which we have been following; that is not the motivation behind our call. We should be aware that at this time it is not the Revolutionary Government of the Armed Forces or any other government which must be supported; it is the destiny of Peru which is at stake, and whatever effort is made to harmonize the national will in order to overcome the present situation, even given disagreements, should be interpreted only as a patriotic action.

Nothing is gained by promoting greater social or political polarization under the pretext of winning votes or imposing ideological programs, because an ambience marked by confrontation and antagonisms only plays into the hands of those extremist groups who do not believe in democracy but who take advantage of it to promote chaos and generate violence. These groups believe only in destruction for destruction's sake. They use the just demands of a people who are currently suffering and deceive them with promises which they could never keep if they had the responsibilities of governance; they apply pressure with absurd demands without realizing that the country does not accept their totalitarian doctrines.

If these groups represent irresponsibility, the democratic political parties and the country as a whole should demonstrate equanimity and a clear, objective attitude. The present moment demands a delineation of positions, so that those who are disposed to work for the achievement of economic recovery and for a correct, democratic solution will come to the forefront and demonstrate with concrete deeds that they are not disposed to accept those who would lead the country into chaos on the backs of the people whom they falsely claim to defend.

In this effort, we want those Peruvians disposed to work for economic recovery to know that they can count on our decided support and that they have the guarantees necessary for them to continue developing their activities within a climate of tranquility, because we will not permit normalcy to be adversely affected or the life of the country to be paralyzed, particularly right now when the true challenge is to work more and produce more in order to install a solid democracy. . . .

The responsibility assumed by the Government of the Armed Forces for the direction of the nation's destiny emanates from and is founded upon an institutional act, and in function of this, our actions are formed and oriented within those prescribed by our statute. Within this reality, which at no time did we try to shirk, the chronology for the transference of power which we planned is stated in writing in the Túpac Amaru Plan of Government. Among various actions, there is the convocation of a Constituent Assembly. The government has no interest whatsoever in promoting conflict with the political organizations which participated in the drafting of the Constitution and less yet in trying to degrade the majesty of the Assembly.

Once general elections have been convoked, and it gives me great pleasure to announce that they will be held on the third Sunday of May, 1980, another step will be taken toward complete democracy. The 28th of July of that same year, the armed forces and the police forces, after saluting the new dawn of the fatherland, will return to their barracks and bases, with their flags on high, to continue fulfilling their fundamental mission: guaranteeing the independence, sovereignty, and territorial integrity of the republic, maintaining internal order, and participating in the economic and social development of the country.

Consistent with these programs, the government, through me as an intermediary, appeals to the patriotism and serenity of the leaders of the political parties to agree upon a dialogue which will allow us to reach an understanding that will facilitate the transfer of power. We believe that it is time to abandon those attitudes which benefit no one and which only tend to aggravate our differences. For that reason, we should provide an example of civility and maturity and should meditate upon the grave responsibility in which we all share.

The Government of the Armed Forces is also disposed to cooperate with the new government as soon as it wins the next electoral contest, so that this new government can, without loss of time, make the contacts necessary to undertake the great tasks that the governing of the country will demand of it. By this attitude, the armed forces want to show that they are not guided by any principles other than the supreme interests of the fatherland and the national will. . . .

Translated, reprinted, and edited from Perú. *La Revolución Peruana*. Segunda Fase, no. 39 (Lima: Oficina Central de Información, 1979).

Note

1. The Túpac Amaru Plan replaced the earlier "Plan Inca" of the "First Phase" of General Juan Velasco Alvarado, 1968–75. Although the Túpac Amaru Plan greatly modified many of the First Phase policies, its most salient feature was that which promised a return to civilian, democratic government. [ED.]

El Salvador

PROCLAMATION OF THE ARMED FORCES
TO THE SALVADORAN PEOPLE
1961

The Armed Forces of the Republic, conscious of their historic responsibility at this present time, and united as never before in their aspiration for salvation and constructive will, consider it their duty to address the Salvadoran people to define publicly their position before the grave economic, social, and political problems which confront the nation.

Immediately after the movement of October 26, 1960, dissociative forces mobilized throughout the republic in a program of agitation designed to undermine and destroy the institutions of the fatherland, aggravating the economic situation and increasing the level of rural and urban unemployment.

The armed forces could do nothing less than confront the emergency of the moment and fulfill their constitutional mandate to guarantee public order and respect for law, in order to contribute effectively to the prodigious national problems. They agreed to depose the governmental junta which had given rise both to the aforementioned situation and to the political confusion, substituting for it a regime which would, at the same time, maintain order and social harmony and would adopt, in the short term, the initial measures destined to improve the conditions of life of the people.

Oriented to attaining these objectives, the armed forces, without commitments to special interests and with the sole aim of serving the fatherland, elected in democratic fashion, through the free and majority vote of all the officers of the military corps, two of their representatives to join the Civilian-Military Directorate which will assume the responsibilities of carrying out, with the collaboration of the citizenry, a program for social reforms and of dictating the measures for a rapid return to constitutional government. To the two military representatives fell the duty of selecting the civilian members of the directorate.

In order to demonstrate their determination to realize these objectives, and so that you understand that the movement of January 25 has not been simply one more coup d'état with neither lofty nor patriotic goals, the armed forces solemnly proclaim to the nation their steadfast decision to insist upon the speedy holding of absolutely free elections during the current year, with the participation of all the legally registered parties, to elect first the municipal councils and then the legislative assembly, which in turn will elect the provisional president who will govern the country to the end of the administrative period begun in September 1956.

The armed forces commit themselves to fight so that in the course of 1961, measures of public benefit will be taken to alleviate the present economic situation and to initiate the development of social reform, focusing primarily on the following objectives:

—Increase the number of jobs and stimulate production through an adequate program of public works.

—Reform the tax system so that its burden is equitably progressive with respect to the income levels of the contributors.

—Promote an increase in agricultural production and raise peasant incomes through a plan of action and a revision of both employment and the land tenure system.

—Augment the construction of rural and urban housing for peasants, laborers, and white-collar workers.

—Extend assistance services—medical, hospital, and sanitary—to the entire nation and progressively develop the social security system until it includes the entire laboring population.

—Intensify the technical education of the peasantry and the workers, with the purpose of facilitating the establishment of new sources of production and improving the level of production in the republic.

In sum, the armed forces intend to fight to make effective the Economic Regimen contained in Title IX of the Political Constitution of 1950, and to carry out the contents of the Act of Bogota in accord with our national possibilities, because the armed forces understand that the only means of winning liberty, security, and social peace is by eradicating misery through the utilization of all those resources capable of revitalizing both the private and public sectors.

In order to attain these objectives, the assistance of all social sectors is needed, particularly those which are economically strong, because they will, in the end, represent the defense of the capitalist and free enterprise system, stimulating national and foreign investment within a climate of respect for private property, credit facilities, and most important, greater and more just benefits for the working classes.

In demonstration of the unity which strengthens them in their goals and responsibility, the armed forces salute the Salvadoran people by affixing their signature of honor to this solemn commitment. They understand that in signing this proclamation which arose from their own breasts, public opinion will be on guard to ensure that the spirit which inspired it is not perverted by ambitions or deceit. They await the collaboration of those citizens of goodwill and profound democratic convictions, so that, with the help of God, an authentic movement of national recovery can be realized.

San Salvador, February 6, 1961

Supreme Command of the Armed Forces:
Col. Aníbal Portillo, Lt. Col. Julio A. Rivera, Lt. Col. Armando Molina, Capt. Major Mariano Castro Morán, Capt. Maj. Oscar Alfonso Rodríguez Simó.

[Below the proclamation appear the names and signatures of all the senior officers of the officer and military corps and regiments of the republic.]

Translated and reprinted from Lt. Col. Mariano Castro Morán, *Función Política del Ejército Salvadoreño en el presente Siglo,* UCA/Editores (San Salvador, 1984), appendix 11, pp. 397–99.

SPEECH BY COLONEL ARTURO ARMANDO MOLINA ON THE OCCASION OF THE DAY OF THE SALVADORAN SOLDIER

On this day, as I gaze out upon the representatives of the various military corps of the republic, I could do nothing less than recall the years 1945–49, when, in the lecture halls of our glorious Military Academy, "Captain General Gerardo Barrios," I learned the reasons which, over the span of my life, have justified my legitimate pride in being a Salvadoran military officer.

I learned, for example, that the armed forces of El Salvador were born to be promoters of the independence and decolonization process, and, from that point forward, they were the very embodiment of the fatherland, defending its integrity against the invasion forces of Iturbide, or in the "National War" of the five Central American countries, or against the filibusters of William Walker, and maintaining until our day a gallant attitude of rejection of any attempt at foreign meddling in the internal affairs of the country.

From their birth, the armed forces, by mandate of the people, assumed the role as depository of the nation's values and of its sacred symbols. And all of its members learned to live and to die for our National Anthem, our Coat of Arms, and our Flag which in its colors are united the desires of achieving greatness and the love of peace of all Salvadorans.

Moreover, in our primary schools and later in our Military Academy, they taught us to respect devoutly the memory of our Founding Fathers and of all our patriots who in war and peace placed their goodwill and intelligence at the service of the republic. From that is derived the intense emotion we feel for the names of General Francisco Morazán, hero of Central America; Captain General Gerardo Barrios, whose *epos* and sacrifice illuminate the efforts to achieve the economic and social development of the country; of General Francisco Menéndez, champion of national education; of General Francisco Malespín, founder of the University of El Salvador; of General Ramón Belloso, who commanded our troops against the filibusters; and of so many others and even of those who governed in more recent times, whose figures, with all their defects and virtues, have begun to reshape history, such as General Maximiliano Hernández Martínez and Lt. Col. Oscar Osorio.

But, above all, I learned that discipline, respect for hierarchy, and honor and veneration for the fatherland were not abstract concepts, but rather norms of conduct which are indispensable to abiding by our oath as soldiers to defend the national sovereignty and to maintain internal security and public order as bases for development.

If we search for explanations for this constant line of greatness and patriotic love over more than 155 years, we would be able to find them in the origin of the armed forces, composed of men of the people with no commitments beyond those of loyalty to their superiors, to the national sentiment, and to the fatherland.

We would be able to find that line in the awareness that the aspirations of the people are converted into objectives of the State and of its institutions, beginning with ours. And it is for this reason that the men in uniform have engaged not only in bellicose battles but also in social battles to improve the conditions of life of our supreme commander, which is the Salvadoran people. Because if loving the fatherland means wanting it to be more just each day and wanting the fruits of the labor of its inhabitants to benefit everyone in proportion to their efforts, then the armed forces have always supported government measures for the socioeconomic development of the country through an orderly, pacific, and constitutional process. The armed forces have always carried on high the flag of liberation and never one of oppression or dictatorship, and even less have they been at the service of private interests who could be opposed to the national interest.

Nevertheless, in recent decades, and with greater intensity in the last few years, our armed forces have been attacked by international subversion and its terrorist groups who consider us, with just reason, to be the strongest barrier against those stateless individuals who carry out the assignments sent to them from the outside, from where they also receive orders, training, and money designed to establish a communist dictatorship in El Salvador. The destruction of the armed forces is one of the essential goals of these ideological mercenaries who have betrayed every national sentiment. In the realization of the objective, they employ the most cowardly and unscrupulous methods: from cowardly, criminal attacks to kidnappings and extortion to the astute exploitation of ambitious politicians or of the anger of frustrated persons who, with shameful goals, dare to prefabricate violations of constitutional procedures, thereby converting themselves into conscious or unconscious allies of subversion against constitutional order.

Nevertheless, for the tranquility of the Salvadoran people, I can state categorically that the armed forces, faithful to their tradition, will always carry out the mandate of Article 112 of the constitution: defend the sovereignty and territorial integrity of the republic, see that the law is obeyed, maintain public order, guarantee constitutional rights, and keep particular vigil to ensure that the norm of alternation of president of the republic is not violated.

And I ought to assure you, in the name of each and every member of our institution, that El Salvador has had, has now, and will have for centuries and centuries, one single army dedicated to fulfilling its duty, to continuing to be the iron barrier mentioned in our National Anthem, and to destroying those who dare to stain our sovereignty like those who take up arms against the Salvadoran people, which is the modern form of invasion attempted by the mercenaries of international subversion.

Present and Future Generations of Soldiers

A few moments ago, we celebrated the solemn ceremony of delivering the banner, which embodies the spirit of our nationality, to the various military corps of the republic, . . . who will have custody of it as a treasure of each one of them.

Since the time of ancient Greece, in a community of sentiments which combined the culture of Athens with the stoicism and bravery of Sparta, across time, the flag has been the symbol of the fatherland, and the soldiers have dedicated their lives to serving it and to defending it. I am sure that the love of God, Union, and Liberty, which constitute the emblem of our National Flag, will be the maximum inspiration to maintain it always on high, in defense of whatever aggression, internal or external, even at the cost of the maximum sacrifice, if necessary.

It is for that blue and white of our flag that I solemnly declare to all Salvadorans that democracy will live as long as the army lives, and as the founder of our institution, General Manuel José Arce, said, "The army will live as long as the Republic lives."

Comrades in Arms

I am fifty-four days away from handing over the constitutional mandate to whomever the Salvadoran people choose as their future governor. This is the last time, then, on the occasion of the Day of the Soldier, that I will speak to you as your commander in chief. And, since one does not express appreciation for the carrying out of one's duty, I only want to state before the nation that you have been loyal and that you have demonstrated a capacity for sacrifice and patriotic love by supporting all the measures taken by the Government of the Republic to benefit the great majority of the people.

What I want to tell you is not only that your commander in chief is proud of each and every one of you, but also that the exemplary behavior which you exhibited during the fifty-eight months and eight days of my government makes me personally even more satisfied for having chosen a military career and for being an officer, particularly a Salvadoran soldier.

Because it is also due to your support, comrades, that in my speeches to the Salvadoran people I have been able to speak always with my head held high with determination, decision, and strength.

First Infantry Brigade,
San Salvador, May 8, 1977

Translated and reprinted from Mensaje al Pueblo Salvadoreño, con Motivo de las Elecciones Presidenciales del 20 de Febrero de 1977, *Mensajes y Discursos del Señor Presidente de la República, Coronel Arturo Armando Molina*, vol. 10, pp. 40–48.

SPEECH BY GENERAL CARLOS HUMBERTO ROMERO
1979

In the fulfillment of a democratic tradition and of my duty as a leader, I appear before the Honorable Assembly in order to present to the Salvadoran people a report of the actions taken, during my second year of governance, in the diverse areas of public administration, as well as a recounting of the most relevant events within our national and international political activities.

I salute the accredited members of the Diplomatic Corps who honor us with their presence in this august place, and I beg them to convey to their respective peoples and governments our cordial and friendly greetings.

The Creative Ability of Our People

Along the road of working to build the future of the fatherland, we have met with diverse, negative factors. Nevertheless, our work has been stimulated and strengthened by the creative ability of our people, by their traditional spirit of industry, and, above all, by that unbreakable determination to overcome and go forward when faced with adversity.

External Confusion and Internal Violence

In the exterior, groups interested in confounding international public opinion have continued their publicity campaigns designed to present a negative image of our country.

With respect to internal order, it is evident that the violence has increased, with the consequent kidnappings, extortions, occupations of embassies and churches, and assassinations and terror, as part of a plan to provoke a violent change in the system and to install a Marxist-Leninist dictatorship in contradiction to our constitution and the democratic vocation of the Salvadoran people.

I repeat that we are categorically against violence, regardless of where it comes from and regardless of the social position or political standing of those who are victims of it, because, above all else, those victims are human beings and because violence will never resolve our problems. I know the peaceful vocation of Salvadorans, and I am convinced that only in a peaceful, law-abiding climate can we achieve the social and economic transformations which the country needs so that the great, marginalized majorities will understand the true meaning of democracy.

Peaceful Solutions with the Patriotic Contribution of Everyone

Our country is living in a difficult period of its history, precisely because of the threat of a cruel, insane, absurd, and inhumane fanaticism which seeks to tear out by the roots our nationalist sentiments and our democratic traditions.

I know the social problems of the country; I know that their causes are profound and complex and that it is undeniably urgent to find a road which will lead us to authentic justice within a climate of peace; but the patriotic contribution of everyone who truly desires peaceful solutions is absolutely essential.

National Dialogue

Salvadoran reality and the responsibility which I have as president moved me to convoke a national dialogue with the goal that through the participation of all representative sectors we could analyze the problems of the country to seek together, with the most absolute respect for the freedom of opinion, the most efficient and advisable solutions to the reality in which we live.

The objective of the national dialogue has been clear from the outset because the inducement for its realization is cloaked in the greatest citizen honesty. The objective is to analyze, with patriotic criteria, our diverse problems, to the end of discovering formulas for solution which will, within the framework of the law, promote social progress and economic development while at the same time strengthening the democratic, republican, and representative system.

We have invited to the dialogue representatives from legally registered entities who, in great numbers, accepted the invitation, and they are witnesses to the responsibility and seriousness which have prevailed during the working sessions.

I want to make it very clear that the national dialogue is a vehicle for serving the country, and only the country, through the free expression of ideas and the elimination of problems in an objective, dispassionate, and impartial manner.

Because of this, I want to recognize publicly those persons who have responded to the call and who are currently working with patriotic vision.

The Historic Repercussion of the Dialogue

And to those who have abstained from attending and contributing to the discovery of the solution which the country needs, I reiterate that the doors of the dialogue are still open so that you can enter at the moment you desire. I only want you to reflect on the fact that your absence constitutes a negative stance, with historical repercussions, because the situation which currently afflicts the nation demands the joining of forces and the leaving aside of personalist or sectarian attitudes, since what is at stake is the very existence of the republic itself. . . .

The National Plan "Well-Being for All" and the Efforts of a People

Domestically, and in spite of the political difficulties and the impact of inflation, the government is carrying forward the implementation of the National Plan "Well-Being for All," to the end of counteracting the adverse factors and improving, at the same time, the standard of living of Salvadorans.

In effect, this plan, together with the unbreakable and decided efforts of our people, has constituted during the last two years the bastion and the most positive factor upon which the country has depended to counter effectively the forces which are impeding the social well-being of Salvadorans. . . .

Agrarian Policy: Make the Rural Dweller Conscious of His Dignity

The distribution of more than 258,500 hectares of land (646,250 acres) has been begun by the Salvadoran Institute of Agrarian Transformation within a program destined to create new farmers. The 258,500 hectares are being delivered to peasants or community associations of peasants. This distribution, which will be carried out in only one year, constitutes the greatest apportionment of land that has ever been effected in the history of the country.

Nevertheless, I ought to reiterate that the simple distribution of land is neither the basis for nor the principal goal of our agrarian policy. Our primary goal is that of raising the standard of living of the peasant family in every way through better education and health, better nutritional indices, and higher incomes. Material progress will always be limited if we do not at the same time realize the most important task of all, which is to give the rural person, on a basis of justice, the consciousness of his dignity as a person.

Impetus to the Production and Commercialization of Basic Grains

Of special concern has been promoting the production of basic food stuffs. For that, there is the notable work of the National Center of Agricultural Technology in assisting the farmers to improve their crops; there are the price supports provided by the Regulatory Institute for Food Distribution, supports which were the highest in the history of that institution; and, finally, there is the credit assistance provided through the Agricultural Development Bank, which granted loans of approximately 175.5 million *Colones* [El Salvador's currency] through its twenty-seven agencies, affecting 5,451 hectares (13,628 acres) of cultivated food and benefiting some 45,000 families of small farmers. . . .

In Spite of the Violence, the Work of the Government Has Proceeded

The climate of extremist violence that everyone knows about has merited my constant concern; and I have been the first to lament its painful results. Nevertheless, the work of our Program of Government has continued its march toward the goal of securing the common good for all Salvadorans.

This account of the work realized in the second year of my government will be duly detailed by the various government ministries in their respective constitutional reports.

Violence as a Product of Fanaticism, Stupidity, and Injustice

I believe that El Salvador has to progress along the roads of civilization and culture, never via the paths of subversion, terrorism, or barbarism.

Violence will never be accepted by Salvadorans as a means of change or political, social, or economic transformation, because violence is a consequence of fanaticism, stupidity, and injustice.

It is necessary to lay bare the true motivations of those who want to make violence a banner of political struggle and who seek to replace the democratic system with a totalitarian dictatorship which is contrary to both liberty and the dignity of man.

To Live in Peace Is a Right of the People

The Salvadoran people have a right to live in peace and to progress with security. It is for this essential objective that the armed forces have carried out and will continue to carry out their constitutional mission with a broad patriotic vision, because their interest as an institution at the service of the people is to strengthen the democratic system and to create the climate of security necessary to promote social justice among all the inhabitants, particularly among families in the rural areas.

The Urgency of Social Transformations and the Preservation of the Democratic System

The armed forces, conscious of the sociopolitical situation in our country, know that integral transformations are urgent but that these should be carried out in a peaceful and orderly fashion and in strict compliance with the law, because only in a State of Law and in an ambience of peace, security, and liberty will we be able to combat effectively the penetration of totalitarian doctrines.

Within that panorama, the armed forces, firmly rooted in republican tradition, have as one of their objectives the preservation of the democratic system of government and of the bases which sustain it, among which are free, universal, equalitarian, and secret elections, through which the citizenry exercises its part in popular sovereignty.

The Armed Forces Guarantee the Right of Suffrage

For that reason, the armed forces, conscious of their historic responsibility and firmly imbued with republican spirituality, guarantee the citizens the constitutional right of suffrage in the next elections, as a manifestation of popular confidence in the fact that the electoral way constitutes a democratic and peaceful solution for those who would question us in the economic, political, and social arenas.

The Increase of Violence and the Suspension of Constitutional Guarantees

This year, unlike any other in our recent history, produced grave altercations in public order, and the impact of the extremist violence brought brief and sorrow to many Salvadoran families. Agents of authority— judges, mayors, teachers, congressmen, and citizens from the most diverse sectors of the nation—fell victim at the hands of criminals.

The irrationality of this bloodbath culminated with the death of my friend Dr. Carlos Antonio Herrera Rebollo, who participated in my government as minister of education, a post in which he always demonstrated the righteousness of his democratic thought and his vocation in service to the country.

Thus, it was in the face of increased violence and disorder that we made use of the resource which the basic law of the republic provides—the suspension of constitutional guarantees—a situation we feel obligated to extend in view of the fact that the conditions which prompted its implementation still exist.

Together in the Crusade against Terrorism

I know that the moral decomposition of the instigators of the violence is so great that they will always be lying in ambush for innocent victims in order to continue their orgy of blood. And in the face of such a hard expectation, I call for the unity of all Salvadorans—without distinction of either political or religious creeds—so that together we can carry out a patriotic crusade against terrorism and violence, whatever may be their origin or motivation.

Distinguished Representatives of the People

The historic moment in which the world lives offers us political and social alternatives which will outline the future of humankind. Each nation, in accord with its traditions and its own reality and based on its aspirations, will have to follow the road it selects.

More than 150 years ago, El Salvador began its independent life as a Sovereign Republic, and her people decided at that time to be free and to work within the democratic system. For this reason, we should promote this system aggressively and with perseverance, every day of every year, through education and the adoption of positive attitudes which will allow the great majority to understand that, even with its imperfections, democracy is still the best system under which humans can live.

Justification of Democracy

Democracy is justified by the values which it defends, such as liberty and the dignity of man. Democracy permits dialogue and the right to dissent. In the totalitarian dictatorships, on the other hand, the individual is obligated to accept, without discussion, the decisions of the State.

Social Justice Should Be Promoted as a Fruit of Democracy

Democracy should be a dynamic concept with real strength, which allows those who live under the system to realize the true dimension of its political and human potential.

It is impossible for those who struggle in misery to comprehend the meaning of democracy. We have to show them that democracy is the system under which man can build his own destiny in an atmosphere of decorum and dignity.

A change of attitude is urgently needed in order to understand that social justice must be promoted in our fatherland as a fruit of democracy and by means of peaceful transformations within the framework of the constitution and the law.

Social Changes: Undelayable Goal

We have to humanize wealth and sensitize consciences so that those social changes can be implemented immediately, not only because they are necessary but also because they are just.

I am confident that my words will be understood in their exact meaning because they represent the result of a serene, responsible, and meditative analysis of the national situation.

A Fatherland with Neither Hatred Nor Violence

It is my highest aspiration that in our beloved fatherland there will exist neither hatred nor violence and that the vast majority of my compatriots can live free of misery, injustice, and fear.

To the dissociative, subversive, and terrorist groups, I must warn you that this people and their armed forces will know how to preserve and strengthen the liberty which the founders of the fatherland bequeathed to us.

United to Achieve Progress and Peace for the Republic

I call upon all sectors of the country, the professionals, private enterprise, the students, the fathers of families, the teachers, the workers, the peasants, indeed all the forces which make up national life, to struggle to better their social conditions, but that they do so within a moral order, within the framework of law, respecting each other's rights, and with an orientation to the democratic system.

I want greatness for my country and well-being for all Salvadorans. Therefore, I ask one more time that we work together to achieve progress and peace for the republic.

Translated, reprinted, and edited from *Mensaje al Pueblo Salvadoreño del Señor Presidente de la República General Carlos Humberto Romero en su segundo año de gobierno* (San Salvador: Secretaría de Información de la Presidencia de la República, 1979).

PROCLAMATION OF THE ARMED FORCES OF
THE REPUBLIC OF EL SALVADOR
1979

A. The armed forces of El Salvador, fully conscious of their sacred duties for the Salvadoran people and in full agreement with the clamor of all the nation's inhabitants against a government which
   1. has violated the human rights of the multitude,
   2. has fomented and tolerated corruption in public administration and in the justice system,
   3. has created a veritable economic and social disaster, and
   4. has profoundly impaired the reputation of the country and of the noble armed forces;

   B. Convinced that the previously mentioned problems are the product of antiquated economic, social, and political structures which have traditionally prevailed in the country and which do not offer to the majority of the inhabitants the minimal conditions necessary to live like human beings (on the other hand, the corruption and lack of ability of the regime provoking distrust in the private sector because hundreds of millions of *Colones* have fled the country, thereby accentuating the economic crisis to the detriment of the popular classes);

   C. Knowing with certainty that each government in turn, likewise the products of scandalous electoral frauds, has adopted inadequate programs of development in which the timid changes in the structure have been blocked by the economic and political power of the conservative sectors which, at all times, have defended their ancestral privileges as the dominant classes, even endangering the socially conscientious capital of the country which has manifested its interest in achieving a just economic development for the population;

   D. Firmly convinced that the previous conditions are the fundamental cause of the economic and social chaos and of the violence the country is currently suffering, violence which can be overcome only with the arrival to power of a government that guarantees the operation of an authentically democratic regime;

   Therefore, the armed forces, whose members have always been identified with the people, decided, based on the right of revolt which all peoples possess when their government fails to carry out the law, to depose the government of General Carlos Humberto Romero and to replace it with a Revolutionary Junta of Government composed primarily of civilians whose absolute honesty and competence will be beyond all doubt. Said junta will assume the powers of state with the end of creating the conditions in our country which will allow all Salvadorans to have peace and to live in accord with the dignity of a human being.

While the conditions necessary to hold truly free elections, where the people can decide their future, are being established, it is of imperative necessity, in view of the chaotic political and social state in which the country lives, to adopt a Program of Emergency which will contain urgent measures intended to create a climate of tranquility and to establish the bases upon which the profound transformations of the economic, social, and political structures of the country will be sustained.

The features of this Program of Emergency are the following:

I. *Cease the violence and the corruption*
   A. Effectively dissolving ORDEN (*Organización Democrática Nacionalista*)[1] and combatting extremist organizations which, by their actions, violate human rights
   B. Eradicating corrupt practices in public administration and in the justice system

II. *Guarantee the existence of human rights*
   A. Creating the ambience propitious for achieving truly free elections within a reasonable time frame
   B. Permitting the formation of political parties of all ideologies in such a manner as to strengthen the democratic system
   C. Granting general amnesty to all political prisoners and to those in exile
   D. Recognizing and respecting the right of all labor sectors to organize
   E. Stimulating freedom of speech in accord with ethical norms

III. *Adopt measures which will lead to an equitable distribution of the national wealth, increasing, at the same time, in an accelerated fashion, the gross national product*
   A. Creating solid bases for initiating a process of agrarian reform
   B. Providing greater economic opportunities for the population through reforms in the financial, tax, and foreign commerce sectors of the country
   C. Adopting protective measures for the consumer in order to offset the effects of inflation
   D. Implementing special development programs whose goals will be to increase national production and to create additional sources of employment
   E. Recognizing and guaranteeing the rights of housing, food, education, and health for all the inhabitants of the country.
   F. Guaranteeing private property within a social function

IV. *Channel, in a positive fashion, the foreign relations of the country*
   A. Reestablishing relations with the sister country of Honduras in the shortest time possible

B. Strengthening ties with the sister people of Nicaragua and its government
C. Tightening the ties which unite us with the peoples and governments of the sister republics of Guatemala, Costa Rica, and Panama
D. Establishing cordial relations with all the countries of the world who are willing to support the struggles of our people and respect our sovereignty
E. Guaranteeing the fulfillment of standing international commitments

In order to obtain the accelerated accomplishment of these goals which the Salvadoran people are justly demanding, the Revolutionary Junta of Government will form a cabinet composed of honest and capable individuals, representatives of diverse sectors, who will put into play all their patriotism in the performance of such lofty functions.

In this moment of true national emergency, we are putting out a special call to the popular sectors and to socially conscious capital so that they can contribute to beginning a new era for El Salvador, an era characterized by the principles of peace and effective respect for the human rights of the entire citizenry.

Translated and reprinted from Lt. Col. Mariano Castro Morán, *Función Política del Ejército Salvadoreño en el presente Siglo*, UCA/Editores (San Salvador, 1984), appendix 14, pp. 412–15.

Note

1. ORDEN (Democratic Nationalist Organization) had been formed in the 1960s with government support to dispense patronage and provide intelligence on subversive activity to the state security apparatus. [ED.]

Guatemala

SPEECH BY COLONEL ENRIQUE PERALTA AZURDIA TO THE PEOPLE OF GUATEMALA
1963

My Fellow Citizens:

In accordance with the self-imposed rule I have always followed in the different posts with which I have been entrusted—the rule of keeping the citizenry informed of my actions—I come before you now to give a report on my four months as head of the government. Before that, however, I want to offer you a most cordial greeting on behalf of all the members of the army and to state that the armed forces, as a whole and in each of its parts, reaffirm the promises they made upon assuming the functions of the government.

I also want to tell you that all the commanders and officers of the army have been constantly informed about the activities of the government and that they are completely satisfied with how these activities have been carried out. Only in the feverish minds of the merchants of politics could enter the idea that the military is going to accept incorrect or dishonest suggestions. Each and every one of them have pledged their honor and their word to the fatherland and have promised that they will act to rescue it from crisis, a crisis which could have taken us only God knows where. Therefore, in the name of the army, which I have the honor to represent, I reaffirm its decision to maintain the current state of affairs until the country gets back on the correct course.

Economic Development

For the first time since the army assumed power, I am addressing all Guatemalans in order to explain the financial policies of the government over which I preside, as well as to explain other general aspects of transcendental importance for the country, both in the domestic and international realms.

One of the army's primary motives for taking over the government was the imperative necessity of rebuilding the shattered national economy, of restoring confidence to the production and labor sectors, and of managing public administration with honesty and efficiency. We are convinced that internal security and political reconciliation are insufficient to assure wellbeing for all Guatemalans. What is lacking is a vigorous action undertaken to foster the economic and social development of the country so that the fruits of progress and prosperity will be justly and equitably distributed among all the inhabitants.

Within the traditional socioeconomic organization of Guatemala, the state has the duty of fostering economic growth and social justice. This is not state socialism, nor a managed economy. It is, clearly and simply, a rational method of acting within the framework which the national and international realities of this century impose upon the evolution of peoples. If we want to avoid violent revolution, it is necessary that we understand our historic responsibility and that we make every effort to offer constructive solutions by means of a socially oriented capitalism.

Operation Honesty

This preamble has been necessary for the Guatemalan people to understand why our government actions have emphasized "Operation Honesty" (the brake on the flight of capital), fiscal equilibrium, and tax reform. Before acting, the government carefully considered the implications of those politico-financial measures, and it is convinced that all of them will contribute to the objective of creating conditions of stability and strength in the national economy based upon a healthy and efficient public administration.

With "Operation Honesty," the government proposes to restore to the coffers of the nation all that has been removed by illicit or fraudulent means, as well as to eradicate those practices which in recent times have totally undermined administrative management. The first actions of this operation have produced edifying results, and we intend to pursue them with determination to the end.

New Fiscal Policy

With the control of currency exchange operations, designed to impede the flight of capital, the government has attempted to stop a national decapitalization of huge proportions. The sacrifice represented by these exchange controls has been imposed in order to strengthen the national economy. This is the reason the government has supported the monetary officials in the exchange regulation. The improvement of Guatemala's foreign commerce during the present year makes us confident that a return to a normal currency exchange system will not be long in coming.

With respect to this, I want to make it clear that the current belief that the banks are dictating the financial policies of Guatemala is completely erroneous. Neither the banks nor public or private sectors are imposing their policies on the government. We are perfectly capable of recognizing when a sector is acting on behalf of the country's interests and when it is acting out of self-interest. The ministers who make up the cabinet have always been willing to discuss any differences in round-table discussions and in public, thereby allowing the people of Guatemala to be the judge. If this has not yet taken place, it is because certain sectors have not accepted our invitation.

With the new fiscal policies initiated the first of July, we have faced squarely the grave decline which the public finances have been suffering for the past five years. The government recently informed the Guatemalan people that the fiscal deficit accumulated over the last five years had risen to the impressive sum of 51 million *Quetzales* [the Guatemalan currency] and that the public debt had reached 88 million *Quetzales*. Faced with the alternatives of either continuing to increase national indebtedness or closing the gap between current public income and expenditures, the government opted to increase some taxes and to create others. It is also worth noting that in the creation of new taxes, several activities which have never paid one cent of taxes have now been included. The continuation of deficit spending policies would have meant a reduction in public investment and the creation of an ever greater burden for future governments.

It is necessary to make it perfectly clear that the increase in taxes does not have as its aim an increase in administrative and bureaucratic expenditures. On the contrary, the government has adopted a strict policy of austerity in its regular expenditures to the end of increasing the allocations for social and cultural programs and augmenting public investments in highways, communications, electrification, housing, rural development, irrigation, etc. With the new income from taxes, it will be possible to balance the 1963–64 budget.

The imposition of an income tax constitutes the basis of a tax reform and will help to correct the inequalities inherent in an anachronistic system of indirect taxes. It is false that an income tax is a socialist policy prejudicial to private investment. On the contrary, the income tax is a determinative instrument in the evolution of modern capitalism. Guatemala is one of the last countries of the Western world to have adopted this tax system. Its implications will be translated not only into a primary source of fiscal revenues, but also as a mechanism for redistributing fairly the incomes of Guatemalans and for developing a stable and healthy economy. . . .

Confidence in Guatemala

The measures adopted are a response to the imperative necessity of rehabilitating public finance, of improving the administration, and of putting the country on the road to stability and strength.

The government expects the nation's industrialists and merchants to abstain from raising prices in the marketplace; seeing the contrary, the government will feel obliged to issue drastic laws to prevent it, because there exists no justification for such action.

The honest and determined stance of the present government has been received favorably in the exterior, which will benefit the general population as much as the capitalist sectors. Such a stance is already reestablishing confidence in Guatemala and will attract the investments necessary for our economic development, which in turn will propitiate a new, healthy, and durable political regime.

In the course of the present century, there have been in our fatherland various sociopolitical movements of a reformist nature, but the regimes which emerged from those movements either have been ephemeral or have quickly degenerated and fallen into the same vices. During the last epoch, there was much speculation about different doctrines, but the condition of the population has not substantially altered. In the last five years, a pseudodemocracy was established which was characterized by disorder, insecurity, and corruption. The army felt obliged to assume power in the midst of precarious economic conditions and a grave fiscal situation; conscious of its historic responsibility, it did so to save Guatemala from a dismal future.

Under the appearance of relative progress, we have actually gone backward with regard to the solution of fundamental problems. The percentage of illiterates has been increasing, and the economic growth of the country has lost ground relative to the increase in population. At this rate, we will arrive at the twenty-first century internationally insolvent and with our very existence threatened.

Administrative Integrity

We have rescued public power from the hands of thieves and have warded off the communist threat. It is necessary now to work to establish solid foundations for the future, because otherwise we will continue to be threatened by Marxism. Two things are needed for this: honest and capable governments which concentrate their energies on the general well-being, and the decided collaboration of the citizenry. The problems of the republic are too grave for the leadership to waste its time on *politiquería* and trivialities or for the well-off classes to resist a few sacrifices.

These classes should understand that the only way to achieve a just and permanent equilibrium is to solve the problems of the population. Otherwise, the efforts of the army will be frustrated and Guatemala will again be at the mercy of negative and destructive forces.

We are adopting the measures necessary for achieving national recovery; we are strengthening the systems of security in order to liberate the inhabitants from the anxiety created by the increase in criminality and the appearance of new types of delinquency; we will continue with the works pending and will initiate others of general utility in order to alleviate the imperative necessities of the people and the situation of the greatest number of pensioners; we will support private initiative and will stimulate capital investments which contribute to economic development and open new sources of jobs; we will support the social conquests and will watch over the interests of the country's inhabitants; and, if everyone, particularly the rich and powerful, gives us their dedicated cooperation, we will have established the basis for an austere, evolutionary, and dynamic regime which will develop the resources of the nation until achieving just standards of living and an economic potentiality that will allow us to resolve thoroughly Guatemala's transcendental social problems.

Politicians, resentful and unsuccessful in their personal ambitions, have taken on the task of spreading a rumor that a plebiscite will be called to perpetuate our power. I can assure you that this is absolutely false and that it is completely opposed to our intent. We will remain in power only long enough to redirect the republic on the basis of order, security, and confidence, so that the people, in exercising their sovereign will, can elect an honest and capable government which will lead the nation with dignity along the road of progress and social justice. . . .

Security and Order

We feel a profound sense of respect for all institutions, public and private, and we recognize and will protect the fundamental rights of man. But this does not mean that disrespect for either authority or disorder will be tolerated, or that demagogues and criminals will enjoy leniency. Security and order are indispensable conditions for the realization of values and for economic and social evolution. Those who disturb the public order will be energetically repressed, and those who attack the security of personnel, property, or institutions of the state will be severely punished. We will be relentless toward both international agitators and those who act under foreign signs. Those who would attempt to take Guatemala into communism will be trampled without pity.

We are living at a decisive moment. We have to rescue our sons from a tragic destiny. It is worth making some sacrifices. We, the military and the civilians who assist us in governing, have pledged our honor and our lives to this goal.

Translated, reprinted, and edited from *Mensaje del Jefe De Gobierno Coronel Enrique Peralta Azurdia al pueblo de Guatemala* (Guatemala City: Publicaciones de la Secretaría de Información, 1963), pp. 1–11.

SPEECH BY CARLOS MANUEL ARANA OSORIO
1974

On a day like yesterday, four years ago, I received from the people of Guatemala the mandate to assume the Presidency of the Republic, and the electors, as much as I, are aware of the reasons why I was elected.

In that period, the country was dominated by political terrorism, and we were threatened with the danger that our democratic system might be destroyed by armed violence from the extreme left. Many homes still weep for their dead, and in the eastern part of the country, the tombs of sacrificed peasants still burn with pain. It would be desirable for many Guatemalans to undertake a retrospective analysis of what occurred then, in order to better appreciate the changes operating in this new Guatemala, free of fear and uncertainty.

The express mandate which the people conferred on me was to end that tragedy and that danger.

In my presidential acceptance speech, I warned that peace in our country was not then, nor is it today, a simple problem of repressing the subversive activity of the extreme left. I also stated that it is indispensable to go to the root causes. Thus it is necessary, at the same time, to know how to differentiate between the armed activity through which communist organizations intend to achieve power and the conditions which move the poorest and most forsaken people to a desire for violent changes and to a clear attack on the institutions.

Interpreting the country's realities thusly, as president, I have fulfilled the mission with which you entrusted me, confronting the violence as much in its illicit armed forms of ideological expression as in the social and economic conditions which enable subversion to flourish.

These have been four difficult and complex years. The national problems which accumulated over such a long time became much more acute due both to the growing population and to our inadequate resources. Such resources were gravely affected by the pressures and consequences exercised over us by the international situation.

In our time, there is not one country, big or small, powerful or weak, developed or underdeveloped, that is not affected by world events. Guatemala's principal markets are the United States, Japan, Germany, and others in the European region; these transfer to our nation all the positive and negative aspects which their economies possess. It is a commonly known fact that our age, more than any other, is characterized by an economy of intense and continuous relationships, of reciprocal actions and interactions. He who tries to deny this is deliberately lying, whether he has a doctorate in economics or lacks even the ability to occupy the most modest post of constable in the smallest village.

During the last three years, three world economic events occurred which led to repercussions in every country and which produced an inflationary process affecting Guatemala. The first was the devaluation of the dollar, which declined 8 percent in 1971, and 10 percent in February 1973. Among other consequences, this forced the revaluation of the Japanese yen, which drove up the prices of those items we import from Japan.

In 1972, the United States sold practically all of its wheat reserves to Russia. Following this sale, there was a worldwide drought which produced an increase in the price of wheat and all other grains. As a result, there was an increase in the price of concentrated foods which are used to feed the livestock whose meat feeds human beings. The consequence was that Guatemala's imports of grains and concentrated foods cost much more.

The third event took place in November 1973, when the Arab-Israeli War precipitated the oil crisis, resulting in price increases which have continued until today, with derivative price increases for all other products.

Nevertheless, the effects of the international economic situation have been smaller and less grave in Guatemala than in countries of comparable development. Despite this, however, my government has been irresponsibly and demagogically criticized and selfishly attacked by politicians of the opposition, attacked demagogically, irresponsibly, and out of self-interest because to a greater or lesser degree, in one way or another, the leaders of the opposition have participated in the government of the republic and in my own government.

As is well known, the principal local leader of the Christian Democratic Party asked for, and received, the support of my government, and his political conduct was, until very recently, one of complete solidarity with the president of the republic. Numerous events and activities of said party were carried out in consultation with the president, which means that Christian Democracy lacks the moral authority to censure the government. Until very recently, I repeat, it acted in consultation with my government, which it considered to be "very good," "excellent." Thus, the change in its way of thinking is nothing more than a matter of momentary, electoral convenience.

On the other hand, the presidential candidate of the opposition served in the current government for three important years, performing delicate functions. During that entire time, he was never heard to make any observation or criticism. But now, now that he has joined the opposition, it turns out that "there are no liberties" and that all of his ex-colleagues in the government are "bad," he being a strange exception, in accord, of course, with his own opinion.

I appeal to your conscience and good judgment, my beloved compatriots, to answer and judge such serpentine conduct.

The same is true of the mayor of Guatemala City, who also spoke recently of the errors of the government. Not even two years ago, this same government provided the guarantees necessary to obtain domestic and foreign loans for the municipality. I authorized those guarantees because the funds were designated for service works for the residents and because what interests me is the well-being of all citizens regardless of their political affiliation.

Now it turns out that he thinks in a manner distinct from the government and that he speaks in a manner quite distinct from the way he spoke to me in private. But I ask: Why does the mayor see straw in another's eye and not the wooden beam in his own? And I also ask: Where are the projects that should have been completed with the funds which the government authorized?

This, then, is the position of my opposition.

In the face of this, I ask all of you who live in the interior of the country: Do you accept as just those attacks by the opposition?

I know that you are answering with a resounding NO, because in each village, in each town, in each city, and in the entire country, there are thousands of Guatemalans who are being helped by my government's projects; there are thousands of families who now have what they never knew existed; there are millions of inhabitants who are receiving the benefits of our works.

As all the people know, I am just a simple and sincere man. I can assure you that, with your support and with the support of the reality, about which no one can lie, in the past years we have carried out physical and social works without precedent in the history of the country.

But if this is not believed, there are the works. They are in full view of everyone. They are at the service of the population of the entire country.

And if that is not sufficient, all Guatemalans know that I have been the only president who, before handing over power, has personally visited each department to verify that the works promised have been carried out; and I have verified that they have been carried out, and the inhabitants of every village know it.

Instead of closing myself up in the National Palace and only superficially seeing the problems and needs of the people, I have traveled to the most distant villages and attended to the popular needs in those places; without sparing any effort, I flew by plane and by helicopter; I rode in vehicles and on mules; I walked on foot by day and night. And I returned some time later to confirm that the projects had been carried out. Those works are there, all over the country, and only political passion or political maliciousness or political lies can deny them.

Because of this, and because I am seriously worried about what the future life of Guatemala might be, I come before you tonight to solicit your greatest serenity and your firmest maturity in electing the new government this Sunday; may your decision be the best for the national interest.

I am also worried about the threat of a socialist regime because it will destroy not only our democratic institutions, but also everything that the people, through me, have built for their well-being.

A National Plan of Development is in process; numerous public works projects and health and education programs are under way; valuable plans are being developed which will bear positive results. But the moment is approaching when we Guatemalans must elect a new government.

Elections constitute the most important characteristic of democracy. The vote is the means through which the people express their sovereign will, and through the vote, political differences are resolved; civic ideals are manifested in the vote, and only through the vote should a new government be created.

As your president, I ask each and every one of the registered voters to go to the polls and exercise the constitutional right of suffrage. I ask all of them, without any discrimination, to vote to elect the government which they believe should govern Guatemala.

I further ask that those determined, responsible citizens who are of clear conscience reject violence and the insolent demagogues of second-class politics and that they vote for the candidates who will guarantee the maintenance of our democracy.

The government will not play games or tricks of any type to pervert the suffrage, nor will it allow any candidate to claim victory until he has been so declared officially by the proper authorities, after receiving the vote totals from the entire republic.

As your president, I ask you to vote for the candidates who promise to ccntinue the work I have carried out. It would be extremely serious for Guatemala if a government was elected which paralyzed or postponed that which we have achieved.

In my capacity as a citizen, I ask my friends, my followers, and also all those who have benefited from my government, to vote for General Kjell Eugenio Laugerud García. And I want to explain clearly and sincerely why I ask you to vote for General Laugerud.

The world in which we live is divided into two political and economic systems: that of socialism and that of democracy. In spite of its faults, the democratic system is the best system of life known today because it is based upon the principles and the objectives for which man has fought since his origin.

Those principles and objectives can be summarized as follows: that every human being has natural rights to liberty, justice, and the opportunity to progress; that he is equal before the law; that the sum of the wills expresses sovereignty; that sovereignty comes from the people; and, that the State should act with the primordial goal of guaranteeing the inhabitants of a nation the natural rights of man, as well as economic well-being, social justice, and peace.

Within the democratic system there exists private property. The family also exists and it should be protected. Intellectual freedom prevails over the dogmas which the State seeks to impose. And, in sum, education, health, and the physical well-being of the inhabitants are not the privileges of a minority, but rights common to all. Finally, the people govern through their representatives, who are elected by the vote.

But democracy has faults, imperfections, and injustices. There is a great deal of poverty, with many illiterates and many sick bodies, and the needy and indigent do not always receive help. In this are to be found the beginnings of groups who propose changes in the institutions. And such groups are then divided among those who seek the progress of the nation through means of violent revolution and those who promote it, develop it, and carry it out through peaceful means.

Guatemala needs peaceful and progressive changes, but it must reject violent changes.

An officer of excellent orientation within the army, a man formed within rigid moral norms, a military commander of great professional virtues, General Laugerud represents the new spirit of the military, as does his clear and unequivocal conviction that our institutions must be reformed.

As a citizen, I ask that you vote for General Laugerud because he will know how to put into practice the principle that the security of the country, its physical and moral progress, as well as its development and social peace, depend upon popular satisfaction.

Popular satisfaction is the product of better justice in the distribution of the riches which the nation can produce. Popular satisfaction is the result of greater equity in the protection of the inhabitants, as much in the areas of health and education as in the opportunities to rise economically, participate in the culture, and guarantee moral values.

I know, I am sure, that General Laugerud has the intellectual capacity, the honesty, the probity, and the determination to stimulate the progress of the country.

I also know that, because of his maturity and his sensitivity, he will lead the government with firmness and with justice, moving toward the realization of the ideal which he calls: "to create well-being for those who do not have it without taking it away from those who do."

I ask, therefore, that you vote for General Laugerud. I ask this because I am sure that he will be the desirable and able governor which Guatemala needs for the upcoming years.

Good night, and may God protect Guatemala and enlighten you to vote this Sunday.

Translated and reprinted from *El Imparcial* (Guatemala City), March 2, 1974.

SPEECH BY GENERAL JOSÉ EFRAÍN RÍOS MONTT
1982

My fellow citizens, in the name of the armed forces, I want to present to you my most cordial greeting and my gratitude for the opportunity you are giving me to enter your homes.

Today, the officer corps of the army, wishing to show its professional spirit, desiring to reintegrate itself within the dignity of a people, and attempting to revive our values, carried out a military movement, over which, by chance, I preside. I preside with a government junta, a government junta which I want to introduce at this time; General Maldonado and Colonel Gordillo are here.

We three make up a junta which is drawing up a political program to present to the Guatemalan people a solution, a reality, a plan of action—a solution to this incomprehensible mode of life we have had from a political point of view and a reality, we are soldiers; in my capacity as general, I have the capability, the responsibility, to act from a political point of view, not for *politiquería* which everyone confounds with politics, but rather in my capacity as general within a strategic concept. Strategy, my fellow citizens, is the origin of every political task, and within that strategy is a policy of security, a policy of defense, an economic policy, a social policy, and a foreign policy.

Therefore, within those parameters, we are going to present to you a program of work; I only wanted to take advantage of this opportunity to tell you, my fellow citizens, that the people of Guatemala are celebrating and that we, the soldiers, full of rejoicing and enthusiasm, are pledging our word to provide political solutions to the political problems, economic solutions to the economic problems, and social solutions to the great social problems which we face.

My fellow citizens, you will understand that in a military movement, a capability is demonstrated, a dignity is demonstrated, but fundamentally, there is a maximum degree of morality. I want to tell you, fellow citizens, that, in the first place, I am trusting in God, my Lord, my King, that he may enlighten me because only He gives and only He takes away authority. I am trusting in my God so that I will not defraud the officer corps or, less yet, a people, a people which has not been respected, a people which has been insulted.

Eight years ago I was deceived; four years ago they deceived us; and now, just a few days ago, they deceived us again. Guatemalans, we are both conscious and convinced that the army is not just the soldiers who wear a uniform, but that all you citizens have the obligation and the responsibility to walk arm in arm with us toward a more tranquil future. I trust that God Our Lord will spread His mantle of mercy on Guatemala; I trust that God Our Lord will enlighten us; and I trust that God Our Lord will permit that you and we can give a new pause to the political business of the nation.

There are many doubts, and in the judgment of you citizens, there are many more; among all of us there is a great deal of concern, but there is also a great deal of seriousness and responsibility.

We want to tell you, fellow citizens, that responsible to you and responsible to our God who will judge us and, above all, responsible to the younger officers who want to rid themselves of the millstone of manipulative commanders, before all of you, we promise fidelity. What we need is that you comprehend and understand that you should help us. We are not suspending any individual rights; we are guaranteeing human rights, but, please, let us make of liberty the expression of responsibility; let us make of liberty a way of life; let us make liberty a citizen task.

At this moment, the political parties have nothing to do. We are going to present them with a declaration, and we are going to see if they are true political parties, because they have been only electoral political parties, not political parties which offer political solutions to a people needing political solutions. For that reason, fellow citizens, we want your comprehension, we want your support, because really, if we do not have your support, the armed forces will have to come out to repair Guatemala. And, hear me well, the subversion cannot continue. The political task is going to be carried out, and it will be done from a political point of view. Arms are only for the army; arms are only for the army. Please, all you civilians who are armed, take your machine guns down from your roofs and surrender them; take the pistols from your belts and replace them with machetes for work. We need work, we need responsibility, we need honorableness.

There is a challenge to Guatemala and we accept that challenge; there is no one who can touch us. We will build a country; we will build a nation; but we will build a country and a nation in which the population is integrated, a territorial reality which should demonstrate humility and identify itself with ideas and ideals, for us, God, and Guatemala, and for you, God, and Guatemala, because only thusly can we work hand in hand for Guatemala.

I want to thank you very much for the opportunity you have given me, and again be reassured, fellow citizens, that the Army of Guatemala, through me, pledges its word of honor, its word as professional soldiers, that it will make every effort possible, even dying, to benefit the political situation of the fatherland. We do not want any more *politiqueros;* we do not want the same faces; we do not want them to come and congratulate us. Do not even come near us. We are professional soldiers, and we are in a political and social position to guarantee you Guatemalans a future within the framework of peace, tranquility, and justice.

Please, you men of subversion, take note of the following: Only the Army of Guatemala should have arms; give up your arms because if you do not, then we will take them away. And, listen well, you will not be found murdered alongside the road; anyone who breaks the law will be shot, but not murdered. We want to respect human rights, because exercising those is the only means of learning to live democratically. For that reason, I would ask you, in the first place, to pray to God, Our Savior, to allow us to continue developing in peace the program we are going to present to you, and, in the second place, for your collaboration, your tranquility, and your peace. The peace of Guatemala does not depend upon armed actions; the peace of Guatemala depends upon you the men, you the women, you the children. Yes, the peace of Guatemala is in your hearts, and once there is peace in your hearts, there will be peace in your homes and peace in the society. Please, no more drinks, no more anything, Work, Guatemala needs work, because if there are no sources of labor, there is no confidence and no authority, and there was none of these before.

Today, with morality, Guatemalans, we state to you, before God, that we pledge the word of the armed forces to guarantee you peace, work, and security.

Translated and reprinted from *Mensajes del Presidente de la República General José Efraín Ríos Montt* (Tipografía Nacional de Guatemala, 1982), pp. 9–10.

SPEECH BY GENERAL OSCAR HUMBERTO MEJÍA VICTORES 1986

To the People of Guatemala:

May the first words of the last message that I deliver to the nation in my capacity as head of state be a cordial and respectful greeting to the high dignitaries from friendly countries who, honoring us with their presence, share with us these transcendental and historic moments in the political life of Guatemala.

Two and one-half years ago, on August 8, 1983, at the decision of the Army of Guatemala, I assumed the position of chief of state, determined to rechannel and strengthen the process of political liberalization which our institution was encouraging.

I accepted the responsibility which was entrusted to me with the firm conviction that the country needed to return to institutional democracy. In name and representation of the Army of Guatemala, I committed myself to generating a process of national reconciliation which would permit Guatemalans to express themselves freely within the framework of an authentically democratic and pluralistic system.

We established as priority goals the return to constitutional government, the pacification of the country, and the elevation of Guatemala anew to the position she deserves in the international community. Concomitantly, we committed ourselves to confronting, within the limits of our possibilities, the grave economic and social crisis which profoundly affected our country. The task of realizing that was difficult and complex, but we undertook it and finalized it with the assistance of distinct social, economic, and political sectors of the country.

The people and the government responded to the challenge which the circumstances raised, and although we must recognize that, above all in the economic and social arenas, we were not able to achieve all the results desired. I can affirm today, in this solemn ceremony, that the pledge I made as a soldier, the pledge of the Army of Guatemala, has been fulfilled.

It is pertinent, on this occasion, to refer in general terms to some of the principal problems which affected Guatemala when we received the government, as well as to the way in which we resolved them. A climate of uncertainty existed at that time, and the people of Guatemala found themselves confused, disoriented, and frustrated in political matters. Above all, the timetable for return to constitutionality was uncertain, and there also existed—and why not point it out—a profound crisis of credibility and confidence. Faced with that situation, we adopted the measures we believed most adequate to restore to Guatemalans faith in their institutions. We lifted the State of Siege which restricted both the free expression of beliefs and the political and labor rights of the citizenry.

The so-called Tribunals of Special Jurisdiction were abolished, and a broad and generous Amnesty Law was issued so that all of those compatriots who had, in one form or another, participated in or collaborated with the terrorist, subversive groups could rejoin their communities of origin and dedicate themselves to their normal occupations. The Supreme Electoral Tribunal was established and given all the support it required. Apropos to this, the corresponding legal measures were issued, and, simultaneously, we initiated a process of frank and sincere consultation with the leadership of all the political parties, as well as with those committees in the process of forming parties and registering them. We listened to their proposals, we analyzed them, and in common accord, we established the stages of the democratization process.

Elections were called to form a National Constituyent Assembly, and I can affirm with deep satisfaction that the Guatemalan people responded as never before, gathering to vote in unprecedented numbers to elect their representatives who would write the new Constitution of the Republic. The results of those elections were respected, and for the first time in a long time, there was no opposition whatsoever to any of the participating political parties. After arduous labor, the National Constituyent Assembly promulgated the Political Constitution of the Republic of Guatemala, which will go into complete effect after this day.

Our Magna Carta, which all Guatemalans should respect and obey, contains norms which guarantee the functioning of a modern state with emphasis on the separation of powers and the protection of human rights.

When we convoked general elections for president, vice president, deputies to the Congress of the Republic, and municipal councils, we reaffirmed the absolute neutrality of the government and we offered to guarantee free and honest elections. Last November 3, the people of Guatemala again went to the polls in an orderly and exemplary fashion. Since none of the presidential candidates obtained an absolute majority of votes, however, we resorted to a system novel in our country, a second round of elections which, fortunately, took place on December 8. These last two elections, just as with the first one, occurred with observers from various countries and international organizations present. We are extremely pleased that all of them, without exception, including the international press, recognized that the elections were impeccably honest.

On another matter, I also ought to mention that we succeeded in pacifying those areas dominated by conflict. With particular vigor, we actuated development programs for rural communities, and the system of inter-institutional coordination functioned efficiently.

I point with particular satisfaction to the foreign policy of my government. In the past, for reasons of a distinct nature, the prestige of Guatemala had been adversely affected, and she found herself virtually isolated from the international community. From the outset of our administration, we established a clear and precise policy of respect for the fundamental principles of international law. With regard to the crisis in our region, we adopted a considered, balanced, and constructive attitude, convinced that we Central Americans should find politico-diplomatic solutions to resolve our differences.

We recognize that the problems are extremely serious and complex, but we are convinced that they can be confronted if we act in good faith and demonstrate an authentic political will to find formulas of conciliation that will assure the peace.

We have firmly supported the efforts of the Contadora Group, and this is a propitious moment to thank Colombia, Mexico, Panama, and Venezuela for their tireless work over the past three years. I also want to recognize the Support Group of Contadora and the member nations of the European Economic Community for their contribution in this area.

We have acted with independence, dignity, responsibility, and realism, and we have restored to the word *sovereignty* its true meaning and dimension. With legitimate pride, I can say that now we are listened to and respected.

Guatemala, like other sister countries of Latin America, has been affected by an acute economic crisis of both internal and external origin. Within the limits of our possibilities, we tried to adopt policies which, on the one hand, contributed to alleviating the social problems and, on the other, contributed to the reactivization of our economy. We sponsored a great national dialogue with the distinct representative sectors of the country, with whom the situation was analyzed with a positive attitude and with a great deal of objectivity.

All of them cooperated and suggested distinct alternatives for overcoming the crisis. In this area, there is a long way to go, but I repeat that it is imperative that there be efforts and sacrifices from everyone; at the same time, we must ensure that the interests of a few do not prevail over those of the majority. In spite of all the obstacles, a certain economic stability has been achieved, and the outlook for the prices of our principal export products allows us to predict better times ahead. Regarding the work of my government, I have provided details in the Record of Works which has been placed in the hands of the National Congress.

Mr. President, Mr. Vice President, Members of Congress, People of Guatemala: Upon completing this message, I want to state publicly my respect for and appreciation to the Supreme Electoral Tribunal, to the National Constituent Assembly, and to the Supreme Court, who have completed, with great ability, the delicate task entrusted to them. Furthermore, I want to express my personal appreciation to my cabinet, to my collaborators, and, above all, to the Army of Guatemala for its loyalty and esprit de corps. I leave with the tranquility produced by having done my duty, and I exhort all Guatemalans to defend the peace and democracy that has cost us so much to win, and to work and act with responsibility in order to achieve those great national objectives. And, in offering my very best wishes for the success of the new government, I reaffirm that we should look to the future with faith and confidence, emphasizing positive over the negative. May everything be well with our beloved fatherland, Guatemala.

Translated and reprinted from a government press release of the Secretaría de Relaciones Públicas, Presidencia de la República, 1986.

6   The Consequences of Military Rule

Policies and Consequences of Military Rule in Latin America

The antipolitical military governments which emerged after 1964 defined for themselves immediate *defensive* missions to rescue their nations from the threat of subversion and chaos. They also identified a range of economic and social objectives to wrest their countries from the verge of economic collapse. In the short term, the military leadership vowed to defeat subversion, prevent a collapse of the institutional order, overcome economic crisis, and prevent the political victory of Marxist groups in their respective societies. In some cases, for example, Argentina, Guatemala, or El Salvador, ongoing urban and rural guerrilla warfare confronted the armed forces with identifiable military targets as well as a political threat. In other cases, for example, Brazil in 1964 or Chile in 1973, populist policies of incumbent governments and direct threats to military discipline by reformist or socialist politicians led to military coups, though no significant internal *military* threat by opposition movements existed.

The defensive aspects of the military programs implied severe repression of political organizations and social movements, suppression of civil liberties and civil rights, and radical transformation of previous political practices. The level of repression corresponded, to some extent, to the military leaders' perceptions of the severity of the populist or revolutionary threat facing their respective nations. In countries where revolutionary guerrilla movements or political violence preceded the military interventions, for example, Guatemala, El Salvador (1972), Argentina (1976), Bolivia (1971), or Uruguay (1971–73), extensive brutalization of opposition leadership and systematic persecution, torture, and assassination became routine instruments of military rule. This also occurred where high levels of popular mobilization or threats by populist governments to military discipline and the prevailing socioeconomic order precipitated military action, such as in Brazil (1964), Bolivia (1971), and Chile (1973). Even when preintervention political mobilization was limited, as in Peru

(1968), or Bolivia (1964), the new military regimes moved quickly to restrict the activities of labor, student, and religious organizations and to limit, suspend, or outlaw the activities of political parties. They also curtailed civil liberties and sought to control the content of the mass media through censoring or closing the opposition press.

The defensive projects of the antipolitical regimes also entailed adoption of new, but ostensibly temporary, decrees or "institutional acts" to serve as the "legal" basis for the military governments. These measures, sometimes dignified as amendments to previous constitutions, varied in language but shared in practice a focus on centralizing authority in the executive branch, and limiting or eliminating the role of traditional legislative and judicial institutions. The emergency measures also provided almost unlimited legal discretion for the government to defend the nation against threats to internal security. The new military leaders based some of their actions on the authority of existing constitutional provisions for states of constitutional exception, for example, state of siege, civil war, or threats to internal security. In most cases, even where existing constitutions provided plausible legal foundations for military action, the new governments also adopted "institutional acts," "revolutionary statutes," or "constitutional acts" to provide the appearance of a legal basis for government action. Nowhere did the military regimes neglect to create *some* immediate, formal rationale for repression and for other regime initiatives. In some cases, the military utilized periodic elections (Guatemala, Brazil, El Salvador) or plebiscites (Chile, Uruguay) in efforts to "legitimize" governments, policies, or new constitutions.

With time, these temporary measures became the foundations of the new institutionality which the military elites and their civilian allies sought to impose after the initial defensive mission was achieved. In no case, however, did these efforts to establish new political institutions and practices survive the eventual demise of military rule. By the end of 1986, only Chile remained subject to the broad constitutional and legislative institutions imposed by the authoritarian regime—though significant remnants of the military government's innovations persisted in Argentina, Bolivia, Brazil, El Salvador, Guatemala, and Peru.

In the social and economic sphere, all the military leadership groups which came to power in the 1960s and 1970s promised to promote economic growth and to overcome the obstacles to economic development which had impeded progress in the region for centuries. Uniformly blaming the plight of their nations on the demagogy, corruption, venality, and incompetence of their civilian predecessors, the military antipoliticians adopted a wide range of economic projects and policies. The diversity of economic programs corresponded to the unique economic problems and resources of an emergent international economic power like Brazil, the impoverished and less developed economies of Peru, Bolivia, El Salvador, or Guatemala, or the more industrialized and complex societies of Chile and Argentina. These economic projects ranged from an emphasis on expansion of the role of the public sector and massive government investments in Brazil, to Chile's post-1973 experiment with the most radical neoliberal program of "privatization" of economic activity and reduction of the role of the public sector ever experienced in Latin America. Neoliberal policies emphasized economic stabilization through monetary controls to decrease growth in money supply, restrictions on credit, reduction of government expenditures and the role of the public sector, and varying degrees of privatization of provision of social services. In addition, neoliberal policies encouraged transfer of public enterprises to the private sector and attraction of foreign investment to stimulate the local economy.

The stabilization programs typically relied upon wage restraints and relaxation of price regulations, which led frequently to real income declines for workers, small farmers, and the growing numbers of unemployed and underemployed. Reductions in public services made health care, educational opportunities, social services, and housing less accessible to the majority of the population. In some cases, university enrollments declined markedly along with the decreasing opportunities in technical and vocational institutions.

Trade policies under neoliberal approaches focused on an economic opening for freer commerce through reduction or elimination of protective tariffs. These measures were adopted to encourage increased efficiency of domestic firms and to reduce the price of imported consumption goods and products used as inputs in local industry and agriculture. Some of the military governments also encouraged foreign investment to spur economic growth. Only in Chile, however, was a more or less "pure" neoliberal approach tested for a period of time; elsewhere, parts or almost all of this model was rejected. For example, the Brazilian and Peruvian military regimes expanded public investments and state enterprises in key economic sectors. They also adopted protective tariffs and exchange controls to shelter domestic industries from foreign competition. Likewise in Argentina, some hesitancy by the military rulers and their civilian advisers to allow massive competition with domestic firms somewhat insulated Argentine producers in comparison with their Chilean counterparts. Despite some movement toward privatization and a rhetoric emphasizing the role of the market in economic policy, the Argentine military regime expanded the role of state enterprises in the economy.

Whatever the *specific* array of economic policies adopted, however, the new military regimes viewed economic modernization and economic growth as an extension of the military mission itself to provide for national security. Economic development and national security were viewed as inseparable. This was made clear in military professional journals, in public policy declarations, and in the considerable attention given to economic issues in military academies and institutions. It was also made clear in the dramatic economic innovations, of all sorts, introduced by military presidents and their civilian technocratic collaborators.

In most cases, important differences existed within the military leadership over the content of economic policy, as well as over the overall character of the new political institutionality to be created. Nevertheless, whether the new policies favored expansion of the public sector and an interventionist state role or an array of neoliberal measures to spur growth and stabilization, in part through reducing the role and size of the public sector, agreement existed that responsibility for directing the economic and social transformation of their nations had passed from the old political class to the military saviours. This occurred very early in El Salvador (perhaps as early as the government of Colonel Osorio in the early 1950s), in the 1960s in Bolivia, Brazil, Peru, and Guatemala, and somewhat later in Uruguay and Chile.

In addition to the short-term defensive projects and the commitment to economic modernization, the military elites gradually defined their intentions to create a new political institutionality to replace the defective democratic systems of the past. According to the military leadership, the old political institutions and practices gave rise to corruption, failed to solve pressing national problems, and allowed the advance of subversive, antinationalistic forces within these nations. The rejection of the old institutions brought forth in their place a variety of antipolitical projects labeled everything from "reorganization of the nation" by General Videla in Argentina, to "constitutionalization" by General Banzer in Bolivia, to "authoritarian democracy" by General Pinochet in Chile. In Brazil and Guatemala, military governments even utilized manipulated elections and the facade of parliamentary institutions to avoid a total departure from the old legitimacy—while adopting new "constitutional" or "institutional" acts that in practice made a tragic mockery of democratic institutions.

Whatever the name given to the new political projects and whatever their detail from country to country, they all proscribed political participation for "subversive" groups and outlawed political movements proclaiming "subversive" ideologies. They all gave to the State a tutorial role in defining and achieving the common interest for a society viewed as an organic community. The new institutionality proposed by the military governments typically introduced exclusionary and demobilizational measures to restrict or prohibit participation by designated political and social forces and to outlaw certain ideological visions of society—especially those of Marxism.

Universally critical of the defects of pluralist liberal democracy, the military regimes sought to eliminate mobilizational politics and autonomous groups which opposed the new economic and political order. In certain cases, for example, Peru, this even included a frontal assault on wealthy landowners, industrialists, and the conservative mass media. In most cases, the left and center of the political spectrum—party, labor, student, and mass organizations—bore the brunt of antipolitics.

A common innovation in these projects, which represented in many respects a reaffirmation of traditional Hispanic visions of politics and society updated to respond to the realities and challenges of more complex industrializing societies, was the reemphasis on the key role of the State in shaping or directing the society and economy, and the new emphasis on the central role of military institutions in controlling, staffing, and managing the State apparatus. Military leaders justified these innovations by noting the historical failure of civilian politicians and the liberal democratic State to provide political order and social harmony, and their failure to orchestrate the economic modernization requisite for development and national security. That is, previous governments had failed to utilize the State, either directly or indirectly, to advance the common welfare—the fundamental purpose of political authority in the philosophical tradition of Hispanic America.

This militarization of the State went further in some cases than in others, but it invariably placed military officers, both active duty and retired, in key policy-making positions in local government, in public enterprises, and in posts in the public administration previously occupied almost exclusively by civilians. In some countries, educational institutions from the primary level to the universities were assigned military directors and the faculties purged of "subversives." In other cases, military administrators even took over the day-to-day direction of farms and plantations, mines, and industrial enterprises. Of course, in every case, civilian advisers, technicians, and supporters collaborated with the military administration's efforts to create a new political system and to respond to the socioeconomic crises confronting these nations.

These changes in political systems and public policy offered military officers new types of economic opportunities and also new temptations. Sometimes military personnel proved susceptible to some of the opportunities for private enrichment and corruption for which they had long condemned civilian politicians. Corruption corroded professional morale and pride in the armed forces. Scandals involving a variety of improprieties tarnished the image of officers and the military institutions from Peru and Argentina to Guatemala. In Bolivia, Guatemala, and Peru, the lure of the narcotics trade further undermined the claims of morality, honesty, and selflessness which the military elites proclaimed so righteously. Military budgets increased, and acquisition of expensive weapons systems added to burgeoning national debts. Military compensation, both for military and nonmilitary government assignments, increased considerably.

Most important, military elites took on the responsibility for their countries' economic performance and the public sector's delivery of goods and services to the population. These responsibilities would prove heavy as increased energy prices, international recessions, renewed inflation, a growing debt burden, and, in the early 1980s, severe economic recession eroded support for the military governments, support previously derived from economic expansion. Resurgence of labor conflict and even political violence further challenged the military governments. These conditions all intensified internal divisions within the military institutions.

Over time, controversies within the armed forces concerning the direction and specific content of social and economic policy weakened the resolve and capabilities of military governments. At times these controversies almost amounted to the functional equivalent of conflicts between political parties and interest groups in a civilian regime. Supporters of rejected policies lost prestige or even career opportunities, whereas proponents of adopted policies furthered both their military and political careers. As these sorts of cleavages permeated the military regimes, solidarity was lost and civilian movements allied themselves with like-minded military factions. Politics reappeared within the armed forces much to the distress of antipoliticians.

Even where impressive economic growth occurred or profound social change modified the old order (as in Brazil and Peru), the military political projects gradually collapsed in the late 1970s and early 1980s. Everywhere, the military governments failed in their self-assigned mission of creating a new political institutionality. Calls for redemocratization became the battle cry of the opposition. Resurgent political parties, student movements, labor unions, and religious organizations all pressured for political liberalization. Even business, commercial, and professional groups who had previously allied themselves with the antipolitical military regimes withdrew their support and urged a return to civilian government. The defection of these groups proved a pivotal turning point for the military regimes in Argentina, Uruguay, Brazil, and Guatemala. Only in Chile did the military-imposed constitution of 1980 survive after 1985. Even in Chile, however, the ultimate failure of the antipolitical project is certain; only the time of its passing remained in doubt when this volume went to press.

Failure to consolidate the new antipolitical institutions did not mean that the antipolitical military regimes failed to alter, and in some cases radically transform, the social, economic, and political realities of their respective countries. The policies and programs of the military governments restructured national economies in a number of ways. In some cases this meant dramatic increases in industrialization, changes in land tenure and agricultural systems, and severe adjustments in occupational and social structure. To finance new economic initiatives and to pay for acquisition of new weapons and materiel, the military governments contracted large debts to foreign commercial banks and international financial institutions. These debts, like the changes in socioeconomic structure, did not disappear when the military leaders withdrew from direct policy-making responsibility.

In other cases, particularly where neoliberal policies emphasizing freer trade were adopted, industrial sectors shrank, as domestic firms could not compete with the wave of imports made possible by removal of tariff and other trade barriers. This led, in turn, to rising unemployment. Increased concentration of income and a relative shift in economic power to financial-banking and commercial conglomerates upset the fundamental configuration of economies based upon import-substitution industrialization since the 1930s and 1940s. The consequences of all these changes, and of others discussed in the case studies which follow, provided immediate challenges for the civilian governments which replaced the military regimes.

The experience of the antipolitical regimes also deeply scarred the political and cultural life of these nations. Conscious of the brutal reality of antidemocratic practices during the decades of military rule, opposition movements which allied to oust the military governments greatly feared a reversion to the recent past. Yet this vivid memory could not produce, in itself, viable political coalitions or fundamental social consensus. A new legitimacy remained to be created even where the symbols and rhetoric of "redemocratization" served as the immediate rationale for transitions from military rule.

Extrication of the military from direct government responsibility coincided almost everywhere with new constitutions or modification of existing constitutions and with new electoral legislation. These new constitutions and electoral laws reintroduced party politics, social and civil liberties, a relatively free press and media, and a renewed struggle to redefine the long-term destinies of the nations of Latin America. New conceptions of democracy and democratization competed with older versions of liberal democracy for support by the recently elected civilian leadership. Ominously, the traditional democratic Left and the old Marxist movements once again challenged the legitimacy of the capitalist order while military leaders and advocates of exclusionary authoritarian politics warily observed the emerging political situation.

Under the extremely unfavorable circumstances of international recession, debt crises, and negative economic growth (1981–85), the new civilian governments replaced the antipolitical military regimes. Yet the transition from military to civilian regimes did not destroy the old military institutions, eliminate their coercive power or influence, or end the support by certain social sectors for authoritarian, nonparticipatory politics. Failure of the antipolitical regimes did not automatically create a new consensus on the nations' political futures. Pressures by students, workers, peasants, business associations, and government employees to meet long-postponed needs for housing, education, improved employment opportunities, and social services exceeded the capabilities and resources of many of these new governments. The threat of renewed social mobilization and political activism—strikes, farm occupations, food riots, urban land invasions, and demands for trials and punishment of the ousted military rulers and their subordinates for human rights violations—all added to the dilemmas facing the new civilian authorities. Eventually the new civilian leaders agreed, either privately or through public policy, to limit the extent of prosecutions of military and police officers for human rights violations during the period of military rule (though selected military leaders were tried and sentenced to prison—most dramatically in Argentina).

The failure of these newly elected civilian governments was possible if only because agreement on the definition of success was not easily forthcoming. The old cleavages emerged quickly: Peronism versus Radicalism in Argentina; Apristas, Communists, the new Right, and a radical Left in Peru, including the rise of Sendero Luminoso and other politico-guerrilla movements; reemergence of traditional political movements and regionalism in Brazil; personalism and ideological divisions in Bolivia reminiscent in some ways of the 1950s, with some of the same political actors; a weak civilian party system in Guatemala, with an ongoing guerrilla struggle; continuing civil war in El Salvador, notwithstanding the victory of a Christian Democratic administration at the polls; and, in Chile through 1987, inability of the Right, Center, and Left to reach any fundamental compromise in order to oust General Pinochet.

If the failure of these new civilian experiments is to be avoided, a clear understanding of the common legacy and idiosyncratic impacts of the antipolitical military regimes is essential. Of course, such an understanding is no guarantee of successful democratization, but, at least, it may draw attention to the risks of reliving the politics of the recent past and of refusing to confront the challenges of the present. The country studies which follow review the recent legacy of military antipolitics for the seven countries on which this volume has focused.

David Rock

Military Politics in Argentina, 1966–73

The advent of the Onganía government marked an important political hiatus. For the first time a military government was in power rejecting the transitional and provisional role of its predecessors and declaring its intention to rule for an indefinite period. The responsibility for change, which had been previously left to the civilians, was now to be carried out by a military regime, if necessary by force and without the encumbrance of having to seek the support of public opinion. As soon as it took power the government moved quickly into an assault on the major institutions which had played an important part in politics in the immediate past. The political parties were abolished and the universities purged of their left-wing and centrist elements. Of the major civilian institutions, which before had been overtly involved in political activities, only the CGT escaped.

In 1967 the Onganía government was in a stronger position than any of its predecessors. The last barrier to its authority, the CGT, was broken. It was now free, it seemed, from the need to bargain with any of the major groups and could implement whatever policies it chose. It now appeared that the complex competing "horizontal" and "vertical" pressures from the past had been finally superseded by a united and purposeful military dictatorship. Simultaneously with the confrontation with the CGT, the government revealed its plans on the economic front. Onganía appointed as minister of the economy a leading member of the neoliberal school, Adalbert Krieger Vasena. He announced a program of diversifying and rationalizing Argentine industry through another major attempt to quicken the flow of foreign investment. It was hoped to overcome the balance-of-payments bottleneck by encouraging the export of industrial products. To prepare for these objectives, a new anti-inflation stabilization program was announced which included a strict incomes policy.

The Krieger Vasena plan posed a threat to two vital political groups. It was opposed first by the smaller domestic entrepreneurs and their leading association, the General Economic Confederation (CGE). There were fears that the stabilization program, as had happened under Frondizi, would trigger a major recession and widespread bankruptcy. Once again there was talk of a "takeover" of Argentine industry by "foreign monopolies."

The Krieger Vasena plan was also opposed by the unions, which saw it as a disguised attack on wages and an attempt to raise the level of domestic savings at the cost of working-class consumption. In 1968 another major division occurred in the ranks of the CGT. Vandor continued in the hope that he could eventually pressure the government into making concessions. He therefore maintained his contacts with members of the administration. He was opposed in this by a rebel CGT group led by a printers' leader, Raimundo Ongaro. Although at first this group had little following, it rapidly evolved into the most vocal source of opposition to the government.

The Onganía government had thus brought about several very significant changes. Added together, these threatened to disrupt and transform the essential pattern of politics, as it had evolved since 1955. In spite of its retention of certain superficial vertical features, the class-based horizontal structure, based on the conflict between Peronism and anti-Peronism, had been the central axis of politics since Perón's downfall. This was now threatened by the military regime which had put all the parties on an equal footing in the ranks of the opposition. In doing so it had abruptly cut the normal channels of communication through which sectional opinions were expressed and the horizontal pattern of politics maintained. For the first time ever Radicals and Peronists found themselves in the same camp. Secondly, the adoption of the Krieger Vasena plan, and its aggressive provisions for eliminating inflation and enhancing the flow of foreign capital, had a similar parallel effect on two key interest groups, the unions and the smaller employers. This not only meant the intensification of the gathering confrontation between "nationalist" and neoliberal groups, but also implied a new common interest between the former and the unions against the government. A third major factor was, in part, a by-product of the first. In suppressing conventional political activities, the Onganía government weakened the capacity of formal political vehicles like the parties and the CGT to act as articulating agents for the major socioeconomic groups. The protests of entrepreneurs tended less to be expressed through the parties, and those of the workers less through a CGT dominated by Vandor. A further stage in the growing atomization of formal political bodies before 1966 was the tendency afterward for new vehicles of political articulation and mobilization to emerge. Examples of this were the growing importance of the CGE, representing the entrepreneurs, and Ongaro's wing of the union movement, representing dissident segments of the working class.

For a little over two years the Krieger Vasena plan seemed highly successful. By 1969 the rate of inflation had fallen to a comparatively negligible amount. Wages were falling, but gradually and without the traumatic shocks of the past. There was no apparent sign of any dangerous buildup of working-class opposition. Fears that the plan would provoke a major recession proved largely unfounded. Unlike Frondizi's stabilization plan in 1959, Krieger's had the advantage of having been introduced during a period of depression. Cyclical forces encouraging economic recovery for a time proved stronger than the deflationary influence of government policy.

However, the *pax onganiana*, and the determined effort it marked to escape from the mould of stagnation which had begun in 1949, eventually failed. Suddenly in May 1969, there was a spate of student unrest in the interior cities of Resistencia, Corrientes, Rosario, and Córdoba. In Rosario and Córdoba these movements quickly and spontaneously evolved into major urban riots. The more significant was in Córdoba, where the students were joined by large numbers of striking auto workers. Only when the army was brought in in strength was the outbreak quashed.

These events destroyed the Krieger Vasena program and led directly to Onganía's downfall a year later. The army, which since 1966 had remained united behind the government, now divided between the adherents of repression like Onganía himself and other groups led by the army commander in chief, General Alejandro Lanusse, which supported a more conciliatory policy in the hope of curbing unrest. The *cordobazo*, as the rebellion in Córdoba became known, remains the central event in contemporary Argentine history. It underlay the fundamental realignment of political forces which culminated in the restoration of Peronism in 1973.

The revolts in the universities were closely associated with pressures deriving from or complementing the central orientation of the Krieger Vasena plan. Since 1966 there had been an effort to "functionalize" the universities by emphasing technical and managerial training, and by restricting their intake in accordance with estimates of demand for different professional qualifications. The revolts of 1969 were triggered by dramatic changes in the food prices charged in university refectories as part of a campaign to rationalize costs. Reactions like this clearly relate to frustrated mobility aspirations among students and were culturally based responses to sudden, violent changes in disposable incomes. This illustrated the chronic political problems produced by twenty years of economic stagnation, combined with the government's praetorian zeal for efficiency.

Similar pressures were apparent among the Córdoba auto workers. Throughout the 1960s the auto industry had been subject to wide oscillations in output, and this made for great insecurity among the workforces.

The flashpoint for the strike in 1969 was the sudden waiving of traditional privileges concerning Saturday afternoon working. But again, this can be a preliminary basis for any general explanation. Any simple Marxist argument along the lines of progressive pauperization cannot be applied literally in this context. As Krieger Vasena remarked soon after his resignation in June 1969, the Córdoba auto workers were among the best paid in the country. It was not that the auto workers were becoming any poorer in the literal sense. The source of their reaction is more explicable in terms of fluctuations in output and intensity of labor.

Further facilitating the links which developed in Córdoba between the students and the auto workers was that many of the students were themselves shift workers in the auto plants. A second point relates to the divisions in the national CGT between Vandor, Alonso, and Ongaro. In Córdoba, this had produced a chaotic situation among the groups in different plants claiming to represent the work force. When the spark came, the different factions proved unable to exercise any form of effective leadership and were simply carried along by events. These conditions of institutional fragmentation, which again relate to government policy and behavior since 1966, seem to have played some part in the central pattern of events.

Although the *cordobazo,* and the other lesser movements, were largely spontaneous and leaderless, it was not long before attempts were beginning to fashion their energies into a new popular opposition front against the government controlled by New Left groups. None of these was ever successful. At first it seemed that Ongaro's group would gain the upper hand. Within a short time a rough alliance had emerged between him and the most active of the Córdoba union leaders, Agustín Tosco of the light and power workers. In 1970, a new radical union, Sitrac-Sitram, emerged among the Córdoba auto workers. It too began to call for the formation of a popular liberation front.

Thus, 1969 saw the emergence of the threatened new popular force. If it lacked a unified leadership and a coherent, shared ideology, it had some of the vertical, cross-class features of the populist alliances of the past. Workers, students, and in some cases businessmen had united in a violent protest against the government. In doing so, they isolated the neoliberal groups which had supported the Onganía government and the Krieger Vasena plan. Onganía's destruction and repression of traditional political institutions in 1966 and the weakening of the unions in 1967 underlay the violence of the reaction in 1969 and its tendency to spawn new, organized groups like the radical Sitrac-Sitram.

This new movement was not Peronist. Neither Perón nor Vandor, who was murdered in mysterious circumstances a few weeks after the *cordobazo,* had played any significant part in its conception or execution. If the new movement sought inspiration in anyone, it was the mythical figure of Ernesto [Che] Guevara. For the first time in twenty years, the division between Peronists and anti-Peronists had been superseded. Instead of dividing society along class lines, the policies of the Onganía government had finally come to unite them.

In 1970 the dangers to the military government posed by the new alliance were increased with a sudden profusion of Marxist and Peronist guerrilla groups. This was a novel phenomenon, and it illustrated the point to which opposition to the military government had escalated. From the end of 1969 onward, the guerrilla groups made a series of spectacular raids on police stations, army outposts, and banks. There was also a spate of kidnappings. The most important was the abduction and execution of former president Aramburu by the Peronist Montoneros group. This event was the signal for an army coup led by General Lanusse against Onganía in June 1970, and his replacement by a former military attaché in Washington, General Roberto M. Levingston.

In 1970 and 1971 the economy again plunged into recession, and, as in the past, this gave a further impulse to unrest. There was a marked slowing of industrial production, coupled with a heavy deficit on the balance of payments. Soon after the abandonment of the Krieger Vasena plan, inflation had again swiftly developed. Unemployment also increased and by the middle of 1971 had reached the same level as in 1967 during the first phase of the Krieger Vasena plan.

On the political front, the most significant events occurred in March 1971. Following the resignation of a popular provincial governor, Bernardo Bas, there was another major uprising in Córdoba, again involving students, middle-class groups, and auto workers. The difference between this and the movement of 1969 was that in 1971 there was much greater control and coordination over it, led in particular by groups like Sitrac-Sitram. It was also widely reported that sections of the leading Marxist guerrilla group, the ERP, were closely involved. The feared links between Marxist guerrillas and popular uprisings appeared to be in an advanced form of gestation. Although this may have been exaggerated, it proved to be the spur to a radical change of policy by the army. Within a week of the movement in Córdoba Levingston's short rule was brought to an end, and Lanusse himself personally took control. The principal aim of his government, constantly reiterated by himself and other members of the administration, was to drive a wedge between "subversion" and the popular uprisings, to eliminate the former and to control the latter.

Lanusse immediately announced presidential elections for March 1973 and called upon the traditional political parties to join with the government in a "Great National Agreement" to save the country from revolutionary anarchy. By restoring the privileges and full legal status of the parties, the agreement marked the final abandonment of the practices followed by Onganía's "Argentine revolution" in 1966. The turnabout on the economic front, which had begun with the downfall of Krieger Vasena in 1969, was now followed in 1971 by a change of equal scope at the political level. These efforts at conciliation did not include the New Left groups. Ongaro, Tosco, and others were imprisoned. Militant unions like Sitrac-Sitram were dissolved by government decree. Under government promptings, the official CGT reacquired the privileges and bargaining power it had lost in 1967. Meanwhile, the war against the guerrillas continued without quarter. In August 1972 a number of imprisoned guerrillas who had been recaptured after an escape attempt were summarily shot in the naval garrison of Trelew. These were the central guidelines of government policy—the revival of the traditional political bodies to fill the institutional vacuum left by Onganía, accompanied by a root-and-branch campaign against the New Left groups.

However, Lanusse's boldest stroke, achieved in the face of bitter opposition among certain groups in the army, was to include the Peronists in his project of reviving the traditional structures and using them as a buffer between the government and the forces of popular unrest. In a further energetic attempt to shift popular attention away from the left, the government began a campaign to persuade the Peronists to join the "Great National Agreement" and then to speculate publicly on the possibility of Perón's return from exile. It was evident that if the old grudges against Perón were far from dead, the government felt that the situation was sufficiently desperate to justify a major change of attitude. In this way the sixteen-year ostracism of Perón suddenly ended.

Reprinted and edited from *Argentina in the Twentieth Century* (Pittsburgh, Pa.: University of Pittsburgh Press, 1975), pp. 207, 209–17.

David Rock

The Military in Politics in Argentina, 1973–83

The unforeseen denouement to Ongania's Revolución Argentina was the rebirth of Peronism on a breadth and scale even greater than thirty years before. In the election of March 1973, the Peronist alliance, the FREJULI (Frente Justicialista de Liberación) was victorious with almost 49 percent of the vote. Far behind trailed the Radicals with a little over 21 percent, with the rest of the vote taken by minority parties. Since Perón's candidacy had been vetoed by the army, the president-elect was Héctor Cámpora, Perón's most recent "personal delegate" in Argentina. Cámpora, typical of those who had served in this office, had no personal base in the movement, serving only as Perón's stalking horse. Cámpora took office toward the end of May, to remain there a mere forty-nine days.

Soon after Cámpora's inaugural latent tensions surfaced in the Peronist movement—products of its recent headlong growth, its extreme heterogeneity, and the power struggle between the Montoneros and the union leaders. Among Cámpora's first acts was to declare a political amnesty and the release of all imprisoned guerrillas. The Montoneros now abandoned clandestine recruiting and made an open bid to broaden their base and capture strategic positions of power. They took control of the Peronist Youth, established front organizations in the universities and among the shantytowns, and were similarly active among the unions, where the union "bureaucrats" promptly began to organize resistance. In June 1973, Perón made ready for his second return to Buenos Aires. An estimated half-million people trekked out from the city to the airport at Ezeiza to meet him. As they waited, pitched battles erupted between armed hirelings of the unions and the Montoneros. Scores of persons, if not hundreds, died in the affray.

Ezeiza highlighted Cámpora's inability to control the movement and to hold at bay its contending forces. By June 1973, many observers, among them the Army leaders, were concluding that only Perón could abate the conflict and achieve stability. In July, Cámpora was unseated after Perón theatrically withdrew his personal support from the government. The presidency passed to Raúl Lastiri, formerly president of the Chamber of Deputies, pending the September presidential elections. Perón received 60 percent of the vote, and on 17 October 1973, the twenty-eighth anniversary of his great triumph in 1945, he began his third elected term as president.

Perón's restoration was an admission of political bankruptcy by a military now prepared to clutch at any straw to contain the radical left. Even so, his reinstatement constituted a quite remarkable change of fortune for Perón, still more so because the country now exuded a sense of deliverance and a sudden optimism rarely seen in recent decades. Yet Cámpora's fall had brought little abatement in political violence. The Montoneros undertook a campaign to annihilate union leaders: in September 1973, they assassinated José Rucci, secretary-general of the CGT. As the Peronists grew increasingly hostile, the ERP began preparing for renewed guerrilla warfare, amassing funds from kidnaps and robberies in late 1973. In January 1974, the ERP mounted a full-scale assault against an Army garrison in the city of Azul. Meanwhile, right-wing violence also increased. By early 1974, most kidnaps and murders of leftist militants were the work of a new secret organization, the Argentine Anticommunist Alliance (*Alianza Argentina Anticommunista*), known familiarly as the "Triple A"; evidence pointed toward the federal police as its guiding hand.

Perón's ability to succeed now also depended on his age and health, for he had resumed the presidency at age seventy-eight. To mask the divisions in his movement, he had chosen his third wife, María Estela Martínez de Perón, "Isabel," as his running mate. Like Cámpora, she had been among his couriers to Buenos Aires and was politically inexperienced. In late 1973, the outcome of the recent political settlement seemed to depend first and foremost on Perón's own ability to survive.

As he had in 1946, Perón took the presidency at a fortuitous moment. In 1973, a world commodity boom brought an unexpected 65 percent increase in export earnings and a swift expansion of the reserves. Wheat prices, for example, which averaged $67 a ton in 1972, climbed to $116 a ton by early 1974; thus, between 1972 and 1973, foreign reserves jumped from $465 million to $1.3 billion. Since the *cordobazo*[1] extreme recession had been staved off by expansionist economic policies. Yet between 1970 and 1972, growth was under 3 percent; in 1973, it climbed to 6 percent. Throughout 1973, inflation steadily declined, from an annual rate of 80 percent in May to only 30 percent by October. As throughout the postwar period, improving economic conditions invariably favored greater political calm, which Perón immediately encouraged. As he took the presidency, he indulged in effusive shows of reconciliation with former political enemies, some of whom he had imprisoned or driven into exile twenty years earlier.

Despite any gestures to the contrary, eighteen years of exile, and the circumstances surrounding his recent return, had done little to develop Perón's ideas. As in 1946, the kernels of his programs were income redistribution in favor of labor, the expansion of employment, and renewed social reform. The new Peronism was to resurrect the IAPI, increase food subsidies, and tax farming; the state would once more control the banks, support native industry, and regulate trade through highly protective tariffs and multiple exchange rates; numerous plans were drafted to trim the influence of foreign corporations and to extend nationalization. Perón remained adept in the exploitation of symbols. During his negotiations with Lanusse in 1972, the embalmed body of Eva Perón was rediscovered in a secret resting place in Italy. Perón brought it back to Argentina and laid new plans for the construction of a national mausoleum.

Another facet of Perón's program in 1973 had its antecedents in the stabilization plan of 1952. To quell inflation, the Peronists proposed that the CGT and the CGE, representing employers, negotiate an agreement on prices and incomes. Under this social compact (Pacto Social), the wage share in national income would rise over a four-year period to roughly the level of the early 1950s; the unions, after receiving an initial large wage boost, would agree to defer new collective bargaining agreements for a two-year period; and price controls would prevail, leaving profits to increase along with the expansion of demand. When the compact was first concluded under Cámpora in June 1973, inflation fell rapidly. In the first year of the agreement, prices rose by only 17 percent.

As recovery continued and inflation fell, public backing for Perón soared. Soon he felt himself strong enough to reinstate the political agenda of his first government—purge the movement, strengthen his personal grip, and eliminate the independent factions. In 1946, his targets were the *laboristas*; in early 1974, the Montoneros and the Peronist Youth. Perón's demeanor toward them had begun to change after the Ezeiza incident in June 1973, and hardened into thinly veiled hostility after Rucci's assassination in September. It now became apparent that Perón had used the left as an instrument for his return to power and that the left, in a mix of blind ingenuousness and opportunism, had allowed him to do so. But his new plan, for which he had enthusiastic backing in both the Army and the GCT, was to destroy it. Soon after taking the presidency, Perón endorsed changes in the penal code providing stiffer sentences for acts of terrorism; however, he ignored the activities of the Triple A. He was also courting the leaders of the CGT, buttressing their authority by reinstating union verticality, another of his once-favored techniques. A new union law in early 1974 proposed the reconstruction of the unions as industry-wide federations under the CGT, which would again enjoy full faculties of intervention in individual unions. To protect and stabilize the present union leadership, the law established a four-year interval between labor congresses.

As Perón closed ranks with the CGT, he began denouncing "infiltrators" in the movement, attacks that were interpreted as the signal for open purges of leftists in the provinces. The internecine conflict became manifest in May 1974, when Perón addressed the crowds in the Plaza de Mayo on Labor Day. Greeted by a barrage of remonstrances from the Peronist Youth and the Montoneros, he retorted angrily and unyieldingly, calling them "callow and stupid" *(imberbes y estúpidos)*. The split in the movement was now public, and each side hastened to marshal its forces. But on 1 July 1974, Perón succumbed to heart failure and died.

With Perón's death, the political settlement of 1973 shattered. His widow assumed the presidency as political and economic crisis, a storm of violence and inflation, reconverged. The Montoneros tried once more to gain a voice in the regime, but when again repulsed, they repudiated Isabel and proclaimed a return to clandestine operations in September 1974. Like the ERP the year before, they sought to finance their campaign by robbery and kidnap, extorting millions of dollars from such escapades. In September the Montoneros abducted Juan Born and Jorge Born, owners of the largest of the grain-exporting houses in Buenos Aires, exacting a ransom estimated somewhere between $20 million and $60 million. Another $14 million was paid for the release of an American oil executive.

Late in 1974, guerrilla warfare resumed with a wave of bombings and assassinations. The chief victims were army and police personnel, and, to a lesser degree, union leaders and politicians who had had a leading role in preparing the elections of 1973. In the next twelve months, the guerrillas' tactics came to include open rebellion. In Tucumán, the ERP began a drive for control of the province; the Montoneros, increasingly active in the east, in October 1975, orchestrated the storming of an Army garrison in the northeastern province of Formosa in which 500 guerrillas took part.

As the guerrilla war grew in scale, resistance stiffened. In the latter half of 1974, the Triple A murdered some seventy of its opponents, mostly prominent leftist intellectuals or lawyers; by early 1975, they dispensed with leftists at the rate of fifty a week. Throughout 1974, the Army sought to stay clear of the conflict, but in early 1975, it intervened in full force. In Tucumán it ruthlessly hunted the guerrillas and initiated reprisals against those suspected of harboring them. The three armed services were now on full war footing; supported by the state security police (Coordinación Federal), each formed espionage networks and clandestine operational units. These forces, which soon dwarfed their adversaries, imposed repression by the use of unchecked, random, indiscriminate violence that struck without warning or warrant. The definition of *subversion* was broadened and became increasingly capricious, encompassing the mildest protest, whether made by the parties, the press, the universities, the legal profession, or the unions. The number of persons who simply disappeared (los desaparecidos) mounted rapidly, with some held hostage to deter the guerrillas; guerrilla actions were answered by the execution of hostages. Corpses were found floating in barrels in the River Plate, or left charred and unrecognizable on refuse dumps; other captives were rumored to have been hurled to their deaths from aircraft. From the prisons came detailed accounts of systematic torture.

Above this sordid contest stood a government whose authority was rapidly deteriorating. Isabel Perón at first made faint gestures toward repairing the rift with the left, but once its grievances focused against her, she left the issue to the armed forces and the police. In November 1974, following the assassination of the Chief of Police Alberto Vilar, the government decreed a state of siege, which gave the Army carte blanche authority to deal with the guerrillas. Isabel Perón meanwhile succumbed to the influence and direction of José López Rega, a member of Perón's personal entourage from Madrid and since May 1973, the minister of social welfare. Under his guidance, she became another Peronist parody, an image of Evita, who sought popular esteem by mimicking the former first lady's public style, oratory, and exploitation of organized charity. López Rega's influence was reflected in the national budget: In 1975, the Ministry of Social Welfare collected 30 percent of all federal appropriations.

The new government's prospects were quickly compromised by renewed economic crisis. In July 1974, outbreaks of hoof-and-mouth disease in Europe incited bans on imported Argentine meat. More important, while the domestic economy expanded, oil prices soared after the Arab-Israeli War in 1973. Argentina's oil bill rose from $58 million in 1972, 3.1 percent of total imports, to $586 million, or 15.1 percent of imports, in 1974. To pay for the oil, and for numerous other imports undergoing similarly sharp price increases, the government resorted to the reserves, which dwindled as fast in 1974 as they had risen during the short-lived export boom the year before. Once the reserves were exhausted, a huge payments deficit mounted. By the end of 1975, export earnings had fallen by 25 percent and the deficit had risen to $1 billion.

The new crisis was not solely exogenous in origin; internal conditions and recent policies also had a major bearing on its germination and intensity. Since Cámpora's administration, wages and public spending had increased sharply, but when commercial conditions altered, the government made no attempt to check the expansion of the economy. For a time, inflation was held at bay by the liquidation of the reserves and by the price freeze imposed by Perón in 1973; by late 1974, however, the sudden rampant growth of the black market illustrated the rising undercurrent of inflation.

Had Perón lived, such conditions would have tested him to the limit; to some extent they were also his doing. Instead, it was Isabel Perón who became ensnared in the classic trap of the Latin American populists. To fight inflation she had to attack wages and consumption; to safeguard her political base she had to hold fast to expansion. Her government lurched first down one road and then down the other, forfeiting control over the economy and suffering a fatal procession of political defections. "Zero inflation" Perón had boasted in early 1974; a year later, prices were rising at three-figure rates. In 1974, consumer prices rose by 24.2 percent; in 1975, by 183 percent. . . .

For more than a year, surging inflation had been accompanied by growing violence—the classic scenario for a coup d'etat. The Air Force attempted one in late December 1975, but failed to win support from the Army. While intensifying the war on the guerrillas, the Army waited until the last vestiges of the government's popular support had crumbled and Peronism lay shattered. At length, on 24 March 1976, the Army abducted the president as a prelude to dissolving the government. Once in power, the Army embarked on the conquest of any lingering resistance to a revolution in government whose aim was the total dismantlement of the Peronist state.

Postscript: The New Autocracy and Its Decline, 1976–82

The junta of 1976, led by General Jorge Rafael Videla, came to power with greater strength and freedom of maneuver than any of its military predecessors. With the collapse of Peronism, the disruption of the unions, and the population at large prostrated by strikes, lockouts, inflation, and terror, only the guerrillas offered organized resistance, but by March 1976, their numbers, too, were declining. In the past two years, their sympathizers had been weeded out of the public administration, the universities, the mass media, and the unions. Their press organs were suppressed; and possession of their literature was declared an act of criminal subversion. Throughout the past six years, both guerrilla bands had failed to obtain a broader popular base, for the Montoneros had little success in penetrating the unions even at the height of the conflict between *verticalistas* and *antiverticalistas*. In 1975, one of their front organizations, the Partido Auténtico, joined with another Peronist group to contest an election in Misiones, but gathered only 9 percent of the vote. The ERP fared no better. In 1975, its forces in Tucumán were eradicated by the Army; that December 80 combatants, all but one secondary or university students, were killed in an attack on an Army garrison at Monte Chingolo, in the province of Buenos Aires. Even so, at the time of the coup, the rebels were still capable of audacious bombings and assassinations.

The last phase of the guerrilla war was its bloodiest and most terrifying: All due process of law was overturned; military patrols infested the country; thousands vanished into the prisons and police torture chambers. During the previous six years, the guerrillas' victims had numbered at most 200 or 300; the price now exacted in retaliation, mostly through "disappearances," was at least 10,000. The repression quite deliberately, it seemed, was arbitrary, uncoordinated, and indiscriminate, which intensified its powers of intimidation. After the coup, the combination of terror and collapsing living standards induced thousands to seek refuge abroad. But by 1978, the Army had crushed the guerrillas. Almost all of those who had failed to escape were tracked down and liquidated. . . .

On taking power in March 1976, Videla declared that the coming of the new junta signaled "the final closing of one historical cycle and the beginning of another." In this spirit, the regime conducted its war on subversion, demolished many of the new institutions created by the Peronists, and quashed all political opposition. A similar iconoclastic elan characterized its approach to the economy. For some five years after the coup, economic management was entrusted to José A. Martínez de Hoz, a member of one of the great landed families and a prominent figure in banking. He immediately attacked hyperinflation and the steep balance-of-payments deficit by an onslaught on consumption and wages. After the coup, the CGT was abolished, strikes were banned, and the war on subversion was broadened to encompass union leaders and workers suspected of plotting resistance. An authoritative report, issued January 1978, on the "disappearances," estimated that fewer than 20 percent of the victims were guerrillas and some 37 percent were factory workers, mostly second-level or shop-floor union leaders.

In 1977, the wage share shrank to only 31 percent of national income, its lowest level since 1935; the near 50 percent plunge in real wages in 1976 was the fastest and steepest ever. . . . Further cuts were enforced through the transfer of state services to the provinces unaccompanied by increased central subsidies. The government, however, was reluctant to provoke open unemployment, lest the guerrillas gain new recruits. At 2.2 percent in February 1978, unemployment was lower than any period since the late 1940s. The income wrested from wage earners in 1976 and 1977 was propelled into farming, which rewarded Martínez de Hoz with a bumper harvest in 1976–77. In 1976, foreign loans helped reestablish the reserves; export earnings increased by 33 percent, imports fell by 20 percent, and the previous year's $1 billion payments deficit became a surplus of $650 million. Meanwhile, the government managed to reduce a heavy public-sector deficit by indexing taxes and freezing salaries among government workers.

With Martínez de Hoz came a commitment not only to restore order in the economy, but also to change and reconstruct it. The minister and the leading members of his team, all extreme market economists, attacked the heavy concentration of economic power in the state and pushed for its dismantlement. They wanted a prolonged attack on inflation by monetary controls. Inefficiencies would be conquered by open competition, and price distortions overcome by ending subsidies, tariff controls, and regulated exchange rates, and by the creation of new financial markets. Through an aggressive pursuit of foreign investment, Martínez de Hoz aimed to broaden the infrastructure for industry and create a rejuvenated, diversified export sector.

Along with wages, manufacturing bore the main brunt of his program. The collapse in demand in 1976 prostrated the wage-good sector of industry: the textile industry; for example, suffered a 50 percent contraction. Industry also had to endure a graduated reduction in tariffs, an end to subsidized exports, new internal terms of trade that favored agriculture, and competition from agriculture for funds in an open capital market. In July 1977, representations against such measures by the CGE were met by the closure of the institution. By the first half of 1979, manufacturing, which had accounted for 38.1 percent of the gross domestic product in the boom year 1974, shrank to 35 percent. Steel output dropped from 4.4 million tons in 1974 to only 3.3 million tons in 1978. Between 1976 and 1978, manufacturing employment declined by 10 percent.

The Army's war on subversion and Martínez de Hoz's program elicited opposite responses from outside observers, who detested the extreme brutalities of the former, but generally praised the latter. In many respects, however, the two policies were complementary and inseparable. The butt for both was the urban sectors: the unions, industry, and much of the middle class. The Army's task, with the war against subversion in part as a pretext, was to shatter their collective bargaining power and their means of resistance; Martínez de Hoz's role was to weaken and ultimately destroy the economy on which they subsisted, for example, by eliminating the state as a major source of employment and the chief agent distributing resources in urban society. If manufacturing survived his onslaught, it was likely to do so in still more concentrated blocs. Even on optimistic assumptions—successful export diversification, conquest of balance-of-payments constraints on growth, and the emergence of an efficient, competitive manufacturing sector—the outlook for the bulk of urban society seemed bleak. . . .

In the event Martínez de Hoz's program was applied only in part, mainly to accomplish short-term recovery, for by 1978, it was losing momentum. If united in the war on subversion, the Videla junta was divided into three broad factions on issues of the longer-term political future. The faction led by Admiral Emilio Massera, which evoked the Army Blues[2] of 1962, and the line initially taken by Lanusse in 1971, urged military populism, a new "Peronism without Perón," that would supersede Peronism, protect against renewed popular outbreaks like the *cordobazo*, and pose a barrier to the revival of the Left. Because the economy precluded rallying popular support by wage and other concessions, the method Perón once used, Massera at first sought to forge popularity by inflating the threat from the guerrillas or "international Marxist conspiracies" and by constructing a reputation as the leading architect of "national defense" against them. But as the internal war subsided, he was obliged to seek alternative instruments in an extreme nationalism. In mid-1977, the decision was announced of a British arbitration on a long-standing dispute between Argentina and Chile for sovereignty over the Beagle Channel in Tierra del Fuego. By and large, the award favored Chile. Massera seized upon Argentine dissatisfaction to foster a climate of military confrontation and used the Beagle Channel as a pretext to prolong the atmosphere of national emergency, a prelude to attempts to penetrate, mobilize, and coopt popular institutions. Using Chile as the new enemy, he hoped to don the mantle of Perón and establish a popular dictatorship— Bonapartism in a raw form. In October 1978, when the dispute with Chile seemed likely to evaporate peacefully, Massera began calling for an invasion of the British-held Falkland Islands.

A second faction in the junta, led by Generals Carlos Suárez Masón and Mario Menéndez, appeared as heirs to the extreme anti-Peronist "gorillas" of the late 1950s and early 1960s. Like the *colorados* of 1962, its members supported indefinite military dictatorship backed by an unrelenting war on the Peronist party, the unions, and all leftist organizations. Theirs was Martínez de Hoz's program pressed to its fullest extreme—a succession of unremitting blows against the defense bulwarks of urban society.

Third was a group led by Videla and General Roberto Viola, who, in May 1978, succeeded Videla as Army commander in chief. The Videla-Viola faction, which recalled Onganía's regime after 1966, envisaged a series of phases by which economic recovery would again serve as the foundation for eventual political liberalization. It thus regarded Martínez de Hoz's program mainly as a short-term plan to achieve recovery and control inflation, and it soon grew uneasy with the minister's more radical proposals—tightening the pressure on manufacturers, the permanent collapse of wages, and the dismantlement of the state sector. . . .

As its standing increased, the Videla-Viola faction became more moderate and further diluted its endorsement of Martínez de Hoz; by late 1979,

Viola publicly criticized low wages. Martínez de Hoz consequently found himself under growing pressure from the junta to accomplish a series of contradictory, if not incompatible, goals: to continue the war on inflation, but at the same time contain the fall in living standards, and revive manufacturing. His inability to touch the public sector, however, deprived him of his main weapon against inflation, and in 1976, the price index rose by around 500 percent. Even after steep drops, inflation remained for much of the late 1970s at more than 150 percent. In 1977 and 1978, the high inflation was due in part to military mobilization and rearmament during the dispute with Chile, but also in part to continuing government deficits provoked by subsidies to public corporations.

In groping for methods to curb inflation, Martínez de Hoz continued the plan of graduated tariff reductions he had adopted in 1976, with the aim of encouraging imports to compete with domestic producers and thus force down prices. Although the policy showed little discernible influence in containing prices, it did impede recovery in the manufacturing sector, which remained in deep depression throughout the late 1970s. Meanwhile, to enhance the long-term competitiveness of manufacturing, Martínez de Hoz sought new foreign investment that would deepen the productive infrastructure and thereby reduce manufacturers' costs.

Recourse to foreign investment under the military regime followed legislation in March 1977 that established new tax benefits and favorable terms for profit remittances, including the removal of all restraints on convertibility. Foreign investment was also facilitated by new liberal banking regulations and high domestic interest rates. Changes in the banking laws, also in early 1977, led to the swift proliferation of new financial institutions known as *casas financieras*. High domestic interest rates strongly motivated the new *financieras* and the traditional banks to an energetic pursuit of funds abroad, and they soon became one of the government's chief means for attracting foreign investment. By 1978, following a marked decline in international interest rates, foreign investment also became available on relatively easy terms. The large and rapidly growing influx of funds financed oil and gas exploration projects, hydroelectricity, and nuclear schemes—exactly the kind of projects that Martínez de Hoz hoped would eventually boost domestic manufacturing. But to accelerate the process still more, in January 1979, he eliminated the stipulation that required the banks and *financieras* to keep in reserve a margin of 20 percent of their funds from abroad. Arguing that major changes in parity would induce still higher rates of domestic inflation, he also instituted "crawling peg" devaluations, which caused the rate of peso depreciation to fall substantially behind the rise in domestic prices.

The new measures of early 1979 complemented those instituted in 1977 to boost foreign investment. . . . An increasingly overvalued peso accompanied by falling tariff duties also meant cheaper imports, which occasioned a growing influx of luxury consumer goods and buying sprees by state corporations. By late 1979, imports were growing three times faster than exports.

In early 1980, the country appeared to have undergone a dramatic change. With the guerrillas vanquished, discernible repression had waned. The troops had returned to the barracks, and the covert police squads, agents of the "disappearances," were no longer active. Although wages and manufacturers' profits remained bitingly low, the press gagged, and the unions cowed, much of the population found solace in speculation and the purchase of cheap imports.

But the storm only appeared to be passing; in truth, the country stood in the eye of another, contrived by Martínez de Hoz. An overvalued peso pumped in foreign investment but swiftly disrupted foreign trade, and in the first half of 1980, the trade deficit reached $500 million. To control the deficit required a steep devaluation, one that would immediately eliminate the high returns earned by foreign investors. Martínez de Hoz knew that in all probability, devaluation—even a rumor of devaluation—would provoke foreign investors into massive withdrawals that would cause the reserves and the peso to collapse, leading the economy into another deep depression.

By 1980, conditions had an inescapable air of 1889–90, with Martínez de Hoz becoming a latter-day Juárez Celman.[3] The first signs of financial strain came in early 1980, with the sudden collapse of the Banco de Intercambio Regional, one of the newer *financieras*, provincial in origin, that had undergone rapid growth. . . .

By October 1980, the financial system was reported "close to collapse," as a multitude of firms struggled to survive by renegotiating their debts through new short-term loans. In early February 1981, after another spate of bankruptcies, a sudden unprogrammed devaluation was followed by capital flight estimated at $2 billion. Between December 1979 and March 1981, Argentina's foreign debt had risen from $8.5 billion to $25.3 billion, from 14 percent to 42 percent of the gross domestic product. Interest charges on the foreign debt were 10 percent of exports in 1979, but more than 30 percent by the end of 1980. In 1980, export values fell in constant dollars by 3.9 percent, while imports grew 43 percent.

On the expiration of Videla's term in March 1981, Viola became president, while Martínez de Hoz resigned. The new president began his tenure still cherishing hopes of political liberalization, but his position was at once imperiled by a financial crisis that soon exploded into a thunderous economic collapse. Further, numerous conflicts still divided the military, and within weeks Viola found himself embroiled with his Army commander, General Leopoldo Galtieri, over concessions to the Peronists, including the liberation of Isabel Perón, held captive for the past five years. In June 1981, when rumors of an impending coup led by Galtieri coincided with a new devaluation, the reserves fell by a reported $300 million in a single day; the financial crisis was now "without historical precedent." In July, amid fears of popular demonstrations triggered by the Peronists, Viola proclaimed a pending "dialogue" with the political parties as a prelude to a political "opening" (*apertura*), an announcement that provoked new friction with Galtieri. . . . In November a new run on the peso proved the end for Viola, whom Galtieri forced to resign in late December. Throughout 1981, the peso depreciated by over 600 percent of its value, the gross domestic product fell by 11.4 percent, manufacturing output by 22.9 percent, and real wages by 19.2 percent.

The Galtieri coup marked the victory of those military factions committed to "firmness and action," qualities they regarded Viola's regime as lacking. Galtieri's outlook appeared to bring together the positions of the Massera and Suárez Masón–Menéndez factions four or five years earlier. He opposed even the slightest new concession to the Peronists and appeared to be preparing an attack against them as the prelude to forming a new mass movement dominated by the generals. But Galtieri's economic policy reinvoked the initial extremes of Martínez de Hoz's program, with pledges to renew the plan to alienate state industries and services into private hands. The regime also renewed the quest for still more foreign investment, aiming for a new partnership with the United States based on the ideological affinities between Galtieri and the Reagan administration. In November 1981, a few weeks before the overthrow of Viola, Galtieri had visited Washington and had reportedly offered the Americans military bases in Patagonia in return for investments in a new gas pipeline and in the oil industry, which were to produce Argentina's first exports of gas and oil. Galtieri also offered technical advisers and military support for the American-backed war against leftist rebellion in Central America.

To his compatriots, Galtieri appeared to be "[a] man of austerity while simultaneously presenting himself as a man of the people"—in essence the reputation Massera had sought in 1977. To test and enhance its popular standing, the government organized public barbecues (*asados*) in the provinces, events that critics dubbed the Gran Asado Nacional, a pun on Lanusse's Gran Acuerdo. But Galtieri's weakness, it was apparent, was a lack of political momentum. He neither sparked popular support nor overcame the persisting divisions in the armed services. In an effort to resolve these problems, Galtieri once more exhumed Massera's ideas and turned to foreign affairs. In late January 1982, Argentina mounted a new campaign against Chile over the Beagle Channel; in February came hints of pending military involvement in Central America; next, a diplomatic offensive against Britain concerning the Falkland Islands and a demand for an acknowledgment of Argentina's sovereignty. This last issue seemed most promising and gained increasing primacy. For if the regime escalated the tension with Chile, it risked a protracted war that could spread elsewhere in Latin America, perhaps ultimately sparking an invasion from Brazil. And if Argentina became too involved in Central America, domestic dissidents would charge that the government was acting as a mercenary to imperialism, a position that might unite the Peronists, prompt the revival of the Left, and incite renewed popular unrest. By comparison, action in the Falklands was "the easiest war of all." As the options were canvassed in early 1982, Galtieri swiftly acquired the reputation of a "trigger-happy warmonger."

In early April 1982, the junta invaded and took the Falkland Islands and their dependencies. It was the first time since 1870 that Argentine forces had engaged in a foreign conflict. In executing the invasion, the junta expected maximum gains and minimum losses, for the "reoccupation" of *"nuestras Malvinas"* was universally popular. Incipient protests against the government were replaced by massive demonstrations of solidarity that gave the junta the instrument of vicarious unity it required. The junta now posed as an agent of national redemption, dismissing its opponents, whatever their grievances, as "traitors" or "antipatriots". . . .

The junta, however, had misjudged. The invasion bought ephemeral domestic peace at the price of a swift and shattering military defeat. The British responded to the invasion by mobilizing their navy and dispatching a task-force flotilla to the South Atlantic. . . . The United States pursued efforts at mediation, but when Argentina resisted pressure to withdraw from the islands pending negotiations, the Americans sided with Britain. The British fleet reached its destination in May, and immediate naval and air encounters bottled the Argentine navy in its ports; the Argentine air force was almost completely destroyed. British troops and marines then landed on the Falklands, securing all their objectives in scarcely a month. Within three months of their arrival, 10,000 Argentine troops had surrendered their weapons and were transported back to the mainland. Galtieri resigned, plunging the services into renewed conflict. The streets of Argentina filled with protesters. . . .

In the aftermath of military defeat, the military regime lost all remaining legitimacy and, divided internally, was unable to resist renewed opposition and mobilization. Human rights demonstrations, tax rebellions, a general strike (December 1982), and popular demonstrations for democracy led General Bignone to announce elections for October 1983. By mid-1983, the military government presided over a contest between Peronists and the Radical Party in which both major contenders for the presidency severely criticized the military regime and the policies of the military government. After the elections, the military leaders opted for an accelerated transfer of authority to the victor, Radical Party candidate Raúl Alfonsín (10 December 1983).

Facing an economic crisis and the challenge of reestablishing civilian government and democratic procedures, President Alfonsín's government tried top-ranking military officers (including ex-President Videla) for their participation in state terror and attempted to reassert civilian control over military institutions, including reforms of military education, demilitarization of some state enterprises, and reduction of military budgets. Whether these measures will succeed—or simply represent part of the ongoing cycle of coups since 1930 (military governments followed by a return to civilian rule followed by another coup)—only time will tell.

Reprinted and edited from *Argentina, 1516–1982: From Spanish Colonization to the Falklands War* (Berkeley: University of California Press, 1985), excerpted from chapter 8.

Notes

1. The *cordobazo* was a mass insurrection of students and workers in May 1969, in the city of Cordoba. The rebels succeeded in occupying the city for a short time before being dislodged by the military. (ED.)

2. The Blues (*azules*) and the *colorados* (see below) are names assigned to factions within the Argentine military, who, at least in theory, differed as to the degree and tenure of military participation in government. Theoretically, the *colorados* were less tolerant of civilians and civilian rule. (ED.)

3. This refers to the economic and political crisis of the last decade of the nineteenth century with the author comparing the policies of Martínez de Hoz to those of former President Miguel Juárez Celman (1886–90), particularly in terms of inflation, monetary devaluation, and an increasing foreign debt. (ED.)

Juan E. Corradi

Military Government and State Terrorism in Argentina

The last one hundred years of Argentine history can be neatly divided in two halves. From 1880 through 1930 it was mainly a success story, a legend of rapid economic growth, of fabulous fortunes made at the top but trickling down the social ladder, of immigration, mobility, and exceptionalism. The country was in the hands of an oligarchy of landowners in dependent association with British capital. But the wealth generated by agrarian exports opened the doors to millions of Southern Europeans that flocked to rapidly growing cities, changed the cultural texture, found new occupations, and entertained new hopes. Social progress turned into political demand, and the general prosperity, coupled with the rulers' liberal bent, allowed the extension of citizenship to a rising middle class. The next fifty years were years of turbulence ending in disappointment. They were marked, overwhelmingly, by the irruption of organized labor as a political force in a context of economic uncertainty and institutional improvisation. Argentina muddled through the industrial era unable to work out satisfactory arrangements of political conviviality. This gave rise to another, darker legend of wasted opportunities, of dereliction from great promises. Nevertheless, Argentina managed to avoid the true tragedies of the century: It did not become enmeshed in serious international conflict; its crises were never catastrophic; its political errings were more colorful than dreadful. Just as it had grown in happy nonchalance, it now seemed to falter blandly. Then suddenly, in the seventies, it caught up with the horrors of our era.

Since the ouster of the first Peronist regime (1955) through 1966, military interventions periodically interrupted the constitutional process in Argentina, but allowed it to resume its course after a while. The political regime was one of exclusionary democracy, characterized by the proscription of the main political force—Peronism—from direct participation. This system was bidimensional: It consisted of an institutional political facade (parties, parliament, and the executive) and a parallel network of negotiations in camera between corporate interests (unions, business groups, landed, financial and trade interests, and so forth), in unstable interface, which was periodically "corrected" by military interventions. The military did not stand above politics, but were part of the political process itself—one of the several actors that brought into the political arena disparate power resources. A second phase began in 1966, when the military seized power with the explicit purpose of suspending politics indefinitely and steering an ambitious program of development in dependent association with transnational capital.

The order of priorities was as follows: economic development first, social recomposition second, and political institutionalization last. However, the destruction of the existing political fabric and the social tensions brought about by the developmental process had puzzling unintended consequences that brought down the regime. The discontent of crucial social actors could not be mediated by institutional mechanisms. Instead, it generated new political alliances (notably a rapprochement between labor and middle-class sectors, between Peronists and former anti-Peronists) and a climate of generalized insurrection that threatened the state and forced the military to retreat to the barracks. A formidable amount of social power had accumulated on the margins of institutions, and the military could neither suppress nor channel it. In addition, the new mobilization carried, in its wake, the first significant anticapitalist challenge in modern Argentine history. The task of defusing the explosive mix fell on none other than Perón, who was the predictable winner of the first truly open elections since 1955. But Perón was the victim of his own success: He could not create a viable political system capable of taming the very forces that brought him back to power. After Perón's death in office (1974), his followers were even less able to control the situation. The Peronist government failed abysmally on all fronts: political stability, economic management, and the maintenance of law and order. The Peronist civilian interlude of 1973–76 was characterized by the progressive subjection of political institutions to a "siege of terror" by leftist and rightist paramilitary groups. It ended with a new seizure of power by the armed forces in 1976. The new dictatorship was the most radical of all military experiments in Argentine history. It was determined to become more impersonal, autonomous, permanent, repressive, and deeply "structural" than anything before.

The military regime installed after the March 24, 1976, coup against the government of Isabel Perón was a response to the prolonged state of war of all against all that had hitherto characterized Argentine politics. It also embodied the "learnings" of military and corporate elites from past failures. The leaders of the armed forces and their business associates proclaimed that their objective was not merely to terminate the untenable disorder of the Peronist years, but to transform the very bases of Argentine society as well. The junta vowed to abolish terrorism, to revitalize the economy by freeing it from the trammels of state guidance, to cut the Gordian knot of stalemated conflict by reducing the number of significant social actors and disciplining the remaining ones. In short, it sought to undo what had been built haphazardly since the onset of industrialization. The vision was baptized, immodestly, a "process of national reorganization," echoing another, founding process of national organization drafted by the political generation of 1837 and carried out by that of 1880 (a process that set the ground rules for Argentine preindustrial growth and modernization until 1930).

Five years later, the first military president, General Videla, finished his mandate and conveyed power to a new president-elect, General Viola. At that point, the regime began to falter. Viola was very soon replaced by the army commander, General Galtieri. After the debacle of the South Atlantic war, the latter was replaced by General Bignone, who presided over a difficult transition to an uncertain civilian rule.

An important restructuration of power took place in Argentina after 1976. It was accompanied by significant changes in ideology. Argentina in 1976 is a particularly complex case in which internal decay produced a movement for the forced reintegration of society around new or partially new patterns of behavior.

The military and civilian elites that seized power in 1976 had a draconian definition of the situation, reeking of medical imagery:"diagnosis," "social pathology," "cancer," "surgery," "extirpation of diseased tissues," and so forth. Civil society was seriously ill. The disease that afflicted the country and which came, as it were, from below, had to be met by decisive action from above. The explicit intention of the government of the armed forces was to close the historic cycle that Peronism had opened in the forties and initiate a new one. The political crisis of the seventies was perceived by both the military and some entrepreneurial elites as a basic threat to stable domination. Their critique went beyond the existing political regime that gave such a prominent place to Peronism: It focused on the social bases of the political system. Illness as political metaphor served to bridge the two major components of ideological inputs to the forced reorganization of society: to articulate the discourse of warriors and the discourse of free-enterprise conservatives.

After 1976, the main feature of the military process that took over Argentine life was the conversion of the previous populist public mores into a state-political practice and discourse in which everything was reduced to a simple dichotomy: the paradigm Friend-Foe. By reducing political rivals to ideological nonexistence, such discourse frames them for "treatment." The construction and maintenance of this order of discourse involves the deployment of particular nondiscursive sanctions which may be characterized as practices of ab-jection (expulsion, confinement, torture, "disappearance," and extermination).

The Terror Process

. . . to wage its war against subversion, the Argentina junta organized and armed many separate units within the armed forces and the police. These units operated with total autonomy and impunity, having a free hand in the selection of their victims. This strategy had several advantages for the government: It became a network very difficult to infiltrate, precisely because of its decentralized, protean nature; it was largely immune to the influence of even well-placed relatives of the victims, and it allowed the central government to disclaim responsibility for violations of human rights. Terror went through an intense phase in Argentina from 1976 through 1979. It then abated, although the repressive apparatus was seemingly still in place, or in a state of latency. During the terror phase, somewhere between 10,000 and 30,000 persons were liquidated. The extermination was largely secret—a fact that makes a precise estimate of the number of victims difficult. They rather belong to a category of nonpersons, between the dead and the living, for which Argentina has become sadly famous: those who have never been heard of again, the *desaparecidos*. Although repression was presented as a war against armed subversion, terror spilled over well beyond the limited zone of counterinsurgency operations. It affected nonviolent opponents of the regime, and also potential and imaginary opponents. It threatened, for a while, to become total. The main categories affected were, in addition to members of guerrilla organizations which were effectively decimated, lower and intermediate union cadres, students, civilian politicians, and professional groups (lawyers, psychiatrists, artists, social scientists, clergy, etc.), as well as relatives of initial victims. The terror process of Argentina has served three main and two subsidiary functions. As part of a "dirty war" against armed insurgency, it eliminated those engaged in or suspected of active hostility to the power structure. It also functioned as a mechanism of deterrence, aimed at intimidating other opponents. It sought to destroy institutional alternatives and postponed the reintegration of the disorganized groups into new organizational patterns. Furthermore, it sought the prophylactic elimination of potential opponents, identified on the basis of an ideological diagnosis of the social "disease." Indirectly, the terror process helped the military to extend control across the country. This thorough penetration of the institutional fabric of society should not be confused, however, with the consolidation of an "authoritarian-bureaucratic" state. It was a narrower and more particularistic seizure of the state apparatus by corporate groups. It was also part of a strategy to transform the country's economic structure *without*, however, strengthening the levers of bureaucratic command over the economy. Rather, the economy was streamlined and forcefully reprivatized.

Like an old kingdom of West Africa, Argentina was governed by both a visible and an invisible government, by dignified military officers managing the administrative machinery of the state and by secret terroristic associations, by hidden executioners, agents from the state *absconditus* that intervened in ordinary life at certain moments, unpredictable to the victims, holding sway by virtue of the widespread fear of their powers and through the extreme violence associated with their acts. The dissociation of the invisible government from the social relations of ordinary life, the withdrawal of the state from the public sphere—a process paralleled and reinforced by the abandonment of social regulation to the "automatic" mechanisms of the market—made systematic terrorism possible. By attributing their acts to the imperatives of national security, the officials were freed from ordinary responsibility for those acts, although they were held responsible to the highest orders of military command. In essence, the state became a quasi-private and violent affair. To the privatization of civil existence under terror corresponds an increasing privatization of state power and violence.

Many allies and critics of the regime have projected an image of it as an authoritarian state representing power externally and social regulation internally—even if the latter was often reduced to mere police regulation, without an intrinsic bond of community among the governed. The acquisition and consolidation of power by the military regime issued not Leviathan but Behemoth. Something resembling a dual state existed in Argentina during these years of intense repression (i.e., a state within which two systems operated). One served as a mark for the other, under the remnants of the constitution—applied only with respect to those provisions that have not been amended by the military government—to which a new body of law has been attached, comprised of laws and decrees, institutional acts and statutes, specific provisions, resolutions and instructions enacted since March 24, 1976. The other served under individual measures in which expediency, arbitrariness, and considerations of military security override all law. But the second system was contained in the first and acted upon it in an utterly destructive way. The seeds of that destruction are often contained in texts that have the semblance of law but none of its substance. For instance, by virtue of the Institutional Act of June 18, 1976, the military junta assumed "the power and responsibility to consider the actions of those individuals who have injured the national interest," on grounds as vague and ill-defined as "failure to observe basic moral principles in the exercise of public, political, or union offices or activities that involve the public interest." The Act led to the enactment of special laws, to the exercise of arbitrary power designed to intimidate particular groups and individuals on the basis of acts committed prior to the existence of such "laws." The generic ground on which laws rest; the discretionary nature of the powers that they grant; the creation and functioning of special bodies to which they grant jurisdictional powers; the application of their provisions on a retroactive basis; the punitive measures which they authorize; the disqualification from holding office; the restriction against practicing one's profession; the confiscation of property; the loss of citizenship, liberty, and life to which they lead, suggest, as in case of Nazi Germany, that "we are confronted with a form of society in which the ruling groups control the rest of the population directly, without the mediation of that rational though coercive apparatus known as the state."

In 1976, the military groups that seized power benefited from the disappointment of large sectors of the population with a nominally democratic system that delivered them to chaos. Yet, after six years of rule, a majority longed again for structures of representation and binding compromise, for something as undramatic as the acknowledgment of social complexity, some measure of democratic participation, and modest economic growth. Coercion and fear appeared to them, in retrospect, as another form of disorder. As mentioned previously, on the level of official ideology, the operating metaphors of law and order were medical, and more precisely, surgical. They correspond to a self-presentation of the regime as punishing definite acts of subversion and breaking up seditious organizations, on the one hand, and as establishing the bases for "sound" economic behavior, on the other. These metaphors provided a common definition of the situation for the military-technocratic elites; they bridged the vision of national security with free-enterprise and technocratic utopias. Yet, behind the manifest discourse, there developed a culture of fear corresponding to the terror process.

Pseudo-Conservatism

The initial years of the Argentine military regime—the years of terror—were characterized by a sense of timelessness at the top and anxiety at the bottom. Democracy remained suspended sine die. Perón had been dead for four years. The guerrilla movement was defeated in a bloody campaign. Terror reached a peak of intensity. Lawlessness became, paradoxically, an official routine. It consumed even the suspect. Mass silence reigned, with one exception: For several months in 1978, Argentines were allowed to pour out on the streets to attend and celebrate the world soccer championship. The outpour of collective enthusiasm was routed to a safe channel, controlled and manipulated by the regime, and acted as a safety valve for suppressed mobilization. The "Here I am" that was shouted in the streets was a nativist identification with the country's glory. Politics and independent culture were frozen, but cheering in the stadiums was allowed. While the regime acknowledged that it held nearly 3,500 political prisoners, while countless others disappeared every day, when the armed forces had seized command of all major institutions and many minor ones, from the general labor confederation to charitable associations, public life returned to a primordial state. The national sport came to mean solidarity on the cheap. It carried, no doubt, populist undertones and reminiscences of another era, but the regime felt confident enough to feign a bond of consensus with the masses and reap political profit from the event. Four years later it would try the experiment again on more dangerous ground, when it decided to occupy militarily the Malvinas Islands, tap nationalist feelings, and manipulate opinion through a brief totalitarian mobilization which backfired after the defeat, resuscitating populist mythology. These two episodes were the closest the regime came to fascism. For most of the time it preferred to combine nativism with an emphasis on discipline in a more quietistic manner, avoiding organized mass mobilization. Because of its predominantly diffuse style, the regime may be called pseudo-conservative rather than fascist. In military circles around power, the sense of a crusade against political and cultural subversion was strong. What guided the crusaders was a notion that culture and politics should be strictly subordinated to small-town morality, religion, and national security. These are supposed to form the core of an "Argentine life style" that is the antithesis of "communism" and a bulwark against it. The simplicities of this official view are not without paradox. The ideas of the moral crusaders are reactive and antimodern, yet Argentine culture is nothing but a by-product of modern enlightenment. In consequence, the ruling ideology produces the disconcerting spectacle of a young country defending old values, a community of recent settlers endorsing traditions they never had, conservatives with little to conserve. In fact, the conservatism of officers (many of them the children and grandchildren of immigrants) who want to stamp out sociology, psychoanalysis, and even some branches of modern mathematics is phony. It is a form of corporate paranoia, a universe plagued with demons and full of ill-digested values. This sense of cultural siege drove these officers to be critical of modern Western culture in the name of a myth of that culture which they pretended to guard against nameless "traitors."

Economics and Desocialization

The central feature of state action is neither compromise nor mobilization, but withdrawal from the pressures of organized social sectors and immunity from popular demands. Liberal economic policies and a free-enterprise ideology are pieces of that political strategy. They are designed to destroy preexisting patterns of economic behavior and political alliance.

Argentine economic liberalism rested on two ground rules: to open the internal to the international market, and to free capital markets. The ostensive purpose of policy was to reduce inflation. Several successive measures were adopted to that effect. They were not successful in terms of the stated objective, but they had several other functions that were perfectly in accordance with the global political vision of the regime. They were: a drastic rollback of real wages (1976–77), a reduction of the money supply (1977–78), a modulated exchange rate that produced a revaluation of the currency (1978–81). Their impact on general economic activity was cyclical until 1979 and persistently recessionary since. This pattern was accompanied by a spectacular increase in the foreign debt, until Argentina became the third-ranking debtor nation in the world, and probably the first in per capita terms.

The foremost victims of these policies were workers with fixed incomes. But other groups were also affected negatively. After 1978, farmers and exporters suffered from the overvalued currency. National industry, which saw increased benefits and expansion in 1977 and 1979, was forced to contract a debt so burdensome that it collapsed in the 1980s. Only some financial sectors did spectacularly well. The period 1976–82 may well look in retrospect as one in which a dependent national economy was ravaged by international finance capital. The political effects were completely in line with the intentions of the power holders. The labor sector was fragmented and its bargaining power significantly reduced. A large number of workers literally disappeared from the social map of Argentina, first through a combination of demographic stagnation, retirement, transfer of personnel to service and self-employed categories, and migration; and then through the increase of unemployment. The national business class was severely affected by the enormous pressures on the international market on which it depended, by debt and bankruptcy. Curiously, its wail has been louder than the protest of the workers. Also disgruntled were the agrarian exporters, although their position remained more solid than that of industrial entrepreneurs. The key to the whole policy was a financial manipulation that channeled resources toward a speculative economy. For some time, the bitter pill of deindustrialization was coated with what came to be known popularly as "sweet money" (*plata dulce*). The prototype of the new *homo oeconomicus* produced by the regime was the anomic speculator. If we now join the new pattern of induced economic action with the effects of political repression, we complete the picture of the social climate generated by the regime. Jointly, they further sapped the sagging public spirit.

The arbitrariness of security procedures, the tales of disappearances, the fear that anyone could be picked up, confined citizens to looking after themselves and their immediate families. Silence, denial, rationalization, mere self-regard became social norms. Everyone tended to become security conscious, metabolizing in the microcosm of the neighborhood, the job, or in the intimacy of family life the brutal thrust coming from above. Politically intimidated, Argentines were also harried by inflation and by the economic strategies to which they had to turn in order to cope. Argentina became a land of wheelers and dealers, of speculators and moonlighters, some making or losing paper fortunes overnight, others running ever faster in order to stand still. The carrot was no less demoralizing than the stick. Imagine individuals who run with their paychecks and pocket calculators to study the day's posted interest rates, then place their earnings in thirty-day, even seven-day instruments, while inflation and interest yields race each other on a three-digit lane. A speculative economy urges the individual to secure maximum value. Everything conspires, from the police state to wild market forces, to turn a person into a maximizing consumer rather than a cooperating citizen, discouraging and eroding feelings of social obligation. The combined timelessness of terror and the high velocity of money, the disorienting abstractions of political and economic processes, explain why traditional social conventions, such as fellowship and civil conviviality, gave way to a pervasive cynicism. . . .

The consequence of institutional failure was an added flow of power to military authorities, and an attempt by the latter to extensively overhaul the status quo. At this juncture the rulers imposed a draconian model of a better system and sought frantically to prevent other groups from developing alternatives. The model was based on a charter myth combining the doctrines of national security and free enterprise. It had clear totalitarian elements, notably the recourse to terror, the attempt to pulverize old structures—albeit through market mechanisms—and the use of ideological controls to dissolve previous identities.

Yet, the project of the power holders also contained a number of contradictions and self-checks. First, there was a tension between the economic and the military "logics" of the regime. The corporate interests of the officers often clashed with the designs of free-market technocrats. Moreover, the radical and autonomous nature of policies deprived the regime of stable alliances among crucial economic sectors. Second, the combination of physical coercion and economic disarticulation managed to stifle organized social political opposition but failed to provide substitute structures of participation and isolated the regime from society. The latter became increasingly opaque to the rulers. This situation in turn made potential opposition less predictable. The lack of early feedback signals from society compounded rather than corrected the strategic and tactical errors of the regime. When these errors were perceived, it was too late. At that point the regime changed course in a fitful manner, trying to escape from one crisis by jumping into another. Thus, when the indication of economic malfunctioning became clear, the rulers switched channels and prepared a mass mobilization for a war which, much to their dismay, actually took place and which they lost. In so acting, they opened a Pandora's box of resentment, retribution, old populist myths, and alternative ideologies.

Reprinted and edited from TELOS 54 (Winter 1982–83), pp. 61–76.

Military Rule in Bolivia after 1964

On November 4, 1964, [Alfredo] Ovando and [René] Barrientos occupied the presidential palace and declared themselves copresidents. But as the crowd gathered outside the palace persisted in shouting their preference for Barrientos, Ovando allowed Barrientos to assume the formal title alone, while he occupied the post of commander in chief of the armed forces.

Barrientos insisted that his assumption of power was not to be regarded as a counterrevolutionary move. In fact, he pledged a restoration to "the true path" of the 1952 Revolution, from which he maintained the Paz government had greviously deviated. But he began his rule with the same ephemeral base of support—military and peasants—that had crumbled beneath Paz; furthermore, like Paz, he looked to the United States as his principal source of economic assistance and, in so doing, accepted the logic of the stabilization plan that called for the containment of the labor left. Although many of the peasants tended to identify with Barrientos because he had an Indian mother and spoke Quechua, he was actually dependent for immediate effective support on alliances with key peasant leaders whose competition among themselves inhibited attempts to mold the peasantry into a power bloc. The peasants failed to constitute an effective counterweight to miners and other workers, and Barrientos was dependent almost exclusively on his military supporters for the imposition of his economic game plan.

In early 1965 the Mining Corporation of Bolivia (Corporación Minera de Boliva—COMIBOL) was placed under the control of a military director. Control Obrero (workers' control), the provision of the nationalization decree empowering union leadership to veto management decisions, was nullified. Miners' pay was halved to the equivalent of about U.S. $0.80 a day, and the COMIBOL work force was cut by 10 percent. The number of subsidized food items in company stores was also sharply reduced. When the miners responded in May 1965 by striking, the military moved into the mines and, after a violent clash, terminated the strike and disarmed the miners' militias. Leaders of the miners' unions were hustled into exile and were soon joined by leaders of other unions that protested the treatment of the miners. [Juan] Lechín was among those exiled, and the Bolivian Labor Central (Central Obrera Boliviana—COB) was effectively dismantled. In September 1965 the mines were placed under permanent military occupation, and the remnants of independent labor organization in most sectors were eliminated.

Meanwhile, with an eye to legitimizing his rule through elections in 1966, Barrientos attempted to construct a new civilian political organization. The organizing cadres for the Popular Christian movement (Movimiento Popular Cristiano—MPC) were to be drawn from right-wing anti-Paz factions of the MNR, and their target group was to be the peasant masses. The organizing campaign was not successful, however, and the MPC remained a phantom party.

Ultimately Barrientos decided on a broad-front tactic. Four small parties with nothing obvious in common—the MPC, PIR, PRA [Partido Revolucionario Auténtico], and the Social Democratic party—plus what the pro-Barrientos peasant leaders had designated the *bloque campesino* (peasant bloc) composed the heterogeneous Frente Barrientista (Barrientista Front). With the bulk of the peasant vote (but with relatively few city dwellers' votes), Barrientos won handily over five lesser-known opponents in the presidential elections of July 3, 1966.

In order not to lose his grip on the power base he had started with, Barrientos frequently increased the salaries and perquisites of the military and continued the process of granting land titles; but most attempts to expand that base beyond its original components proved futile. Cultivation of the urban middle class was difficult as the laissez faire drift of the Barrientos government, offering greater privileges to foreign investors, ran against the nationalistic grain, which was strong in that sector. Most labor organizations remained implacably opposed to his government, and students and teachers became increasingly alienated.

The killing of Ernesto "Che" Guevara in 1967 and the defeat of the guerrilla movement he had led might have consolidated support for Barrientos within the military, but an incident the following year aroused the ire even of a number of military officers. In August 1968 Antonio Argüedas, former minister of government and a close personal friend of Barrientos, announced that he had been an agent of the United States government and that agents of that government had penetrated all levels of the Bolivian government. The importance of the incident lay not so much in what was said (the rumor mill had been circulating the same information for a long time) as in who had said it because Argüedas had been the man in charge of the government's large-scale crackdown on labor, students, and other leftist groups. Nationalistic indignation was aroused, and a cloud of suspicion enveloped the government.

By 1969 Barrientos had dropped many of the formalities of constitutional government and was relying more and more on coercive measures to contain potential opposition. Moreover, as had not been uncommon in Bolivian political life, he was being publicly criticized by his own vice president, Luis Adolfo Siles Salines. Many Bolivians believed at that time that the tenure of Barrientos depended more on the military than on any other political base.

The tenure issue was eliminated rather than resolved when the president was killed in a helicopter crash on April 27, 1969. Ovando was in Washington at the time of the crash, and the vice president, Siles Salines, received permission from the army high command to assume his mandate.

Elections had been scheduled for July 1970, and it appeared for a few months that Ovando might wait for an electoral mandate and assume the presidency by constitutional means. The death of Barrientos, however, initiated a great deal of political activity and maneuvering among the various political parties and forces. The fluidity of the situation became particularly apparent in July when the popular mayor of La Paz, General Armando Escobar Uria, announced his candidacy for the presidency. On September 27, 1969, however, calling for national pacification and a true nationalist political program, Ovando dismissed Siles Salines and moved into the presidential palace. He installed a new ideologically eclectic and regionally diverse civil-military cabinet, which he described as representative of the national left, annulled the elections scheduled for 1970, and dismissed the Congress. Attempting to harness the political energy contained in the issue of economic nationalism in general and anti-Americanism in particular for the provision of immediate popular support for his new government, Ovando proceeded to nationalize the Bolivian Gulf Oil Company and to nullify the Petroleum Code. He also imposed restrictions on capital movement, gave the state mining bank a monopoly over mineral exports, withdrew the army from the mining camps, and publicly criticized what he viewed as the emphasis the United States placed on military assistance as opposed to economic assistance.

In adopting this populist-nationalist stance, Ovando had rejected his own past associations and allies, who had advocated the acceptance of international economic and military assistance, gambling that sponsorship of popular measures would provide him with a new and stronger power base. But the popularity of his policies did not translate into widespread political support for his presidency. Thus, lacking organized backing from the populist-leftist-nationalistic sector, he had to turn again to those advocating international cooperation in economic and military affairs. Lechín was again exiled for several months, and a miners' hunger march in December 1969 was denounced as subversive. In February 1970 United States military assistance, which had been temporarily suspended, was reinstated, and in September 1970 an agreement in principle was reached with the Bolivian Gulf Oil Company for financial compensation.

By mid-1970 failure to convert populist rhetoric into real benefits for the masses and concessions he had made to the right had chipped away much of the diffuse popular support Ovando had originally enjoyed. Thus, he was left in the untenable position of posing as a leftist whose base of support was the predominantly rightist military. Ambivalence and a power vacuum at the highest levels of government seemed to invite conspiracy from both right and left.

In October the situation deteriorated. The first move against the Ovando government came from the right. On October 4 General Rogelio Miranda led a revolt of the La Paz garrison, forcing Ovando's resignation and claiming the presidency for himself. He was, in turn, forced by some of the more moderate conservatives among his colleagues to step down in favor of a junta. The junta had hoped to unify the armed forces, but a group of younger, more nationalistic officers under the leadership of General Juan José Torres González had different ideas. This group, with some support from students and the Bolivian Labor Central (Central Obrera Boliviana—COB), plus the armed muscle of the air force, were enough to topple the junta and install Torres in power on October 7.

From the start Torres faced many of the same problems that had plagued Ovando, but, having been dismissed in July as commander in chief of the armed forces, he was not associated with some of the more damaging compromises of Ovando's last months in office, and he enjoyed more organized support from the nationalistic left. The Workers' Political Commando (Comando Político de los Trabajadores), for example, organized in October to back Torres, embraced the PRIN [Partido Revolucionario de la Izquierda Nacional], the POR (Partido Obrero Revolucionario), the Siles Suazo splinter of the MNR, and the Moscow-oriented wing of the PCB [Partido Comunista de Bolivia].

This support made it possible for Torres to weather the first attempt to unseat him. He had held office only three months when it took place. Participants in the abortive coup, led by Colonel Hugo Banzer Suárez, commander of the elite Colegio Militar in La Paz, were isolated within hours as a mass demonstration by workers and students suggested that Torres's faction of the military had strong popular support. Civilian demonstrators had urged Torres to distribute arms to them as a hedge against future coup attempts by right-wing military elements, but Torres, mindful that he had no control over these groups, refused.

Torres made a serious, but ultimately futile, attempt to win the full confidence of the left. He tolerated the organization in July 1971 of the People's Assembly. The majority of the delegates to this two-week session represented the trade unions, although peasant organizations and students were also represented and six leftist parties were allowed two delegates each. Neither the MNR, the largest political party, nor the military was represented. The assembly lacked the means to implement its program, and proposals to establish a people's militia and to reinstitute trade union control over COMIBOL, among others, served only to unite in opposition the disparate elements who saw their interests threatened by the assembly.

Even more provocative to opponents of the Torres government in general and to the military hierarchy in particular was the emergence of the Military Vanguard of the People (Vanguardia Militar del Pueblo—VMP). A manifesto published by this group in August 1971 noted that the lower ranks of the army were the proletarians in a class-stratified institution and proposed the replacement of the existing hierarchy with a popular army at the service of the people. The VMP, a secret society of junior officers organized on a cellular basis, was active only in La Paz. By publicizing its intentions while lacking a firm base, the VMP merely gave premature warning to its opponents.

In deference to his civilian supporters, Torres had purged a number of right-wing officers from the military, but he was apparently unwilling or unable to allow the predominance of the military among the country's institutions to be undermined. As he wavered between the irreconcilable pressures of the military and the unions, the minimal control he had exercised over each of these groups was eroded.

Meanwhile, Banzer and his principal collaborators, exiled following the abortive coup in January, had returned surreptitiously and were being harbored by military colleagues in Santa Cruz. By August, rumors had spread throughout the country that Banzer, supported by such diverse entities as Bolivian Gulf, the Brazilian government, and the FSB [Falange Socialista Boliviano], was plotting a coup. The government apparently placed credence in these rumors because on August 18, 1971, Banzer and a number of his colleagues were arrested by the police in Santa Cruz. The remaining conspirators proceeded to organize a demonstration and to occupy the town square, the major radio stations, the university, and the trade union headquarters. By nightfall, effective control of Santa Cruz was in the hands of the insurgents, and military garrisons all over the lowlands were declaring their support for the insurrection.

Within a couple of days the garrisons of the Altiplano were wavering in their support of the central government. Workers and students in La Paz organized a large demonstration in favor of Torres and demanded weapons to defend his government. Those supporting Torres had few weapons to distribute. Nevertheless, the violence and loss of life accompanying this change of government was greater than at any time since the 1952 Revolution. In the final confrontation only one military regiment, the Colorado Regiment, of La Paz, was willing to fight to preserve the government. Many workers, students, and other civilians, however, some with and some without weapons, attempted in vain to hold out against the insurgents. Street fighting in La Paz reportedly left some 200 dead and 500 to 700 wounded.

On August 21 Torres retreated to the Peruvian embassy, and Banzer emerged from imprisonment to assume the presidency. Before dawn on the morning of the following day tanks rolled through the streets of La Paz, their loudspeakers announcing that Bolivia had been saved from communism. The last of the serious fighting took place on August 23, when armored-car units and air force fighter planes attacked students at the Higher University of San Andrés, in La Paz. The Banzer government announced that 7 students had been killed; other sources maintained that casualties were several times that number. About 300 students were arrested. All of the country's universities were closed thereafter for more than a year while faculties and student bodies were purged of opponents of the government and a new university reform decree eliminating university autonomy was drawn up.

The power base of the new government consisted of an alliance of groups drawn together for the most part by their fear of Torres's radicalism and their commitment to order, anticommunism, and private enterprise. In addition to Banzer's military allies, the major components of the Nationalist Popular front (Frente Popular Nacionalista—FPN), as the new ruling coalition was called, were the FSB and the core of the MNR, under the leadership of Paz. Considering the family background (the landowning class of Santa Cruz) of the new president and his consistently conservative stance, the collaboration of the FSB with his government was not surprising. The involvement of the MNR has been seen in part as a consequence of the nearly total exclusion of that party from the government of Torres, particularly in its later days. Paz was invited to return from exile, but he did not assume a formal position in the government.

The two parties were allocated five ministries each, and at the departmental level one party was to nominate the prefect and the other, the mayor. The military retained the ministries of defense, government, and agriculture, and the ministries of industry and of hydrocarbons were filled with representatives of private enterprise. One of the most notable shifts in the power structure was that of regional base; almost half the cabinet members were natives of Santa Cruz.

The precariousness of the collaboration of such traditional foes as the FSB and the MNR was apparent from the start, as fistfights erupted between members of the two groups at the swearing-in ceremonies for the cabinet.

Both parties suffered internal dissension as a consequence of their collaboration with each other and with the military. The MNR leaders were constrained by the military in their efforts to mobilize their traditional popular base, and the FSB had never had a mass base, so both parties were, to a degree, dependent on the pleasure of the military for their continued participation in government.

The new minister of government, Colonel Andrés Selich, head of the ranger unit that had been specially trained by United States military advisers to deal with guerrilla movements, launched a pacification program in which he enjoyed considerable autonomy of action. Predictably, public employees were among the first groups to be purged, both because they had served a government considered radical and because all available patronage was needed to undergird the new government. Other groups that were targets of the government ministry's campaign were labor and student leaders, worker-priests, and journalists. Within a month of the coup d'état, for example, more than 100 journalists had vanished from their former posts.

By early 1972 the visibility of the rangers and the zeal and apparent lack of discrimination with which Selich had pursued his campaign against those he considered communist subversives had provoked sharp protests from the church and appeared to have brought the shaky government coalition to the verge of disintegration. The presbyterial council of the diocese of La Paz called on the government ministry to end the repression, and the bishop of Corocoro expressed outrage over the unexplained invasion and search of his house by the police. MNR leaders in the government were antagonized by the arrests of many members of their rank and file; and the detention of former vice-president Nuflo Chávez Ortiz and of Paz's son, an international civil servant, aroused extreme indignation.

More importantly, the elite status and virtual autonomy of the rangers were resented by many in the upper echelons of the regular military hierarchy. The rangers were far better paid, fed, and equipped than other military units and wore a distinctive uniform. Moreover, many in the upper echelon of the regular military ranks perceived that close ties existed between Selich and the United States military assistance group. At a birthday celebration in December 1971 for a newly appointed commander in chief of the armed forces, the rangers were openly accused of being mercenaries under foreign control.

Banzer announced the dismissal of Selich that same month. Initially, Selich held out in the ministry and threatened to shoot anyone who tried to remove him. He was finally assigned to diplomatic exile in Paraguay and later was forcibly retired from the army. Nevertheless, rumors that he was plotting a coup persisted. The seriousness of such threats to the government could not be reliably ascertained. The majority of subversive plots that the government reported to have uncovered in the course of 1972, however, were attributed to leftist groups.

The semipublic bickering and dissembling within and between the parties in the governing coalition that continued throughout 1972 appeared to enhance the power of Banzer vis-à-vis the civilian leaders, but in July he acquiesced to MNR pressure and permitted the legalization of labor unions (though not of the major federations). The devaluation of the peso from about 12 to 20 to $1 (U.S.) in October, however, sparked a new crisis. A general strike shut down business activity in the capital, and demonstrations resulted in clashes between strikers and police and in large-scale arrests of labor leaders. On November 23, Banzer, stating that he had uncovered a leftist plot to overthrow the government, declared a state of siege.

In December Banzer announced that his government had uncovered another massive plot, in this case to assassinate him and "Vietnamize" Bolivia. The plotters were said to be components of a front group known as the Anti-Imperialist Revolutionary Front (Frente Revolucionaria Anti-imperialista—FRA). More than twenty Bolivian organizations, including virtually every party to the left of the MNR, were listed as components. Also listed among the plotters were about a dozen leftist organizations from other parts of the hemisphere, including three composed of Chile's Mapuche Indians. The plot was said to be funded by Cuba and supported by the People's Republic of China (PRC) and the Soviet Union and to include an attack by a 7,000-man guerrilla army that was in training in Chile.

A reinvigorated campaign to round up subversives followed this announcement. By January 1973 the number of political prisoners, many of whom were held in special camps in remote areas, was estimated by some sources at more than 1,500. As had been true in several other Latin American countries, the thoroughness of the antisubversive net was such that even personal libraries of suspects were examined for literature that might be considered subversive.

It was announced in January that the coalition of the Christian Democratic party (Partido Demócrata Cristiano—PDC), formerly the PSC, and the PRA had entered into an opposition pact with the Siles Suazo faction of the MNR, known as the Nationalist Revolutionary Movement of the Left (Movimiento Nacionalista Revolucionario de la Izquierda—MNRI). In early February the coalition appealed to the armed forces to restore constitutional order and guarantee free elections. The armed forces high command responded that "when the social and economic objectives (of the government) are achieved, the political conditions necessary to enter into an institutionalization process will be studied."

The reappearance in Bolivia of Colonel Selich in May 1973 set off a chain of events that resulted in the most severe crisis that the Banzer government had yet confronted. Suspected once again of masterminding a plot to overthrow the government, Selich was arrested on May 14. It was announced on the following day that Selich had died as a consequence of falling down a flight of stairs while attempting to escape. The original official version of the event met with considerable skepticism, and on May 18 a new official version was released. Government Minister Alfredo Arce Carpio announced at that time he had discovered that Selich had been beaten to death by overly zealous interrogators.

The announcement provoked outrage from both military and civilian sectors, and the FSB threatened to withdraw its support from the government if Arce were not removed from office. President Banzer discouraged precipitous action by his opponents by posting army vehicles and troops around the National Palace, while acquiescing to FSB demands and accepting Arce's resignation. The commander in chief of the armed forces, General Joaquim Zenteno Anaya, also resigned, claiming that Banzer's coalition was inoperative, and the president himself took charge temporarily of that vacated post. Meanwhile, President Banzer was reportedly sharing his power to a greater extent with other military officers.

Reprinted and edited from United States Government, *Area Handbook for Bolivia,* 2d ed. (1974), pp. 239–46.

James Dunkerley

The Military and Bolivian Politics, 1971–83

Hugo Banzer Suárez ruled Bolivia for almost exactly seven years. His regime was the country's longest in over a century, spanning the bulk of a decade in which open political activity was the exclusive prerogative of the military and its closest collaborators. The August coup and the dictatorship built upon it radically altered public life, which for the majority was subordinated to the risky negotiation of daily and civic affairs. Banzer certainly encountered opposition, but inside the military he was able to contain it with adroit manoeuvre; popular discontent and resistance, on the other hand, was repressed without quarter. This drove many sectors of the population into an anguished resignation that was abetted by the parlous state of the left, for much of this period entirely preoccupied with the arduous and painfully slow tasks of reorganization. Banzer's ability to uphold this system of rigid control was due principally to the unequivocal support he enjoyed for several years from Washington, from an economically expanding and politically ambitious Brazil, and from the dominant agro-industrial interests of Santa Cruz, now the dynamo of the economy as a result of a massive increase in the price of oil and the boom in export agriculture. The matrices of Bolivia's economy were transformed almost to the same degree as the country's politics, these alterations being trumpeted so loudly that it seemed to many that a new era had indeed arrived.

This illusion was greatly bolstered by the advent of similar regimes throughout the southern cone of Latin America. The coups of June and September 1973 in Uruguay and Chile established governments that were even more extreme than Banzer's and acted from their inception with a radicalism and confidence that lent substance to ambitions to hold sway for at least a decade and possibly to the end of the century. The shift to the right in Peru with the 1975 overthrow of the ailing Velasco by General Morales Bermúdez was less emphatic but marked a general trend which was fully confirmed by the establishment of General Videla's institutional regime in Buenos Aires in March 1976. A Southern Cone Model emerged, characterized by the prohibition of independent and union activity, an authoritarian garrison state, the pugnacious celebration of "western christendom" and "nationalism," and corporativist systems of social organization. Repression was generalized and extraordinarily harsh; the left was defeated on a regional scale with the death and "disappearance" of tens of thousands. Economic management was handed over to the enthusiastic acolytes of Milton Friedman and the "Chicago School" of free-marketeers who dismantled the apparatus of protectionism, pared down state enterprise, scythed through welfare expenditure, and made a frontal assault on wages. Although in the medium term the results were in every case disastrous, it should not be forgotten that some spectacular immediate returns were registered by local financial groups, as well as foreign capital.

If Bolivia did not exhibit the extremes evident in the large neighboring states, it was largely because the ecological limits to her economy were simply too tight. Following his *"autogolpe"* of November 1974, Banzer dispensed with the services of his civilian allies, founded an exclusively military administration, and introduced a string of corporativist decrees similar to those promulgated by General Pinochet in Chile. The model of an "organic regime" was fully embraced with a formal but not inconsequential realignment of the ideology of August 1971. This system was to remain firmly intact for a further three years. Its eventual collapse, which only became visible at the end of 1977, was most obviously underpinned by economic factors and pressure from the Carter administration, but it was also accelerated by the resurgence of political forces that reformed and took advantage of unexpected opportunities with great rapidity. Thus, despite its remarkable longevity, the Banzer regime was by a long margin the first of the southern cone dictatorships to crumble, its "New Bolivia" proving to be too threadbare a construction to endure once economic expansion was exhausted and external patronage removed.

"Paz, Orden, Trabajo"

Banzer was a talented career officer to whom political extravagance was alien. His political skills, which were not for some time fully appreciated by his peers, centered on an ability to control the armed forces through a diligent management that frequently required decisive pre-emptive action but was generally based on negotiation. He was not overly encumbered with novel ideas, never very popular with his colleagues, neither physically nor personally imposing, and only over time did he develop into a capable public speaker. The new president was the grandson of German immigrants, the son of a senior but undistinguished commander in the Chaco

War, and well-connected with the influential expatriate business community in his home town of Santa Cruz. Aged only forty-four when he came to power, Banzer had graduated as a sub-lieutenant in the immediate aftermath of the 1946 counter-revolution when anti-militarist sentiment was rife. As a lieutenant he survived the purges of 1952 and was promoted rapidly under the MNR, becoming a colonel at the age of thirty-five after attending a number of advanced courses in the U.S. An expert in logistics, he served as Barrientos' minister of education and then as attache in Washington. Trenchantly conservative in outlook but without party affiliation, respected by his colleagues, trusted by the North Americans, and feted by the *cruceño* bourgeoisie, the diminutive Machiavellian was in almost every sense the perfect leader for the new Bolivian counter-revolution.

The trinity of "peace, order, work" became the leitmotif of Banzer's rule and was seen by many as confirming its fascist character. However, in August 1971, neither Banzer nor the military as a whole felt able to advance without the support of the country's most powerful parties of tradition and historic antagonists: the Falange and the MNR. Both parties were given four seats in the new cabinet, in which seven out of fifteen members came from Santa Cruz. The FSB's leader Mario Gutiérrez was made foreign minister in recognition of his party's role in the August rebellion, but Víctor Paz, who before the end of the month was declaring with entirely misplaced confidence that "I am the caudillo of Bolivia and people believe in me," preferred to manage his party's affairs without taking up a government position. In a move that was soon to provoke some institutional discontent, Banzer signed a pact with the two parties to form the Frente Popular Nacionalista [FPN], by which the military formally became part of a political movement. The CEPB was also included in this new front, which was financed by "donations" of 1 percent of all state salaries, deducted at source. . . .

The response from Washington was predictable. John Connally brought Nixon's "warmest wishes" to La Paz and praised Banzer's "great courage." In Washington itself, newly appointed ambassador Colonel Valencia went to the White House to hear the U.S. president promise close cooperation "throughout the 1970s," indicating that both sides had expectations of a prolonged rule. Indeed, for a number of years the rising price of tin proved to be virtually the only fly in the ointment; in 1973, following a period of steady increases, Nixon finally decided that it had reached a point that merited the reduction of the U.S. stockpile from 232,000 tons to 40,500 tons, starting with a sale of 18,500 tons at the end of the year. The threat to the Bolivian economy was very great and had been anticipated for some time, but Banzer was in no position to challenge the sales, particularly since his regime was benefiting from unprecedented amounts of U.S.

aid. Between 1942 and 1970, Bolivia received a total of $6.7 million from the U.S. for "administration and government"; over the sixteen months between August 1971 and December 1972, Banzer collected a total of $32 million under this head. In his first year of office, military assistance from Washington was double that for the period 1968 to 1970, with total U.S. AID loans exceeding $60 million; the grants of military aid for 1973 and 1974 were three times as great as any previously made by the U.S. to a Latin American country. The scale of this support from Washington prompted a congressional debate in which Defense Secretary Melvin Laird was unable to determine any reason for such largesse other than "domestic insurgency," since it was now publicly accepted by the Pentagon that Cuba no longer threatened a country like Bolivia. Banzer was, of course, especially privileged because until mid-1973, Bolivia was the most critical strategic redoubt for U.S. interests in the southern cone.

Similar geographical interests lay behind Brazil's policy toward the regime. Brasilia was traditionally concerned to counter Argentina's interests in the *altiplano,* and this it could now do without great difficulty by favoring Santa Cruz, which lay firmly within its economic and political orbit. Less than a month after the coup, Brazil granted Bolivia $10 million in credits for machinery to build a railway between the eastern capital and the border town of Corumba. Over the following years, annual grants averaged $46 million, underpinning a series of economic agreements by which Bolivia was to provide her giant neighbor oil, gas, rubber, manganese, and iron ore at preferential rates. The terms of some of these agreements were so generous that opposition to them extended well beyond the now embattled friends of Buenos Aires, obliging Banzer to qualify somewhat the enthusiasm with which he had initially embraced the new alliance. Although Bolivian oil and gas were for a time of more than minor interest to Brazilian economic planners, the country offered only a limited export market, and one should not underestimate the more strategic motivations of the Brazilian military. These encompassed not only control over a zone of manifest political importance, but also the forging of inroads through to the Pacific seaboard. This latter objective was naturally hampered by Chilean possession of Bolivia's coastal territory, but with a compliant regime in La Paz, Brasilia's influence in that sector was markedly increased; once Pinochet came to power the possibility of an accord between governments of similar ideological disposition was further enhanced. The Brazilian generals made few efforts to conceal such aims; in 1972, the "Superior School of War" published a document which stated that, "The armed forces ought to intervene in instances of border disputes between other countries of the continent with concern for national interests, the ramifications of armed conflict, and the activity of international communism, whether it be in the country itself or in other countries." If

Banzer and his colleagues were alarmed by this untempered interventionist ethic, they made little show of resisting it in practice. In April 1974, Bolivia passed to Brazil 12,000 square kilometers, including the villages of San Ignacio and Palmarito (population: 3,000) in a revision of the border. In 1976, a further 27,000 square kilometers were lost in similar style; a year later the island of Suárez in the Beni changed hands, this time through direct Brazilian occupation. In several zones of the northeast, progressive colonization by Brazilian nationals reached such a point that by 1974, the Bolivian chancellery was obliged to request its Brazilian counterpart to restrict the flow, since national sovereignty was at risk. There was no reply.

The compliant nature of the Banzer government in its relations with the U.S. and Brazil was complemented by its severe treatment of dissidents inside the country. Both legal and de facto repression exceeded that imposed by Barrientos, being particularly fierce in the opening phase of the regime. Banzer appointed Selich as his first minister of interior, closed the universities for six months, reinstated the death penalty, and did nothing to curb those in his camp who proclaimed that "for every nationalist who is killed, ten extremists must die." After the fall of San Andrés on 23 August, armed resistance was minimal and posed no threat whatsoever, but "communist subversion" was almost always cited as the reason for arrests, deportations, and the closure of newspapers or radio stations; those people who died at the hands of the military were invariably described as "subversives" or "Castro-communists."

By supreme decree 09875 (7 September 1971), the regime formally declared the 1967 constitution to be in force, "in every respect which does not contradict the spirit and nature of the Nationalist Government and its actions." Having conferred upon itself the right to act unconstitutionally, the government only bothered to legalize the death penalty and the right to hold suspects for an indefinite period (supreme decree 10295, 3 June 1972). In the immediate aftermath of the coup, Selich was given free rein to liquidate opponents, two of the most important of whom were Alcides and Félix Sandoval Morón, shot in police stations in Santa Cruz, where the populist clan was still feared by the vested interests that had suffered at its hands in the 1950s. On some occasions, such as when he accused Torres of leading the ELN and Ovando of masterminding its operations from Madrid, Selich's imagination proved to be a little too fertile, even for the purposes of constructing a rationale for repression. Mostly, however, he acted with absolute disregard either for life or the external impact of gratuitous killing. When, in November 1971, a pro-Torres army captain and ten other prisoners persuaded five of their guards at the Alto Madidi concentration camp to help them capture a plane and flee to Peru, Selich bombed and strafed the camp before closing it down.

By January 1972, Selich was acting so zealously and had concentrated so much power in his ministry that Banzer, fearing a coup attempt, sent him to Asunción as ambassador. Four months later he was removed from that post. This did not, however, signal any relaxation on the part of the regime, as was vividly illustrated in May 1973, when Selich himself was arrested in La Paz by officers who had previously worked for him, interviewed by the new minister, and then beaten to death. The official version that he had thrown himself down a flight of stairs "during a nervous attack" convinced nobody and caused outrage in the military, which forced a public inquiry. Perhaps the greatest irony of Selich's fate was that his death provided one of the best documented revelations of how the system he had instituted undertook its operations.

The work begun by the defunct colonel was continued by Colonels Mario Adett Zamora and Juan Pereda Asbun, who, as ministers of interior, controlled the much-feared Departamento de Orden Político (DOP), the main instrument of political control. For most of the *banzerato* the DOP was headed by Colonel Rafael Loayza, whose principal henchman, Abraham Baptista, had been a vigorous chief of police under Barrientos. Captain Carlos Mena was another prominent officer who showed great appetite for the department's work, but many of its most infamous operatives—Guido Benavides, Fernando "Mosca" Monroy, "Danger" Salamanca, and Daniel Torrico, who at the weekends transformed himself into the popular wrestler 'Mr. Atlas'—were civilians recruited from the lower ranks of the FSB or the criminal fraternity. A large part of the DOP's activity was organized around the jails, interrogation centers, and concentration camps at Madidi, Achocalla, Chonchoroco, Viacha, and the Titicaca island of Coati, which, like Madidi, had to be closed down for a while when sixty-seven prisoners escaped to Peru after overpowering their guards during a football match in November 1972. Although most people who fell into the hands of the repressive state apparatus in Bolivia were eventually accounted for—unlike in Chile and Argentina, where the verb "to disappear" acquired a sadly transitive form—it is hard to enumerate the effects of repression with any precision. However, the copious documentation collected by various human rights organizations yields a figure of 200 as the minimum for those killed between October 1971 (after the initial offensive) and December 1977. Some 14,750 people were jailed for "offenses against the state," almost every one of them without semblance of judicial process. . . .

These figures may appear very moderate when compared to the horrific statistics of persecution for the other states of the southern cone, but it should be borne in mind that Bolivia had a population of less than six million people, most of whom still lived in the countryside. In the urban and industrial centers where political and public life was concentrated, the impact was considerable. Yet, since these circles were in relative terms very limited, there was no exodus comparable to that from countries with big urban conurbations or large middle classes, such as Uruguay, Chile, and Argentina, whence refugees streamed into Europe on a scale not seen since the 1930s. In these countries one of the predominant characteristics of repression was the . . . imposition of a blanket control, enabling Banzer to enforce the highly unpopular economic measures required of his government by the IMF. The first of these was implemented on 27 October 1972, when the regime devalued the peso by 67 percent in order to obtain a $24 million loan from the Fund. The devaluation increased the cost of living by 39 percent over the following year, while wage rises were limited to between 10 and 20 percent, resulting in a minimum loss of earning power of 19 percent. Following traditional practice, Banzer announced the measure on a Friday evening to delay popular mobilization and allow time for troops to occupy the center of La Paz over the weekend, when a full stage of siege was declared. Nevertheless, on the Monday afternoon, after a series of meetings which led to the declaration of an eight-hour protest strike, several hundred workers took to the streets of the capital. This first open demonstration against the "fascist, anti-worker dictatorship" was suppressed quickly and with maximum force. According to the government, clashes with the troops left fourteen people wounded, but up to twenty deaths were reported in the foreign press.

The popular economy suffered an even more severe blow when, in decrees first announced in October 1973, but eventually delayed until 20 January 1974, Banzer removed or substantially reduced state subsidies on a range of basic goods and services. The subsidy on flour alone amounted to $20 million a year, the withdrawal of which would represent a considerable saving for the state. In the event, this commodity was one of the last badly hit, the price rise introduced in January in order "to bring it into line with the world market . . . and reduce contraband" being limited to 150 percent. The cost to the consumer of cooking oil, eggs, sugar, coffee, meat, rice, and pasta rose by an average of 219 percent. Fully aware that inflation to such a degree required wage compensation if public order was to be maintained, the regime decreed a complicated system of bonuses for the industrial labor force, but this covered only half the rise in prices. In the towns, the response to this measure was stronger than that of October 1972. The day after it was declared, more than a hundred factories in La Paz came out on a thirty-six-hour strike. Two days later, a national factory workers' strike received the support of the miners and bank workers. Housewives protested outside the presidential palace, brandishing pots and pans, and there were a number of clashes between students and the police. Seventy people were arrested, the church issued an extraordinarily strong condemnation of the decrees, and the CEPB stated flatly that it could not afford to pay the stipulated wage bonus. Yet it was in the countryside that the removal of price subsidies produced the gravest crisis.

The spontaneous mobilization that took place in the upper Cochabamba valley after the introduction of the price rises stemmed from the fact that the *campesinos* received no compensatory bonus at all and were prohibited from increasing the market price of their produce. Moreover, many did not produce the goods affected and, like the urban workers, were obliged to purchase them at the new prices, which was nigh-on impossible in January when stocks from the last harvest were exhausted and the next still far from ripe. Trouble began early on the morning of the 22nd when, adhering to the strike call, workers at the large Manaco shoe factory at Quillacollo, fifteen kilometers from Cochabamba, held a protest march. This soon drew the support of other factories and became so large that the local detachment of police had to withdraw. The next day demonstrators attempted to blow up three bridges, and then held a public meeting at which demands were raised for the withdrawal of the decrees, freedom for all political prisoners, the devolution of "intervened" radio stations, and the dispatch of a government commission to discuss terms. As a result of the symbiosis between town and country in Cochabamba, news of the Quillacolla events was soon known in most of the valley. On the 24th, the road to Santa Cruz was blocked. The next day blockades extended from kilometer 20 as far as the turning to Sucre at kilometer 126. Despite extremely heavy rain, some 20,000 peasants congregated at the major points at which the highway was barricaded. Their demands for the removal of the decrees and that Banzer come immediately to negotiate with them were presented first to the minister of agriculture, Colonel Alberto Natusch Busch, on the 25th, and then to the newly designated military "inventor," General Pérez Tapia, on the 28th. Refusing either to make a deal with subordinates or to go to La Paz, the *campesinos* insisted upon Banzer's presence as the only condition for lifting the barricades. The president's response was curtly to reject "any dialogue under pressure," declare a state of siege, and send the Tarapacá to reinforce local troops.

Early on the 29th, the *campesino* leaders held a further meeting with General Pérez, the talks lasting until mid-afternoon. On returning to Cochabamba, Pérez was surprised to encounter a column of six tanks and eight armored cars moving toward the first roadblock. Having made some progress in his discussions, he ordered the column to halt but was informed that Banzer had commanded a complete "mopping up of the subversives." The regime later announced that Pérez had been taken hostage and was only released on the 30th after action by the armored column.

What was soon dubbed "The Massacre of the Valley" began at the village of Tolata at 5 P.M. on the 29th. When the column approached, the *campesinos* gathered round thinking that Banzer had finally arrived. The commanding officer ordered them to disperse. First there was silence and then a woman threw a stone at the leading tank. The attack that followed combined the use of fighter aircraft with the automatic weapons of the armored vehicles but was described by the high command as "a simple dissuasive action." One conscript later told a priest, "We have seen mounds of corpses, *campesinos* stacked up like wood." Another counted some thirty covered trucks traveling to the airport from Tolata, and said that after the attacks, some soldiers refused to go on while others had deliberately fired into the air. Later that night some 700 peasants were attacked at a bridge near Epizana, fifteen corpses were found, and twenty people "disappeared." The next day military operations produced more casualties, but the remaining roadblocks were cleared without further loss of life.

The total death toll was estimated at between 80 and 200, one factor in the uncertainty being ignorance of the fate of 65 people who had "disappeared." There were no military casualties. Tolata was Banzer's San Juan and described by the church as "another My Lai." It effectively terminated the alliance between the military and the *campesinado* for, although the *Pacto* continued to be signed every year by official leaders, it now patently lacked any credibility among the rural masses. The president's response was to claim that the protest had been planned by the Cubans in league with the exiled Chilean socialist leader Carlos Altamirano. Two days after the Tolata killings, Banzer gave a speech to tame peasant leaders from the *altiplano* in which he persisted in his theory, stating, "To you, *campesino* brothers, I am going to give direction as your leader: I authorize you to kill the first agitator that goes into the *campo,* I take full responsibility. If you don't kill them, bring them here so that they can deal with me personally. I will give you a reward." In practice, Banzer had already dispensed with many of Barrientos' methods in upholding the alliance with the peasantry since it no longer played the crucial role of ten years before. With the working class in full retreat and the armed forces greatly strengthened, the regime could exist with neutrality rather than popularity in the countryside. The appointment of hard-liner Natusch, who had declared, "we will be totally radical" with the Cochabamba protesters, was one indication of this new approach. Neither Natusch, a *beniano,* nor Banzer, a *cruceño,* spoke an indigenous language or cared to cavort in populist style. The president rarely made rural tours, and when he gave speeches seldom deviated from bland celebrations of "nationalism" and warnings about its opponents: "I have heard that you don't like politicians. I don't like them either because they come to cheat you. The Communists want to take away your land, to give it to the state; the politicians just want to cheat you. They only want peasant votes in order to get into office, where they forget about their false promises. . . ."

Managing the Boom

Banzer's economic strategy had two main goals: the attraction of direct foreign investment by removing all but the most minimal constraints on capital, and the fostering of rapid, export-led growth centered on Santa Cruz. The privatization of chunks of the large infrastructural state sector was recognized to be unattractive to private enterprise except in a very few areas, and it was only in the exploitation of oil and gas that this made appreciable headway. By the end of 1974, the extent of economic expansion appeared to vindicate the strategy. However, the real cause of substantially increased export earnings was not a restructured manufacturing sector dynamized with fresh foreign capital, but massive leaps in the price of oil, supported by a subsidiary boom in agro-industry that was fueled by even shorter-term price fluctuations and an over-abundance of credit. The complete mismanagement of this transient "loophole" in the terms of trade meant that when price advantages were reduced, the Bolivian economy was plunged into a crisis comparable only with that of 1956. The principal features of this crisis were, as elsewhere in Latin America, the accumulation of a massive foreign debt and persistent inflation.

The failure to attract foreign investment did not stem from any lack of effort on the part of the government. The September 1971 investment law freed capital movement to enable substantial repatriation of profits, removed tariffs not only on capital goods (which in this case included vehicles of all description), but also on primary materials, abolished taxes on production and manufactured exports, and laid down exceptionally generous terms for the assessment of capital depreciation. With the removal of key tariffs, the tax level on imports fell from 10.2 percent in 1972 to 5.6 percent in 1978. The loosening of credit was no less emphatic: Over the same period, local bank loans rose from Bs1.3 billion to Bs5.0 billion, while foreign lending was considerably more generous. Yet, over these six years, the liquidity coefficient (the relation of money in circulation to the value of production) increased from 0.2 percent to 0.8 percent, indicating that the large sums of money being made available were not being matched by increased output. One central reason was that foreign capital simply did not arrive, total direct external investments over the *banzerato* amounting to only $96.8 million, of which more than 65 percent came from just three firms: Atlas Copco Andina in metallurgy, Sociedad Aceitera de Oriente in agro-industry, and Sheraton Hotels. However generous and politically stable it might have been, the Banzer administration proved unable to persuade foreign capital that Bolivia had ceased to be a high-risk zone. More critically still, it was hindered by the fact that the country had a very small internal market and a low level of internal and regional integration, which, despite the availability of cheap labor, meant unacceptably high production costs. Thus, the comparatively high export of capital during the 1970s was not primarily accounted for by repatriated profits, as might at first seem natural from the terms of the investment law. These were only $70 million (12 percent), while the much larger figure of $314.4 million (88 percent) left the country in the form of interest payments on the government's escalating borrowing. Yet, the policy of opening up the economy did not just fail to "take off" since the removal of import controls actively prejudiced the interests of a highly vulnerable local industrial sector. Although between 1971 and 1978, imports of consumer goods rose only marginally, from 20.1 to 21.5 percent of the total, those of capital goods fell substantially from 49.1 to 42.8 percent, while primary materials that were frequently in competition with local products rose from 29.6 to 35.0 percent.

When set against such a picture, the government's policy of dynamizing the economy of Santa Cruz seemed to be an unqualified success. . . . The Banzer regime also enjoyed a remarkably favorable situation with regard to the market in tin. After stagnation in the 1950s and a sluggish, uneven rising trend in the 1960s, tin prices registered an increase that was significantly more moderate than that for oil but still critical for an economy which continued to depend on the industry for 70 percent of its foreign currency earnings. Between 1972 and 1978, the price rose from $1.69 to $5.72 a pound. Yet, as with petrol, increased export value—from $113 million in 1972 to $374.4 million in 1978—corresponded solely to the price rise and not to greater production, which in fact fell (from 30,277 tons in 1971 to 29,697 tons in 1978).

The most marked characteristic of the organization of mining in this period was the officially sponsored ascendancy of the twenty-five larger firms of the private sector organized in the Asociación de Mineros Medianos (ANMM). Between 1973 and 1976, the value of Comibol's exports rose by 55 percent, while taxes on its operations increased by 99 percent; over the same period the ANMM's revenue from foreign sales rose by 76 percent, but its taxes by only 26 percent. Rates of profit as a consequence varied widely, Comibol's falling by 107 percent and the ANMM's growing by 27 percent. Boosted not only by favorable government treatment, but also by price rises for subsidiary minerals in which it had obtained a sizable share of control (tungsten: 70 percent; antimony: 100 percent; copper: 65 percent), the ANMM increased its labor force by 80 percent and accounted for a fifth of national mineral production. The dominance of an aged state operation mortgaged to foreign banks was placed under acute challenge by private companies which were almost without exception linked to international firms (U.S. Steel, W. R. Grace, IMPC, etc.). In this respect, one of the first and most telling of Banzer's appointments was that of Guillermo "Willy" Gutiérrez Vea Murguia to the executive directorship of the national investment institute. Gutiérrez was head of the Avicaya mining company, linked to the Grace group, but more importantly, he had been a senior adviser to Aramayo and was the Rosca's leading candidate in the 1951 elections. His appointment strongly suggested a desire to return to the days before Comibol existed.

However serious their consequences, none of the features of the regime's policy summarized above were to have such a profound and lasting effect on the country's economy as the Banzer government's recourse to loans since, in the absence of any meaningful direct foreign investment, the policy of rapid growth had to be financed by foreign debt. This was, of course, not an abnormal course for a Latin American state in the 1970s, but the scale of Bolivia's borrowing was for a country of its size and productive capacity appreciable even by the unenviable standards of the regime. In 1971, the foreign debt stood at $782.1 million; by the end of 1978, it had risen to $3,101.8 million. This increase of $2,319.7 million was not, moreover, matched by a corresponding rise in exports, the debt service rising from 17.3 to 32.0 percent of export value over the same period. Furthermore, the cost of this credit became progressively higher as international agencies and foreign states drew away from lending to be replaced by private banks, which imposed more stringent terms. In 1971, less than 4 percent of the debt was with private banks; by 1978, they controlled 43.1 percent. In 1972, Bolivia's debt service—the return of principal and payment of interests and commissions—was 36.7 percent of the amount borrowed, whereas in 1978 it was returning 66 percent to the lenders. Between 1971 and 1978, the average annual debt service was over half the sum borrowed. As is now widely appreciated, such a situation leads to yet further borrowing to cover balance of payments deficits and to regenerate production. With the exception of 1974—the year blessed by the oil price rise—every year of Banzer's rule ended with a balance of payments deficit on the current account; and yet the objective of accelerated growth had scarcely been attained: the average growth rate to 1977 was 5.3 percent, compared to 5.5 percent over the 1960s. The 1975 five-year plan had projected a rate of 8 percent per annum for 1978, 1979, and 1980; the figures registered for these years by the UN's Comisión Económica para América Latina (CEPAL) were 2.8, 2.8, and 1.2 percent, respectively.

In terms of both the form in which it was generated and its consequences, such growth was manifestly not co-substantial with genuine development. It did, though, provide a veneer of modernization. The short-run commodity booms prompted an increase in speculative activity, an expansion in the size and average income of the professional middle class (state spending on services quadrupled), and—in line with the need to accommodate and cater to the new consumerist aspirations of this stratum—a rise in urban construction. While Santa Cruz grew outward, La Paz expanded both outward and upward, with the progressive emergence of ugly but prestigious tower-blocks populated by a young middle class escaping the constraints as well as the support structure of the parental home. Those who directed and funded this activity built themselves opulent suburbs, such as Calacoto and Cota Cota in La Paz, where a conspicuous and competitive consumption was concretized on a scale that would be the envy of many a European executive. With the advent of cocaine, these redoubts of the elite were supplemented with even more extravagant examples of spacious, *arriviste* architecture.

The government celebrated such tangible transformation of the landscape as progress incarnate, but it would be more accurate to describe it as just one side of inflation. For the great mass of urban dwellers, as well as a peasantry now substantially integrated into the money economy, neither housing nor any other item of expenditure became cheaper, better in quality, or more plentiful. Banzer's economic team were profligate free marketeers but, as we have seen, only one side of the market was free. For seven years Bolivia experienced nothing that appertained to "free collective bargaining" and registered the lowest number of strikes for three decades; there might be discussion over the form and degree of the rise in the cost of living but dreary accusations of "wage-push" inflation were patently devoid of any validity. The impact of the principal factors in the rise of the cost of living—the 1972 devaluation and the 1974 removal of subsidies—has already been outlined; they contributed to an average inflation rate of a little over 30 percent per annum. According to the COB, this was accompanied by a drop in the wage-earners' share of national income from 47 to 31 percent. The miners' real wages, which have been the object of a close study, fell by at least 14 percent. Figures for the overall loss of earning power vary very widely indeed, the lowest acceptable figure being between 8 and 10 percent, the highest around twice this.

The computation of economic statistics such as these is rarely free of trouble, but the margins of error are not so generous as to make the obscure mathematics employed by the government believable. In 1976, it assessed per capita GOP at $600 a year, in 1977 at $729. The World Bank, on the other hand, estimated the 1975 figure to be $360, but in 1979 its local director voiced the opinion that the official figures on which its estimates were based were highly inflated; at the time the Bank was making available to Bolivia soft loans reserved exclusively for countries with a per capita GOP of less than $280 a year. Furthermore, the Bank—

against which charges of radicalism would be extraordinarily hard to sustain—concluded that "Bolivia has one of the most deformed income distributions in Latin America. . . ."

"Nueva Bolivia" in Retreat

Although the boom of the 1970s was short-lived, growth rates slumped disastrously, and the level of inflation crept ever upward, these factors underlay the decline and eventual overthrow of Banzer's regime rather than directly causing it. The full extent of the crisis accumulating over the decade was only to become clear later, and the principal fissures in the edifice of the dictatorship were primarily of a political and superstructural nature. By their very nature, dictatorial regimes encourage the primacy of democratic demands in opposition, but in the case of Bolivia the weakness of any parliamentary tradition tended to disaggregate the movement for constitutionality into the defense of the most salient freedoms it guaranteed, rather than any system *tout court.* Thus, for a long time badly weakened forces sought to gain ground tactically and chip away at the edifice of the dictatorship; there was minimal agreement over a broad strategy of how and with what it should be replaced. This was clear at the very end of its days, when a rank-and-file movement for a complete political amnesty broke the momentum of the *banzerato* but was channeled without greater difficulty into electoralism: There seemed to be no ready alternative, even though by taking such a route, Banzer gained considerable advantage in making his retreat. The enthusiasm of the major political formations for this strategy and the importance of elementary democratic liberties served to dazzle the working class and peasantry. The form in which Banzer's extended rule was eclipsed soon proved to be of more than passing importance; indeed, it provided the framework for the apparently endless political crisis that followed.

The first consolidated assault on the system was mounted by the FSTMB and was resolutely syndicalist in character. In January 1975—only two months after the *autogolpe* Siglo XX—Catavi staged a fortnight-long strike in demand for the return of the local radio stations closed down by the regime. The action not only achieved its aim but also indicated that although national union federations no longer had any formal existence and plant unions were in the hands of the *coordinadores,* rank-and-file organization remained intact and the *Comites de Bases* led by the left enjoyed broad support. Over the following eighteen months, the impetus given by this partial victory encouraged mobilization on the question of wages, which, as we have seen, were badly affected in the mining sector. Proscribed FSTMB leaders returned quietly to the country and began to organize a national union congress in order to formulate strategy. Although it was illegal, the regime made no move to suppress this meeting, which eventually took place at Corocoro on 1 May 1976. The main demand was for a rise of some 200 percent on the daily basic pay of $1.75. The government refused to accept the figure of $4 as the minimum necessary to sustain a family of four and offered increases of between 30 and 50 percent. Although the PCB argued strongly against any precipitate strike and urged piecemeal tactical moves, the congress was swayed by a radical bloc of the PRIN, POR, and MIR that succeeded in winning support for issuing an ultimatum to the government that if there was no satisfactory response within thirty days, a national miners' strike would be called.

While the Corocoro congress was still under way, news arrived in Bolivia of the assassination of General Zenteno in Paris by a previously unknown-of "Che Guevara International Brigade." There was no discernible grief in the popular sectors, but no great jubilation either, for it was widely believed that the killing was the work of the right, a suspicion confirmed by police leaks to Le Monde which implicated the regime and Zenteno's own embassy staff. Two weeks later another Bolivian general was killed in exile, but this time the impact inside the country was considerably greater: The victim was Juan José Torres, gunned down in Buenos Aires early on 1 June. Soon after the Videla coup (24 March), Torres had been threatened by the Bolivian military attaché, and he was clearly at risk in the new "internal war" being waged by the Argentine security forces, which had kept a continuous watch on his flat. The death of this popular figurehead was immediately linked to Banzer, and dynamized an already tense situation. Black awnings and flags appeared in the popular quarters of the towns, and in Siglo XX, 20,000 people attended a demonstration of protest and remembrance on 3 June. In what was perhaps the most completely cynical gesture of his rule, Banzer declared public mourning and sent an aircraft to Buenos Aires with the offer to the ex-president's wife of bringing back the corpse. However, when Emma Obleas insisted that Torres' body be laid in state at San Andres and the FSTMB offices and then interred in the cemetery at Siglo, Banzer, who had suggested a rapid and discreet burial, felt obliged to withdraw his generous proposal. President Echeverría brought this macabre incident to a close by offering "asylum" to Torres' remains in Mexico, where they remained until June 1983.

Torres' death and the spontaneous demonstrations of protest that followed it terminated the regime's cautious attitude to the strike call. On 9 June, the reoccupied FSTMB offices were raided, their occupants arrested, and six of the federation's national leaders deported to Chile, where General Pinochet had them interned in an isolated camp in the south. Siglo XX came out on strike the next day, and as troops invested the camp and began a house-to-house search the strike leaders took refuge inside the mine, using shafts and exits only the miners knew. The government immediately closed the *pulperías* and threatened to cut the electricity. Within a few days the stoppage had spread to the other camps and received the support of the factory workers, who came out for twenty-four hours. All the Comibol camps were occupied by the army, two workers being shot dead in Siete Suyos; press censorship was imposed. . . .

The Banzer regime had initially been shaken but, as its tactics showed, still possessed the strength to overcome any opposition. The failure of the strike did not vindicate a policy of negotiation but simply emphasized the unequal balance of forces. In mid-1976 it seemed certain that Banzer's mandate to himself to rule until 1980 would be fulfilled to the day and hour of his choosing.

It was only with the confidence bred of such supremacy that the president could possibly have embarked upon his celebrated diplomatic adventure with Pinochet to negotiate an exit to the sea. The recuperation of the coast lost after the War of the Pacific in 1880 had always been an issue to unite the most extreme political protagonists, being of the utmost importance to the armed forces, which nurtured the memory of heroic defeat as a core institutional myth and preparation for recovery as a rationale for generous budget allocations. The fact that there existed an enormous imbalance between the military capacities of the two countries did very little to weaken this ideology of revindication. (On occasions this was backed up with spectacular military imagination, such as when it was proclaimed that the carburetors of Chilean tanks would not function on the *altiplano*—a fact that may not have unduly concerned Pinochet's air force, for which La Paz represented a magnificent target. During 1978 and 1979, when Chile had serious border disputes with Argentina and Peru, and was indeed on the verge of war, opportunist jingoism enjoyed a marked revival, especially because the latter year was the hundredth anniversary of the outbreak of the war. Even as late as 1982, a senior air force officer privately declared that the acquisition of fifty-three military aircraft he sought to buy from Belgium would not only give him parity with the Chileans, but also enable the FAB to "bomb the shit" out of the pleasant little coastal town of Arica, which had in fact belonged to Peru before 1880.) Banzer was, therefore, taking the bull by the horns in seeking a diplomatic settlement, which, from the very start, implied recognition of Chilean sovereignty over much of the disputed territory and would very probably entail further concessions on the part of the dispossessed Bolivians. . . .

For three years, Banzer had juggled over-confidently with an issue that he could not control; his image as a "nationalist" was badly tarnished, relations with a valuable ally wrecked on the rocks of needed rivalry, and dissent inside the armed forces increased, especially amongst the junior officers. . . .

The adoption of human rights as a major feature in aligning U.S. foreign policy toward the Third World marked a critical shift in the relationship between Washington and La Paz. One certainly does not have to believe the rhetoric of this policy or imagine that Carter himself, Linowitz, Vance, or Brzezinski had any great affinity with liberalism to accept that their erratic pursuit of the issue contributed to the dislocation of U.S. hegemony in several important zones. Perhaps the most striking instance was Iran, but Latin America was the region most consistently affected. In Central America, Somoza was deprived of the total support he needed to resist the Sandinistas in the 1978–79 civil war. Guatemala was put into quarantine and the overthrow of the regime of General Romero in El Salvador (October 1979) actively encouraged, having infinitely more disastrous consequences than the State Department could possibly have imagined at the time. Only the signing of the Panama Canal treaty in September 1977 produced a result that approximated the objectives of the policy. In contrast to the cases of South Korea, Indonesia, and the Philippines, the dictatorships of South America were put under pressure to limit their excesses, modify their methods, and proceed with a modicum of liberalization. This was met with an outburst of pugnacious nationalism in both Argentina and Chile, the latter selected for special attention for a while at least because of the sheer arrogance of its secret police (DINA) in slaughtering Allende's ambassador to the U.S., Orlando Letelier, and a North American colleague in Washington, an event which drew public attention to the fact that the Nixon administration had played an important part in the 1973 coup. The Brazilian regime reacted with less virulence since it was already embarked upon an extremely graduated *apertura* after many more years of unchallenged control. Bolivia, on the other hand, was not only a much less significant regional power, but also a great deal more vulnerable in economic terms. Exhibiting a palpable loss of internal dynamism and unity—but not to such a degree that any relaxation sponsored by the U.S. seemed likely to exceed the carefully controlled limits envisaged for "redemocratization"—the Banzer regime presented a relatively unproblematic target for the human rights policy. This, though, was no guarantee of success; over the following five years, the State Department found itself continually obliged to intervene in Bolivian affairs in order to sustain a policy that was first marginalized by Carter himself and then entirely reversed (except for Poland and Afghanistan) by Reagan. This was in part because redemocratization proved so persistently vulnerable and in part a result of the emergence of a new complicating factor: cocaine.

The first step in persuading Banzer to consider a gradual withdrawal was taken by Assistant Secretary of State Terence Todman, who visited La Paz in May 1977 and held "secret discussions" with the president. Todman was heavily lobbied by human rights organizations, but it appears that he made little headway since the government's activity remained unchanged and Banzer reconfirmed that elections would not be held until 1980. Nevertheless, the pressure applied by the U.S. embassy over this period must have convinced Banzer that a change in tactics would not necessarily prejudice his wider strategy. Early in September, he flew to Washington to attend the signing of the Panama Canal treaty and talk with Carter. It seems likely that this meeting was decisive since, on 30 September, the president declared that elections might well be brought forward. This was the first time in three years that such a possibility had been admitted, the reason being advanced by Banzer revealing his major worry: "We want the Armed Forces to withdraw at the opportune moment and not when they might be exhausted by the exigencies of politics. . . . If tomorrow or the day after we start to have a political carnival, there will be no elections."

However guarded, such a statement changed the tempo of public life completely. A rapid tour of the garrisons secured support for such a move, the success of which now depended almost entirely upon containing popular mobilization. On 9 November, Banzer announced that elections would be held in July of the following year, although he made no move to lift the restrictions that impeded the political campaign he had to all intents and purposes declared open. This was not surprising; the military last sponsored elections to succeed an institutional regime in 1940. There was no experience of the tactical problems this entailed and no established system as, for example, in El Salvador or Guatemala, whereby the military could guarantee an acceptable result while formally permitting open competition. As a consequence, the nine months following the announcement of the poll were characterized by ill-organized and frenetic efforts to obtain a victory at all costs and with little concern as to the wider effects of clumsy manipulation. As Banzer declared toward the end of the campaign, "We support *continuismo* and we are satisfied because we have just embarked upon the task of economic development and it is logical that we should continue the work we have just begun."

Perhaps the only perspicacious move that Banzer made in his efforts to secure this *continuismo* was to hold back from standing as a candidate himself. On 6 December, his minister of interior, the air force general Juan Pereda Asbun, was declared "the candidate of nationalism" with full support from the government and the armed forces. This was, in fact, not quite the case, since the army was less than happy at the prospect of an air force officer taking charge, and the candidature of Colonel Alberto Natusch Busch had been canvassed in some barracks as an alternative. Banzer's choice of Pereda as his dauphin was surprising insofar as he was an extraordinarily poor speaker—experiencing great difficulty in pronouncing virtually the only word that could not plausibly be omitted from his anodyne speeches: *constitucionalizacion*—and being about as uncharismatic as it is possible to be outside the British diplomatic service. These qualities were, though, excellent in a man who could be handed formal power and yet not be expected to wield it independently. Pereda, a *cruceño* and long one of Banzer's most faithful acolytes, had patently been chosen not as a genuine institutional successor, but as an interim "front man" so that the president himself could continue to direct affairs from behind the throne. Both the strategy and the man selected to realize it proved to be calamitous; but this was certainly not predictable at the end of 1977, and once the step had been taken, the army threw itself behind Pereda and the Unión Nacionalista del Pueblo (UNP) created to run his campaign.

Following the declaration of Pereda's *oficialista* candidature, Banzer made the first move in rolling back the restrictions in force since August 1971 and enshrined in the decrees of November 1974. On 21 December, he duly announced an amnesty, but in terms so limited as to cast grave doubt on the possibility of any genuine opponent returning to the country, let alone contesting the election. The measure expressly prohibited the return of 348 "political dissidents," including Juan Lechín, Marcelo Quiroga, Hernán Siles Zuazo, and many leftist militants, as well as two children aged eight and twelve, one person who had been killed by the police several years before, and a number of people who were paid the dubious honor of having their names listed twice. In real terms, the result of the "amnesty" was that thirty-three people were released from prison and nineteen of these sent for trial; nobody sacked for political or union activity, including 950 miners dismissed after the 1976 strike, was entitled to redress.

The popular response to this artless maneuver took an unexpected form but rapidly proved to be uncontainable. In what seemed a misguided move during the Christmas holiday, when they could expect little publicity, the wives of four exiled miners (Aurora de Lora, Nelly de Paniagua, Angelica de Flores, and Luzmila de Pimentel) entered the offices of Archbishop Manrique together with their children on 28 December and declared themselves on indefinite hunger strike until their demands for a general and unrestricted amnesty, work for all those who had been fired, and the withdrawal of the troops from the mines were met in full. Initially, the hunger strike appeared to be no different from any other staged by desperate individuals with a particular grievance, but circumstances dictated that within days it was transformed into a mass movement at the center of national affairs. On 31 December, a second group formed from representatives of APDH, the university, and the Unión de Mujeres de Bolivia (UMBO) began to fast in the offices of *Presencia,* replacing the wives' children who had become ill. The editor of the paper, Huáscar Cajías, was less than cordial in his response to this, but given that Manrique had given full support to the action, he could scarcely eject the occupants. From that point on, the strike spread rapidly: After six days, 61 people had joined; after fourteen, some 500 were fasting; and at its end (18 January), over 1,000 were on strike in all of the country's major cities, with a great many more lending active support. On 6 January, the regime—which had put the armed forces on a "state of emergency" and steadfastly refused to meet with ex-president Luis Adolfo Siles, who had been elected as a mediator by the strikers—organized a counter-demonstration which all public servants were obliged to attend. The torrential rain that persisted throughout that day proved to be a great deal more inconvenient for those who had turned out simply to admire Pereda's oratorical skills than for the thousands of dragooned civil servants who gratefully and none-too-slowly vacated the Plaza Murillo. The demonstration of mass support for the government and its mumbling candidate dissolved before Pereda's eyes and had later to be reconstructed for the press through the employment of creative photography. On the 16th, the regime's *coordinadores* in La Paz declared a twenty-four-hour strike against the fast—a measure that amounted to a general lockout—and the police forbade the movement of vehicles in the city. This was made a pyrrhic victory when the rank-and-file union committees announced that their support for this stoppage was to express solidarity with the hunger strike and not repudiation of the action. A number of police posts were attacked and one schoolchild was shot dead by police. On the same day, Banzer had reluctantly begun to negotiate with the strikers' representatives, but in the face of their intransigence and the loss of order on the streets, he opted to suspend the talks and resort to force. Early on the 17th, police raided a number of sites occupied by the strikers. In La Paz, some fifty heavily armed men charged into the offices of *Presencia* in military formation, and, with much shouting, began to order the strikers out, only to be brought to a halt by a young doctor who informed the irate commander that she would hold him and his superiors entirely responsible for any harm that befell people who had taken nothing but water for twenty days and could not be moved without ambulances. After some delay, during which the officer conferred with the ministry, and those on fast gave a barely audible rendition of "Viva Mi Patria Bolivia" to an audience of now shame-faced policemen, ambulances were fetched and the "prisoners" transferred to clinics around the city.

The use of repression succeeded only in increasing the popularity and vindicating the cause of those against whom it was directed. Under the new rules of the game, Banzer could scarcely expect to derive any benefit from the sight of half-starved individuals being manhandled by troops in helmets and flak jackets. Moreover, there was a ready stock of volunteers to replace those who were removed. After a stormy cabinet meeting, the president went on television at midnight on the 17th to declare a full amnesty and the "resolution" of the strike. However, those on fast refused to halt their action until they received written guarantees against persecution, which took a further day to extract from the regime. The final agreement granted all their demands except the removal of the troops from the mines. This was a key issue, but the strike could clearly not continue without loss of life and had already gained all the concessions that could feasibly be expected of such a tactic. It was lifted on the evening of the 18th. Although it was to be some time before it was fully evident, the hunger strike was the single most important factor in bringing the *banzerato* to an end and laying the basis for mass mobilization over the coming period.

From January, the regime was thrown onto the defensive and forced into increasingly frantic maneuver to control the election. At a meeting of 160 senior officers early in April, Banzer tried to gain support for a suspension of the poll or, failing that, the launching of his own candidature. This move came to naught because a majority of the officer corps now considered that such a manifest reversal of the *apertura* would lead to even greater opposition. Thus, although thirty-five people were arrested for staging a prohibited May Day demonstration and San Andrés University was closed for a month after student protests against the regime's refusal to respect autonomy, the campaign went ahead. . . .

The media were directed with great clumsiness in favor of Pereda. Although the miners' radio stations and a few others kept up generally objective commentaries, many stations were suborned into favoring the "candidate of nationalism." The programmers of the state-controlled television channel were particularly partisan and access for the opposition was strictly limited; Quiroga's one election address was cancelled "for technical reasons" four days before it was due to be transmitted. With the exception of *Presencia,* the newspapers were either disposed to favor *oficialismo* anyway or sufficiently cowed either by direct threat or by the political use of advertising accounts into limiting their coverage. However, it was in the mechanism of the vote itself that the regime exercised most effort to bring Pereda home. Under the existing system, voting was by different colored ballot papers, with each slate responsible for delivering its papers to the polling stations. Since Bolivia's roads are so few and tightly controlled by the traffic police (*transito*) at the *trancas* outside each town, the confiscation of opposition papers was a relatively easy matter and took place on a wide scale over the week before the poll; at many stations no opposition ballots were available at all. In some places—Apilla Pampa (Cochabamba), Concepcion (Santa Cruz), Mineros (Santa Cruz)— no vote took place on 9 July; but most of the identifiable fraud took the traditional form of stuffing boxes, exchanging them, or simply "losing" them. One of the most notable cases involved was the dumping of a number of boxes into Lake Titicaca, which was immediately brought to the notice of the overworked international team observing the count. At those centers where opposition observers were not intimidated, or it proved difficult to "fix" the count, the UNP was easily overhauled by the UDP. A computation of 60 percent of the vote from the provinces of La Paz gave Pereda 15,223 votes against 139,236 votes for Siles and 12,847 votes for Paz. On this basis, the UDP would have scored a total of 232,000 (74.9 percent) in the department against 25,371 for the UNP (8.2 percent), but the official result gave Pereda 194,946 votes (52.9 percent), well ahead of Siles' 124,192 (33.7 percent). In no department did the turnout fall below 84 percent, a miracle in a country with such appalling communications and insufficiently explained by the provision of beer, sandwiches, and a free ride in army lorries for those *campesinos* prepared to vote for *el general*. In Santa Cruz, the turnout was an impressive 100.9 percent, but this did not compare with Chuquisaca's achievement of 104 percent. At the other end of the scale, the official result in San Luis (Tarija) gave Pereda 300 votes but Víctor Paz only 2, denying him the support not only of his home town but also of a large section of his family, which is not small and had been conspicuous by its presence at the voting stations.

In the event, the fraud was so blatant that it defeated its own purpose. The FSTMB threatened to strike if it was not investigated; the PDC, MNRH, and UDP agreed not to recognize the result, and Siles embarked upon his traditional hunger strike. The international team was unanimous in its opinion that there had been widespread malpractice. Banzer, who, even prior to the poll had given up all hopes in Pereda and considered the staging of the election a lost cause, put as much distance between himself and the UNP as possible and seemed set to sacrifice his heir. Pereda, who had naturally pronounced himself the victor long before the count was over, was now induced by his advisers to steal a march on the opposition and ask the CNE for an annulment because of the irregularities, although the fact that they had been conducted in his favor was not deemed worthy of extensive consideration. Confronted with universal repudiation of an exercise that was designed primarily to impress, such a move was virtually the only one open to the UNP. On 19 July, the CNE, itself at the heart of the fraud, duly obliged. That same day, Banzer signaled his complete break with Pereda by announcing that if the CNE had no winner to declare, he would hand power over to a military junta on 6 August. On the 20th, Pereda, fully aware that, with no electoral victory to his name he was of minimal value to Banzer, visited the garrisons of Cochabamba and Santa Cruz. The next day he declared himself in rebellion "against international communism" and immediately received the support of the Rangers and the FAB. Twenty hours of stalemate followed as Banzer held on to the allegiance of the La Paz garrison but made little progress in limiting support for the coup outside the capital. In the end, the FAB's threat to bomb him out of the palace forced Banzer to concede the day on the established rationale of averting bloodshed between brothers. After making a prolonged and lachrymose speech on television, he retired unmolested to his home. For three hours a junta of service commanders held power until Pereda flew in to don the presidential sash, finally obtained by the preferred methods of his fraternity.

Following the overthrow of Banzer, Bolivia plunged into political chaos. Between July 1978 and July 1980, two further general elections were staged, five presidents held office (none of them as a result of victory at the polls), and of the cluster of coups under almost constant preparation, four were essayed in practice, one failing and three successful. This chronic instability reflected both the inability of the constitutionalist camp to wrest initiative from those who wished to sustain the *banzerato* and the incapacity of the forces of the right fully to suppress the *apertura*. Even though General García Meza's coup of 17 July 1980 seemed, in the first instance, to have decided the issue firmly in favor of dictatorship, this regime was also to run out of steam within the space of a year. We can, however, divide the last four years of the period under study into two phases—after July 1980 the contest for power became almost exclusively an institutional affair. Until July 1980, the same structural crisis took the form of much more open encounters between badly divided political forces of all the major social classes.

The very existence of constitutional democracy was at the heart of the conflict, in part simply because it was abhorrent to powerful sectors of the right, but largely because the principal political formations failed to provide anything resembling a coherent alternative to the Banzer model. The natural competition of party politics quickly decomposed into stagnant sectarianism, reflecting not just the lack of an indigenous parliamentary tradition and the ambiguous legacy of the MNR era, but also a lack of confidence and unity in the ruling class. The dominant bloc fought shy of the modicum of risk involved in a popular front (UDP), covered its bets by patronizing two variants of reactionary civilianism (Víctor Paz and Banzer), neither of which was sufficiently distanced from the policies of the last decade to attract majority backing, and yet was reluctant to pledge itself to outright dictatorship in view of the growing fissures inside the armed forces and the defensive strength of the popular movement. The parliamentary left was less divided, but very far from strong, the UDP failing to capture the sympathies of an overwhelming majority as it became increasingly immersed in partisan maneuver and desisted from mobilization that might jeopardize the balance of forces on which constitutionalism depended for its survival. As a consequence, the popular front encountered a growing apathy among the masses which showed up to some degree in increased support for the PS-1, but was evident less in terms of numbers of votes than in a broader disenchantment with parliamentarianism. The great popular mobilizations of this period were against dictatorship and assaults on the popular economy, but not in support of any specific political front. In each case the cause of constitutionalism was pursued by rolling back the initial gains in the streets and workplaces. Exhausted and confused, the populace gave the UDP a clear majority in June 1980, but was in no state to resist García Meza's coup that followed the victory.

The process of polarization that spanned the two years between Pereda and García Meza was neither uniform nor inexorable; it followed shifts in the balance of forces both within and between the democratic and authoritarian camps. However, the confusion of this period was constantly underpinned by the economic crisis aggravated by Banzer, and it served to emphasize that however internally divided they might be, the principal political forces in Bolivia remained the military and the COB. The crisis of constitutionalism was, therefore, not simply conjunctural, not just a case of bad timing, wrong politics, or collective ineptitude, but the result of a social structure that allowed minimal space for those who wished to uphold the formal division of powers and reverse the 150 years' dominance of the executive over the legislature. Such objectives are not achieved overnight, by grasping good opportunities, or by courtesy of more or less benevolent foreign sponsors. This is particularly the case in Bolivia, a country that is economically backward but politically advanced; constitutionalism was weak not because it was nascent, a stage about to be achieved, but because it had never represented an adequate means of control for the ruling class or a historic source of liberties for the masses. Here the distinction between finite democratic rights and the complete apparatus of electoralism is critical: While the system owed the strength of its mystique to its incorporation of such rights, these had invariably been obtained in practice by collective action and within the orbit of a direct, popular democracy rather than that of parliamentarianism. In this context, it is possible to view the project of formal democracy as a kind of tactical option for both sides, emerging at the end of the 1970s precisely because the military had lost its political dynamism and the organized working class was still too disoriented to provide a coherent alternative. There was a political vacuum.

The Delinquent Dictatorship

Several days after taking power, General García Meza gave an interview to a Chilean magazine in which he stated, "I will stay in power for twenty years, until Bolivia is reconstructed. My government has no fixed limits and in this sense I am like General Pinochet." Given the efficiency of the coup, the extremely tight and violent control imposed in its aftermath, and the apparently comprehensive defeat of the constitutionalist camp, such a claim was treated seriously. Banzer had, after all, ruled for seven years, and García Meza had begun his rule in an equal, if not more consolidated and confident, manner. Yet, García Meza's regime lasted one year and eighteen days and was within six months wracked with contradictions, hemmed in and destabilized by external repudiation, debilitated by dissent within the military, and unable to eliminate the passive resistance that began to take an increasingly open form as the government lurched from one crisis to the next. The three short-lived administrations that followed suffered the same fate as they attempted first to sustain the project of July 1980 and then to conduct a measured retreat. By mid-1982, the endeavor to impose an organic dictatorship and eradicate all vestiges of the democratic interlude had collapsed completely.

The roots of the crisis that drained this militarist exercise of any potential were the same as those which had undermined constitutionalism: a severe and escalating fiscal crisis of the state inherited from Banzer and worsened by decreasing production and falling prices for the country's core exports; substantial disunity inside the dominant bloc; and an inability to complement the political defeat of the left with a complete destruction of its syndicalist foundations. However, the form taken by the political emergency between July 1980 and October 1982 was quite distinct from that which had preceded it, reflecting above all else the weakness and lack of unity inside the armed forces. It proved impossible to sustain a right-wing regime on anti-U.S. policies for any length of time, and even after these were first tempered and then reversed, the effects of a fifteen-month boycott imposed by Washington continued to erode legitimacy, restrict foreign assistance, and encourage internal competition. The same was true of the initial, ill-conceived assault on the Andean Pact that further blackened the regime's reputation. Furthermore, while receipts from the cocaine trade were substantial and facilitated the funding of a sizable informal apparatus of control, the purchase of loyalty in the upper echelons of the military, and the accumulation of impressive personal fortunes, they could not compensate for the collapse of the legal economy, service the foreign debt, or finance state operations as a whole for any length of time. At its peak, income from cocaine was perhaps four times greater than that from traditional exports, but a great deal of it did not return to Bolivia and much of that which did fueled largely nonproductive activity or conspicuous consumption. In some cases—the plantation zones of La Paz and Cochabamba, and the commercial entrepots of the Beni—short-term regional booms occurred, but because of its outlaw status, the trade failed to revive general business confidence. While cocaine capital did not in general derive from a process of primitive accumulation, the rules of competition in this sector were loose and not unlike those of early capitalism, exaggerating the historical tendency of the Bolivian state to be a site for plunder.

The working through of this process allied to the exceptional violence, extreme capriciousness, and lack of any serious strategy or social support on the part of the García Meza government determined its downfall. During the two years of military rule, there were no less than six open attempts at a coup d'etat, an even greater number of strikes than over the five previous years, and five different presidents. After García Meza himself was finally prized from power early in August 1981, a junta of commanders managed amid constant bickering to cling to office for a month. The eventual resolution of their institutional differences in the appointment of the army commander General Celso Torrelio Villa as president proved to be highly inconclusive. Torrelio was a García Meza appointee, a front man unable to meet the most minimal conditions for holding high office, save the fact that he represented the army. His very weakness ensured the continuation of the existing structure of power and the protection of those sectors that had flourished under García Meza and Arce Gómez, but it was an inadequate defense against both competitors from those factions and the more consolidated institutionalist currents regrouping inside the military. Unwilling to preside over a meaningful *apertura* and unable to contain the challenges of officers such as Faustino Rico Toro, identified both with *narcotráfico* and the extreme right wing, Torrelio simply held the fort until his presence in the palace served no useful purpose for any faction. His replacement in July 1982 by General Guido Vildoso Calderón marked a shift to a more agile and perspicacious policy of negotiation on the part of an institution that continued to inflict repression and persist in empty, stentorian claims to a mandate for power, but which had been badly buffeted by working-class action, weakened by sharp domestic divisions, and was clearly seeking sanctuary in the barracks. Thus, in October 1982, the armed forces handed power back to the constitutionalist camp, Hernán Siles Zuazo, and the UDP, retrieving the office denied them in August 1980.

This withdrawal signified a formal victory of democracy over dictatorship, was widely and enthusiastically celebrated as such, and certainly represented a shift in the balance of forces and the quality of everyday life. Nonetheless, it did not mark a new era in the country's economic fortunes

and soon proved to have compelled very few alterations in the comport-
ment of the civilian political elite. The crisis continued amid growing
popular discontent, renewed squabbling over the spoils of office, and a
crippling lack of concrete policy and leadership. The considerable advantages gleaned from military exhaustion, international goodwill, and a
regional retreat on the part of the forces of authoritarianism sustained the
Siles administration for a number of months, but could not suppress the
profound conflicts within Bolivian society, still less, resolve them.

Reprinted and edited from *Rebellion in the Veins: Political Struggle in Bolivia, 1952–1982*
(London: Verso Editions, 1984), pp. 201–94, excerpted from chapter 6.

Riordan Roett

The Post-1964 Military Republic in Brazil

After 1964, the Brazilian political system experienced a number of institutional modifications. A series of unique, extra-constitutional decrees, known as Institutional Acts, were utilized during the early years of the Military Republic to reorganize political life.

The Institutional Acts were a significant and interesting event in Brazilian political life. These documents constituted the justification for military intervention and also provided a political framework within which major institutional and structural reforms were made. While not canceling the Constitution, whether that of 1946 or 1967, the acts superseded and restricted the purview of that document. . . . They represented a running commentary on the inadequacies of the 1946 Republic, as well as formal notification to the nation that the changes introduced in 1964 were to be considered permanent. . . .

After 1964, seventeen Institutional Acts and more than one hundred Complementary Acts were issued. The Complementary Acts spelled out the specific intent of the more general principles involved in the Institutional Acts. It is clear from the working of the acts that they were decreed by the armed forces acting in a dual role: that of the representatives of the movement of March 31, the Revolution, a role which has a life of its own apart from any institutional or constitutional restraints, and as the executive power of the Brazilian government.

The 1967 Constitution emerged, in part, from a feeling that the changes brought about by the early Institutional Acts and the Complementary Acts required incorporation into the Constitution; the 1946 document no longer served the needs of the nation. With the First Constitutional Amendment of October 1969, it became clear that the 1967 Constitution was an impermanent statement to be ignored when required by the interests of the armed forces in their efforts to restore the status quo to Brazil. Not until the mid-1970s would a slow process of juridical normalization begin with the cancellation of the Institutional Acts. Indeed, by then they had accomplished their purpose. The regime, in the late 1970s, turned to other means to maintain its control over political life, such as the unilateral establishment of the electoral rules for 1982 and the promulgation of a new National Security Law which, the opposition argued, gave the regime power similar to that embodied in the Acts.

Institutional Act No. 1, April 9, 1964

The presidency of Brazil was declared vacant on the night of April 1, 1964, by the president of the Senate. The president of the Chamber of Deputies was sworn in as acting president on April 2. The nation—and the civilian political elite—waited.

After a week of negotiation over the course of the March 31 coup, the armed forces decided to act unilaterally. The political initiative passed to the military; it remained in their hands throughout the second half of the 1960s. On April 9, the three military ministers issued an Institutional Act which would become known as Institutional Act No. 1 when others appeared. The act did not rest on any constitutional justification; its authority derived from the moral force of the Revolution itself. No further justification was deemed necessary by the armed forces.

The preamble of the act states the reason for its issuance:

The successful Revolution invests itself with the exercise of the Constituent Power, which manifests itself by popular election or by Revolution. This is the most expressive and radical form of the Constituent Power. Thus, the successful Revolution, like the Constituent Power, is legitimized by itself. The Revolution dismisses the former government and is qualified to set up a new one. The Revolution holds in itself the normative strength inherent to the Constituent Power, and establishes judicial norms without being limited by previous norms.

The act vastly strengthened the powers of the chief executive. While the 1946 Constitution remained in force, it was subject to modification by the act. The president received the power to propose amendments to the Constitution, which the Congress had to consider within thirty days; only a majority vote, as opposed to the two-thirds vote stipulated in the 1946 Constitution, was needed for approval. Only the president could submit expenditure measures to Congress, and the Congress could not increase the amount stipulated in the bills. The power to declare a state of siege without congressional approval was given to the president, and the executive was granted the power to suppress the political rights of "political undesirables" for a period of ten years.

The act decreed that the election of the new president to replace President Goulart and of the vice president would be by an absolute majority of the Congress, to take place within two days of the promulgation of the act. On April 11, 1964, General Humberto Castello Branco, a leader of the March 31 coup, was elected president. The date for the election of Castello Branco's successor, who was to assume office in January 1966, was set for October 3, 1965.

Article X of the Act, which gave the president the right to revoke legislative mandates and to suspend political rights, was to expire on June 15, 1964. The military government moved quickly to revoke the mandates of those members of Congress identified with the defeated left. By the deadline, former president Goulart, as well as six governors and more than 40 members of Congress, plus some 300 individuals active in political life, had had their rights suspended. Under Article VII, which gave the president the power to expel people from the civil service without regard for existing legislation guaranteeing employment, it is estimated that approximately 9,000 people were fired by November 9, the cutoff date stated in the act.

As the military became accustomed to its new political role, it was clear its task would not be completed by January 1966, when the presidential term of Castello Branco would terminate. In July 1964, a constitutional amendment extended the president's term of office until March 15, 1967; new presidential elections were set for November 1966.

With the decision to extend the president's term, implying a military commitment to retain power for an indefinite period, a number of events in 1965 helped to determine the political strategy of the regime. The first was the election, in the mayoral race in São Paulo in March 1965, of a candidate backed by former president Quadros. The victory of a man identified by some as a representative of the populist tradition in Brazilian politics (even though a military officer) provided the impetus required for a move away from the economic emphasis of the Revolution into the political arena.

On July 15, 1965, two laws dealing with elections and political parties were announced. These represented the first substantive revision of the pre-1964 political rules of the game. The Electoral Code reduced the number of parties by increasing the minimum requirement that parties had to meet to achieve or maintain legal status. Electoral alliances were forbidden; candidates were required to reside in the area they sought to represent; voters were required to choose legislators from the same party in order to strengthen party discipline; and the running mates of successful gubernatorial and presidential candidates were automatically elected. These reforms were an attempt to deal with one of the problems perceived by the military as most debilitating in the pre-1964 era: the weak and diffuse multiparty system. It was hoped that these reforms would introduce some coherence into the political system.

The Political Party Statute stipulated stringent procedures for the organization of new political parties. Individuals were forbidden to run for more than one office in any election. Residence and party membership requirements were specified for candidates. It was hoped that this law would help to control the problem of representation, so abused before 1964, when there were few requirements linking a candidate to his constituency.

Also promulgated on July 15 was an Ineligibilities Law. It prevented former ministers in the Goulart government (those appointed after the January 1963 plebiscite) from candidacy. Its primary purpose was to prevent the candidacy of several prominent anti-regime politicians in the upcoming state elections.

Although the three proposals were submitted to Congress for consideration, two became law without final action of that body. When the time period for consideration expired, the president, using the authority granted to him by the Institutional Act, acted unilaterally. The Political Party Statute was passed by the Congress, but fourteen items introduced during floor debate were vetoed by the president. It appeared in the form in which it was originally submitted to the Congress.

The gubernatorial elections of October 1965 were a critical event in the unfolding of the military regime. Despite the warning and fears of many members of the armed forces, the Castello Branco government determined to hold open, competitive elections. Two candidates identified as opponents of the regime (Israel Pinheiro in Minas Gerais and Negrão de Lima in Guanabara), both supported by former president Kubitschek, were victorious.

Immediately the military hardliners pressed the government to annul the elections. In order to fulfill his promise to allow the inauguration of all candidates elected, President Castello Branco promulgated Institutional Act No. 2. With the publication of the second act, the military regime made a basic decision to restructure national politics to try to ensure that the legacy of the 1946 Republic would be effectively neutralized. The elections seem to have been the determining factor in the decision of Castello Branco and the moderate wing of the military that the unity of the armed forces was more important for the future development of Brazil than was the constitutional principle of direct elections.

Institutional Acts Nos. 2, 3, and 4

Institutional Act No. 2 determined that only the president could create new positions in the civil service; further restricted the time allowed to Congress to consider legislation before it became law automatically; increased the number of members of the Supreme Court (which had been viewed as a last holdout against the more blatantly unconstitutional actions of the Revolutionary government); reserved the right of nomination of all federal judges to the president of the Republic; reorganized the Supreme Military Tribunal; stipulated that civilians accused of crimes against national security were to be submitted to military justice; decreed the indirect election of the president and vice president by an absolute majority of the federal Congress; permitted the president to declare a state of siege for 180 days to prevent "the subversion of internal order"; extended the right of the Revolution to suspend individual political rights for ten years; established restrictions on the activities of those whose political rights were removed; gave the president the right to intervene in the states of the federation, for other than the reasons stipulated in the Constitution, in order to assure the execution of a federal law and in order to prevent or punish the subversion of order; abolished existing political parties and canceled their registration; excluded from judicial competence all acts of the Supreme Revolutionary Command and of the federal government in the first and second acts and in the complementary acts to follow, plus resolutions, passed since March 31, 1964, of state assemblies that cancelled the mandates of legislators; and gave the president the power to recess Congress, legislative assemblies, and chambers of municipal councilors. The second act was to remain in force until March 15, 1967, the date of the inauguration of Castello Branco's successor. . . .

The complementary acts announced through 1965 and 1966 served to implement or elaborate on the institutional acts. Perhaps the most notorious complementary act promulgated during this time was the 23rd, of October 20, 1966; it confirmed the growing centralization of power in the hands of the military and strengthened the determination of the government to allow little, if any, organized opposition to its plans. It was preceded by the removal of six federal deputies from office on October 12 and a break with the government by the ARENA congressional leadership. Complementary Act No. 23 decreed the recess of the federal Congress until November 22, 1966—after the scheduled elections. The act stated that there existed in the Congress "a group of counterrevolutionary elements whose objective was to disturb the public peace and upset the coming election of November 15, thus compromising the prestige and the authority of the legislative power. . . ." A precedent had been established, allowing the executive power to quiet the legislative branch successfully whenever it suited the government's needs.

With the indirect election by the National Congress of Marshal Costa e Silva to succeed Castello Branco, the succession issue was settled. Costa e Silva ran unopposed; attempts by the MDB to launch a rival candidacy had failed. Federal senators and deputies, state deputies, mayors, and municipal councilmen were selected in direct elections on November 15. ARENA won overwhelmingly, electing senators from fifteen states and approximately two-thirds of the new deputies.

Institutional Act No. 4 of December 7, 1966, convoked an extraordinary meeting of Congress to vote and promulgate a new constitution. The preamble of the fourth act stated that it had become necessary to give the country a new constitution that would "represent the institutionalization of the ideas and principles of the Revolution." The Constitution was promulgated on January 24, 1967. It further strengthened the executive power and weakened any hope of opposition groups to use the constitution to justify opposition to the regime.

The Costa e Silva Government

The Failure of the Opposition to Unite
With the inauguration of President Costa e Silva on March 15, 1967, the Revolution entered a new phase. The early efforts at controlling inflation seemed to be working; the needed structural reforms of the political system had been undertaken; and the crisis of confidence within the military seemed to have been overcome with the acceptance by Castello Branco of the Costa e Silva candidacy. The main political event of the first year of the second military government was the discussion about the formation of a united front of opposition forces.

The only significant attempt to organize a united political front against the military regime occurred between 1966 and 1968. Former governor Carlos Lacerda of Guanabara, who saw his presidential ambitions destroyed by the military, assumed his traditional role in Brazilian politics and took the offensive against the regime. When former presidents Kubitschek and Goulart were contacted, they evinced some interest in a united opposition movement.

In September, Lacerda met with Goulart in Montevideo and signed a pact with his former political enemy to proceed with the organization of the front. Upon his return, the executive committee of the MDB announced that it would not support the front; ex-president Jânio Quadros let it be known that he would not join the movement. The ex-president of the PTB, Lutero Vargas, attacked the idea in October. And in a speech that received widespread publicity, Interior Minister Albuquerque Lima condemned the front as an attempt to take Brazil back to the days before 1964.

By early 1968, the movement to form a united opposition front appeared badly fragmented. By the end of 1968, Lacerda had his political rights cancelled, and the moving force behind the front collapsed into silence. The movement was declared illegal; moreover, members of Congress supporting it were expelled from the Congress and banned from political activity for ten years. . . .

The Crisis of December 1968

Throughout the last half of 1968, it became apparent that the division within the regime had deepened between those who supported a moderate, semi-constitutional policy favoring limited civilian participation and the hardline nationalists who argued for military preeminence in all matters. The president seemed to favor a more moderate line; the leading proponent of a rigorous, nationalist development policy, carried out by the military, was the interior minister, General Alfonso Albuquerque Lima.

Albuquerque Lima had a large following among the younger members of the officer corps. He believed in the necessity of prolonged military rule in order to modernize Brazil, a task the civilian politicians in the 1946–64 period had failed miserably in achieving. For him, modernization meant structural reform of things such as the land-tenure system, the development and integration of the Amazon, the necessity of reducing regional imbalance, and so on. The general believed that a great nation like Brazil could no longer ignore its underdeveloped regions; such a policy of neglect threatened national security and modernization.

The two positions were brought into confrontation over the issue of a speech made on the floor of the Congress by Deputy Márcio Moreira Alves. He urged Brazilians to boycott military parades on Independence Day and asked that parents not allow their daughters to date military personnel. The nationalists found this address disgraceful and expected that the government would take appropriate action against the deputy. President Costa e Silva attempted to utilize legal channels to convince the Congress to remove Alves' congressional immunity, but the Congress balked.

In late October, a group of captains of the First Army stationed in Rio de Janeiro issued a manifesto. The document took note of their sacrifices for the Revolution, including their state of near-poverty amidst the plenty enjoyed by some. The message was unmistakable—the government was not responding to the basic needs of the nation. The modernization of the country required firm and decisive leadership; abrasive and insolent disregard for national priorities from civilians was not to be tolerated.

On December 12, 1968, the Congress met to consider the insistent request of the government that it lift Alves' immunity. Of the members of Congress, 216 voted against the government, 141 in favor, and 15 cast blank ballots. The government's demand had been rejected. In the face of this blatant disrespect for military authority, the government moved quickly to regain control of a rapidly deteriorating situation.

Institutional Act No. 5, December 13, 1968

The fifth act stated that the "revolutionary process unfolding could not be detained." The very institutions given to the nation by the Revolution for its defense were being used to destroy it, said the preamble of the act. The fifth act empowered the president to recess the national congress, legislative assemblies, and municipal councils by complementary acts. These bodies would convene again only when called by the president. In addition, the president could decree intervention in the states when in the national interest and without regard for the constitutional restrictions on intervention; he could suspend political rights of any citizen for ten years and cancel election mandates without regard for constitutional limitations. The national state of siege was prolonged; the confiscation of personal goods illicitly gained was allowed; the right of habeas corpus was suspended in cases of political crimes and crimes against national security and the social and economic order; and the restrictions to be placed on those who lost their political rights were increased and more explicitly designated.

Complementary Act No. 38, of December 13, 1968, decreed the recess of Congress. With the closing of the legislature, the regime had determined the immediate future of the Revolution of March 31, 1964. It would be a period of outright military rule without the inconvenience of elected, civilian interference. The economic planning process, which represented the only significant accomplishment of the regime, would continue unfettered. The possibilities for "humanizing" the Revolution gave way to the necessity of internal security, that is, precluding overt opposition from civilian political groups, and development, to be determined by the military regime and its civilian supporters. The issuance of the act seemed to secure the leadership of the president within the regime. Albuquerque Lima's abrupt departure in January 1969 indicated that the government felt sufficiently in control to eliminate his symbolic presence in the cabinet.

The first eight months of 1969 saw a flurry of revolutionary legislation. Institutional Act No. 6 (February 1, 1969) amended the 1967 Constitution (Article 113) and stipulated that the Supreme Court would consist of eleven members nominated by the president. It also said that the Supreme Military Tribunal would be responsible for trying all those accused of national security crimes. . . .

All of the institutional acts confirmed the assumption of supreme legislative power by the military regime. . . . The acts and the promulgation of political decisions by means of the acts affirmed the willingness of the regime to pursue its twin themes of security and development.

The President Incapacitated

Two dramatic events in August and September of 1969 demonstrated both the potential vulnerability and the military's predominance in the 1964 regime: the incapacitation of President Costa e Silva and the kidnapping of U.S. Ambassador C. Burke Elbrick in Rio de Janeiro.

A massive stroke incapacitated President Costa e Silva in late August. By the 1967 Constitution, Vice President Pedro Aleixo, a civilian from Minas Gerais and old-line member of the defunct UDN, was next in succession. It was clear that the armed forces would determine if the constitutional succession would be observed. Within forty-eight hours of the president's illness, Institutional Act No. 12 (August 31, 1969) was issued. The military had decided against the Constitution. The ministers of the navy, the army, and the air force promulgated the act "in the name of the president of the Republic . . . temporarily impeded from exercising his functions for reasons of health." The document stated:

The situation that the country is experiencing . . . precludes the transfer of the responsibilities of supreme authority and supreme command of the Armed Forces, exercised by his excellency, to other officials, in accordance with the constitutional provision.

As an imperative of National Security, it falls to the ministers of the Navy, of the Army and of the Air Force to assume, for as long as the head of the Nation is incapacitated, the duties given to his excellency by the constitutional documents in force.

The Nation can have confidence in the patriotism of its military chiefs who, in this hour, as always, will know how to honor the historic legacy of their predecessors, loyal to the spirit of nationalism, the Christian formation of its people, contrary to extremist ideologies and violent solution, in moments of political or institutional crises.

The act, relatively short in length, stipulated that military ministers would act on behalf of the president, that the previously published institutional and complementary acts would remain in full force, and that all the acts and complementary acts would be beyond judicial purview.

The new act demonstrated the willingness of the armed forces to violate the Constitution they themselves had promulgated in 1967. No mention was made of the vice president; none was required, really. It was clear that the ministers represented the general will of the military in assuming supreme command of the nation.

The U.S. Ambassador Disappears

On Thursday, September 4, 1969, U.S. Ambassador Elbrick was taken at gunpoint from his limousine in Rio de Janeiro. His kidnappers left a note in which they identified themselves as members of revolutionary movements; it demanded the release of fifteen political prisoners held by the regime in exchange for the life of the ambassador. A note found in the ambassador's car, addressed "to the Brazilian people," stated:

With the kidnapping of the Ambassador we want to demonstrate that it is possible to defeat the dictatorship and the exploitation if we arm and organize ourselves. We show up where the enemy least expects us and we disappear immediately, tearing out the dictatorship, bringing terror and fear to the exploiters, the hope and certainty of victory to the midst of the exploited.

The demands of the kidnappers were that their manifesto be published and that the fifteen prisoners be taken to Algeria, Chile, or Mexico, where they would be granted political asylum. A time limit of forty-eight hours was stated. The manifesto ended with a warning to the regime from the terrorists: "Now it is an eye for an eye, and a tooth for a tooth."

The government, in the hands of the military ministers, responded immediately. The fifteen political prisoners were rounded up from their places of detention and placed aboard a plane for Mexico; the manifesto appeared in the Brazilian newspapers. The list of prisoners included some of the leading critics and opponents of the regime. Amidst rumors that members of the officer corps were "unhappy" over the government's decision, Institutional Act No. 13 (September 5, 1969) appeared. It empowered the executive to banish from the national territory any Brazilian considered dangerous to national security.

Institutional Act No. 14, issued the same day, stated: "[It is considered] that acts of adverse psychological warfare and revolutionary or subversive war, that disturb the life of the country and maintain it in a climate of intranquility and agitation, deserve more severe repression. . . ." The act amended the Constitution (Article 150) and established the penalties of death, perpetual imprisonment, banishment, or confiscation of goods for those guilty of participating in psychological, revolutionary, or subversive war against the state.

The Urban Guerrilla Movement in Brazil

The kidnapping of the U.S. Ambassador dramatically publicized the existence, previously deemphasized by the regime, of a network of guerrilla bands operating in the cities of Brazil. The movement posed a most serious threat to the stability of the regime during the 1967–69 period. By challenging the authority of the government, the terrorist groups hoped to weaken the support for the military from the middle and upper urban sectors. If the government could not secure public order, what else justified its continuation? The terrorists had begun to have a real impact on the public mind with a series of daring bank robberies—more than a hundred by the end of 1969—and public bombings.

The terrorist groups stemmed from dissident elements of the Moscow-oriented Brazilian Communist party (PCB), led for decades by Luis Carlos Prestes. The first breakoff had been with the formation of the revolutionary Communist Party of Brazil (PC do B) with a decidedly Maoist or Fidelist orientation. Other fragments represented Trotskyite and Marxist variants.

The more prominent of the groups was the National Liberating Alliance (ALN) founded early in 1967, led by former Communist party deputy Carlos Marighella. Committed to terrorist and guerrilla warfare, Marighella became the mastermind of the movement; the ALN combined within its ranks a number of smaller terrorist bands who looked to Marighella for leadership and ideological inspiration.

A group that worked closely with the ALN but maintained its own identity was that led by ex-captain Carlos Lamarca. Called the Popular Revolutionary Vanguard (VPR), it merged with another group called the National Liberation Command (Colina) in June-July 1969 to form the Armed Revolutionary Vanguard (VAR), referred to as VAR-Palmares. Palmares was the site of an unsuccessful slave revolt in the late nineteenth century in the Brazilian Northeast. The VPR, in turn, resulted from a fusion of other fragmented terrorist groups. Under Lamarca's daring leadership, the VAR-Palmares became a romantic symbol of protest against the regime and attracted many students to its ranks. Disillusioned by military rule, they accepted Lamarca's leadership in, and Marighella's ideological justification for, armed insurrection. A pamphlet entitled "The Mini-Manual of the Urban Guerrilla" by Carlos Marighella, which appeared in the middle of 1969, offered a sophisticated and incisive summary of the bankruptcy of the regime and the necessity of undermining it by urban revolutionary warfare.

The movement was not a monolithic entity. It was splintered and represented antagonistic views of Brazilian society, ranging from reformist to revolutionary-anarchistic. A congress of VAR-Palmares, held in September 1969 to debate the future of the organization, resulted in further fragmentation of that group. The murder of Marighella in São Paulo on November 26 weakened the revolutionary left considerably. The loss of Marighella and the continuing fragmentation of the radical left was accompanied by increasing effectiveness on the part of the regime. In the state of Guanabara, the Center of Operations of Internal Defense (CODI) brought together all the civilian police and armed forces units working on security. A similar movement in São Paulo, Operation Bandeirante (OBAN), united all federal and state police units. OBAN was successful in uncovering clandestine groups of many of the terrorist organizations and by the end of 1969 had made more than 400 arrests.

By 1972, it seemed that this challenge to the regime had been effectively counteracted. The terrorist groups had not weakened the regime in the eyes of its strongest supporters, the middle and upper sectors. On the contrary, these groups interpreted the guerrilla movement as added justification for strong and effective government. The promptness and humaneness with which the government dealt with the kidnappings of foreign diplomats (in contrast with the Guatemalan government, which had refused to negotiate with similar terrorists who then murdered the West German ambassador to Guatemala) reassured the international community that the regime was willing and able to release political prisoners without severely undermining its internal support. The death of Carlos Lamarca in a gun battle with security police in September 1971 deprived the guerrillas of their principal leader.

While the period following the 1964 Revolution had witnessed strong and often arbitrary conduct by the Military Republic, the opening of the guerrilla offensive legitimated the expansion and consolidation of a complex security and intelligence network. At both the state and federal levels, a series of coordinating institutions either emerged or were reorganized to confront and destroy the subversive offensive and its adherents. Given the diversity of Brazil, the differences in state police and federal military jurisdictions, the level of perception of threat by individual security and military commanders, and the operation of "private" groups such as the infamous "Death Squads" in São Paulo, the challenge of coordinating intelligence efforts was overwhelming. Inevitably, local and state excesses occurred that were unknown or overlooked at the national level. As the armed forces became deeply involved in cooperating with police and security units working within each of the four army regions, allegations of direct military involvement in torture and interrogation sessions grew. . . .

Constitutional Amendment No. 1, October 20, 1969

As the regime surmounted the challenge to its authority represented by the kidnapping of the U.S. ambassador, it became clear that the president's incapacitation was permanent. The country confronted the task of selecting its fifth chief executive in the 1960s.

The immediate issue concerned the constitutional succession—would Vice President Aleixo be allowed to assume the presidency? The answer of the armed forces emerged on October 14, 1969, with the announcement of Institutional Act No. 16. The high command of the armed forces—that is, the three service chiefs—promulgated the document:

. . . considering that the superior interests of the country require the immediate and permanent filling of the office of the President of the Republic; . . . considering that Institutional Act No. 12 (of August 13 [31], 1969) . . . attributes to the military ministers the right to substitute for the President of the Republic in his temporary incapacitation. . . . Article 1. The position of the President of the Republic is declared vacant. . . . Article 2. The position of Vice President of the Republic is also declared vacant. . . .

By using an institutional act, with Congress in recess, the prerogatives of that body were exercised by the executive power. By precluding the constitutional succession of the civilian vice president, the military prepared the way for the creation of a more rigidly authoritarian government to succeed Costa e Silva.

The internal dynamics of the selection process for the new chief executive are not fully known. It is commonly accepted that the officer corps of the three services was polled. At the time there were approximately 118 army generals, 60 admirals, and 61 air force brigadiers. These, plus other command officers (an estimated total of about 13,000 men), were asked to nominate those men thought most qualified to replace Costa e Silva. General Emílio Garrastazu Médici, a supporter of the stricken president and commander of the Third Army located in the state of Rio Grande do Sul, ranked highest. He was followed in popularity by General Orlando Geisel and General Alfonso Albuquerque Lima, the former interior minister. It is reliably reported that Albuquerque Lima had prepared a program of action which he discussed with the officer corps on trips to the various command posts before the final selection was made by the high command of the armed forces. In the end, General Médici received the military nomination for the presidency. Admiral Augusto Hamman Rademaker Grunewald, then serving as navy minister, received the vice presidential nomination.

The sixteenth act stipulated that the elections for president and vice president would be held by the Congress on October 25, 1969; those elected would take office on October 30; their term of office would terminate on March 25, 1974. (The act also clearly reserved the right of legislation to the military ministers even though the Congress had been convened.)

The political parties were given the right to nominate candidates for the offices. ARENA nominated Médici and Rademaker; the MDB did not offer nominations. The candidates of the Revolution were solemnly elected to the vacant positions by the Congress on October 25, 1969.

Institutional Act No. 17 of October 14, 1969, gave the president the power to transfer to the reserves any military officer guilty of violating the cohesion of the armed forces. The preamble of the act stated that "the Armed Forces as institutions that serve to sustain the constituted powers of law and order, are organized on a basis of the principles of hierarchy and discipline. . . ." The act can be interpreted as a warning to those officers in disagreement with the decision of the military high command in passing over Albuquerque Lima in favor of Médici. Also, the act gave to the new president "legal" means of imposing the military's will on the armed forces without having to resort to other forms of coercion or intimidation.

The sixteenth and seventeenth acts were followed by another unilateral decision of the military commanders: Constitutional Amendment No. 1 of

October 17, published in the Official Diary on October 20 and in effect as of October 30. The effect of the amendment has led some political observers to refer to the amendment as the 1969 Constitution, even though 95 percent of the 1967 document remained. The amendment, among other changes, reduced still further the powers of the Congress. . . .

The amendment represented the determination of the military to ensure a presidential succession unmarred by dissent or protest. It provided the new chief executive with all the power required for governing and controlling the nation. By moving to promulgate these decisions before the election of General Médici, the military high command assumed collectively the responsibility for the political decision to emasculate the 1967 Constitution. . . .

With the consolidation of internal security and a period of dramatic economic growth following the stabilization period of 1964–67, a new developmental emphasis emerged in the Médici government's domestic program. While the unity of the armed forces was by no means guaranteed, a combination of skillful administration, popular and pragmatic policies, and luck indicated that a majority of the officer corps were willing to support the Médici government's initiatives in the social and economic arenas. . . .

The Post–1964 Economic Performance of Brazil

The Castello Branco government (1964–67) quickly moved to implement a stabilization program to correct the internal and external disequilibria of the postwar period. The expectation was that a draconian program of stabilization would yield high growth rates by the end of the decade. New policy initiatives included restrictive fiscal and monetary measures; a restriction on real wages; the creation of compulsory social security funds which were deposited in the BNDE and in a newly established housing bank (BNH); a "crawling peg" system in 1968 to keep the *cruzeiro* from becoming overvalued; the introduction of a procedure of indexing by which the principal and interest on debt instruments were adjusted to reflect the current rate of inflation, which encouraged savings and noninflationary financing of government deficits; tax and credit incentives for investments in underdeveloped regions and in sectors earmarked for growth, such as exports and capital markets; and the initiation of large government investment projects, principally in infrastructure, with the financial support of the World Bank, the U.S. Agency for International Development, and the Inter-American Development Bank.

The economic reforms, led by Planning Minister Roberto Campos and Finance Minister Octávio Bulhões, worked. While the 1964 to 1967 years resulted in low rates of GDP growth (an average of 3.9 percent p.a.) and of industrial expansion (3.6 percent p.a.), inflation began to drop—from 87 percent in 1964 to 27 percent in 1967. With the direction of economic affairs in the hands of Antônio Delfim Netto after 1967, and using the Campos-Bulhões stabilization program as a foundation, manufacturing grew impressively from 1967 to 1973 at an average rate of 12.9 percent p.a. The average import ratio of the manufacturing sector increased from an all-time low of 6 percent in 1964 to 7 percent in 1967 and 10.3 percent in 1971. As a result, the share of industry in GDP, which had remained constant at 26 percent between 1960 and 1967, jumped to 30 percent in 1972. Overall, GDP grew at an average annual rate of about 11.5 percent, while the industrial sector and the manufacturing industries expanded at rates of 13.2 and 13.9 percent, respectively.

In addition to the measures taken by the government after 1964, the economic strategy of the Military Republic was aided by a high degree of idle capacity in the manufacturing sector. Also highly relevant was the international environment—a period of rapid economic growth in the industrial world which opened markets for Brazilian exports—and a high level of capital investment in Brazil. Total exports increased from $1.9 billion in 1968 to $6.2 billion in 1973, while manufactured exports grew from $0.4 billion to $2.0 billion, reaching average annual growth rates of about 27 percent and 38 percent, respectively. As a result, the share of manufactured exports in total exports grew from 20.3 percent in 1968 to 32.4 percent in 1973. In the same time period, the share of total exports in GDP rose from 5.2 percent to 7.6 percent.

Brazil's economic expansion was directly related to higher levels of capital investment. Much of that investment came from state company expenditures, but a significant contribution was made by foreign capital. Indeed, the *dependencia* (dependency) school of thought argued that Brazil's—and Latin America's—freedom of action was being severely limited by the role of the multinational corporations in the 1960s and 1970s.

In Brazil, total investment in manufacturing increased nearly four times between 1970 and 1979, growing at an average annual rate of about 15.5 percent in real terms. Significantly, the distribution of investment has been highly concentrated in a reduced number of industries. The share of total investment in metallurgy, transport equipment, and chemical products added up to 47.3 percent in 1969, 62.2 percent in 1975, and 63.5 percent in 1979.

The share of equity in government firms increased from 18.5 percent in 1971 to 22.5 percent in 1979. The share of domestic private firms also increased from 47.1 percent in 1971 to 55.0 percent in 1979, while the share of foreign firms decreased from 34.4 percent to 22.5 percent. These changes in the structure of ownership reflect the significant expansion and diversification of the activities of the public enterprises. . . .

To a remarkable degree between 1964 and 1973, the government achieved many of its economic objectives. Financial markets were reformed; there was a steady decline in the government budget deficit; a new capital market law increased the use of the stock market; and tax incentives were employed to influence the allocation of resources among regions and sectors given priority by the government. Infrastructure projects were begun, and a program to diversify Brazil's exports was successfully undertaken.

The 1973 Oil Shock

As a result of the Arab-Israeli conflict of 1973, world oil prices rose precipitously in 1973–74. Brazil, which imported more than 80 percent of its petroleum needs, was highly vulnerable. The new government of President Ernesto Geisel (1974–79) had a long and complicated agenda it wished to accomplish during its five years in office. Of highest priority was the process of *abertura* (political liberalization). Of importance, also, was an increase in the standard of living of the working class, which had been deliberately suppressed in the preceding decade to finance the rapid diversification of the economy through forced savings and holding down real wages in the industrial sector. The option of introducing measures that would slow the economy was unacceptable to the Geisel administration. The government decided to maintain the ambitious—and expensive—development goals of the Second National Development Plan (1975–79), released in September 1974.

Within a year, it became clear that the financial burden of the import bill was growing rapidly. From 1973 to 1974, Brazil's import bill rose from $6.2 billion to $12.6 billion. The only way to meet Brazil's import expenses, from the government's perspective, was to borrow abroad. Eurodollars were plentiful in this period. Demand for loans was low in the industrial countries because of the oil-induced recession. By the end of 1977, Brazil's net debt had risen to $32 billion. Debt servicing required 51.2 percent of that year's exports. Few observers pointed out that 72 percent of the debt accumulated by the end of 1977 would be repayable by 1982.

The government took a lenient stand with regard to industrial pressure to raise prices in response to rising production costs, linked to energy and labor costs. While price controls were in force throughout the 1970s, the enforcement agencies were lenient in allowing increased costs to be passed along through price adjustments. By the late 1970s, the government faced a serious inflationary spiral. . . .

In spite of increasing inflation and the general decline in world ecoomic conditions, the Brazilian economy had performed very well during the 1970s. The World Bank reported that:

in 1979, manufacturing accounted for 28.0 percent of Brazilian GDP, up from 26 percent in 1960, and the overall industrial sector accounted for 38 percent of GDP. These are very high figures for developing and industrialized countries' standards alike, reflecting a very advanced stage of industrialization of the economy. Brazil's share of manufacturing in GDP is only exceeded by 5 and equaled by 2 of the 76 developing countries for which data are presented in the 1982 World Development Report. Even more noticeable, only 4 of the 18 industrialized countries exceed Brazil's share of manufacturing in GDP.

This was impressive performance indeed. Equally important, in terms of the overall process of development, the share of industrial sector employment among the economically active population increased from 12.9 percent in 1960 to 23.2 percent in 1976. During this period, manufacturing industry was the main source of employment within the industrial sector; its share among the economically active population increased from 8.6 percent to 15.0 percent. . . .

Direct municipal elections in November 1972 saw ARENA win majorities in mayoral and city council elections in some 4,000 municipalities. In Manaus, Natal, and Pôrto Alegre, the MDB won majorities, but ARENA carried the other nineteen state capitals. There were no elections for mayors in the state capitals or in "zones of national security" such as the Amazon and border municipalities.

In June 1973, President Médici announced the selection of General Ernesto Geisel, the head of the state petroleum company, as his choice in the January 1974 presidential elections. Geisel was a former aide to President Castello Branco. In addition to his reputation as an administrator, he had the good fortune that his brother served as war minister in the Médici cabinet. Because of his identification with the Castello Branco wing of the armed forces, it was hoped that his election would signal the possibility of liberalization of the Military Republic.

In December 1973, President Médici reported to the nation that the economic growth rate that year had surpassed 10 percent. Exports rose, foreign investment continued to flow into the country, and the economy promised to continue to expand and diversify. Shortly thereafter, the head of the National Petroleum Council announced that from September 1973 to February 1974, the price Brazil paid for crude oil had risen 350 percent. The inauguration of General Ernesto Geisel as the fourth president of the Revolution took place on March 15, 1974.

The Fourth Government of the Military Republic:
General Ernesto Geisel (1974–79)

Geisel emerged as the key figure in the post-1964 Military Republic. His commitment to authoritarian liberalization—that is, innovation directed and determined at the apex of the political system—profoundly changed Brazil. The five years of the Geisel government witnessed a determined movement away from the grandiose overtones of the Médici team with its emphasis on *grandeza* (greatness), the building of monumental public works projects, and its disdain for civil liberties or human rights. Slowly, but inexorably, Geisel charted a course of liberalization that won increasing support from all sectors of Brazilian society, including the armed forces. When he transferred power to his chosen successor, General João Figueiredo, in March 1979, Geisel had earned the respect of the Brazilian nation for his honesty and probity.

Geisel demonstrated his desire to separate himself from the Médici government in the organization of his cabinet and palace advisory team. His chief political advisor in the palace was the head of his civilian household, General Golbery do Couto e Silva, a disciple of General Castello Branco and a key architect of the coming liberalization. Golbery had been one of the founders of the National Intelligence Service (SNI) after the Revolution and served as president of Dow Chemical of Brazil as well. General João Figueiredo, chosen to direct the SNI, was a military officer who had worked with both the Castello Branco–Geisel and the Costa e Silva–Médici groups since 1964. His selection was seen as a guarantee that the SNI would be conducted as a professional operation. The key economics positions went to Mário Henrique Simonsen, a well-known economist and banker, who became the Finance Minister, and João Paulo de Reis Velloso, a holdover from the Médici group, who retained the post of Planning Minister. Other appointments appeared to indicate a preference for either competent technocrats or civilian political leaders with prior governmental experience.

In order to better administer the array of complex programs that the Revolution had initiated, decision making under Geisel tended to gather issues around three cabinet-level groups: the Economic Development Council (CDE), chaired by the president, which formulated economic policy; the Social Development Council (CDS), also chaired by the president, which established national policy in the social assistance, health, and welfare areas; and the National Security Council (CSN), previously a principal mechanism for armed forces participation in decision making, but, under Geisel, increasingly an advisory body with little effective veto power over national policy. Reis Velloso and the Planning Secretariat coordinated and reconciled the work of the various councils and attempted to identify priorities within the government's national development plans.

The 1973 oil price shock had a strong impact on the Brazilian economy, although the brunt would not be felt until the end of the decade—at the time of the selection of Geisel's successor, SNI chief General João Figueiredo. The Brazilian economic team, led by Finance Minister Mário Henrique Simonsen, decided to exploit Brazil's comparative advantage and continue to grow. Foreign borrowing escalated—but at relatively low rates of interest. Markets held up, and the trade balance was generally good. Brazilian exports continued to diversify. As Velloso had provided the continuity from the Médici to the Geisel government, so Simonsen would briefly serve as Planning Minister in the Figueiredo administration—and begin to realize the dangers of rising inflation, a growing oil bill, and increasingly rising debt levels. His efforts in 1979 to dampen the economy met with strong resistance, and he was replaced by Antônio Delfim Netto, the miracle worker of the Costa e Silva and Médici periods.

Believing that economic, trade, and investment matters should be left to the technocrats, Geisel, Golbery, and their collaborators concentrated on the political liberalization process. The decision taken in the mid-1960s to allow direct elections for members of Congress and for municipal posts had posed no difficulty through the early 1970s. ARENA, the government party, was returned to office with wide majorities. Some intimidation was involved, of course; many able candidates of the opposition had lost their political rights; many Brazilians actually believed that the government deserved their electoral support; and others became apathetic about voting specifically and about politics in general, and chose not to participate.

By the mid-1970s, with the first economic shock of the increase in petroleum prices, and the emergence of societal pressures for liberalization, elections suddenly took on a different meaning:

As Brazilian society became more polarized and consciousness levels were raised during the second phase of the post-64 period, the opposition MDB party was strengthened by being the only available electoral channel for the public expression of disapproval. Thus, the 1974, 1976, and 1978 elections were increasingly viewed as "plebiscites" by the revolutionary government.

In the relatively free elections for Congress on November 15, 1974, the MDB made a strong showing. Of the 22 Senate seats available, the MDB carried 16, for a total of 20 seats in the new Senate (61 percent of the vote in the Senate elections were for MDB candidates and only 39 percent for those of ARENA). The MDB elected 172 deputies to the Chamber, compared with 192 for ARENA (the MDB had only 87 deputies in the previous Congress).

On the state level, the MDB victory was equally impressive. Before the election, the opposition controlled only one state assembly, that of the state of Guanabara (the city of Rio de Janeiro, basically); after the election it had taken six state assemblies, including São Paulo and Rio Grande do Sul. The results of the 1974 election were viewed by many as a plebiscite on the 1964 Revolution—and the regime had either lost or been taught a lesson, or both.

While the election results heartened civilian supporters of liberalization, they created problems for Geisel in dealing with the armed forces. Repeatedly, warnings were issued by both mid-rank officers and members of the high command that electoral politics were precisely what the 1964 Revolution wanted to end. The conservative viewpoint was that elections generally resulted in corruption and subversion. Geisel clearly thought otherwise, but he had to move with care. Using carrot and stick methods with both the armed forces and the opposition civilian forces, he tried to give something to both groups—without losing sight of his principal goal. In dismissing the commander of the Second Army in January 1976, for example, he had used a stick against the army and offered the opposition a carrot; he repeated that tactic with the dismissal of Army Minister Frota in October 1977. But the conservative elements of the regime required a "carrot" also, and everyone waited to see how Geisel would react.

Throughout 1975 and 1976, Geisel reacted by publicly cautioning those supporting liberalization to move with care. More concretely, he did not hesitate to use the powers of Institutional Act No. 5 to cancel the political rights of state deputies, federal deputies, and senators charged with corruption, challenging the government, or other vague mistakes. The message was clear—if there was going to be liberalization, Geisel would orchestrate it. To counterbalance his military critics, the president moved military officers frequently, "exiling" those he believed openly hostile to his plans and neutralizing those who appeared uncertain in their support. . . .

In mid-1977, Geisel had an opportunity to offer a carrot to the hardline authoritarians. The Congress had proven recalcitrant in providing a two-thirds majority required to pass a judicial reform bill; Geisel, without warning, recessed the Congress. He then proceeded to promulgate, without political consultation, what became known as the "April Package" of reforms, all of which were seen as regressive. The package canceled the planned direct election of state governors in 1978; they would be selected indirectly by electoral colleges, the majority of which ARENA controlled. The new decree changed the pattern of voting in congressional elections and returned to the old rule whereby the number of deputies was decided not by how many voters a state had, but how large the population was. This meant that in states with large populations, but small numbers of eligible literate voters, ARENA would do well. The Falcão Law was extended to other elections. The law had been first utilized in the November 1976 elections. It excluded the use of radio and television in electoral campaigns, which again worked against the opposition candidates who were the newer candidates in most cities and states, and less well-known to the public. The term of the presidency was extended to six years—beginning with Geisel's successor. And the famous "bionic" senators were created—each state was given a third senator, to be elected by the state assembly, thereby guaranteeing ARENA a solid majority in the federal Senate.

To make it perfectly clear that he was in charge, Geisel proceeded in July 1977 to cancel the political rights of Alencar Furtado, the popular and effective leader of the MDB in the Chamber of Deputies. The party leader, in what was a rare television appearance by an opposition figure, had bitterly attacked the Geisel government. Geisel's decision to act, combined with the April Package of reforms, made it clear by June 1977 that the presidential palace remained very much in charge.

The spring and summer of 1977 were seasons of political turbulence in Brazil. Students, intellectuals, businessmen, church groups, lawyers, and opposition civilian leaders all joined in decrying the regressiveness of the April Package and demanding a stronger commitment to liberalization. An intriguing question is whether or not Geisel and his collaborators deliberately used the April Package to goad the broad forces of the opposition into action. Why? To demonstrate to the hardline opponents of liberalization that only widespread repression would end the demand for a return to a state of law. Geisel correctly gambled that there were elements in the armed forces opposed to liberalization—but they were not willing to kill their fellow citizens to prevent it from happening. . . .

On December 1, 1977, meeting with members of ARENA, President Geisel made the surprise announcement that he was planning a series of important institutional changes in the 1964 regime. The time had come, he stated, to move ahead with liberalization. The institutional acts were to be replaced with new legislation and new political parties, as well as by other reforms that were to be introduced in 1978. . . .

There were other indications that the process of liberalization was accelerating. In May 1978, the first massive strike since 1964 took place in the São Paulo industrial suburbs. . . . Both the private sector and the government responded hesitantly to this new challenge to the authoritarian regime—particularly given the economic importance of the region for the national economy. But as the strike mentality spread beyond São Bernardo to schools, hospitals, banks, and other public service sectors, the government realized that it no longer controlled workers in Brazil as it had in previous decades. No one emerged satisfied from a messy series of negotiations. The unions prepared for the April 1979 wage negotiations and utilized the time to seek unity in labor ranks and to set out a practical and just agenda of demands.

In June of 1978, the progressive leadership of the São Paulo business community issued a manifesto in which it called for a return to democracy. The government decided to lift prior press censorship which had been in force since 1964. In the same period, at the government's urging, the Congress began to consider a series of government-inspired measures to liberalize the authoritarian regime. Among the most important were the abolition of the institutional acts; the restitution of habeas corpus; the restoration of political liberties, after ten years, to those prosecuted under the provisions of the institutional acts; limitations on the president's power to close Congress; and the creation of new political parties. It was made clear that Geisel, in return, would neither accept any revision of the April 1977 Package nor any change in the application of the Lei Falcão, which regulated political use of radio and television in campaigns. Even with these changes, Congress remained relatively weak. It had no authority over the budget process and could modify neither the National Security Law nor the existing labor legislation, for example. After a series of heated sessions in Congress, the legislation passed in September 1978, but only after the presidential palace implied a return to tighter controls if the president's proposals were not passed as proposed.

In October, the government submitted a new national security law to Congress which incorporated the basic security measures contained in the various institutional acts. The National Security Law was a vital control mechanism for the process of authoritarian liberalization. It was intended to replace the fifth institutional act and to reassure skeptics on the right that the liberalization was indeed controlled from the top. It became law in 1979.

After a spirited presidential campaign, waged throughout Brazil, the ARENA-controlled electoral college convened on October 15, 1978, and, as expected, chose General João Figueiredo as President Geisel's successor. Figueiredo pledged himself to the process of liberalization. . . .

The Fifth Government of the Military Republic: General João Figueiredo (1979–85)

João Figueiredo assumed the presidency at a difficult moment in Brazilian history. The economic fortunes of the country were poor. The second oil price shock of 1979 and the consequent world recession hurt Brazil badly. The new Planning Minister Mário Henrique Simonsen attempted to halt policies of growth and spending, but soon resigned in frustration. His replacement, Agriculture Minister Antônio Delfim Netto, sparked a national commitment to continued growth and expansion that would ultimately end in the debt crisis of 1982–83.

Figueiredo retained not only Simonsen from the Geisel government but also kept General Golbery as his chief political advisor. Senator Petrônio Portella, a wise and experienced member of ARENA, received the post of Minister of Justice with instructions to work out the liberalization process. The cabinet was the usual mix of former military officers and technocrats and evidenced an obvious bias toward those with a commitment to the president's program of authoritarian liberalization. In his first months in office, Figueiredo was confronted with a series of challenges. Of these, two were most significant. One came from organized labor, a second emerged from the growing pressures for accelerated liberalization.

The Labor Unions

The May 1978 strike and its settlement had been the first experiment since 1964 with strikes and collective bargaining. The government had not interfered. The situation was different in 1979:

The May 1978 stoppages had created a new climate in which rank-and-file mobilizations were rife, and in the city of São Paulo the old union leadership had faced serious opposition during the annual wage-settlement negotiations in November 1978. The new leaders wanted to undermine the power of the pro-government elements in the unions even further. For the government, the annual negotiations would be a test of the degree to which democratization could be kept under control.

At midnight on March 13, two days before Figueiredo's inauguration, a massive strike erupted in the southern industrial belt of São Paulo, centered on the city of São Bernardo and the large auto plants. The metal-workers' union had refused to recognize the agreement negotiated a short time before between the manufacturers and the union leadership. Negotiations continued. Following a threat of government intervention, the union leaders agreed to put forward a proposal for a return to work pending further negotiations over the following forty-five days. Mass meetings of more than 90,000 workers rejected the compromise. The three opposing unions were then taken over by the Minister of Labor, Murillo Macedo.

To avert further polarization, a truce was arranged. The Ministry of Labor promised to withdraw from the unions in which it had intervened and the workers promised to return to work. Negotiations would continue for a new wage and work package. The final determination afforded neither party a clear victory. . . .

Pressures and Counter-Pressures to Liberalization

By mid-1980, the broad outlines of the regime's authoritarian liberalization were in place, and new parties were formed. Political amnesty had drawn exiled political leaders back to Brazil, and they were now actively involved in the new party structure. Habeas corpus had been restored, strengthening the integrity of the judicial system. Press freedom continued, and government censorship of radio and television diminished. The government had determined to restore direct elections in November 1982 for the country's governorships, an important move to revitalize the federal system. The bionic senators were to disappear when their terms ended in 1986, thereby removing a point of embarrassment for the government. The government also promised to consider revisions in the Falcão Law and to review congressional pressure to restore some of its powers.

In April 1980, the government confronted organized labor in São Paulo once again. After massive strikes, the government intervened and arrested a large group of labor leaders, including Lula. The strike failed, but again the government was warned that labor militancy had become a fact of life in Brazil. In a series of intricate feuds within the Brazilian Communist Party (PCB), longtime leader Luís Carlos Prestes, one of the *tenentes* of the 1920s, was removed in May 1980 and replaced by Giocondo Dias. The feuding on the left pleased the regime and indicated that neither the communists nor the other Marxist groups actively involved in politics would pose a threat to the liberalization process. Brazil had welcomed Pope John Paul II in July 1980, and his successful visit had pleased the Church, the government, and the people.

The Papal visit had another side, however. A resurgence of rightwing terrorism disturbed the apparent peaceful evolution of liberalization. A prominent member of the Roman Catholic community in São Paulo, and a close collaborator in the Church's human rights effort, Dr. Dalmo Dallari of the University of São Paulo law faculty, was kidnapped, beaten, and stabbed on July 2 by unknown assailants. Dallari had been arrested with others during the metalworkers' strike. Newspaper stands selling opposition material were firebombed. In September 1980, a secretary of the Brazilian Bar Association was killed by terrorist bombs in Rio de Janeiro; seven others were injured. Rumors circulated that rightist military officers were linked to the violence in an effort to intimidate Figueiredo from proceeding any further with authoritarian liberalization.

In September 1980, more than one million university students and 40,000 professors declared a nationwide strike which closed one half of the country's universities. Their demand was for increased government spending on education and training. The government confronted a challenge in December 1980 with the publication of a nationalist manifesto in São Paulo, signed by a former government minister and high-ranking army officers.

In retrospect, 1981 was a year of potential crisis for the process of authoritarian liberalization—but the crisis was overcome, thus permitting the holding of the November 1982 national elections. With press freedom guaranteed and habeas corpus in effect, there arose increasing pressure to identify those responsible for the repression of the early 1970s. The armed forces high command became increasingly nervous about such investigations and communicated its feeling to the presidential palace.

The country was shocked in May 1981 by the explosion outside the Rio Center, a convention hall in Rio de Janeiro, of two bombs on the evening of a May Day concert for working-class Brazilians. An army sergeant died and a security agency captain was badly wounded when the bombs exploded in their car. It was generally understood that the security agencies of the armed forces were involved in the tragic event. Figueiredo confronted a delicate and potentially serious situation. If he pushed for an investigation and prosecution, he would create a direct challenge to the conservative members of the military leadership. If he ignored the incident, his credibility was at stake. Political party leaders rallied around the president and met with him. After a desultory investigation, the case was declared closed although it was made clear in the press, and informally in political circles, that the presidential palace was divided on the government's response. The cautious decision not to confront the military was viewed as a judgment by Figueiredo about his level of support in the armed forces and his desire to continue to proceed with liberalization.

As a result of differences over the Rio Center incident and about the strategy of the government in pursuing *abertura,* General Golbery suddenly resigned in August 1981. There were rumors of differences with Planning Minister Delfim Netto and also with the SNI chief, General Octávio de Medeiros. The president acted quickly and called Professor João Leitão de Abreu from the Supreme Court to take Golbery's place as head of the civilian household and chief political coordinator for the government. Many commentators noted that the Médici team was back in place with different jobs—Delfim in planning, Figueiredo as president, and Leitão as chief advisor to the president. All three had held high positions in the Médici government in the early 1970s.

The second shock to the political system was the unexpected incapacitation of President Figueiredo in September with a heart attack. After a short period of doubt, it was decided to allow the civilian vice president, Aureliano Chaves, to become acting president in Figueiredo's absence. Apparent pressures by the conservatives in the regime to name an army officer as acting president failed. Supporters of the *abertura* warmly welcomed the decision. Chaves' conduct in office was exemplary. The vice president had strengthened the hand of those who argued that a civilian successor to Figueiredo was both possible and desirable, and he had enhanced his own chances to become that candidate.

President Figueiredo returned to the palace in late 1981, determined to see through a crucial phase of the process of authoritarian liberalization—

the national elections of November 1982. Taking firm control of the PDS, he initiated a series of electoral reforms (called "counter-reforms" by many in the opposition). . . .

The Political Implications of the Economic Crisis, 1982–83

With the elections completed in November 1982, the Figueiredo administration turned to the pressing financial problems that Brazil confronted. The crisis over the Mexican foreign debt, in August-September 1982, and the uncertainty about Argentina's capacity to repay, had a negative impact on Brazil's image in the international banking community. By December 1982, Brazil had agreed to negotiate with the International Monetary Fund as a prerequisite to receiving further loans from the private commercial banks.

As Congress organized in March 1983, the economic crisis and the deteriorating social conditions of millions of Brazilians who were without employment, hungry, and sick, became a dominant theme in its debate. In addition, President Figueiredo's desire to postpone discussion of his successor until 1984 was frustrated. As soon as the elections in November were over, the presidential race opened. With the social and economic difficulties confronting the government, 1983 became a year of intense national discussion about Brazil's future. . . .

From 1983 to 1985, deteriorating economic conditions—skyrocketing inflation, rising unemployment, exacerbation of the debt crisis, and imposition of austerity measures in response to negotiations with the IMF— intensified the demands by Brazilians for a return to civilian government through the electoral process. Support by middle class and business groups who had long backed the military regime now eroded and divisions within the armed forces further weakened the military government. As President Figueiredo's term came to an end, Brazil returned to "civilian" government admidst an economic and political crisis more severe (e.g., inflation of over 200 percent per annum) than the circumstances of 1964 which prompted the coup against President Goulart. Nevertheless, the economic and political legacy of two decades of military rule was stamped indelibly on Brazilian society.

Reprinted and edited from *Brazil: Politics in a Patrimonial Society*, 3d ed. (New York: Praeger Publishers, 1984), pp. 125–78.

Scott Mainwaring

The Transition to Democracy in Brazil

On January 15, 1985, Brazil elected a new president, seventy-four-year-old Tancredo Neves, a moderate career politician who had been one of the important leaders of the opposition to the military regime which took power in 1964. Tancredo died before assuming office, but the elected vice-president elect, José Sarney, took over the Executive Office on March 15, 1985, bringing to an end twenty-one years of military rule. . . .

This article analyzes the transition to democracy in Brazil. Starting from the viewpoint that political liberalization was initially a choice made by the military regime in 1974, the analysis examines why the regime undertook that path and then traces the main characteristics of the transition during two periods: (1) March 1974–October 1983, and (2) October 1983–January 1985. The latter period, which is examined in greater detail, is distinctive for the extent to which the regime lost its ability to dictate, or respond effectively to, political change. The following section then discusses the reasons behind the rapid erosion of regime power during the 1983–85 period.

Liberation from Above: The Initial Impulse

In March 1974, President Ernesto Geisel and Chief of Cabinet Golbery do Couto e Silva announced their intention to promote a slow, gradual, and careful process of political liberalization. This was not the first time the military regime had announced such an intention. Presidents Castello Branco (1964–67), Costa e Silva (1967–69), and Médici (1969–74) had publicly stated their desire to do so, yet none was able to implement this goal. Furthermore, during the course of the *abertura*, there was a conflict between the push for liberalization and the tightening authoritarian controls. Nevertheless, it is possible to date the *abertura* from March 1974 because, despite oscillations and regressions, from that time on, the general movement was toward a more liberal political system.

Why did the military decide to open up the regime? In contrast to earlier coups, where the military had returned power to civilians after a short interregnum, in 1964 the predominant thrust was toward a long-term intervention. Nevertheless, most leaders of the regime never envisioned military rule as a stable, permanent solution; the military was to restore order and eventually return power to civilians. The regime defined itself according to Western values, including that of democracy. Despite thousands of incidents of torture and political assassination, the regime always maintained some significant institutions typical of liberal democracy. In contrast to the recent authoritarian regimes of Uruguay, Argentina, and Chile, the Brazilian regime closed Congress only twice (1968–69 and 1977), both times for relatively short intervals. Also, in contrast to the other bureaucratic-authoritarian regimes of the Southern Cone, a party system functioned throughout the entire authoritarian period. The opposition party, the MDB (Movimento Democrático Brasileiro), was created by the government in 1965. During the most repressive years, 1969–74, the MDB had difficulty in functioning as an independent opposition voice, but it always served as a channel for some opposition demands and, after 1974, became increasingly autonomous and important.

During 1968–74, some nationalistic, far-right elements of the military initiated moves designed to increase the break with democratic institutions. Despite these efforts, and in contrast to the experience of other such regimes (Argentina, Uruguay, Chile), their initiatives were consistently defeated. The continued existence of democratic institutions throughout the authoritarian period would later prove important to the liberalization process. Despite the fact that such institutions may have served the military mostly as a facade, or as a way to facilitate continuation of civilian support, the existence of parties, elections, and a constitution offered the domestic opposition space in which to maneuver and provided at least a minimal continuity of democratic practices and leaders. . . .

An important backdrop to the *abertura* was the continuing state of tension generated by the conflicting pressures to open up the regime on the one hand, and to keep it closed on the other. However, mere existence of such pressures does not sufficiently explain why the liberalization process grew after 1974 when it had failed to do so earlier. Four factors were crucial to the decision to liberalize at that time.

First, since World War II, authoritarian regimes in the West have had trouble in devising the appropriate symbols or discourse which could win them widespread *legitimacy* [emphasis added, ED.]. Initially, the Brazilian regime constructed symbols of legitimacy which were almost exclusively negative: anti-Communism, anti-corruption, and anti-chaos. At the outset such symbols were very effective in winning the support of much of the population, particularly the middle and upper classes. To remain credible for the long haul, however, there must be a universally recognized and accepted threat of communism, corruption, or chaos. If an authoritarian regime should extirpate these "evils," then its *raison d'être* disappears; conversely, if the regime fails to combat its enemies, it loses credibility owing to its inefficiency. Paradoxically, it is precisely when the authoritarian regime meets its goals of restoring peace and order most successfully that the challenge to its legitimacy is apt to be greatest. Regimes able to defeat the Left and invigorate the economy will probably enjoy broader support than those regimes less successful in meeting stated objectives, but they will often face more pressures, both internal and external, to open up the political system. After all, how do you justify repression when there is no visible and plausible enemy?

The Brazilian government under President Médici turned to more positive symbols for legitimacy, such as the themes of efficiency, economic growth, and national aggrandizement. However, legitimacy based exclusively on performance is also precarious. Democratic legitimacy is based largely on *procedure,* even though performance and charisma may play important roles. Procedure provides a more stable base for legitimacy than efficiency because it requires mere acceptance of the rules of the game in order to survive. When legitimacy is based on performance, a regime may encounter crisis when performance declines. At the same time, a continued outstanding economic performance can shift public attention away from the previous focus on economic life, and toward a deeper concern with other aspects of sociopolitical life. Thus, in the contemporary West, where democratic norms and procedures have widespread legitimacy, either good or bad performance can undermine legitimacy based on efficiency.

In the Brazilian case, it was precisely those sectors which benefited most from the years of the "economic miracle" which were the most vocal in demanding a return to democratic rule: the population of the large and developed cities, and the middle class. In 1964, these sectors had led the demonstrations against João Goulart: in 1984, they led the demonstrations for direct elections. By 1974, when the *abertura* began, the disaffection of middle-class Brazil was already apparent. Such prominent institutions as the Brazilian Press Association and the Order of Brazilian Lawyers played a major role in opposing the authoritarian abuses. The Catholic Church, which essentially endorsed the coup in 1964, had become an outstanding source of opposition. Even some leaders of the industrial bourgeoisie of São Paulo began to call for a move toward democracy. Furthermore, in the 1974 elections, the opposition trounced the government party in the largest, most developed states. The signs of disaffection and of decreasing legitimacy were most visible in the same sectors from whom the regime had derived legitimacy during its earlier years.

The outstanding ideologue of the military regime, General Golbery do

Couto e Silva, recognized the need for legitimacy as the main motive for promoting political liberalization. In a major speech at the Escola Superior da Guerra (Superior War College), Golbery argued that the extreme concentration of power had created the threat of a "black hole," a vacuum resulting from the gap between the major decision centers and civil society. Although he did not refer explicitly to the notion of legitimacy, Golbery's speech indicated an acute awareness of the problem.

A *second* factor which contributed to the decision to liberalize was the fact that the close identification between the military and the government, necessary during the most repressive phases of authoritarian rule, had created problems for the military. There was an ongoing tension between the military as an institution and the military as government. As an institution fundamentally oriented toward national defense, the military required the kind of discipline and unity which was threatened by political divisions. Yet, as the holder of power, the armed forces were constantly being politicized and subjected to internal divisions.

These divisions were especially apparent during the presidential successions, which almost always present dilemmas for authoritarian regimes. Unlike democratic systems, which have clearly stipulated procedures for determining presidential succession, authoritarian regimes lack defined mechanisms for transferring executive power, and because power is usually concentrated in the hands of the executive, the issue of who controls the succession takes on great importance.

The Brazilian regime was exceptional in the way it institutionalized presidential successions; still, every succession created serious tension within the armed forces. From 1965 until 1967, there were conflicts between soft- and hard-liners as to who would succeed Castello Branco. In 1969, this scenario was repeated when President Costa e Silva died. Although hard-liners took over during the Médici presidency (1969–74), the group headed by General Golbery do Couto e Silva immediately began to plan ways of returning to power—which it did. During Geisel's presidency (1974–79) the Minister of the Army, General Silvio de Frota, attempted to undermine the *abertura* and become the next president. In 1978, the opposition party chose a dissident general to run for president. Even though Geisel and Golbery did not propose to relinquish power to civilians, both were aware that political liberalization, which by its very nature would allow greater separation between the military and the government, could alleviate some of these tensions.

Third, by 1974 the military had decimated the Left, had control over popular movements, and faced a weak opposition. Peasant movements, severely repressed in 1964, had never recovered. The labor movement had been silenced since suppression of the strikes at Osasco and Contagem in 1968; no major strike occurred again until 1978. The opposition party had suffered many key losses due to the repression, and ARENA (Alianca Renovadora Nacional), the government party, had easily won the 1970 elections. This situation led the regime to believe that it could successfully control a liberalization process, given the regime's strength, and the opposition's weakness and moderate character. The regime opted to liberalize, therefore, not because of weakness, but because of its strength.

This relative weakness of the opposition, and relative capacity of the regime to control the political situation, were distinctive marks of the liberalization process in Brazil during the early phases of the *abertura,* which made it differ radically from the situation in Argentina and Bolivia in the early 1970s, where active, powerful opposition groups were able to mobilize to topple military governments.

This weakness of the Brazilian opposition, however, by no means implied that the regime enjoyed sufficient support to govern without repression and without frequent manipulation of electoral laws. From 1974 until late 1983, political liberalization was characterized by the curious situation which enjoyed the support of powerful political actors, of a steadily increasing (though fluctuating) opposition, yet was unable to topple the regime.

Fourth, the economic situation fostered the regime's belief that it could afford to liberalize. Some authors automatically attributed the *abertura* to the end of the economic miracle. In fact, even though the 1973 oil crisis affected the Brazilian economy adversely, this argument is difficult to sustain. The main architects of the *abertura,* Geisel and Golbery do Couto e Silva, had planned an orderly and controlled liberalization even before the effect of the oil crisis became apparent. Furthermore, the Brazilian economy was one of the fastest growing in the world from 1967 to 1974. Inflation, which had almost reached 100 percent when Castello e Branco took over in April 1964, had been reduced to 20 percent. Finally, despite the deceleration in the rate of economic expansion after 1974, the Brazilian Gross Domestic Product (GDP) continued solid growth (7 percent per annum) until 1980, even though this growth increased the external vulnerability of the economy, thus restoring order along the economic, as well as the political, front.

Political Liberalization, 1974–83

Even though the decision to liberalize originated with the authoritarian regime, it created a new dynamic between the regime and its opponents. Liberalization implied redefining the rules of the game in such a way as to enhance the role of the opposition. Thus, the 1974–83 period inaugurated a stage of constant struggle and negotiation between regime and opposition, constant efforts by the latter to expand the cause of democracy, and constant attempts by the former to contain it.

It is worth illustrating this point at some length to indicate the flavor of the transition during those nine years. As part of its decision to allow greater political freedom, the regime decided to allow more competitive elections in 1974, anticipating a victory which would confirm its legitimacy. In 1970, under the aegis of the "miracle," the government party, ARENA, had demolished the MDB, creating the expectation that it would win subsequent elections. Yet the opposite happened: The opposition fared far better in 1974 than it had in 1970, claiming many key victories. In the Senate, the opposition won sixteen out of twenty-two disputed seats. The government overestimated its own strength and underestimated that of the opposition, especially in the developed urban areas where the regime was soundly trounced. Demographic trends, notably a rapid growth of large cities, indicated that the regime would likely encounter trouble in the 1978 elections.

Following a pattern which would be repeated over the years, the regime used a combination of coercion and ingenuity to reassert authority and its ability to control the liberalization process. In April 1977, President Geisel closed Congress to promulgate new electoral legislation which enabled the government to maintain control of the Senate and Chamber of Deputies in the 1978 elections.

Beginning in 1978, the regime faced challenges at both the institutional and popular levels. As the political arena opened wider, the opposition demanded restoration of basic civil liberties, especially freedoms of the press and of speech, amnesty for political exiles, and an end to torture. While the opposition successfully generated discussion of these issues, the regime took the initiative in responding to them. During his presidency, Geisel reduced the incidents of torture despite resistance from the hardliners. In 1979, the regime granted amnesty to exiles and abolished institutional Act No. 5, responsible for eliminating important civil liberties. Also in 1979, the regime took the initiative in reforming the artificially imposed two-party system, created in 1965. The opposition had long been demanding party reform, but the regime seized upon the issue as a means to divide the opposition. Ironically, though perhaps typically, when the reform finally came, it garnered more support among government leaders than among the opposition party. Equally instructive was the fact that the government included dissolution of the opposition party as part of the reform. Even measures taken in the name of liberalization (or democracy) were often imposed in manipulative fashion.

An unexpected challenge came from popular movements. After years of being virtually dormant as far as the public was concerned, popular movements surged back with surprising vitality between 1977 and 1980.

Most publicized was the auto workers movement of Greater São Paulo, which staged major strikes in successive years between 1978 and 1980. Throughout the country, peasant unions emerged stronger than at any time since 1964 and more numerous than ever. Neighborhood associations and local movements for urban services also blossomed all over the country.

The government responded to these movements with varying degrees of repression, cooptation, and concessions. Aware that its political future depended upon maintaining as much public support as possible, the government attempted to make new inroads into the popular sector. Significant in this regard was the reformulation of wage policy in 1979 designed to favor the poorest workers. Traditional mechanisms, such as housing projects, left behind during the most repressive period, resurfaced, but, in other cases, the regime made clear that it wished to impose limits upon popular movements. Every year repressive measures were employed against the auto workers' strikes while violence against peasants was rampant in the Amazon region.

In urban areas, these policies often succeeded in containing the challenges posed by popular movements. The regime prevented the movements from becoming a determining element in the political process, even though it had to reformulate its own policies and style of decision making to do so. In the poorest states, the government managed to retain its popular support. By 1982, urban popular movements were on the decline, a result of the economic crisis, the attention commanded by the political parties, and government ability to marginalize these movements. In many rural areas, especially frontier regions, private and public repression remained the norm.

Every step in the *abertura* provided new possibilities for the opposition and new dilemmas for the regime. The latter designed the 1979 party reform in such a way as to maximize its own prospects in the 1982 elections. Its strategy was to divert the opposition into several parties, assuming that a large, malleable centrist party would emerge. By 1981, it was apparent that the government would fare quite poorly under the new electoral laws and party situation. The centrist Popular Party (PP for Partido Popular) proved to be more combative than the regime expected. Furthermore, the largest opposition party, the PMDB (Partido do Movimento Democrático Brasileiro), proved significantly stronger than the government had anticipated. As a result, in November 1981, the regime once again turned to authoritarian means to impose changes in the electoral laws, this time to prevent party alliances during the 1982 elections.

The 1982 elections marked a new point in the *abertura*, since significant decision centers were at stake for the first time. These elections, for state governors, were the first since 1965 and resulted in a stalemate. The opposition won most of the major states: Rio de Janeiro, São Paulo, Minas Gerais, as well as a number of smaller states. The opposition-controlled states accounted for 60 percent of Brazil's population and 75 percent of her GDP. The opposition also far outpolled the government in terms of popular votes for governors.

Nevertheless, the government could claim some significant victories, too. It elected governors of two important states, Rio Grande do Sul (in the far south) and Pernambuco (in the northeast), and it won a majority of states (twelve out of twenty-two). Thanks to the continuous tampering with electoral laws and despite having a minority of the popular vote, the PDS (Partido Democrático Social, the government party) elected a majority of representatives for the electoral college which would determine the presidential election of January 1985. Many observers assumed that, by getting the majority of the electoral college votes, the regime had virtually wrapped up the 1985 elections, two years and two months before it took place. Indeed, if the regime had played its cards well, it probably could have wrapped up the 1985 election, thereby prolonging its control of the executive office until 1989 or 1991.

More than eight years after beginning the *abertura,* the regime still retained a relatively strong position. This does not mean that it was consistently able to impose its will throughout the 1974–83 period. Indeed, it generally failed to control the events of political change to the degree it would have liked. Yet, what was remarkable about the Brazilian *abertura* was the regime's ability to respond to new situations in ways enabling it to remain in power and to limit the nature of the political change.

Even though state policies reflected the dialectic between the regime and opposition, the regime was able to ensure significant continuity in both policies and leadership during this period. For example, sporadic repression continued against popular movements and against the Left during the Figueiredo administration. Indeed, in some rural areas, especially the Amazon, the level of violence even escalated after 1978. Figueiredo employed clientelistic practices and generally excluded the popular sectors from the decision-making sphere.

The continuity of leadership during this period is remarkable, as is the regime's ability to institutionalize regular presidential succession. Such key figures as Presidents Figueiredo, Geisel, and Médici, Chiefs of Cabinet Leitão de Abreu and Golbery do Couto e Silva, and Cabinet members Delfim Neto, Jarbas Passarinho, and Mário Andreazza, to mention only a few, played leading roles in lengthy chapters of the regime's history. In many cases, the same figures responsible for leading the *abertura* had also been responsible for implementing policy during the most repressive years.

This ability of the military government to provide continuity in policies and to limit the nature of political change made the Brazilian *abertura* singularly slow and protracted. . . . Over time, the opposition's ability to affect the political arena increased significantly; yet, until 1983, the opposition was incapable of toppling the regime, either electorally or through mass mobilization.

The Struggle for Democracy, October 1983 to January 1985

Beginning with October 1983, the political process changed in significant ways in relation to the first nine years of the *abertura*. After years of responding successfully to a wide amalgam of challenges, the regime lost its ability to control the presidential succession, paving the way to an earlier transition to democracy than most observers expected. Indeed, it lost its very ability to formulate a coherent, articulate political strategy during this final period in power. Whereas, in November 1982, the government seemed almost certain to win the presidential election of January 1985, when the score was finally tallied, it suffered an ignominious defeat. The regime's decline and the opposition's ascension can be subdivided into three short periods.

Regime Erosion: October to December 1983

Throughout almost its entire course, the regime had been able to count on the government party (ARENA until 1979, PDS afterwards). The party had always been the submissive partner of a tandem—a party of the regime, not a regime of the party, a party *of* the government, but not a party *in* government. Generally, the government party supported the regime, and it was not terribly consequential even when it didn't: The regime imposed its will on the party. This situation changed in the second half of 1983. In July, a liberal faction within the PDS won 35 percent of the votes in the election for the Executive of the PDS. This liberal faction had already clashed with Figueiredo, and the strength of this group, coupled with eroding cohesion within the PDS, led Figueiredo to threaten to resign from the party.

The debate over wage policy, in the midst of the severe recession which began in 1980 and reached a low point in 1983, proved to be the issue which provoked a PDS revolt. In July 1983, as part of the stabilization plan sponsored by the International Monetary Fund (IMF), the government presented a new wage policy which would have resulted in enormous erosion of real earnings of vast sectors of the society. Congress rejected successive government proposals, under PDS leadership, despite government pressure on its own behalf. It took the government several months to get a proposal finally approved.

Another blow to PDS unity and ability to control the presidential succession occurred in late December. In his end-of-year speech, President Figueiredo announced that he would not coordinate the party's campaign after having previously agreed to do so, in May 1983. Coordinating the campaign was difficult in light of the profound divisions within the party, yet his decision to abdicate from the task of choosing a successor probably affected adversely the party's chances of reestablishing some degree of internal cohesion. This decision seemed to strengthen the candidacy of Paulo Maluf, thereby increasing the feeling of the opposition that it could not negotiate the choice of the next president. Figueiredo's decision marked a profound change from past practices. Previous military presidents had indicated, and actively campaigned for, their personal choice for president—and, in the cases of Castello Branco (1964–67), Médici (1969–74), and Geisel (1974–79), they had won. It was within this context of gradual erosion of the government's ability to manage the political and economic situation, and of increased tension between the PDS and the government, that the campaign for direct elections began.

Mobilization of the Opposition: January to April 1984

The opposition parties had long proposed direct elections for president, but the massive public campaign for direct elections began only in January 1984. The first demonstration took place in Curitiba, the largest city of the southern state of Paraná, on January 12, with approximately 30,000 people present. Over the next three and one-half months, there were literally hundreds of demonstrations all over the country in favor of direct elections. Never before in Brazilian history had so many people demonstrated for anything. The largest masses gathered in Rio (about one million people on April 10, 1984) and São Paulo (over one million people on April 16, 1984). Even occasional warnings by military leaders that demonstrations for direct elections could endanger the *abertura* failed to diminish the opposition's resounding success in mobilizing the Brazilian population. As early as January 25, when 200,000 people gathered in the rain in São Paulo, even some PDS Congressional leaders announced their support for direct elections.

As the campaign for direct elections accelerated, the regime began to disintegrate visibly, and an increasing number of PDS members began to support direct elections, including, on February 8, Vice President Chaves himself. Before the turn of the year, the PMDB presented an amendment in Congress for direct elections which seemed to have no chance of passing. The opposition needed the support of two thirds of both houses in order to win. This meant getting 320 votes in the Chamber of Deputies and 46 in the Senate, although the opposition parties controlled only 244 seats in the Chamber and 24 in the Senate. But what the regime had dismissed as impossible in January, when the campaign began, began to seem quite plausible by mid-March. Several PDS members in the Congress predicted that the Amendment for Direct Elections would pass.

It is difficult to overstate the impact of the campaign for direct elections. The campaign's success gave the opposition a confidence it had not known since 1968 and led to an unprecedented crisis within the regime. As the campaign proceeded, many PDS leaders came to feel that the regime needed to negotiate a way out. Led by Aureliano Chaves, Chief of Cabinet Leitão de Abreu, the (PDS) head of the Chamber of Deputies, and the Ministers of the Air Force and the Navy, this group reckoned that if the regime elected the next president under the conditions then prevailing, the country would enter into an unprecedented political crisis. This faction felt that, at the very least, the regime needed to reduce the mandate of the next president to a maximum of four years. Another faction, led by the Chief of the National Information Service, the Minister of the Army, the Minister of Justice, and the other two candidates for president, fiercely opposed this kind of negotiation. They believed that the regime could weather one more crisis, after which things would return to normal.

Throughout 1984, tensions between these factions remained high, with leaders of the groups insulting one another publicly in a way unprecedented for the authoritarian regime. The Minister of the Navy was fired in late March as a result of his outspoken views on behalf of the more liberal faction in these conflicts. In mid-April, Theodorico Ferraco, a PDS Deputy from Rio, described the government as a group of "a half dozen irresponsible people who are leading the country." Meanwhile, Vice President Chaves, who had previously announced his support for direct elections, recommended that they be held in 1984.

The Electoral College: April 1984 to January 1985

As the date approached (April 25, 1984) for voting on the amendment to reestablish direct elections for president, regime intransigents won out. President Figueiredo declared emergency measures to be in effect in Brasília and ten nearby cities to abort the possibility of demonstrations. In addition, he mobilized all the support he could muster in Congress to defeat the amendment. When roll call finally came, the amendment fell 22 votes short of the 320 needed to pass the Chamber of Deputies.

As the campaign for direct elections went on, the PDS set about attempting to find a candidate for president. The three main candidates were Vice President Aureliano Chaves, Minister of the Interior Mário Andreazza, and Federal Deputy Paulo Maluf, ex-Governor of São Paulo. Aureliano Chaves, the most liberal of the three, had the most popular support by far, but he lacked support within the party machine. Andreazza was Figueiredo's preferred candidate, and, during the early stages, it appeared he had good chances of winning. However, by April the most likely winner seemed to be Maluf, who was anathema to the moderate factions of the party as being notorious for egregious corruption.

With these possibilities in mind, the moderate factions began to flirt with the idea of supporting Tancredo Neves, even though he was not officially a candidate. Two days following defeat of the amendment for direct elections, eight of the nine governors from the impoverished northeast, all PDS leaders, pledged their support to Tancredo, an avalanche of defections. In mid-June, when it appeared certain that Maluf would win the PDS convention, not only did the President of the PDS resign, but the Governor of Rio Grande do Sul, also from the PDS, announced his preference for Tancredo over Maluf. The last week of June, these defections were consecrated by the formation of the Liberal Front, headed by moderate PDS leaders who supported Aureliano Chaves and had voted for Tancredo, who increasingly appeared to be the likely opposition candidate, regardless of whom the PDS nominated. Consequently, the opposition seemed to have a good chance of winning the election, a situation which paved the way for increasing acceptance of indirect elections except for most of the PT (Partido dos Trabalhadores) and the PDT (Partido Democrático Trabalhista).

From this point on, unity within the PDS became progressively eroded. Aureliano Chaves withdrew his candidacy and began to work openly for Tancredo, an old political rival. Some regime moderates continued to put their hopes on Andreazza, but the PDS convention, held the second week of August, closed that question: Maluf won, 493 to 350, leading some of Andreazza's coterie to defect to the enemy camp. Among the most important of these was the ex-Governor of Bahia, António Carlos Magalhães, who, in September, gave an unprecedented lambasting to the Minister of the Air Force for having called the PDS defectors traitors. Maluf's victory implied virtual defeat for the PDS in the January election.

Meanwhile, Tancredo Neves embarked upon construction of a broader network of support, aiming his campaign at both the members of electoral college and the public at large. Equally important, Neves was busy persuading the military not to intervene. The success of his campaign on all fronts is undeniable: By January 15, he came out ahead, 480 to 180, in the electoral college, and averted the possibility of a coup. Through this double victory, he became the first civilian elected to the presidency since 1960. . . .

Erosion of consensus in the upper echelon of the regime. The leaders of the military government had always experienced some internal tensions, usually between the hard-line and the moderate authoritarian factions. These tensions were generally accentuated during periods of debate over the presidential succession. Nevertheless, until 1982, the level of agreement and unity, both within the armed forces and within the government, was striking. Conflicts notwithstanding, all the presidential successions were handled in ways which managed to avoid crises for the regime.

In 1983–84, the presidential succession provoked an unresolvable crisis. For the first time, the regime found itself unable to agree upon an acceptable candidate. The major leaders were split not only over whom to choose for president, but over whether to shorten the mandate for the next president, and whether to hold direct elections in future presidential contests. Ex-President Geisel and Chief of the Cabinet Leitão de Abreu supported Vice President Chaves; Figueiredo supported Andreazza; and ex-Chief of the Cabinet Golbery supported Maluf. Chaves' supporters generally favored a negotiated settlement with the opposition, including a reduction of the presidential mandate and an assurance that the next presidential election would be direct. The supporters of Andreazza and Maluf generally preferred a hard-line approach: Impose a PDS victory now, and make concessions later. But, whereas Maluf's supporters urged Figueiredo to play a neutral role in the succession question, Andreazza hoped the president would force his nomination to go through. Equally significant in revealing the profound schisms within the upper echelons of the regime were the tensions evident between the president and the vice president. Even though Chaves served as interim president on two occasions when Figueiredo underwent his operations, the president never seemed to trust, or work with, his running mate, and the friction between the two was exacerbated during the campaign for direct elections.

Inability of President Figueiredo to lead the regime. Despite their different styles and orientations, all previous military presidents had come across as effective leaders. When Figueiredo took office in 1979, it appeared that he would carry on this tradition. The new president seemed enthusiastic, and his proposal of carrying out the *abertura* appealed to the media. However, Figueiredo's charisma wore off, and he increasingly appeared ill-suited for executive office. In a major speech in January 1985, Figueiredo asked the nation to forget him—hardly a request befitting a president who hopes to be remembered as an effective leader.

Nowhere was Figueiredo's ineffectual leadership more apparent than in the presidential succession process. In May 1983, Figueiredo agreed to coordinate the PDS procedure for choosing the next president. Seven months later, however, he decided against it, contrary to the practice of all his predecessors in the military presidency. Coordinating the presidential succession obviously was more difficult in a time of open political competition, but this reversed decision revealed a vacillation uncharacteristic of previous administrations. Effective leadership and campaigning on behalf of one of the candidates, particularly if Figueiredo had opted for Chaves, could have helped the regime avoid some of the schisms which emerged.

Particularly salient in this regard was Figueiredo's persistent refusal to support his own vice president. Early in 1984, it was clear that, in terms of popular support, Aureliano Chaves far outdistanced both Maluf and Andreazza. In fact, surveys showed Chaves as leading all potential candidates in a direct election for president. Although history can always devise strange twists of fate, it seems likely that, had the regime chosen Aureliano as its candidate for president, or negotiated with the opposition to agree upon Chaves, it would have been able to elect one of its own for president. Figueiredo was the only person in a position to enhance Chaves' chances significantly and he consistently refused to do so.

Increasing tension between moderate sectors of the PDS and the government. Even though ARENA and PDS leaders sometimes expressed frustration at their marginalization from the decision-making process, few major conflicts between the regime and the government party had occurred prior to 1983. ARENA/PDS leaders had consistently gone along with the regime, a situation which broke down in October 1983 when the party rejected successive wage packages proposed by the government, providing a forecast for the even greater tensions which surfaced during the presidential succession. Throughout the entire process, friction between the moderate sectors and more intransigent groups was sharp. These strained relations culminated in the decision of moderate PDS Congressional leaders to abandon the party to help create the Liberal Front and to vote for Tancredo Neves. . . .

Unity of the Opposition

After the 1979 party reform, the opposition parties frequently had difficulties in creating alliances against the regime. The regime had promoted party reform as a method to divide the opposition, and this strategy proved successful to a significant extent.

The campaign for direct elections overrode these party disputes and served to unite the opposition parties. This unity of the opposition parties was an important component in the success of the campaign for direct elections. It helped generate the perception of a national consensus on the issue—a fact supported by surveys which showed that, by early 1984, over 80 percent of the population wanted the chance to vote for president. The virtual unanimity of the opposition also denied the government a legitimate interlocutor upon whom it could rely. After the Amendment for Direct Elections was defeated on April 24, this unity of the opposition parties dissolved.

The gap between social movements and opposition parties also narrowed during the campaign for direct elections. The social movements mobilized people to participate in the demonstrations. While the primary responsibility for success of the campaign must go to the opposition parties, social movements played an important secondary role. This relative unity between social movements and opposition parties also eroded in the months following the defeat of the Amendment for Direct Elections.

Finally, Tancredo Neves was able to do something that perhaps no other opposition figure could: win the support of significant parts of the left, center-left, and much of the center-right, while proving acceptable to the military. Support of part of the left and center-left was indispensable in making possible an alliance between the PMDB and PDT, as well as part of the PT, during his campaign. Support of the center-right, which included mostly PDS people who defected to the Liberal Front, was necessary for his electoral victory. Finally, the fact that Neves proved acceptable to the majority of military leaders avoided an authoritarian objection or complication. A more progressive leader might have induced a military veto.

Notes on the Erosion of the Regime, 1983–85

The erosion of regime power during its last year and a half was the result of a combination of legitimation problems, which were fundamentally structural, and of government choices. For the most part, the regime handled the transition with unusual political perspicacity, avoiding the precipitous decline in legitimacy and increase in political mobilization which usually accompany transitions in the wake of regime collapse. It would be misleading to suggest that the regime suffered a direct, steady decline in legitimacy after 1974. Its level of support followed a pattern somewhat akin to that of the *abertura* as a whole: periods of decline, followed by other periods during which the regime renewed its appeal on the basis of its initiatives. Yet the pattern of gradual decline is clear. The government party, ARENA, won 50.5 percent of the votes for federal deputies in 1966, 48.4 percent in 1970, 40.9 percent in 1974, and 40.0 percent in 1978; its successor, the PDS, won only 36.7 percent in 1982.

The difficulty that contemporary Western authoritarian regimes have in developing formulas for legitimacy which are effective over the long term has already been noted. In Brazil, this difficulty became more acute the longer the regime was in power. It became easier for the opposition to denounce the authoritarian measures still being employed. At the same time, it became increasingly difficult to justify these measures. There was no opposition in sight, since that would be "disloyal" to the regime, and it became increasingly evident that most of the society yearned for a return to democracy. Between 1974 and 1985, the regime attempted to find new legitimacy formulas as electoral politics became more central. Yet it could not win elections without resorting to vast manipulation of electoral laws. These *casuismos*, to use the Brazilian lexicon, kept the government in power, yet, along with other authoritarian measures, they clearly prevented the government from regaining legitimacy through its attempts to restore democracy.

These *casuismos* were profoundly ambivalent in their effects. In the short run, they helped the regime retain power, but their long-term efficacy was dubious, for they were instituted in authoritarian fashion and had an anti-democratic intent. Geisel closed Congress to impose the April 1977 electoral package, which created "bionic" senators (one third of the Senate), elected indirectly to assure an ARENA victory. In December 1979, in another blatant measure, the government dissolved the MDB to enhance its own electoral prospects, using party reform to divide the opposition. Two years later, the November 1981 package also contained flagrantly manipulative measures, such as imposing a straight party vote and not allowing party identification on the ballots. All these measures provided the opposition with ammunition with which to attack the regime's authoritarian character. The government was moving toward democratic rule in its attempts to regain legitimacy, but this very move only served to expose its authoritarian character the more. By the early 1980s, electoral manipulation seemed to have a limited future. The question was not whether the regime would be able to perpetuate itself in power *ad infinitum*, via electoral manipulation; rather, it was what would be the outcome for the regime if the system were to become more democratic. The adverse impact of the *casuismos* and other such measures became so apparent that, by early 1984, even some leading figures in the regime (notably Aureliano Chaves) decided to support direct elections for president.

By 1983, the economic crisis combined with a wave of corruption scandals to shrivel public confidence in the regime even further. When the military took power in 1964, the armed forces had used the twin issues of economic crisis and corruption to justify the overthrow of Goulart. When the same problems erupted during the Figueiredo administration, they rebounded against it. After basing their claim to legitimacy on the principle of efficiency, the regime's credibility was severely undermined by the severity of the domestic economic problems, and they appeared lame in attributing the cause to international factors beyond their control. The international conjuncture certainly contributed to the crisis—but this did little to convince most Brazilians that the regime was efficient, given the indications to the contrary.

The economy entered deep, prolonged recession in 1980, but it was not until after the November 1982 elections that the severity of the debt crisis became apparent. After having denied the need to do so, the government announced, immediately after the elections, that it would resort to IMF loans and accept its stabilization program. This action represented a political defeat for the regime, since it involved making concessions to a foreign institution. Worse, the stabilization program exacerbated the economic crisis.

Never before in Brazilian history had the economy suffered through such a deep recession or such a high inflation rate. Between 1980 and 1984, per capita income fell approximately 15 percent. By 1983, the inflation rate was well over 200 percent per annum. Meanwhile, the foreign debt increased from $6.6 billion in 1971 to approximately $100 billion by 1984. It became apparent that some of the 1970s growth had been purchased at the price of an increasing external debt. Under other circumstances, the economic crisis could have led to an authoritarian stance, hence, more rigid, but, given the "tired" nature of the Brazilian regime by 1983, and the deep desire on the part of a divided society to restore democracy, the opposite occurred. A series of disclosures of massive fraud, embezzlement, and corruption within enterprises linked to the armed forces darkened the regime's public image further.

Even though the gradual erosion of regime legitimacy was clearly visible, the regime's displacement from power in January 1985 was not inevitable. In retrospect, there may well be a temptation to read backwards into the events of October 1983 to October 1984 the unavoidable demise of an old regime *in extremis*. Nevertheless, a balanced analysis would have to emphasize both the strengths, as well as the vulnerabilities, of the Brazilian regime in 1983. Considering everything it had experienced and the length of the *abertura,* the Brazilian regime's capacity to remain in power while promoting political liberalization stands out as exceptional.

While the slow decline in legitimacy set the stage for the more rapid erosion of 1983–84, it was choices by both the regime and the opposition which ultimately determined the latter's victory—and the return to democracy—in January 1985. If the regime had played its cards better, or if the opposition had played its cards worse, the former could have won the January 1985 election. In this sense, political choice and leadership played a decisive role in enabling the transition to take place when it did.

Perhaps most significant in this regard was President Figueiredo's refusal to support Aureliano Chaves as his successor. If the president had done so, it is likely that Aureliano would have won both the PDS convention and the January election. At one point, Figueiredo considered holding primary elections within the party as a means of determining the candidate. If this had happened, everything indicates that Chaves would have won. The PDS's ultimate choice, Maluf, was by far the worst in terms of regime unity and popular support.

For the opposition, the most important choice was that of Neves as the candidate to run against the PDS. As became clear during the course of the campaign, Neves had an ability to placate the military and to win support from former PDS leaders that probably no other opposition candidate possessed. In this sense, the decision of progressive opposition leaders to accept Tancredo was an important one. While this decision helped pave the way for the March 1985 transition, other factors, in particular the decisive voice of ex-regime supporters and marginalization of the progressive sectors of the opposition, also marked the early days of the new democratic regime.

From Elite-Led Transition to Elitist Democrats

October 1983 ushered in a new period in the democratization of Brazil, with characteristics which differed markedly from those of the previous years of *abertura*. We could describe the 1974–82 years as a "transition from above" and the 1983–85 period as a "transition through withdrawal." The critical difference between the two kinds of transition lies in the regime's ability to influence the transition (greater in transitions from above) and in the degree of discontinuity in the political process (lesser in transitions from above).

Nevertheless, it would be misleading to overstate the extent to which the post–October 1983 period represented a rupture in the political process. Even though regimes which effect transitions through withdrawal lack legitimacy and the support of civil society, they still retain enough power to impose some limits on the kind of transition that takes place. This ability may erode over time—the political world is always dynamic and fluid—but it is almost certain to mark the first years of democratic rule. In this sense, it is significant that, even though it suffered a major legitimacy problem by late 1984, the Brazilian regime did not collapse. Equally significant is the fact that the opposition, despite a considerable degree of unity among main opposition parties and the social movements, was incapable of overthrowing the regime. Only by allying with significant and substantial parts of the regime was the opposition able to come to power. Without creation of the Democratic Alliance, a coalition composed of parts of the PMDB, the PFL (Partido do Frente Liberal) and the PDS, the opposition could not have won the 1985 election. This means that the left has been excluded, while the center-right, and even parts of the right, have been included. This alignment of forces became clear in the naming of the Cabinet. Progressive sectors of the PMDB complained of *continuismo* (i.e., a basic continuity in policies despite the changes in names and faces). The PDT and PT complained also, even though the latter was embroiled in internal disputes severe enough to threaten its very existence. . . .

Although post–October 1983 characteristics differ from those of the preceding liberalization period, the Brazilian transition is relatively cautious. Even before March 15, 1985, it was apparent that major changes would be confined to political institutions, while there would be minimal change in the socioeconomic order. The elitist negotiations between the PMDB, the Democratic Front, the Democratic Alliance, and the Armed Forces systematically excluded popular participation. Considering the length of the elite political domination of Brazil, this fact is hardly earth-shaking. Yet, considering the important role played by the popular mobilizations of early 1984 to reverse authoritarianism, the return to politics as usual was a disappointment to progressive segments of the society—including sectors of the PMDB. . . .

The transition took an unexpected twist when Tancredo Neves died before he could assume office. The new president, José Sarney, embodied the fragile side of the Brazilian transition. Until June 1984, Sarney had been president of the PDS, and, along with his PDS colleagues, had helped bury the Amendment for Direct Elections. The fact that an old regime leader became president of the New Republic was revealing of the compromises made to depose the military regime. . . . The painfully slow transition involving so many elements of continuity from the military was sure to mark the new democracy.

Reprinted and edited from *Journal of Interamerican Studies and World Affairs* 28, no. 1 (Spring 1986), pp. 149–79.

Brian Loveman

Antipolitics in Chile, 1973–87

Background to the Military Coup

In 1970, Dr. Salvador Allende, presidential candidate of the Unidad Popular coalition, won a plurality—but not a majority—of votes from the Chilean electorate. Consequently, and in accord with Chilean electoral laws and constitution, the Chilean Congress was called upon to vote for the president, and it selected Dr. Allende as the country's new president. Soon thereafter, a wave of opposition to his administration developed among business and middle-class sectors: Rightist political movements and parties, entrepreneurial associations, some white-collar unions, as well as groups representing both commercial interests and those of small business. Eventually this opposition determined that "the government of Allende was incompatible with the survival of freedom and private enterprise in Chile, [and] that the only way to avoid their extinction was to overthrow the government."

Gradually this opposition movement spread and consolidated, supported in part by external funding and covert political intervention, to create a conspiratorial Comando Gremialista (the term *gremio* was applied broadly in Chile to include professional and occupational associations) which incorporated truckers, merchants, retailers, industrialists, agricultural landowners, white-collar professionals, and women's groups. These groups eventually took their protests to the streets and highways of Chile, mounted an explosive media campaign against the government, and generally created a climate of instability and tension throughout the country.

For almost three years, Chile became increasingly polarized politically as the Allende government sought to implement a controversial program labeled "the Chilean road to socialism." Polarization was abetted and exacerbated by chaotic economic conditions, which included hyper-inflation. Opposition members of Congress accused the government of violating the Chilean constitution and of planning to install a totalitarian regime, and they called upon the military forces to "re-establish the rule of the constitution and the law . . . in order to guarantee institutional stability, civil peace, security, and development." Under the pressure of these appeals, combined with its own fervent anti-Marxism and the threat to its integrity posed by Leftist leaders who were urging enlisted personnel to mutiny and engage in subversion, the military finally acted by instituting a brutal coup d'etat on 11 September 1973.

Political Mission of the Military Regime

Above all else, the new military government blamed Chile's crisis on "politics" and politicians who had betrayed the nation, engaged in demagogy, and allowed Soviet-inspired Marxists to gain control of the Chilean state. According to General Pinochet, speaking at the University of Chile in 1979, the harsh military action of 1973 was "intended to repudiate the totalitarian action of the Soviets, enthroned in a government obedient to their desires, which had practically destroyed the democratic foundations [of Chilean society], through spiritual and material violence." Further, "administrative corruption and economic chaos had corroded the harmony and democratic institutionality of the country. . . . we bordered upon fratricidal war." Only by destroying the old order, by rejecting liberal democracy in its Chilean variant, by purging the politicians and "extirpating the Marxist cancer," could Chile be saved from the brink of disaster and create a new institutionality to guarantee political stability, economic recovery, and growth.

Thus, on the one hundredth anniversary of the founding of the city of Antofagasta, General Pinochet declared, "The Supreme Government has established as its most important objective the creation and consolidation of a new institutionality, founded on a real democracy, a democracy vigorously defended from its enemies." In 1981, the military government imposed upon Chile the new constitution approved the previous year in a managed plebiscite. This new constitution codified many of the political practices and emergency decrees through which the military dictatorship sought to construct a new basis of political legitimacy. Major features of the constitution included permanent proscription of all parties and movements spreading doctrines undermining the family, advocating violence, or adopting a conception of society, state, or juridical order of a totalitarian character or based on class conflict (Art. 8); outlawed all groups "contrary to morality, public order, and national security" (Art. 15); provided for a number of "states of constitutional exception"—internal and foreign war, internal commotion, emergency and public calamity, which, in turn, allow the president of the country to declare "state of assembly," "state of siege," "state of emergency," or "state of catastrophe." These states of constitutional exception authorized suspension, for various periods of time, of civil liberties and constitutional guarantees concerning freedom of association, assembly, press, and other political liberties, including the rights of workers to organize and engage in collective bargaining. In some cases, the constitution authorized the president to expel citizens from the national territory (Arts. 39–41).

Most importantly, the authors of this constitution sought to institutionalize antipolitics or what General Pinochet called "authoritarian democracy." The constitution limited participation of class-based, ideologically motivated, or merely interest-oriented political groups, parties, or movements, and founded a military-tutored administrative state. The key concept in the new constitution was national security; every citizen was obligated to "honor the fatherland, defend its sovereignty, and contribute to the preservation of national security and the essential values of Chilean tradition" (Art. 22). Almost all rights of Chilean citizens specified in the constitutional text were limited by the requirements of national security (Art. 19). While national security itself was nowhere precisely defined, the constitution assigned the armed forces the mission to "guarantee the institutional order of the republic" (Art. 90). In this sense, the armed forces became the dominant political force in the new institutionality. This role was further enhanced by creation of a National Security Council dominated by military commanders and responsible for a number of advisory and policymaking tasks (Arts. 95–96).

The constitution also provided *each* of the armed forces with direct representation on regional development councils which appointed mayors, thereby controlling or monitoring municipal administration (Arts. 101–108). Provisions for eventual election of a new congress and participation of newly defined political parties (contingent upon approval of a new law regulating political parties, which through 1986 was not forthcoming) explicitly included designees of the National Security Council as senators (ex-commanders of each of the four military forces) (Art. 45). Thus, the new constitution clearly provided for a *permanent* militarization of Chilean politics intended to exorcise the evil of "politics" from the political process.

Without hesitancy or chagrin, General Pinochet called this new institutionality "authoritarian democracy." On the second anniversary of the 1980 constitution's implementation (March 1983), General Pinochet declared:

I hereby notify politicians anxious to regain power that we will not tolerate any limits on our exercise of authority beyond that established by the constitutional text. . . . *When government and opposition speak of a "return to democracy," they are not referring to the same thing.* Between one and the other conception are profound differences that no one should ignore. Confronted by the totalitarian threat, and in order to never return to the vices of the past, the government over which I preside is designing, within the context established by the constitution, a political system which delivers the administration and government of the regions and communes to intermediate social entities, decontaminated from the virus of partyism. . . . Without doubt, we Chileans will not at this date allow ourselves to be misled by false visions of apparent redemption, nor by the demagogic deception of politicians from the past.

Regime and Opposition, 1973–80

Not only did the government and the opposition refer to different concepts when they spoke of return to democracy in the Chile of 1986, but the opposition in Chile remained divided, fragmented, disoriented, frustrated, and subject to episodic regime terror. Most importantly, it was an opposition unable to agree on a viable legitimate alternative, either as a form of government, a socioeconomic strategy, or even a short-term coalition to manage the transition from direct military dictatorship to some form of limited democracy with military participation, as in Brazil or the Philippines.

In short, the opposition in Chile included many oppositions: opposition to specific policies or programs of the military government; opposition to the personal dictatorship of General Pinochet; opposition to military rule; opposition only to *certain aspects* of the authoritarian model (e.g., restrictions upon "democratic" groups versus "Marxist" groups); opposition to the authoritarian model and the constitution of 1980; opposition focused on a restoration, or partial restoration, of Chilean multiparty democracy; opposition to the military regime, liberal democracy, and capitalism which carried some vague "socialism" as its political objective; opposition which still favored the ultimate establishment of a political system based on Marxist-Leninist principles. Both within and among these different types of opposition to the military government existed shifting viewpoints, commitments, and alliances, as well as old-fashioned personal rivalries and factional strife.

In a sense, the ultimate failure of the military programs and policies since 1973 was that not only had *all* pre-coup political movements, groups, parties, and ideologies survived, but that new radical movements and organizations had come into being. This occurred despite state terrorism, recurrent purges, deportation of visible leaders, assassination of exiles, and brutalization of the population. However, the failure of military government to eliminate its opposition left Chilean society and politics almost as polarized and politicized in 1986 as it had been in 1973. By the early 1980s, most Chileans favored a "return to democracy," but with widespread disagreement over the precise definition of "democracy" and, among the forces of the political center and right, over the extent to which leftist political parties and movements should be allowed to participate in any post-Pinochet political process.

A public opinion survey reported by the Chilean weekly *Hoy*, in 1983, found that 21.6 percent of respondents believed that the best government formula for solving national problems was "the current government"; another 15 percent preferred a government without Pinochet but including military participation or directed by a leading rightist politician; 24.2 percent desired a "new government formed by the opposition but without communists"; and 22.7 percent preferred a "new government formed by opposition elements without exclusions." At the same time, over 75 percent of the respondents favored "reestablishment of full democracy" before 1989 (almost 60 percent favoring this alternative by 1985) in clear opposition to the provisions of the 1980 constitution. Merely recognizing that the Constitution of 1980 enjoyed little domestic support from the majority of Chileans, and that it could not survive much beyond Pinochet himself, did not, in and of itself, provide any viable political alternative to the present government (as had occurred in quite different ways in Argentina, Uruguay, Peru, and Brazil in the early 1980s). In this sense, the political opposition to the military government in Chile which evolved after 1973 reflected, in all its aspects (focus, organization, tactics, ideological diversity, inability to transcend its pre-1970 historical legacy, etc.), both the concentrated ferocity and power of the dictatorship on the one hand, and the multiple divisions within "the" opposition on the other.

Immediate Responses to the Coup

Initial opposition to the military regime began with a courageous, but disorganized, resistance in factories, workplaces, homes, streets, and centers of detention. This took the form both of physical resistance to violence by the military and of organizational efforts to survive the immediate repression of leaders of the political parties associated with the Popular Unity coalition, including leaders in the labor movement. Because the political left was not organized to offer effective military resistance, it was unable to mount any sustained counterattack to the military coup or to the first repressive measures instituted by the junta. The labor movement found itself similarly ill-equipped to withstand the harsh measures imposed upon it. These included the outlawing of Chile's major labor confederation, the Central Única de Trabajadores (CUT), and its affiliates, the military occupation of CUT headquarters, dissolution of two of the largest rural labor federations, as well as attacks upon organizations made up of workers in the public sector, such as teachers and government employees.

Initially, a segment of the labor movement did support the anti-Marxist and anti–Popular Unity pogrom carried out by the military within the various sectors of organized workers. With the exception of a small minority, most of the Christian Democratic leadership, the political right, the *gremialistas,* and most nonpartisan professional associations also supported military repression of the left. The hierarchy of the Catholic Church, at odds with Popular Unity over proposed educational reforms, called on the Chilean population to cooperate with the new regime in restoring order, even though the Permanent Committee of the Episcopal Conference lamented the violence and bloodshed of the coup.

Only slowly, and with painful moderation, did the majority of Chilean political forces begin to challenge the most extreme measures of the military government. Vocal opposition to the coup itself was rare among non–Popular Unity parties, professional associations, Church leaders, and even trade unionists—with the exception of the Movimiento de la Izquierda Revolucionaria (MIR) and smaller revolutionary groups. This meant that, at least at first, opposition focused on the junta's national security enforcement practices (later generically labeled "human rights abuses") and on specific policy decisions, for example, reductions in public services and public employment, elimination of price controls on a variety of products, or the ending of subsidies to public enterprises. This latter type of opposition occurred among the civilian technicians cooperating with the military government, as well as among certain producer groups, unions, and the political parties in "recess" (the National party, Christian Democratic party, and smaller non–Popular Unity parties).

The outlawing and "dissolution" of parties and movements of the left, along with the murder, "disappearance," detention, or exile of thousands of leaders and cadres, precluded significant public policy debate from these sources. The military government tolerated no serious opposition to its "emergency measures," which overturned the Constitution of 1925, nor to its economic and social policies, even when the government was not always united internally as to specific objectives or methods.

The Church as an Umbrella for Opposition to Military Government

The hierarchy of the Catholic Church, and a number of other religious groups in Chile, were perceived as opponents of the Popular Unity coalition, or at least as groups hostile to particular policies of the

Allende administration. The military government sought, and received, the sanction of the Church in the immediate aftermath of the 1973 coup; Brian Smith reported that twenty-four of the twenty-seven bishops interviewed in his study indicated they believed the coup was necessary. However, the desire of the military to acquire the support of the Church as a source of legitimacy, and the willingness of the Church leadership to collaborate in the "work of reconstruction," also worked to provide Church functionaries and affiliates with a limited degree of insulation from the frontal assaults then being launched against other organizations, such as unions, political parties, and political movements. Over time, although it remained internally divided regarding its role vis-à-vis the new regime, the Church came to provide a fragile umbrella of protection for a variety of human rights, research, social service, and anti-regime activities.

Established shortly after the coup, the National Committee to Aid Refugees (CONAR), composed of a number of various religious groups, created a nucleus around which an active opposition to the government's severe repression was able to organize. In October 1973, the Committee of Cooperation for Peace (COPACHI) began to provide legal services, food, economic aid, medical assistance, places of refuge, and comfort to victims of the state terror unleashed by the military and the new secret police apparatus, Dirección Nacional de Inteligencia (DINA). Gradually, a national network of safe houses and underground resistance to the regime emerged, frequently in Church buildings or in the homes of people courageous enough to risk their lives to spare others from torture or death. This network won thousands of small victories against the military government, but its willingness to collaborate with Popular Unity and Mirista leaders and cadres soon brought down the wrath of the regime. Some religious leaders withdrew from COPACHI after clear evidence of its links to underground and clandestine activities was publicized; in December 1975, Cardinal Silva, under pressure from both conservative and moderate Catholics, as well as from General Pinochet himself, dissolved the organization while at the same time congratulating it for its humanitarian efforts.

Shortly thereafter, Cardinal Silva established the Vicariate of Solidarity, the single most important umbrella organization, which provided social services to the growing number of Chilean poor and also sought to oppose the human rights abuses of the government. From 1976 to 1986, this Church-supported entity was the foundation of moral and legal resistance to the military dictatorship, just as Church-based community organizations provided at the local level a framework for opposition meetings and planning which the military government attacked on an episodic basis.

While religiously based organizations could mediate certain government policies and challenge human rights abuses openly, neither the hierarchy of the Catholic Church nor its local organizations presented a serious threat to regime policies in other areas or constituted an opposition coalition capable of reforming or overthrowing the military government. Church declarations (such as *Nuestra Convivencia Nacional,* 1977, or *Humanismo Cristiano y Nueva Institucionalidad,* 1978) explicitly praised multiparty democracy and described politics as a noble art consistent with human nature, offering a direct refutation of the regime's derogation of politics and politicians. Even with substantial international support, however, Church work and organization was no substitute for an explicit political opposition which could offer a proposal for transition together with a long-term political program—whether of democratic restoration or some other vision of Chile's political future. The Church functioned primarily as a source of moral opposition to the military dictatorship. It also served as an umbrella which offered partial protection to a gamut of community organizations, research centers, human rights groups, and loosely organized action groups for the opposition. It was unable and unwilling, as was to be expected, to assume the role normally ascribed to other agents in the political process (such as political parties, professional and interest-based associations, or labor) to build coalitions or to elaborate political programs. The Church also suffered from internal division, as some bishops continued to give staunch support to the military government. In addition, significant political cleavages persisted in the wider Catholic community of Chile, with hard-core, conservative, Catholic-inspired organizations (such as Opus Dei, the Society for the Defense of Tradition, Family, and Property (TFP), and the Asociación de Católicos Anticomunistas) condemning politicization of the Church and defending the military's repression in aggressive fashion.

Nevertheless, some Church leaders, and groups under their auspices, managed to achieve many of the goals which Manuel Antonio Garretón has identified as the measure of "the value and success of opposition forces" under authoritarian regimes (i.e., creation of "breathing spaces" or *espacio político*; maintenance of hope in an alternative; creation of gradual inroads in the regime itself; and organization/support of diverse forms of resistance). Perhaps even more important, the Church's international ties, and the regime's desire to maintain the fiction of its "western and Christian" identification, enabled the Church to play a limited, but crucial, role in opposing the practices, policies, and political objectives of the government.

Universities, Students, and Intellectuals

University students have played a colorful and vital role in Chilean politics since the beginning of the twentieth century. Student movements, aligned with major political parties or groups, have pressured governments for a wide range of social and political reforms as well as for democratization of the university system. Perhaps the most celebrated case occurred in July 1931, when protests by university students helped to precipitate the street demonstrations and general strike which ousted the dictatorial government of General Carlos Ibáñez.

From the 1930s through the 1960s, Chilean universities not only produced new generations of political leaders, but expanded their enrollment in relation to the total population. Politics has always been an essential element of university life, including competition for control of faculty and student organizations by supporters of the country's parties and revolutionary movements. During the Unidad Popular administration, Chilean universities, like most other national institutions, reflected, in microcosm, the political and ideological conflict extant in the larger society.

In line with its efforts to depoliticize Chilean society, the military dictatorship quickly moved against the universities in 1973 to "purify" (*depurar*) the faculties and eliminate any Marxist influence. Military administrators took over control of the universities and gradually introduced "modernizations" designed to emphasize professional education on the one hand, and to diminish the role and prestige of the humanities and social sciences on the other. Decreased levels of support for both students and universities, together with tightened standards of admission, significantly reduced the opportunities for higher education in Chile.

In the 1980s, university enrollment was down by over a third, in absolute numbers, from 1973. Some institutions were affected by the government's programs more drastically than others—most notably the Universidad Técnica del Estado, which had been perceived as perhaps the most politicized, but also the least elitist, of the Santiago institutions of higher learning. Competition for the reduced number of university admissions, combined with the narrower, more technical curriculum and, of course, the systematic purges of politically unacceptable faculty and students, dramatically altered Chilean university life.

In the case of both students and professors, political organization became not only difficult, but dangerous, after 1973. Expulsions from the university for political activity severely dampened overt challenges to the military government from the campus. Penetration of the institutions by secret police and by informants practically destroyed whatever effective intellectual and organizational opposition might have emanated from the university community. While individual faculty members spoke out occasionally, and small groups of students voiced opposition to government policies (especially in the two major Catholic universities) from time to time, Chilean universities, on the whole, failed to generate significant resistance to the military dictatorship until after 1984.

Unlike the purged universities, the expanding number of "independent" research institutes, and loosely connected groups of impoverished scholars and technicians, emerged as a source of intellectual revitalization and, eventually, vocal sources of opposition to the regime. The military's insistence on "decentralization" and "privatization" spawned a surprising number of relatively autonomous research centers. Often associating members or supporters of the same political party (even here sectarianism seemed to survive all efforts of the military to end politics in Chile), these groups produced clandestine films documenting the outrages of the dictatorship, as well as solid investigations of Chile's history and the impact of the military regime. Many individual scholars also contributed to the growing public debate over military policies and the timing of "re-democratization." However, none of these groups had a mass base or influence sufficiently widespread to challenge General Pinochet's hegemony seriously; at will, the general's apparatus censored, imposed self-censorship, shut down, or allowed the reopening of, magazines, periodicals, or newspapers critical of the regime. Nevertheless, these groups of intellectuals, students, and professionals stubbornly and courageously refused to submit to the military dictatorship, thereby offering technical, political, and moral critiques which undermined General Pinochet's credibility, if not his ability to apply devastating repression when overly annoyed by members of the country's intellectual community.

Political Parties and Opposition to the Military Regime

Prior to the military coup of 1973, the Chilean political party system was highly institutionalized, and penetrated almost all spheres of society. In high schools, universities, unions, peasant cooperatives, local community organizations, and even mothers' clubs, partisan political cleavages mirrored the programs, ideologies, and symbols of national party organizations. In addition, most of the major parties had their own newspapers and theoretical journals; some even controlled radio stations. Parties thus served as the major political instruments in Chilean society, articulating class and interest group positions, representing social movements in Congress, formulating alternative policies and programs, providing government leaders, and competing for the policymaking positions within the state bureaucracy.

Since the 1930s, a relatively stable ideological spectrum, from the revolutionary left to the radical right, characterized this party system, with coalition governments, including all but the most "fringe" elements at one time or another. Expansion of the suffrage and post-1958 electoral reforms made for highly competitive elections, accompanied by varying degrees of revolutionary, populist, millenarian, and clientelistic appeals. In the fashion typical of political parties in Western democracies, Chilean party leaders often promised more than they could deliver, engaged in personal and intraparty conflicts, made and unmade coalitions, and hewed, more or less consistently, to certain programmatic and underlying ideological commitments.

Identified as principal targets in the military mission of depoliticizing Chilean society, the initial response of party leaders varied considerably—generally in accord with their role prior to the coup. In almost all cases, however, divisions emerged within the parties that had opposed the Unidad Popular government as well as within the parties of the Popular Unity coalition itself. Even within the National party (formed in the 1960s by a merger of the old Conservative and Liberal parties, who represented the institutionalized right of Chilean politics), some dissenting voices were heard at the outset. The immediate response of the various parties and movements to the coup set the tone for more than a decade of the political debate, reaction, and anti-regime activities.

Movimiento de Izquierda Revolucionaria (MIR).

MIR which had predicted a coup all along and criticized the naiveté of a "peaceful road to socialism," declared that neither the left nor socialism nor revolution had been defeated but that a "reformist illusion" had come to its end. MIR advocated armed resistance and confrontation with the "fascist gorillas" (the military). After 1973, notwithstanding penetration by military security, torture, murder, imprisonment of its cadres, and the loss of much of its leadership by 1976, MIR persisted in its revolutionary struggle against the dictatorship—with only limited symbolic victories and without, apparently, gaining the support of much more of the Chilean population than it had in 1973. For MIR, particular policies of the government or the personality of Pinochet mattered much less than the character of the regime, the impossibility of peaceful restoration of "democracy," and the ultimate objective of a socialist revolution in Chile.

Partido Comunista de Chile (PCCH)

Unlike the MIR, the Chilean Communist Party (PCCH) had vocally and repeatedly called for moderation by the more impatient or more revolutionary members of the Popular Unity coalition. The PCCH rejected the *via armada* and sought some reconciliation with the Christian Democrats to defuse the crisis of 1973. Nevertheless, the Communist Party was fiercely attacked by the military government; party, union, peasant, and community leaders were arrested, tortured, and "disappeared."

Facing relentless persecution, the Communist Party went underground and established a directorate in exile. In 1976, almost the entire internal leadership was captured, but by then the party had created a clandestine apparatus. Supported morally and financially by a nucleus of leaders living in Moscow, the Communist Party, against heavy odds, managed to sustain linkages to workers, peasants, students, and community organizations, and to make its presence felt in a growing *public* opposition to the military government (1983–85).

Whereas the Communist Party initially blamed Mirista "ultra-leftism" for the isolation of the working classes and the strong middle-class support of the coup, the circumstances of military dictatorship gradually moved the PCCH into a tactical alliance with the MIR and a segment of the Socialist party which favored armed confrontation of the Pinochet government. However, this did not mean giving up traditional political tactics, nor even, at least until 1980, abandoning efforts to forge a new Center-Left opposition coalition. Meeting in 1977, the party's Central Committee adopted a "program for the reconstruction of Chilean society," which combined nationalistic economic measures with calls to create new democratic institutions. Once again, this program appeared to seek an alliance with the political center, in particular with the Christian Democrats, in order to end the dictatorship. As in the past, however, the Christian Democrats refused to join an alliance with the PCCH.

In 1980, several important Communist leaders publicly acknowledged the need for *all* types of struggle against the military regime. Both internal and external circumstances contributed to the radicalization of Communist opposition tactics. Growing desperation and militancy among the unemployed of Santiago's shantytowns, the evident ineffectiveness of center/left political movements to overcome the dictatorship, and the need to reestablish the party's credibility as an efficacious opponent of the Pinochet government, all influenced the decision to incorporate armed struggle into the overall resistance strategy. After approval of the 1980 constitution, which seemed to presage at least nine more years of General Pinochet's authoritarianism, armed struggle seemed to many Communists to be an essential, but not exclusive, revolutionary tactic. External events only reinforced these tendencies. The victory of the Sandinistas over the Somoza dictatorship in Nicaragua made armed struggle even more feasible, despite the obvious differences between Chile and Nicaragua. Likewise, the strong support given to Pinochet by the new Reagan administration in the United States discouraged the non-Marxist opposition and reversed whatever pressure for change in regime policies that had been exerted by the Carter administration through its human rights emphasis. Lack of any viable internal alternative to the dictatorship, and loss of hope that U.S. pressure would advance a rapid transition to democracy, made the Communist call for armed struggle all the more understandable—even if unlikely to succeed. Despite its dismal prospects, Communist advocacy of armed struggle only aggravated the difficulty of forging a broad-based opposition coalition against the military government.

The revival of a strategy of armed struggle only served to vindicate General Pinochet's allegation of Soviet imperialism and Marxist terrorism, however, particularly when combined with overt demonstrations of external ties, such as party leaders in Moscow, short-wave broadcasts into Chile from the Soviet Union, and repeated statements of support (both published and broadcast) from the Cuban government of Fidel Castro. On the other hand, the party's ability to maintain a clandestine organization, to recruit new cadres, and to take such a dramatic initiative against the regime may have restored credibility to its historical claim as vanguard of revolutionary struggle in Chile.

In practice, however, the Communist Party was divided, not only with regard to the principal means of struggle to be used against the military government, but also with respect to the relative importance of the external leadership vis-à-vis the internal, clandestine leadership. A group called the Frente Patriótico Manuel Rodríguez (FPMR), representing the armed action element of the party, took responsibility for a number of attacks on military targets, as well as acts of economic sabotage. This raised questions as to the degree of control the party exercised over this group, indeed, questions as to whether a PCCH shift to a more accommodationist line could even be imposed on those favoring armed struggle. Certainly early similar groups in Guatemala, Venezuela, Colombia, and El Salvador eventually rejected party directives and control.

Moreover, permanent repression of the party by the military government meant that an entire generation of cadres had been trained under conditions unique for Chilean Communists, thereby creating a potential source of conflict between Communist youth and those generations of cadres accustomed to a more traditional role for the party in Chilean politics. For the moment, however, refusal of the "democratic" opposition even to consider cooperation with the Communists, plus the military regime's persistent focus on the Communists as Chile's principal enemies, gave the Communist Party no choice but to resist government policies, and to seek destruction of the authoritarian regime, by *all* means available.

Partido Socialista de Chile (PSCH)

Unlike the relative unity of the Chilean Communist Party, the Chilean Socialist Party contained a wide range of social democratic, socialist, Marxist, Leninist, and even Trotskyist groups which periodically coalesced and divided in response to the political moment and the strength of party leadership. After 1973, the always-fragmented Socialist Party splintered into a number of personalist and ideologically hostile factions. Debates over the cause of the coup and the proper goals of the party under the dictatorship from 1973 to 1986 left two major factions—one headed by Clodomiro Almeyda (accepting the thesis of using all means, including armed struggle, against the dictatorship and allied tactically with the Communist Party), and the other identified with Ricardo Lagos, Carlos Briones, and Ricardo Núñez (favoring a moderate line and allied with Social Democrats and the Christian Democrats). Each of these two major factions was subdivided, in turn, into a number of personalist and "ideological" groups, which, when combined with disputes over the power of internal versus exiled leadership, greatly weakened the Socialists as a principal force in the opposition to the military regime.

Some socialists and other small groups (e.g., factions of the Movimiento de Acción Popular Unitaria or MAPU, Izquierda Cristiana, and a segment of the Radical Party) sought to forge a new ideological consensus called the Convergencia. In the early 1980s, the Convergencia represented a middle ground between the MIR and PCCH on the one hand, and the Almeyda Socialists and the other major anti-regime coalition, the Alianza Democrática (AD) (composed of the major non-Marxist anti-government parties and some groups which had belonged to the Popular Unity coalition) on the other. Unable to translate minimal ideological consensus into a viable organization, the Convergencia failed to assume a permanent niche in the political landscape. Even with the creation of a "socialist bloc" (*bloque socialista*) consisting of a somewhat more compatible coalition of socialists and leftist Catholics committed to "socialism, democracy, and popular participation," the Socialist Party itself failed to reunite and lost considerable influence in the labor movement, among student groups, and in other traditional organizational spheres penetrated by political activity. Nevertheless, the multiple voices of an always ambiguous socialist political movement were not silenced; key socialist leaders offered plans to reverse policies of the regime and to overthrow the political institutions imposed by the dictatorship. With small numbers of socialists involved in armed struggle and many others collaborating with a variety of "unarmed" opposition groups in a range of tasks, the military regime failed as much in its efforts to eradicate Chilean socialism as it had in its attack on MIR and the Communist Party. Whether Social Democrats and moderate socialists in partnership with the Alianza Democrática (until the end of 1986), or revolutionary socialists aligned, after 1983, with the PCCH in the Movimiento Democrático Popular (MDP), socialism, however fragmented, remained a significant force in Chilean politics.

Democracia Cristiana (DC)

In contrast to the Popular Unity parties, most of the Christian Democratic leadership initially endorsed the military coup and called upon supporters to "contribute to the new government their technical, professional, or functional cooperation." Expressing their regret for the departure from democratic doctrine, constitutionalist traditions, and also the use of violence, party leaders nevertheless declared that the coup was "primarily the consequence of the economic disaster, the institutional chaos, the armed violence, and the profound moral crisis to which the deposed government led the nation." A minority of Christian Democrats rejected this position from the outset, categorically condemning the overthrow of President Allende even while reaffirming the culpability of the far left and the "sectarian dogmatism" of the Popular Unity coalition.

While the majority of Christian Democrats generally approved of the coup, they also expected a gradual (one- to three-year) restoration of a modified democratic system which would allow ex-President Frei to be reelected to the presidency. As the main source of opposition to the Popular Unity coalition, and with strong links to groups in the labor movement, to peasant organizations, professional and business associations, government employees, and community groups, the Christian Democrats contained the possibility of being able to pose a threat to the military regime. Likewise, their newspapers, radio station, and a variety of newsletters and communications to party-linked social organizations presented the military government with a potentially serious dilemma.

Gradually, the full scope of the military political program pushed the Christian Democrats into more and more public opposition. Christian Democratic union leaders, technicians, government bureaucrats, and even businessmen, became a source of visible and vocal opposition—first to government policies and programs, later to the military dictatorship and General Pinochet himself. By 1977, this stance so irritated the military government that *all* political parties were "dissolved." In the meantime, Christian Democratic leaders were harassed, imprisoned, exiled, and even made into targets for assassination. Within the labor movement, among peasant and student groups, and in community organizations, the close ties between Christian Democrats and Popular Unity cadres sometimes caused their fates to be joined in prison camps or "disappearances."

For the Christian Democrats, however, the major thrust of their position was to end the military government and to restore Chilean democracy, or at least a modified version of it which would include a limited role for the Marxist left. In addition, Christian Democrats criticized major policy initiatives of the military regime. Technocratic and programmatic critiques by leading Christian Democrats served to rally public opinion and focus attention on the deleterious effects of government policy for various social sectors; they also served to recruit to the opposition some members of the pro-military coalition who had become inured to various aspects of the radical neo-liberal economic program implemented after 1975. This bridge to the political right undermined the unity of those groups most closely associated with the coup: *gremialistas*, professional associations, industrialists, and even some agricultural interests. Since the most important source of legitimacy for the military government, after the initial nationalistic anti-Marxist bombast, was the efficacy of its economic program, Christian Democratic efforts to attack specific policies and programs on technical and performance grounds began to create chinks in the solid pro-military coalition of 1973, particularly as the economic policies proved to be disastrous in many ways.

The multifaceted opposition of the Christian Democrats—to government policy, to the human rights abuses, to the authoritarian constitution—still failed to overcome the contradictions inherent in seeking to restore democracy without the participation of key groups in Chile's recent political history. Although ex-President Frei's death, in 1982, brought forth a massive demonstration against the military regime, it also emphasized the party's inability to form a coalition capable of both uniting the opposition and *convincing the military* to seek a new political option.

Emergence of Opposition on the Political Right

The traditional political right in Chile, composed of the National Party, the Radical Democrats (a splinter of the Radical Party), and a few members of the Radical Party, provided the principal civilian support for the military coup and also staffed government ministries and policymaking positions under the military government. In addition, right-wing groups (such as Patria Libertad) and many *gremialista* and professional organizations welcomed the coup and actively supported attacks on the parties of the Unidad Popular, as well as against organized labor, working class, and community organizations.

In some cases, individual party members did oppose the assault on Chilean democracy. Certain of these individuals participated in the "Group of 24," a constitutional study group made up of representatives from many political parties, which sought alternatives to the military constitution of 1980. Similarly, other members of the political right expressed their resistance to the militarization of Chilean politics, opposed specific government policies, and lobbied for a transition to a less authoritarian regime. In general, however, the political right not only supported the military government, but worked actively to secure the long-term political objectives of depoliticizing Chilean society and preventing a return to the "demagoguery" and politics (*politiquería*) of the past.

Even among these groups, however, the abuse of civil liberties combined with the economic disasters resulting from the combination of neoliberal economic policies with the international recession of the early 1980s gradually eroded support for the increasingly personalist administration of General Pinochet. Fragmentation of the political right paralleled fragmentation of the left. An array of "nationalists," *gremialistas*, "liberals," "conservatives," and the old National Party attempted to define their position with respect to the Pinochet government, military rule, legitimacy of the 1980 constitution, and the type of post-Pinochet government which would be most desirable. The so-called "Group of 8," a loose alliance of diverse elements on the political right who supported the military government, dissolved in 1984; personalist, ideological, and tactical considerations destroyed the fragile coalition.

The severe economic recession (1981–85), which witnessed concomitant collapse of major financial institutions, numerous business bankruptcies, a burgeoning foreign debt, as well as a decline in living standards for much of the population, significantly undercut support for the Pinochet administration. Groups and individuals who had originally railed vociferously against President Allende, including leading *gremialista* figures and persons with close associations to the early years of the military dictatorship, began to criticize particular aspects of government policy in the 1980s. Many called either for more rapid transition to full implementation of the 1980 constitution than that prescribed in the "Transitory Dispositions" (which included the possibility of Pinochet's "reelection" for a term to last until 1997) or for return to a restricted democracy. Certain rightist individuals and movements sought to distance themselves from the incumbent government sufficiently so as to appear eligible to participate in any transition coalition formed when Pinochet might pass from the scene. While this opposition helped weaken the regime's base of support, it still did not represent a fundamental rejection of the authoritarian model nor did it indicate backing for *full* restoration of the former multiparty system.

A significant number of Chileans on the right managed to deny to themselves the high cost in human rights imposed by the dictatorship. They considered themselves to be both anti-Marxist *and* in favor of democracy. Yet mobilizing opposition to the Pinochet government on the right appears to be a key element for ending his personalist administration. Support of these groups, together with that of *both military officers* and the Christian Democrats, will be necessary if even a small move in the direction of redemocratization in Chile is to be managed. Despite economic difficulties faced by many financial, industrial, commercial, and agricultural groups as a result of the international recession and of government policy, the unwillingness of these groups to risk a "return to chaos" (the Popular Unity years of which General Pinochet constantly reminds them) limits severely both the extent, and pace, of change *within* the regime, as well as any movement toward a change *of* government. Persistent anti-democratic and authoritarian tendencies within these groups, plus fear of the past, continued to undermine efforts to forge a center-right coalition capable of either ousting Pinochet or transforming the government from within.

Labor Movement Opposition

The history of Chile's major labor organizations was tied inextricably to the development of class- and interest-based political movements and parties. All the principal labor unions, federations, and confederations, including the quasi-unions in the public sector among government employees and teachers, were arenas of political competition and played an overt role in national politics. The largest national confederation, the Central Única de Trabajadores (CUT), had actually been a part of the Popular Unity coalition and had designated ministers in President Allende's cabinet. These realities made labor an obvious target for immediate repression by the military government, not to mention a target for the military's objectives of depoliticizing Chilean society over the long term as well.

In 1973, the military junta lost no time in attacking the major labor organizations of the country, considering them instruments of the political parties and of the Marxist movements which had produced the crisis. In its first months of power, the military dictatorship (1) suspended the processing of all labor petitions; (2) suspended the right to strike and to bargain collectively; (3) first nullified the legal status of the CUT and then dissolved it; (4) allowed layoff of workers involved in "interruption or paralyzation" of work; and (5) declared a "recess" of all *juntas de conciliación* (mediation boards), and assigned military officers to hear labor disputes. The military government also (6) prohibited union elections; (7) declared that, if any union officer had to be replaced, seniority would determine the identity of the new officer unless that worker belonged to a proscribed organization or movement (i.e., any leftist party); and (8) outlawed any union meeting held without prior notification to, and approval by, the police as to its time and place. This so-called emergency measure remained in effect until 1979.

Systematic, crushing purges of the old union leadership, combined with infiltration of unions by the new secret police, demoralized workers and allowed imposition of wage and price policies which significantly eroded real wages. Economic policies which removed protective tariffs for most Chilean industry only served to increase unemployment, thus adding to the workers' ills.

Labor's initial responses to policies of the military government were halting but evidenced, nonetheless, a determination to resist to the best of its ability. By January of 1974, the Central Nacional de Trabajadores

(CNT), which joined together workers from Christian Democratic and *gremialista* movements, including those of public employees, maritime workers, bank employees, health workers, and even some from the federation of metalworkers, attempted to obtain government recognition of its status as a legitimate voice of labor. Desirous of coopting the non-Marxist labor organizations, if possible, and thereby obtaining international support for its programs, the military junta gave these groups a public forum by recognizing them as spokesmen for organized labor.

By excluding almost all Marxist and Popular Unity elements, the CNT failed to garner any immediate mass support. Inevitable conflicts arose between the *gremialistas* (most of whom supported the military government) and the Christian Democrats (who saw their role as one of responsible labor opposition) and undermined the possibility of forging any long-term alliance capable of defending the interests of the working class, despite the fact that the *gremialistas*, too, found themselves at odds with government labor policy from time to time. By and large, even the most conservative of white collar, and public employee, organizations eventually found themselves in the position of seeking to reverse government *policies*, while the rest of the work force recognized much more rapidly the necessity of opposing the dictatorship and working for a return to democracy.

In the meantime, the outlawed CUT established an overseas directorate in Paris, while parties of the deposed Popular Unity coalition undertook sufficient clandestine activity to assure the continued presence of the political left within the labor movement, even though they were temporarily unable to respond to the military repression in a more direct way. During 1974, illegal strikes challenged the dominance of the military but also brought harsh persecution of union leaders.

The government response came from the Minister of Labor, who declared, at the May 1st Labor Day celebration (in 1975), that whereas "September 11 detained Marxism, it did not destroy it; now we must destroy Marxism." However, a month later, in June, a number of labor federations which had previously been affiliated with the CUT (including some Christian Democratic leaders who had rejected cooperation with the government) formed a loosely structured alternative to the CNT: the Coordinadora Nacional Sindical (CNS). This new organization represented an ideologically pluralistic effort, by organized labor, to resist government policies.

Emulating, in some ways, the labor policies of the Ibáñe. dictatorship (1927–31), the military government tried to control organized labor by establishing, in 1976, a National Gremialist Secretariat and also by sponsoring an official National Unity Labor Front. Under the provisions of Decree Law 198, the government removed opposition leaders from their positions within key federations or national unions and replaced them with supporters of the regime. The government also sponsored parallel unions within firms or economic sectors where labor opposition remained strong, for example, among copper workers, port workers, and the National Electricity Industry (ENDESA). In 1977, the government attempted to create official federations of chemical, railroad, and metallurgical workers, rejecting requests to hold meetings on the part of existing labor organizations. The military government tried again, in 1978, to create an official new labor organization called the Unión de Trabajadores de Chile (UNTRACH). While this group sometimes opposed the government's labor and social security policies in an effort to recruit rank and file support, it usually avoided questioning the government's legitimacy or overall program. Nevertheless, even under these severe conditions, organized labor refused to succumb. Strikes in the copper mines, among railway and port workers, in factories, and in service industries, confirmed the survival of a heterogeneous opposition to government *policies*. Government employees, teachers, shopkeepers, and truckers—in some cases led by the very people who had been the most violent opponents of the Popular Unity government—joined the opposition to government policies even though, at the same time, some of these same leaders still sought "a responsible military officer" to head a transition government.

As in the case of the Church, the external support for labor's demands acted as a constraint on government policy. Threatened by an international boycott, including, significantly, a threat by the AFL-CIO to stop the import of Chilean goods into the United States, the military government moved to institutionalize a new industrial relations system. Beginning with Decree Law 2200 (1978), and followed by a series of decrees purporting to reform the 1931 Labor Code, the military government rewrote the Chilean industrial relations code. Adopted after 1978 as part of the government's so-called "labor plan," the new system made it much easier to dismiss workers without cause and restricted union activity with respect to collective bargaining and strike actions (only plant unions or, in agriculture, only unions in individual farms could present labor petitions and engage in collective bargaining), in contrast to the old system of unions organized by economic sector, by region, or by locality.

In the new 1980 constitution, further restrictions were placed on union activity and relationships between labor and political parties, emphasizing the long-term objectives of depoliticizing the labor movement and weakening labor as a national or regional political force. In the same year, the government eliminated the traditional system of labor courts, even dissolving the old *colegios profesionales* (essentially, professional associations of doctors, lawyers, pharmacists, journalists, etc.), and replacing them with *gremialista* associations.

All these measures were resisted, to some degree, by the various labor and professional associations. Militant and public opposition by the CNS leadership led to arrest of the organization's president and secretary-general. Released shortly thereafter, these same leaders were again taken prisoner in June after the CNS presented a "national petition" making a number of economic and political demands on the government—and thus engaging in an illegal act under the terms of the new constitution and labor laws.

In the meantime (April 1981), certain key Christian Democrats, who opposed both the policies of the military government and the resurgence of influence by the left within the labor movement (the CNS), formed the Unión Democrática de Trabajadores (UDT). The UDT challenged the government's "labor plan" and also called for renewed political party activity and a legitimate *political* role for labor. At the same time, however, the UDT rejected unity with the CNS and leftist union organizations—reflecting the continuing ideological and organizational splintering of the Chilean labor movement.

In some ways the labor movement, despite its fragmentation, temporarily replaced the outlawed ("dissolved") political parties as the major visible political opposition to the dictatorship. General Pinochet responded angrily to the national petition (formulated by the CNS and signed by over 400 labor leaders) by labeling the CNS "a front organization for international communism" and threatening the leadership with prosecution under Article 8 of the new constitution which prohibited the propagation of "totalitarian ideas" or concepts of "class conflict." When a number of ex-politicians, including prominent Christian Democrats, signed declarations of support, they were sent into exile.

Repression of the leadership did not curtail union activity. Strikes occurred among metalworkers, in the shoe and leather industry, and in some large textile firms. Employers retaliated with widespread dismissals of union leaders; and the government retaliated with more violence. In early 1982, the president of the national association of public employees, Agrupación Nacional de Empleados Fiscales (ANEF), and the vice president of the UDT, Tucapel Jiménez, was assassinated.

By mid-1982, the effects of the international recession and Chile's debt crisis pushed unemployment up to 20 percent, thereby producing a desperate situation for millions of Chilean workers and growing impoverishment for even middle sector and professional groups. These unfavorable economic conditions made mobilization of labor for strike actions or political protests quite difficult. Nevertheless, labor protest and activity continued to challenge government policies. In some cases, labor organizations assumed a visible anti-regime role in seeking to oust General Pinochet and abrogate the Constitution of 1980.

Late the same year, the military government retaliated by prohibiting unions from receiving outside funds and, during the first half of 1983, by arresting numerous labor leaders. Still seeking the illusive unity which has eluded Chilean labor since the 1930s, labor leaders created a new umbrella organization in 1983: the Comando Nacional de Trabajadores (CNT). The new CNT attempted to organize a "national strike," but was unsuccessful in this effort. Undaunted, the panoply of independent, *gremialista*, Christian Democratic, and traditionally leftist labor organizations continued to oppose government policies and often figured prominently in the overall political opposition to the military regime. Thus, in 1984, in an open letter addressed to General Pinochet and signed by ten leaders of the CNT, the labor coalition called for a return to the pre-1973 constitution, an abrogation of the military government's "labor plan," and a reversal of government economic policies—in short, it called for a comprehensive change in regime and government policy.

As public protests against the government mounted, in 1984–85, the CNT, CNS, and UDT sought to coordinate opposition to the regime. At the plant level, individual unions returned to represent worker demands for improvement in wage and working conditions. Sectoral federations and confederations also renewed their "bread and butter" demands, along with their participation in the growing opposition to the Pinochet government (1984–87). As was true of political parties, however, dissension and ideological fragmentation continued to plague the labor movement. Despite almost universal opposition to government labor policies, the new labor decrees, and parts of the 1980 constitution, labor proved unable to unify sufficiently either to provide the social base for a transition government or to arrive at a consensus as to Chile's political future. Labor's opposition to the Pinochet government and its policies was even more apparent than was that of other professional and occupational groups (*gremialistas*); nevertheless, labor unity, even when confronted by military dictatorship, remained an elusive, perhaps impossible, goal.

Community Organizations, Pobladores, Urban and Rural Poor

That segment of the opposition to the military regime's policies/objectives most difficult to identify and to measure, particularly in regard to impact, resides in the multitude of community organizations, shantytowns, rural cooperatives, and seemingly dormant rural labor organizations, women's groups, and local committees. This component of the opposition came into existence shortly after the 1973 coup and has continued to function, more or less efficiently, well into the 1980s. Many of these groups maintained tenuous connections to political parties, national labor confederations, and Church-related associations. Others operated practically in isolation for long periods of time, serving either as buffers against government repression or as sanctuaries for those persecuted by the government. A detailed history of this resistance awaits future research after the fall of the dictatorship.

Of great significance for the military, particularly for the potential they offered for violent resistance to the dictatorship, were the thousands of *pobladores* in the urban shantytowns on the perimeter of Santiago. Repeated confrontations between police and *pobladores*, including recurrent police raids on the *poblaciones*, radicalized many shantytown dwellers and created the possibility, and the fear, that they might erupt at any time into spontaneous rioting or demonstrations or insurrection. In fact, fear of unleashing this stored-up hatred of the *pobladores* acted as an effective brake on the initiatives of the "democratic" opposition whose (predominantly middle class) constituencies dreaded the possible consequences of popular violence.

While the urban poor of the *poblaciones* had long constituted a dilemma for Chilean political leaders, the misery imposed by the military government's economic policies and political repression hardened political attitudes among these groups of the population. Moreover, the dismantling of the industrial sector of the economy as a result of neo-liberal trade and economic policies, and the loss of land and employment opportunities by rural workers as a result of reversing the agrarian reforms of 1964–73, transformed Chile's occupational and social structure. Large numbers of semi-employed, peddlers, dayworkers, and the "self-employed" formed an important new element in Chilean society.

The military government introduced several programs intended to alleviate the impact of massive unemployment, most notably the Minimum Employment Program (PEM)—which expanded from 19,000 participants to over 200,000 in 1982—and the Program for Heads of Household (POJH)—which was instituted in 1982. Thus, almost 8 percent of the labor force was "organized" into government make-work programs. By the 1980s, the workers of PEM and POJH had begun to protest against low government wages and limited benefits, while shantytown dwellers organized clandestine resistance committees to oppose the military regime.

Periodic sweeps through the *poblaciones* by military and police forces fostered hostility toward both the military government and its civilian allies. In the countryside, rural workers and dispossessed smallholders, including *campesinos* deprived of the gains only recently acquired through the agrarian reform programs of the two previous governments, patiently awaited the fall of the military government and worked slowly to rebuild the rural labor and cooperative organizations broken up by the regime during the 1970s. Despite efforts of those most marginalized by the regime to combat its gravest injustices, the combination of the exigencies of daily existence plus the systematic coercion of the government rendered most unlikely the success of any mass-based insurrection on the model of Nicaragua, notwithstanding warnings to that effect by conservative academics in the United States.

The Armed Forces as a Source of Opposition

In order to carry out the military coup of 1973, the *golpistas* purged high-ranking officers who appeared most likely to resist the military takeover. Significant numbers of officers were killed, imprisoned, or retired. Enlisted personnel who refused to participate in the coup also suffered execution, incarceration, or other punishment. Later, General Prats, a potential challenger to Pinochet's personalist control, was assassinated in Buenos Aires. Consolidation of General Pinochet's hegemony through creation of the DINA (now the CNI) further alienated certain sectors within the armed forces. Likewise, the forced departure of Air Force General Leigh from the junta, in 1978, revealed the existence of internal disagreements over policy, nature of the regime, as well as the timetable for restoring democratic government.

Despite some resentment over General Pinochet's increasingly personalized rule and relegation of the Navy and Air Force to secondary roles, most officers and enlisted personnel benefited substantially, both economically and in improved social status, during the 1970s. "Retirement" into the private sector provided military officers with lucrative executive opportunities. Combined with unheard-of modifications in the personnel and retirement systems, these gains by the military and their families made them much more dependent upon the patronage and good graces of Pinochet himself. The national police (*carabineros*) also gained status and benefits when they were transferred out of the Ministry of Interior and "elevated" to co-equal status with the other armed forces.

Perhaps even more importantly, the example of Argentina's treatment (prosecution) of military commanders following restoration of democracy in that country—and the explicit threat by the Chilean opposition also to prosecute military and police torturers when the opportunity presented itself—served to engender a kind of defensive solidarity among many officers within the armed forces. Restoration of civilian government not only threatened prospects for career advancement and present benefits, but it also raised the specter of criminal prosecution for a large number of Chile's military personnel.

These changes within the armed forces represented double-edged swords, inasmuch as the growing personalization of the regime, and of the army hierarchy, also meant a certain *deprofessionalization* of the career system. Resistance to these developments began to interfere with the loyalty to Pinochet of some military officers and even to raise questions as to the desirability of continuing direct participation by the military in the national government. This reluctance did not indicate any rejection of authoritarianism or a change of heart regarding leftist politics and politicians, so much as a sincere concern for the military institutions and future of Chile from the standpoint of a highly nationalistic and patriotic military elite.

By 1985, some officers had become aware that, to minimize damage *to the military institutions*, it might well be to the advantage of the military to extricate itself from government. However, this still left the problem of finding a civilian coalition capable both of (1) providing an alternative to Pinochet, and (2) guaranteeing compliance with any agreement negotiated to transfer power to a democratic civilian government. In this sense, the deep ideological divisions rending the Chilean opposition and the lack of an obvious candidate to succeed Pinochet served to restrain the more concerned military officers from seeking some sort of gradual accommodation with civilian parties and movements.

Prior to 1986, however, these various considerations on the part of the military had failed to present any serious challenge to the Pinochet administration, although they did presage difficulties for the general in the short term and decreased the likelihood of sustaining his personalist administration beyond 1989.

During 1986, selected military officers began to criticize the government openly, influenced on the one hand by Pinochet's seemingly more erratic and arbitrary behavior, and on the other hand by the spreading perception (shared by conservative civilians as well) that Pinochet was losing the support of the U.S. Embassy—a development which placed in jeopardy the massive economic support Chile receives from the U.S. and international agencies. This concern within the military took a sharper turn late in 1986, in spite of an attempt to assassinate the general in early September in which a number of his military escort were wounded or killed. Pinochet's response to these signs of disaffection (the assassination attempt, the dissidence within the military, civilian calls for his ouster) was to unleash a new campaign of murder, detention, and terror against his opponents. In the first part of October, he replaced the army representative on the junta with the director of secret police and retired a number of generals. At present, Pinochet appears to retain the upper hand, but the public dissent of leading military officers, particularly those in the Navy and Air Force, and an increased emphasis on hastening adoption of a law to legalize and regulate political parties (provisionally approved early in January 1987) may signal a move toward military exit from a monopolistic political role.

Ultimately, only military acquiescence in the removal of Pinochet or a decision by a group of officers to extricate the armed forces from direct responsibility for governing Chile, appeared likely to allow a change of government. This fact made even more important the ability of civilian parties and movements to expand quiet contacts with military leaders and to forge a civilian coalition which represented, at least for the immediate future, only a *limited threat to the military institutions*—for, unlike their Argentine counterparts, the Chilean military appear unlikely to provoke their own self-destruction by engaging in an ill-advised war against a foreign power.

In effect, the non-Marxist civilian opposition still needed the assistance of the military to establish the sort of coalition government they had hoped to create in 1973—with the ouster of President Allende. However, such assistance would have its price, primarily the capability of responsible political leaders to assure control of the transition process (i.e., their ability to direct and contain the mobilization of society, to prevent any "return to chaos," and to guarantee that transition government would not carry in its wake trials of military personnel or attacks on the autonomy of their institutions).

The Military Junta's Economic Policies

Consolidation of the junta's political power coincided with the gradual development of a new economic program. At first, the economic program had an "emergency" character, focused upon halting hyperinflation and divesting the public sector of the many enterprises acquired from 1970 to 1973. To achieve these objectives, the government devalued the currency, removed price controls from most commodities, postponed scheduled wage increases, freed interest rates for capital market transactions, and modified tax laws in order to encourage domestic and foreign investment. Over 200 firms in the public sector were returned to private owners and public expenditures and employment were reduced greatly.

The increased oil prices associated with the first "oil shock" of 1973 sharply reduced prices for Chilean exports, while rising interest rates and balance of trade problems limited the success of the government program. Unemployment increased dramatically while inflation, though reduced, continued over 300 percent per year. In response, the junta and its civilian advisers decided to introduce an even more profound "shock treatment" to halt inflation and create conditions for economic recovery.

What followed included 15 to 25 percent reductions in government expenditures (but not in the realm of national security) and drastic reductions in the size and role of the public sector; a 10 percent increase in income taxes, tightened monetary policy, loss of perhaps 80,000 government employees, and a decline of some 25 percent in industrial production in 1975. However, inflation did decline significantly—from 300 percent per year in 1974 to 84 percent in 1977—and the government's fiscal deficit practically disappeared by the end of 1975.

In a sense, the government program was tremendously successful. The cost, however, was massive unemployment and underemployment, declines in real wages of 40 percent, and a grim impoverishment of millions of Chileans. The junta claimed this sacrifice was necessary, in the short term, to stabilize the economy and create the conditions that would permit long-term recovery and growth without inflation.

The emergency measures and the "shock treatment" merged eventually into a coherent neo-liberal program for restructuring the Chilean economy. This program included privatizing most of the entrepreneurial activities of the government (including banks, insurance companies, exporting firms, major industrial firms); returning much of the agricultural land and assets affected by the previous administrations' land reform programs—and then abolishing the land reform agency (CORA); and opening the economy to private investment and international trade. Taken together, these programs resulted in concentration of financial and productive assets in the hands of a small number of new diversified financial groups which came to dominate the Chilean economy.

The "shock treatment" restructured the Chilean economy. The recovery which followed was based primarily upon improved prices for Chilean products, increasing levels of exports from the agricultural, mining, and industrial sectors, and significant inflows of foreign credit and investment. A wave of financial and real estate speculation fueled a short-lived "boom," with new construction projects in the private and public sector and spectacular nominal increases in the value of urban land, commercial developments, and stock prices giving credence to government claims of success. Reduced import duties made possible a frenzy of consumption that seemed to justify the military junta's enthusiasm.

Macroeconomic indicators also seemed to confirm the success of the junta's policies. Inflation went down to only 30 percent in 1979; budget deficits were low and domestic production increased notably. Diversification of markets and product lines for exports contributed to positive balances of payments after 1978. Worldwide economists discussed the "Chilean miracle" and advocates of free market economics held up Chile as vindication of their theories. In an official publication (*Chile: 1980 Economic Profile*), the government declared that Chile had "boldly embarked on a course to revitalize its weakened economy, replacing protectionism with free-market policies" and that "A diversified economy capable of functioning at an internationally competitive level has now been established, thereby assuring economic stability and offering excellent opportunities for domestic and foreign investors."

Opponents of the military government suggested that the "miracle" was only economic recovery from the artificial depression imposed by the "shock treatment." They also noted that unemployment remained over 15 percent, that the gains in consumption were concentrated among the top 20 percent of income earners, and that a growing foreign debt and wild real estate and financial speculating augured disaster.

Between March 1981 and the end of the year, a combination of domestic and international factors confirmed the predictions of the doomsayers. Financial panic and economic collapse followed as international recession, the onset of the debt crisis (short-term foreign debt more than tripled from 1979 to 1982), and the unraveling of the financial pyramids built by the financial conglomerates plunged the country into its worst depression since the 1930s. Rising interest rates and reductions in the inflow of foreign loans and investments which had fueled the "boom" made it impossible to continue the debt service. Declines in copper prices (over 40 percent from 1980 to mid-1982) and prices for other Chilean exports contributed to a growing balance of payments deficit. As the economy collapsed, the government was forced to bail out the financial and banking conglomerates (1983). The political opposition sarcastically labeled the process "the Chicago road to socialism," thereby mocking the junta's reliance on University of Chicago–trained economists and economic theory.

The collapse of the "economic miracle" which began in 1981 caused widespread political realignment. Bankruptcies, declining standards of living, and even middle-class unemployment pushed small business operators, professionals, and other supporters of the junta into the camp of the opposition. Leaders of the *gremios*, Chamber of Commerce, professional organizations, and trade associations which had most fiercely attacked the Popular Unity government of Salvador Allende now called the Pinochet administration "the worst government in the country's history." If they had not been outraged by the human rights violations and political repression of the junta, they experienced directly the economic depression in the early 1980s.

Pragmatic and adroit, General Pinochet modified the "free-market" approach enough to ameliorate somewhat the economic collapse. New tariffs, new subsidies, new government programs for employment, construction, and investment all evidenced the general's willingness to depart from economic purity in order to achieve political goals. Holding on in the face of political challenges by a growing opposition, General Pinochet took advantage of the international economic recovery after 1985. The drop in oil prices and interest rates from 1985 to 1987, combined with economic recovery in the United States, Europe, and Japan, provided a breathing space for the Chilean government by bolstering the Chilean economy. A new surge of foreign investment and expansion of exports renewed confidence in the economy; enthusiastic government policy-makers reaffirmed the validity of the "free market" and export-driven economic model—though the government had clearly recognized the political necessity of departing significantly from a "pure" market approach.

Social Mobilization, Political Stalemate

The collapse, after 1981, of the "Chilean miracle," an economic boomlet which provided the Pinochet government with a certain amount of social support, was followed by five years of growing opposition activity among all strata of society. A so-called opening (or *apertura*) from 1983 to 1985 produced numerous calls for restoration of democracy, for opposition forces to unite, and for Pinochet to end his personalist rule. Strikes and protest days, even days of "prayers for life," gave the appearance that the dictatorship was losing some of its control. By mid-1984, hopes were high that the military regime was destined for a quick end; daring headlines in opposition media declared, in bold print, "He doesn't want to leave," and in smaller print, "We'll have to throw him out." By August 1985, a significant element of the opposition had hammered out a "National Accord for Transition to Full Democracy" which included agreements on the need for a new constitution (or at least reforms sufficient to destroy the main provisions of the 1980 constitution); a social and economic plan to reactivate the economy, to create jobs, and to redistribute income; and an active state role to reshape the Chilean economy. The Acuerdo also called for an immediate end to states of constitutional exception, for reestablishment of civil liberties and civil rights, for restoration of university autonomy, for an end to political banishment and exile including restoration of citizenship to those deprived of Chilean nationality by decree of the military government.

High hopes for the Acuerdo crumbled before General Pinochet's reaffirmation of the 1980 constitution as the basis of Chilean political life at the same time that the political left was declaring that the Acuerdo was no substitute for armed struggle as the way to achieve a revolutionary transformation of Chilean society. During the next year, new efforts were made to mobilize the civilian opposition which resulted in creation of a "Civic Assembly" (Asamblea de la Civilidad)—still one more attempt to unite opposition groups and movements in an effective way to overcome the dictatorship and achieve "democracy now." Prospects for the Civic Assembly seemed little better than those of previous attempts to forge broad-based civilian opposition coalitions. Chilean society remained severely fragmented, both ideologically and along class lines; the persistent lack of consensus and intense polarization which had preceded the military coup in 1973, combined with the repression of the regime, inhibited successful mobilization against the dictatorship.

This inability of the opposition to resolve the differences (historical, personal, and ideological) which divided them from one another (not to mention the *internal* cleavages in most groups as well) left the military itself as the pivotal arbiter of the government's fate. Lacking viable civilian allies, however, opponents of General Pinochet within the armed forces were understandably hesitant to take steps to end the general's reign.

Reprinted and edited from *Journal of Interamerican Studies and World Affairs* 28, no. 4 (Winter 1986–87), pp. 1–38.

Stephen M. Gorman

Antipolitics in Peru, 1968–80

Whether the nearly twelve years of military rule in Peru between October 1968 and July 1980 are labeled a "revolution," a "so-called revolution," or a simple "military dictatorship," one fact remains inescapable: The reforms and programs of the armed forces during that period profoundly altered Peruvian society. The military that overthrew President Fernando Belaúnde Terry in 1968 set out to completely restructure social, political, and economic relations in the country. The objective was to promote urban industrial expansion, head off growing political activism among the lower classes, and strengthen the role of the state as an agent of national development and social reconciliation. Peru's military leaders endeavored to create a corporate social order that would be characterized by moral solidarity, social discipline, centralized authority, and hierarchically integrated self-managing socioeconomic units. The fact that the military failed in many of these objectives, and progressively turned away from reformist policies after 1975, does not alter the fact that the military regime nevertheless intentionally changed the nature of Peruvian political life.

The military's intervention into politics in 1968 is somewhat unique within both Latin American politics generally and Peruvian history in particular. In the first instance, although different military factions had been involved in at least eleven coups d'etat since the election of Peru's first civilian president in 1872, only once before, in 1962, had the armed forces acted as an *institution* to seize control of the state. On that occasion the military limited its role to convening and supervising "honest" elections, and little more.[1] But in 1968 the armed forces took power with the objective of instituting far-ranging reforms with no intention of returning government to civilian hands in the foreseeable future. Secondly, although the military adopted a political program that had been articulated by progressive sectors of the emerging middle class for more than three decades, the armed forces did not govern as the representative of any specific social class. This is not to suggest that certain groups did not benefit more than others from the military's policies, but this was largely incidental to the broader goals of national development and political stability pursued by the armed forces. Finally, the Peruvian military acted out of extreme nationalism and vigorously attacked the nefarious forms of political, economic, and even cultural neo-imperialism that were considered largely responsible for the country's underdevelopment and international dependency. Certainly, other Latin American military regimes have adopted similar anti-dependency objectives, most notably in Brazil since the early 1970s, but most of these regimes originally came to power in response to perceived internal communist threats. But for the Peruvian military, the breaking of the linkage between North American imperialism and Peru's ruling oligarchy was an important motivating consideration in the overthrow of the civilian government. . . .

The twelve years of military rule (the *docenio*) are normally divided into the First Phase, corresponding to the presidency of Juan Velasco Alvarado (1968–75), and the Second Phase, corresponding to the presidency of Francisco Morales Bermúdez (1975–80). In point of fact, however, there was a brief period between the overthrow of Velasco in August 1975 and the Lima riots of July 1976 which stands apart from both phases. The First Phase was a period of reformism while the Second Phase is considered rather reactionary, since President Morales Bermúdez presided over the emasculation of many earlier reforms. Morales Bermúdez himself originally characterized the Second Phase as a period of "consolidation" intended to rationalize the reforms that had been effected under Velasco. Throughout the first year of his regime, the emphasis actually appears to have been on consolidating earlier revolutionary gains during a period of economic difficulties. Only after the Lima riots and an attempted right-wing coup within the armed forces in July 1976 were liberal officers purged from the government and a systematic assault initiated against many of the progressive reforms of the earlier period. This shift in governmental policy apparently resulted from the failure of many reforms to produce the results intended by the military. . . .

The military assumed power with an ideology that claimed to understand the past errors of civilian governments that had produced Peru's underdevelopment and international dependency, including the nature of the country's subordinate integration into the global capitalist system. Yet, the military rulers proceeded to predicate the success of revolutionary reforms on the expansion of the country's integration into the international market (albeit with some diversification of products, trading partners, and marketing techniques). The result economically was that the generals' approach to development failed in much the same fashion as civilian regimes before them, but on a grander scale.

Ideology and Goals

One of the important characteristics of the Peruvian military is that its officer corps has not been drawn from the upper classes. In fact, officers after the turn of the century were drawn increasingly from the middle and lower-middle classes, especially in the case of the army. Thus, the armed forces, dominated by the army, were not strictly speaking an extension of the ruling classes, although they frequently acted in defense of upper-class interests prior to 1968. The essentially middle-class composition of the army officer corps rendered it especially susceptible to the reformist currents that gained steadily after the early 1930s. Because of early hostilities between the army and the main carrier of progressive middle-class reformism, the Peruvian Aprista Party (or APRA), however, the army was inhibited from embracing the dominant reformist ideology for some time.[2] But with the establishment of the Center of High Military Studies (CAEM), an indirect process of officer indoctrination in middle-class progressivism was initiated under the aegis of military professionalization.

Among the courses offered at CAEM were many dealing with the political history and socioeconomic conditions of Peru. A significant number of the civilian instructors brought in to offer such courses were, at least indirectly, influenced by the writings of Peru's early socialist José Carlos Mariátegui (1895–1930) and the political platform advanced by APRA. New officers became ever more sensitive to the political and economic corruption of the national oligarchy, the domination of the country by foreign economic interests, and the superficiality and decadence of Peru's purely formal democracy and personalistic political parties. All of this promoted a rejection within the army of the sterility of civilian rulers. The final step in the gradual politicization of CAEM officers was the conceptualization of national development as an integral dimension of national defense. If development was indeed essential to a strong national defense, and if civilian politicians were, as the army came steadily to believe, incapable of promoting development, then the army would be compelled to assume the direction of the state in order to fulfill its own mission of national defense.

Without implying that the following goals were universally held within the armed forces, or clearly and consciously understood by the entire circle of military rulers at the outset of the revolution, we can nevertheless identify four major concerns that oriented the military after 1968: (1) Social Justice, (2) Popular Participation, (3) National Independence, and (4) Development.

Social Justice was a primary and all-inclusive goal of the military revolutionaries, but it was defined in only the vaguest manner. Generally, Social Justice combined a concern for the material well-being of individuals with the teachings of Catholicism. As such, it was analogous to Christian Humanism. But its main emphasis was on the collectivity over the individual, and social responsibility over personal interest. General Velasco Alvarado explained early in the revolution that the military leaders were "humanist revolutionaries" who were intent on moralizing Peruvian society with a set of values completely different from "those that sustain capitalism or communism." The goal of the revolution was to create a society that would "reprieve" man as part of a broader collectivity.

The concept of Social Justice precluded social conflict, which was considered to be a by-product of social stratification based on the special privileges and monopoly over wealth enjoyed by an egotistical minority. Accordingly, Social Justice required that all people share *equitably* (although not necessarily *equally*) in both the wealth and "destiny" of the country. This would be possible only when there arose "free citizens" occupying their "just place in society." It should be stressed that this was not a call for strict egalitarianism since it did not propose a leveling of society, but only a more "just" distribution of social wealth.

Finally, Social Justice imposed certain limitations on formal or legal rights, including property ownership. Stated Velasco, "The Revolution recognizes the legitimacy of all those rights whose observance does not signify perpetuating injustice. . . ." Conversely, the military government refused to respect certain formal rights whose observance "would signify, necessarily, condemning the majority to eternal poverty. . . ." This clearly encompassed property rights. The notion of Social Justice assumed that property might be held in private ownership, but that this would not relieve it of its social obligations. In other words, the right of private property in the productive sectors was conditioned on the use of that property to promote socially beneficial ends.

Participation of the masses in the revolution was another important component of the military's ideology. But participation was redefined and placed within a moral and economic context instead of an essentially political one. That is, participation was not understood in electoral terms. Elections were considered the window dressing of the purely *formal democracy* which had worked only to the advantage of elites in Peru prior to 1968. In a speech to the nation on the 148th Anniversary of Peruvian Independence, Velasco made it clear that the military had no intention of respecting the institutional norms of the civilian political system, including elections, since these had merely permitted the privileged few to deceive and manipulate the vast majority. Not only did participation as defined by the military reject the need for national elections, but it also excluded the need for intermediaries such as political parties. Intermediaries were considered unnecessary, in the first instance, because the national leaders were "interpreters" of popular aspirations, not mere representatives of it. The government and people were *one and the same* (Velasco, in *El Comercio*, July 29, 1969), and thus the functions which political parties purportedly perform to link government and people were superfluous in the case of revolutionary Peru.

What the military meant by participation was the right and duty of all citizens to share in the burdens and benefits of Peruvian development. Also, individuals were to be allowed a wider and more meaningful participation in the operation of social and economic institutions that directly touched upon their own immediate lives, such as neighborhood councils, workers' councils in factories, or other *localized* units. Yet, such grass roots participation was not intended to serve as a process of reconciliation between opposing interests. The military argued that true participation could only take place within a context of moral solidarity, which meant that it could not occur in the presence of competing interests or values. Consequently, the revolutionary goal of promoting participation had

as its end the construction in [Peru] of a social democracy of full participation, that is to say, a system based on a moral order of solidarity, not individualism; on an economy fundamentally self-managing, in which the means of production are predominantly social property . . . ; and on a political order where the decision-making power, far from being monopolized by the political and economic oligarchies . . . [is grounded in] social, economic, and political institutions directed, without intermediation or with a minimum of it, by the men and women that form them.

The organic and solitary definition of true participation, thus, entailed a *progressive depoliticization of Peruvian society* [emphasis added, ED.]. . . .

National Independence was another important objective of the Peruvian revolution, which was dedicated to breaking the country's political, economic, and military dependency on North America. Dependency was defined as the subordination of national will to "imperialist" interests. For the military, subordination occurred whenever national decision makers yielded to foreign pressures or influence. The oligarchy prior to the revolution was considered to have been the active agent of imperialism, and therefore bore primary responsibility for the dependency of Peruvian society. The military promised to resist any and all forms of foreign political influence in the formulation of Peru's domestic and foreign policies.

Nationalism meant, preeminently, national liberation. It required that the government conduct its foreign affairs in strict relation to the national interest, and not in accordance with such outmoded international configurations as the East-West split. Nationalism also meant cultural and intellectual emancipation. A nationalist ideology, for instance, could only be based on, and understood in reference to, the unique heritage of a particular people. Appropriately, Velasco insisted that the Peruvian revolution was neither capitalist nor communist, but predicated on strictly indigenous values and ideas.

Most significantly, nationalism and the struggle against dependency was taken to mean that Peru should join with the vanguard of underdeveloped nations in pressing for a restructuring of the international political and economic order. To assert the country's new independence, Peru's military leaders broadened diplomatic and commercial ties to include many communist bloc nations, and turned away from the United States as the country's chief arms supplier. Lastly, National Independence presupposed national development oriented toward the satisfaction of domestic needs and greater international economic equality with trading partners.

National Development, which was the fourth major revolutionary objective, was intended both as a justification of the revolutionary process (the end that would justify the means), and as a condition that would facilitate the realization of the other revolutionary goals (Social Justice, National Independence, etc.). First and foremost, development required the construction of a modern industrial society, supported by a modern and efficient agrarian sector. Production had to be oriented both toward increasing internal consumption and improving Peru's competitiveness in the international finished goods market. The military realized that foreign capital would be necessary for development, but would have to be closely controlled to insure that it benefited Peru as much or more than it benefited foreign investors. It would also require a greater mobilization of Peru's own domestic resources which would be channeled to the industrial sector. Consistent with these two principal requirements, the revolutionary leaders redefined the rules for investment and altered the incentives to encourage greater private investment in specific areas of production, while reserving certain "key" industrial sectors to the state.

Underlying the military's approach to development was a strong belief that the state should play a larger role in industrialization and exercise tighter supervision of foreign capital to direct it into those economic activities most beneficial to Peru. But even while the state was to expand its economic role, the military still intended to rely heavily on private domestic investment, for which reason it was predisposed to permit increasing profits in modern industries to stimulate the accumulation of capital for further investment. Agrarian reform to stimulate greater production for domestic consumption, and price controls to hold down the cost of living for urban workers (and hence the cost of labor for industrialists), were integral elements of the military's approach to national development. And in a more general context, the military assumed that complete development would ultimately require national integration in the broadest possible sense. Only through a simultaneous process of economic, cultural, political, and linguistic integration would it be possible to fully mobilize human and material resources and build a modern industrial society.

It should be reemphasized that the four principal objectives of the revolution outlined above evolved gradually over the first year or so of the military regime. In other words, the military did not take power with a clear conceptualization of purpose, but rather came slowly to define its political program through the actual exercise of power. Toward the end of the Velasco period, one of the president's close advisors argued that the military had been pursuing a detailed secret plan of government almost from the outset. But the actual conduct of the military government between 1968 and 1975 strongly suggests that many reforms were ad hoc responses to unanticipated developments, while others (like the agrarian reform and creation of so-called Industrial Communities) may actually have been part of a "grand strategy."

The First Phase of the Revolution

Under Velasco, the military government committed itself to creating a "pluralistic" economy and a "Social Democracy of Full Participation." These duel objectives required some far-reaching economic reforms and a comprehensive reordering of the national political environment. On the economic side, a variety of different forms of economic organization were promoted in industry and agriculture, the state assumed a greater role in planning the economy and stimulating industrial expansion, and workers were provided with varying degrees of participation in profits and management. On the political side, the government endeavored to reduce (and eventually eliminate) the role of unions and political parties in the society, depoliticize higher education and increase technological training, and deprive the upper class of its traditional monopoly over political resources (such as control of information). Naturally, economic and political reforms overlapped and were highly interdependent. Nevertheless, it is possible to differentiate between primarily economic and political reform measures in the following discussion for purposes of clarity. While all of the important reforms cannot be reviewed here for reasons of space, we can identify the major programs initiated by the military during the revolution's First Phase.

Economic Reforms
The goal of promoting national development within a context of economic pluralism took the form of recognizing different ownership patterns and organizational forms throughout the economy. The four chief economic sectors that emerged were State Property (involving a government monop-

oly over certain business, financial, and commercial activities of special importance to Peruvian development), Reformed Private Property (involving worker participation in the profits and management of private industrial firms), Unreformed Private Property (in which companies with less than six employees or $250,000 in annual sales remained essentially unaltered), and Social Property (modeled after Yugoslav worker ownership of industries). Aside from promoting a variety of organizational forms throughout the economy, the military government attempted to restructure the overall economy itself by channeling a greater share of national resources to the modern industrial sector, providing increased opportunities for private capital accumulation, and expanding agricultural production for both export and internal consumption. One of the first and most important moves the Velasco government undertook to stimulate development was agrarian reform.

Agrarian reform. On June 24, 1969, the Velasco regime decreed a comprehensive agrarian reform intended, among other things, to increase production in order to generate surplus capital for investment in the urban-industrial sector. The reform applied to most coastal properties above 150 hectares and sierra holdings above 35 to 55 hectares (with regional variations). While expropriated holdings were compensated for with bonds payable over twenty to thirty years, the actual value of compensation was "sharply reduced by inflation and lax law enforcement." Although some observers perceived the reform as an attempt by the military to head off peasant unrest in the highlands, the pattern of application suggested that increasing productivity was the primary motivation for the law. The large export-oriented coastal estates were expropriated almost immediately, while the provisions of the reform were applied only gradually to the highlands on a regional basis.

The reform originally called for transferring roughly 11 million hectares (out of a national total of perhaps 21 to 23 million hectares of agricultural land) to some 340,000 rural families (out of perhaps 700,000 rural families). Through subsequent decrees, expropriated properties were organized along four primary lines, depending on the size, productivity, and previous organization of the holdings. Large, profitable coastal estates were constituted as Agricultural Production Cooperatives (CAPs), while the best sierra holdings were organized as Social Interest Agrarian Societies (SAISs). Fully 76 percent of expropriated properties were eventually organized into CAPs or SAISs, while the remainder were distributed as individual plots in either Campesino Cooperatives or Campesino Communities (both of which suffered from a scarcity of government assistance and credit). While the peasants in CAPs and SAISs were guaranteed a dominant voice in the management of their cooperatives, conflicts between cooperative members and state-appointed technocrats were frequent over such questions as the allocations of surpluses toward reinvestment or increased pay. Other conflicts concerned the demands of large numbers of peasants who failed to qualify as beneficiaries of the reform because they had been non-tenant laborers on highland haciendas or only temporary or part-time employees on coastal estates before the reform. Finally, a considerable amount of land escaped expropriation in the highlands because government delays allowed owners to carry out their own parcelation of holdings among family members and/or others. . . .

The agrarian reform suffered from a certain ambiguity of purpose from the outset. The "developmentalist" officers viewed the reform as a measure to increase agricultural productivity, while so-called radical officers favored the reform as a means of income redistribution (that would mobilize popular support behind the military regime). The revolutionary rhetoric that accompanied the declaration of the reform aroused the expectations of landless sierra peasants, but in practice, the government concentrated on increasing productivity on the already highly efficient coastal estates rather than meeting the demands of highland peasants for the swift and complete expropriation of haciendas. The percentage of Agrarian Bank loans allocated to the agro-export sector increased during the First Phase, and the bulk of public investment in agriculture went toward large-scale irrigation to benefit coastal estates. The fact that most part-time agricultural laborers and non-tenant peasants failed to benefit from the agrarian reform led to serious labor tensions along the coast and land invasion in the highlands.

Partly in response to tensions in the countryside, the military government created the National Agrarian Confederation (CNA) as "the one legitimate organ of expression of farm interests." Established in 1972 by Decree Law 19400, the CNA did not hold its first national convention until late 1974. The CNA was intended to join together all individuals who worked in the agricultural sector to both communicate their interests to government and coordinate regional and national agricultural policies. However, the CNA was "basically a mechanism to enhance the labors of the government" since peasant interests were to be defended by the CNA only to the extent that they were "compatible with the national interest as determined by the Military Government." Although problems continued to disrupt government policies in the countryside even after the formation of the CNA, as the expectations unleashed by the agrarian reform contributed to growing political instability, the situation remained within manageable limits throughout the Velasco period. And although the agrarian reform did not measure up to all of the rhetoric that surrounded its initiation, it nevertheless qualified as one of the most important changes effected by the military.

Reformed private property. The First Phase government attempted to stimulate industrial expansion and harmonize worker-owner relations through the introduction of a series of reforms in 1970. The General Law of Industries (D.L. 18350) required private companies with more than six employees or $250,000 in gross income to reinvest 15 percent of their profits in the name of the workers as a group until workers acquired 50 percent ownership, provide participation in management proportionate to worker ownership in the company, and distribute another 10 percent of net profits directly to individual workers. This was followed by Decree Law 18384, which established the organizational form of the Industrial Communities in each firm through which workers were to share in profits. Finally, Decree Law 18471 in November 1970 significantly tightened the conditions under which industrial workers could be fired or laid off. . . .

Regardless of the intentions of the reform to reconcile the interests of labor and management, worker unrest increased. During the two years preceding the reform of industrial property (1968–69), there had been 735 strikes involving over 200,000 workers (about 10 percent of the labor force), while during the two years following the measure (1971–72), there were 786 strikes involving 292,000 workers (about 15.4 percent of the labor force). More important, the severity of strikes increased. During the period 1968–69, a total of 7.3 million man hours were lost through strikes. This increased to 17.2 million man hours during 1971–72. What also changed was the cause of strikes. Whereas in 1968–69, 23.1 percent of all strikes involved layoffs and firings, 17.7 percent involved pay demands, and 15.9 percent involved contract disputes, in 1971, fully 35 percent of all strikes involved pay demands, while the other two issues declined in importance. Certainly not all of these strikes affected the Reformed Private Property Sector, but they do reflect the intensification of labor conflicts in the better organized sectors of the economy which industrial reforms failed to stem.

Even together with a modified form of Industrial Communities (CIS) for State Enterprises (in which workers received bonds instead of stock), industrial reform measures benefited only a minority of Peru's modern work force. In 1972, there were roughly 53,100 workers in mining, 485,200 workers in manufacturing, and 171,700 workers in construction, which together represented 16.2 percent of Peru's labor force. Yet, by the end of the reform period in 1975, only approximately 200,000 workers belonged to CIS, representing less than 4.3 percent of Peru's economically active population. These workers, who were organized into more than 3,500 CIS by the close of the Velasco period, came to pose something of a political challenge to the military government after 1973 when the Ministry of Industry and Tourism sponsored the First National Congress of Industrial Communities. Although the government had not intended to form a permanent national body to aggregate and communicate the interests of CIS (as it had done in the agricultural sector with the formation of the CNA), the workers themselves formed the autonomous National Confederation of Industrial Communities (CONACI) in October 1973 which called upon the government to (1) convert all reformed property to Social Property, (2) increase worker participation in management, and (3) cancel the agrarian debt owed to former land owners. By mid-1974, CONACI had become a serious embarrassment to the regime because of its efforts to push the revolution further left than the generals desired to go. The military responded with an effort to divide CONACI and bring it back within the ideological parameters of the revolution.

The state sector. The expansion of the Peruvian government's direct involvement in the economy under Velasco has been characterized by many observers as a form of "state capitalism." Aside from its other economic reforms, the military created a heterogeneous state sector composed of a collection of industrial, financial, and commercial enterprises. The First Phase government did not intend to either replace or discourage private domestic and foreign investment. Rather, state investment in certain "strategic" areas of the economy was intended to guarantee a rapid development of the industrial infrastructure (e.g., steel production) and promote the expansion of the domestic market. Major export activities were also nationalized to insure that export earnings were maximized to finance the military's ambitious industrial investment program. Finally, the creation of a state sector was intended to break up certain monopolies held by domestic and foreign capitalists in Peru which acted as obstacles to what the military perceived as the inherent dynamism of the economy. Thus, while foreign investment was still encouraged, it was no longer allowed to freely choose the area and scope of its activities. It was expected to be consistent with, and contribute to, the government's developmental strategies.

Two primary characteristics of the state sector were that it was formed primarily on the basis of existing (mostly foreign) industries, and grew largely out of the pursuit of other objectives, such as the rationalization of a particular area of production or the reduction of external dependency. While the military became intent on centralizing what it perceived as strategic economic activities, it nevertheless remained committed to a notion of "economic pluralism" and had no intention of moving toward a completely state-managed economy. The state sector firms that emerged during the First Phase of the revolution fell into three major categories. In the first group were state enterprises formed from expropriated foreign holdings (including PETROPERU, ENTROMIN, HIERROPERU, ENTELPERU, and ENAFER). These state enterprises gave the government dominant control over the important extractive industries (oil, copper, iron) and public services (electricity and rail transportation). In the second group were formerly domestically owned industries taken over after economic collapses. The fishmeal industry is the chief example, which was converted into the state enterprise PESCAPERU in 1973 at a time when the sector was in severe decline. The third group was made up of already existing and newly created state enterprises, like the steel firm SIDERPERU.

Apart from these primarily extractive and manufacturing firms, the government assumed a dominant position in marketing and credit. Through the purchase of stock, the government came to control most of the banking industry. State monopolies were also created in the foreign marketing of minerals and other products, the domestic wholesale of basic foodstuffs, and industries oriented to processing primary exports to increase the value added.

The military had intended to have the state augment private investment, not replace it. But the rhetoric of the revolution created a climate of uncertainty in the business community that discouraged both domestic and foreign private investments in the economy. Thus, the state's share of fixed investment rose from 29.8 percent in 1968 to 44 percent in 1973. Over the long run the military rulers expected primary exports (especially oil and copper) to finance state investments in heavy industry. But over the short run, the government turned to private international credit which, as it happened, was readily available at reasonable terms during the early 1970s. Indeed, it was the abundance of private credit during this period that allowed the Peruvian government to escape almost completely the effects of the cutoff of official bilateral credits and aid from the United States. The cutoff was in retaliation for the uncompensated expropriation of the International Petroleum Company in 1968, and was not ended until the 1974 Greene Agreement between Peru and the United States resolved all outstanding claims against the revolutionary government.

Even with heavy foreign borrowing, however, the rate of fixed capital formation by the close of the Velasco period remained virtually the same as during the early 1960s. And the growth of industrial output generally, and manufacturing in particular, remained virtually unchanged between the periods 1961–70 and 1971–75. What did change was the economy's dependence on state investment and the country's external public debt (which began to increase almost exponentially). The expansion of the state sector also brought the government into an employer-employee relationship with a sizable proportion of the Peruvian work force. This eventually posed serious political difficulties for the government after 1974 when the military began to react to the first signs of economic crisis by "rationalizing" state-controlled industries (i.e., reducing labor costs).

Social property. As early as July 1971, President Velasco let it be known that the Revolutionary Government's reorganization of property ownership would not stop with the formation of agrarian cooperatives, Industrial Communities, and the expansion of the state sector. He announced that an entirely new form of property—Social Property—would be created as the foundation for Peruvian socialism. It was not until August 1973, however, that the government finally issued a draft law of Social Property for public comment. After eight months of sometimes intense public debate, resulting in the deportation of certain leading critics, the Law of Social Property (D.L. 20598) was decreed on April 30, 1974. This law provided for the formation of a Social Property Sector composed of Social Property Enterprises (EPSs) which, it was planned, would come to constitute the dominant form of production in the country over the course of twenty or thirty years.

The Social Property Sector was to be presided over by the National Commission of Social Property (CONAPS) which would be responsible for approving the creation of individual EPSs, supervising their early operations, and coordinating policy for the sector as a whole. While EPSs could be formed in any economic field either from scratch or through the conversion of an existing company upon the request of its workers, preference was initially given to the establishment of entirely new firms. To provide state capital for the formation of EPSs, the government set up the National Fund of Social Property (FONAPS) to finance the growth of the new sector. Finally, the law provided for a national Social Property Sector Assembly to consist of EPS representatives elected through regional associations. This national assembly was to meet biannually: in November to plan programs for the sector for the coming year, and in April to evaluate the performance of the sector during the previous year.

The government devoted considerable time and effort to detailing the structure and function of the sector since it was supposed to become the priority area for future public investment. . . . The introduction of Social Property received an enthusiastic response from most workers and leftist intellectuals, but was bitterly opposed by business leaders who feared that it threatened the concept of economic pluralism and was intended to subvert private property. The success of Social Property, however, was jeopardized from the outset by two major difficulties. First, by 1974–75, the military government's investment resources were already severely strained which in turn limited the expansion of the new sector. Second, the high concentration of production in the various branches of modern industry in Peru where EPSs were to be formed threatened the economic viability of the new firms. Their competitiveness within such monopolistic conditions could not be guaranteed even with state-imposed restrictions on the expansion of existing private manufacturers. As a result, demands increased toward the end of the First Phase for the conversion of *existing* companies into EPSs, rather than the formation of new enterprises. These and other problems delayed the expansion of the sector, and by the close of the Velasco period, only a handful of EPSS were in operation (with perhaps another one hundred in various stages of planning or formations). The actual growth of the Social Property Sector failed to satisfy the expectations that the reform aroused workers and intellectuals, and the government's commitment to the social property concept waned quickly after 1975.

Political Reforms
While the military's basic approach to development reflected a high degree of confidence in technocratic solutions to economic problems, its approach to the representative duties of government was influenced by a deep distrust of politics and politicians. Labor unions, to the extent that they were traditionally either the creatures of political parties in Peru or, at a minimum, politically oriented, were also highly suspect in the military's eyes. The traditional political system in Peru had operated on the basis of the marginalization of the highland rural population and the segmentary incorporation of different urban and coastal groups by political parties that became their patrons.

The client-patron relationships that developed between the various political parties and their constituencies led to a situation in which the national interest was neglected in favor of particularistic interests. When, as often happened, competing narrow interests could not be reconciled and a consensus for action arrived at, the situation gave rise to the stagnation of the national governmental process. Politics was overwhelmingly a forum for sectarian competition between essentially personalistic political parties. Thus, the military committed itself to the complete depoliticization of Peruvian society. . . . The following measures, although in no way comprehensive, stand out as some of the more important political reforms enacted by the First Phase government to restructure the political environment and foster the growth of a corporatist society in Peru.

Mobilization and participation. The military, or at least a certain faction within the military, was interested in mobilizing support for revolutionary reform and increasing lower-class participation in restructuring Peruvian society. . . . Three options were open to the government: It could create its own revolutionary political party, work through one of the existing political parties (such as the pro-government Communist Party), or attempt to completely redefine the nature and process of mobilization and participation. The military opted for the third alternative and established . . . the National System for Support of Social Mobilization (SIN-AMOS). The law establishing SINAMOS (D.L. 18896) in June 1971 and the subsequent statute (D.L. 19352) outlining its organization and procedures in April 1972 assigned the agency a number of responsibilities. The most important duties of SINAMOS were to (1) train and organize the popular classes at the local level to promote the implementation of national policies, (2) elaborate a corporatist definition of participation in which individuals would cooperate in localized activities directed from above by the government, (3) coordinate self-help activities among the poor, and (4) undercut the traditional role of political parties as integrative agents for "marginalized" groups.

SINAMOS was given a wide field of operations, including the cooperatives formed by the agrarian reform, the Industrial Communities formed by the Industrial Law, and, most importantly, the squatter settlements (*pueblos jóvenes*) surrounding Lima. To facilitate its manifold responsibilities, SINAMOS was given a dual organizational structure. Alongside a variety of functional departments (dealing with rural organization, labor organization, community development, etc.), the government created a pyramidal national structure with a central office at the top, ten regional offices (presiding over two to five departments), and numerous zonal offices (ideally presiding over about two provinces each). Finally, at the lowest level, were the actual field operatives—or "contact points"—of SINAMOS who initiated or coordinated community activities. . . .

SINAMOS was beset with difficulties almost from the outset. In the first instance, the formation of the agency was a response to the autonomous formation of Committees for the Defense of the Revolution that sprang up around Lima and throughout the country in 1970. . . . Some military hardliners wanted these committees disbanded, while other officers viewed them as an opportunity to expand the revolution's base of support. Whether this is true or not, SINAMOS was also an attempt to overcome the military's lack of grass roots structures within the society by which the popular classes could be linked to the government, and give substance to the military's rhetoric of "participation." . . . SINAMOS programs throughout most of the society were visible failures by late 1973; with some notable exceptions, such as in the *pueblos jóvenes* of the Lima/Callao areas. . . .

SINAMOS encountered opposition from virtually every political sector: Government technocrats resented its efforts to interject politics into economic planning, the target communities feared its manipulative potential, and the political parties and unions opposed the efforts of SINAMOS to deprive them of popular leadership. Most significantly, SINAMOS was unable to control many of the mass-based groups it helped bring into existence. Paradoxically, although the military originally created SINAMOS to undercut the appeal of unions, by 1974–75, the government virtually abandoned SINAMOS and in turn attempted to compete with unions directly by forming state-sponsored syndicates in a variety of economic sectors.

Education. The military considered the rationalization and modernization of Peruvian higher education essential to national development, and therefore moved quickly to impose major university reforms. In a highly controversial move, the government issued Decree Law 17437 in February 1969 in a sudden and unexpected manner. The law reduced student participation in university governance from one third to one fourth, reorganized faculties into disciplines, and attempted to depoliticize student politics by setting academic standards for election to student organizations and barring reelections. Most threateningly, the law effectively abolished the traditional autonomy of Peruvian universities by placing them under the supervision of a National Council of the Peruvian University (CONUP) that was placed under the authority of the Ministry of Education. Because of intense reaction from practically all university groups, especially students and professors, the Velasco regime made progressive modifications in the law throughout the remainder of the year. Finally, in November 1969, the government attempted to mollify the university community by appointing an Educational Reform Commission under the supervision of the Ministry of Education to write a new comprehensive educational reform proposal with public input.

It took the Reform Commission until September 1970 to publish its first report for public comment, which sparked considerable public debate. As far as possible, the commission—sometimes under direct pressure from President Velasco himself—endeavored to incorporate the demands of important groups into a new reform proposal. By early 1971, the commission had produced a draft law, but this was not released for public comment until December. After still further modifications in the law in response to pressures and demands from both within and without the universities, the Velasco government finally issued its General Law of Education (D.L. 19326) in March 1972 (more than thirty-four months after the military's first educational reform initiative). . . .

Conflict between the government and the educational community continued at all levels after 1972. In higher education, two major issues of conflict concerned pay for teaching and non-teaching personnel (which failed to keep pace with inflation) and the alleged interference of CONUP in university self-governance. Both the pro-government Revolutionary Students of Peru (formed with the assistance of SINAMOS) and the more radical Student Federation of Peru (FEP) criticized or opposed the reformist measures of CONUP. And the National Federation of Teachers of the Peruvian University (FENDUP) vigorously attacked the government's "rationalization" program in education. Within lower education, popular opposition to the government on a wide range of issues became increasingly radical. In 1970, the strongest teachers' union had been the National Federation of Educators of Peru (FENEP), whose membership was split between followers of the pro-government General Confederation of Peruvian Workers (CGTP) and left-wing Apristas. The Apristas withdrew and formed the Sole Syndicate of Workers of Peruvian Education (SUTEP), which adopted an extremely militant opposition to the military regime.

When the government sponsored elections in the educational establishment in 1973, SUTEP emerged as the dominant teachers' union. The Velasco regime reacted by withdrawing recognition from SUTEP and forming a government-sponsored Syndicate of Educators of the Peruvian Revolution (SERP). The continued dominance of SUTEP among educators, however, led the government to seek a dialogue with the union in July 1974. The "dialogue" came to an end, however, shortly after SUTEP's Secretary General, Horacio Zevallos, labeled the military's education reform as an attempt to promote the interests of the country's "dependent bourgeoisie" at a national congress in November. By early 1975, SUTEP had formulated a political program calling for the overthrow of the existing "bourgeoisie government" and its replacement by a proletarian regime, total opposition to the General Law of Education because of its bias in favor of "power groups," and the formation of a united front to resist the manipulative agencies of the military government (such as SINAMOS and the Ministry of Education).

In reality, the military's approach to education became ever more equivocal after 1973 as opposition mounted to reforms. At times the government adopted a hard-line policy, as with the promulgation of Decree Law 20201 in October 1973 that authorized the Minister of Education to dismiss any instructor suspected of "subversion" without appeal over the course of a year. At other times, the government (acting through CONUP) struggled to appease student and teacher demands, especially during the first half of 1975. In spite of its obvious disappointment with the response to its reforms, the Velasco government continued to attempt to effect major changes in education right up to the end of the First Phase. For example, in May 1975, Decree Law 21156 established the Indian language of Quechua as one of the official languages of the country, mandated obligatory instruction in the language by the 1976 school year, and gave the judicial system until January 1977 to acquire the capacity to conduct proceedings in the language when requested by defendants.

Information and the press. The Velasco government enjoyed generally good relations with the Peruvian press during its first year in power, but the increasing tempo of reforms invariably caused tension between the military and the wealthy owners of the leading national dailies. The government's first effort to exercise control over the press came in December 1969 with Decree Law 18075. This law imposed stiff penalties for libel against government officials and state entities, and prohibited either foreigners or Peruvian nationals living abroad from owning newspapers. As the government's treatment in the press worsened, more direct measures were taken. In March 1970, two important dailies (*Expreso* and *Extra*) were expropriated and turned over to their workers (who were under the influence of the pro-government Communist Party). The papers, which belonged to Manuel Ulloa (who had served as a minister in the Belaunde government) were accused of defending the interests of foreign capitalists and the Peruvian oligarchy. In 1971, a third important daily came under indirect military influence when the government purchased the stock of the Banco Popular after the collapse of the financial empire of one of the nation's leading oligarchic families. The bank had served as the holding company for the diverse investments of the Prado family, including the Lima daily *La Cronica*. The paper was renamed *La Nueva Cronica* and placed under the management of an editorial council sympathetic to the revolution. Finally, in January 1972, the government issued Decree Law 19270 that gave the workers in each paper the first option to purchase their dailies, should the owners be forced to sell under the provisions of Decree Law 18075 of 1969.

The crux of the growing conflict between the government and the independent press was that practically all of the leading dailies were owned by extremely wealthy individuals who were deeply involved in the political and economic issues on which their papers editorialized. Indeed, with the exception of *El Comercio* (which was the primary investment of the Miró Quesada family), the leading papers had been purchased by members of the oligarchy precisely in order to protect their investments in other areas of the economy. In other words, left-wing accusations that the national dailies were little more than political organs for the upper class had a great deal of substance. Nevertheless, the rights of the private owners of the press were defended by the more moderate members of the revolutionary government (especially the representatives of the navy), and the efforts by radical officers to take more decisive actions against the press precipitated a political crisis within the Velasco regime between late 1973 and early 1974. Only after these moderates were purged from the inner council of the Velasco regime did the revolutionary government proceed with its plan for guaranteeing "popular control" of information.

In a preliminary move, the government created the National Information System (SINADI) in March 1974 to monitor all mediums of communication to (1) guarantee "truth" in reporting on government programs, (2) "harmonize" reporting with the objectives of the national development plan, and (3) modify the content of news to insure that it "serve culture." The system was placed under the administration of a Central Office of Information (OCI), whose director was given ministerial rank. The major offensive was contained in Decree Law 20680, issued secretly on July 23, 1974, and put into effect dramatically a few days later. Under its provisions, all national dailies (papers with a circulation of more than 20,000 or distribution in more than half of the departmental capitals) were expropriated. Each of the expropriated papers was assigned to a different sector of the population whose government-recognized participatory organizations were to elect the civil associations that would oversee the editorial policies of each daily. *La Nueva Cronica,* in turn, was placed directly under the authority of the oci as the official government press. The law brought about the expropriation of the five remaining major dailies (*La Prensa, El Comercio, Correo, Ultima Hora,* and *Ojo*) which, together with *Extra* and *Expreso,* were designated as the representatives of different socio-economic groups such as urban labor, campesinos, the service sector, and professional organizations. . . .

While the papers remained generally supportive of the revolutionary government up through mid-1975, they nevertheless exhibited considerable editorial independence. As the government encountered increasing financial difficulties and important reforms failed to meet the growing expectation of the population, this editorial independence became increasingly intolerable to the First Phase regime. Finally, during the last month of the Velasco government, the military reacted to what it perceived as a radicalization of the press with the first of many purges of "subversive" journalists. The Second Phase government subsequently tightened press controls and, finally, completely abandoned the idea of a socialized press in Peru.

The Second Phase and the End of Revolutionary Change

Although many of the reforms of the First Phase were either incomplete or poorly executed, a considerable redistribution of national resources was accomplished benefiting the lower classes. The new or increased responsibilities of the central government in industrialization, public welfare, and other areas, however, placed severe strains on the treasury. With the onset of the international recession induced by increasing energy prices in early 1974, Peru began to encounter serious balance of payments problems. Many of the Velasco-era development projects had been financed with private foreign credit, which was to be repaid with the earnings from expanding primary exports. The international recession that set in early in 1974 placed the Velasco regime in a difficult posture: On the one hand, the revolutionary government had become committed to extensive public expenditures, while on the other hand, it needed to come to terms with international creditors who began to press for austerity measures to stabilize the Peruvian economy. The political situation was further complicated by President Velasco's deteriorating health and increasingly personalistic style of rule.

By mid-1975, a coalition of conservative officers within the army had formed around Velasco's Prime Minister, General Francisco Morales Bermúdez. Morales Bermúdez, who was next in line for the presidency on the basis of military seniority, favored conservative fiscal policies to improve the country's national accounts, but otherwise professed support for the objectives of the revolution. In a well-coordinated putsch on August 29, 1975, Velasco was overthrown without bloodshed when the country's five regional army commanders issued an Institutional Manifesto naming Morales Bermúdez president. The action was quickly endorsed by the air force and navy, and encountered virtually no opposition from the popular organizations created by the revolution.

Morales Bermúdez announced that the coup merely signaled a change in personnel, and not a rejection of the goals of the revolution. The government would continue to pursue the objectives of the First Phase, only without "personalismo" or "desviaciones" (personalism or deviations). Nevertheless, the so-called Second Phase reordered government priorities, reduced the influence of reformist officers in decision making, and began to stress the themes of labor discipline and sacrifice. The Second Phase government attempted to "rationalize" First Phase programs, which usually entailed increasing the profitability of public enterprises by adopting wage or employment policies injurious to the working class. Also, a succession of austerity measures (that actually began under Velasco) were imposed that reduced public welfare expenditures and generally raised the cost of living. During its first year, the Morales Bermúdez government kept most of the working class organizations in line by stressing that Peru's economic difficulties were the result of the collapse of the international capitalist system. The seemingly antipopular policies of the government, it was explained, were only temporary expedients to deal with a transitory crisis. The political space of the Second Phase regime, however, was narrowing as a disproportionate amount of the burdens of the austerity measures fell on the very groups to which the revolution had originally looked for support. By mid-1976, it was clear that the piecemeal austerity measures adopted over the previous year were insufficient to either satisfy Peru's foreign creditors or stabilize the economy. In order to obtain a refinancing of the foreign debt, attract foreign investment, and stimulate exports, drastic action was required. In late June 1976, the ministerial cabinet finally agreed on a set of policies that the ranking reformist officer in the government was forced to announce on national television on June 30. Although numerous reformist officers had been forced into retirement after the Morales Bermúdez coup, enough remained in the Second Phase government to block some of the more onerous policy demands of the most conservative generals. These holdovers from the First Phase were grouped behind General Jorge Fernández Maldonado Solari, who served as Prime Minister and Commander of the Armed Forces by virtue of seniority. The ability of the conservative generals to maneuver Maldonado into announcing the austerity measures, which he certainly had fought against in the cabinet, was probably designed to blunt the public's reaction and direct resentment away from the president.

The austerity package was draconian. It provided for a 12.4 percent cut in government investment in state enterprises, a 12.8 percent reduction in the national budget, a steep increase in consumer prices, and a devaluation of the national currency by 44.4 percent. To help offset the effects of these actions, it was also announced that wages would be increased by 10 to 14 percent. The wage increases, however, did not come close to covering the rise in the cost of living. One immediate effect of the policies was a dramatic increase in the cost of gasoline, which was not compensated for by a corresponding increase in public transportation fares. To protest this fact, the Lima/Callao transportation cooperatives went on strike the following day. The transportation strike, in turn, sparked three days of rioting that required a full-scale military operation to contain. The violent popular reaction, which was largely directed against government institutions, profoundly altered the military's attitude toward the masses and appeared to confirm the fears of conservative generals that the First Phase had created revolutionary organizations that the government could not be sure of controlling. Many of the organizations created during the First Phase (such as the CNA, CONACI, the Confederation of Workers of the Peruvian Revolution, etc.) joined together in the Front for the Defense of the Revolution that functioned simultaneously as a source of political support for the government and a powerful pressure group designed to push reforms through to completion. As late as June 24, 1976, the Front had remained committed to the military government, but bitterly resisted the conservative orientation of certain officers. In a public communique, the Front declared:

We believe that the world economic crisis and its consequences in Peru, together with the imperialist's and reactionary right's offensive ... have disrupted the rhythm of the advance of the Revolution in the past ten months. But we are sure that the earlier transforming orientation will be regained shortly, without deviations or foreign influences of any kind. Therefore, we are in the same trench of battle as the Armed Forces, supporting the President of the Republic, General Francisco Morales Bermúdez, and remain confident that he will keep the Revolution on the same road that the People and Armed Forces have been following heretofore. (*El Comercio*, June 24, 1976)

Three days later, reacting to rumors that a major austerity package was under consideration in the cabinet, the coordinating committee of the Front issued another communique, stating:

Whoever has proposed such measures to the government has not considered the suffering of our people, the future of the Revolution and of the country, and therefore we are not in agreement with such policies.

As an alternative, a number of countermeasures were proposed that would attack what the Front termed the capitalist infrastructure of the country, and place the major burdens for contending with the economic crisis on the upper classes. The austerity program unveiled on June 30, therefore, represented a major political defeat for both the remaining reformist officers in the government and the mass-based organizations created under Velasco. Popular support for the military government after the rioting virtually evaporated and the armed forces found themselves politically isolated.

The final blow to the Peruvian revolution came later in the month of July when a power struggle ended in a complete purge of reformist officers from the government. During the rioting in Lima between July first and third, the conservative commander of the Center for Military Instruction (CIMP) ignored standing orders and deployed his troops to protect upper-class suburbs instead of seizing communications centers. General Bobbio Centurión, a strong supporter of austerity measures, incorrectly assumed that mobs were about to attack Lima's upper-class residential districts and took defensive actions without authorization from General Maldonado. Afterward, on July 9, Maldonado used the incident to demand Bobbio Centurión's early retirement. The commander of Lima's second most important military garrison then declared himself in rebellion (expecting support from the arch-conservative navy). After a brief battle, Bobbio Centurión was placed under arrest and sent into exile after the five regional army commanders and the Joint Chiefs of Staff issued a pronouncement in support of the existing government.

Although the power struggle appeared to have been won by Maldonado, the declaration of the armed forces against Bobbio Centurión was not so much an endorsement of the reformists in the government as an attempt to maintain the outward appearance of military unity and discipline. In reality, Maldonado's actions against Bobbio Centurión solidified the right-wing officers within the armed forces who then forced Maldonado and the other remaining reformist officers into early retirement later the same month. By August 1976, the revolutionary process was over in Peru, and a wide range of First Phase programs were either terminated or, at best, ignored. As Henry Pease Garcia and Alfredo Filomeno observed: "1976 is thus a year of redefinition of the military political project.

At times, the government appeared to be a new regime, distinct from the one that ran the state during the previous eight years." The attack on revolutionary programs was swift. Just five days after Maldonado's forced retirement on July 16, the government announced that the conditions for transferring the socialized press to complete citizen control did not yet exist, and the papers would therefore have to remain under the administration of government representatives. (Gradually, the military came full circle on the notion of a socialized press and favored the return of the Lima dailies to their former owners.) The following month, in a major address, President Morales Bermúdez declared that the term *socialism* would be dropped from the government's vocabulary because it was a vague and confusing word that merely discouraged private investment in the country. By mid-1977, the government began negotiations with the International Monetary Fund in an effort to appease foreign creditors and investors, which the First Phase government had pledged would never again influence Peruvian decision making. Finally, the government adopted a policy of "labor discipline" to replace the earlier policy of "labor stability," meaning that employers were given a freer hand to dismiss workers for reasons of either profitability or discipline.

The slackening and eventual termination of revolutionary change after the overthrow of Velasco prevented some programs (like Social Property) from ever getting off the ground, and others (like agrarian reform) from expanding their beneficiaries. The case of the agrarian reform is particularly interesting, since it is generally considered to have been the single most important consequence of the revolution. The 1969 agrarian reform had originally aimed at transferring up to eleven million hectares of land (well below the total arable land in Peru) to some 340,000 rural families. Yet, in June 1976, the Morales Bermúdez government declared the agrarian reform at an end (with one year permitted for resolution of all pending cases), with only 6.7 million hectares having been distributed among 269,437 families: 4.9 million of it as CAPS and SAISS. All told, a total of seven million hectares were distributed by the close of the revolution, leaving as much as twelve million hectares unaffected. And even if the original target of 340,000 families had received land (which they did not), those benefited would still have represented only a fraction of an agricultural work force that was calculated in excess of 1.5 million in 1972. In essence, the armed forces simply lacked the resources and resolve to carry through to completion the reforms begun in the First Phase.

In July 1977, President Morales Bermúdez declared that the military would sponsor elections to return government to civilians. The armed forces had exhausted their political capital and seriously damaged their institutional prestige and solidarity. But the military's withdrawal from power proved to be slow and painful. Elections were held for a Constituent

Assembly in 1978 that drafted a new constitution which was promulgated the following year. In May 1980, general elections were held for the national legislature and the presidency. During the three years between the announcement of elections and the actual surrender of power by Morales Bermúdez in July 1980, the military found it necessary to rely on openly repressive measures to contend with growing labor militancy. The armed forces ended up devoting their last three years of rule to brutalizing the popular classes in whose name they assumed power in 1968.

Reprinted and edited from *Post-Revolutionary Peru: The Politics of Transformation* (Boulder: Westview Press, 1982), pp. 1–32.

Notes

1. The following is a list of military coups in Peru since 1872:

1883   General Miguel Iglesias
1886   General Andres A. Cáceres
1914   Colonel Oscar R. Benavides
1930   General María Ponce
1930   Comandante Luis M. Sánchez Cerro
1931   Comandante Gustavo Jiménez
1948   General Manuel A. Odría
1962   General Ricardo Pérez Godoy
1968   General Juan Velasco Alvarado
1975   General Francisco Morales Bermúdez

In addition, there were three notable civilian coups:

1879   Nicolás de Piérola
1895   Nicolás de Piérola (called a revolution)
1919   Augusto B. Leguía

2. The historical rivalry between the military and APRA dates from the 1931 presidential election and an Aprista uprising that followed. Aprista supporters in Trujillo attacked a military garrison and killed a number of soldiers. The military responded with mass executions.

William M. LeoGrande and Carla Anne Robbins

Oligarchs and Officers:
The Crisis in El Salvador

El Salvador is burdened with one of the most rigid class structures and worst levels of income inequality in all of Latin America. For over a century, the social and economic life of the nation has been dominated by a small landed elite known popularly as "the 14 families" (*Los catorce*), though their actual number is well over fourteen. The family clans comprising the oligarchy include only a few thousand people in this nation of nearly five million, but until recently, they owned 60 percent of the farmland, the entire banking system, and most of the nation's industry. Among them, they received 50 percent of national income.

The tensions inherent in such a social structure are exacerbated in El Salvador by severe population pressure on the land. With over 400 people per square mile, population density is the highest in Latin America. Over 200,000 peasants are landless—a more severe imbalance of land and labor than in Mexico. Unlike most of its neighbors, El Salvador has no undeveloped territory for surplus agricultural labor to colonize; cultivation already extends up the slopes of even active volcanoes. Illegal emigration to less populous Honduras acted as a safety valve for the potentially explosive situation in the countryside until the 1969 "soccer war" closed the border. An expanding manufacturing sector offered another alternative to rural laborers in the decades after World War II, but the war with Honduras also pushed the economy into a recession from which it has never fully recovered.

The dominance of the oligarchy and the persistence of rural poverty produced an immense potential for class conflict. For decades, the oligarchy's primary political objective has been to prevent this latent conflict from erupting into class war. Despite its economic preeminence, the Salvadorean oligarchy has exercised political hegemony indirectly. The military has ruled El Salvador since 1931, and the history of the nation's governance has largely been a history of the twists and turns in the political alliance between oligarchs and officers.

This alliance was forged in 1932 when the armed forces took control of the government to suppress a massive peasant uprising. The insurrection, endorsed but by no means controlled by the Salvadorean Communist Party, was crushed at a cost of some 30,000 dead. The psychic scars left by this abortive revolution and its suppression disfigured the nation's political culture in ways that are still evident. For the oligarchy, the growth of even moderate opposition has always raised the specter of 1932. A strong current of belief persists among the oligarchs that the threat of revolution can only be effectively met as it was in the 1930s—by bloody suppression.

The military has shared the oligarchy's fear of revolution, though it has occasionally opted for reform rather than repression as a more reliable bulwark against the Left. The coup that has come to be known as the "revolution of 1948" brought to power a coalition of young military officers with a modernist vision. Motivated not only by the fear of radical revolt but also by their desire to see El Salvador develop economically, this modernizing military embarked upon a program of "controlled revolution": moderate reforms (none of which challenged the dominance of the oligarchy) blended with heavy doses of political repression for radical opponents. The oligarchy tolerated such reformism because it promised modernization without structural change, and because an authoritarian regime centered in the armed forces seemed to offer security against the Left.

This practical partnership between oligarchs and officers gave birth to an electoral system that was largely a charade. Moderate opponents could vent their views in periodic elections, but control of the government was reserved for the military's own political party, the Revolutionary Party of Democratic Unity (PRUD). Perpetual electoral victory for the PRUD was guaranteed by the military's power to count the ballots.

The developmentalist program of the military modernizers stimulated economic growth, but yielded no improvement in equity. With economic growth came demographic growth of the urban middle and working classes, both of which bridled at the military's monopoly on politics. At issue was whether the military and its oligarchic partners would allow the creation of a system of politics (i.e., an institutional process for reconciling the conflicting political demands of the nation's significant social groups). The oligarchs preferred the security of authoritarianism to the uncertainty of electoral competition.

The officers were less unanimous. In 1960, a rising tide of civil unrest disrupted the prevailing political consensus within the armed forces. Alarmed at the regime's unwillingness to open the political process and fearful that such rigidity could lead to revolution, progressive officers joined with civilian opposition leaders to depose the PRUD government. The new government promised to accelerate the pace of social reform, offering a program similar to what the Peruvian armed forces would propose eight years later. Such reforms were beyond the oligarchy's threshold of tolerance; it mobilized its conservative supporters within the armed forces, who toppled the new government by counter-coup after only three months.

The political system built after the counter-coup was a carbon copy of what had gone before. The PRUD was dissolved, but then resurrected as the Party of National Conciliation (PCN). Like its progenitor, the PCN was dedicated to modest reform and political liberalism within the confines of military rule. The PCN also reestablished the military's working partnership with the oligarchy; its program of social reform left unscathed the socioeconomic foundations of oligarchic power.

The deterioration of the Salvadorean economy in the wake of the 1969 war with Honduras set the stage for political turmoil in the 1970s. The proximate cause, however, was the same as it had been in 1960—the military's determination to maintain its monopoly on politics (by electoral fraud if necessary) rather than relinquish power to its civilian opponents. Despite its electoral facade, the Salvadorean polity in 1970 was no closer to having an open political process capable of producing the orderly resolution of political conflict than it had been a decade before.

By 1970, Christian Democrats (PDC) had become the principal focus of opposition. Indeed, the PDC's strength virtually preempted any growth on the far Left. In the late 1960s, when virtually every government in Latin America faced guerrilla challenges inspired by the Cuban revolution, in El Salvador there were none.

The opportune time for a "centrist solution" to El Salvador's socioeconomic ills came in 1972 when the Christian Democrats stood at the summit of their popular support. By all informed accounts, the PDC won the 1972 presidential election. The PCN was able to snatch victory from the jaws of electoral defeat only through blatant fraud and brutal suppression of the resulting protests. As if acting from the script written a decade earlier, the progressive wing of the armed forces joined with PDC leaders to attempt a coup. Unlike 1960, however, the attempt failed, leaving conservative officers in control of the military.

Even the pretense of political liberalism was jettisoned forthwith. The Christian Democrats became the principal target of government repression, which destroyed the party's effectiveness as an electoral opposition, and with it the viability of electoral opposition per se. Most of the PDC's leadership was driven into exile and most of its rank and file was driven to the Left. The PDC contested the presidency once more in 1977, but the result was a foregone conclusion.

The government's assault on the center also created the far Left. Three guerrilla organizations began operating during the 1970s and expanded as the center was demolished. The Popular Forces of Liberation (FPL) was founded in 1970 by radical university students and dissident Communist Party members. A year later, another group of dissident communists joined with radicals from the Christian Democrats to form the Revolutionary Army of the People (ERP), which split in 1975, leading to the creation of the Armed Forces of National Resistance (FARN).

The most impressive gains on the Left were made by the "popular organizations." Begun at mid-decade, these coalitions of peasant, worker, and student unions pressed demands for immediate social improvements by staging mass demonstrations and acts of civil disobedience. There are three major popular organizations: the Popular Revolutionary Bloc (BPR); the United Popular Action Front (FAPU); and the Popular Leagues of the 28th of February (LP-28), named for the day in 1977 when security forces killed over 100 demonstrators. Though their demands and tactics are similar, political differences among the popular organizations prevented them from mounting any joint actions until early 1980. Most of those differences centered upon the proper long-term strategy for bringing the Left to power, and also reflected rivalries among the armed groups with which the popular organizations are affiliated.

The growth of the Left terrified the oligarchy, which responded by financing death squads on the Right (e.g., the White Warriors' Union, the White Hand, the Falange, and others). Local political activists, including peasant leaders, trade unionists, and priests, were the principal targets of the death squads during the late 1970s. As in other nations, the paramilitary Right is widely suspected of having links to the government's security forces.

As the 1977 presidential election approached, the second reign of the military modernizers showed unmistakable signs of decay. The government's sporadic attempts to enact a modest agrarian reform law between 1973 and 1976 were blocked by the influence of the oligarchy and the Defense Minister, Humberto Romero. The moderate opposition, led by the Christian Democrats, was in retreat under the drumfire of repression, while both the armed and popular wings of the Left were gaining strength. The oligarchs, meanwhile, were funding their private paramilitary minions. In the face of this growing crisis, the PCN signaled its determination to hold fast rather than compromise by nominating the conservative General Romero for the presidency. He won, of course.

With Romero's election, the regime of the military modernizers became, in effect, a regime of military conservators. Despite popular demands for access to the political process, the authoritarian military regime refused to create a political order it could not control. By its refusal, it produced instead political disorder which no one could control. The rapid deterioration of El Salvador's moribund polity began in earnest after Romero's election.

As so often happens with regard to Latin America, the United States did not become very concerned about El Salvador until the crisis was well under way. A small nation of little strategic importance or economic interest, El Salvador had seldom attracted much attention in Washington. Bilateral relations were ordinarily governed by regional policies which the United States fashioned in response to exigencies elsewhere. The result has not always been wholly sensible. When counterinsurgency was thought to be an antidote to Cuban-style revolution, and the United States lavished security assistance on Latin America, El Salvador received some four million dollars worth between FY 1961 and FY 1970, even though it had no revolutionaries to speak of. It did, however, have a military government which inevitably perceived the flow of arms as an endorsement.

Military assistance to El Salvador was interrupted when Congress began introducing human rights concerns into the allocation of U.S. foreign assistance. In early 1977, El Salvador joined Guatemala, Brazil, and Argentina in rejecting further arms aid because critics in the United States found their human rights records dismal. Previously authorized aid continued to flow to El Salvador, but no new authorizations were made until 1979. Concomitantly, economic aid was cut by half, from approximately $20 million to $10 million.

El Salvador first attracted high-level attention in the Carter Administration in June 1977, when one of the right-wing death squads, the White Warriors' Union, accused the Salvadorean Catholic Church of promoting communism, and threatened to kill all the Jesuits in the country. Since several activist priests had already been assassinated, the threat was not taken to be an idle one. Under pressure from U.S. church groups and members of Congress, the Carter Administration launched an intensive campaign to convince General Romero that El Salvador's relations with the United States depended upon preventing the prospective massacre. To underscore its concern, the United States vetoed a $90 million Inter-American Development Bank loan to El Salvador.

The effort was an apparent success. The slaughter of the Jesuits never materialized (though half a dozen more priests were assassinated over the next two years); the activities of the death squads subsided temporarily (reinforcing suspicions that they were operating with official sanction); and the Romero government itself began to ease official repression. In the hope of reinforcing what it took to be liberalization, Washington granted approval for the loan in October.

Unfortunately, this change in policy, intended as an incentive, was interpreted as irresolution. Less than a month later, the government responded to the assassination of industrialist Raúl Molinas Canas by passing the draconian Law for the Defense and Guarantee of Public Order. The Public Order Law effectively made it illegal to oppose the government in any fashion whatsoever. It instituted Press censorship, banned public meetings, outlawed strikes, made it a crime to disseminate information that "tends to destroy the social order," and suspended normal judicial procedures for such offenses. Mere suspicion was specified as grounds for arrest. The day after this law's passage ended any pretense of democracy in El Salvador, U.S. Ambassador Frank J. Devine, speaking to the Salvadorean Chamber of Commerce, endorsed the right of governments to do whatever is necessary to maintain public order.

Far from restoring stability, the Public Order Law accelerated the spiral of political violence and institutional decay. The clandestine guerrilla organizations proved to be beyond the reach of the government's security apparatus or the paramilitary Right, so the brunt of the repression fell upon the more accessible moderates. The remnants of the PDC and the social democratic National Revolutionary Movement (MNR) were silenced, leaving only the courageous Archbishop Oscar Romero (no relation to the President) as a public spokesman for the moderate Left. Even the church was vilified by government propaganda, and the death squads resumed their assassination of priests.

The radical Left met the wave of official violence with a counterwave. The armed groups stepped up the bombings, assassinations of government officials, and kidnappings of businessmen, both foreign and domestic. The popular organizations began a campaign of occupying government offices and foreign embassies to demand the release of prisoners arrested under the Public Order Law.

Frustrated at its inability to control the growing popular opposition, the military government made one major attempt to demolish its largest foe, the Popular Revolutionary Bloc. Following a March 1978 street demonstration that ended in violence, the government unleashed the largest of the paramilitary rightist groups, ORDEN, on the peasants of San Pedro Perulapan, a stronghold of Bloc support.[1] In San Pedro, ORDEN conducted a reign of terror akin to that unleashed by Somoza's National Guard in 1975. The effect was also similar; it further radicalized the rural population, widened the gulf between the government and its moderate opponents, and attracted widespread international condemnation. In late 1978 and early 1979, a series of human rights reports from Amnesty International, the International Commission of Jurists, the Organization of American States, and the U.S. Department of State unanimously condemned the Romero government for its systematic torture, murder, and persecution of political dissidents.

When the mediation efforts in neighboring Nicaragua brought the political crisis there to a temporary stalemate in early 1979, the Carter Administration turned its crisis diplomacy to the burgeoning conflict in El Salvador. Abandoning its embarrassing silence on the effects of the Public Order Law, Washington began urging Romero to reduce the level of official violence. As a conciliatory gesture aimed more at Washington than at the opposition, Romero agreed to lift the law in late February. The effect was negligible; political violence from neither the government's security forces nor the paramilitary Right abated.

The fall of Somoza in Nicaragua in July conjured up images of Central American dominoes in Washington and prompted a major review of U.S. policy toward the region. Advocates divided roughly into two camps. Those seeking a restoration of military aid to El Salvador, Guatemala, and Honduras argued that the prospects for order would best be ensured by reinforcing the existing military regimes, even at the expense of human rights. The opposing view, which ultimately prevailed, held that the an-ciens régimes of Central America had become obsolete and could not be sustained in the long run. Rather than enlisting on the side of military dictatorships that faced eventual extinction, this view ran, the interests of the United States would be better served by policies aimed at managing the inevitable social and economic change. Implicitly, such management meant—as it had under the Alliance for Progress—a search for "openings to the center" and policies to promote the center while containing the Left.

Rent by escalating political violence, El Salvador moved quickly to the top of the policy agenda. The Carter Administration resolved not to repeat the mistakes it had made in Nicaragua, where it failed to break fully with Somoza and enlist wholeheartedly on the side of the moderate opposition until the eleventh hour—several hours too late. Washington pressured General Romero to move El Salvador's political conflicts back into the electoral arena where the Christian Democrats and the social-democratic MNR could retrieve the political initiative from the Left.

Romero responded with promises of reform, including a pledge that the 1980 congressional elections would be internationally supervised to en-sure fairness. But he was adamant in his refusal to reschedule the presiden-tial election, which was not due until 1982. Convinced that the tattered fabric of El Salvador's polity would not hold together until 1982, the United States was not satisfied. Neither was the opposition. Even the moderates refused to confer with the government on its promised reforms until the violence of the security forces was ended. Romero would not or could not end it.

By trying to accommodate the United States, Romero undercut his own support on the Right. As order unraveled, so did the partnership between the oligarchy and the armed forces. The government's obvious inability to contain the Left was, in effect, a failure to meet its part of the implicit political bargain struck between the oligarchy and the conservative PCN. Romero's willingness even to suggest a relaxation of repression while the Left was gaining ground signaled to the oligarchs that the government could no longer be trusted to provide for their security. Since the government was no longer reliable, the oligarchs took their defense into their own hands, and violence from the paramilitary Right escalated sharply. That the oligarchs still had allies within the military was confirmed by the fact that, despite Romero's promises, the behavior of the security forces did not change. By the fall of 1979, El Salvador was descending into chaos.

On October 15, 1979, the Romero government was ousted in a bloodless coup led by two young and apparently progressive colonels. Charging Romero with corruption, electoral fraud, and human rights violations, the colonels committed their new government to a thorough reform of the nation's "antiquated economic, social, and political structures." The oligarchic system, they charged, had not offered the people even "the minimal conditions necessary to survive as human beings."

The colonels moved quickly to establish a popular base by inviting the moderate opposition into the government. Three moderate civilians joined the colonels in a ruling junta, and the cabinet was drawn almost entirely from the centrist political parties. In a dramatic break with the past, the junta also called for support from the country's previously excluded militant Left, saying that the Left "must understand that the government is no longer their enemy." To gain such support, the junta promised an ambitious program of reforms drawn largely from the Common Platform, a list of demands issued in September by a coalition that included all the major centrist parties and one of the Left's popular organizations, the Popular Leagues. The junta pledged to end the repression, create a democratic political system, and institute a wide range of economic policies aimed at improving the plight of the poor. Most important, it promised agrarian reform.

The popular response to these proposals was mixed. Though the moderate opposition parties joined the new government immediately, Archbishop Oscar Romero was more cautious in his endorsement. Acknowledging the junta's good will, he warned that the nation's new rulers could rally popular support only by demonstrating that their "beautiful promises are not dead letters."

On the Left, reaction to the coup was even more equivocal. Two of the armed groups greeted the new government with calls for insurrection; they refused to believe that the military would or could break with the past and displace the oligarchy. By the end of the first week, however, the government's attempts to create an opening to the Left began to have an effect. Encouraged by the junta's support of the Common Platform and its promises to bring Leftists into the government, the Popular Leagues and the Revolutionary Army of the People gave the government conditional endorsement. Though they never offered explicit support, the leftist FAPU and FARN were also impressed by the government's apparent commitment to real change. Finally, in early November, the Popular Revolutionary Bloc and the Popular Forces of Liberation agreed to suspend their attacks on the government for thirty days to give it an opportunity to make good its promises.

The junta did not use the time well. The pledge to investigate human rights abuses led to no arrests; the pledge to reorganize the government's security apparatus led only to a cosmetic reshuffling of personnel; and the pledge to conduct an agrarian reform led nowhere. In fact, the government could not even rein in its own security forces. Though the colonels had condemned the Romero government's indiscriminate use of lethal force against civilians, the practices of the police and National Guard did not change noticeably after October.

As the weeks passed, it became clear that more than mere indecision lay behind the junta's failure to act. The issue of the "disappeared" was indicative of the new government's dilemma. Despite its initial promise to discover the whereabouts of some 300 political activists, two weeks after coming to power, the junta claimed that it could not find any of the missing. The junta dared not look too closely at the excesses of the Romero regime for fear of what it might find; senior police and military officials were almost certainly culpable in the disappearances. Such a discovery would have shattered the fragile unity of the armed forces—something the progressive officers refused to risk. The same predicament confronted the progressives at every turn because the conservatives objected to every major reform.

This political stalemate revealed in bold relief the historic dilemma of Salvadorean politics. In a closed political system that had never allowed significant civilian participation, public policy was the exclusive preserve of the armed forces. Reforms were inevitably constrained by the government's need to preserve at least a rough political consensus within the officers' corps. The oligarchy, of course, defended its interests through its links with the conservatives in the military. Bound together with their conservative compatriots by institutional loyalty, progressive officers could alter the status quo only in ways the conservatives were willing to tolerate—a tolerance ordinarily defined by the conservatives' fear of the Left. This, of course, was why three decades of military modernizers had failed to produce any significant change in El Salvador's outmoded social structure. It was also why the October junta failed. On every important issue, the progressives caved in to conservative resistance rather than risk a split in the armed forces.

The government's paralysis destroyed any chance it may have had to build a popular base on the Left or the Center-Left. By December, all three of the popular organizations and their armed wings had gone back on the offensive, and even the moderates within the government had become deeply discouraged. In a final effort to break the deadlock in the armed forces, two of the junta's three civilian members issued an ultimatum: either Defense Minister José Guillermo García (the leading conservative) would resign or they would. Forced to choose openly between their commitment to change and their loyalty to the armed forces, the progressive officers chose loyalty. Backed by a majority of senior officers and local garrison commanders, García stood fast.

On January 3, less than three months after its birth, the Center-Left government collapsed when two of the junta's three civilian members resigned along with the entire cabinet (except for García, of course). In presenting their resignations, the civilians blamed conservative resistance for the government's impotence and its inability to build a popular base of support. The most dramatic demonstration of disillusionment with the junta and the possibility of peaceful change came at a press conference called by the former Education Minister, Salvador Samayoa. Samayoa explained that he had resigned to "fight for total liberation." He then picked up an AK-47 machine gun and walked out of the room, escorted by two masked gunmen.

Despite the government's failure to win the trust of the Left or to retain the cooperation of the Center-Left, the colonels pressed onward. Within a week, the Christian Democrats rejoined the government, justifying their decision on the grounds that there was no other alternative to civil war. A new junta was formed and a new round of reform proposals was issued, including promises to nationalize the banks and expropriate the large landed estates.

Superficially, the new junta seemed hardly distinguishable from its predecessor; in Washington, it has been portrayed as a centrist government of progressive officers and moderate civilians committed to significant social change. Indeed, the January junta even carried out (albeit reluctantly and under intense U.S. pressure) some of the promises the October junta left unfulfilled. Yet the new government's strategy for resolving the current political crisis was profoundly different. The October junta sought to combine structural change with a political opening to the Left, which was guardedly willing to let the government prove its sincerity. The junta failed when it was unable to overcome the conservative officers' resistance to reform. The new junta's strategy was to assuage the Right's fear of reform by combining it with repression of the Left. The goal of building a Center-Left social base for the government was abandoned. Instead, the government sought to consolidate, as best it could, a political consensus for reform within the armed forces—even if the means of doing so left it utterly isolated from the civilian populace. In this sense, the new government in El Salvador was no different from the military modernizers of the past. The reforms it advocated may have been more extensive, but its approach to politics was a familiar one—an authoritarian regime centered in the armed forces and buttressed by repression of those who dared to challenge the military's hegemony.

Even the effectiveness of the junta's reform program was problematic. Though the junta nationalized the banks and expropriated several hundred of the largest private estates, its reforms were accompanied by a state of siege and wave of repression as intense as any undertaken by the Romero regime. In the countryside, conservatives in the security forces used the repression to obviate the agrarian reform and to terrorize the peasantry. In the cities, the security forces used the state of siege to wage war against the opposition. In the first few months of 1980, the number of people killed in political violence was nearly a thousand, the vast majority of whom were killed either by the police or the paramilitary Right.

The strategy of reform with repression destroyed what little chance the January junta might have had to build a popular base of support. The reforms alienated the Right, and the repression alienated everyone else. The PDC, a partner in the government, was deeply divided over the junta's strategy for governing. In March, several leading Christian Democrats, including junta member Héctor Dada, resigned from the government on the grounds that reform and repression were mutually exclusive. Before he was assassinated on March 24, even Archbishop Romero had begun to suggest that insurrection against the repressive regime was justified.

The conservatives in the armed forces may have been momentarily won over to the cause of reform, but the oligarchy was not. The oligarchs and their supporters on the far Right denounced the government as Marxist, and the death squads launched a new campaign of political assassination. Their targets were not only members of the Left, but also leaders of the moderate opposition and of the government itself.

On the Left, the climate of repression forged unprecedented unity. In January, all the major popular organizations created the Revolutionary Coordinator of the Masses to plan joint strategy, and in March, the political parties and trade unions of the Center-Left formed a coalition of their own, the Democratic Front. In April, the Left and Center-Left came together in a grand coalition when the Revolutionary Coordinator joined the Democratic Front to produce the Revolutionary Democratic Front (FDR). Shortly thereafter, the FDR forged an alliance with the armed groups, who had joined together in the Farabundo Martí Front for National Liberation (FMLN), thereby forming the FDR-FMLN.

The strategy of reform with repression left the January junta desperately isolated and precariously dependent upon the support of the United

States. When rightists in the armed forces sought to depose the government in late February and again in May, there was no significant social or political group in El Salvador which the government could rally to its defense. Only the United States preserved it.

After January 1980, the moderation of the Salvadoran government was more chimerical than real. The key difference between the junta formed in January and its predecessor lay in its strategy for resolving the nation's political crisis. While the October junta sought to create a political opening to the Left, the January government sought to defeat the Left militarily. At the insistence of the United States, the government grudgingly undertook some social reforms, the most touted of which was the agrarian program. But this strategy of "reform with repression," as Archbishop Oscar Romero characterized it before he was assassinated by the far Right, proved to be considerably more repressive than reformist.

Under the stewardship of Ambassador Robert White, the United States pursued four interrelated objectives during 1980: (1) to pressure the government into implementing social reforms designed to undercut the Left's popular support; (2) to urge the government to reduce the level of official terrorism by reigning in its own security forces, even if that required the removal of some rightist officers; (3) to protect the government from a coup by the extreme Right; and (4) to entice the moderate Left away from its alliance with the guerrillas, thus opening the way for a negotiated settlement that would leave the radicals isolated on the political periphery. It was White's judgment that the government was not under any immediate danger of military defeat by the guerrillas, and so he opposed any significant increase in U.S. military aid.

As the Carter Administration came to a close, it was clear that this reformist strategy had failed. The agrarian program, the cornerstone of an otherwise modest package of reforms, was at a standstill. The level of official violence had risen dramatically rather than subsiding, and there was no evidence whatsoever that the government was making a very serious effort to curtail it or to bring its perpetrators to justice. The extreme Right had not overthrown the government, but the government had moved so far to the right that its extremist opponents were quiescent.

The pivotal issue was whether the Christian Democratic politicians and the progressive military officers could win control of the armed forces away from the Right. Such control would have allowed the moderates to remove extremist officers from command positions, punish those guilty of political murder, crack down on the death squads, and thereby curb the repression which took the lives of some 10,000 people, 80 percent of them unarmed civilians killed by the security forces.[2]

Not only were the moderates unable to restrain the security forces, they were unable even to maintain the little influence they had. The right-wing coup that Robert White labored so diligently to prevent occurred slowly, by degrees, not in the streets, but in the high councils of the officers corps. As the rightist officers lost patience with reform, they slipped quietly into agreement with their more extreme compatriots, becoming convinced that the only way to meet the challenge of the Left was with violence—another *matanza* if that was what it took.

During 1980, the same rightist officers who blocked the reform program of the October 15 government consolidated their hold on power by reducing the Christian Democrats and the progressive officers to impotence. The steady stream of resignations by Christian Democrats over the year stood as testimony of the rightist character of the regime. Almost without exception, each letter of resignation told the same story—frustration with the intransigence of the Right and the inability of the moderates to circumvent them.

The progressive officers fared worse than the Christian Democrats, perhaps because they represented a more serious rival to the Right. In midsummer, the Right began a campaign to systematically strip the progressives of their command positions, demoting them or reassigning them to diplomatic posts. Shortly thereafter, several of the most prominent progressives were assassinated by death squads. In November, shortly after a failed assassination attempt against him, the leading progressive, Adolfo Majano, was removed from the five-member junta by a vote of the officers corps. Majano was later arrested and sent into exile. The progressive faction of the corps, which was powerful enough in 1979 to overthrow the Romero government, ceased to be a significant political force.

Without allies in the military, the Christian Democrats served at the pleasure of the rightist officers. The appointment in November of Christian Democratic leader José Napoleón Duarte as president of the junta did not constitute a significant realignment of political forces. The leadership shuffle that placed Duarte in the presidency left the senior military command basically intact, which prompted one diplomat to describe Duarte as an "adornment."[3]

Duarte may have had his own political agenda, but he did not have the political power to carry it out. Like the agrarian reform, the restructuring of government came at the insistence of the United States. The Carter Administration needed it to preserve the fading centrist image of its client in the wake of the murders of the four North American religious women, and the Salvadoran officers agreed to it in order to mollify the State Department. But the reorganization did not alter the structure of power in El Salvador. The government remained a military regime with a civilian facade.

Nothing demonstrated this more clearly than the practices of the government itself. The violence of the security forces accelerated in 1980.

Despite the pleas of the Christian Democrats, the reign of official terror was much worse than under the openly reactionary government of General Humberto Romero. Not one person was arrested for the thousands of political murders of Salvadorans for which the extreme Right took "credit" in 1980.[4] Officers on the extreme Right who were caught plotting to overthrow the government were not punished. Major Roberto D'Aubuissón, who led a coup attempt in May, was placed under arrest by Majano, then released on a vote from the senior commanders of the armed forces. The Vice Minister of Defense, Nicolás Carranza, was also implicated in the plot, but was not removed from his post until November 1980.

El Salvador as Test Case

Central America became the first test of Reagan's new foreign policy. The Salvadoran guerrillas, anticipating that Reagan would seek massive increases in military aid for the regime in San Salvador, launched a "final offensive" on the eve of Reagan's inauguration, hoping to present the new president with a fait accompli. Though the offensive failed, Reagan entered the Oval Office with Central America dominating the headlines.

Secretary of State Alexander Haig, anxious to establish himself as the "vicar" of foreign policy, announced that El Salvador would be the administration's "test case" in the struggle against international communism. This translated into a policy providing massive military assistance to the Salvadoran armed forces so they could defeat the guerrillas of the FDR-FMLN on the battlefield rather than having to accept a negotiated settlement that would give the opposition a share of political power.

Between 1980 and 1987, U.S. military assistance to El Salvador totaled three quarters of a billion dollars, rising frum $10 million in 1980 to a peak of over $180 million in 1984. Over 100 U.S. military advisors were in El Salvador coordinating every phase of the war, from strategic planning at General Staff headquarters to tactical advice for battalions in combat. U.S. military units based in Honduras flew intelligence-gathering missions over the Salvadoran countryside, and CIA operatives led Salvadoran troops on long-range reconnaissance patrols into guerrilla-held territory.

In its efforts to win a military victory, the Reagan Administration confronted not only the problem of how to strengthen the Salvadoran armed forces, but also how to consolidate a regime that was badly divided between the far Right and the Center-Right. Moreover, the administration also had to defuse domestic congressional and public resistance to the escalating U.S. military involvement.

Strengthening the armed forces was, from the outset, the first priority; when it came into conflict with the other objectives, it invariably prevailed.

Over the years, the Pentagon's assessment of what would be required to win the war expanded exponentially, yet the administration was always prepared to provide whatever resources the Pentagon requested.

The State Department, more than any other agency, saw political consolidation of the regime as essential to long-term stability. When Reagan came to office, the regime in San Salvador was exceptionally weak because it was trying to battle both the Left and the far Right. Reagan sought to strengthen it by reincorporating the far Right. To achieve this, the United States had to deemphasize reforms and human rights, shift its own political investment from the Christian Democrats to the armed forces, and pressure the Christian Democrats to allow greater rightist participation in the government.

This had to be accomplished, however, without producing a regime so dominated by the Right that the Christian Democrats would be driven out of it, thereby alienating the U.S. Congress. In effect, Reagan's strategy was to modernize the Salvadoran oligarchy, clean up its image, and give it back a share of power. Assistant Secretary of State Thomas O. Enders, who was the principal architect of policy toward Central America until 1983, sought to consolidate the regime around a Center-Right coalition within which the balance of power would be determined by elections. Washington would use its influence with the military to effect limited reforms sufficient to assure continued congressional funding for administration policy.

These efforts would buy time for large-scale U.S. military aid to give the Salvadoran army the upper hand on the battlefield, eventually limiting the guerrillas to isolated pockets of resistance in depopulated northern provinces. Seeing the hopelessness of the war, the Center-Left politicians of the FDR might be enticed to break with the "Marxist-Leninists" in the FMLN and join an electoral process controlled by the government. The most recalcitrant fighters would remain in the hills, but without domestic or international legitimacy, they could eventually be eradicated. At the State Department, this scenario was dubbed the "Venezuelan solution" because of its superficial similarity to the way in which the insurgency there was defeated in the 1960s.

The 1982 Salvadoran elections were intended to strengthen the position of civilian politicians, particularly the Christian Democrats, relative to the armed forces, thereby increasing the legitimacy of the Salvadoran regime both at home and abroad. In particular, the Reagan Administration hoped the election would bolster support for its policy in congress.

The unexpected electoral victory of the extreme Right coalition led by Roberto D'Aubuissón's ARENA party threatened to produce a government headed by D'Aubuissón and excluding the Christian Democrats, who he referred to as "the right wing of the communist party." Because such a regime would have been unacceptable to the U.S. Congress, the Reagan administration was compelled to intercede. Washington appealed to the armed forces, which were totally dependent on U.S. military aid to fight the war. The military responded by imposing Alvaro Magana, an apolitical banker, as provisional president. They also insisted that the Christian Democrats remain in the government, and that the agrarian reform be retained.

In this way, the extreme Right was prevented from capturing control of the regime, but the dominant political role of the armed forces was reinforced rather than diminished. The resulting Government of National Unity was hardly unified. Because it included parties with diametrically opposed policies—ARENA and the Christian Democrats (PDC)—it was paralyzed from the moment of its creation. President Magana had no political base of his own, serving at the de jure pleasure of the Constituent Assembly and the de facto pleasure of the armed forces. With ARENA members in charge of the agricultural ministries, the agrarian reform was strangled administratively, even though the military blocked the effort of the rightist majority in the Constituent Assembly to repeal it.

Deprived of electoral victory by the military, the extreme Right moved to strengthen its position in the officers corps. D'Aubuissón's immediate target was Defense Minister José Guillermo García, who was a valuable asset for the United States because he was willing to cooperate (however reluctantly) with Washington's political strategy for El Salvador. He allowed the agrarian reform to go forward in 1980, he prevented the Constituent Assembly from electing D'Aubuissón president in 1982, he blocked the repeal of the agrarian reform, and he pressed for the indictment of military personnel guilty of killing the U.S. churchwomen in 1980 and the U.S. labor advisors in 1981. By 1982, García had become vulnerable within the officers corps precisely because he was so willing to do the bidding of the U.S. Embassy, particularly regarding the prosecution of fellow officers.

This vulnerability was exacerbated by the army's inability under García's leadership to contain the insurgency. From 1981 to 1983, the FMLN held the military initiative, determining the pace of the war, when and where battles would be fought, and how large they would be. Each year, the FMLN's offensives grew larger and more successful, while the government searched in vain for a formula to halt the guerrillas' advance.

The Salvadoran army generally ignored the advice proffered by U.S. military advisors, conducting large sweeps rather than the small unit operations. It did this because its regional commanders were incompetent and corrupt. They were appointed to their posts because of their loyalty to Minister of Defense García, rather than their skill. They generally had no combat experience and no desire to risk getting any. Their jobs were sinecures, and they could reap more profit in graft from large maneuvers than from small patrols.

The Pentagon tried to get García to replace these crooks with officers willing to engage the FMLN in combat, but he would not. The regional commanders were García's base of political support within the military— critical allies in García's struggle with extreme rightist officers who supported D'Aubuissón.

In early 1983, the extreme Right assembled a broad coalition within the officers corps to force García's ouster. A similar move had failed the previous fall because García enjoyed the support of the U.S. Embassy. But by January, the deteriorating military situation had become the priority of U.S. policy makers, and García's refusal to replace provincial commanders of proven incompetence led Washington to seek his removal as well. After a minor mutiny by provincial commander Sigifredo Ochoa and Air Force Commander Juan Rafael Bustillo, García resigned.

The political upheavals within the armed forces damaged its ability to wage the war. With the military's attention diverted by internecine struggles, it failed to respond effectively to guerrilla offensives in October 1982 and January 1983. The guerrillas were able to consolidate their control over large portions of the countryside, and army morale plummeted.

With García gone, the army launched a new counterinsurgency strategy heralded as the key to winning the war. The National Plan, modeled on the CORDS program from Vietnam, was begun in San Vicente and Usulután departments in early 1983. Large numbers of elite, U.S.-trained troops from the "rapid response" battalions would be concentrated in the department to drive out the FMLN. Then the army would organize and arm local residents in a militia that would prevent the FMLN from returning. The elite troops would move on to another department, and the process would be repeated until the entire country had been pacified.

In San Vicente, the FMLN simply withdrew in the face of the army's advance, and stepped up operations in other departments which were lightly defended. Suspicious of the loyalty of local residents, the army was unwilling to distribute arms to a militia for fear the people would join the guerrillas. When the elite battalions moved on to Usulután, they left the department in the hands of the static defense forces that had been there all along. The FMLN moved back in, and the situation returned to the status quo ante. In Usulután, the FMLN effectively resisted the army's offensive, and after a few months, the effort to pacify the department was abandoned.

As El Salvador moved toward presidential elections in 1984, the officers corps was divided into roughly three political factions. Between a quarter and a third of the officers identified with the extreme Right. Like their civilian allies, the oligarchs, they were strong rightist nationalists, unhappy with the United States for its emphasis on human rights, agrarian reform, and the need to keep the PDC in the government. This group wanted U.S. military aid with no strings, so they could use it to exterminate the Left once and for all. If U.S. aid was available only with onerous conditions, they preferred not to have it. They looked to the pacification strategy used in Guatemala as a model—massive violence against all "subversives" and their potential supporters.

A second faction was composed of younger officers trained by the United States who held field commands and carried the brunt of the war. They were ideologically close to the extreme Right, but regarded themselves as more professional. They called themselves "Praetorians." The Praetorians were distinguished from the far Right by their combat skills (they had contempt for rightist officers in the security forces who only shot at people who could not shoot back), their lack of clear established ties to the oligarchy, and their recognition that U.S. military aid was indispensable. Consequently, they were more willing to accept a working partnership with the U.S. Embassy, even if that meant some policy concessions to ease U.S. sensibilities.

A third faction, the least cohesive of the three, was composed of the remnants of factions defeated in the internal political struggles of the past—a few remaining reformist officers once associated with Majano, some pro-PDC officers associated with Colonel Abdul Gutiérrez, who was defeated by García in 1982, and the García faction itself, defeated by the alliance between the rightists and the Praetorians in 1983.

In the spring of 1984, Christian Democratic candidate José Napoleón Duarte was elected President of El Salvador (with some help from the Central Intelligence Agency) on a campaign platform promising social and economic reform, and a negotiated end to the war. In November, Duarte proposed a "dialogue" with the FDR-FMLN—an initiative that was controversial both within El Salvador and abroad. Neither the armed forces nor the United States was particularly happy with the proposal. Two meetings between Duarte and representatives of the FDR-FMLN were held inside El Salvador in subsequent months, at La Palma and Ayagualo. No specific accords were reached at these meetings, however, and no date was set for a third conference.[5]

The Salvadoran armed forces were divided over the wisdom of the dialogue. Their acquiescence was a necessary condition for the talks to go forward, but those within the military who favored negotiations (mostly the Praetorians around Chief of Staff Adolfo Blandón) faced stiff resistance from the Right (led by Air Force Commander Bustillo). Just prior to Duarte's second meeting with the opposition, there were reports of an abortive coup d'etat. It was averted at the last moment by the U.S. Ambassador's warning that a coup would mean the end of U.S. aid, and by

Duarte's pledge to make no concessions in his upcoming meeting with the FDR-FMLN leaders. Two years later, the army aborted a third dialogue session in the town of Sesori by occupying the area with troops shortly before the meeting was scheduled to begin.

The attitude of the United States toward the dialogue was also equivocal. While Washington could not publicly oppose a peace initiative, it worried that negotiations would legitimize the opposition. The administration's displeasure with Duarte led it to favor a coalition of rightist parties in the 1985 legislative elections rather than Duarte's Christian Democrats, on the theory that continued rightist control of the assembly would hold Duarte in check. The PDC won the elections nevertheless, but its victory did not resolve the central problems of the economy, the war, and the political predominance of the armed forces.

The one major success that the Salvadoran government could claim was in the human rights field, where the number of murders by rightist death squads declined significantly in 1984 and 1985, reducing the most gruesome and visible stain on the regime's human rights record. A few months before the 1984 Salvadoran presidential election, Vice President George Bush traveled to El Salvador to warn the armed forces that significant increases in U.S. aid depended upon immediate action to reduce the murderous activity of the paramilitary Right. The army, facing a difficult situation on the battlefield, took the threat seriously and moved to curtail the death squads. No one was tried or arrested for politically motivated murder, but certain rightist officers were transferred and the number of killings gradually subsided.

The reduction of death squad activity led to a revival of dissident politics. As Duarte's campaign promises were unfulfilled and the economy continued to deteriorate, urban political activity began to reemerge from the quiescence of the early 1980s. That quiescence had been due primarily to the physical elimination of thousands of urban activists by the death squads and the government's security forces in the years between 1980 and 1983, when some 50,000 noncombatant civilians were killed. There was little Duarte could do to calm the new urban movement; he had neither the resources nor the power to meet its demands for reform and dialogue, and he could countenance its repression only at the risk of sacrificing his own domestic political base and his international reputation.

The military situation was hardly more stable. A sharp increase in U.S. military aid followed Duarte's election in 1984, allowing the army to expand from its 1980 size of 15,000 to almost 60,000 by 1987. Much of the U.S. aid went to pay for aircraft and helicopters to give the armed forces greater firepower and mobility.

Yet the army's greatest success was not at engaging the guerrillas, but at depopulating those areas of the countryside under guerrilla control. As in

Guatemala, depopulation was accomplished by a combination of air attacks and infantry sweeps. Although this forced depopulation damaged the logistical base of the guerrillas, it also created an ever-expanding dependent population of internal refugees living at government expense— an added strain on El Salvador's already moribund economy.

The FMLN was forced to alter its military strategy by the growing air power and mobility of the army. Rather than concentrating their forces for major engagements, the guerrillas dispersed into small units to fight a "war of attrition." The success of the guerrillas' small unit tactics was difficult to assess, but they continued to inflict significant numbers of casualties on the army. They also retained the capacity to launch major operations, as demonstrated by the 1984 assault on Cerrón Grande dam, the 1985 attack on the La Unión infantry school, the 1986 attack on the garrison at San Miguel, and the 1987 destruction of the counterinsurgency base at El Paraíso. But such dramatic engagements were the exception rather than the rule. The FMLN, which had clearly held the initiative in the war through 1983, was at best fighting the army to stalemate in 1987.

There is no doubt that greater political space existed in El Salvador in 1987 compared to the early 1980s. The decrease in death squad activity was the key factor in providing expanded opportunities for political activity. Dissidence was no longer its own death warrant. But despite the revival of urban political action, and despite the regular holding of elections, the Salvadoran armed forces continued to be the ultimate political authority. Civilian politicians could make no fundamental decisions without military approval, and the officers remained the final arbiters of political conflict.

Civilians could hold office and engage in political activity because the military allowed them this latitude. Some officers accepted the new civilian role because they believed it was a necessary change, and that repression of the sort that characterized the early 1980s played into the hands of the FDR-FMLN. Other officers accepted the civilians because continued U.S. military assistance was tied directly to continued de jure civilian rule, and U.S. aid was indispensable to the war effort.

Ironically, the Christian Democrats were allowed to share power with the army because of the FDR-FMLN. Were it not for the insurgency, it is doubtful that the officers corps, now dominated almost entirely by rightists of one stripe or another, would have tolerated civilian authority. In order to defeat the guerrillas, the army collaborated with the Christian Democrats, but it would not give them the power to actually resolve the central dilemmas of the Salvadoran crisis: the continued economic dominance of the oligarchy and the war.

The FDR-FMLN seemed to have lost some of the political support it commanded in the late 1970s before its urban infrastructure was decimated by the death squads, and it lost the military initiative that it held in the early 1980s. Nevertheless, it continued to hold the loyalty of a significant portion of the populace and to fight the armed forces to a stalemate. In 1987, just as in 1980, the FDR-FMLN was a veto group on the Salvadoran political scene. No government could hope to reestablish order and revive the economy without coming to terms with it. Eight years of large-scale military aid from the United States had not altered this basic fact of Salvadoran political life. The only alternative to a protracted war, which would continue to bleed the economy and unravel the social fabric, is a negotiated peace.

Reprinted and edited from *Foreign Affairs* 58 (Summer 1980), pp. 1084–1103. Updated for this volume by Professor LeoGrande.

Notes

1. ORDEN (short for the Democratic Nationalist Organization) was created in 1968 as a civilian auxiliary to government security forces in the countryside, and grew quickly to a membership of between 50,000 to 100,000.

2. Legal Department of the Archdiocese of San Salvador, *Repression Carried out by the National Army . . . the Military Corps of National Security . . . and Paramilitary Organizations*, 4 vols. (San Salvador, November 1980).

3. Raymond Bonner, *Weakness and Deceit: U.S. Policy and El Salvador* (New York: New York Times Book Co., 1984), p. 220.

4. Two Salvadoran enlisted men were arrested for the killings of the two U.S. labor advisors and Rodolfo Viera, and five enlisted members of the National Guard were eventually convicted of killing the U.S. churchwomen.

5. For a discussion of the negotiations and the prospects for peace, see Terry Lynn Karl, "After La Palma," *World Policy Journal* 2, no. 2 (Spring 1985), pp. 305–30.

George Black

Military Rule in Guatemala

Three generals ruled Guatemala during the 1970s: Carlos Arana Osorio (1970–74), Kjell Laugerud García (1974–78), and Romeo Lucas García (1978–82). Arana, they say, was the cunning old fox, Laugerud the insipid reformer, Lucas the psychotic tyrant. But these epithets, reducing waves of terror and intervals of reform to a leader's whims, mask the logic and continuity of the military regimes. After twelve years of their rule, a deep political crisis engulfed Guatemala's ruling class.

Capitalist modernization in the 1960s had segmented the bourgeoisie into agrarian, industrial, financial, and commercial fractions, the rhythm of their formation dictated above by the needs of transnational capital. Conflicts between the MLN and the newer, more dynamic groups were often rancorous. But otherwise, cotton growers and bankers, traders and cattle ranchers, lived in relative harmony until the mid-1970s—as long, that is, as the economic boom lasted.

More important than the internecine disputes of the rich was the changing relationship between the armed forces and the bourgeoisie as a whole. Starting with Arana, the military developed its own economic interests. Brought into government initially as coercive protector of the established order, its senior officers used state power as a launching pad into agroexporting, industry, finance, and real estate. In the process, they became Guatemala's strongest political force. Internal cohesion promoted loyalty to the military caste and squashed any tendency within the ranks toward Peruvian-style reformism.

Military rule neutralized still further the ineffectual parties, and the armed forces filled the vacuum with their own quasi-party structures. A clique of high-ranking officers functioned as a central committee in all but name. The chief of staff held veto power over cabinet appointments.

Though the armed forces encroached on many key areas of the economy and the state through Mafia-like methods, the bourgeoisie was not unhappy with the alliance. The military's extreme laissez-faire approach to economic management, sustained growth rates, and a denial of political reforms provided a large enough pie for most of the bourgeoisie, even if the military's slice grew dramatically. With blind complacency, the ruling class believed that its economic growth model was eternal. If the political system remained unchanged, the Garden of Eden would continue to bring forth its fruits in abundance.

Like the Garden of Eden, this was ultimately a fantasy world. The fires of class conflict were stoked by suffocating repression and the refusal to open up the political system. Rapid capitalist development brought profound changes in class structure, and agroexporting expansion fueled rural inequalities. Violence, escalating into naked terror during the periods 1966–68, 1970–73, and 1978–82, proved the only means of defending the status quo.

Increasingly, that terror hit the center of the political spectrum. Christian Democrats and social democrats were fair game for the death squads if they threatened to become more than an ineffectual adornment to the military version of pluralism. The fast-growing middle class—never allowed more than crumbs from the rich men's table—stood alienated from the military regime.

Pacification and Growth

Widespread distaste for the brutality of his counterinsurgency campaign of 1966–68 had put Arana in mothballs for a year as ambassador to Nicaragua. But after cementing strong ties to Nicaraguan dictator Anastasio Somoza, he was recalled to be the military's presidential candidate in the 1970 elections. Washington duly signaled its pleasure at Arana's election by dispatching $32.2 million in economic aid during 1972, the second highest annual figure ever to Guatemala.

Defeat of the guerrillas had done nothing to mitigate social tensions, and the bourgeoisie made it clear to Arana that pacification was top on their agenda. So did the U.S. corporations which had invested in Guatemala over the previous decade. With over $200 million in direct investments, the U.S. transnationals far outweighed national industrial capital—most industries employing more than fifty workers were foreign-owned.

By the time of Arana's inauguration, winds of change were blowing through the economy. The limited import-substitution industry of the common market period was grinding to a halt, and after the 1969 Honduras–El Salvador war, regional trade was in disarray. Richard Nixon's arrival to the White House in January 1969, backed by Cuban exile and Sunbelt investors, paved the way for their invasion of Central America. Their instincts were well-suited to rapid-profit speculation in tourism, real estate, and new forms of agribusiness export (fruit, flowers, vegetables, and, later, cardamon).

State power gave Arana—never the most fastidious of operators—a unique platform. Partnership with foreign capital, always attractive, became overtly criminal. Corruption was the norm in government. The 1973 budget granted Arana $12,000 a month in presidential "expenses" and allocated him $1.6 million more a year in confidential discretionary funds.

Though graft was nothing new, Arana raised it to new heights. What *was* qualitatively different was the systematic use of the state apparatus for the enrichment of the bloc in power—senior military officers and their closest civilian and bureaucratic allies.

Arana's abrasive style did not endear him to economic competitors, but Guatemala's first Five Year Development Plan (1971–75) held out hopes for generating enough wealth to go around. Arana's authoritarian design to modernize the economy argued that not even the solid growth rates of the 1960s were adequate. A booming economy should aim for sustained annual growth rates of 7.8% through the 1970s.

The New Infrastructure

To provide energy and communications for the large, foreign-based corporations, and to open up the virgin farmlands of the north, large-scale infrastructural projects got underway by 1974. The second Development Plan (1976–79) gave even greater emphasis to such projects under Laugerud's direction. Three hydroelectric plants alone—Chixoy and Chulac in the highlands and Aguacapa on the south coast—cost well over $1 billion. Add to this a 1.2-billion-barrel-per-day oil pipeline from the Mexican border to the Caribbean, a small oil refinery in Baja Verapaz, a new Pacific port complex at San José, and a $1 billion national highway system, and the concept was awesome.

Chixoy was the pearl of the program. After an initial injection of $7.8 million from the Central American Economic Integration Bank in November 1974, international cash flowed into a project whose 300,000 kw generating capacity was the largest in the region. The World Bank supplied $145 million in 1975 and the Inter-American Development Bank $105 million in 1976—that bank's largest-ever single loan. U.S. representatives eagerly argued the case for both loans. . . .

As well as infrastructure, the transnational corporations gained financial benefits. Legislation put through in 1975 gave them a 100% tax exemption on profits for five years, and a one-year exemption from import taxes on machinery, plant, fuel, and spare parts.

By the end of the 1970s, 193 U.S. companies had taken advantage of the "favorable investment climate," 52 of them in agribusiness. Direct investment amounted to $260 million, the largest figure in Central America, and

33 of the world's top 100 firms had established local operations. This was in striking contrast to El Salvador, where only 6 are present.

The Army's Political Model

While Arana kept his bargain with foreign capital, he redrew the rules of the political game at home. Bodies began to appear along roadsides in a new wave of terror. In January 1971 alone, 483 people disappeared: not only nameless peasants and workers, to be hastily buried in graves marked XX, but even national figures—intellectuals, trade union officials, moderate party leaders—who had agreed to the military's political rule book. The gunning down in 1971 of Adolfo Mijango López, wheelchair-bound leader of the social democratic Revolutionary Democratic Union (URD), set the tone. Revolutionary opposition was clearly unacceptable, but the political process would now exclude anyone whose views were left of what the armed forces deemed the center.

The military took full control of the electoral machinery, narrowing down the spectrum of "tolerable" opponents. And by opening new agencies like the Army Bank to rationalize its economic holdings, the military showed that its ascent to riches under Arana was no short-term whim. Instead, it served notice that it intended to remain in power, shaping a system under which its economic and political status could never be challenged.

Down the Slippery Slope

No matter how disdainful of public opinion, any ruling group has to find ways of legitimizing its power. The creeping political crisis of the Guatemalan bourgeoisie in the 1970s lies in its failure to build and hold together a viable social base.

Arana, Laugerud, and Lucas each took office at the head of a differing right-wing coalition. Each promised change, Arana offering "Bread and Peace"; Laugerud, "gradual civic reform"; Lucas depicting himself as "the Center-Left Soldier." None could deliver. The ritual of elections, which only the Right could contest and only the Army could win, degenerated into farce. Each new president burned his bridges to left, right, and center. The military continued to use a list of 72,000 proscribed opponents, drawn up in 1954, adding new names constantly.

General Kjell Laugerud García, a career officer of Norwegian extraction, took office in 1974. Arana had promised that he would use "all the might that goes with holding power" to ensure the election of his hand-picked successor. The previous year had brought an upsurge of working class mobilization throughout Central America, and strikes in Guatemala by electricity, railroad, and communications workers, teachers and students. The military high command was united in its belief that "the Army is the only force capable, morally and materially, of governing Guatemala."

By election time the military was sure that the Arana bloodbath had done its job. The economy was booming; the Army not only had ascended to state power, but had become the dominant economic fraction of the ruling class. The military puppet masters could now afford the illusion of electoral pluralism, knowing that they pulled the strings of centrist and reformist participation. However, the rules were clear: A civilian candidate would not be permitted to win.

Two parties dropped their original civilian nominees in favor of military officers. Against Laugerud's civilian-military coalition, the Revolutionary Party fielded Colonel Ernesto Paiz Novales, and a coalition of Christian and social democrats backed former Chief of Staff General Efraín Ríos Montt.

To Arana's horror, Ríos Montt took 45 percent of the vote, clearly unacceptable. An Army recount showed Laugerud with a healthy 5.5 percent winning margin. General Ríos Montt, though raging at "a regime of absolute illegality," was outmanned and outgunned. As a military man, he understood military realities. After a closed-door meeting with the incoming president—during which money allegedly changed hands—he accepted diplomatic exile in Madrid.

Secure in its fraudulent victory, the Army shored up its political defenses. Since 1970, Mario Sandoval Alarcón's MLN had been its main electoral ally. As president of Congress under Arana, Sandoval had fortified his position, channeling state funds to his paramilitary supporters. But tha Army felt increasingly unhappy with the marriage. Economically, the rural oligarchy had been eclipsed by the modernizers; politically, the MLN's warrior-monk image was a liability. By 1974, Arana had broken much of the MLN's free-lance terror machine. Within the military, Laugerud chiseled away at MLN support in the officer corps.

Nonetheless, the fascists' organized power base was an undeniable asset, and Laugerud selected Sandoval as his vice president. In no time, the combative MLN leader was denouncing his boss because of a modest rural cooperative program designed to win peasant support. Anti-communist bonds notwithstanding, Laugerud judged that new political alliances would be more expedient. The military's Democratic Institutional Party (PID) made overtures to the emasculated Revolutionary Party (PR) and the right wing of the Christian Democrats. The MLN's marginalization from affairs of state finally provoked a split in the party in 1975.

Also crucial to Laugerud's rightist alliance was the Organized Aranista Central (CAO). First conceived as an electoral machine in 1970, the CAO had taken on a life of its own as a personal vehicle for Arana's ambitions of long-term political power. Throughout, Arana remained the power behind

Laugerud's throne. His CAO crony, Luis Alfonso López, was corruptly "elected" president of Congress in 1976 amid a bribery scandal, and, according to one Army officer, Arana "was in the *Casa Presidencial* almost every day." During the Laugerud administration, Arana used his influence to further extend his financial tentacles into meat packing, fisheries, timber, construction, vehicle importing, cement works, publishing, broadcasting, and breweries. . . .

Open the Door an Inch. . .
Laugerud's attempt to stabilize military rule embraced a series of tactics. First, consolidate the PID-PR-CAO power axis, squeezing out the MLN. Then separate off the right wings of the Christian Democrats and social democrats, exposing what the generals insisted was a handful of "communists directed, financed, and incited by the Cuban government." Opening some space for democratic activity, settling strikes by negotiation, and lowering the tenor of repression might win over key leadership of the labor unions and isolate the radical Left. Sustained economic growth, boosted by the post-1976 earthquake construction boom, gave the generals confidence to proceed with their plans.

Their confidence was ill-founded; their reforms too little, too late. Inflation, a new phenomenon during 1973, was eroding workers' already meager living standards. The 1974 election fraud told the mass movement that even basic democratic freedoms could not be reclaimed within the framework imposed by the armed forces. Urban tensions erupted.

EVOLUTION OF DOMESTIC CONSUMER PRICE INDEX (1961–1981)

Year	(avg.) 61–65	(avg.) 66–70	1971	1972	1973	1974	1975
Inflation	0.1%	1.5%	–0.5%	0.5%	10.0%	16.0%	13.1%

Year	1976	1977	1978	1979	1980	1981
Inflation	10.7%	12.6%	7.9%	11.5%	12.0%	12.4%

Sources: United Nations Economic Survey of Latin America (1979); Inter-American Development Bank Annual Report (1981); Boletín Estadístico del Banco de Guatemala; This Week in Central America and Panama.

Union leaders and Army alike were taken aback by the sheer scale of an angry movement which, thought moribund, now burst onto the streets. The funeral of a murdered activist could trigger a teeming protest by thousands chanting, "We don't want elections, we want revolution." Striking mine workers from the remote highland town of Ixahuacan found their 300-kilometer march to the capital in 1977 joined by 100,000 united peasant and worker sympathizers. A powerful National Committee of Trade Union Unity (CNUS) crystalized around a 1976 strike at the local

Coca Cola franchise, EGSA, and a devastating earthquake the same year, whose main impact hit urban slum dwellers and highland peasants.

This should not suggest that the entire mass movement became instant revolutionaries. True, the Christian Democrats and fellow reformist parties lost credibility by reaffirming electoral methods after 1974. But they and many of their working-class followers believed that the Laugerud opening, though limited, could be pushed. If not in time for the 1978 elections, a restoration of democracy could surely come by 1982.

Laugerud's reforms were too lukewarm to neutralize the Left, but enough to allow it some space in which to reorganize. As the mass movement swelled in size and confidence, its positions grew more radical. The National Workers' Federation (CNT), largest member of CNUS, severed its ties to the Christian Democratic Latin American Workers' Federation (CLAT). The militant new Committee of Peasant Unity (CUC) registered sweeping successes among south and coast plantation workers. After the earthquake, church groups working in the Indian highlands and foreign aid–financed urban slum projects became an explosive new ingredient in opposition to the regime. Even modest community demands—a new standpipe to the barrio, a drainage system, electric light—took on threatening political dimensions. And a revived guerrilla movement began to inflict stinging blows on the Army.

. . . Slam It Shut Again

Under pressure from his right flank, Laugerud backtracked. Far from stabilizing the regime, his tactics had only succeeded in undermining it further. Real reforms were unacceptable to the agroexporting class, MLN supporters, and Army loyalists alike, and token reforms only opened a Pandora's box. Locked in the classic agrarian mentality of those whose products are shipped straight overseas with little regard for the demands of a local market, the bunker vision of the Right only hardened in response to the U.S. State Department's 1977 designation of Guatemala as a "gross and consistent violator of human rights."

By Lucas García's inauguration in 1978, the armed forces and the rest of the bourgeoisie faced starkly drawn options: thoroughgoing reforms or the full weight of state terrorism against all opponents. Unable to countenance the political repercussions of reform, the regime took the only recourse it knew. . . .

Lucas García: The Descent Into Anarchy

Lucas came to power in March 1978 on a record low voter turnout. The MLN—real winners of another flagrantly fraudulent election—protested, but Arana's goon squads and the military high command intervened to uphold Lucas' election. Like Laugerud, Lucas was the protege of ex-president Arana—reputedly because Arana saw him as the most unintelligent and pliable member of the high command.

Lucas showed some early base of support among the middle class, but in any organizational sense that support was extremely shallow. Since elections were a charade, the Democratic Institutional Party (PID) and the Revolutionary Party (PIR), which formed the core of Lucas' electoral alliance, were not effective political instruments, but merely platforms for patronage and enrichment.

The centrist opposition parties were badly split. Opportunistic leaders wanted to gain a stake in the political process; other activists felt their middle-class base might still be brought in from the cold. Lucas shrewdly capitalized on their confusion. The military dangled the carrot of legal registration in front of the FUR, which obliged by tacitly endorsing Lucas' win and keeping aloof from the new, broad-based Democratic Front Against Repression. Christian Democrats, now divided into feuding left and right wings, had spent the 1970s flirting with the idea of building a "centrist alliance" with the PID. Rebuffed in 1974, they nonetheless again fielded a military candidate in 1978, General Ricardo Peralta Méndez.

Lucas' vice-presidential running mate was the experienced centrist, Francisco Villagrán Kramer, who had severed his earlier links to the reformist parties. Villagrán Kramer offered Lucas a last veneer of respectability and a last bridge to Washington. By now, Congress had suspended military aid to Guatemala. His own aim, the Vice President told a U.S. reporter, was "to avoid a Custer's Last Stand in Guatemala." He was predictably labeled a Marxist by the MLN, and accused by his eventual successor, Colonal Oscar Mendoza Azurdia, of being "an agent of both the United States and the Soviet Union."

The MLN remained the single largest party, with twenty out of sixty-one deputies. But its estrangement from the military power center was complete. MLN decline was exemplified by the enforced choice of retired Colonel Enrique Peralta Azurdia as its presidential candidate. No serving Army officer would accept the albatross of an MLN nomination.

Death Wish?

The October 1978 bus-fare riots had dispelled any remnant hopes of reform under Lucas. His initial hesitation about whether to crush or accommodate the strike exasperated the fiercely right-wing police chief, Colonel Germán Chupina. The colonel, given to hiring out his Mobile Military Police as vigilantes to private businessmen, assigned police provocateurs to inflame the throngs, and thus justify blanket repression. The new Secret Anti-Communist Army, a death squad repeatedly linked to Chupina's office, issued a death list of forty prominent opposition figures, and set about the job of killing them. Terror escalated to unheard-of levels. Ten corpses a day appeared, hideously disfigured by torture, along the roadsides, in storm drains, under viaducts.

Hombres desconocidos (unknown men). Every Guatemalan knows the words; thousands have experienced their meaning. Those who knock on the door at dead of night and speed off in unmarked Cherokee station wagons, dragging away "communists" whose mutilated bodies will later be left on public display.

The first death squad, the National Anti-Communist Organization, took up operations in 1960. And during the peak years of counterinsurgency (1966–68), the squads bloomed like poisonous flowers. They adopted flamboyant names—An Eye for an Eye, Purple Rose, The Hawk of Justice. They mutilated their victims' faces and genitals and boasted of their exploits in apocalyptic communiques. The New Anti-Communist Organization announced publicly that it would cut off the tongue and left hand of its enemies. Open publication of death lists and victims' photographs added to a national psychosis of terror.

In the countryside, security forces, private landowners, and MLN thugs used terror in ways which made one group indistinguishable from the others. Since military commissioners were authorized to bear arms such as machine guns (normally restricted to the Army), many farmers and businessmen simply took out credentials as commissioners to set up their own hit squads. In other cases, officers would use the death squads as enforcers for their private rackets and fiefdoms within the police force.

Fifteen years of this had provided the right climate for private enterprise to reap the harvest of economic growth. The violence was never concealed, especially in the years when the fascist MLN shared power. Even though the first mass disappearances and killings of the 1960s had been quickly tied to Army and national police headquarters and to the La Aurora Air Force base, the Army continued to depict the death squads as a spontaneous "civic response" to the Antichrist of communism, a conscious strategem to offer seemingly independent corroboration of its own harsh rule.

By the late 1970s, any distinction between institutional terror—exercised by the state on behalf of the ruling class—and free-lance terror from extra-legal groups of the bourgeoisie had blurred into meaninglessness. So had the pretense that death-squad killings were the result of fictitious encounters between "extreme Left" and "extreme Right." The war against communism, Arana argued, prefiguring a line which Argentine generals would later echo, was a dirty business. Innocent people would get hurt. A 1981 Amnesty International report laid to rest any remaining idea that the death squads were independent of the top echelons of the Army and security forces by tracing the chain of command all the way to Lucas' office.

The Psychosis of Terror

The major death squad of the Lucas period, the Secret Anti-Communist Army (ESA), faced a new target—an organized mass movement. The ESA's scale of operations was awesome: 311 peasant leaders killed during 1980, 400 University of San Carlos students and teachers butchered in four months.

Democratic Socialist Party leader Alberto Fuentes Mohr described the death squads' tactics: "Every single murder is of a key person—people in each sector or movement who have the ability to organize the population around a cause." It was his last interview; only days later, he was gunned down in the street. Within weeks, FUR leader Manuel Colom Argueta was also dead, his murder agreed on at a March 1979 meeting between senior Army officers and high-ranking representatives of the private sector.

A decade earlier, Regis Debray had written of the effects of the terror: "Administered in large enough doses over a long enough period, it has an anaesthetic effect . . . the obscene becomes commonplace, the abnormal normal." By 1980, the obscenity was still a commonplace, but the anaesthetic had worn off. A mass movement revived both in its psychology and its clandestine organization managed to survive the rampant terror. The exhaustion of state terror as an effective means of domination knocked another pin from under the fast-crumbling Lucas regime. . . .

The Garrison State

Since the 1970s, the military's role had changed, overstepping its "normal limits" and invading spheres of activity customarily reserved for civil society or the civilian state apparatus. Overlap between the military's coercive role and its ownership of key means of production has severely distorted the function of the state.

The military caste has special privileges. Officers enjoy access to special stores where luxury consumer imports are sold at discount prices. Military entrepreneurs have moved into hotel and real estate speculation on the shores of beautiful Lake Atitlán, Guatemala's prime tourist attraction.

More worrisome than this new wealth is the machinery created for its acquisition and protection—an array of institutions fusing the armed forces with the state. Military men run forty-six semiautonomous state institutions. Military-controlled agencies include a pension and investment fund—the Institute for Military Social Security (IPM) and the Army Bank. The IPM put up some of the capital for Arana's foundation of the Army Bank in 1972, but even more was siphoned out of public funds. A $5 million appropriation launched the bank, whose charter called for it to open credits for cattle raising, industry, and real estate development. Since then, it has become a financial monster with active capital of $119.2 million in 1981. In 1981, Lucas' Congress approved a further $20 million injection of state funds.

Together with the Bank of America, the Army Bank co-financed the luxury 800-unit Santa Rosita military housing project. IPM funds, in collaboration with the South African Trade and Project Management Service, financed the military-owned Cementos Guastatoya, infringing a long-agreed civilian sector monopoly over the lucrative cement industry. IPM money has also bought the Army a profitable, multistoried parking building in downtown Guatemala City.

This growing domination of the economy by those who wield state power is in no sense state capitalism: The overall trend remains toward the privatization of the economy. Rather, the military has chosen to own what it identifies—through economic self-interest and its particular concept of national security—as key areas of economic life. The profits from these enterprises find their way into the pockets of senior officers and into consolidating the military as an institution.

Fiddling While Guatemala Burns

. . . The Guatemalan military state has proved too voracious to even mediate *intra*-class disputes. The military, now an independent economic power, has used the political-economic levers at its command only for self-enrichment, not to maneuver a stable bourgeois consensus behind its rule. If coffee exporters asked for a tax break, for example, they were likely to be given a tax *increase*, to fatten state revenues for the military's pet projects.

When the effectiveness of terror and the sustained growth of the economy both evaporated under Lucas, previously masked tensions in the ranks of the private sector exploded. With recession sharpening capitalist competition for shrinking profit margins, the individual private sector chambers clamored for special treatment. They found instead that the military only insisted on being cut in on all the most profitable enterprises.

Businessmen excluded from the corridors of power began to mutter that Guatemala was being "Somozanized." The corrupt government bureaucracy—stuffed with self-seeking military officers and technocrats—showed neither inclination nor capacity for pulling the economy out of its nose dive. Plunder replaced planning. By 1981, the military and its immediate right-wing allies were isolated, fast losing control.

A gaping rift even developed between Arana, founding father of the militarized state, and Lucas. . . . Arana, too, now felt the chill winds of economic competition. Through his increasingly vocal party, he proposed the unrestrained machinery of the free market as a path to economic recovery. His harsh Chilean-style monetarism, blaming economic ills on state intervention, sounded like a coherent long-term alternative to many disenchanted businessmen.

Some U.S. policy makers also saw the attraction. Lucas' wild bloodletting, and his willful ruination of the economy, antagonized the Carter administration. Arana, long a favorite son for his counterinsurgency skills, now also offered economic appeal to his backers in the upper echelons of the CIA, Pentagon, and Republican Party.

The Disintegrating Military

Military expansionism affected not only the country's economic base. . . . The military also moved into direct control of culture and education. Army grants pay for young officers to study the "subjects of the future"— electronics, mining, and petroleum engineering. Since 1978, there has been ambitious talk of a military university. In 1979, the armed forces established their own Department of Radio and Television. They also own Channel 5 of Guatemalan television. Control of the press and restrictions on the dissemination of information have tightened.

Ultimately, the military elite have even allowed the legendary cohesion within their own ranks to crumble. Decomposition is rapid. Their monopoly of power has been accompanied by corruption on a massive scale. Even within the officer class, there is potential here for cracks: Generals and colonels control what captains and lieutenants cannot yet aspire to. In the most celebrated case of Mafia-style activity—an arms-buying racket controlled by eight generals—runaway sums were involved. Young officers reported that between 1975 and 1981, the Guatemalan military registered $175 million worth of arms purchases from Israel, Italy, Belgium, and Yugoslavia. The generals reported the value of the sales as $425 million, salting away the difference in private bank accounts in the tax haven of the Cayman Islands. . . .

As the final guarantee of its power, the Guatemalan Army has always been able to resort to its monolithic internal cohesion. The fragmentation of military unity under Lucas was something new, a further Achilles' heel of the military state.

Reprinted and edited from *Report on the Americas* "Garrison Guatemala," 17, no. 1 (Jan./ Feb. 1983), pp. 9–26, published by North American Congress on Latin America.

Editors' note. With the election of President Reagan in 1980, the shift of the United States back to a hard-line anti-Communist foreign policy greatly encouraged the Guatemalan military. To meet the resurgent guerrilla challenge and to end the personalism and corruption of General Lucas García's administration, junior officers and their sympathizers carried out a coup in 1982. The new government, headed by General Ríos Montt—a member of a non-Catholic charismatic Christian sect—pledged to end the guerrilla menace and to carry out socioeconomic reforms. Like several of his predecessors in the 1960s, Ríos Montt achieved some early military successes against the EGP guerrillas. The regime declared victory in 1983. Despite the renewed repression and apparent military victories of the

Ríos Montt regime, the Guerrilla Army of the Poor called for an "agrarian, anti-imperialist, and anti-capitalist revolution." It was clear, in light of the last quarter century of struggle, that General Ríos Montt's victory could be no more permanent than the "victories" of Peralta Azurdia, Méndez Montenegro, Arana Osorio, and the military governments in the decade 1970–80. Indeed, Ríos Montt himself was overthrown in mid-1983 by more traditional officers who disliked his evangelical religious affiliation and cronyism.

In 1985, following the trends established by Peru, Bolivia, El Salvador, Argentina, Uruguay, and Brazil, the military government headed by General Humberto Mejía Victores held elections and allowed a civilian candidate, Vinicio Cerezo Arévalo, to assume the presidency. As in the past, however, the army remained the most important political force in Guatemala.

Acknowledgments

Grateful acknowledgment is made to the publishers and authors of the following selections for their permission to reprint the following sections in whole or in part:

"An Overview of the European Military Missions in Latin America," by Frederick M. Nunn. *Military Affairs* 39 (February 1975): 1–7.

"The Rise of Modern Militarism in Argentina," by Marvin Goldwert. *Hispanic American Historical Review* 48, no. 2 (May 1968): 189–205.

"The Influence of the German Armed Forces and War Industry, 1880–1914," by Warren Schiff. *Hispanic American Historical Review* 52, no. 3 (August 1972): 436–55.

"Origins of the 'New Professionalism' of the Brazilian Military," by Frank D. McCann, Jr. *Journal of Interamerican Studies and World Affairs* 21, no. 4 (November 1979): 505–22.

"Emil Körner and the Prussianization of the Chilean Army," by Frederick M. Nunn. *Hispanic American Historical Review* 50, no. 2 (May 1970): 300–322.

"Military Professionalization in Peru," by Víctor Villanueva. Translation of chapter 5 ("Los Militares Vuelven a Sus Cuarteles") of *Ejército peruano: del caudillaje anárquico al militarismo reformista* (Lima: Librería-Editorial Juan Mejía Baca, 1973), pp. 122–33.

"The Military and Argentine Politics," by Robert A. Potash. Adapted from chapters 1, 2, 3, 4, and 8 of *The Army and Politics in Argentina, 1928–1945: Yrigoyen to Perón*, with the permission of the publishers (Stanford, Calif.: Stanford University Press, 1969). © 1969 by the Board of Trustees of the Leland Stanford Junior University.

"An Overview of the Bolivian Military in National Politics to 1952," by William H. Brill. From *Military Intervention in Bolivia: The Overthrow of Paz Estenssoro and the MNR* (Washington, D.C.: Institute for Comparative Study of Political Systems, 1967), pp. 5–9.

"The Military and Brazilian Politics to World War II," by Ronald M. Schneider. From *The Political System of Brazil: Emergence of a Modernizing Authoritarian Regime, 1964–1970* (New York: Columbia University Press, 1971), pp. 37–48. Reprinted by permission of the publisher and the author.

"The Military in Chilean Politics, 1924–32," by Frederick M. Nunn. First published as "A Latin American State Within the State: The Politics of the Chilean Army, 1924–1927," *The Americas* 27, no. 1 (July 1970): 40–55.

"The Military in Peruvian Politics," by Víctor Villanueva. Translation of chapters 3–5 of *El Militarismo en el Perú* (Lima: T. Scheuch, 1962), pp. 52–107.

"The Guatemalan Military and the Revolution of 1944," by Kenneth J. Grieb. *The Americas* 32, no. 4 (April 1976): 524–43.

"Guerrilla Warfare in Underdeveloped Areas," by W. W. Rostow. *Marine Corps Gazette* 46, no. 1 (January 1962): 46–49.

"Post-Vietnam Counterinsurgency Doctrine," by Col. John D. Waghelstein. *Military Review* 65, no. 5 (May 1985): 42–49.

"Military Politics in Argentina, 1966–73," by David Rock. From *Argentina in the Twentieth Century,* ed. David Rock (Pittsburgh, Pa.: University of Pittsburgh Press, 1975), pp. 207, 209–17. Reprinted by permission of the University of Pittsburgh Press. © 1975 by the University of Pittsburgh Press.

"The Military in Politics in Argentina, 1973–83," by David Rock. Excerpted from chapter 8 of *Argentina, 1516–1982: From Spanish Colonization to the Falklands War* (Berkeley: University of California Press, 1985). © 1985 by the Regents of the University of California.

"Military Government and State Terrorism in Argentina," by Juan E. Corradi. First published as "The Mode of Destruction: Terrorism in Argentina," *Telos* 54 (Winter 1982–83): 61–76.

"The Military and Bolivian Politics, 1971–1983," by James Dunkerley. Excerpted from chapter 6 of *Rebellion in the Veins: Political Struggle in Bolivia, 1952–1982* (London: Verso Editions, 1984).

"The Post-1964 Military Republic in Brazil," by Riordan Roett. From *Brazil: Politics in a Patrimonial Society,* rev. ed. (New York: Praeger Publishers, 1978), pp. 133–69. Abridged and reprinted with permission of the author and the publisher.

"The Transition to Democracy in Brazil," by Scott Mainwaring. *Journal of Interamerican Studies and World Affairs* 28, no. 1 (Spring 1986): 149–79.

"Antipolitics in Chile, 1973–1987," by Brian Loveman. First published as "Military Dictatorship and Political Opposition in Chile, 1973–1986,"

Journal of Interamerican Studies and World Affairs 28, no. 4 (Winter 1986–87): 1–38.

"Antipolitics in Peru, 1968–1980," by Stephen M. Gorman. From *Post-Revolutionary Peru: The Politics of Transformation* (Boulder: Westview Press, 1982): pp. 1–32.

"Oligarchs and Officers: The Crisis in El Salvador," by William M. LeoGrande and Carla Anne Robbins. *Foreign Affairs* 58 (Summer 1980): 1084–1103. Updated for this volume by Professor LeoGrande. Reprinted by permission of *Foreign Affairs*. Copyright 1980 by the Council on Foreign Relations, Inc.

"Military Rule in Guatemala," by George Black. First published as "The Decade of the Dinosaurs" and "Lucas Garcia: The Descent into Anarchy," *Report on the Americas* "Garrison Guatemala," 17, no. 1 (Jan./Feb. 1983): 9–26. Published by the North American Congress on Latin America.